PHILOSOPHICAL FOUNDATIONS
OF
NEUROSCIENCE

D1500508

Advance reviews of *Philosophical Foundations of Neuroscience*:

'This remarkable book, the product of a collaboration between a philosopher and neuroscientist, shows that the claims made on behalf of cognitive science are ill-founded. The real significance of impressive recent developments in the study of the brain, they allege, has been clouded by philosophical confusion in the way in which these results have been presented. The authors document their complaint in a clear and patient manner. . . . They disentangle the confusions by setting out clearly the contrasting but complementary roles of philosophy and neuroscience in this area. The book will certainly arouse opposition. . . . But if it causes controversy, it is controversy that is long overdue. It is to be hoped that it will be widely read among those in many different disciplines who are interested in the brain and the mind.' *Sir Anthony Kenny, President of the British Academy (1989–1993)*

'Overall the book provides the most thorough critical survey of the ruling theories of mental phenomena as they figure in contemporary science. The attention to detail is meticulous, and the philosophical analysis outstandingly lucid. Contemporary scientists and philosophers may not like Bennett and Hacker's conclusions, but they will hardly be able to ignore them. The work is a formidable achievement.' *John Cottingham, Professor of Philosophy, University of Reading*

'Contemporary neuroscience is an exciting, ebullient field and its practitioners are not much given to self-doubt. This dissection of the field by Bennett and Hacker ought to provoke some misgivings. Arguing for a sharp distinction between conceptual analysis of our everyday psychological concepts on the one hand and empirical, neuroscientific investigation on the other, Bennett and Hacker conclude that many neuroscientists – and some of their philosopher friends – have ignored or muddied that distinction at their peril. In particular, they argue that the misuse of psychological concepts in the interpretation of neural processes does not lead to testable or even false claims, but to nonsense. Neuroscientists, psychologists and philosophers will be challenged – and educated – by this sustained and well-informed critique.' *Paul L. Harris, Professor, Human Development and Psychology, Harvard University*

'This book was simply waiting to be written. The reductionist agenda in biological science has generated so many conceptual difficulties that someone, sometime, had to analyse these problems in depth from outside the reductionist viewpoint. The key to understanding these confusions lies in an analysis of the logical conditions for ascribing mental and psychological properties. This is not easy. I wish I had had the benefit of the relatively easy path that Bennett and Hacker have provided.' *[From the Foreword by] Denis Noble CBE, Professor of Cardiovascular Physiology, Oxford University*

PHILOSOPHICAL FOUNDATIONS OF NEUROSCIENCE

M. R. Bennett and P. M. S. Hacker

350 Main Street, Malden, MA 02148-5018, USA
108 Cowley Road, Oxford OX4 1JF, UK
550 Swanston Street, Carlton South, Melbourne, Victoria 3053, Australia
Kurfürstendamm 57, 10707 Berlin, Germany

First published 2003 by Blackwell Publishing Ltd

Library of Congress Cataloging-in-Publication Data

Bennett, M. R.
Philosophical foundations of neuroscience / M.R. Bennett and P.M.S. Hacker.
p. cm.
Includes bibliographical references and index.
ISBN 1-4051-0855-X (hbk. : alk. paper) – ISBN 1-4051-0838-X (pbk. : alk. paper)
1. Cognitive neuroscience–Philosophy. I. Hacker, P.M.S. (Peter Michael Stephan) II.
Title.

QP360.5 .B465 2003
612.8′2′01–dc21

2002028110

A catalogue record for this title is available from the British Library.

Set in 10/12pt Bembo
by Graphicraft Limited, Hong Kong
Printed and bound in the United Kingdom
by TJ International Ltd., Padstow, Cornwall.

For further information on
Blackwell Publishing, visit our website:
http://www.blackwellpublishing.com

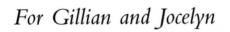

For Gillian and Jocelyn

Contents

Foreword

This book was simply waiting to be written. The reductionist agenda in biological science has generated so many conceptual difficulties that someone, sometime, had to analyse these problems in depth from outside the reductionist viewpoint. That a neurophysiologist and a philosopher should combine to do so is also a sign of the times. As biology moves on to address the complexity and extraordinary subtlety of life, now that it has broken it down into its smallest pieces, we will find this kind of combination of skills and ways of thinking even more necessary. As the authors make clear, philosophy (at least in the analytical form practised here) and empirical science are not in opposition. Rather they deal with different kinds of question. Yet, since a conceptual scheme is necessary to any fruitful experimentation, we cannot avoid asking both kinds. Keeping a clear head while we do so is not as easy as it may seem!

I must issue a warning: this book is *highly* controversial. Some of my scientific colleagues will strongly challenge, and will surely be deeply provoked by, the claim that neuroscience has frequently and systematically confused conceptual and empirical questions. To them I would say, first, that the authors clearly recognize the brilliance and phenomenal achievements of the scientists whose conceptual work they analyse. This is emphatically not a book debunking experimental science, any more than the fact that most physiologists now dismiss the dualist philosophy of Sherrington or Eccles detracts in any way from recognizing the immense significance of their scientific achievements. We find it perfectly possible to admire the experimental and associated analytical skills while wincing when we see how completely trapped they were in their outdated and indefensible philosophical position.

Second, I would appeal for some patience and humility. Patience, because as a physiologist who has interacted with (and published with) professional philosophers of various persuasions for over 40 years,[1] I have to say that I find scientists unthinkingly debunking

---

[1] See, for example, Noble, D. (1989), What Do Intentions Do? In: *Goals, No Goals and Own Goals*, eds Alan Montefiore and Denis Noble, London: Unwin Hyman; and Noble, D. (1991), Biological Explanation and Intentional Behaviour. In: *Modelling the Mind*, eds W. H. Newton-Smith and K. Wilkes, Oxford: Oxford University Press.

philosophy more often than the other way round. Humility, because the issues are of the utmost social importance. Some of the claims of reductionist science are not only conceptually incorrect or even unintelligible, they have major social implications. The words we use, the concepts by which we analyse and present biological discovery, deeply affect the way in which we see ourselves as human beings. For that reason, if for no other, a critical debate is necessary. The authors of this book have thrown down a major challenge in that debate.

The controversial nature of this book arises because the particular reductionist philosophical position it criticizes is very widely held today within the scientific community (and also by some well-known philosophers). Moreover, for most of them, this position is a *methodological* necessity, perceived to be the only paradigm for science to successfully explain things. The first reaction to the counter-argument, as presented here, will be to protest that somehow science is being (unnecessarily?) circumscribed; that some problems are, as it were, being taken from its grasp. I would argue the other way. The first step to scientific progress is to ask the right questions. If we are conceptually confused, we will ask the wrong questions. The authors illustrate this in detail with many examples.

It is hard to escape the confines and confusions of the culture in which one finds oneself. The history of philosophy shows that, just as much as the history of science. The central appeal of this book is to throw off the remaining legacy of the Cartesian confusions, first expressed as a duality of mind and body, but latterly expressed as a duality of brain and body. The authors show that, although the first required belief in a non-material substance, while the latter is wholly materialistic, many of the conceptual problems (essentially those of the 'ghost in the machine') are the same. For our dualist predecessors the ghost was an actual immaterial substance, for us it is 'the "I"' (or 'inner eye' or whatever) that 'sees' the qualia that 'form our experience'. This is what may lead us to ask which group of cells, or even which neurone(!), is doing the 'seeing'. The point here is that simply replacing 'I' or 'inner eye' by the brain or a part of the brain doesn't avoid the problem.

The key to understanding the confusions here lies in an analysis of the logical conditions for ascribing mental and psychological properties. This is not easy. It involves one of the most difficult of twentieth-century philosophical ideas, that of the 'private language argument': what it is to say things like 'I feel pain' or 'I see red'. I struggled through the ramifications of this argument many years ago before writing my own contributions to the philosophy of biology. I wish I had had the benefit of the relatively easy path that Bennett and Hacker have provided. Even those who fundamentally disagree with their arguments (and I look forward to seeing them engage in debate) must surely acknowledge that this is a sustained and valuable exposition of an important and influential philosophical position.

Although I would describe that position as philosophically radical (in the correct sense of that word: going back to basic roots and eradicating those that shouldn't be there), it is often dismissed by scientists as conservative because it may appear to restrict using language in new ways. Yet, they would argue, science cannot advance without doing that. And what better way to achieve it than to start with metaphor or *façons de parler*, consolidate with dead metaphor (metaphors that become part of everyday language – constructivists argue that that is the way language evolved) and finally end up with a change in our conceptual scheme? Indeed, why not, if that is what will enlighten us, lead us into new conceptual territory, formulate new theories. But there is a simple test for whether that could work in any particular case. For each such metaphorical (or similar) change in use or meaning, or novel piece of terminology (such as 'qualia' or 'memes'), imagine stating its opposite, and then ask whether any conceivable experiment could test empirically between the two. The deep problem for many 'novel' concepts and language uses in reductionist approaches is that this test totally fails. The novel use of language is then not so much a scientific as a political or social tool. If you doubt this, try imagining an experiment to test between the existence or non-existence of qualia. Or for whether or not the brain makes representative maps (which are *not* homunculi incidentally). Or for brain states that 'explain' rational thought (rather than being a necessary physical basis for its existence). Surely we should only introduce new terminology where, as with quarks and black holes, we provide the empirical criteria for determining their existence?

Perhaps the problem for many scientists is to imagine what would happen if we abandoned the universality of the reductionist approach. For sure, the nature of science would change. But so it should! We would have to recognize that causation and explanation do not always run upwards from lower to higher levels. And, surely, at a time when we have already come to understand the extent to which causation runs in the opposite direction (higher-level states in biological systems even influence something as fundamentally lower-level as gene expression), how can we possibly imagine that we will progress without recognizing the validity of explanations at all levels? One of the criteria for determining the level at which explanation succeeds is to ask what can sensibly be ascribed at different levels. It does not make sense to look for explanations at levels lower than that for the applicability of the relevant predicates.

This is particularly true of rational behaviour, including the use of language. The argument is basically very simple. We cannot, coherently, deny our own rationality. Otherwise we would have difficulty meaning what we say or being convincing in saying it, which is precisely what happens in the sad cases of those mentally ill people who nevertheless are aware of, but can't help, their irrationality. If we really could succeed in 'reducing' rational behaviour simply to molecular or cellular causation then we would no longer be able meaningfully to express the truth of what we had succeeded in doing. But, thankfully, no such reduction is conceivable. We know what it is to be rational, and what it is to lose that capacity. That knowledge has nothing to do with the question whether there exist specific and causally sufficient neural states and interactions while I am writing this review, for example. Of course they do. And, if we can discover them, they may well provide a complete explanation for the mechanisms of my brain while thinking and writing. The main claim of anti-reductionism in science is that such a complete explanation of mechanisms at one level does not necessarily explain what exists and happens at higher levels. Indeed we may need to know about the higher levels in order to explain the lower-level data that form an input to the mechanisms involved (which is what must be the case in writing this review! – one of the inputs was my reading this book, but the book is not thereby 'inside' my brain).

The most spectacular case of this need for higher-level understanding in modern biology is, of course, the genome, whose sequences will only be understood eventually in terms of higher-level function (genes don't come with functional names attached – nor do neurones!).

I started my life in physiological research as a fully paid-up member of the reductionist club. In the 1960s you couldn't get much more reductionist than to discover ion channels in excitable cells and then to simulate their activity in a bottom-up approach. I did for heart cells what Hodgkin & Huxley did for nerve cells. It is through trying to extend this approach to higher physiological levels that I have come to see the conceptual and computational problems that arise in practice. I have written elsewhere on the impossibility of a completely bottom-up reconstruction of living systems.[2]

Concurrently I also interacted extensively with professional philosophers (of different schools of thought – including those who would support the reductionist agenda). Coming to adopt an integrationist agenda was not an easy road, either scientifically or philosophically. But it is a far richer position. The integrationist does not deny the validity or immense achievements of successful reduction. For some reason (political, social, philosophical?) reductionists seem to need to claim universality for their approach. This book will give them some cause to re-think that position – or so I would hope.

Denis Noble CBE FRS hon FRCP
Professor of Cardiovascular Physiology at Oxford University
Secretary-General, International Union of Physiological Sciences (1993–2001)

---

[2] Noble, D. (2002), Biological Computation. In: *Encyclopedia of Life Sciences*, http://www.els.net, London: Nature Publishing Group. Noble, D. (2002), The Rise of Computational Biology. *Nature Reviews Molecular Cell Biology*, 3, 460–3. See also Novartis Foundation (2002), *In Silico Simulation of Biological Processes*. Novartis Foundation Symposium, vol. 247, London: John Wiley.

Acknowledgements

Many people have assisted us in writing this book, and we have benefited from their advice, critical comments and constructive suggestions. We are grateful to Dr Hanoch Benyami, Professor Jonathan Dancy, Professor John Dupré, Dr Hanjo Glock, Professor Oswald Hanfling, Professor Paul Harris, Dr Tim Horder, Professor Andrew Parker, Professor Herman Philipse, Dr John Richardson, Wolfram Schmitt and Professor Stuart Shanker for their helpful comments on one or more (sometimes many more) chapters of the book. We are especially indebted to Dr John Hyman and Professor Hans Oberdiek, who read and commented constructively on the whole text. We thank Sir Anthony Kenny, Professor Sir Peter Strawson and Professor Georg Henrik von Wright for their encouragement and moral support throughout the writing of this book. We are grateful to Jean van Altena for copy-editing our typescript with her characteristic skill, tact and good humour.

Chapters 1 and 2 are a rewritten version of a review article entitled 'The motor system in neuroscience: a history and analysis of conceptual developments', published in *Progress in Neurobiology*, 67 (2002), pp. 1–52. Parts of chapters 3, 4 and 5 were published in an article entitled 'Perception and memory in neuroscience: a conceptual analysis', in *Progress in Neurobiology*, 65 (2001), pp. 499–543. Parts of chapter 10 were published in an article by Hacker entitled 'Is there anything it is like to be a bat?' in *Philosophy*, 77 (2002), pp. 153–70. We thank the editors of these journals for permission to republish this work.

M. R. Bennett, *University of Sydney*
P. M. S. Hacker, *St John's College, Oxford*

Introduction

Philosophical Foundations of Neuroscience presents the fruits of a cooperative project between a neuroscientist and a philosopher. It is concerned with the conceptual foundations of *cognitive* neuroscience – foundations constituted by the structural relationships among the psychological concepts involved in investigations into the neural underpinnings of human cognitive, affective and volitional capacities. Investigating logical relations among concepts is a philosophical task. Guiding that investigation down pathways that will illuminate brain research is a neuroscientific one. Hence our joint venture.

If we are to understand the neural structures and dynamics that make perception, thought, memory, emotion and intentional behaviour possible, clarity about these concepts and categories is essential. Both authors, coming to this investigation from very different directions, found themselves puzzled by, and sometimes uneasy with, the use of psychological concepts in contemporary neuroscience. The puzzlement was often over what might be meant by a given neuroscientist's claims concerning the brain and the mind, or over why a neuroscientist thought that the experiments he had undertaken illuminated the psychological capacity being studied, or over the conceptual presuppositions of the questions asked. The unease was produced by a suspicion that in some cases concepts were misconstrued, or misapplied, or stretched beyond their defining conditions of application. And the more we probed, the more convinced we became that, despite the impressive advances in cognitive neuroscience, not all was well with the general theorizing.

Empirical questions about the nervous system are the province of neuroscience. It is its business to establish matters of fact concerning neural structures and operations. It is the task of *cognitive* neuroscience to explain the neural conditions that make perceptual, cognitive, cogitative, affective and volitional functions possible. Such explanatory theories are confirmed or infirmed by experimental investigations. By contrast, conceptual questions (concerning, for example, the concepts of mind or memory, thought or imagination), the description of the logical relations between concepts (such as between the concepts of perception and sensation, or the concepts of consciousness and self-consciousness), and the examination of the structural relationships between distinct conceptual fields (such as between the psychological and the neural, or the mental and the behavioural) are the proper province of philosophy.

Conceptual questions antecede matters of truth and falsehood. They are questions concerning our *forms of representation*, not questions concerning the truth or falsehood of empirical statements. These forms are presupposed by true (*and* false) scientific statements and by correct (*and* incorrect) scientific theories. They determine not what is empirically true or false, but rather what does and what does not make sense. Hence conceptual questions are not amenable to scientific investigation and experimentation or to scientific theorizing. For the concepts and conceptual relationships in question are *presupposed* by any such investigations and theorizings. Our concern here is not with trade union demarcation lines, but with distinctions between logically different kinds of intellectual inquiry. (Methodological objections to these distinctions are examined in chapter 14.)

Distinguishing conceptual questions from empirical ones is of the first importance. When a conceptual question is confused with a scientific one, it is bound to appear singularly refractory. It seems in such cases as if science should be able to discover the truth of the matter under investigation by theory and experiment – yet it persistently fails to do so. That is not surprising, since conceptual questions are no more amenable to empirical methods of investigation than problems in pure mathematics are solvable by the methods of physics. Furthermore, when empirical problems are addressed without adequate conceptual clarity, misconceived questions are bound to be raised, and misdirected research is likely to ensue. For any unclarity regarding the relevant concepts will be reflected in corresponding unclarity in the questions, and hence in the design of experiments intended to answer them. And any incoherence in the grasp of the relevant conceptual structure is likely to be manifest in incoherences in the interpretation of the results of experiments.

Cognitive neuroscience operates across the boundary between two fields, neurophysiology and psychology, the respective concepts of which are categorially dissimilar. The logical or conceptual relations between the physiological and the psychological are problematic. Numerous psychological concepts and categories of concepts are difficult to bring into sharp focus. The relations between the mind and the brain, and between the psychological and the behavioural, are bewildering. Puzzlement concerning these concepts and their articulations, and concerning these apparent 'domains' and their relations, has characterized neurophysiology since its inception (we shall begin our investigations in chapter 1 with a historical survey of the early development of neuroscience). In spite of the great advances in neuroscience at the beginning of the twentieth century at the hands of Charles Sherrington, the battery of conceptual questions popularly known as the mind–body or mind–brain problem remained as intractable as ever – as is evident in the flawed Cartesian views embraced by Sherrington and by such of his colleagues and protégés as Edgar Adrian, John Eccles and Wilder Penfield. Brilliant though their work unquestionably was, deep conceptual confusions remained – as we show in chapter 2. Whether the current generation of neuroscientists has successfully overcome the conceptual confusions of earlier generations, or whether it has merely replaced one conceptual entanglement by others, is the subject of our investigation in this book.

One such tangle is evident in the persistent ascription of psychological attributes to the brain. For, while Sherrington and his protégés ascribed psychological attributes to the mind (conceived as a peculiar, perhaps immaterial, substance distinct from the brain), contemporary neuroscientists tend to ascribe the same range of psychological attributes to the brain (commonly, although not uniformly, conceived to be identical with the mind). But the mind, we argue (§3.10), is neither a substance distinct from the brain nor a substance identical with the brain. And we demonstrate that ascription of psychological attributes to the brain is incoherent (chapter 3). Human beings possess a wide range of psychological powers, which are exercised in the circumstances of life, when we perceive, think and reason, feel emotions, want things, form plans and make decisions. The possession and exercise of such powers define us as the kinds of animals we are. We may enquire into the neural conditions and concomitants for their possession and exercise. This is the task of neuroscience, which is discovering more and more about them. But its discoveries in no way affect the conceptual truth that these powers and their exercise in perception, thought and feeling *are attributes of human beings*, not of their parts – in particular, *not of their brains*. A human being is a psychophysical unity, an animal that can perceive, act intention-ally, reason and feel emotions, a language-using animal that is not merely conscious, but also self-conscious – not a brain embedded in the skull of a body. Sherrington, Eccles and Penfield conceived of human beings as animals in whom the mind, which they thought of as the bearer of psychological attributes, is in liaison with the brain. It is no advance over that misconception to suppose that the brain is a bearer of psychological attributes.

Talk of the brain's perceiving, thinking, guessing or believing, or of one hemisphere of the brain's knowing things of which the other hemisphere is ignorant, is widespread among contemporary neuroscientists. This is sometimes defended as being no more than a trivial *façon de parler*. But that is quite mistaken. For the characteristic form of explanation in contemporary cognitive neuroscience consists in ascribing psychological attributes to the brain and its parts *in order to explain* the possession of psychological attributes and the exercise (and deficiencies in the exercise) of cognitive powers by human beings.

The ascription of psychological – in particular, cognitive and cogitative – attributes to the brain is, we show, also a source of much further confusion. Neuroscience can invest-igate the neural conditions and concomitants of the acquisition, possession and exercise of sentient powers by animals. It can discover the neural preconditions for the possibility of the exercise of distinctively human powers of thought and reasoning, of articulate memory and imagination, of emotion and volition. This it can do by patient inductive correlation between neural phenomena and the possession and exercise of psychological powers, and between neural damage and deficiencies in normal mental functions. What it *cannot* do is *replace* the wide range of ordinary psychological explanations of human activities in terms of reasons, intentions, purposes, goals, values, rules and conventions by neurological explanations (reductionism is discussed in chapter 13). And it *cannot* explain how an animal perceives or thinks by reference to the brain's, or some part of the brain's, perceiving or thinking. For it makes no sense to ascribe such psychological attributes to anything less than the animal as a whole. It is the animal that perceives, not parts of its brain, and it is human beings who think and reason, not their brains. The brain and its activities *make it possible* for *us* – not for *it* – to perceive and think, to feel emotions, and to form and pursue projects.

While the initial response of many neuroscientists to the accusation of conceptual confusion is to claim that the ascription of psychological predicates to the brain is a mere *façon de parler*, their reaction to the demonstrable fact that their explanatory theories *non-trivially* ascribe psychological powers to the brain is sometimes to suggest that this error is unavoidable due to the deficiencies of language. We confront this misconception in chapter 14, where we show that the great discoveries of neuroscience *do not require* this misconceived form of explanation – that what has been discovered can readily be described and explained in our existing language. We demonstrate this by reference to the much discussed phenomena resultant upon commissurotomy, described (or, we suggest, misdescribed) by Sperry, Gazzaniga and others (§14.3).

In Part II we investigate the use of concepts of perception, memory, mental imagery, emotion and volition in current neuroscientific theorizing. From case to case we show that conceptual unclarity – failure to give adequate attention to the relevant conceptual structures – has often been the source of theoretical error and the grounds for misguided inferences. It is an error, a *conceptual* error, to suppose that perception is a matter of apprehending an *image* in the mind (Crick, Damasio, Edelman), or the production of a *hypothesis* (Helmholtz, Gregory), or the generation of a *3-D model description* (Marr). It is confused – a *conceptual* confusion – to formulate the binding problem as the problem of combining data of shape, colour and motion to form *the image* of the object perceived (Crick, Kandel, Wurtz). It is wrong, *conceptually* wrong, to suppose that memory is always of the past, or to think that memories can be *stored* in the brain in the form of the strength of synaptic connections (Kandel, Squire, Bennett). And it is mistaken, *conceptually* mistaken, to suppose that the investigation of thirst, hunger and lust is an investigation into the emotions (Rolls) or to think that the function of the emotions is to inform us of our visceral and musculoskeletal state (Damasio).

The initial reaction to such critical remarks may well be indignation and incredulity. How can a flourishing science be fundamentally in error? How could there be unavoidable conceptual confusion in a well-established science? Surely, if there are problematic concepts, they can easily be replaced by others that are unproblematic and that serve the same explanatory purposes. Such responses betoken a poor understanding of the relation between form of representation and facts represented, and a misunderstanding of the nature of conceptual error. They also betray ignorance of the history of science in general, and of neuroscience in particular.

Science is no more immune to conceptual error and confusion than any other form of intellectual endeavour. The history of science is littered with the debris of theories that were not simply factually mistaken, but conceptually awry. Stahl's theory of combustion, for example, was *conceptually* flawed in ascribing, in certain circumstances, negative weight to phlogiston – an idea that made no sense within its framework of Newtonian physics. Einstein's famous criticisms of the theory of electromagnetic aether (the alleged medium by which light was thought to be propagated) were directed not only at the results of the Michelson–Morley experiment, which had failed to detect any effect of absolute motion, but also at a conceptual confusion concerning relative motion involved in the role ascribed to aether in the explanation of electromagnetic induction. Neuroscience has been no exception – as we show in our historical survey. It is true enough that the subject is now a *flourishing* science. But that does not render it immune to conceptual confusions and entanglements. Newtonian kinematics was a flourishing science, but that did not stop

Newton from becoming entangled in conceptual confusions over the intelligibility of action at a distance, or from bafflement (not remedied until Hertz) over the nature of force. So too, Sherrington's towering achievement in explaining the integrative action of synapses in the spinal cord, and thereby eliminating, once and for all, the confused idea of a 'spinal soul', was perfectly compatible with conceptual confusions concerning the 'cerebral soul' or mind and its relation to the brain. Similarly, Penfield's extraordinary achievements in identifying functional localization in the cortex, as well as in developing brilliant neurosurgical techniques, were perfectly compatible with extensive confusions about the relation between the mind and the brain and about the 'highest brain function' (an idea borrowed from Hughlings Jackson).

In short, conceptual entanglement *can* coexist with flourishing science. This may appear puzzling. If the science can flourish despite such conceptual confusions, why should scientists care about them? Hidden reefs do not imply that the seas are not navigable, only that they are dangerous. The moot question is how running on these reefs is manifest. Conceptual confusions may be exhibited in different ways and at different points in the investigation. In some cases, the conceptual unclarity may affect neither the cogency of the questions nor the fruitfulness of the experiments, but only the understanding of the results of the experiments and their theoretical implications. So, for example, Newton embarked on the *Optics* in quest of insight into the character of colour. The research was a permanent contribution to science. But his conclusion that 'colours are sensations in the sensorium' demonstrates failure to achieve the kind of understanding he craved. For, whatever colours are, they are not 'sensations in the sensorium'. So in so far as Newton cared about *understanding* the results of his research, then he had good reason for caring about the conceptual confusions under which he laboured – for they stood in the way of an adequate understanding.

In other cases, however, the conceptual confusion does not so happily bracket the empirical research. Misguided questions may well render research futile (examples will be examined in relation to mental imagery (§6.3.1) and voluntary movement (§8.2)). Rather differently, misconstrual of concepts and conceptual structures will sometimes produce research that is by no means futile, but that fails to show what it was designed to show (examples will be discussed in relation to memory (§§5.2.1–5.2.2) and to emotions and appetites (§7.1)). In such cases, the science may not be flourishing quite as much as it appears to be. It requires conceptual investigation to locate the problems and to eliminate them.

Are these conceptual confusions *unavoidable*? Not at all. The whole point of writing this book is to show how to avoid them. But, of course, they cannot be avoided while leaving everything else intact. They *can be* avoided – but if they are, then certain kinds of questions will no longer be asked, since they will be recognized as resting on a misunderstanding. As Hertz put it in the wonderful introduction to his *Principles of Mechanics*: 'When these painful contradictions are removed, . . . our minds, no longer vexed, will cease to ask illegitimate questions.' Equally, certain kinds of inferences will no longer be drawn from a given body of empirical research, since it will be realized to have little or no bearing on the matter which it was meant to illuminate, even though it may bear on *something else*.

If there are problematic concepts, can they not be replaced by others that serve the same explanatory function? A scientist is always free to introduce new concepts if he finds existing ones inadequate or insufficiently refined. But our concern in this book is not with the use of new technical concepts. We are concerned with the misuse of old, non-technical concepts – concepts of mind and body, thought and imagination, sensation and perception, knowledge and memory, voluntary movement, and consciousness and self-consciousness. There is nothing inadequate about these concepts relative to the purposes they serve. There is no reason for thinking that they need to be replaced in the contexts that are of concern to us. What are problematic are neuroscientists' misconstruals of them and the misunderstandings consequently engendered. These are remediable by a correct account of the logico-grammatical character of the concepts in question. And this is what we have tried to supply.

Granted that neuroscientists may not be using these common or garden concepts the way the man in the street does, with what right can philosophy claim to correct them? How can philosophy so confidently judge the clarity and coherence of concepts as deployed by competent scientists? How can philosophy be in a position to claim that certain assertions made by sophisticated neuroscientists *make no sense*? We shall resolve such methodological qualms in the following pages. But some initial clarification here may remove some doubts. What truth and falsity is to science, sense and nonsense is to philosophy. Observational and theoretical error result in falsehood; conceptual error results in lack of sense. How can one investigate the bounds of sense? Only by examining the use of words. Nonsense is often generated when an expression is used contrary to the rules for its use. The expression in question may be an ordinary, non-technical expression, in which case the rules for its use can be elicited from its standard employment and received explanations of its meaning. Or it may be a technical term of art, in which case the rules for its use must be elicited from the theorist's introduction of the term and the explanations he offers of its stipulated use. Both kinds of term can be misused, and when they are, nonsense ensues – a form of words that is excluded from the language. For either nothing has been stipulated as to what the term means in the aberrant context in question, or this form of words is actually excluded by a rule specifying that there is no such thing as . . . (e.g. that there is no such thing as 'east of the North Pole'), that this is a form of words that has no use. Nonsense is also commonly generated when an existing expression is given a new, perhaps technical or quasi-technical use, and the new use is inadvertently crossed with the old – for example, inferences are drawn from propositions containing the new term which could only licitly be drawn from the use of the old one. It is the task of the conceptual critic to identify such transgressions of the bounds of sense. It is, of course, not enough to show that a certain scientist has used a term contrary to its ordinary use – for he may well be using the term in a new sense. The critic must show that the scientist intends using the term in its customary sense and has not done so, or that he intends using it in a new sense but has inadvertently crossed the new sense with the old. The wayward scientist should, whenever possible, be condemned out of his own mouth. We address methodological qualms in detail both in chapter 3, section 3, and in chapter 14.

The final misconception against which we wish to warn is the idea that our reflections are unremittingly negative. All we are concerned with, it might be thought, is criticizing.

Our work may appear at a superficial glance to be no more than a destructive undertaking that promises neither assistance nor a new way forward. Worse, it may even appear to be engineering a confrontation between philosophy and cognitive neuroscience. *Nothing could be further from the truth.*

We have written this book in admiration for the achievements of twentieth-century neuroscience, and out of a desire to assist the subject. But the *only* ways in which a conceptual investigation can assist an empirical subject are by identifying conceptual error (if it obtains) and by providing a map that will help prevent empirical researchers from wandering off the high roads of sense. Each of our investigations has two aspects to it. On the one hand, we have tried to identify conceptual problems and entanglements in important current theories of perception, memory, imagination, emotion and volition. Moreover, we argue that much contemporary writing on the nature of consciousness and self-consciousness is bedevilled by conceptual difficulties. This aspect of our investigations is indeed negative and critical. On the other hand, we have endeavoured, from case to case, to provide a perspicuous representation of the conceptual field of each of the problematic concepts. This is a constructive endeavour. We hope that these conceptual overviews will assist neuroscientists in their reflections antecedent to the design of their experiments. However, it cannot be the task of a conceptual investigation to propose empirical hypotheses that might solve the empirical problems faced by scientists. To complain that a philosophical investigation into cognitive neuroscience has not con-tributed a new neuroscientific theory is like complaining to a mathematician that a new theorem he has proved is not a new physical theory.

It is improbable that many neuroscientists will wish to read a 450-page conceptual investigation from cover to cover. Consequently, we have tried to make our chapters on select psychological concepts as self-contained as possible. We have done this in the hope that the book will serve as a conceptual reference work for cognitive neuroscientists who wish to check the contour lines of the psychological concept relevant to their investigation. This has, of course, meant that there is a degree of repetition between certain chapters. This is, we hope, warranted by the objective.

The chapters of the book are accompanied by italicized marginalia indicating the subject under discussion in the correlated paragraph or paragraphs. The purpose of this is to facilitate surveyability, to make it easier to follow the steps in the argument, and to assist in locating arguments. The section headings in the table of contents are accompanied by the italicized names of neuroscientists (and occasionally philosophers who concern them-selves with neuroscientific and cognitive scientific matters) whose theories are either discussed in some detail or mentioned *en passant* in the course of the chapter. This will, we hope, help the reader to locate the themes and discussions that are of specific interest with ease.

Part I

Philosophical Problems in Neuroscience: Their Historical and Conceptual Roots

1

The Early Growth of Neuroscientific Knowledge: The Integrative Action of the Nervous System

The conceptual framework for early investigations into the biological basis for human sensory, volitional and intellectual capacities was set by Aristotle's philosophical writings on the *psuchē*. The early growth of neuroscientific knowledge was dominated by the question of how the contraction of muscles involved in voluntary movements of limbs is effected. However, Aristotle's own rudimentary investigations, which led him to believe that the blood vessels initiate muscle contraction, were a false start. It was, above all, Galen's much later discoveries of the nerve supply to muscles from the spinal cord that made it clear that it is the nerves that carry out this function. Galen's work initiated 2,000 years of enquiry into how the spinal cord and brain are involved in voluntary movement and into the reflex origins of some movements. The identification of motor and sensory spinal nerves, the role of the spinal cord in reflex movements, and the relationship between the action of the brain and the spinal cord in voluntary and reflex movement were all resolved by experiments. These involved observations on muscles and limbs following lesions to different parts of the nervous system. In this way a conception evolved of how the functions of the brain, spinal cord and nerves are integrated to give the final motor output.

The conceptual framework within which neuroscientific knowledge grew originated in Aristotelian thought, but it was subsequently transformed by the Cartesian revolution in the seventeenth century. In this chapter we shall adumbrate the development of ideas concerning the neural basis of animate functions, concentrating increasingly upon what Sherrington, the greatest of neuroscientists, called 'the integrative action of the nervous system', as it applies to movement. This sketch of the history of the slow growth of knowledge about the nervous system and its operations will display some of the conceptual difficulties encountered by natural philosophers over the centuries as they grappled with the problems concerning the biological foundations of characteristic powers of animate beings in general, and humans in particular. As we shall see, the roots of current conceptual difficulties in cognitive neuroscience are buried deep in the past. Grasping this aspect of our intellectual and scientific heritage will help to bring current conceptual problems into sharp focus. These problems are the principal concern of this book.

It might be asked why we do not concentrate more on the role of the great sensory systems, such as vision, in our historical sketch of the integrative action of the nervous system. The reason is that the early neuroscientists took up the challenge of understanding the motor system first, for it allowed experimentation which they could undertake to test their ideas with the techniques then available. This was not the case with the sensory systems. These pioneers saw the need to integrate their account of the sensory systems into their evolving knowledge of muscular contraction and movement. This led them to speculate on the relationship between vision and motor performance. It did not, however, add much to our understanding of how vision occurs, a subject that had to wait for techniques that became available only in the nineteenth and especially the twentieth centuries.

1.1 Aristotle, Galen and Nemesius: The Origins of the Ventricular Doctrine

Aristotle's conception of the psuchē   Aristotle is the first great biologist whose treatises and observational data survive. His philosophical world picture shaped European thought until and, in certain respects, beyond the scientific revolution of the seventeenth century. So although his knowledge of the nervous system was almost non-existent, his fundamental conceptions of animate life are indispensable to an understanding of the reasoning of the early scientists, such as Galen and Nemesius, who probed the nature of the nervous system and its role in determining the cognitive, cogitative, affective and volitional powers of man. Moreover, as we shall see, Aristotle's conception of the nature of man, of the relation between organs and functions, between the body and the distinctive capacities that constitute what he called 'the *psuchē*' was profound. The Aristotelian conception of the *psuchē* and the Cartesian conception of the mind, which displaced it in the seventeenth century, constitute in certain respects two fundamentally different ways of thinking about human nature, which have informed neuroscientific reflection on the integrative action of the nervous system throughout the ages.

The psuchē *as the form of the natural body*   Aristotle ascribed to each living organism a *psuchē*. The *psuchē* was conceived to be *the form of a natural body that has life*.[1] It was also characterized as *the first actuality of a natural body that has organs* (*DA* 412^{b}5–6). Aristotle's technical terminology needs elucidation.

In its common meaning, 'psuche' signified 'breath' or 'life breath' (which one 'expires' at the moment of death or in a faint), as did the later Latin term 'anima', by which it was translated. It is linked with the idea of wind and of vital power. It was a pre-Aristotelian philosophical innovation to detach *psuchē* from such associations. It was an Aristotelian

---

[1] Aristotle, *De Anima* 412^{a}20. Subsequent references to this treatise in the text will be flagged '*DA*'.

innovation to link it firmly to all organisms as *the principle of life that informs each living being*. Although 'psuche' is commonly translated as 'soul', it is important to realize that, as used by Aristotle, 'psuche' has none of the religious and ethical connotations of our term 'soul'. *Psuchē* is 'the principle of animal life' (*DA* 402ᵃ7–8), and indeed of vegetal life too. For plants, no less than animals, have a *psuche*. It would be equally misleading to translate 'psuche' as 'mind', since the mind and mental powers are not associated, as *psuchē* is, with growth, nutrition or reproduction, which characterize all forms of living things. Nor is *psuchē* essentially linked with consciousness, as is the Cartesian conception of the mind. The term 'psuche', which, in conformity with tradition, we shall in the sequel translate as 'soul', is a *biological concept* – not a religious or an ethical one. It will be important to keep this in mind not only in regard to Aristotle, but also in respect of neuroscientific debates in the seventeenth and eighteenth centuries on the existence of a 'spinal soul' (see §1.4).

Form distinguished from matter   Aristotle introduced the distinction between form and matter to provide the theoretical apparatus necessary for describing persistence through change. Substances, irrespective of whether they are space-occupying things of a given kind (such as a rock, a tree, a horse, an axe or a man) or whether they are partitioned quantities of stuff of a certain kind (of water, bronze, wine or cheese, which may occur as a drop, a nugget, a bottle or a slice) undergo change. The change may be 'accidental' or 'substantial' ('essential'). 'Accidental change' is a change to the non-essential properties ('accidents') of a given substance. It is the acquisition of a new attribute or the loss of an existing attribute – as when a tree grows taller, an axe becomes blunter, a man becomes fatter, and as when a pool of water becomes warm, or a certain quantity of gold melts. Accidental change is compatible with the continued identity of the substance. Substantial change occurs when a substance changes its essential properties, as when wine turns to vinegar, or milk to cheese, and equally, when a living creature dies. Substantial change is incompatible with the continued existence of the substance in question – if the wine changes into vinegar, then there is no more wine, and if a horse dies, it ceases to exist, and only its remains, a dead body, are left behind. Aristotle introduced the notion of *matter* as a technical term to pick out *that which has a capacity for substantial change*, and *form* to pick out *that which makes a certain matter into the kind of substance it is*. Accordingly there are both *accidental forms* (e.g. the accidental forms of the different colours which a thing may acquire or lose, while remaining the very same thing), and *substantial forms* (e.g. of wine or vinegar, of a plant or of a man). When a substance undergoes accidental change, it retains its substantial form through change.

Form and matter are not parts of a thing   It is important to realize that although individual things of any given kind are said to be both form and matter, form and matter are not *parts* of a thing. Matter cannot exist without form – its form may change, accidentally or essentially, but it must have some form or other. Equally, form cannot exist without matter – for the form of X-ness to exist is just for there to be some substance that is X. It may well be argued that this conceptual apparatus is well suited to discussing stuffs and their transformation (e.g. milk to cheese), and perhaps also (with adjustment) to investigating things and their constitutive stuffs (e.g. a sword and the steel from which it is made), as well as (with different adjustments) things and their constitutive parts (e.g. a house and the bricks of which it is made). It is questionable whether it is very well suited to being extended to the description of things and their capacities.[2] Be that as it may, Aristotle did so extend it in characterizing the soul as the form of the living body, and in simultaneously conceiving of the soul as the first actuality of the living body.

The psuchē *of a creature is constituted by its first actualities*

The actualities (*entelechiai*) of a substance are those things which it is or is doing at a given time. Among its actualities are (rather confusingly) its powers (i.e. the active and passive potentialities which it actually possesses). Such powers may be possessed without being exercised at a given time – the sighted do not become blind when they sleep, and English speakers do not cease to know English when they are silent. Aristotle refers to the unexercised dispositional power (*hexis*) of an animal as a first actuality (e.g. being sighted, knowing English), by contrast with the exercise of a dispositional power (the actual activity of, for example, watching something or speaking English), which he refers to as a second actuality (*energeia*). When the soul is said to be the actuality of the body, it is so only as first actuality. For a living creature has a soul – that is, possesses its distinctive defining powers – when it is asleep no less than when it is a wake.

The psuchē *or soul is neither part of a living being nor an additional entity related to it*

So, the phrase 'to have a soul' does not signify a relation of possession between an agent and an entity, as does 'to have a car'. Furthermore, the soul does not stand to the body as the brain does, for it is not a part of the body. How, then, should these things be conceived? Aristotle gives a pair of analogies. The matter of an axe is the wood and iron of which it is made. Its form is its capacity to chop. The axe's first actuality is its power to chop wood, which it possesses inasmuch as its constituent matter has been appropriately fashioned into blade and handle. Its power to chop cannot exist independently of the matter (wood and iron) or the parts (handle and blade) of which it consists. (But, of course, an axe is an inanimate artefact, and inanimate things have no soul.) Similarly, Aristotle suggests, we can compare the relationship between an animal and its soul with the relationship between an eye and the power of sight. If the eye were an animal, as it were, then its soul would be sight (*DA* 412^{b}18); although, of course, the eye is not an animal, but a part of an animal – and accordingly, while it has a function, it has no soul.

The psuchē *or soul, as first actuality of a living body with organs, consists of its defining functions*

The soul consists of the essential, defining functions of a living thing with organs.[3] The essential functions of a living being can be exercised only because of its possession of organs, which confer upon it the potentiality of exercising the functions of life appropriate to the kind of living being it is. It is by the use of its organs that its second actualities are exhibited.

---

[2] For a discussion of this point, see J. L. Ackrill, 'Aristotle's definition of *psuchē*', repr. in J. Barnes, M. Schofield and R. Sorabji (eds), *Articles on Aristotle*, vol. 4: *Psychology and Aesthetics* (Duckworth, London, 1979), pp. 65–75.

[3] We disregard here Aristotle's formulation 'of a natural body *that has life potentially*' (*DA* 412^{a}20).

Nutritive, sensitive and rational soul distinguished

Aristotle distinguished a hierarchy of three kinds of soul in nature. The *nutritive soul* is the fundamental principle of biological life as such. It 'is the most primitive and widely distributed power of soul, being indeed that one in virtue of which all are said to have life' (*DA* 415ª23–6). It consists of the powers of growth, nutrition and reproduction. Plants possess only a nutritive soul. Their various organs (roots, leaves, stamens, etc.) enable them to exercise the essential functions of vegetal life. Animals have not only nutritive powers, but also powers of perception, desire and locomotion. They are accordingly said to possess a *sensitive soul*. The possession of a sensitive soul presupposes possession of the powers of a nutritive soul, but not vice versa. Mankind, however, is unique in nature in possessing not only the powers of a nutritive and a sensitive soul, but also the powers of a rational soul. These are thought (reasoning) and will (rational volition).

The psuchē *or soul is neither an agent nor an entity, but the essential, defining powers of a living thing*

The *psuchē*, therefore, is not an 'inner agent' – the subject of experience and the originator of action, animating the body but independent of it. It is not a substance or part of a substance. It is, Aristotle insists, 'not a body but something of a body' (*DA* 414ª20–1). In general, the form of a thing is not a kind of entity. It is not made of anything, and for a form to exist just is for a thing thus *in-formed* to exist. So too, the *psuchē*, which is the form of the living creature, is neither material, like the body or brain, nor immaterial, like a ghost. Body and soul 'make up' an animal, not as chassis and engine make up a car, but 'just as the pupil and sight make up an eye, so in this case the soul and body make up an animal' (*DA* 413ª1–2).[4] To have a soul is not to possess something or to be related to something, it is to be, as it were, 'en-souled' (*empsuchos*).

The Aristotelian and Cartesian conceptions of the soul contrasted

Precisely because Aristotle did not conceive of the soul as a separate entity from the body, but rather as the powers of the living being, he did not make the mistake of attributing to the soul the exercise of the distinctive powers of the creature whose soul it is. Indeed, he noted that 'to say that the soul is angry is as if one were to say that the soul weaves or builds. For it is surely better not to say that the soul pities, learns or thinks, but that the man does these with his soul' (*DA* 408ᵇ12–15).[5] This observation marks a crucial divide between the Aristotelian conception and the later Cartesian one, inasmuch as Descartes ascribed all psychological functions to the mind (see §1.2). It also marks a crucial divide between Aristotelian thought and contemporary conceptions, inasmuch as current neuroscientists (and others) ascribe a multitude of psychological (especially cognitive and volitional) functions to the brain (see §3.1). To do so is in effect to ascribe to a part of an animal attributes which it makes sense to ascribe only to the animal as a whole.

Aristotle's conception was altogether different from that of his teacher Plato, who did indeed conceive of the soul as an entity separate from the body. Within the framework of

---

[4] It should be noted that Aristotle held that a sightless eye is no more an eye than a painted eye, just as a corpse is no more an animal than a statue.

[5] Note that when Aristotle says that we do these things *with* our soul, this is *not* like doing something with our hands or eyes, but rather like doing something with our talents and abilities.

Platonic and, much later, of Cartesian dualism, the pressing – and indeed insoluble – problem is to give a coherent account of the relationship between these two entities, and also to explain the essential unity of a human being. These questions cannot arise within the Aristotelian biological framework of thought. Indeed, Aristotle sapiently explains, 'we can dismiss as unnecessary the question whether the soul and the body are one: it is as though we were to ask whether the wax and its shape are one, or generally the matter of a thing and that of which it is the matter' (*DA* 412^{b}6–7). In short, to speak of the soul or *psuchē* of a creature is to speak of that creature's essential powers. A thing of a given kind will retain its soul as long as it can continue to exercise its characteristic functions. To destroy its powers to engage in its essential activities is to destroy the thing itself.[6]

Aristotle's conception of the sensus communis   In his account of perception, Aristotle distinguished the five senses (sense-faculties) and sense-organs that correspond to (four of) them. Of course, the different sensory powers are all powers of a single unified being, the animal, with a single unified perceptual power. The senses are, Aristotle wrote, 'inseparable, yet separate in account' – that is, a different account is needed of the operations and mechanisms of each, but they are all constitutive elements of a unified perceptual power, and the sense-organs are all parts of a connected apparatus that he thought to be centred on the heart. The animal actually perceives only when the impulses initiated by impact on a sense-organ or any part of the body sensitive to touch are transmitted by the blood to the central sensorium in the heart. Aristotle in effect allocates to the heart the unifying functions which we allocate to the brain.[7] He characterized this locus of our perceptual capacities as a 'controlling sensory organ'[8] – wrongly so, for we do not perceive with the 'sensorium' (no matter whether it be the heart or the brain) in the sense in which we see with our eyes and hear with our ears, and it is not a *sense-organ* in the sense in which the eyes and ears are.

----

[6] We disregard here the complexities, and incoherences, that arise with regard to Aristotle's distinction between the active and passive intellect and the intimation that the active intellect may be capable of existing without a body (*DA* 429^{a}18–29, 430^{a}18–25). These passages were crucial for the later scholastic synthesis of Aristotelian philosophy of mind with Christian doctrine concerning the immortality of the soul.

[7] For his reasoning, see *De Partibus Animalium* 647^{a}22–34. In this respect he differed from the Hippocratic tradition. The Hippocratic lecture on epilepsy noted that 'It ought to be generally known that the source of our pleasure, merriment, laughter and amusement, as of our grief, pain, anxiety and tears, is none other than the brain. It is especially the organ which enables us to think, see and hear, and to distinguish the ugly and the beautiful, the bad and the good, pleasant and unpleasant. . . . It is the brain too which is the seat of madness and delirium, of the fears and frights which assail us, often by night, but sometimes even by day; it is there where lies the cause of insomnia and sleepwalking' ('The sacred disease', §17, in G. E. R. Lloyd (ed.), *Hippocratic Writings* (Penguin Books, Harmondsworth, 1978). The Hippocratic insight is wonderful; the physiological reasoning is, however, no less erroneous than Aristotle's reasoning in support of his different hypothesis.

[8] Aristotle, *De Somno* 455^{a}21. This is the Barnes translation; an alternative translation of the sentence in which this term appears is 'For there exists a single sense-faculty, and the master organ is single'.

Aristotle emphasized that although we have different sense-faculties, and although some objects of sense (the so-called *proper sensibles*, e.g. colour, sound, smell, taste) are uniquely discovered by a given sense-faculty (e.g. colour by sight, sound by hearing), others, the so-called *common sensibles* (e.g. motion, shape, size, number, unity), are discernible by more than one sense. The latter fact is one among a number of not wholly perspicuous reasons for postulating a 'primary faculty of perception' or 'primary capacity for sense', which he occasionally refers to as the 'common sense'[9] (and which later writers right down to the eighteenth century refer to as the 'sensus communis').

The sensus communis *– a master organ for unifying sensibles in perception*

The *sensus communis* is required, it seems, to explain how we can perceive common sensibles *by* perceiving proper sensibles (we could not see shape if we could not also see colour), and perceive them as unified attributes. For although we perceive shape, for example, both by sight and by touch, sight and touch are severally ways of detecting one and the same attribute: namely, shape (for we do not perceive, as it were, two distinct attributes, visual shape and tactile shape). Moreover, although when we perceive, say, a rose, we perceive different proper sensibles with our different sense-organs and their corresponding faculties, we perceive them as unified qualities of a single object.[10] This, according to Aristotle, is a further reason for assuming a 'single sense-faculty' and a 'master organ' – the heart. (Arguably, what we have here is a foreshadowing of contemporary neuroscientists' preoccupation with the so-called binding problem, but without their Cartesian and Lockean confusion of supposing that the sensorium must produce an internal image or representation.[11]) Other reasons for which a *sensus communis* is held to be needed are as follows:

(i) We do not see that we are seeing or hear that we are hearing. Nevertheless, Aristotle held, we do perceive that we are seeing or hearing – and that is one of the functions of the common sense.[12] (Some contemporary neuroscientists and neuro-psychologists engaged in the investigation of 'blind-sight' assign to some part of the brain the function of a self-monitoring device to fulfil the same function.[13]) However, the reasoning is faulty, since we do not *perceive* that we see or hear; rather, when we see or hear, we can *say* that we do so – but not because we in any sense perceive that we

---

[9] His term is *aisthēsis koinē*, which occurs only in *De Anima* 425ª27, *De Memoria* 450ª10, and *De Partibus Animalium* 686ª27.

[10] Aristotle, *De Sensu* 449ª5–11.

[11] See, e.g., F. Crick, *The Astonishing Hypothesis* (Touchstone, London, 1995), p. 22; A. Damasio, *The Feeling of What Happens* (Heinemann, London, 1999), p. 320; E. Kandel and R. Wurtz, 'Constructing the visual image', in Kandel, Schwartz and Jessell (eds), *Principles of Neural Science* (Elsevier, New York, 2001), p. 492. For a discussion of the binding problem, see §4.2.3.

[12] Aristotle, *De Somno* 455ª15–20.

[13] e.g. Lawrence Weiskrantz, *Blindsight: A Case Study and Implications* (Oxford University Press, Oxford, 1986), and *idem*, 'Varieties of residual experiences', *Quarterly Journal of Experimental Psychology*, 32 (1980), pp. 365–86. See below §14.3.1.

do. This form of self-awareness needs elucidation, but arguably not by this route (see chapter 12).

(ii)   By means of the sense of sight, we discriminate white from red, and by means of taste, we distinguish sweet from sour. But, Aristotle curiously observes, we also discriminate white from sweet and red from sour – and that neither by sight nor by taste.[14] So, he infers, there must be some master faculty of perception which is employed to fulfil this function (*DA* 426[b]).

(iii)   Since sleep affects all the sense-faculties (i.e. we do not see, hear, taste, smell or feel while asleep), waking and sleeping must be affections of one single unifying sense-faculty and controlling sense-organ.[15]

Finally, Aristotle also allocated to the *sensus communis* the functions of (a) apprehension of time; (b) image formation by the imagination, or *fantasia*; (c) memory (which, in his view, presupposes both (a) and (b)); and (d) dreaming.[16] Items (b) – (d) are all functions which presuppose antecedent perception, but do not require any current use of a perceptual organ. They are, as it were, processes involving 'decaying sense' (or, as we might put it, 'brain traces' or 'engrams').

In these early reflections on the human faculties, on the conceptual structure necessary to describe them and their exercise, and in these arguments on the need for a *sensus communis*, we can see the beginnings of systematic scientific thought on the integrative action of the nervous system.

Two further points before we leave Aristotle:

The conception of pneuma   First, like Empedocles, Aristotle believed that there were four sublunary elements: earth, water, air and fire. To this list he added a further supra-lunary element, 'the first element' or 'the first body', subsequently called 'the aether', from which heavenly bodies are constituted. The sublunary elements naturally move rectilinearly (upwards or downwards). The motion of the first element, or aether, differs: it is (a) eternal, and (b) circular. There is some suggestion that Aristotle may have given some sublunary role to the first element in his biology. In *De Generatione Animalium*, he wrote:

> Now it is true that the faculty of all kinds of soul seems to have a connection with a matter different from and more divine than the so-called elements . . . All have in their semen that which causes it to be productive; I mean what is called vital heat. This is not fire nor any such force, but it is the breath (*pneuma*) included in the semen and the

---

[14] The argument is curious, inasmuch as it is unclear in what sense he thinks we *discriminate* white from sweet. To be sure, we possess the faculties to see white things and distinguish them from other coloured things, and to taste sweet things and distinguish them from things with other tastes, and we (language-users) also possess the concepts of white (and other colours) and sweet (and other gustatory qualities). But we do not *discriminate* white things from sweet things; nor do we need any further organ to differentiate white from sweet (for what would it be to confuse them?).

[15] Aristotle, *De Somno* 455[a].

[16] Aristotle, *De Memoria* 450[a]9–14.

foam-like, and the natural principle in the breath, being analogous to the element of the stars. (736^{b}29–737^{a}1)

It is difficult to know what to make of this (let alone how it is meant to be applied to the soul of plants). Cicero, writing some centuries later on the basis of lost works of Aristotle, claimed that

> He thinks that there is a certain fifth nature, of which mind is made; for thinking, foreseeing, learning, teaching, making a discovery, holding so much in memory – all these and more, loving, hating, feeling pain and joy – such things as these, he believes, do not belong to any one of the four elements. He introduces a fifth kind, without a name, and thus calls the mind itself '*endelecheia*', using a new name – as it were, a certain continual, eternal motion.[17]

Aristotle appears, therefore, to have associated the capacities which constitute the soul with a 'divine' element that is incorruptible, which is a kind of vital heat or breath (*pneuma*) present in semen and responsible for generation. This pneuma was converted in the heart in to *vital pneuma*, which was then conducted along blood vessels to muscles, where it effected contraction. The concept of *pneuma*, as we shall see, was to have a long, confused history throughout the struggle to clarify the integrative action of the nervous system.

Second, it is noteworthy, and relevant to the conception of the 'spinal soul' that preoccupied neuroscientists in the eighteenth century (see §1.4), that Aristotle observed that 'certain insects go on living when divided into segments'. This shows, he argued, that 'each of the segments has a soul in it identical in species, though not numerically; for both of the segments for a time possess the power of sensation and local movement. That this does not last is not surprising, for they no longer possess the organs necessary for self-maintenance' (*DA* 411^{a}17ff.) The reasoning is that since the two halves of the insect continue to display sensitivity and capacity for motion, each half must have its own sensitive (and motor) soul. It is important (and relevant to the eighteenth-century debate on the spinal soul) that Aristotle did *not* think that the whole insect consists of a single 'master soul', as it were, and apart from that, two additional souls, one in each half of its body. Rather, the whole insect has a certain range of capacities, and if it is cut in half, the two halves will then have a certain more limited range of capacities.

Galen: motor and sensory centres   Aristotle's ideas had to be modified with the discovery by Galen (130–200) and his students in the second and third centuries AD that nerves arising from the brain and the spinal cord are necessary for the initiation of muscle contraction.

---

[17] Cicero, *Tusculan Disputations* 1.10.22, quoted by D. Furley, 'Aristotle the philosopher of nature', in D. Furley (ed.), *From Aristotle to Augustine*, vol. iv of *Routledge History of Philosophy* (Routledge, London, 1999), p. 16. Cicero's 'endelecheia' is the same as the *entelecheia* mentioned earlier. Note that Cicero must surely be mistaken in ascribing to Aristotle the view that the soul is *made* of anything.

They changed the Aristotelian account so that the *vital pneuma* was delivered by blood vessels to the brain and converted there to *psychic pneuma*, the composition of which was unclear, whence it was conducted along nerves to be transmitted to muscles. Thus, 'The nerves which in consequence enjoy the role of conduits, carry to the muscles the forces that they draw from the brain as from a source.'[18] This allowed the muscles to contract, probably as a consequence of their ballooning as they filled with the *psychic pneuma*.[19]

Galen distinguished motor from sensory nerves

Hence Galen introduced the idea of *motor nerves* derived from the spinal cord.[20] As a consequence of his observations on injured chariot drivers, he also distinguished *sensory* from *motor nerves*. These were differentiated in terms of their relative 'hardness', motor nerves being 'hard' and sensory nerves 'soft'.[21] The hard motor nerves were uniquely associated with their origins in the spinal cord, the soft sensory nerves with the brain.[22]

Using the term 'soul' in an Aristotelian sense, Galen considered that there was a 'motor soul' and a 'sensory soul', which were not to be considered as two different entities but as two different functions or principles of activity.[23] According to this conception, and given the assumed relationship between the relative hardness/softness of nerves, the motor/sensory differentiation and the fact that the hardest nerves are found uniquely associated with the spinal cord (caudal), the idea of two separate souls or principles of activity, one associated with the spinal cord and one with the brain is natural (although it is unlikely that Galen succumbed to this temptation). It was to have considerable vogue in the eighteenth century to explain the existence of continuing spinal cord reflexes in decorticate animals. However, by then the conception of the soul had changed and had become entwined with that of consciousness.

Galen: the functional localization of the rational soul in the ventricles   This association of the pure sensory nerves with the brain, and the fact that these nerves were very soft, carried with it important implications for brain function.[24] It is clear that Galen associated the whole brain, and not just the ventricles, with the mental capacities of humans. In *On the Usefulness of the Parts of the Body* he states: 'In those commentaries I have given the demonstrations proving that the rational soul is lodged in the enkephalon; that this is the

---

[18] C. Galen, *Du Movement des muscles*, sect. I, ch. 1, French translation. by C. Daremberg, in *Oeuvres anatomiques, physiologiques et médicales de Galen* (Ballière, Paris, 1854–6), vol. 2, p. 323.

[19] For further detail, see M. R. Bennett, 'The early history of the synapse: from Plato to Sherrington', *Brain Research Bulletin*, 50 (1999), pp. 95–118.

[20] C. Galen, *Des Lieux affectés*, sect. IV, ch. 3, tr. Daremberg in *Oeuvres*, vol. 2, p. 590; C. Galen, *Utilité de parties du corps*, sect. IX, chs 13–14, tr. Daremberg in *Oeuvres*, vol. 1, pp. 593–7; see also W. H. L. Duckworth, *Galen on Anatomical Procedures*, (ed.) M. C. Lyons and B. Towers (Cambridge University Press, Cambridge, 1962), pp. 22–6.

[21] C. Galen, *Utilité de parties du corps*, sect. IX, ch. 14, tr. Daremberg in *Oeuvres*, vol. 1, pp. 597f.

[22] C. Galen, *Hippocrates librum de alimento commentarius*, sect. III, ch.1, in K. G. Kühn (ed.), *Opera Omnia Claudii Galeni* (Cnobloch, Leipzig, 1821–33), vol. 15, p. 257.

[23] C. Galen, *De Symptomatum Differentis*, sect. VII, in Kühn (ed.), *Opera Omnia*, vol. 7, pp. 55–6.

[24] C. Galen, *Utilité de Parties du Corps*, sect. VIII, ch. 6, tr. Daremberg in *Oeuvres*, vol. 1, pp. 541–3.

part with which we reason; that a very large quantity of psychic pneuma is contained in it; and that this pneuma acquires its own special quality from elaboration in the enkephalon' ('enkephalon' is a cognate of 'enkephalos', meaning 'that which is in the head'). So Galen attributed to the brain those functions in perception that Aristotle had attributed to the heart. However, this did not distinguish between the respective roles of the cortex and the ventricles. Galen did not ascribe to the cortex any special function with regard to the higher mental powers such as reasoning, for he observed that donkeys have a highly convoluted brain. Consequently, he thought that the cerebral convolutions could not be associated with intelligence. Instead, he identified the ventricles, rather than the cortex, as the source of such powers as reasoning.[25] Galen enjoyed absolute authority for more than a millennium. It therefore comes as no surprise that the association of the ventricles with higher mental functions was elaborated in detail in the following centuries.

Nemesius: the formal attribution of all mental functions to the ventricles   It was Nemesius (*c.* 390), the bishop of Emesa (now Homs) in Syria, who developed the doctrine of the ventricular localization of all mental functions, rather than just the intellectual ones. Unlike Galen, he allocated perception and imagination to the two lateral ventricles (the anterior ventricles), placing intellectual abilities in the middle ventricle, reserving the posterior ventricles for memory. Hence the idea that imagination/perception, reasoning and memory are to be found in the lateral, third and fourth ventricles respectively.

Nemesius claimed that this localization was based not on a whim but on solid evidence, for he states that

> The most convincing proof is that derived from studying the activities of the various parts of the brain. If the front ventricles have suffered any kind of lesion, the senses are impaired but the faculty of intellect continues as before. It is when the middle of the brain is affected that the mind is deranged, but then the senses are left in possession of their natural function. If it is the cerebellum that is damaged, only loss of memory follows, while sensation and thought take no harm. But if the middle of the brain and the cerebellum share in the damage, in addition to the front ventricles, sensation, thought, and memory all founder together, with the result that the living subject is in danger of death.[26]

In relation to the anterior ventricles, he states:

> Now, as organs, the faculty of imagination[27] has, first, the front lobes of the brain and the psychic spirit contained in them, then the nerves impregnated with psychic spirit that proceed from them, and, finally, the whole construction of the sense-organs. These organs of sense are five in number, but perception is one, and is an attribute of the soul.

---

[25] C. Galen, *Des Lieux affectés*, sect. IV, ch. 3, tr. Daremberg in *Oeuvres*, vol. 2, p. 590.

[26] Nemesius, 'The nature of man', in *Cyril of Jerusalem and Nemesius of Emesa*, tr. and ed. William Telfer (Westminster Press, Philadelphia, 1955), pp. 341–2.

[27] Presumably by the word 'imagination' here Nemesius means sensibility.

> By means of the sense-organs, and their power of feeling, the soul takes knowledge of what goes on in them.[28]

This localization of the various mental functions in the ventricles became known as the ventricular doctrine.

The soul taken as spiritual substance rather than as first actuality   It is noteworthy that Nemesius conceived of the soul in very different terms from Aristotle and his followers. Nemesius, as a Christian, was more influenced by Neo-Platonism than by Aristotelian philosophy (he was attracted by the doctrine of the pre-existence of the soul, and also by metempsychosis). He did not conceive of the soul as the form of the body, but as a separate, indestructible spiritual substance, linked with the body in a 'union without confusion' in which the identity of each substance is fully preserved. Consequently, he did not attribute perception and cognition to the human being (i.e. to the whole animal), but rather to the soul. The attribution of psychological attributes to a subordinate part of a living creature deviates importantly from the Aristotelian conception. As we shall see, the tendency to explain how a living being perceives, thinks, feels emotions, etc. by reference to a subordinate part of that being's perceiving, thinking, feeling emotions, etc. runs like a canker through the history of neuroscience to this very day.

One thousand years of the ventricular doctrine   The ventricular doctrine for the localization of psychological functions, established in the first centuries of the first millennium, was still accepted and promulgated by scholars at the beginning of the second millennium. Thus Avicenna (Abu Ali al-Husain ibn Abdullah ibn Sina), a great physician and philosopher working in the years 980–1037, could write that:

> [T]he sensus communis is located in the forepart of the front ventricle of the brain. It receives all the forms which are imprinted on the five senses and transmitted to it from them. Next is the faculty of representation, located in the rear part of the front ventricle of the brain, which preserves what the sensus communis has received from the individual five senses even in the absence of the sensed object. Next is the faculty of sensitive imagination in relation to the animal soul. This faculty is located in the middle ventricle of the brain. Then there is the estimative faculty located in the far end of the middle ventricle of the brain. Next there is the retentive and recollective faculty located in the rear ventricle of the brain.[29]

Ventricular localization still held sway during the Quattrocento in Italy. Physicians like Antonio Guainerio (d. 1440) ascribed problems with memory in some patients to 'an excessive accumulation of phlegm in the posterior ventricle so that the "organ of memory" was impaired'.[30] The doctrine was still being taught in the best teaching centres at the

---

[28] Nemesius, 'Nature of Man', pp. 321 and 331f.

[29] F. Rahman, *Avicenna's Psychology* (Oxford University Press, Oxford, 1952), p. 31.

[30] A. L. Benton and R. Joynt, 'Early descriptions of aphasia', *Archives of Neurology*, 3 (1960), pp. 205–22. See also Antonio Guainerio's *Opera medica* (Antonio de Carcano, Pavia, 1481).

beginning of the sixteenth century, as is indicated by illustrations produced in the 1494 edition of Aristotle's *De Anima*. Leonardo da Vinci (1452–1519) went to great trouble to determine the first accurate description of the ventricles, given their presumed importance in the mental life of humans. In order to achieve this (circa 1506), he injected molten wax into the cavities in cattle. His drawings provide detail of a kind unmatched in accuracy, although they still ascribe the mental faculties to the different ventricles. In these drawings Leonardo's only deviation from the doctrine laid down by Nemesius 1,100 years earlier was to localize perception and sensation in the middle ventricle rather than in the lateral ventricles, a change which Leonardo made on the ground that most sensory nerves converged on the midbrain rather than more anteriorly.

Andreas Vesalius (1514–64) comments on the dominance of the ventricular doctrine when he was at the University of Louvain in 1503. He gave detailed, accurate drawings of the human ventricles in 1543 and accompanied these in his *Fabrica* with descriptions of how psychic pneuma is generated in the ventricles and then distributed to the nerves in ways that are not much different from those suggested by Galen.[31] Although Vesalius subscribed to the conception of ventricles as the origins of the psychic pneuma, following Galen, he was sceptical about the idea that psychological functions originate in the ventricles. His writings on this are important, for they prepare the way for Thomas Willis, who, a century later, was to provide the definitive shift of attention away from the ventricles to the substance of the brain itself in the search for the physical basis of psychological functions. Vesalius noted that as the shape of the ventricles is much the same in a variety of mammals, including humans, it is difficult to associate psychological powers such as reasoning, which demarcate humans from other mammals, with the ventricles.[32]

1.2 Fernel and Descartes: The Demise of the Ventricular Doctrine

Fernel: the origins of 'neurophysiology' The concepts of *physiology* and *neurophysiology* originated at the time of Vesalius. Although some have credited Aristotle in his biological writings as having dealt with physiological subjects and have conceived of Galen's *On the Use fulness of the Parts* as the earliest separate treatise dealing with human physiology, it is the sixteenth-century physician and scholar Jean Fernel (1495–1558) who should be credited with the first formal treatment of physiology. Fernel's *De naturali parte medicinae*, published in Paris in 1542, contains the word 'physiologia' for the first time. In it, physiology was first defined: 'Physiology tells the causes of the actions of the body.'[33] Fernel distinguishes anatomy, which indicates only *where* processes take place, from physiology, which studies *what* the processes or functions of the various organs are. The book

---

[31] A. Vesalius, *De humani corporis fabrica* (Basel, 1543), bk. VII, ch. i, p. 623.
[32] Wolf Singer, Vesalius on the Human Brain (Oxford University Press, Oxford, 1952), p. 40.
[33] J. Fernel, *De naturali parte medicinae* (Simon de Colines, Paris, 1542); see *Physiologia*, bk. II, Praefatio.

was renamed *Physiologia* in the 1554 edition, and was soon regarded as the major treatise on the subject, a position it held for more than a century.

Aquinas's influence on Fernel   Fernel's empirical observations, as well as his general reflections, are accommodated within the framework of late medieval Aristotelian thought as modified by Christian thinkers (in particular Thomas Aquinas's great synthesis). Like Aristotle, Fernel holds that plants and animals have a soul (*anima*), or principle of life. Possession of a rational soul (i.e. a soul that includes the powers of the intellect and will) is distinctive of man. Unlike Aristotle, but like Aquinas, Fernel conceived of the rational soul of man (as distinct from his nutritive and sensitive soul) as separable from the body, and as immortal.[34] It is, to be sure, far from clear whether the Aristotelian conception of the *psuchē* as the 'form' or 'first actuality' of the body – that is, as an array of powers and capacities (second-order powers) – can be coherently married with Christian doctrines concerning the immortality of the soul. But that was precisely what Aquinas had endeavoured to do (and in the course of his endeavour, he had reified the intellect, treated form as separable from matter, and confused the incorporeality of powers (which are abstractions) with the alleged incorporeality of the soul, conceived as a *non-physical part* of a human being).[35] Other scholastic philosophers also contributed to the attempted synthesis of Christianity with Aristotelian philosophy. Fernel was heir to this confused tradition.

'Physiology' as the study of organ function: Fernel   Physiology, according to Fernel, is concerned with the processes that produce a healthy body and soul. He comments that 'In all animate beings, and most in man, the body has been created for the sake of the soul (*gratia animae*). It is for that soul not only a habitation (*diversorium*) but an adjusted instrument for use by its (the soul's) inherent powers.'[36] This was an Aristotelian doctrine. As we have noted, the relation of the soul to the body, according to Aristotle, is analogous to the relation of sight to the eye. The eye exists for the sake of sight (*DA* 412^{b}17–24); that is its point and purpose. So, too, the body exists for the sake of the soul – that is, for the sake of the powers and capacities of which the soul consists. Without these, and their actualization in the behaviour of the living animal, there would be no point to the existence of the body (*DA* 415^{b}15–21; *De Partibus Animalium* 645^{b}19). The explanation of the actions of the parts of an organism must be in terms of their contribution to the optimal functioning of the whole of which they are the parts.

---

[34] Aquinas, capitalizing on Aristotle's obscure remarks about the active intellect, argued that 'the intellectual principle which is called the mind or intellect has an operation through itself (*per se*) in which the body does not participate. Nothing, however, can operate through itself (*per se*) unless it subsists through itself, for activity belongs to a being in act . . . Consequently, the human soul, which is called the intellect or mind, is something incorporeal and subsisting' (*Summa Theologiae* I, 76, 1).

[35] For a discussion of Aquinas's philosophy of psychology, see A. J. P. Kenny, *Aquinas on Mind* (Routledge, London, 1993).

[36] Fernel, *Physiologia*, bk. VI., ch. 13.

Fernel conceived of perception as produced by the transmission of images from the sense-organs to the common sensorium in the brain, where they are apprehended by the internal sense. Memory and imagination are two subordinate faculties of the sentient soul, and they enable the sentient animal to apprehend what is pleasant or unpleasant, beneficial or harmful. Appetite causes a movement towards a pleasing or beneficial object, or a movement away from a displeasing or harmful one. This is effected by the contraction of the brain forcing the animal spirits from the front ventricle into the fourth (rear) ventricle, and thence down the spinal cord and out along the nerves into the muscles.

The idea of an organ (muscle) reflex   All this was received doctrine. What is important for our present concerns is Fernel's observation that some of our acts occur without the action of the will or intent or any other directive of the mind. Such behaviour, he held, is exemplified by certain movements of the eyes and eyelids, of the head and hands during sleep, as well as by the movements associated with breathing. According to Fernel, these muscular movements do not involve an act of will, and therefore can be regarded as reflexes. Fernel was emphatic that muscular movement can occur without the will initiating a voluntary act; that is, there are motor acts in which thinking plays no part.[37] This insight marks the beginning of an investigation that was completed only with the work of Sherrington in the twentieth century.

Physiologia went through several editions and had an influence that lasted for a century. However, it could not continue as the definitive text in physiology beyond the middle of the seventeenth century, inasmuch as the Aristotelian concepts and conceptions on which it was based were no longer held to be viable. What, above all, made them obsolete was the rise of Keplerian physical astronomy and Galilean mechanistic physics. The spectacular success of the new physics led to the rapid demise of Aristotelian teleological science, and to the replacement of teleological explanations of natural phenomena by mechanistic explanations. This was equally evident in the advances in the biological sciences as in those of the physical sciences. First, Harvey showed that the heart was a mechanical pump. Secondly, Descartes argued persuasively that the activities of the body, the subject matter of physiology, could be considered in purely mechanical terms.

Descartes: the beginning of the end of the ventricular doctrine   Descartes (1596–1650) marks a profound upheaval in European thought. Although some aspects of his philosophy are still rooted in scholastic Aristotelian thought (and others in Augustinian thought), the novelty of his philosophical reflections is the starting point for modern philosophy. Much of his neuroscientific research proved wrong, but it provided a crucial impetus and shift of direction for neuroscience. Descartes agreed with the Aristotelian scholastics that the intellect can operate independently of the body, that the soul or mind is incorporeal, that it can exist independently of the body, and that it is immortal. However, he broke with them radically over the following four matters.

---

[37] Ibid., bk. IX., ch. 8, p. 109a.

Four marks of the Cartesian trans-formation of the conception of the mind or soul

First, he held that the mind is the *whole soul*. The scholastics, by contrast, conceived of the mind (understood as the intellect) as merely a part of the soul (the immortal part that is separable from the body). The other parts of the soul – namely, the nutritive and sensitive functions – are to be conceived, according to the scholastics, in Aristotelian fashion, as the form of the body. Descartes disagreed radically. Unlike Aristotle, he conceived of the soul not as the principle of *life*, but as the principle of *thought* or *consciousness*. The functions of the Aristotelian nutritive soul (nutrition, growth, reproduction) and of the sensitive soul (perception, physiologically conceived, and locomotion) are *not* essential functions of the Cartesian mind, but of the body. All the essential functions of animal life are to be conceived in purely mechanistic terms. This was to have profound effects on the further development of neurophysiology.

Secondly, Descartes redrew the boundaries of the mental. The essence of the Cartesian mind is not that of the scholastic-Aristotelian rational soul – that is, intellect alone – but rather *thought* or *consciousness*. A person is essentially a *res cogitans*, a thinking thing – and Descartes extended the concepts of thought and thinking far beyond anything that Aristotle or the scholastics would have ascribed to the rational soul. The functions of the rational soul, according to the scholastics, included the ratiocinative functions of the intellect and the deliberative-volitional functions of the will (rational desire), but excluded sensation and perception, imagination and animal appetite (concupiscence). By contrast, Descartes understood *thought* as including 'everything which we are aware of as happening within us, in so far as we have awareness of it. Hence *thinking* is to be identified here not merely with understanding, willing, imagining, but also with sensory awareness.'[38] Thought, therefore, was, in a revolutionary step, defined in terms of consciousness – that is, as that of which we are immediately aware within us. And consciousness was thereby assimilated to self-consciousness inasmuch as it was held to be impossible to think and to have experiences (to feel pain, seem to perceive, feel passions, will, imagine, cogitate) without knowing or being aware that one does. The identification of the mental with consciousness remains with us to this day, and casts a long shadow over neuroscientific reflection (we shall investigate the contemporary debate concerning consciousness and self-consciousness in Part III).

Thirdly, he held that the union of the mind with the body, though 'intimate', is a union of two distinct substances. Contrary to scholastic thought, according to which a human being is a unitary substance (an *ens per se*), Descartes intimated that a human being is *not* an individual substance, but a composite entity. The person (the *ego*), on the other hand, is an individual substance, and is identical with the mind. To be sure, *because* the

---

[38] Descartes, *Principles of Philosophy*, I-9. Repr. in *The Philosophical Writings of Descartes*, vol. 1, trans. J. Cottingham, R. Stoothoff and D. Murdoch (Cambridge University Press, Cambridge, 1985), p. 195. Subsequent page references to this translation will be abbreviated 'CSM'. References to the canonical *Oeuvres de Descartes*, ed. Ch. Adam and P. Tannery, rev. edn (Paris: Vrin/C. N. R. S., 1964–76) will also be given in the form 'AT' followed by volume and page numbers – here AT VIII A, 7. Sphen references are given by section number.

human mind is united with the body, it has perceptions (psychologically understood). But perceptions thus understood are conceived of as modes of thought or consciousness, produced by the union of the mind with the body. Indeed, it is precisely by reference to the intimate union of mind and body that Descartes explained the non-mechanical perceptual qualities (i.e. colours, sounds, tastes, smells, warmth, etc.) as being produced in the mind in the form of ideas consequent upon psychophysical interaction. Similarly, the mind, *because* it is united with the body, can bring about movements of the body through acts of will. Hence neuroscience must investigate the forms of interaction between the mind and the brain that produce sensation, perception and imagination (which are 'confused' forms of thought), on the one hand, and voluntary movement on the other.

Fourthly, just as he conceived of the mind as having a single essential property – namely, thought – so too he conceived of matter as having a single essential property – namely, extension. He conceived of the principles of explanation in the physical and biological sciences alike as purely mechanical, save in the case of the neuropsychology of human beings, who are unique in nature in possessing a mind.

Descartes contributed substantially to advances in neurophysiology and visual theory.[39] Although his theories proved to be largely wrong, they were essential steps on the path to a correct understanding. Moreover, his conviction that fundamental biological explanation at the neurophysiological level will be in terms of efficient causation has been triumphantly vindicated by the development of neurophysiology since the seventeenth century.[40]

The ventricles conceived as the source of 'animal spirits'; animal spirits conceived as 'neural transmitters'

Descartes replaced the conceptions of Aristotle and Galen, in which the psychic pneuma was generated in the ventricles, with the hypothesis that the ventricles are the site of generation of corpuscles or particles that directly participate in mechanical phenomena. These are the animal spirits that are conducted by nerves and transmitted to muscle cells, and so effect action. As to the origin of these corpuscles: 'The parts of the blood which penetrate as far as the brain serve not only to nourish and sustain its substance, but also and primarily to produce in it a certain very fine wind (that is "composed of very small, fast-moving particles"), or rather a very lively and pure flame, which is called the *animal spirits*.'[41] This is an unfortunate name as it is not an apt descriptive term for components of a mechanical theory, for the word 'spirit' can be interpreted as a principle of life that animates the body or as the active principle of a substance extracted as a liquid. However, Descartes is quite explicit that 'animal spirits' are material: namely, 'a certain very fine air or wind,'[42] and that

> what I am calling 'spirits' here are merely bodies; they have no property other than that of being extremely small bodies which move very quickly, like the jets of flame that

---

[39] Descartes, *Optics*, CSMI, pp. 152–75; AT VI, 81–146.
[40] Bennett, 'Early history of the synapse'.
[41] Descartes, *Treatise on Man*, CSMI, p. 100; AT XI, 129.
[42] Descartes, *Passions of the Soul*, I-7.

come from a torch. They never stop in any place, and as some of them enter the brain's cavities, others leave it through the pores in its substance. These pores conduct them into the nerves, and then to the muscles. In this way the animal spirits move the body in all the various ways it can be moved.[43]

Descartes thus argued that the flow of animal spirits from the ventricles (in the case of motor action) involved the opening of particular valves in the walls of the ventricles, with a consequent flow of spirits into the appropriate motor nerve and contraction of muscle. In the case of involuntary behaviour associated with, for example, a pinprick, this would lead to a tension on just those filaments which open the appropriate valves in the walls of the ventricles to release the animal spirits into the motor nerves that contract the muscle to move the limb away from the point of the indentation.

Transmission involves inhibitory and excitatory processes
Descartes used the word 'reflex' only once in developing his conception of non-human animals as automata, although it is implied throughout his descriptions of animal behaviour and human non-volitional reactions. Although Descartes does not quote Fernel's *Physiologia* in his *Treatise on Man*, it is clear that his development of the doctrine of mindless motor behaviour in humans and animals has for its foundations the concept of the reflex first enunciated by Fernel.[44] *Treatise on Man* argues that such motor behaviour requires not only an excitatory process, but also an inhibitory one, a speculation that was later to be confirmed experimentally by Sherrington and analysed at the cellular level by his student John Eccles. Descartes then argued that the excitatory and inhibitory processes, when acting together, allow animals and the bodies of human beings (when functioning independently of the intervention of the mind) to be described as automatons.

These suggestions of Descartes's about the mechanism of reflex or involuntary movement, involving as they do the animal spirits stored in the ventricles, raise the question of the mechanism of voluntary movement. Here Descartes departed fundamentally from the ventricular doctrine. He denied that the ventricles are the seat of the sensitive and rational (including volitional) powers of human beings. He also denied that non-human animals have any sensitive powers *in the sense in which human beings do*, inasmuch as they lack consciousness. And he held that the human mind or soul interacts with the body in the pineal gland, which he incorrectly placed inside the ventricles.[45]

The pineal gland as locus for the sensus communis and point of interaction of mind and body
It is interesting to note the reason (or part of the reason) why Descartes concluded that the pineal gland is the locus of the *sensus communis* and of interaction between the body and the soul. It was because it is located *between* the two hemispheres of the brain and is not itself bifurcated. Consequently, he reasoned, it must be in the pineal gland that 'the two images coming from a single object through the two eyes, or the two impressions coming from a single object through the double

---

[43] Ibid., I-10.

[44] C. S. Sherrington, *Man on his Nature*, 2nd edn (Cambridge University Press, Cambridge, 1953), p. 151.

[45] Descartes, *Passions of the Soul,* I-31.

organs of any other sense [e.g. hands or ears] can come together in a single image or impression before reaching the soul, so *that they do not present it with two objects instead of one*.'[46] These images or figures 'which are traced in the spirits on the surface of the gland' are 'the forms of images which the rational soul united to this machine [i.e. the body] will consider directly when it imagines some object or perceives it by the senses'.[47]

It is noteworthy that Descartes warned that although the image generated on the pineal gland does bear some resemblance to its cause (immediately, the retinal excitation; mediately, the object perceived), the resultant sensory perception is not caused by the resemblance. For, as he observed, that would require 'yet other eyes within our brain with which we could perceive it'.[48] Rather, it is the movements composing the image on the pineal gland which, by acting directly on the soul, cause it to have the corresponding perception.

Descartes's conceptual error of attributing seeing to the soul rather than to the person or living being

The warning was apt, but the caution insufficient. Descartes was, of course, wrong to identify the pineal gland as the locus of a *sensus communis*, and wrong to think that an image corresponding to the retinal image (and hence to what is seen) is reconstituted in the brain. These are factual errors, and it is noteworthy that they still have analogues in current neuroscientific thought – in particular, in the common characterization of the so-called binding problem (discussed below, §4.2.3). But Descartes was right to caution that whatever occurs in the brain that enables us to see whatever we see, our seeing cannot be explained by reference to *observation* of such brain events or configurations. For, as he rightly observed, that would require 'yet other eyes within our brain'. Nevertheless, he was confused – *conceptually* confused – to suggest (i) that images or impressions coming from double organs of sense must be united in the brain to form a single representation *in order that the soul should not be presented with two objects instead of one*; (ii) that the soul 'considers directly' the forms or images in the brain when it perceives an object; and (iii) that it is the soul, rather than the living animal (human being), that perceives. The first error presupposes precisely what he had warned against, for only if the images or impressions were actually *perceived* by the soul would there be any reason to suppose that the 'two images' would result in double vision or double hearing. The second error is the incoherence of supposing that in the course of perceiving, the soul or mind 'considers' anything whatsoever (no matter whether forms or images) *in the brain*. And the third is the error of supposing that it is the *soul* or *mind* that perceives. We have already noted the much earlier occurrence of this confusion in Nemesius. The confusion is a form of a *mereological fallacy* (mereology being the logic of the relations between parts and wholes). For it consists in ascribing to a part of a creature attributes which logically can be ascribed only to the creature as a whole. The particular form which this mereological fallacy took in Descartes consisted in ascribing to the soul attributes which can be ascribed only to the whole animal. We shall discuss this matter in detail in chapter 3.

---

[46] Ibid., I–32, italics added.
[47] *Descartes, Treatise on Man*, CSM I, p. 106; AT XI, 119.
[48] *Descartes, Optics*, CSM I, p. 167; AT VI, 130.

By the middle of the seventeenth century, Descartes had replaced the ventricular doctrine localizing psychological functions in the ventricles of the brain with his idiosyncratic interactionist doctrine localizing all psychological functions in the pineal gland, which he conceived to be the point of interaction between mind and brain. This is how he met Vesalius's objection that it is difficult to reconcile the idea that the different ventricles are associated with different cognitive and cogitative powers when the ventricles of humans are so similar to those of other mammals. Furthermore, he had replaced psychic pneuma by animal spirits as the medium through which the pineal gland produces its effects. This amounted to replacing the fluid derived from the *pneuma* described by Aristotle with mechanical corpuscles that possessed special properties. However, his contemporaries were soon to point out that the pineal gland is not inside the ventricles and, furthermore, that since other mammals possessed this gland, his response to Vesalius was inadequate.

Descartes's primary contribution   Nevertheless, Descartes had made the fundamental contribution of opening up all animal activity to mechanical analysis – that is, to what became physiology and neuroscience. Furthermore, by associating the psychological capacities of humans with the pineal gland, he had moved consideration of their physical dependence from the ventricles (filled now with particles of the animal spirits rather than with the psychic pneuma of Galen) to the matter of the brain – in his case the pineal gland. This shift of attention from the ventricles to the substance of the brain became definitive as a result of the work of a young man who was but twenty-nine when Descartes died, Thomas Willis.

1.3 The Cortical Doctrine of Willis and its Aftermath

Thomas Willis: the basis of psychological functions in the cortex As a consequence of his observations on patients with neurological problems, who subsequently died and so could be examined postmortem, the Professor of Medicine at Oxford, Thomas Willis (1621–75) reached the conclusion that the psychological attributes of humans are functionally dependent on the cortex and not the ventricles. This he argued at length and with great force in his classical work, *De anima brutorum*[49] and in his *Cerebri anatome, cui accessit nervorum descriptio et usus*,[50] the persuasive power of which was greatly assisted by the magnificent drawings made from Willis's sketches by the young Christopher Wren. Willis gave the first cortical theory of the control of the musculature and of reflex control. He assigned to man and to all other animals ('brutes') a system of particles found throughout

---

[49] T. Willis, *De anima brutorum* (Thomas Dring, London, 1683). English translation by S. Pordage: *Two Discourses Concerning the Soul of Brutes, which is that of the Vital and Sensitive of Man* (Scholars' Facsimiles & Reprints, Gairiesville, FL, 1971).

[50] T. Willis, *Cerebri anatome, cui accessit nervorum descriptio et usus* (Thomas Dring, London, 1681); for translation, see Tercentenary Facsimile Edition, *The Anatomy of the Brain and Nerves*, Tr. S. Pordage, ed. William Feidel (McGill University Press, Montreal, 1965). Subsequent references in the text to this volume are flagged '*ABN*' followed by the page number.

their bodies which he called 'the Corporeal Soul'. 'This soul . . . arises together with the body out of matter rightly disposed. It cannot be perceived by our senses, but is only known by its effects and operations. If the body or this soul is hurt in such a way that the particles of the soul disappear from the concretion . . . the body being made soulless tends to corruption' (*ABN* 6f.). Willis now explained in detail the role of the vital spirits (or vital liquor) of the blood circulated in the heart and vessels and that of the animal spirits (or animal liquor) of the brain and nerves – the term 'spirits' being taken in the Cartesian sense: namely, as the distillation of a liquor. The animal spirits are derived from the vital spirits (*ABN* 22f.). The corporeal soul is associated with both of these liquors.

Animal spirits from the cortex activate muscles through the nerves

The role of the animal spirits in integrating the activity of the cortex and the movement of muscle is then spelt out:

> We have shown that the *Animal Spirits* are made in the cortex of the brain and cerebellum, whence they descend and flow into the middle and marrowy parts where they are kept in sufficient amounts to be used for the various purposes of the Soul. Animal Spirits flow from there to the oblong and spinal marrow, and thence into the nerves and nervous shoots, activating and expanding these. Finally, sufficient amounts of *Animal Spirits* are distilled from the ends of the nerves implanted in the muscles, membranes and viscera, and so activate them, the organs of sense and motion. (*ABN* 24)

In brutes, the cortex lies in a reflex arc from sensation or perception to motor act

How is the flow of the animal spirits in and from the cortex to muscles initiated? To answer this, Willis first describes how the flow of animal spirits occurs in the brain when an organ of perception is excited (*ABN* 38). He then links an animal's perceiving something with a subsequent motor act. This description places the cortex in a reflex arc from sensation to motor act, and it is clear that Willis thought that in all animals other than man, all motor acts are reflex, for he comments that 'because brutes or men, whilst they as yet know not things, want spontaneous appetite. So long therefore, they being destitute of the internal principle of motion, move themselves or members, only as they are excited from the impulse of the external object, and so sensation preceding motion, is in some manner the cause of it' (*ABN* 59). The reflex nature of many motor acts is emphasized in his comments on the behaviour of some animals when they are cut in pieces (*ABN* 17).

Human acts of will are possible due to interaction of soul and body in the cortex

But what of volitional acts that man alone performs? Here Willis invokes the idea of the rational soul, which is immortal (*ABN* 39). To carry out a volitional act, we must be aware of the object towards which the act is directed (*ABN* 58). Willis identifies the rational soul in the brain as doing the perceiving, which he spells out in detail (*ABN* 59). The rational soul, he held, beholds this image in the corpus callosum.[51] His conception of the formation of an *internal representation* upon

---

[51] Willis, *Two Discourses Concerning the Soul of Brutes*, pp. 43f.

the corpus callosum is reminiscent of Descartes's idea that an image of what is seen must be produced on the surface of the pineal gland, where it is 'presented to the soul'. And Willis's supposition that the rational soul 'beholds the image of the thing there painted' at least approximates the very error that Descartes warned against (and then partly succumbed to): namely, of explaining how the human being can see an object by appealing to the soul's seeing or apprehending a representation of the object in the brain.

So, volitional acts are initiated by the rational soul, located in the corpus callosum, after the animal spirits have delivered 'the images or representations of all sensible things' from the common sensory:

> [N]othing seems more probable than that these parts [corpora striata] are that common sensorium that receives and distinguishes all the appearances and impressions and transfers them in suitably ordered arrangement into the corpus callosum, represents them to the imagination presiding there, and transmits the force and instinct of those spontaneous movements begun in the brain into the nervous appendix for performance by the motor organs.[52]

Willis then associated the functions of perception, memory and volition with the cerebral cortex. In particular he associated these functions with the gyri of the cortex, so that animal spirits move between the gyri. The gyri, he held, were much more numerous in humans than in other animals because of the superior intellectual powers of human beings (*ABN* 65–8).

Willis explicitly subscribes to the Cartesian idea of an immaterial soul or mind, that perceives and performs acts of will initiating motor action and that interacts with the body. Like Descartes (and many others), he held that because the rational soul is immaterial, therefore it has no parts. Having no parts, it is indestructible, for all destruction is decomposition into parts. The important difference between Willis and Descartes is that Willis locates the point of causal interaction between the mind or rational soul and the body in the cortex – namely, in the corpus callosum – and not, like Descartes, in the pineal gland, incorrectly located in a ventricle. However, just as Descartes was left with the insoluble problem of explaining the interaction of the mind with the pineal gland, so Willis was left with the problem of the explaining the interaction between the immaterial rational soul and the material corporeal soul in the corpus callosum. So no explanation is provided as to how the bond is formed between the rational soul and the corporeal soul, which are placed in a state in which they can interact by God at birth: 'That this immortal soul (the Rational Soul), for as much as it cannot be born, as soon as all things are rightly disposed for its reception, in the humane formation of the child in the womb, it is created immediately of God, and poured into it' (*ABN* 41f.).

The result of Willis's work was to move attention completely away from the ventricles for the first time in over 1,000 years and to centre both research and speculation on the cortex as the biological basis of the psychological attributes of humans.

---

[52] Ibid.

The cortex 100 years after Willis   The revolution due to Willis ultimately led to a focus on the relationship between the cortex and those nerve trunks that could be argued to be intimately related to it. For the century after Willis there was no advance regarding the problem of functional localization in the brain. In 1784 Jiri Proc. hàska (1749–1820) did not go much beyond Willis:

> Since, however, the Sensorium commune, by certain laws peculiar to itself and without the consciousness of the mind, reflects sensory impressions into motor, and because we have declared the Sensorium commune to be comprised of the spinal marrow, medulla oblongata, and the whole origin of the nerves, it follows that, with the exception of the Sensorium commune, the cerebrum and cerebellum and their parts are the organs of the faculty of thought.[53]

Mistichelli and du Petit describe the decussation of the pyramids and identify motor function of pyramidal fibres in cortex   However, there was one remarkable contribution during this period, by Domenico Mistichelli (1675–1715) and Francois Pourfour du Petit (1664–1741). They both described the decussation of the pyramids – that is, the crossing over of nerves from left to right and right to left at the spinomedullary junction called the pyramid.[54] Their remarkable work also placed the origins of the pyramidal fibres in the cortex, and du Petit went further, identifying the fibres as motor in function. Du Petit, a military surgeon, observed that contralateral motor paralysis followed a wound to the cerebral cortex. On the basis of these observations, he explained movement by the passage of animal spirits from the cortex, through the striatum and basal ganglia, and then across the pyramids to muscle. He gave the first explicit description of the motor cortex's controlling movement through the pyramidal tract. This prescient work has a remarkably modern ring to it.

1.4 The Concept of a Reflex:
Bell, Magendie and Marshall Hall

The spinal cord can operate independently of the enkephalon   It had been noted since time immemorial that cutting off the head of a snake did not stop its movements in response to a touch for some days. However, a thorough study of the ability of the spinal cord to mediate the contraction of muscle and movement in the absence of the enkephalon was not made until the investigations of Alexander Stuart (1637–1742). In his Croonian

[53] J. Proc.hàska, 'De functionibus systemis nervosi, et observationes anatomico-pathologicae', in *Adnotationum Academicarum* (W. Gerle, Prague, 1784), tr. T. Laycock, as 'A dissertation on the functions of the nervous system', in *Unzer and Procháska on the Nervous System* (Sydenham Society, London, 1851), pp. 141–3.

[54] D. Mistichelli, 'Trattato dell'Apoplessia' (Roma, A de Rossi alla Piazza di Ceri), tr. C. D. O'Malley, in E. Clarke and C. D. O'Malley, *The Human Brain and Spinal Cord* (University of California Press, Berkeley, 1968), pp. 282–3.

Lecture to the Royal Society of London in 1739, Stuart described experiments in which he first cut off the head of a frog and then used a blunt instrument to bring pressure on the medulla, resulting in the movement of the limbs. From these experiments he concluded that compression had forced the animal spirits out of the spinal cord into the nerves to the muscles.[55] In this way Stuart thought that he had provided experimental evidence for the flow of animal spirit from the spinal cord to the muscle as the agent which initiated contraction.

The problem of how animals can continue to function at some level in the absence of the enkephalon was taken up next by Robert Whytt (1714–66) in his works *Essays on the Vital and Involuntary Motions of Animals* and *Observations on the Sensibility and Irritability of the Parts of Man and Other Animals*, written about 1751 in Edinburgh.[56] Whytt was not able to accept the mechanical principle that both Descartes and Willis had advanced: namely, that the reflex does not require the intervention of a soul to initiate it. He wrote: '*The motions performed by us in consequence of irritation*, are owing to the original constitution of our frame, whence the soul or *sentient principle*, immediately, and *without any previous ratiocination,* endeavours by all means, and in the most effectual manner, to avoid or *get rid of every disagreeable sensation* conveyed to it by *whatever hurts or annoys the body*.' It is important to note that this conception of the soul is more Cartesian than Aristotelian in inspiration. For it is a principle of sentience (and so of consciousness). Whytt anticipated Sherrington on the stretch reflex: 'Whatever stretches the fibres of any muscle so far as to extend them beyond their usual length, excites them into contraction about in the same manner as if they had been irritated by any sharp instrument, or acrid liquor.'[57]

Idea of a spinal cord reflex   The idea of a 'soul' or sentient principle operating in the nervous system that remains after loss of the enkephalon was taken up by Prochàska. He resurrected the notion of the 'Sensorium commune' which had been associated with the lateral ventricles in the ventricular doctrine, but was now attributed by Prochàska to the brain and spinal cord.[58] This work of Prochàska, in clearly associating sensory reception and motor action at the spinal cord level greatly helped in the development of the idea of a reflex. This connection is made explicit in his comment that: 'As, therefore, *the principal function of the Sensorium commune consists in the reflection of sensorial into motor impressions,* it is to be observed, that this reflection takes place whether the mind be conscious or unconscious of it.'[59] But he too failed to resolve the problem.

The problem of how the brain and spinal cord participate in the integrative action of the nervous system which accompanies behaviour arose, as we have seen, with the discovery of nerves and their origins in the brain and spinal cord by Galen and his

---

[55] A. Stuart, Lecture III of the Croonian Lectures, *Proceedings of the Royal Society*, 40 (1739), p. 36.
[56] R. Whytt, 'An essay on the vital and other, involuntary, motions of animals' (1751), repr. in Alexander Walker, *Documents and Dates of Modern Discoveries in the Nervous System* (1839), pp. 112–22; facsimile ed. P. Cranfield (Scarecrow Reprint Corp., Metuchen, NJ, 1973).
[57] Ibid., p. 120.
[58] Procháska, 'A dissertation', p. 123.
[59] Ibid., pp. 127–9.

Galvani's discovery of animal electricity makes redundant the supposition of a cortical store of animal spirits for motor action

followers. They retained the Aristotelian notion of vital pneuma generated in the heart, but were now required to modify Aristotle's ideas by their discovery of spinal nerves and the importance of the integrity of these nerves for motor behaviour. Galen suggested that when vital pneuma enters the brain it is converted into psychic pneuma. Thence it passes down both the cranial nerves and spinal cord and out of the spinal nerves to activate muscles. Galen conceived of psychic pneuma as a fluid that either flowed along hollow tubes in the nerves or provided the substrate for the flow of a potency, somewhat akin to the modern conception of an action potential. Descartes, as we have seen, refined Galen's conception, describing the vital pneuma as composed of fine blood particles which, on reaching the brain, are converted into even finer particles. He named these 'animal spirits'. The discovery by Willis of reflexes raised the problem of how animal spirits might participate in the integrative actions of the nervous system that accompany reflexes. This difficulty was exacerbated by the realization that reflexes could be performed by decorticate animals. For in this case how could the production of animal spirits, dependent on the integrity of the brain, participate in reflex generation by spinal cords with their attached motor nerves *in the absence of the brain*? The solution was provided by Luigi Galvani (1737–98). He showed that nerves could conduct electricity in a way similar to that whereby metallic wires conduct voltaic electricity, and that the potential for generating this electricity in the nerves could be found in the nerves themselves.[60] His key experiment to show that nerves conduct electricity was to suspend a frog's exposed spinal cord/leg preparation in a sealed jar by means of a wire passed through the spinal cord and then through a seal at the top of the jar; lead shot was present in the bottom of the jar. A wire was then strung across the ceiling to pick up the charge from a frictional machine and convey it to the wire from which the spinal cord was strung. This apparatus unequivocally demonstrated that when the machine sparked, the legs twitched. From this Galvani concluded that the spinal cord and its attached nerves conduct electricity.[61] These discoveries showed that there was no need for a store of animal spirits in the brain derived from psychic pneuma and used by the spinal cord and its attached nerves to control organs. Both spinal cord and nerves possessed the ability to generate the electricity needed to initiate reflexes independently of the brain.

Bell and Magendie: identification of sensory and motor spinal nerves   We have seen the confusion that was still present in the eighteenth century concerning the idea of reflexes and the extent to which Whytt had to invoke a conception of the soul in relation to the function of the spinal cord in order to explain reflex action. This difficulty was to remain until a demarcation emerged between the sensory and motor functions of the posterior and anterior roots of the spinal cord at the beginning of the nineteenth century. This was due to Charles Bell (1774–1842), who identified the anterior roots

---

[60] For more detail, see Bennett, 'Early history of the synapse', pp. 103–5.
[61] L. Galvani, 'De viribus electricitatis in motu musculari commentarius', *De Bononiensi Scientiarum et Atrium Instituto atque Academia commentarii*, 7 (1791), pp. 363–418.

as motor, and to François Magendie (1783–1855), who was responsible for the idea that the posterior roots are sensory. Much controversy attended the attribution of these discoveries.[62]

It is striking that the arguments for the claim that the anterior roots are motor in function did not involve any reference to the action of either the soul or a sensorium commune. The reason why debate on these issues came to be based on experimental observations alone, without any such reference, is clear. Bell's and Magendie's experiments did not involve disruption of the spinal cord or removal of the brain, so questions as to how reflexes could be elicited without the brain did not arise. Rather, their research centred on the effects of cutting nerves that lead from the brain and spinal cord to the peripheral parts of the body. Bell had satisfied himself by dissection that the anterior and posterior roots were continuous with particular columns of the spinal cord that were connected to the brain. So there was no conflict between the idea that the soul resides only in (or interacts only with) the brain and the fact that severing the roots produced the effects observed. In an incisive passage, Bell seems also to have understood correctly the integrative power of the spinal cord in decapitated animals: 'the spinal marrow has much resemblance to the brain, in the composition of its cineritious and medullary matter. In short its structure declares it to be more than a nerve, that is, to possess properties independently of the brain.'[63] In this passage the requirement of a soul or a sensorium commune in the spinal cord is abandoned, even though animals without brains are being considered.

Bell does not seem to have made any reference to the posterior roots possessing a sensory function. This may be explicable by the fact that most of his work was carried out on stunned rabbits. It was Bell's contemporary, Magendie, who first distinguished between motor and sensory nerves in relation to the anterior and posterior roots. In its proceedings for 1822, the French Academy of Science announced: 'Monsieur Magendie reports the discovery he has recently made, that if the posterior roots of the spinal nerves are cut, only the sensation of these nerves is abolished, and if the anterior roots are cut, only the movements they cause are lost.'[64] These experiments established the sensory nature of the posterior nerves.

---

[62] C. Bell, 'Idea of a new anatomy of the brain; submitted for the observations of his friends', repr. in G. Gordon-Taylor and E. W. Walls, *Sir Charles Bell, His Life and Times* (Livingstone, Edinburgh, 1958), pp. 218–31; idem, 'On the nerves; giving an account of some experiments on their structure and functions, which lead to a new arrangement of the system', *Philosophical Transactions of the Royal Society*, 111 (1821), p. 398.

[63] C. Bell, 'On the functions of some parts of the brain, and on the relations between the brain and nerves of motion and sensation', *Philosophical Transactions of the Royal Society*, 124 (1834), pp. *idem*, 471–83; 'Continuation of the paper on the relations between the nerves of motion and of sensation, and the brain; more particularly on the structure of the medulla oblongata and the spinal marrow', *Philosophical Transactions of the Royal Society*, 125 (1835), pp. 255–62.

[64] F. Magendie, 'Expériences sur les fonctions des racines des nerfs rachidiens', *Journal Physiologie expérimentale ct de pathologie*, 3 (1822), pp. 276–79; repr. with trans. in Walker, *Documents and Dates*, pp. 88, 95.

The experiments of Bell and Magendie provided the grounds for what became known as the Bell–Magendie hypothesis of spinal roots, which is best stated in Magendie's words: 'it is sufficient for me at present to be able to advance as positive, that the anterior and posterior roots of the nerves which arise from the spinal marrow, have different functions, that the posterior appear more particularly destined to sensibility, whilst the anterior seem more especially allied to motion'.[65]

Marshall Hall: isolating sensation from sensing in the spinal cord Bell and Magendie had avoided becoming caught up in the controversies as to whether the spinal cord contained a soul capable of initiating motion independently of the cerebrum. This, as we have seen, was because the experiments they performed involved only cutting the spinal nerves. Nevertheless, the apparent problem remained of how sensibility (i.e. the ability to feel a sensation) could be associated (as it seemed that it had to be associated) with the isolated spinal cord. This problem was largely dissolved by Marshall Hall (1790–1857) in the 1830s. He gave a full communication to the Royal Society in 1833 entitled 'On the reflex function of the medulla oblongata and medulla spinalis', in which he concluded that 'there is a property of the sentient and motor system of nerves which is independent of sensation and volition; – a property of the motor nerves independent of immoderate irritation; – a property which attaches itself to any part of an animal, the corresponding portion of the brain and spinal marrow of which is entire'.[66]

The spinal cord as a reflex centre – the true spinal marrow: Hall makes the supposition of a spinal soul redundant By 1837 Hall had given an account of the spinal cord as containing a reflex centre that operated in a non-sentient and non-volitional manner by contrast with the nerves of sensation which pass up to the brain and the motor nerves of volition that pass down from the brain. These conclusions were revolutionary inasmuch as they stated clearly that sensory nerves exist that do not produce sensations and that motor nerves exist that do not merely mediate volitional acts. So reflex acts do not require a nervous arc from muscle to brain and then from brain to muscle, as Charles Bell had thought. Rather, the reflex arc required

1   a nerve leading from the point or part irritated to and into the spinal cord marrow,
2   the spinal marrow itself,
3   a nerve or nerves passing out of or from the spinal marrow; all in essential relation or connection with each other.[67]

This work laid the foundations for, and in some respects anticipated, Sherrington's work later in the century. Following Hall, the notions of a spinal soul and a spinal Sensorium

---

[65] Ibid., p. 91.

[66] M. Hall, 'On the reflex function of the medulla oblongata and medulla spinalis', *Philosophical Transachoris of the Royal Society,* 123 (1833), pp. 635–65; *idem,*'These motions independent of sensation and volition', *Proceedings of the Committee of Science, Zoological Society,* 27 Nov. 1832, repr. in Walker, *Documents and Dates,* p. 138.

[67] M. Hall, 'Synopsis of the diastaltic nervous system or the system of the spinal marrow and its reflex arcs, as the nervous agent in all the functions of ingestion and of egestion in the animal economy', Croonian Lectures (Mallett, London, 1850).

communis were, by and large, abandoned. In 1831 Johannes Muller confirmed the Bell–Magendie law experimentally.

In 1890 Michael Foster (1836–1907) published the fifth edition of his great work *A Textbook of Physiology*, in which he gave a succinct account of the relationship between spinal reflexes and the brain. Yet even in the last decade of the nineteenth century the idea of a spinal cord soul still lingered and was considered by Foster in his *Textbook* to be worthy of consideration, as in his comments that:

> We may thus infer that when the brainless frog is stirred by some stimulus to a reflex act, the spinal soul is lit up by a momentary flash of consciousness coming out of the darkness and dying away into the darkness again; and we may perhaps further infer that such a passing consciousness is the better developed the larger the portion of the cord involved in the reflex act and the more complex the movement.[68]

1.5 Localizing Function in the Cortex: Broca, Fritsch and Hitzig

Broca: the cortical area for language; Fritsch and Hitzig: the motor cortex   Although the first experiments indicating a specialized area of the cortex for motor control were reported by Fritsch and Hitzig in 1870, it could be claimed that the first evidence for cortical specialization was that reported by Paul Broca (1824–80) in 1861 for speech. In that year Broca reported the results of an autopsy on the cortex of one of his patients, a Monsieur Leborgne, who had suffered from loss of speech (aphasia). Broca found a lesion in the left anterior (frontal) lobe, which, he suggested, was the language area of the cortex. Subsequently it became known as Broca's area.[69]

There was little progress in the understanding of the function of the cortex for nearly 200 years, between the death of Thomas Willis in 1675 and, as we shall see, the experiments of Fritsch and Hitzig around 1870. For example, the leading French physiologist of the day, Marie-Jean-Pierre Flourens (1794–1867), claimed, as a consequence of his researches on pigeons (*c.* 1824), that the cortex was concerned only with perception, intellectual abilities and the will, not with motor action.[70] He showed in 1858 that the motor action involved in respiration could be delimited to the medulla, and did not involve the brain. Furthermore, according to Flourens, these functions of the cortex could not be ascribed to different areas of the cortex, for this acted as a whole. All sensations, all

---

[68] Michael Foster, *A Textbook of Physiology* (Macmillan, London, 1890), p. 912. The Cartesian roots of this conception of the spinal soul are here evident in its association with consciousness.

[69] P. Broca, 'Remarques sur le siège de la faculté du language articulé, suivies d'une observation d'aphémie (perte de la parole)', *Bulletins de la Société Anatomique* (Paris), 6 (1861), pp. 330–57, 398–407; (tr. as 'Remarks on the seat of the faculty of articulate language, followed by an observation of aphemia', in G. von Bonin, *Some Papers on the Cerebral Cortex* (Charles C. Thomas, Springfield, IL, 1960), pp. 49–72.

[70] M. J. P. Flourens, *Recherches experiméntales sur les propriétés et les fonctions du système nerveux dans les animaux vertèbrés* (Ballière, Paris, 1823).

perception and all volition, he argued, occupy concurrently the same seat in these organs. The faculty of sensation, perception and volition, he therefore concluded, is essentially one faculty.

Discovery of the motor cortex:
Fritsch and Hitzig

It was not until the second half of the nineteenth century that progress was made on the motor control functions of the cortex. In 1870 Gustav Fritsch (1838–91) and Edouard Hitzig (1838–1907) published their monumental work 'Über die elektrische Erregbarkeit des Grosshirns' (1870), in which they described the results of their experiments on stimulating the brains of dogs with galvanic currents, which led them to the idea of a 'motor cortex'. In these experiments, the exposed cortex of dogs was excited at different sites with levels of electrical stimulation just detectable when applied to the human tongue. They found areas on the surface of the cortex that gave rise to muscular contractions involving the face and neck on the opposite side of the dog to the hemisphere being stimulated, as well as forepaw extension and flexion. On unilateral ablation of the forepaw area of the cortex, they observed that sensation was unaffected, but that the dog possessed impaired motor activity and posture. On this they commented:

> A part of the convexity of the hemisphere of the brain is motor, another part is not motor. The motor part, in general, is more in front, the non-motor part more behind. By electrical stimulation of the motor part, one obtains combined muscular contractions of the opposite side of the body. These muscle contractions can be localized on certain very narrowly delimited groups by using very weak currents. The possibility to stimulate narrowly delimited groups of muscle is restricted to very small foci which we shall call centers.[71]

This led them not only to the hypothesis that a discrete area of the cortex possessed a motor function, but also to the generalization that other functions might also be localized in specific areas of the cortex. This conception of cortical localization was the first major advance in our understanding of cortical function since the time of Willis.

Somatotopic organization of motor
cortex: Jackson and Ferrier

Following this work of Fritsch and Hitzig on dogs, John Hughlings Jackson (1835–1911) reached similar conclusions concerning the existence of a motor cortex in humans, based on his observations on patients with epilepsy reported in 1863: 'In very many cases of epilepsy, and especially in syphilitic epilepsy, the convulsions are limited to one side of the body; and, as autopsies of patients who have died after syphilitic epilepsy appear to show, the cause is obvious organic disease on the side of the brain, opposite to the side of the body convulsed, frequently on the surface of the hemisphere.'[72] Of particular interest was the temporal pattern of contraction across muscle groups during

---

[71] G. Fritsch and E. Hitzig, 'Über die elektrische Erregbarkeit des Grosshirns', *Archiv für Anatomie, Physiologie and wissenschaftliche Medicin, Leipzig*, 37 (1870), 300–32; tr. as 'On the electrical excitability of the cerebrum' in von Bonin, *Some Papers on the Cerebral Cortex*, pp. 73–96.

[72] J. H. Jackson, 'Convulsive spasms of the right hand and arm preceding epileptic seizures', *Medical Times and Gazette*, 2 (1863), pp. 110–11.

seizures in spreading epilepsy. This led Hughlings Jackson to speculate that the motor cortex must be organized along somatotopic lines, so that the hands, face and feet, which possess the greatest capacity for specialized movement, are allocated the largest area in the motor cortex. These brilliant suggestions of Hughlings Jackson were confirmed by the work on primates by David Ferrier (1843–1928) in 1874. Using alternating current stimulation of discrete sites on the cortex, he was able to delineate clearly the area of the cortex that produces the twitching of muscles, as well as movements that in some cases resembled attempts at walking. On introducing small lesions into the motor area of the cortex which he had mapped, Ferrier showed that, in some cases, these resulted in a paralysis of the opposite hand and forearm, and in another case, to the paralysis of the biceps muscle. By contrast, these animals showed normal sensitivity to touch and noxious stimuli. Such observations clearly pointed to a somatotopic organization of the motor cortex.[73] This work on primates was subsequently confirmed and extended by Victor Horsley (1857–1916), who, in 1887, showed that the precentral gyrus was predominantly motor, and the postcentral sensory, so that the motor cortex was to be found exclusively anterior to the Rolandic fissure.[74]

Caton's and Beck's discovery of electrical phenomena in the cortex support the idea of a motor cortex   In 1875 Richard Caton (1842–1926) discovered that electrical oscillations could be recorded through two electrodes placed on the surface of the cortex of a monkey, and that these oscillations were altered by sensory stimulation, anoxia and anaesthesia. Caton comments that:

> In every brain hitherto examined, the galvanometer has indicated the existence of electrical currents on the areas shown by Dr Ferrier to be related to rotation of the head and to mastication, negative variation of the current was observed to occur whenever those two acts respectively were performed. Impressions through the senses were found to influence the currents of certain areas; e.g. the currents of that part of the rabbit's brain which Dr Ferrier has shown to be related to movements of the eyelids, were found to be markedly influenced by stimulation of the opposite retina by light.[75]

---

[73] D. Ferrier, 'The localization of function in the brain', *Proceedings of the Royal Society*, 22 (1873–4), pp. 228–32; *idem*, 'Experiments on the brain of monkeys', Croonian Lecture (2ond ser.), *Philosophical Transactions of the Royal Society*, 165 (1876), pp. 433–88; *idem*, *The Function of the Brain* (Smith Elder and Company, London, 1876).

[74] C. E. Beevor and V. Horsley, 'A minute analysis (experimental) of the various movements produced by stimulating in the monkey different regions of the cortical centre for the upper limb, as defined by Professor Ferrier', *Philosophical Transactions of the Royal Society*, 178 (1887), pp. 153–67; idem, 'A further minute analysis by electrical stimulation of the so called motor regions (facial area) of the cortex cerebri in the monkey (*Macacus sinicus*)', *Philosophical Transactions of the Royal Society*, 185 (1894), pp. 39–81; *idem*, 'A record of the results obtained by electrical excitation of the so-called motor cortex and internal capsule in an orang-outang (*Simia satyrus*)', *Philosophical Transactions of the Royal Society*, 181 (1890), pp. 129–58.

[75] R. Caton, 'The electrical currents of the brain', *British Medical Journal*, 2 (1875), p. 278; *idem*, 'Interim report on investigation of the electric currents of the brain'. *British Medical Journal*, 1 (1877), Suppl. L, pp. 62–5; *idem*, 'Researches on electrical phenomena of cerebral grey matter', *Transactions of the Ninth International Medical Congress*, 3 (1887), pp. 246–9.

The electrical changes due to stimulation of the retina with light were later confirmed by Adolf Beck (1863–1942), adding credence to Caton's observations on the localization of electrical activity during motor acts of the kind predicted by Ferrier's work.[76]

1.6 The Integrative Action of the Nervous System: Sherrington

It is to Charles Sherrington (1857–1952) at the end of the nineteenth and the beginning of the twentieth century that one must turn to find an experimental plan for elucidating the mechanisms of the 'true spinal marrow'. The thoroughness and methodical nature of Sherrington's researches on the subject are at a new level. These were not dependent on technical advances at the time so much as on the brilliance and clarity of his thinking, coupled with a formidable and indefatigable capacity for experiment. Sherrington first elucidated the spinal origin of the efferent nerves innervating a particular muscle.[77] In 1905 his experiments indicated that stimulation of the afferent nerves of a particular muscle could produce contraction of that muscle independent of contraction of opposing muscles of the joint.[78] In 1910 he published his great paper, nearly 100 pages long, on 'Flexion-reflex of the limb, crossed extension-reflex, and reflex stepping and standing'.[79] In this he first describes the flexion-reflex and identifies the extension reflex as well as the crossed-extension reflex. This work, together with his earlier papers of 1897 and 1907, laid down the conceptual scheme for the analysis of the role of the spinal cord in stepping and standing. In doing this, Sherrington completed the research programme initiated eighty years earlier by Marshall Hall, with the consequence that the notion of a 'spinal soul' was finally eliminated from further consideration.

Although Ferrier in 1886 had first located the motor cortex in primates as a distinct area, it was Grunbaum and Sherrington in 1902 who first gave a detailed description of the spatial extent of this area on the cortex of primates.[80] They noted that the 'motor' area does not at any point extend behind the sulcus centralis. In this Sherrington and Grunbaum clearly distinguished for the first time the motor area from the area behind the sulcus centralis that we now know as somatosensory.[81] Their method of unipolar Faradization

[76] A. Beck, 'Die Bestimmung der Localisation der Gehirn- und Rückenmarkfunktionen vermittelst der elektrischen Erscheinungen', *Centralblatt für Physiologie*, 4 (1890), pp. 473–6.

[77] C. S. Sherrington, 'Notes on the arrangement of some motor fibres in the lumbo-sacral plexus', *Journal of Physiology*, 13 (1892), pp. 621–772.

[78] C. S. Sherrington, 'On reciprocal innervation of antagonistic muscles: Seventh Note', *Proceedings of the Royal Society*, B 76 (1905), pp. 160–3; *idem*, 'On reciprocal innervation of antagonistic muscles: Eighth Note', *Proceedings on the Royal Society*, B 76 (1905), pp. 269–97.

[79] C. S. Sherrington, 'Flexion-reflex of the limb, crossed extension-reflex, and reflex stepping and standing', *Journal of Physiology*, 40 (1910), pp. 28–121.

[80] A. S. F. Grünbaum and C. S. Sherrington, 'Observations on the physiology of the cerebral cortex of some of the higher apes (preliminary communication)', *Proceedings of the Royal Society*, 69 (1902), pp. 206–9.

[81] Ibid.

(alternating current) stimulation of the cortex allowed for much finer localization than had been possible with the double-point electrodes used up to this time.[82] Their classic paper, published at the beginning of the twentieth century, established without equivocation the conception of a motor cortex and therefore that different parts of the cortex, are specialized for different functions.

The notion of a 'spinal soul' had been put to rest, largely through Sherrington's detailed elucidation of spinal reflexes. However, the relationship between the soul and the cortex, or between the mind and the brain, still bedevilled Sherrington, as it had neuroscientists and philosophers for more than two millennia. Sherrington engendered similar concern for it amongst his protégés. We shall now turn to their reflections on this issue and see the extent to which their deepening knowledge of cortical function illuminated the problem.

---

[82] Ibid.

2

The Cortex and the Mind in the Work of Sherrington and his Protégés

2.1 Charles Sherrington: The Continuing Cartesian Impact

Sherrington's work left the role of the mind and its relation to the cortex problematic

As we have seen, it was the brilliant research of Sherrington that finally revealed the true nature of the spinal cord as a reflex centre and the role of the cortex in the generation of reflexes. He also clarified the beautiful specificity of the localization of function within the motor and somatosensory cortex. However, although the notion of a 'spinal soul' no longer figured in neurophysiology, the question of whether a 'cortical soul' existed remained moot. Or, to put it more perspicuously, the question of the relationship between the mind and the cortex remained deeply puzzling. Sherrington considered this question, tackling it in his usual methodical manner by first considering it in a historical setting through the work of Jean Fernel and the beginnings of the conception of physiology and neurophysiology. Later, he took up the problem at length in *Man on his Nature*, his Gifford Lectures of 1937/8.[1]

Sherrington's dualism

Sherrington studied Fernel carefully, and read extensively in the works of philosophers, from Aristotle onwards. But, as we shall see, his grasp of philosophical problems and his understanding of the differences between scientific problems and philosophical ones were infirm. Despite acquaintance with Aristotle's *De Anima*, he failed to see the depth and fruitfulness of the Aristotelian conception of the *psuchē* and its bearing on the essentially conceptual questions

---

[1] We shall be critical of Sherrington's ideas, but it must be remembered that his Gifford Lectures were influential and much admired in their day by great scientists. Erwin Schrödinger observed that 'The book is pervaded by the honest search for objective evidence of the interaction between matter and mind. I cannot convey the grandeur of Sherrington's immortal book by quoting sentences: one has to read it oneself' (quoted by J. C. Eccles in his Gifford Lectures, *The Human Mystery* (Routledge and Kegan Paul, London, 1984), pp. 4f.).

that plagued him. He noted Aristotle's 'complete assurance that the body and its thinking are just one existence', and that 'the "oneness" of the living body and its mind together seems to underlie the whole [Aristotelian] description as a datum for it all'.[2] Nevertheless, Sherrington did not probe the Aristotelian philosophical doctrine properly. Instead, he moved towards a Cartesian dualist conception of the relation between mind and body, unsurprisingly encountering the same insoluble problems as Descartes had. Using the term 'energy' to signify matter as well as energy, Sherrington held that 'evolution has dealt with . . . us as compounded of "energy" and "psyche", and has treated in us each of those two components along with the other. The two components are respectively, on our analysis, an energy-system and a mental system conjoined into one bivalent individual' (*MN* 250). 'Energy', or matter, and mind are, he thought, 'phenomena of two categories' (*MN* 251).

Sherrington's conception of mind   'Energy', in his view, is perceptible, spatio-temporally locatable, subject to the laws of physics and chemistry. Mind, by contrast, is 'invisible', 'intangible', without 'sensual [sensory] confirmation' (*MN* 256). Sometimes Sherrington states that mind is 'unextended';[3] at others he states that since mind has a location, it is inconceivable to him that it should lack a magnitude or be without extension. 'Accepting finite mind as having a "where" and that "where" within the brain, we find that the energy-system with which we correlate the mind has of course extension and parts . . . Different "wheres" in the brain correlate with different mental actions . . . We have to accept that finite mind is in extended space' (*MN* 249f.). On the other hand, he remarks, more sapiently than he evidently realized, that the mind is not 'a thing' (*MN* 256). He conceived of mind as the agent of thought, the source of desire, zest, truth, love, knowledge, values – of all, as he put it, 'that counts in life' (*MN* 256). It is, he wrote, 'the conscious "I"'.[4] But this is misconceived. The mind is no more located in the head or brain than is the ability to walk or talk. It is neither extended, nor an unextended point, any more than the ability to score a goal is either extended or an unextended point. The mind is not 'the conscious "I"', since there is no such thing as 'an I', any more than there is such a thing as 'a you' or 'a he' (see below, §12.4). I am not my mind – I *have* a mind, not as I have a car, or even as I have a head or a brain, but rather as I have eyesight or the ability to think.

Sherrington's conception of the   How we should conceive of the conceptual relationships
relation between mind and body   between mind, body (and brain) and person is a deep
                                     philosophical problem – the character of whose solution
we have intimated, and shall discuss below (see, e.g., §3.10). Sherrington was exceedingly unclear about the issue, not fully realizing that this is not an empirical problem at all, but

---

[2] C. S. Sherrington, *Man on his Nature*, 2nd edn (Cambridge University Press, Cambridge, 1953), p. 189. Subsequent references in the text to this work will be flagged '*MN*'.

[3] 'So our two concepts, space-time energy sensible [perceptible] and insensible [imperceptible] unextended mind, stand as in some way coupled together, but theory has nothing to submit as to how they can be so', quoted by J. C. Eccles and W. C. Gibson in *Sherrington – his Life and Thought* (Springer Verlag, Berlin, 1979), p. 143, without a reference.

[4] Quoted ibid., p. 142.

a purely conceptual one. Sometimes he seems to accept the mistaken idea that the mind has a body,[5] even though, to be sure, it is not *minds* that 'have bodies', it is *human beings*.[6] At other times he seems to go so far as to claim that the body (or at any rate parts of the body) has (or have) a mind – a part of the body that is sensitive has 'mind only lent it, in the form of sensation by proxy' (*MN* 187). But this is confused. What would a body do with a mind? *People* have minds as, indeed, they have bodies. 'So much of the body as feels, has its sensations done for it' by the brain, Sherrington argued, and so too, 'the body's thinking seems to be done for it, namely in the brain' (*MN* 187), presumably by the mind. Here too he was confused, since the brain does not 'do' sensations – there is no such thing as 'doing' sensations. But *we* have sensations *in* various parts of our sensitive body (parts that hurt, throb, itch, etc.) – and we would have no sensations but for the normal functioning of the brain and the nervous system (see §4.1). Similarly, *the body* has no thinking to do – there is no such thing as one's body thinking. It is people who think, and their thinking is not done for them by their brain – they have to do their own thinking (see §6.2). There is no such thing as the brain's thinking anything – although, of course, human beings would not be able to think but for the normal functioning of their brain. (That, to be sure, does not imply that one thinks *with* one's brain, in the sense in which one walks with one's legs or sees with one's eyes.)

Sherrington on the mind–brain nexus: misunderstandings of Aristotle

Given this confused dualism, the question of the relation between the two entities cannot but arise. Sherrington asserted that no one doubts that there is, as he put it, 'a liaison' between brain and mind. But 'The "how" of it we must think remains for science as for philosophy a riddle pressing to be read' (*MN* 190).

> In all those types of organism in which the physical and the psychical coexist, each of the two achieves its aims only by reason of a *contact utile* between them. And this liaison can rank as the final and supreme integration completing its individual. But the problem of how the liaison is effected remains unsolved; it remains where Aristotle left it more than two thousand years ago. There is, however, one peculiar inconsistency which we may note as marking this and many other psychological theories. They place the soul in the body and attach it to the body without trying in addition to determine the reason why, or the condition of the body under which such attachment is produced. This, however, would seem to be a real question.[7]

---

[5] 'I have seen the question asked "why should the mind have a body?" The answer may well run, "to mediate between it and other minds"' (*MN* 206).

[6] The phrase 'to *have* a body' *is* indeed curious and misleading. We do not say of insentient things that they have a body (trees, for example, do not have bodies). We ascribe bodies only to ourselves and sometimes to higher animals. Only what leaves a corpse or remains behind when it dies can be said to have a body (we do not say of a dead fish, for example, that it is the corpse or the remains of a fish – the remains of a fish would be a half-eaten fish). The use of the phrase earmarks not an empirical truth of some kind, but an attitude towards certain kinds of sentient creatures – paradigmatically towards human beings.

[7] C. S. Sherrington, *The Integrative Action of the Nervous System* (Cambridge University Press, Cambridge, 1947), p. xxiii.

It is curious to find Sherrington writing this, since he knew that the question of how the mind can interact with the body is *not* a question that can arise for Aristotle. Within the framework of Aristotelian thought, as we have seen (§1.1), the very question is as senseless as the question 'How can the shape of the table interact with the wood of the table?' Aristotle manifestly did not leave this as a problem within his philosophy. The problem arose within the framework of Plato's dualist philosophy, which was contested by Aristotle but nevertheless informed Neoplatonism and, via St Augustine, came to dominate Christian thought. To be sure, Thomas Aquinas adopted Aristotelian psychology and strove, with questionable coherence, to adapt it to Christian theology. But Platonic dualism remained the most natural conception for popular Christianity, and it informed the Renaissance form of Neoplatonism. The relationship between mind and body is highly problematic for any form of dualism, and with the seventeenth-century dominance of Descartes and the corresponding decline in the influence of Aristotelian philosophy, the problem of inter-action came on to the agenda again, and has remained there ever since.

Sherrington on the irreducibility of the mental

Sherrington contributed nothing towards its solution. He noted that science was impotent to solve the problem:

> Life . . . has resolved itself into a complex of material factors; all of it except one factor. There science stopped and stared as at an unexpected residue which remained after its solvent has dissolved the rest. Knowledge looking at its world had painfully and not without some disillusions arrived at two concepts; the one, that of energy, which was adequate to deal with all which was known to knowledge, except mind. But between energy and mind science found no 'how' of give and take. . . . To man's understanding the world remained obstinately double. (*MN* 200)

Life and the processes of life, Sherrington observed, were explicable by physics and chemistry, but 'thought escapes and remains refractory to natural science. In fact natural science repudiates it as something outside its ken' (*MN* 229). This is, of course, untrue. For psychologists can and do study thinking – which is not in any sense 'outside its ken'. But it is evident that what Sherrington meant was that thinking and thought are not *reducible* to physics and chemistry. 'For myself', he wrote, 'what little I know of the how of the one [i.e. the brain] does not, speaking personally, even begin to help me toward the how of the other [i.e. the mind]. The two for all I can do remain refractorily apart. They seem to me disparate; not mutually convertible; untranslatable the one into the other' (*MN* 247). On the matter of strict reducibility, at any rate, he is quite right (see below, §13.1).

Sherrington on mind–body interaction

Sherrington's conception of the interaction between mind and body was Cartesian (although without the Cartesian commitment to the interactionist role of the pineal gland).

> I would submit that we have to accept the correlation, and to view it as interaction; body ⇒ mind. Macrocosm is a term with perhaps too medieval connotations for use here: replacing it by 'surround', then we get surround ⇆ body ⇆ mind. The sun's energy is part of the closed energy cycle. What leverage can it have on mind? Yet through my retina and brain it is able to act on my mind. The theoretically impossible

happens. In fine, I assert that it does act on my mind. Conversely my thinking 'self' thinks it can bend my arm. Physics tells me that my arm cannot be bent without disturbing the sun. My mind then does not bend my arm. If it does, the theoretically impossible happens. Let me prefer to think the theoretically impossible does happen. Despite the theoretical I take it that my mind *does* bend my arm and that it disturbs the sun. (*MN* 248)

'Reversible interaction between the "I" and the body', he concluded, 'seems to me an inference validly drawn from evidence' (*MN* 250). This is a deep confusion – for it is not 'the "I"' that moves my arm when I move my arm; nor indeed is it my mind. *I* do so – and I am neither my mind, nor am I a 'self', an 'ego', or 'an "I"'. I am a human being. And it is not 'my thinking self' or my mind that thinks it can bend my arm; rather, I, *this* human being, think that I can bend my arm, and usually do so when asked.

Sherrington was admirably candid in confessing his bafflement. But he did not realize that the root of the trouble is conceptual confusion – not empirical ignorance. And he was not aware of the revolution in philosophy that was taking place at that very time in Cambridge that would have enabled him to disentangle his confusions. His predicament was not unlike Descartes's, 300 years earlier. Writing in his old age to Princess Elizabeth of Bohemia, who asked him how a thinking soul could move the animal spirits, the great philosopher and scientist confessed that 'I may truly say that what your Highness proposes seems to me the question people have most right to ask me in view of my published works'.[8]

2.2 Edgar Adrian: Hesitant Cartesianism

Adrian's achievement

Edgar Douglas Adrian (1889–1977) was a much younger contemporary of Sherrington, with whom he shared the Nobel Prize in 1932. Adrian's work is in certain respects complementary to Sherrington's. For it gives an account of the electrical activity in both motor and sensory nerve fibres that accompany reflex and other integrative actions of the nervous system. Adrian showed that there is only one kind of action potential in nerve fibres, no matter whether these are motor or sensory ones. Furthermore, he showed that the force of contraction and the intensity of sensation are graded as a consequence of different frequencies of action potential firing in the nerves as well as changes in the number of nerve fibres that are firing. He later turned his attention to the origins of electrical oscillations in the brain, and established that the Berger rhythm comes from the occipital part of the cortex.

His reluctance to speculate

The question 'How is the brain related to the mind?' puzzled Adrian no less than it puzzled others. But, unlike Sherrington, he was disinclined to speculate upon the nature of the mind, or upon the question of how brain activities are related to mental phenomena. His reflections on such questions are therefore relatively few, and expressed with considerable caution. Nevertheless,

---

[8] Descartes, letter to Princess Elizabeth of Bohemia, dated 21 May 1643.

it is worth surveying them briefly, for they raise questions that still bewilder neuroscientists. Though Adrian did not commit himself to Cartesian dualism, Cartesian elements do creep into his cautious and tentative remarks, as we shall see.

The 'man-machine' and the ego   In his lecture on consciousness in 1965, Adrian observed that, in general, natural scientists prefer to remain uncommitted on such questions as the relationship between mind and matter. However, he admitted, it is difficult for physiologists to maintain such Olympian detachment. Any neuroscientist concerned with studying the sense-organs and the central nervous system can hardly avoid the problems that have always arisen in trying to relate physical events and activities in the body to mental activities. The problem can be put most starkly by reflecting on the fact that one might, according to Adrian, build a mechanical human being that behaved exactly as we do. For the 'universal Turing machine', he observed wittily, can 'turn its band to any problem', and a 'man-machine' might be programmed to do anything we can do. What would be missing, however, 'is ourself, our ego, the I who does the perceiving and the thinking and acting, the person who is conscious and aware of his identity and his surroundings'.[9] We are convinced, Adrian remarked, that we have an immediate awareness of ourselves, and that this is one thing that a machine could not copy.

Adrian's hesitant Cartesianism   This thought is, to be sure, Cartesian through and through. What differentiates man from *mechanical animate nature* is, according to Descartes, consciousness. Descartes assimilated consciousness to self-consciousness. For he held that thought, which is the essential attribute of mind, is defined as 'everything which we are aware of as happening within us, in so far as we have an awareness of it'. Notoriously, Descartes held that the foundation of all knowledge was each person's consciousness of his own thoughts, and hence his indubitable knowledge of his own existence. In this respect, Adrian followed Descartes. For, he observed,

> I used to regard the gulf between mind and matter as an innate belief. I am quite ready now to admit that I may have acquired it at school or later. But I find it more difficult to regard my ego as having such a second hand basis. I am much more certain that I exist than that mind and matter are different.
>
> Apart from those who are insane, 'out of their mind', one does not come across people who do not believe in their own individuality, though there are many who do not believe in the separation of mind and matter. Belief in one's own existence seems to depend very little on deliberate instruction.[10]

Moreover, Adrian continued, 'in the study of the human ego, introspections are almost all we have to guide us'. 'Introspections', presumably, reveal to us the sensory, perceptual and emotional contents of consciousness. This (mis)conception conforms with the venerable philosophical tradition that stems from Descartes and the British empiricists (see §3.6). It is

---

[9] E. D. Adrian, 'Consciousness', in J. C. Eccles (ed.), *Brain and Conscious Experience* (Springer Verlag, Berlin and New York, 1966), p. 240.
[10] Ibid., p. 241.

a general (mis)conception that is still characteristic of much neuroscientific reflection on these matters, especially among those neuroscientists who think that 'qualia' are the mark of conscious life – a feature that seems irreducibly 'mental' (for a detailed discussion of qualia, see §§10.3–10.3.5).

Adrian's confusions about the ego   Adrian was exceedingly hesitant to commit himself to any firm doctrine concerning the nature of what he called 'our ego'. He quoted the neurologist Francis Schiller, who claimed in 1951 that consciousness is a 'logical construction', and the ego 'a convenient abbreviation, an abstract of the multiplicity of objects from which it is developed' – this, Adrian averred, 'seems to me a reasonable position to have reached'.[11] For, he thought, 'the physiologist is not forced to reject the old fashioned picture of himself as a conscious individual with a will of his own', for the view embraced acknowledges some kind of validity to the introspective as well as to the physiological account, while admitting that the two are incompatible. What that implies, Adrian claimed, is that in the fullness of time the two accounts will have to be reconciled. But it would, he held, be absurd to suppose that the scientific account will not be altered.

It is noteworthy that this (essentially Russellian) conception is actually at odds with the Cartesian view of the ego of which Adrian previously approved. It is probable that Adrian had no clear grasp of the Russellian term of art 'logical construction'. For if consciousness is a logical construction and the ego a convenient abbreviation, then the immediate awareness of the self that Adrian endorses is as much of an illusion as an immediate acquaintance with the average man (the average man being uncontroversially a logical construction). Confusions concerning the 'ego' and the 'self' will concern us in chapter 12.

2.3 John Eccles and the 'Liaison Brain'

Eccles's achievement   After studying medicine at Melbourne University, John Eccles (1903–97) went to Oxford in 1925 as a graduate student to work with Sherrington, who was at that time engaged in research with Liddell on the characteristics of the myotatic reflex and with Creed on the flexion reflex. Eccles's first experimental work was done with Creed. It was on the subject destined to dominate his research for over forty years: the mechanism of inhibitory synaptic transmission. After completing his D.Phil. in 1929, he joined Sherrington's research group, and developed a technical improvement of the torsion myograph in preparation for a collaboration concerned with research on the flexion reflex and inhibition. These experiments were to see the last flowering of Sherrington's scientific genius at the age of seventy-five. The work on the ipsilateral spinal flexion reflex introduced Eccles to the technique of stimulating nerves first with just a threshold conditioning volley, then at later intervals with a subsequent test volley in order to tease out the time course of the central excitatory and inhibitory states. This approach, when applied to the mechanism of transmission in the

---

[11] Ibid., p. 246.

spinal cord, gave a very precise measure of the time course of the central excitatory and inhibitory states, or, as we now know, the excitatory and inhibitory postsynaptic potentials. This was shown by Eccles and his colleagues some twenty years later, when they made the first intracellular recordings of postsynaptic potentials in motoneurones. Subsequent studies of inhibitory synaptic transmission using intracellular electrodes were carried out by Eccles and his colleagues at successively higher levels of the central nervous system. These provided a functional microanatomy of the synaptic connections to be found in the cerebellum, the thalamus and the hippocampus. In this way Eccles completed the research programme described by Sherrington in *The Integrative Action of the Nervous System* half a century earlier.

Eccles's interest in the mind–brain problem

Eccles had entered the field of neuroscience as a result of an inspirational experience he had had at the age of eighteen that changed his life and aroused in him an intense interest in the mind–brain problem.[12] In the 1970s, evidently stimulated by the work done by R. W. Sperry and his colleagues in the 1960s on the results of hemispherectomy, he turned at last to these philosophical questions of his youth, first in *The Self and its Brain* (1977), a book he wrote with Karl Popper, and subsequently in his Gifford Lectures of 1977–8, published in 1984 as *The Human Mystery*. He opened his Gifford Lectures with a handsome tribute to Sherrington's Gifford Lectures forty years earlier. Eccles remarked that the general theme of *Man on his Nature* had been the defence of a form of dualism – a doctrine that was, by the 1970s, antipathetic to established philosophy. Nevertheless, it was a doctrine that Eccles deeply admired and, moreover, believed to have been given experimental confirmation by Kornhuber's work on the electrical potential generated in the cerebral cortex prior to performing an intentional action and by Sperry's work on split-brain patients. Hence, he aimed, in his own Gifford Lectures, to defend Sherrington's conception, to 'define the mind–brain problem more starkly,'[13] and to bring to bear on the problem these most recent findings in neuroscience.

Popper's influence

The general framework for Eccles's reflections was furnished by Popper's revival of a misconceived idea of the great nineteenth-century mathematical logician Gottlob Frege.[14] Frege distinguished between the perceptible 'outer world' of physical objects, the private 'inner world' of mental entities, and a 'third realm' of thoughts (propositions) that are imperceptible by the senses, but nevertheless public and shareable. Popper followed suit, distinguishing between World 1 of physical things, World 2 of mental things, and World 3 of thoughts, theorems, theories and other *abstracta*. The conception is confused, since although we distinguish material objects from mental states, and both from propositions or theorems, these do not collectively constitute 'worlds' in any sense whatsoever. Furthermore, neither mental states

---

[12] J. C. Eccles, in K. R. Popper and J. C. Eccles, *The Self and its Brain* (Springer Verlag, Berlin, 1977), p. 357.
[13] Eccles, *Human Mystery*, p. 3. Subsequent references in the text to this book will be flagged '*HM*'.
[14] Gottlob Frege, 'The thought', in his *Collected Papers on Mathematics, Logic and Philosophy* (Blackwell, Oxford, 1984), pp. 351–72.

nor propositions are denizens of a distinct 'world'. There is only *one* world, which is described by specifying whatever is (contingently) the case. We do indeed talk of people's mental states of cheerfulness or depression, or of their having toothache. But this does not imply that cheerfulness, depression or toothache are peculiar mental entities that exist in an 'inner world'. These nominals ('cheerfulness', 'depression', 'toothache') merely provide an indirect way of talking of people *being* cheerful or depressed and of their tooth's hurting – it introduces no new entities, merely new ways of talking about existing entities (e.g. about people and how things are with them). Similarly, we talk of propositions, theorems and other *abstracta* – but this too only *appears* to introduce new entities, and is really no more than a convenient way of talking about what is or might be said, asserted, or proved, etc. There is absolutely no need to succumb to Platonism and conjure new entities into existence and new worlds for them to inhabit. All talk of expressions standing for 'abstract entities' is a misleading way of saying that expressions that look as if they stand for concrete entities do not do so at all, but rather fulfil quite different functions. To be sure, this does not mean that there are no mental states, no cheerfulness, depression or anxiety, or that there are no propositions, no theories or theorems. On the contrary, it means that there are – only they are not kinds of entities.

Popper's three-world doctrine impressed Eccles, and he formulated his dualism in terms of it. World 1, the material world of the cosmos, he declared, consists of mere material things and of beings that enjoy mental states. The latter, being a subset of the entities in World 1, he refers to collectively as 'World 1_M'. This 'world' stands in reciprocal causal interaction with World 2 by means of what he terms 'the liaison brain' (*HM* 211).

The impact on Eccles of Kornhuber's research on readiness potential Research done by Kornhuber and his colleagues on changes in electrical potential antecedent to a voluntary movement had revealed that the so-called readiness potential began up to 800 milliseconds before the onset of the muscle action potential, and led to a sharper potential, the pre-motion positivity, beginning at 80–90 milliseconds prior to the movement. The patterns of neuronal discharges eventually project to the appropriate pyramidal cells of the motor cortex and synaptically excite them to discharge, so generating the motor potential (a localized negative wave) just preceding the motor pyramidal cell discharge that initiates the movement. The question on which Kornhuber's research seemed to throw light was: 'How can willing of a muscular movement set in train neuronal events that lead to the discharge of pyramidal cells of the motor cortex and so to the activation of the neuronal pathways that lead to the muscle contraction?' (*HM* 214).

It is striking that Eccles took these discoveries to betoken empirical confirmation of mind–brain interaction of a kind (but in a different location) that had been envisaged by Descartes. He argued as follows:

> What is happening in my brain at a time when the willed action is in the process of being carried out? It can be presumed that during the readiness potential there is a developing specificity of the patterned impulse discharges in neurons so that eventually there are activated the pyramidal cells in the correct motor cortical areas for bringing about the required movement. The readiness potential can be regarded as the neuronal counterpart of the voluntary intention. The surprising feature of the readiness potential is

its very wide extent and gradual build up. Apparently, at the stage of willing a movement, there is a very wide influence of the self-conscious mind on the pattern of module operation. Eventually this immense neuronal activity is moulded and directed so that it concentrates onto the pyramidal cells in the proper zones of the motor cortex for carrying out the required movement. The duration of the readiness potential indicates that the sequential activity of the large numbers of modules is involved in the long incubation time required for the self-conscious mind to evoke discharges from the motor pyramidal cells. . . . It is a sign that the action of the self-conscious mind on the brain is not of demanding strength. We may regard it as being more tentative and subtle, and as requiring time to build up patterns of activity that may be modified as they develop. (*HM* 217)

Cartesian problems recapitulated:
1. Interaction

So, Eccles conceived of what he called 'the dualist-interactionist hypothesis' as helping to 'resolve and redefine the problem of accounting for the long duration of the readiness potential that precedes a voluntary action' (*HM* 217).

Descartes, as we have noted, conceived of the mind as operating upon the pineal gland to generate the minute fluctuations in the animal spirits (the equivalent of neural transmitters) in the ventricle in which he thought the pineal gland was suspended. This, he held, enabled the acts of will of the mind to affect the motions of the animal spirits, which are then transmitted to the muscles. But the question of *how* an immaterial substance could actually interact causally with a material object such as the pineal gland to produce the appropriate minute motions was left totally unanswered. In much the same way, Eccles thought that the 'self-conscious mind' interacts causally with the pyramidal cells of the motor cortex, gradually (rather than instantaneously) getting them to discharge. But the question of *how* an immaterial entity such as the mind can interact causally with neurons was left equally unanswered.

2. Reifying the mind

Both thinkers erred in conceiving of the mind as an entity of some kind. Had they heeded Aristotle in thinking of the mind not as an entity but as an array of powers or potentialities, they would have been much closer to the truth, and would not have become enmeshed in insoluble problems of interaction. For it patently makes no sense to ask how one's abilities to do the various things one can do interact with one's brain.

3. Misconceptions about the will

Both thinkers erred in imagining that voluntary movements are movements produced or caused by antecedent acts of will.[15] For although there are such things as acts of will – namely, acts performed with great effort to overcome one's reluctance, aversion or difficulties in acting in adverse circumstances – obviously the vast majority of our ordinary voluntary actions involve no 'act of will' in this sense at all. We shall examine this conception in chapter 8.

Eccles was further confused over the object of the alleged act of will, which is variously characterized as (i) a muscular movement, (ii) an action or (iii) a movement of a limb.

---

[15] This error is still common among neuroscientists, and informs the research of Benjamin Libet and his colleagues that we discuss below (see §§8.1–8.2).

Confusions about the object of the alleged act of will

It is, of course, possible to intend to move – for example, to flex a muscle; but that is something we rather rarely intend to do, and although the movement of muscles is involved in all our positive, physical acts (by contrast with acts of omission and mental acts), what we intend, and what we voluntarily perform, are actions (such as raising our arm, writing a letter, saying something, picking up a book, reading a book, and so on), and not the constitutive muscle movements of these actions, of which we are largely unaware. But it is easy to see why a neuroscientist who is attracted to dualism should confuse the objects of the will. For, according to the dualist conception, the mind has causally to affect the brain, and the causal powers of neural events in the brain causally affect muscle contraction.

Problems of volitional interaction between mind and brain

This raises yet a further insoluble problem for the dualist. The 'self-conscious mind' is supposed to influence the pattern of module operation, gradually moulding and directing it so that it concentrates on the pyramidal cells in the proper zones of the motor cortex for carrying out the intended movement. But how does the 'self-conscious mind' know which pyramidal cells to concentrate on, and how does it select the proper zones of the motor cortex? For it would need such knowledge in order to execute such actions. And it is certainly not knowledge of which the self-conscious mind is conscious. To these questions there can be no answers, any more than the nineteenth-century innervationist ideo-motor theories of voluntary movement, favoured by such eminent scientists as Helmholtz and Mach (and psychologists such as Bain and Wundt), could answer the question of how the mind, in addition to having images of kinaesthetic sensations that allegedly accompany voluntary movements, directs the currents of energy going from the brain to the appropriate muscles. (There must be appropriate feelings of innervation – of 'impulse' or 'volitional energy', they thought, otherwise the mind could never tell which particular current of energy, whether the current to this muscle or the current to that one, was the right one to use.)

Eccles's conception of the implications of Sperry's discoveries about results of split-brain operations

A second piece of empirical research encouraged Eccles in his advocacy of interactionist dualism. Sperry's discoveries concerning the capacities of split-brain patients were striking. He himself took them to vindicate some form of mind–brain interactionism:

> Conscious phenomena in this scheme are conceived to interact with and to largely govern the physiochemical and physiological aspects of the brain process. It obviously works the other way round as well, and thus a mutual interaction is conceived between the physiological and the mental properties. Even so, the present interpretation would tend to restore the mind to its old prestigious position over matter, in the sense that the mental phenomena are seen to transcend the phenomena of physiology and biochemistry.[16]

---

[16] Quoted by Eccles, without a reference, in Popper and Eccles, *Self and its Brain*, p. 374.

It is therefore unsurprising that Eccles thought that Sperry's work had dramatic implications. 'It is my thesis', he wrote, 'that the philosophical problem of brain and mind has been transformed by these investigations of the functions of the separate dominant and minor hemispheres in the split-brain subjects' (*HM* 222). The 'most remarkable discovery', Eccles held, was that all the neural activities in the right hemisphere 'are unknown to the speaking subject, who is only in liaison with the neuronal activities in the left [dominant] hemisphere'. To be sure, the right hemisphere is 'a very highly developed brain', but it 'cannot express itself in language, so is not able to disclose any experience of consciousness that we can recognize'. The dominance of the left hemisphere, he argued, is due to its verbal and ideational abilities, and 'its liaison to self-consciousness (World 2)' (*HM* 220). For what Sperry's work shows, Eccles averred, is 'that only a specialized zone of the cerebral hemispheres is in liaison with the self-conscious mind. The term liaison brain denotes all those areas of the cerebral cortex that potentially are capable of being in direct liaison with the self-conscious mind.'[17]

Eccles's conception of the liaison brain and Descartes's conception of the pineal gland compared

Descartes thought that the pineal gland was the point of contact of the mind and the brain, and that the mind apprehends what is before the eyes of the body in virtue of the images that come from the two eyes and are united on the pineal gland. Eccles thought that the liaison brain was the point of contact with the mind, where the nerve impulses from the sense-organs are, in some sense, made available to the mind. But there is an interesting difference between the two doctrines. Descartes thought that the pineal gland itself – that is, a part of the brain – fulfils the task of the Aristotelian and scholastic *sensus communis*, the task of synthesizing and unifying the data of the separate senses. In this respect, his thought was more up to date than Eccles's, since contemporary neuroscientists think likewise that the 'binding problem' is solved by the brain (rather than by the mind).[18] For Singer's discoveries[19] of coherent oscillatory firings in disparate parts of the brain concomitant with perceptual experience suggest that the simultaneity of these manifold neuronal activities and their connections to other areas of the cortex are necessary conditions for a perceiver to have the kind of unified perceptual experience we have. Eccles, by contrast, defended what he called 'the strong dualist hypothesis' that

> the self-conscious mind is actively engaged in reading out from the multitude of active modules at the highest levels of the brain, namely in the liaison areas that are largely in the dominant cerebral hemisphere. The self-conscious mind selects from these modules according to attention, and from moment to moment integrates its selection to give

---

[17] Ibid., p. 358.

[18] See, e.g., F. Crick, *The Astonishing Hypothesis* (Touchstone, London, 1995), pp. 22, 232, and E. Kandel and R. Wurtz, 'Constructing the visual image', in Kandel, Schwartz and Jessell (eds), *Principles of Neural Science* (Elsevier, New York, 2001), pp. 492, 502. (The binding problem is discussed in §4.2.3 below.)

[19] A. K. Engel, P. R. Roelfsema, P. Fries, M. Brecht and W. Singer, 'Role of the temporal domain for response selection and perceptual binding', *Cerebral Cortex*, 6 (1997), pp. 571–82.

unity even to the most transient experience. Furthermore, the self-conscious mind acts upon these modules, modifying the dynamic spatio-temporal patterns of the neuronal events. Thus the self-conscious mind exercises a superior interpretative and controlling role upon the neuronal events both within the modules and between the modules.

A key component of the hypothesis is that the unity of conscious experience is provided by the self-conscious mind and not by the neuronal machinery of the liaison areas of the cerebral cortex. Hitherto it has been impossible to develop any neurophysiological theory that explains how a diversity of brain events comes to be synthesized so that there is a unified conscious experience . . . My general hypothesis regards the neuronal machinery as a multiplex of radiating and receiving structures (modules). The experienced unity comes, not from a neurophysiological synthesis, but from the proposed integrating character of the self-conscious mind. I conjecture that in the first place the *raison d'être* of the self-conscious mind is to give this unity of the self in all its conscious experiences and actions. (*HM* 227f.)

How does the mind engage in this activity of synthesis (or 'binding')? Eccles suggested that the mind

plays through the whole liaison brain in a selective and unifying manner. The analogy is provided by a searchlight. Perhaps a better analogy would be some multiple scanning and probing device that reads out from and selects from the immense and diverse patterns of activity in the cerebral cortex and integrates these selected components, so organizing them into the unity of conscious experience. . . . Thus I conjecture that the self-conscious mind is scanning the modular activities in the liaison areas of the cerebral cortex. . . . From moment to moment it is selecting modules according to its interests, the phenomena of attention, and is itself integrating from all this diversity to give the unified conscious experience. (*HM* 229)

Four flaws in Eccles's conception

The metaphors are striking, and have echoes in current neuroscientific theory.[20] Nevertheless, Sperry's discoveries

---

[20] So, for example, Crick called his theory of attention 'the searchlight hypothesis', since, he claimed, the reticular complex and the pulvinar promote only a small proportion of the activity of the thalamus on its way to the cortex, and this activity can be likened to a searchlight that lights up a part of the cortex. Crick suggested that the thalamic reticular complex and the pulvinar interact with the brain stem and with cortical mechanisms to reach a salient decision as to which neuronal groups that are active will be 'brought into consciousness' by the spotlight of attention (F. Crick, 'Function of the thalamic reticular complex: the searchlight hypothesis', *Proceedings of the National Academy of Science USA*, **81** (1984), pp. 4586–5490). Similarly, the notion of a scanning device or 'monitor' in the brain has been invoked by Weiskrantz in connection with his investigations of blind-sight. In his view, the awareness that a normally sighted person has of whether he sees something in his visual field and of what he sees results from the operation of a neural monitoring system. Conscious experience, according to Weiskrantz, is the product of the monitoring function of the brain (L. Weiskrantz, 'Neuropsychology and the nature of consciousness', in C. Blakemore and S. Greenfield (eds), *Mindwaves* (Blackwell, Oxford, 1987), pp. 307–20). It is interesting that whereas Crick and Weiskrantz apply these metaphors to the brain, Eccles applied them to the mind.

have none of the dramatic implications that Eccles imputed to them. There are four flaws in Eccles's conception to which we wish to draw attention.

1. The phenomena resultant upon hemispherectomy were misdescribed
First, the phenomena were misdescribed. It is not just the neural activities of the right hemisphere that are unknown to the subject – *all* the activities of the brain are unknown to subjects, who do not, after all, perceive their own brains (and, even if they could, do not have electron microscopes for eyes). It is true that the right hemisphere cannot 'express itself in language', any more than the right leg – because there is no such thing as *a part* of a human being expressing itself in language (see §§3.1–3.4). So the left hemisphere cannot 'express itself in language' either. The right hemisphere is not able 'to disclose any experience of consciousness' that we can recognize, because there is no such thing as a subordinate part of a person being conscious. As will be argued in detail in chapter 3, it is only human beings (and other animals) who are conscious (or unconscious), and conscious *of* (or not conscious of) various things – not their subordinate parts. The left hemisphere is equally lacking in 'any experience of consciousness'. Finally, the left hemisphere has no 'verbal and ideational abilities', although the verbal and ideational abilities of normal human beings are causally dependent upon the normal functioning of the left hemisphere.[21]

2. The 'self-conscious mind' is not an entity of any kind
Secondly, the so-called self-conscious mind is not an entity of any kind, but a capacity of human beings who have mastered a reflexive language. They can therefore ascribe experiences to themselves and reflect on the experiences thus ascribed (see §12.6). But the 'self-conscious mind' is not the sort of thing that can intelligibly be said to be 'in contact with' the brain (let alone with something denominated 'the liaison brain').

3. Incoherence in Eccles's hypothesis
Thirdly, Eccles's main hypothesis is unintelligible. If the self-conscious mind were, *per impossibile*, 'actively engaged in reading out' from areas in the dominant hemisphere and 'selecting from these modules according to attention', then the self-conscious mind would have to perceive or be aware of the neural modules in question (otherwise how could it 'read them out'?), and know which ones to select for its purpose (otherwise the wrong ones might constantly be selected). Or, to put matters more lucidly, for any of this story to make sense, human beings would have to be aware of the neural structures and operations in question, and, from moment to moment, decide which ones directly to activate, and, of course, have the capacity to do so. But we possess no such knowledge and no such capacity.

4. The very notion of the self-conscious mind presupposes the unity of experience
Finally, it is confused to suppose that the *raison d'être* of the 'self-conscious mind' is to engender the unity of the self and, as our contemporaries would put it, 'solve the binding problem'. For any talk of a person, or of a being, as having a mind already presupposes the unity of experience and cannot be invoked to explain it.

---

[21] Neuroscientists' misdescriptions of split-brain patients' abilities and their exercise is examined and rectified in §14.3 below.

Eccles's errors cannot be rectified by substituting the brain for his conception of the 'self-conscious mind'

Eccles's dualism was misconceived. Contemporary neuroscientists are eager to dissociate themselves from his doctrines and to dismiss his ideas as silly. This is misguided. Eccles had the courage to face difficult problems and to pursue his ideas about them to their logical conclusions. That his ideas are wrong is true, and much can be learnt from the errors in question. It is, however, a sad mark of how little many neuroscientists have learnt from Eccles's struggles that they apparently believe that the problems that Eccles's interactionist dualism was designed to answer can be solved by substituting the brain for Eccles's 'self-conscious mind'. Problems regarding how the mind can bring about movements of the muscles and limbs by acts of will are not solved by supposing, as Libet does, that it is the brain that decides what muscles and limbs to move. Although it is misguided to suppose that the mind is in liaison with the left hemisphere, it is no less misconceived to suppose, as do Sperry, Gazzaniga and Crick, that the hemispheres of the brain know things, have beliefs, think and guess, hear and see. For these are functions of human beings and other animals, not of brains or half-brains (which enable human beings to exercise those functions). And, as we have noted, although it is confused to suppose that the mind scans the brain, it is equally confused to suppose that the brain must scan itself in order to generate awareness or self-consciousness – as if it lay in the nature of self-consciousness that it necessarily involves a self-scanning process, if not of the mind, then of the brain. In short, the lessons that *can* be learnt from Eccles's failure have largely yet *to be* learnt. We shall endeavour to show this in some detail in later chapters.

2.4 Wilder Penfield and the 'Highest Brain Mechanism'

Penfield's training

Wilder Penfield (1891–1976) was born in Spokane, Washington. After graduating from Princeton in 1913, he won a Rhodes Scholarship to Oxford and entered the School of Physiology there to begin his medical studies under the inspiring influence of Sherrington. He followed Sherrington's interest in histology and, in particular, in neurocytology. After obtaining his BA in physiology at Oxford, he went to the Johns Hopkins Medical School, where he finished his medical degree in 1918. His first research concerned changes in the Golgi apparatus of neurons after axonal section. In 1924 he began to study the healing processes of surgical wounds in the brain. On Sherrington's advice, he spent some time in Madrid working with Pio del Rio-Hortega, learning to use the histological methods of his brilliant teacher Ramón y Cajal. To this end, surgical specimens of brain scars were collected from patients who had been operated on for post-traumatic epilepsy.

Penfield's achievement

Penfield was aware of the studies on cortical localization in the primate brain that Sherrington had carried out, and which have been described above. In 1928, he went to Breslau to work with Otfrid Foerster, to learn his method of gentle electrical stimulation of the cortex of epileptic patients while they were under local anaesthesia during the excision of epileptogenic scar tissue. During these procedures he learnt the method of operating under local anaesthesia, using electrical stimulation to identify the sensory and motor cortex to guide the surgical excision. This technique was to be used to singular effect by Penfield in Montreal, where, in 1934, he established the famous Montreal Neurological Institute at McGill University, which was devoted to the study and surgical treatment of focal epilepsy. Such stimulation made it possible to locate exactly the position of the sensorimotor cortex and of the cortex subserving speech, so that these vital areas could be spared during the surgical excision. In some instances the stimulation might activate the more excitable epileptogenic cortex and reproduce a portion of the patient's habitual seizure pattern. This enabled the surgeon to identify the site of the physiologically deranged epileptic focus. Penfield's mastery of these procedures was subsequently summarized in a series of monographs on brain surgery for epilepsy.

Penfield noted in 1938 that stimulation of certain parts of the temporal cortex in patients occasionally excited the vivid recall of previous experiences. It became evident that almost half of the patients afflicted with epilepsy had seizures that could be shown to originate in one or other of the temporal lobes. This work on temporal lobe epilepsy led to very important observations regarding the hippocampus and memory function, as well as the localization of the cortex subserving the latter. By 1951 Penfield, together with Milner, had shown that removal of one hippocampus on the medial aspect of the temporal lobe resulted in severe memory disorder in patients who were later found to have damage to the hippocampus on the opposite side. Thus the bilateral loss of function of the hippocampus led to the complete inability of these patients to remember any post-operative occurrence. This memory loss was not accompanied by any loss of intelligence or attentive capacity. Penfield's analyses of the electrical stimulation of the cortex of 1,132 conscious patients undergoing brain surgery greatly extended our knowledge of functional localization, especially with regard to memory and to that most human of capacities, speech.

Penfield's methodological commitment

Already in his student days, Penfield had had a 'sense of wonder and a profound curiosity about the mind'. When he turned from the study of the animal to the human brain, his 'planned objective', he later wrote, was 'to come to understand the mechanisms of the human brain and to discover whether, and perhaps how, these mechanisms account for what the mind does'.[22] Studying under Sherrington, he came to 'the realization that the brain was an undiscovered country in which the mystery of the mind of man might some day be explained'. He was, of course, fully aware of Sherrington's views on the relation of mind and brain. In the final paragraph of the foreword to his great book *The Integrative Action of the Nervous System* (1906), Sherrington had remarked, 'That our being should consist of two fundamental elements offers, I suppose, no greater inherent improbability than that it should rest on one only'. Penfield, however, took the view that the neuroscientist should endeavour to explain the behaviour of animals, including humans,

---

[22] W. Penfield, *The Mystery of the Mind: A Critical Study of Consciousness and the Human Brain* (Princeton University Press, Princeton, 1975), p. 1. Subsequent references in the text to this volume will be flagged '*MM*'.

on the basis of neuronal mechanisms alone. Only if that failed, he thought, should one have recourse to alternative forms of explanation. And throughout his career as a neurosurgeon, he retained this methodological commitment.

Penfield on the mind Towards the end of a long life dedicated to neurosurgery and neurology, Penfield published a small volume entitled *The Mystery of the Mind*. This was, he wrote, 'the final report of my experience' – an overview of what he had achieved in respect of his youthful objective. 'The nature of the mind', he averred, 'presents the fundamental problem, perhaps the most difficult and most important of all problems' (*MM* 85). What he wished at last to do, he wrote in the preface, was to 'consider the evidence as it stands, and ask the question *Do brain mechanisms account for the mind? Can the mind be explained by what is now known about the brain?*' (*MM*, p. xiii). Referring explicitly to the above-quoted remark of Sherrington's, Penfield judged that 'the time has come to look at his two hypotheses, his two "improbabilities". Either brain action explains the mind, or we must deal with two elements' (*MM* 4). Despite his methodological commitment, Penfield found himself driven towards a Cartesian view not unlike that of his great teacher. 'For my own part', he wrote,

> after years of striving to explain the mind on the basis of brain-action alone, I have come to the conclusion that it is simpler (and far easier to be logical) if one adopts the hypothesis that our being does consist of two fundamental elements. . . . Because it seems to me certain that it will always be quite impossible to explain the mind on the basis of neuronal action within the brain, and because it seems to me that the mind develops and matures independently throughout an individual's life as though it were a continuing element, and because a computer (which the brain is) must be programmed and operated by an agency capable of independent understanding, I am forced to choose the proposition that our being is to be explained on the basis of two fundamental elements. This, to my mind, offers the greatest likelihood of leading us to the final understanding toward which so many stalwart scientists strive. (*MM* 80)

What led him to this conclusion? Two features in particular had impressed Penfield. First, given his specialization in epilepsy cases, he was, unsurprisingly, impressed by the phenomena of epileptic automatism. Second, he was powerfully struck by the responses elicited from patients in reaction to electrode stimulation during surgery.

Penfield's interpretation of epileptic automatism A patient, suffering an epileptic seizure that has induced automatism, will often continue to execute whatever more or less stereotypical tasks he was engaged in. He will, however, be in a fugue condition – that is, after recovery he will remember nothing of what he has done during the seizure. Penfield interpreted automatism as showing that the epileptic seizure disconnected the mind from what, following Hughlings Jackson,[23] he called 'the brain's highest mechanism' (a precursor of Eccles's 'liaison brain'). He took it that the brain, during the period of automatism, is controlling the behaviour of a 'human

---

[23] J. H. Jackson, 'On the anatomical, physiological and pathological investigations of epilepsies', *West Riding Lunatic Asylum Medical Reports*, 3 (1873), pp. 315–19.

automaton' in accordance with antecedent 'programming' by the mind. Just as the pro-gramming of a computer comes 'from without', so too the programming of the brain, which is, Penfield claimed, a biological computer, is effected by the mind via the brain's highest mechanism. Purpose comes to it from outside its own mechanisms. Short-term programming obviously serves a useful purpose, making possible automatic continuation of routine tasks, and this is visibly and strikingly manifest during periods of such epileptic seizures.

> That this highest mechanism, most closely related to the mind, is a truly functional unit is proven by the fact that epileptic discharge in gray matter that forms a part of its circuits, interferes with its action selectively. During epileptic interference with the function of this gray matter . . . consciousness vanishes, and with it goes the direction and planning of behaviour. That is to say, the mind goes out of action and comes into action with the normal functioning of this mechanism.
>
> The human automaton, which replaces man when the highest brain-mechanism is inactivated, is a thing without the capacity to make completely new decisions. It is a thing without the capacity to form new memory records and a thing without that indefinable attribute, a sense of humour. The automaton is incapable of thrilling to the beauty of a sunset or of experiencing contentment, happiness, love, compassion. These, like all awarenesses, are functions of the mind. The automaton is a thing that makes use of reflexes and skills, inborn and acquired, that are housed in the computer. (*MM* 47)

Though Penfield ventured no testable hypotheses about how this interaction occurs, he claimed that the highest brain mechanism is, as it were, the mind's executive. It accepts directions from the mind, and passes them on to the various mechanisms of the brain (*MM* 84). The mind directs the brain in action. It has no memory of its own. But the contents of the stream of consciousness are recorded in the brain (as seems evident from the inadvertent retrieval of long-lost memories during cortical stimulation of the brain during operations). So, when the mind needs to retrieve a memory, in a flash it opens the files of remembrance in the brain through the highest brain mechanism (*MM* 49).

Penfield's interpretation of phenom-ena consequent on electrode cortical stimulation — Reflection on some of the phenomena consequent on cortical stimulation during operations led Penfield to sim-ilar conclusions. So, for example, a patient, whose 'speech cortex' was interfered with by an electrode, exhibited exasperation when he could not identify a picture of a butterfly. On withdrawal of the electrode, he said, '"Now I can talk. Butterfly. I couldn't *get* the word "Butterfly", so I tried to *get* the word "moth"'!' It is interesting to see how Penfield construed and explained this temporary impairment of the patient's normal identificatory capacities.

> It is clear that while the speech mechanism was temporarily blocked he could perceive the meaning of the picture of a butterfly. He made a conscious effort to 'get' the corresponding word. Then, not understanding why he could not do so, he turned back for a second time to the interpretative mechanism . . . and found a second concept that

he considered the closest thing to a butterfly.[24] He must then have presented that to the speech mechanism, only to draw another blank. (*MM* 52)

According to Penfield, concepts are stored away in the mind's concept mechanism in the brain, from which the mind selects the concept it requires. That concept is then presented in the stream of consciousness, and if the mind approves of the selection, the highest brain mechanism flashes this non-verbal concept to the speech mechanism, which, when functioning normally, will present to the mind the word that is appropriate for the concept (*MM* 53).

Penfield was equally impressed by the fact that when neural stimulation to the brain caused a hand movement, the patient invariably responded, 'I didn't do that. You did.' And equally, when cortical stimulation caused vocalization, the patient said, 'I didn't make that noise. You pulled it out of me.' It was striking that no form of electrical stimulation to the cortex could induce a patient to believe or to decide (*MM* 77). It is not surprising that Penfield drew the conclusion that belief and volition are functions of the mind.

The mind and its interaction with the brain via 'the highest brain mechanism'

A man's mind, Penfield concluded, is the person (*MM* 61). It is the mind that is aware of what is going on, that reasons and decides, and understands (*MM* 75f.). The person walks about the world [*sic*], depending always upon his 'private computer' (i.e. his brain), which he programs continuously (*MM* 61). The highest brain mechanism is the meeting place of mind and brain, the psychophysical frontier (*MM* 53). The mind, in making decisions, causes the highest brain mechanism to send neuronal messages to other mechanisms in the brain, and data stored in the brain are admitted to consciousness. How is interaction effected? Here Penfield speculated that there must be a second form of energy (other than the electrical energy that is used by the highest brain function to innervate the nervous system) which is available to the mind. This, he conjectured, must be made available to the mind in its waking hours by the highest brain mechanism.

> The mind vanishes when the highest brain mechanism ceases to function due to injury or due to epileptic interference or anaesthetic drug. More than that, the mind vanishes during deep sleep.
>
> What happens when the mind vanishes? There are two obvious answers to that question; they arise from Sherrington's two alternatives – whether man's being is to be explained on the basis of one or two elements. (*MM* 81)

Penfield thought it preposterous to suppose that the mind is merely a function of the brain, and so ceases to exist when it 'vanishes' in sleep or epileptic automatism and is re-created afresh each time the highest brain mechanism functions normally. Rather, he concluded, the mind is 'a basic element', and has a 'continuing existence'. 'One must assume', he wrote, 'that although the mind is silent, when it no longer has its special

---

[24] Penfield obviously meant that it was the closest approximation to the concept of a butterfly.

connection to the brain, it exists in the silent intervals and takes over control when the highest brain mechanism goes into action' (*MM* 81). So, the highest brain mechanism switches off the power that energizes the mind whenever one goes to sleep, and switches it on again when one awakens.

Is the explanation improbable?, Penfield queried.

> It is not so improbable, to my mind, as is the alternative expectation [explanation] – that the highest brain mechanism should itself understand, and reason, and direct voluntary action, and decide where attention should be turned and what the computer must learn and record, and reveal on demand. (*MM* 82)

Penfield's neo-Cartesianism

Penfield's neo-Cartesianism is no advance over that of Sherrington and Eccles. But if we are to learn anything from his errors, we must not simply dismiss them as misguided and move on to other matters. That will merely ensure that we learn nothing from his endeavours. We must ask what went wrong, what drove one of the greatest neurosurgeons and neurologists of all times to embrace such a misconceived view of the mind and brain?

Shared presuppositions
1. The Cartesian conception of the mind

It should be noted that there are at least two fundamental presuppositions that Penfield shared with Sherrington and Eccles. The first was a Cartesian conception of the mind.

Like Descartes, Penfield conceived of the mind as an independent substance (or, as he puts it, 'a fundamental element' that has 'continuing existence'). Like Descartes, he identified the person with the mind, rather than with the living human being. Like Descartes, he took the mind to be the bearer of psychological attributes,[25] and consequently conceived of human beings as subjects of psychological predicates only derivatively. And like Descartes, he took the mind to be a causal agent that can bring about changes in the body by its actions.

2. The assumption that the question of whether brain mechanisms can account for the mind is an empirical one

The second presupposition is that the question which so deeply disturbed him – namely, whether brain mechanisms account for the mind, whether the mind can be explained by reference to what is known about the brain – is an empirical question. Like Sherrington, Penfield conceived of the matter as a choice between two different empirical hypotheses. Either we can explain everything the mind does – for example, thinks and believes, reasons and concludes, has wants, forms intentions and purposes, and decides to act – by reference to neural states and events, or we must conceive of the mind as an independent substance in immediate causal interaction with the brain, and hence with the body. The choice between these two hypotheses is to be determined by the evidence that supports them severally and by their relative explanatory powers.

Both presuppositions are misconceived. The mind, as we have already intimated, is not a substance of any kind. Talk of the mind is merely a *façon de parler* for talk about human

---

[25] Indeed, to explain what the mind or spirit is, Penfield quoted *Webster's Dictionary*: 'the element . . . in an individual that feels, perceives, thinks, wills and especially reasons' (*MM* 11).

Criticisms of Penfield's presuppositions: 1. Misconceptions about the nature of the mind

powers and their exercise. We say of a creature (primarily of a human being) that it *has a mind* if it has a certain range of active and passive powers of intellect and will – in particular, conceptual powers of a language-user that make self-awareness and self-reflection possible. The idioms that involve the noun 'mind' have as their focal points thought, memory and will. And they are all readily paraphrasable into psychological expressions in which the word does not occur (we shall discuss this matter in some detail in §3.10).

A person is not identical with his mind. A mind is something (but not some *thing*) a person is said to *have*, not to *be*. In having a mind, an animal (that is thereby also a person, and a bearer of rights and duties) has a distinctive range of capacities. And it is obvious both that an animal cannot be identical with an array of capacities, and that if a human being loses enough of those distinctive capacities, he can cease to be a person (and exist only in a 'vegetal state'). It is not the mind that is the subject of psychological attributes, any more than it is the brain. It is the living human being – the whole animal, not one of its parts or a subset of its powers. It is not my mind that makes up its mind or decides; it is not my mind that calls something to mind and recollects; and it is not my mind that turns its mind to something or other and thinks – it is I, *this* person. Hence, too, the mind is not a causal agent that brings about changes in the body and its limbs by its actions. On the contrary, it is human beings that deliberate, decide and act, not their minds.

2. Whether the brain can 'account for' the mind is not an empirical question

Consequently, Penfield's second presupposition is misguided. Whether we can 'account for the mind' in terms of the brain alone, or must account for the (supposed) activities of the mind (e.g. thought, reasoning, wants and purposes, intentions and decisions, voluntary and intentional actions) by reference to the mind itself, conceived of as an independent substance and therefore causal agent, is not a matter of choice between two empirical hypotheses. If these were empirical hypotheses, then either could in principle be true; that is, both would present intelligible possibilities, and it would be a matter of empirical investigation to discover which is actually the case. But that is not how it is at all.

It is neither the brain nor the mind that is the subject of psychological attributes

First, it is not the mind that thinks and reasons, wants things and has purposes, forms intentions and makes decisions, acts voluntarily or intentionally. It is the human being. We do indeed characterize a person as having a clear, rigorous or decisive mind. But these are merely ways of characterizing the person's *dispositions* in respect of thought and will. If we want to understand why a normal person reasoned the way he did, thought what he did, has the goals and purposes that he has, and why he decided as he did, formed such-and-such intentions and plans, and acted intentionally, no neurological account will clarify for us what we wish to be clarified. To this extent Penfield was right. Where he was wrong was in the supposition that what we need is an explanation in terms of the activities of the person's mind – where the latter is conceived of as an agent with causal powers. Rather, what we want is an explanation in terms of the person's reasoning, hence too by reference to what he knew or believed, and, in the case of practical reasoning, by reference to his goals and purposes. And if our explanation renders his reasoning intelligible, no further information about neural events in his brain can add anything. All a neural explanation could do would be to explain how it was *possible* for the person to reason cogently at all (i.e. what neural formations must be in place to endow a human being with such-and-such intellectual and volitional capacities), but it cannot rehearse the reasoning, let alone explain its cogency.

Neither the causal agency of the brain nor the causal agency of the mind explains intentional action

Similarly, if we are puzzled by a person's actions, if we wish to know why A signed a cheque for £200, no answer in terms of brain functions is likely to satisfy us. We want to know whether A was discharging a debt, making a purchase, donating money to charity, or betting on a horse – and once we know which of these is the case, we may also want to know what A's reasons were. A description of neural events in A's brain could not possibly explain to us what we want to have explained. If we wish to know why A caught the 8.15 a.m. to Paris, a description of neural events cannot *in principle* satisfy our need for an explanation. But the answer that he had a committee meeting there at 2.00 p.m. that was to decide upon such-and-such a project for which A is responsible may give quietus to our curiosity. If A has murdered B, we may wish to know why. We may be given a reason, and still remain dissatisfied, wishing to understand more – but the 'more' we wish to understand is most probably A's motive, not what neural events occurred at the time of the killing. We want to know whether he killed B out of revenge or out of jealousy, for example, and that requires a quite different narrative from anything that neuroscientific investigation could produce. Explanation of action by redescription, by citing agential reasons, or by specifying the agent's motives (and there are other forms of explanation of related kinds) are not replaceable, even in principle, by explanations in terms of neural events in the brain. This is not an empirical matter at all, but a logical or conceptual one. The type of explanation is categorially different, and explanations in terms of agential reasons and motives, goals and purposes, are not reducible to explanations of muscular contractions produced as a consequence of neural events (see chapter 13). But equally, such explanations are not couched in terms of the activities of the mind, conceived as an independent substance with causal powers of its own. In this sense, Penfield's dilemma is a bogus one. He was perfectly right to think that one cannot account for human behaviour and experience in terms of the brain alone, but wrong to suppose that the idea that one might be able to do so is an intelligible empirical hypothesis as opposed to a conceptual confusion. He was also wrong to suppose that the alternative is accounting for human behaviour and experience in terms of the causal agency of the mind, and wrong again in thinking that that too is an empirical hypothesis. There is no need whatsoever to impale oneself on either of the horns of Penfield's dilemma.

The hypothesis that mind–brain interaction can explain human behaviour is logically incoherent

Once these presuppositions are jettisoned, it becomes easier to see why the explanation of human behaviour in terms of the interaction of the mind (conceived as an independent substance) and the brain is misconceived. It is not a false empirical hypothesis, but a conceptual confusion. For inasmuch as the mind is not a substance, indeed not an entity of any kind, it is not *logically possible* for the mind to function as a causal agent that brings about changes by acting on the brain. This is not an empirical discovery, but a conceptual clarification. (But it is equally mistaken to suppose that substituting the brain for the Cartesian mind is any less confused. That too is not an empirical hypothesis, but a conceptual muddle, which likewise stands in need of conceptual clarification.)

Neither epileptic automatism nor electrode stimulation of the brain support dualism

Consequently, Penfield was mistaken to think that what so impressed him – namely, the phenomena of epileptic automatism and the various facts that characterize electrode stimulation of the brain – constitute empirical support for a dualist hypothesis. Epileptic automatism does not show that the mind has become disconnected from the 'highest brain mechanism' to which it is normally connected, and by which it is supplied with energy of an as yet unknown form.[26] What it shows is that during an epileptic seizure, as a consequence of the abnormal excitation of parts of the cortex, the person is temporarily deprived of some of his normal capacities (including memory, the ability to make decisions, emotional sensitivity and a sense of humour), while other capacities, in particular capacities for routine actions, are retained. The phenomena are indeed striking, but they amount to a dissociation of capacities that are normally associated, not to a disconnection of substances that are normally connected. They do not show that the brain is a computer or that the mind is its programmer. The brain is no more a computer than it is a central telephone exchange (the previously favoured analogy), and the mind is no more a computer programmer than it is a telephonist. It is perfectly true that the capacity to continue routine tasks unreflectively is useful (and the expression 'short-term programming' is an apt *metaphor* here). It is also true that the purposes pursued by a person are not the purposes of the person's brain. But it does not follow from this that they are the purposes of the person's mind. They are the purposes of the person – and they are to be understood in terms of facts about human life, social forms of life, antecedent events, current circumstances, agential beliefs and values, and so forth, not in terms of neural events and mechanisms. But it is, of course, true that, but for the normal functioning of the brain, a human being would not have, and would not be able to pursue, the normal kinds of purposes that we do pursue.

The various phenomena that characterize electrode stimulation of the brain are similarly misconstrued by Penfield. The case of interference with the 'speech cortex' does not show that there is any such thing as a 'concept mechanism' in the brain that stores non-verbal concepts that can be selected by the mind and then presented to the speech mechanism to be matched to the word that represents the concept. That is picturesque mythology, not an empirical theory. Words are not names of concepts, and do not stand for concepts, but rather express them. Concepts are abstractions from the use of words. The concept of a cat is what is common to the use of 'cat', 'chat', 'Katze', etc. The common features

---

[26] It is striking to compare Penfield's conception of this matter with Descartes's remarkable simile in his *Treatise on Man*: 'when a *rational soul* is present in this machine [namely, the body] it will have its principal seat in the brain, and reside there like the fountain keeper who must be stationed at the tanks to which the fountain's pipes return if he wants to produce, or prevent, or change their movements in some way' (AT XI, 131). Here the tank is the ventricle in which the pineal gland is allegedly suspended, the pipes are the nerves, and the water the animal spirits.

of the use of these words is not something that can be stored in the brain or anywhere else independently of a word (or symbol) that expresses the concept. The patient whom Penfield describes could not think of the word 'butterfly' with which to identify the object in the picture presented to him. He knew that the object belonged to a class which resembles a different class of insects (viz. moths), and tried, equally unsuccessfully, to think of the word for members of the second class. This temporary incapacity is incorrectly described as knowing the concept but being unable to remember the word for it. The supposition that the mind might be presented with non-verbal concepts from which to choose presupposes that there is some way of identifying non-verbal concepts and distinguishing one from the other independently of any words or symbols that express them. But that makes no sense.

It is certainly interesting that Penfield found that electrode stimulation could not induce either belief or decision. But this does not show that believing and deciding are actions of the mind, any more than it shows that they are not actions of the brain. It is true that they are not actions of the brain – but that is not an empirical fact that might be shown to be the case by an experiment. Rather, there is no such thing as the brain's believing or deciding (any more than there is such a thing as checkmate in draughts). But it is also true that they are not actions of the mind either. My mind does not believe or disbelieve anything – *I* do (although, to be sure, that is no action). Nor does it decide – it is human beings that decide and act on their decisions, not minds.

That the exercise of mental powers is a function of the brain does not show that behaviour and experience are explicable neurally

Penfield objected vehemently to the suggestion that the mind is a function of the brain, and supposed that if it were, then the mind would cease to exist during sleep or epileptic automatism. The suggestion is unclear, but one may surely say that the distinctive capacities of intellect and will of a creature that has a mind are a function of the creature's brain (and of other factors too). It does not follow (as Penfield evidently feared it would) that the behaviour and experience of such a creature in the circumstances of life is explicable in neural terms. But nor does it follow that the mind ceases to exist during sleep or epileptic seizure – any more than one's knowledge and beliefs, intentions and projects, cease to exist when one is asleep. Penfield was rightly impressed by the fact that 'the mind develops and matures independently throughout an individual's life as though it were a continuing element' (*MM* 80). But he was misled by his unquestioned assumption that the mind is a kind of agent. Had he thought of the mind in more Aristotelian terms as a set of powers or capacities, he would have been closer to the truth, and less prone to conceptual illusion. For the continuous possession of capacities is not interrupted by sleep or even by epileptic automatism, even though the agent cannot exercise some of his normal capacities during the seizure. And the developing unity of a person's mind is not the development of a substance distinct from the human being himself, but rather the emergence of a determinate character and personality, an intellect with certain distinctive characteristics and a will with a coherent array of preferences – all of which are traits *of the person*.

Penfield thought that a form of Cartesian dualism is more probably correct than what he conceived to be the alternative: namely, ascribing understanding, reasoning, volition and voluntary action, as well as deciding, to the brain itself. It is very striking and

What Penfield thought the less plausible alternative to dualism is the view currently favoured

important that the strategy that Penfield conceived to be altogether improbable is precisely the route that is currently adopted by the third generation of neuroscientists, who ascribe psychological functions to the brain. This is the subject of the next chapter.

3

The Mereological Fallacy
in Neuroscience

3.1 Mereological Confusions in Cognitive Neuroscience

Ascribing psychological attributes to the brain

Leading figures of the first two generations of modern brain-neuroscientists were fundamentally Cartesian. Like Descartes, they distinguished the mind from the brain, and ascribed psychological attributes to the mind. The ascription of such predicates to human beings was, accordingly, derivative – as in Cartesian metaphysics. The third generation of neuroscientists, however, repudiated the dualism of their teachers. In the course of explaining the possession of psychological attributes by human beings, they ascribed such attributes not to the mind but to the brain or parts of the brain.

Neuroscientists assume that the brain has a wide range of cognitive, cogitative, perceptual and volitional capacities. Francis Crick asserts:

> What you see is not what is *really* there; it is what your brain *believes* is there. . . . Your brain makes the best interpretation it can according to its previous experience and the limited and ambiguous information provided by your eyes. . . . the brain combines the information provided by the many distinct features of the visual scene (aspects of shape, colour, movement, etc.) and settles on the most plausible interpretation of all these various clues taken together. . . . what the brain has to build up is a many-levelled interpretation of the visual scene. . . . [Filling-in] allows the brain to guess a complete picture from only partial information – a very useful ability.[1]

So the brain *has experiences, believes* things, *interprets* clues *on the basis of information* made available to it, and *makes guesses*. Gerald Edelman holds that structures within the brain 'categorize, discriminate, and recombine the various brain activities occurring in different kinds of global mappings', and that the brain 'recursively relates semantic to phonological sequences and then generates syntactic correspondences, not from preexisting rules, but by treating rules developing in memory as objects for conceptual manipulation'.[2] Accordingly,

---

[1] F. Crick, *The Astonishing Hypothesis* (Touchstone, London, 1995), pp. 30, 32f., 57.
[2] G. Edelman, *Bright Air, Brilliant Fire – On the Malter of the Mind* (Penguin, Harmondsworth, 1994), pp. 109f., 130.

the brain *categorizes*; indeed, it 'categorizes its own activities (particularly its perceptual categorizations)', and *conceptually manipulates rules*. Colin Blakemore argues that

> We seem driven to say that such neurons [as respond in a highly specific manner to, e.g., line orientation] have knowledge. They have intelligence, for they are able to estimate the probability of outside events – events that are important to the animal in question. And the brain gains its knowledge by a process analogous to the inductive reasoning of the classical scientific method. Neurons present arguments to the brain based on the specific features that they detect, arguments on which the brain constructs its hypothesis of perception.[3]

So the brain *knows* things, *reasons* inductively, and *constructs hypotheses* on the basis of arguments, and its constituent neurons are *intelligent*, can *estimate probabilities*, and *present arguments*. J. Z. Young shared much the same view. He argued that 'we can regard all seeing as a continual search for the answers to questions posed by the brain. The signals from the retina constitute "messages" conveying these answers. The brain then uses this information to construct a suitable hypothesis about what is there.'[4] Accordingly, the brain *poses questions, searches for answers*, and *constructs hypotheses*. Antonio Damasio claims that 'our brains can often decide well, in seconds, or minutes, depending on the time frame we set as appropriate for the goal we want to achieve, and if they can do so, they must do the marvellous job with more than just pure reason',[5] and Benjamin Libet suggests that 'the brain "decides" to initiate or, at least, to prepare to initiate the act before there is any reportable subjective awareness that such a decision has taken place'.[6] So brains *decide*, or at least 'decide', and *initiate voluntary action*.

Psychologists concur. J. P. Frisby contends that 'there must be a symbolic description in the brain of the outside world, a description cast in symbols which stand for the various aspects of the world of which sight makes us aware'.[7] So there are *symbols in the brain*, and the brain *uses*, and presumably *understands, symbols*. Richard Gregory conceives of seeing as 'probably the most sophisticated of all the brain's activities: calling upon its stores of memory data; requiring subtle classifications, comparisons and logical decisions for sensory

---

[3] C. Blakemore, *Mechanics of the Mind* (Cambridge University Press, Cambridge, 1977), p. 91.

[4] J. Z. Young, *Programs of the Brain* (Oxford University Press, Oxford, 1978), p. 119.

[5] A. Damasio, *Descartes' Error – Emotion, Reason and the Human Brain* (Papermac, London, 1996), p. 173.

[6] B. Libet, 'Unconscious cerebral initiative and the role of conscious will in voluntary action', *Behavioural and Brain Sciences*, **8**, (1985), p. 536.

[7] J. P. Frisby, *Seeing: Illusion, Brain and Mind* (Oxford University Press, Oxford, 1980), pp. 8f. It is striking here that the misleading philosophical idiom associated with the Cartesian and empiricist traditions, namely talk of the 'outside' world, has been transferred from the mind to the brain. It was misleading because it purported to contrast an inside 'world of consciousness' with an outside 'world of matter'. But this is confused. The mind is not a kind of place, and what is idiomatically said to be *in* the mind is not thereby spatially located (cp. 'in the story'). Hence too, the world (which is not 'mere matter', but also living beings) is not *spatially* 'outside' the mind. The contrast between what is in the brain and what is outside the brain is, of course, perfectly literal and unobjectionable. What is objectionable is the claim that there are 'symbolic descriptions' in the brain.

data to become perception'.[8] So the brain *sees, makes classifications, comparisons,* and *decisions.* And cognitive scientists think likewise. David Marr held that 'our brains must somehow be capable of *representing . . . information . . .* The study of vision must therefore include . . . also an inquiry into the nature of the *internal representations* by which we *capture this information* and *make it available as a basis for decisions* about our thoughts and actions.'[9] And Philip Johnson-Laird suggests that the brain 'has access to a partial model of its own capabilities', and has the 'recursive machinery to embed models within models'; consciousness, he contends, 'is the property of a class of parallel algorithms'.[10]

Questioning the intelligibility of ascribing psychological attributes to the brain

With such broad consensus on the correct way to think about the functions of the brain and about explaining the causal preconditions for human beings to possess and exercise their natural powers of thought and perception, one is prone to be swept along by enthusiastic announcements – of new fields of knowledge conquered, new mysteries unveiled.[11] But we should take things slowly, and pause for thought. We know what it is for human beings to experience things, to see things, to know or believe things, to make decisions, to interpret equivocal data, to guess and to form hypotheses. We understand what it is for people to reason inductively, to estimate probabilities, to present arguments, to classify and categorize the things they encounter in their experience. We pose questions and search for answers, using a symbolism – namely, our language – in terms of which we represent things. But do we know what it is for *a brain* to see or hear, for *a brain* to have experiences, to know or believe something? Do we have any conception of what it would be for *a brain* to make a decision? Do we grasp what it is for a brain (let alone a neuron) *to reason* (no matter whether inductively or deductively), to *estimate probabilities,* to *present arguments,* to *interpret data* and to *form hypotheses* on the basis of its interpretations? We can observe whether a person sees something or other – we look at his behaviour and ask him questions. But what would it be to observe whether a brain sees something – as opposed to observing the brain of *a person* who sees something. We recognize when a person asks a question and when another answers it. But do we have any conception of what it would be for a brain to ask a question or answer one? These are all attributes of human beings. Is it a new *discovery* that brains also engage in such human activities? Or is it a linguistic innovation, introduced by neuroscientists,

[8] R. L. Gregory, 'The confounded eye', in R. L. Gregory and E. H. Gombrich (eds), *Illusion in Nature and Art* (Duckworth, London, 1973), p. 50.

[9] D. Marr, *Vision, a Computational Investigation into the Human Representation and Processing of Visual Information* (Freeman, San Francisco, 1980), p. 3, our italics.

[10] P. N. Johnson-Laird, 'How could consciousness arise from the computations of the brain?', in C. Blakemore and S. Greenfield (eds), *Mindwaves* (Blackwell, Oxford, 1987), p. 257.

[11] Susan Greenfield, explaining to her television audiences the achievements of positron emission tomography, announces with wonder that for the first time it is possible *to see thoughts.* Semir Zeki informs the Fellows of the Royal Society that the new millennium belongs to neurobiology, which will, among other things, solve the age-old problems of philosophy (see S. Zeki, 'Splendours and miseries of the brain', *Philosophical Transactions of the Royal Society,* B **354**, (1999), p. 2054). We shall discuss this view in §14.4.2.

psychologists and cognitive scientists, extending the ordinary use of these psychological expressions for good theoretical reasons? Or, more ominously, is it a conceptual confusion? Might it be the case that there is simply *no such thing* as the brain's thinking or knowing, seeing or hearing, believing or guessing, possessing and using information, constructing hypotheses, etc. – that is, that these forms of words make no sense? But if there is no such thing, why have so many distinguished scientists thought that these phrases, thus employed, do make sense?

Whether psychological attributes can intelligibly be ascribed to the brain is a philosophical, and therefore a conceptual, question, not a scientific one

The question we are confronting is a philosophical question, not a scientific one. It calls for conceptual clarification, not for experimental investigation. One cannot investigate experimentally whether brains do or do not think, believe, guess, reason, form hypotheses, etc. until one knows what it would be for a brain to do so – that is, until we are clear about the meanings of these phrases and know what (if anything) *counts* as a brain's doing these things and what sort of evidence would support the ascription of such attributes to the brain. (One cannot look for the poles of the Earth until one knows what a pole is – that is, what the expression 'pole' means, and also what counts as finding a pole of the Earth. Otherwise, like Winnie-the-Pooh, one might embark on an expedition to the East Pole.) The moot question is: does it make sense to ascribe such attributes to the brain? Is there any such thing as a brain's thinking, believing, etc.? (Is there any such thing as the East Pole?)

In the *Philosophical Investigations*, Wittgenstein made a profound remark that bears directly on our concerns. '*Only of a human being and what resembles (behaves like) a living human being can one say: it has sensations; it sees, is blind; hears, is deaf; is conscious or unconscious.*'[12] This epitomizes the conclusions we shall reach in our investigation. Stated with his customary terseness, it needs elaboration, and its ramifications need to be elucidated.

The point is not a factual one. It is not a matter of fact that only human beings and what behave like human beings can be said to be the subject of these psychological predicates. If it were, then it might indeed be a discovery, recently made by neuroscientists, that brains too see and hear, think and believe, ask and answer questions, form hypotheses and make guesses on the basis of information. Such a discovery would, to be sure, show that it is not only of a human being and what behaves like a human being that one can say such things. This would be astonishing, and we should want to hear more. We should want to know what the evidence for this remarkable discovery was. But, of course, it is

---

[12] L. Wittgenstein, *Philosophical Investigations*, ed. G. E. M. Anscombe and R. Rhees, tr. G. E. M. Auscombe (Blackwell, Oxford, 1953), §281 (see also §§282–4, 357–61). The thought fundamental to this remark was developed by A. J. P. Kenny, 'The homunculus fallacy' (1971), repr. in his *The Legacy of Wittgenstein* (Blackwell, Oxford, 1984), pp. 125–36. For the detailed interpretation of Wittgenstein's observation, see P. M. S. Hacker, *Wittgenstein: Meaning and Mind, Volume 3 of an Analytical Commentary on the Philosophical Investigations* (Blackwell, Oxford, 1990), Exegesis §§281–4, 357–61, and the essay entitled 'Men, minds and machines', which explores some of the ramifications of Wittgenstein's insight. As is evident from chapter 1, he was anticipated in this by Aristotle (*DA* 408^b 2–15, quoted on p. 15 above).

not like this. The ascription of psychological attributes to the brain is not warranted by a neuroscientific discovery that shows that, contrary to our previous convictions, brains do think and reason, just as we do ourselves. The neuroscientists, psychologists and cognitive scientists who adopt these forms of description have not done so as a result of *observations* which show that brains think and reason. Susan Savage-Rambaugh has produced striking evidence to show that bonobo chimpanzees, appropriately trained and taught, can ask and answer questions, can reason in a rudimentary fashion, give and obey orders, and so on. The evidence lies in their behaviour – in what they do (including how they employ symbols) in their interactions with us. This was indeed very surprising. For no one thought that such capacities could be acquired by apes. But it would be absurd to think that the ascription of cognitive and cogitative attributes to the brain rests on comparable evidence. It would be absurd because we do not even know what would show that the brain has such attributes.

The misascription of psychological attributes to the brain is a degenerate form of Cartesianism

Why, then, was this form of description, and the forms of explanation that are dependent upon it, adopted *without argument or reflection?* We suspect that the answer is: as a result of an unthinking adherence to a mutant form of Cartesianism. It was a characteristic feature of Cartesian dualism to ascribe psychological predicates to the mind, and only derivatively to the human being. Sherrington and his pupils Eccles and Penfield cleaved to a form of dualism in their reflections on the relationship between their neurological discoveries and human perceptual and cognitive capacities. Their successors rejected the dualism – quite rightly. But the predicates which dualists ascribe to the immaterial mind, the third generation of brain neuroscientists applied unreflectively to the brain instead. It was no more than an apparently innocuous corollary of rejecting the two-substance dualism of Cartesianism in neuroscience. These scientists proceeded to explain human perceptual and cognitive capacities and their exercise by reference to the brain's exercise of *its* cognitive and perceptual capacities.

The ascription of psychological attributes to the brain is senseless

It is our contention that this application of psychological predicates to the brain *makes no sense*. It is not that as a matter of fact brains do not think, hypothesize and decide, see and hear, ask and answer questions; rather, it makes no sense to ascribe such predicates *or their negations* to the brain. The brain neither sees, *nor is it blind* – just as sticks and stones are not awake, *but they are not asleep either*. The brain does not hear, but it is not deaf, any more than trees are deaf. The brain makes no decisions, but neither is it indecisive. Only what *can* decide can be indecisive. So, too, the brain cannot be conscious; only the living creature whose brain it is can be conscious – or unconscious. *The brain is not a logically appropriate subject for psychological predicates.* Only a human being and what *behaves* like one can intelligibly and literally be said to see or be blind, hear or be deaf, ask questions or refrain from asking.

Our point, then, is a conceptual one. It makes no sense to ascribe psychological predicates (or their negations) to the brain, save metaphorically or metonymically. The resultant combination of words does not say something that is false; rather, it says nothing at all, for it lacks sense. Psychological predicates are predicates that apply essentially to the whole living animal, not to its parts. It is not the eye (let alone the brain) that sees, but *we* see *with* our eyes (and we do not see with our brains, although without a brain functioning normally in respect of the visual system, we would not see). So, too, it is not the ear that hears, but the animal whose ear it is. The organs of an animal are parts of the animal, and psychological predicates are ascribable to the whole animal, not to its constituent parts.

Neuroscientists' ascription of psycho-logical attributes to the brain may be termed 'the mereological fallacy' in neuroscience

Mereology is the logic of part/whole relations. The neuro-scientists' mistake of ascribing to the constituent *parts* of an animal attributes that logically apply only to the *whole* animal we shall call 'the mereological fallacy' in neuro-science.[13] The principle that psychological predicates which apply only to human beings (or other animals) as wholes cannot intelligibly be applied to their parts, such as the brain, we shall call 'the mereological principle' in neuroscience.[14] Human beings, but not their brains, can be said to be thoughtful or thoughtless; animals, but not their brains, let alone the hemispheres of their brains, can be said to see, hear, smell and taste things; people, but not their brains, can be said to make decisions or to be indecisive.

It should be noted that there are many predicates that *can* apply both to a given whole (in particular, a human being) and to its parts, and whose application to the one may be inferred from its application to the other. A man may be sunburnt, and his face may be sunburnt; he may be cold all over, so his hands will be cold too. Similarly, we sometimes extend the application of a predicate from a human being to parts of the human body; for example, we say that a man gripped the handle, and also that his hand gripped the handle; that he slipped, and that his foot slipped. Here there is nothing logically awry. But psycho-logical predicates apply paradigmatically to the *human being (or animal) as a whole*, and *not* to the body and its parts. There are a few exceptions, such as the application of verbs of sensation like 'to hurt' to parts of the body – for example, 'My hand hurts', 'You are hurting my hand'.[15] But the range of psychological predicates that are our concern – that is, those that have been invoked by neuroscientists, psychologists and cognitive scientists in

---

[13] Kenny ('Homunculus fallacy', p. 125) uses the term 'homunculus fallacy' to signify the conceptual mistake in question. Though picturesque, it may, as he admits, be misleading, since the mistake is *not* simply that of ascribing psychological predicates to an imaginary homunculus in the head. In our view, the term 'mereological fallacy' is more apt. It should be noted, however, that the error in question is not merely the fallacy of ascribing to a part predicates that apply only to a whole, but is a special case of this more general confusion. As Kenny points out, the misapplication of a predicate is, strictly speaking, not a fallacy, since it is not a form of invalid reasoning, but it leads to fallacies (ibid., pp. 135f.). To be sure, this mereological confusion is common among psychologists as well as neuroscientists.

[14] Comparable mereological principles apply to inanimate objects and some of their properties. From the fact that a car is fast, it does not follow that its carburettor is fast, and from the fact that a clock tells the time accurately, it does not follow that its great wheel tells the time accurately.

[15] But note that when my hand hurts, I am in pain, not my hand. And when you hurt my hand, you hurt me. Verbs of sensation (unlike verbs of perception) apply to parts of the body; i.e. our body is sensitive, and its parts may hurt, itch, throb, etc. But the corresponding verb phrases incorporating nominals, e.g. 'have a pain (an itch, a throbbing sensation)' are predicable only of the person, not of his parts (in which the sensation is located).

their endeavours to explain human capacities and their exercise – have no literal application to parts of the body. In particular, they have no intelligible application to the brain.

3.2 Methodological Qualms

Methodological objections to the accusation that neuroscientists are guilty of a mereological fallacy

If a person ascribes a predicate to an entity to which the predicate in question logically could not apply, and this is pointed out to him, then it is only to be expected that he will indignantly insist that he didn't 'mean it like that'. After all, he may say, since a nonsense is a form of words that says nothing, that fails to describe a possible state of affairs, he obviously did not *mean* a nonsense – one *cannot* mean a nonsense, since there is nothing, as it were, to mean. So his words must not be taken to have their ordinary meaning. The problematic expressions were perhaps used in a special sense, and are really merely homonyms; or they were analogical *extensions* of the customary use, as is indeed common in science; or they were used in a metaphorical or figurative sense. If these escape routes are available, then the accusation that neuroscientists fall victim to the mereological fallacy is unwarranted. Although they make use of the same psychological vocabulary as the man in the street, they are using it in a different way. So objections to neuroscientists' usage based upon the ordinary use of these expressions are irrelevant.

Things are not that straightforward, however. Of course, the person who misascribes a predicate in the manner in question does not intend to utter a form of words that lacks sense. But that he did not mean *to utter* a nonsense does not ensure that he did not do so. Although he will naturally insist that he 'didn't mean it like that', that the predicate in question was not being used in its customary sense, his insistence is not the final authority. The final authority in the matter is *his own reasoning*. We must look at the consequences he draws from his own words – and it is his inferences that will show whether he was using the predicate in a new sense or misusing it. If he is to be condemned, it must be out of his own mouth. So, let us glance at the proposed escape routes that are intended to demonstrate that neuroscientists and cognitive scientists are not guilty of the errors of which we have accused them.

First objection (Ullman): the psychological predicates thus used are homonyms of ordinary psychological predicates, and have a different, technical, meaning

First, it might be suggested that neuroscientists are in effect employing homonyms, which mean something altogether different. There is nothing unusual, let alone amiss, in scientists introducing a new way of talking under the pressure of a new theory. If this is confusing to benighted readers, the confusion can easily be resolved. Of course, brains do not literally think, believe, infer, interpret or hypothesize, they think★, believe★, infer★, interpret★ or hypothesize★. They do not have or construct symbolic representations, but symbolic representations★.[16]

---

[16] See Simon Ullman, 'Tacit assumptions in the computational study of vision', in A. Gorea (ed.), *Representations of Vision, Trends and Tacit Assumptions in Vision Research* (Cambridge University Press, Cambridge, 1991), pp. 314f., for this move. He limits his discussion to the use (or, in our view, misuse) of such terms as 'representation' and 'symbolic representation'.

Second objection (Gregory): the psychological predicates thus used are analogical extensions of the ordinary expressions

Secondly, it might be suggested that neuroscientists are extending the ordinary use of the relevant vocabulary by analogy, as has often been done in the history of science – for example, in the analogical extension of hydrodynamics in the theory of electricity. So, to object to the ascription of psychological predicates to the brain on the grounds that in ordinary parlance such predicates are applicable only to the animal as a whole would be to display a form of *semantic inertia*.[17]

Third objection (Blakemore): neuroscientists' ascription of psychological attributes to the brain is figurative or metaphorical, since they know perfectly well that the brain does not think or use maps

Finally, it might be argued that neuroscientists do not *really* think that the brain reasons, argues, asks and answers questions just as we do. They do not really believe that the brain interprets clues, makes guesses or contains symbols which describe the outside world. And although they talk of there being 'maps' in the brain and of the brain's containing 'internal representations', they are not using these words in their common or vulgar sense. This is figurative and metaphorical speech – sometimes even poetic licence.[18] Neuroscientists, therefore, are not in the least misled by such ways of speaking — they know perfectly well what they mean, but lack the words to say it save metaphorically or figuratively.

Reply to the objection that neuroscientists are using the psychological vocabulary in a special technical sense

With regard to the misuse of the psychological vocabulary involved in ascribing psychological predicates to the brain, all the evidence points to the fact that neuroscientists are not using these terms in a special sense. Far from being new homonyms, the psychological expressions they use are being invoked in their customary sense, otherwise the neuroscientists would not draw the inferences from them which they do draw. When Crick asserts that 'what you see is not what is *really* there; it is what your brain *believes* is there', it is important that he takes 'believes' to have its normal connotations – that it does not mean the same as some novel term 'believes★'. For it is part of Crick's tale that the belief is the outcome of *an interpretation* based on previous *experience* and *information* (and not the outcome of an interpretation★ based on previous experience★ and information★). When Semir Zeki remarks that the acquisition of knowledge is a 'primordial function of the brain',[19] he means knowledge, not knowledge★ – otherwise he would not think that it is the task of future neuroscience to solve the problems of epistemology (but only, presumably, of epistemology★). Similarly, when Young talks of the brain's containing knowledge and information, which is encoded in the brain 'just as knowledge can be recorded in books or computers',[20] he means knowledge, not knowledge★ – since it is knowledge and information, not knowledge★ and information★, that can be recorded in books and computers. When Milner, Squire and

[17] The phrase is Richard Gregory's; see 'The confounded eye', p. 51.
[18] See C. Blakemore, 'Understanding images in the brain', in H. Barlow, C. Blakemore and M. Weston-Smith (eds), *Images and Understanding* (Cambridge University Press, Cambridge, 1990), pp. 257–83.
[19] S. Zeki, 'Abstraction and idealism', *Nature*, 404 (April 2000), p. 547.
[20] Young, *Programs of the Brain*, p. 192.

Kandel talk of 'declarative memory', they explain that this phrase signifies 'what is ordinarily meant by the term "memory"',[21] but then go on to declare that such memories, not memories★, are 'stored in the brain'. That presupposes that it makes sense to speak of storing memories (in the ordinary sense of the word) *in the brain* (for detailed discussion of this questionable claim, see §5.2.2 below).

Reply to Ullman: David Marr on 'representations'

The accusation of committing the mereological fallacy cannot be that easily rebutted. But Simon Ullman may appear to be on stronger grounds when it comes to talk of internal representations and symbolic representations (as well as maps) *in the brain*. If 'representation' does not mean what it ordinarily does, if 'symbolic' has nothing to do with symbols, then it may indeed be innocuous to speak of there being internal, symbolic representations in the brain. (And if 'maps' have nothing to do with atlases, but only with *mappings*, then it may also be innocuous to speak of there being maps in the brain.) It is extraordinarily ill-advised to multiply homonyms, but it need involve no conceptual incoherence, *as long as the scientists who use these terms thus do not forget that the terms do not have their customary meaning.* Unfortunately, they typically do forget this and *proceed to cross the new use with the old*, generating incoherence. Ullman, defending Marr, insists (perfectly correctly) that certain brain events can be viewed as representations★ of depth or orientation or reflectance;[22] that is, that one can correlate certain neural firings with features in the visual field (denominating the former 'representations★' of the latter). But it is evident that this is not all that Marr meant. He claimed that numeral systems (roman or arabic numerals, binary notation) are representations. However, such notations have nothing to do with causal correlations, but with representational conventions. He claimed that 'a representation for shape would be a formal scheme for describing some aspects of shape, together with rules that specify how the scheme is applied to any particular shape',[23] that a formal scheme is 'a set of symbols with rules for putting them together',[24] and that 'a representation, therefore, is not a foreign idea at all – we all use representations all the time. However, the notion that one can capture some aspect of reality by making a description of it using a symbol and that to do so can be useful seems to me to be a powerful and fascinating idea.'[25] But the sense in which we 'use representations all the time', *in which representations are rule-governed symbols, and in which they are used for describing things*, is the *semantic* sense of 'representation' – not a new homonymical causal sense. Marr has fallen into a trap of his own making.[26] He in effect conflates Ullman's representations★, which *are* causal correlates, with representations, which are symbols or symbol systems with a syntax and meaning determined by conventions.

---

[21] Brenda Milner, Larry R. Squire and Eric R. Kandel, 'Cognitive neuroscience and the study of memory', *Neuron*, 20 (1998), p. 450.

[22] Ullman, 'Tacit assumptions', pp. 314f.

[23] Marr, *Vision*, p. 20.

[24] Ibid., p. 21.

[25] Ibid.

[26] For further criticisms of Marr's computational account of vision, see §4.2.4 below.

Reply to Ullman: Young on 'maps' and Frisby on 'symbolic representations'

Similarly, it would be misleading, but otherwise innocuous, to speak of maps in the brain when what is meant is that certain features of the visual field can be mapped on to the firings of groups of cells in the 'visual' striate cortex. But then one cannot go on to say, as Young does, that the brain makes use of its maps in formulating its hypotheses about what is visible. So, too, it would be innocuous to speak of there being symbolic representations in the brain, as long as 'symbolic' has nothing to do with semantic meaning, but signifies only 'natural meaning' (as in 'smoke means fire'). But then one cannot go on to say, as Frisby does, that 'there must be a symbolic description in the brain of the outside world, a description cast in symbols which stand for the various aspects of the world of which sight makes us aware'.[27] For this use of 'symbol' is evidently semantic. For while smoke means fire, inasmuch as it is a sign *of* fire (an inductively correlated indication), it is not a sign *for* fire. Smoke rising from a distant hillside is not a description of fire cast in symbols, and the firing of neurons in the 'visual' striate cortex is not a symbolic description of objects in the visual field, even though a neuroscientist may be able to infer facts about what is visible to an animal from his knowledge of what cells are firing in its 'visual' striate cortex. The firing of cells in V1 may be signs of a figure with certain line orientations in the animal's visual field, but they do not *stand for* anything, they are not symbols, and they do not describe anything.

Reply to the second objection (Gregory), that, in ascribing psychological attributes to the brain, neuroscientists are not committing the mereological fallacy, but merely extending the psychological vocabulary analogically

The thought that neuroscientific usage, far from being conceptually incoherent, is innovative, extending the psychological vocabulary in novel ways, might seem to offer another way of side-stepping the accusation that neuroscientists' descriptions of their discoveries commonly transgress the bounds of sense. It is indeed true that analogies are a source of scientific insight. The hydrodynamical analogy proved fruitful in the development of the theory of electricity, even though electrical current does not flow in the same sense as water flows, and an electrical wire is not a kind of pipe. The moot question is whether the application of the psychological vocabulary to the brain is to be understood as analogical.

The prospects do not look good. The application of psychological expressions to the brain is not part of a complex theory replete with functional, mathematical relationships expressible by means of quantifiable laws as are to be found in the theory of electricity. Something much looser seems to be needed. So, it is true that psychologists, following Freud and others, have extended the concepts of belief, desire and motive in order to speak of *unconscious* beliefs, desires and motives. When these concepts undergo such analogical extension, something new stands in need of explanation. The newly extended expressions no longer admit of the same combinatorial possibilities as before. They have a different, importantly related meaning, and one which requires explanation. The relationship between a (conscious) belief and an unconscious belief, for example, is not akin to the relationship between a visible chair and an occluded

---

[27] Frisby, *Seeing*, p. 8.

chair – it is not 'just like a conscious belief only unconscious', but more like the relationship between √1 and √–1. But when neuroscientists such as Sperry and Gazzaniga
speak of the left hemisphere making choices, of its generating interpretations, of its
knowing, observing and explaining things – it is clear from the sequel that these psychological expressions have not been given a new meaning. Otherwise it would not be
said that a hemisphere of the brain is 'a conscious system in its own right, perceiving,
thinking, remembering, reasoning, willing and emoting, *all at a characteristically human
level*'.[28]

It is not semantic inertia that motivates our claim that neuroscientists are involved
in various forms of conceptual incoherence. It is, rather, the acknowledgement of the
requirements of the logic of psychological expressions. Psychological predicates are predicable only of a whole animal, not of its parts. No conventions have been laid down to
determine what is to be meant by the ascription of such predicates to a part of an animal,
in particular to its brain. So the application of such predicates to the brain or the hemispheres of the brain transgresses the bounds of sense. The resultant assertions are not false,
for to say that something is false, we must have some idea of what it would be for it to be
true – in this case, we should have to know what it would be for the brain to think,
reason, see and hear, etc., and to have found out that as a matter of fact the brain does not
do so. But we have no such idea, and these assertions are not false. Rather, the sentences
in question lack sense. This does not mean that they are silly or stupid. It means that no
sense has been assigned to such forms of words, and that, accordingly, they say nothing at
all, even though it looks as if they do.

Reply to the third objection (Blake-more), that applying psychological predicates to the brain is merely metaphorical	The third methodological objection was raised by Colin Blakemore. Of Wittgenstein's remark that 'only of a living human being and what resembles (behaves like) a living human being can one say: it has sensations; it sees; is blind; hears; is conscious or unconscious', Blakemore

observes that it 'seems trivial, maybe just plain wrong'. Addressing the accusation that
neuroscientists' talk of there being 'maps' in the brain is pregnant with possibilities of
confusion (since all that can be meant is that one can map, for example, aspects of items
in the visual field on to the firing of cells in the 'visual' striate cortex), Blakemore notes
that there is overwhelming evidence for 'topographic patterns of activity' in the brain.

> Since Hughlings Jackson's time, the concept of functional sub-division and topographic
> representation has become a *sine qua non* of brain research. The task of charting the brain
> is far from complete but the successes of the past make one confident that each part
> of the brain (and especially the cerebral cortex) *is* likely to be organized in a spatially
> ordered fashion. Just as in the decoding of a cipher, the translation of Linear B or the
> reading of hieroglyphics, all that we need to recognize the order in the brain is a set of

---

[28] Roger Sperry, 'Lateral specialization in the surgically separated hemispheres', in F. O. Schmitt and
F. G. Worden (eds), *The Neurosciences Third Study Programme* (MIT Press, Cambridge, MA., 1974),
p. 11, (italics added). For detailed examination of these forms of description, see §14.3 below.

rules – rules that relate the activity of the nerves to events in the outside world or in the animal's body.[29]

To be sure, the term 'representation' here signifies merely systematic causal connectedness. That is innocuous enough. But it must not be confused with the sense in which a sentence of a language can be said to represent the state of affairs it describes, a map to represent that of which it is a map, or a painting to represent that of which it is a painting. Nevertheless, such ambiguity in the use of 'representation' is perilous, since it is likely to lead to a confusion of the distinct senses. Just how confusing it can be is evident in Blakemore's further observations:

> Faced with such overwhelming evidence for topographic patterns of activity in the brain it is hardly surprising that neurophysiologists and neuroanatomists have come to speak of the brain having *maps*, which are thought to play an essential part in the representation and interpretation of the world by the brain, just as the maps of an atlas do for the reader of them. The biologist J. Z. Young writes of the brain having a language of a pictographic kind: 'What goes on in the brain must provide a faithful representation of events outside it, and the arrangements of the cells in it provide a detailed model of the world. It communicates meanings by topographical analogies.'[30] But is there a danger in the metaphorical use of such terms as 'language', 'grammar', and 'map' to describe the properties of the brain? . . . I cannot believe that any neurophysiologist believes that there is a ghostly cartographer browsing through the cerebral atlas. Nor do I think that the employment of common language words (such as map, representation, code, information and even language) is a conceptual blunder of the kind [imagined]. Such metaphorical imagery is a mixture of empirical description, poetic licence and inadequate vocabulary.[31]

Whether there is any danger in a metaphorical use of words depends on how clear it is that it is merely metaphorical, and on whether the author remembers that that *is* all it is. Whether neuroscientists' ascriptions to the brain of attributes that can be applied literally only to an animal as a whole is actually merely metaphorical (metonymical or synecdochical) is very doubtful. *Of course*, neurophysiologists do not think that there is a 'ghostly cartographer' browsing through a cerebral atlas – but they do think that the brain *makes use* of the maps. According to Young, the brain *constructs hypotheses*, and it does so *on the basis* of this 'topographically organized representation'.[32] The moot question is: what inferences do neuroscientists draw from their claim that there are maps or representations in the brain, or from their claim that the brain contains information, or from talk (J. Z. Young's

---

[29] Blakemore, 'Understanding images in the brain', p. 265. It should be noted that what is needed in order to recognize the order in the brain is *not* a set of *rules*, but merely a set of regular correlations. A rule, unlike a mere regularity, is a standard of conduct, a norm of correctness against which behaviour can be judged to be right or wrong, correct or incorrect.

[30] Young, *Programs of the Brain*, p. 52.

[31] Blakemore, 'Understanding images in the brain', pp. 265–7.

[32] Young, *Programs of the Brain*, p. 11.

talk) of 'languages of the brain'? These alleged metaphorical uses are so many banana skins in the pathway of their user. He *need not* step on them and slip, but he probably will.

Blakemore's confusion
Just how easy it is for confusion to ensue from what is alleged to be harmless metaphor is evident in the paragraph of Blakemore quoted above. For while it may be harmless to talk of 'maps' – that is, of *mappings* of features of the perceptual field on to topographically related groups of cells that are systematically responsive to such features – it is anything but harmless to talk of such 'maps' as playing 'an essential part in the *representation* and *interpretation* of the world by the brain, just as the maps of an atlas do for the reader of them' (our italics). In the first place, it is not clear what sense is to be given to the term 'interpretation' in this context. For it is by no means evident what could be meant by the claim that the topographical relations between groups of cells that are systematically related to features of the perceptual field play an essential role in the brain's *interpreting* something. To interpret, literally speaking, is to explain the meaning of something, or to take something that is ambiguous to have one meaning rather than another. But it makes no sense to suppose that the brain *explains* anything, or that it apprehends something as *meaning* one thing rather than another. If we look to J. Z. Young to find out what he had in mind, what we find is the claim that it is on the basis of such maps that the brain 'constructs hypotheses and programs' – and this only gets us deeper into the morass.

More importantly, whatever sense we can give to Blakemore's claim that 'brain maps' (which are not actually maps) play an essential part in the brain's 'representation and interpretation of the world', it *cannot* be '*just as the maps of an atlas do for the reader of them*'. For a map is a pictorial representation, made in accordance with conventions of mapping and rules of projection. Someone who can read an atlas must know and understand these conventions, and read off, from the maps, the features of what is represented. But the 'maps' in the brain are not maps, in this sense, at all. The brain is not akin to the reader of a map, since it cannot be said to know any conventions of representations or methods of projection or to read anything off the topographical arrangement of firing cells in accordance with a set of conventions. For the cells are not arranged in accordance with conventions at all, and the correlation between their firing and features of the perceptual field is not a conventional but a *causal* one.[33]

––––––––––

[33] Just how confusing the failure to distinguish a rule from a regularity, and the normative from the causal, is evident in Blakemore's comments on the Penfield and Rasmussen diagram of the motor 'homunculus'. Blakemore remarks on 'the way in which the jaws and hands are vastly over-represented' ('Understanding images in the brain', p. 266, in the long explanatory note to Fig. 17.6); but that would make sense only if we were talking of a map with a misleading method of projection (in this sense we speak of the relative distortions of the Mercator (cylindrical) projection). But since all the cartoon drawing represents is the relative number of cells causally responsible for certain functions, *nothing* is, or could be, 'over-represented'. For, to be sure, Blakemore does not mean that there are more cells in the brain causally correlated with the jaws and the hands than there ought to be!

Blakemore's suggestion that neuroscientists use metaphorical and figurative language because of the poverty of the English language and lack of adequate concepts is a point which we shall examine later (§14.2).[34]

3.3 On the Grounds for Ascribing Psychological Predicates to a Being

The conceptual commitments associated with the mereological principle

We have bluntly asserted the mereological principle in neuroscience, insisting that it is a logical principle, and therefore not amenable to empirical, experimental confirmation or disconfirmation. It is indeed a convention, but one that determines what does and does not make sense. Its application – for example, to psychological concepts – could, in principle, be changed by stipulation, but not without changing a great deal else, thereby altogether changing the meanings of our words and the structure of a multitude of familiar concepts. For the principle that psychological concepts apply to the animal as a whole and cannot be applied to its parts is held in place by a ramifying network of conceptual connections. In this section we shall investigate further the conceptual commitments that are involved in the application of psychological predicates. This will clarify the conceptual incoherences that result if those commitments are not respected, as indeed they are not in much current neuroscientific reflection.

We typically recognize the applicability of psychological attributes to others non-inferentially

We ascribe pain to a person or an animal on the basis of their behaviour (including their verbal behaviour). If a person injures himself and screams or groans, if he assuages his injured limb, limps, or nurses his injury, grimaces and exclaims 'Ow', 'It hurts', or 'I have a pain', we take such pain-behaviour in these circumstances to be justifying grounds or evidence for ascribing pain to the person. This does not mean that we normally *infer* that a person is in pain from such observed evidence. We typically recognize immediately that a person has hurt himself, we see and hear that he is in pain, can see the pain in his face. But it is the person's pain-behaviour that warrants our immediate pain-ascription, and it is by reference to such evidence that we might answer the question 'What grounds did you have for taking him to be in pain?' Similarly, we say of an animal or a human being that they perceive something in their field of perception if, for example, they respond to what is visible (or audible, etc.) in appropriate ways. So, evidence that a dog sees a cat is that it responds to what is visible to it – for example, follows the cat with its eyes, displays interest in the visible behaviour of the cat, chases it and responds to its movements by adjusting its pursuit to the visible twists and turns of the fleeing cat. Likewise, we ascribe a given belief to a human being if, for example, he asserts that such-and-such is the case, or avers that he believes that things are

---

[34] There are other methodological objections that have been elaborated by Quinean philosophers of science. They carry weightier philosophical baggage, and will be considered separately, in §14.1. Readers who would like to examine our further arguments may wish to jump forward.

thus-and-so, or if he acts and explains his doing what he is doing by reference to the reasons that things are thus-and-so – that is, by reference to what he knows or believes to be so. We do not *infer* that A believes such-and-such from the fact that he said so, we normally take him to believe what he says he believes; but our grounds for ascribing to him this belief are that he said what he said.

The evidential grounds for the ascription of psychological attributes to others are not inductive, but rather criterial; i.e. the evidence is logically good evidence

The primary grounds or evidence for the ascription of psychological predicates to another are behavioural. It is the behaviour *of that being* in appropriate circumstances. This, however, is not *inductive evidence*. Inductive evidence is determined by correlation of concomitant phenomena. So it presupposes non-inductive identification of the phenomena that are observed to be correlated as a matter of fact. But pain and pain-behaviour are not correlated as a matter of brute fact. It is not an empirical discovery that when people are in pain, they groan, cry out and assuage their injury. Nor is it an intelligible possibility that pain might systematically be correlated with smiling and laughing, as opposed to being correlated with crying and groaning – that is, with pain-behaviour. Similarly, it is not an empirical discovery that when a creature sees, it responds to *visible* objects, uses *its eyes* to *follow* them, cannot see when its eyes are closed, or when it is pitch dark. Rather, the primary warrant for the ascription of psychological predicates to another person or to an animal is *conceptually* bound up with the meaning of the relevant predicate. Pain-behaviour is a criterion – that is, *logically* good evidence for being in pain – and perceptual behaviour (appropriate to the object perceived and to the perceptual modality involved) is a criterion for the animal's perceiving. That such-and-such kinds of behaviour *are* criteria for the ascription of such-and-such a psychological predicate is partly constitutive of the meaning of the predicate in question.[35]

Criterial evidence for the ascription of psychological attributes to others is defeasible by countervailing evidence

Though non-inductive, the behavioural criteria for assigning such a psychological attribute to another person are, like inductive evidence, capable of being overridden by countervailing evidence. So the support of such evidence does not *entail* the presence of the psychological attribute for which it is evidence. For the logical relation of entailment, as exemplified by the proposition that A is a bachelor entailing the proposition that A is unmarried, is not defeasible; that is, addition of further propositions cannot undermine the entailment relation. But a person may display (apparent) pain-behaviour without being in pain: he may be acting on the stage or pretending to be in pain in order to deceive. If we have evidence that he is doing one or the other of these, this evidence defeats the criterial support given by his apparent

---

[35] This does not mean that the psychological predication is equivalent in meaning to the behavioural description the truth of which warrants its ascription. It is not only possible but common for people to be in (mild) pain, thinking or intending something, and not exhibit the fact that they are. And it is also possible for people to pretend or dissimulate, i.e. to exhibit such-and-such behaviour, yet *not* be in such-and-such a psychological state. We are not defending a form of behaviourism; and the conceptual nexus we are insisting upon is an a priori evidential, but not a reductive, one.

pain-behaviour. A person may say that he thinks or believes something, but he may be lying; he may sincerely aver that he intends to do something or other, but he may be deceiving himself. However, if the criteria for a person's being in pain, believing or intending something *are* satisfied on an occasion and are *not* defeated by countervailing evidence in the circumstances, then we are warranted in asserting that he *is* in pain, *does* believe or intend.

The criterial grounds for the ascription of a psychological predicate are partly constitutive of the meaning of that predicate

The criterial grounds for ascribing psychological predicates to another person are *conceptually* connected with the psychological attribute in question. They are partly constitutive of the *meaning* of the predicate. So the normal ascription of psychological predicates to others does not involve an inductive identification. However, given the possibility of such normal non-inductive identifications, the possibility of inductive (non-logical) identification becomes available through inductively correlating subjects' having certain psychological attributes with other phenomena – for example, neurophysiological events in their brain. But any inductive correlation presupposes the criterial nexus that is partly constitutive of the psychological concept in question. Moreover, if such inductive evidence conflicts with the normal criteria for the ascription of a psychological predicate, the criterial evidence over-rides the inductive correlation. So, for example, if a person avows that he is not in pain, yet evidence from PET or fMRI suggests that he is, the latter is defeated by the agent's sincere utterance, and the inductive correlations of the data from PET and fMRI with the subject's being in pain need to be re-examined.

The brain does not satisfy the criteria for being a possible subject of psychological predicates

These evident logical features should give us pause. We do not, outside the neuroscience or psychology laboratory, ascribe pain to the brain. Though neural phenomena are well correlated with an animal's or a person's being in pain, the brain does not exhibit *pain-behaviour* – it does not moan or groan, assuage its broken arm, shed tears or grimace, for there is no such thing as a brain's engaging in such activities. The observed neural phenomena that are concomitants of a person's suffering pain, for example, are not forms of *pain-behaviour*. They are *inductively* correlated with being in pain. The correlation is an empirical discovery, which presupposes the concept of pain and its nexus with criterial, non-inductive evidence for the application of the concept of pain *to a living creature* (not to its brain).

Similarly, outside the laboratory, we do not ascribe thinking or believing to the brain, but to the person who thinks or believes, and says what he thinks or believes, or acts, and can be seen to act, on the basis of thinking or believing this or that. We do not observe a brain in a brown study, but *Le Penseur* sunk in thought. We do not see the brain's credulity, but the person's belief (or disbelief) may be written all over his face as he listens to another's tale. What we can do is correlate a person's thinking of this or that with localized brain activity detected by PET or fMRI. But this does not show that the brain is thinking, reflecting or ruminating; it shows that such-and-such parts of a person's cortex are active when the *person* is thinking, reflecting or ruminating. (What one sees on the scan is not the brain thinking – there is no such thing as a brain thinking – nor the person thinking – one can see that whenever one looks at someone sunk in thought, but not by looking at a PET scan – but the computer-generated image of the excitation of cells in his brain that occurs *when* he is thinking.) Again, *this* correlation is inductive, not criterial, and it requires antecedent identification of the person's thinking and reflecting by reference to behavioural criteria. It presupposes the *concept* of thinking, *as determined by the behavioural criteria that warrant ascription of thought to a living being.*

A second explanation of why scientists are tempted to ascribe psychological attributes to the brain is the array of Cartesian and empiricist misconceptions to which many of them are committed

This seems obvious enough on reflection. The moot question is: why are we tempted to think otherwise? Why have so many scientists (and philosophers) been convinced to the contrary? What is the source of the temptation to ascribe consciousness, seeing and hearing, thinking and believing, feeling and wanting, etc. to the brain? We have conjectured one explanation: namely, that on the rebound from Cartesianism and classical empiricism, scientists and philosophers unthinkingly transposed psychological attributes from the mind to the brain. But there is a deeper explanation, which will shed light on how such questionable transposition could have been executed without question, argument or evidence.

Although the ascription of psychological attributes to others rests on (is justified by reference to) behavioural, criterial evidence, the application of psychological predicates to oneself does not. One does not say that one is in pain on the grounds that one is groaning and assuaging one's injured limb. One does not express a belief, admit or confess that one believes this or that on the basis of the evidence of one's own behaviour, and one does not wait to hear what one says in order to find out what one thinks. So how is it that we can say what we are feeling or perceiving, what we think or believe, what we want and intend?

Misconceptions concerning 'the inner' and 'the outer'; private ownership of experience; privileged access; direct as opposed to indirect knowledge of the inner; and introspection

It is profoundly tempting to draw the contrast between the mental and the behavioural in a misguided way. Behaviour belongs to the public domain, and is evident to anyone appropriately situated to observe it – it is, we might say, the 'outer'. By contrast, the mental appears to belong to a special, private domain, accessible only to its subject. It is, we are inclined to think, the 'inner' – and we speak accordingly of people's 'inner (mental) life'. According to this picture (and it is, after all, merely a picture, a metaphor), each person has *access* to his own mind. We are further inclined to think of experiences as items owned or possessed by their subject – a temptation fostered by the fact that we speak of *having* pains, perceptual experiences, thoughts, beliefs, etc. And we are inclined to say such things as 'You can't have my pain' or 'Only I can have my pain'. Thinking thus, we suppose experiences to be essentially privately and inalienably owned – that different people cannot have the *same* experience, they can have only a *similar* experience. If so, then each person not only has access to his own mind, he has *privileged access* to it and to the mental events and processes that go on in it. And this seems obvious, for, to be sure, *other* people must rely on my behaviour, on what I do and say, in order to discern what I am feeling or thinking. So, it seems that they know how things are with me *indirectly*. What they directly perceive is merely *outward* behaviour. But I have *direct access* to what is *inner*, to my own mind. I am *conscious* of how things are with me.

The faculty whereby I have such direct access to mental states, events and processes is *introspection* – and it is because I can introspect that I can say how things are with me *without observing what I do and say.*

This array of ideas is fundamental to classical empiricism. Woven into strands of the Cartesian legacy, *it is part of the received conception shared by most contemporary neuroscientists.* Since it was bound up with Cartesians and British empiricists ascribing psychological attributes to the mind, small wonder that contemporary neuroscientists, sharing this picture but rejecting the conception of the mind as an immaterial substance, should be tempted to ascribe psychological attributes to the brain. According to their conception, the 'access' which introspection gives each person to his own mental states and processes *is* a partial and limited access to processes going on in his brain.[36]

3.4 On the Grounds for Misascribing Psychological Predicates to an Inner Entity

Four misconceptions concerning the logical character of experience and its ascription

This powerful picture, partly Cartesian and partly British empiricist, has dominated thought about the mind for centuries. It fosters a very important *misconception* of the logical character of experience and its ascription. We shall clarify this by spelling out four questionable conceptual commitments of this tempting picture. These are widely accepted among neuroscientists, cognitive scientists and psychologists, as well as some philosophers.

1. Misconceptions about privacy, conceived as private ownership of experience

(1) The mental is a private domain, to be contrasted with the public domain of behaviour and physical phenomena. So, for example, Antonio Damasio holds that consciousness is an 'entirely private, first-person phenomenon which occurs as part of the private, first-person process we call mind'.[37] Edelman and Tononi concur that 'privateness' is 'one of those fundamental aspects of conscious experience that are common to all its manifestations'.[38] Stephen Kosslyn and Kevin Ochsner hold that having mental images 'is a quintessential private event', and hence 'notoriously difficult to study' – images being 'internal representations' in the mind of a person.[39] The idea is rendered clearer with the assistance of a philosopher, John Searle: 'Subjective

---

[36] e.g., Crick observes that 'There is general agreement that people are not conscious of all the processes going on in their heads . . . While you may be aware of many of the results of perceptual and memory processes, you have only limited access to the processes that produce this awareness' (*Astonishing Hypothesis*, pp. 19f.).

[37] A. Damasio, *The Feeling of What Happens* (Heinemann, London, 1999), p. 12.

[38] G. M. Edelman and G. Tononi, *Consciousness: How Matter Becomes Imagination* (Allen Lane, The Penguin Press, London, 2000), p. 23.

[39] S. M. Kosslyn and K. N. Ochsner, 'In search of occipital activation during mental imagery', *Trends in Neuroscience*, 17 (1994), p. 290.

conscious states have a first-person ontology because they exist only when they are experienced by some human or animal agent'; furthermore, even if two people experience the same phenomenon, say a concert, each person's experience is distinct from each other person's experience. They may be qualitatively identical (as your penny may be qualitatively identical with mine), but they are nevertheless numerically distinct.[40] As the great logician Gottlob Frege wittily put it, you can't have my pain, and I can't have your sympathy.[41] Every experience, every conscious state, needs an owner, and each experience or mental state has only one owner. The mental is privately and inalienably owned.

2. Misconceptions about introspection conceived as a form of inner perception

(2)   This private domain can be apprehended by means of introspection, which is a faculty akin to perception. William James held that introspection 'means, of course, the looking into one's own mind and reporting there what we discover. *Everyone agrees that we there discover states of consciousness.*'[42] Introspection is sometimes held to be the *only* reliable indicator of the occurrence and character of the inner, conceived as conscious experience. According to Benjamin Libet, 'any behavioural evidence which does not require a convincing introspective report cannot be assumed to be an indicator of conscious, subjective experience'.[43] Nicholas Humphrey, in a similar vein, has claimed that 'conscious experience is the set of subjective feelings which, at any one time, are available to introspection';[44] elsewhere he has compared introspection to an 'inner eye', comparable to other sense-organs.[45]

3. Misconceptions about privileged access and epistemic privacy

(3)   The domain of private experience is accessible directly only to the subject; others have only indirect access. So, for example, J. R. Searle held that 'My present state of consciousness is a feature of my brain, but its conscious aspects are accessible to me in a way that they are not accessible to you. And your present state of consciousness is a feature of your brain and its conscious aspects are accessible to you in a way that they are not accessible to me.'[46] Libet too thinks that a 'Conscious experience, as an awareness of some thing or some event, is directly accessible only to the individual having that

---

[40] J. R. Searle, 'Consciousness', *Annual Reviews*, 23 (2000), p. 561.

[41] G. Frege, 'The thought', repr. in *Collected Papers on Mathematics, Logic and Philosophy* (Blackwell, Oxford, 1984), p. 361.

[42] W. James, *The Principles of Psychology* (Holt, New York, 1890), vol. 1, p. 185.

[43] B. Libet, 'The neural time-factor in perception, volition and free will', repr. in his *Neurophysiology of Consciousness* (Birkhäuser, Boston, 1993), p. 368.

[44] N. Humphrey, *Consciousness Regained* (Oxford University Press, Oxford, 1984), pp. 34f.

[45] N. Humphrey, 'The inner eye of consciousness', in Blakemore and Greenfield (eds), *Mindwaves*, pp. 379. It is striking and bizarre that *here* Humphrey holds that what the 'inner eye' of consciousness has as its field of view is *the brain itself*. On such a conception, introspection should make PET and fMRI partly dispensable.

[46] J. R. Searle, *Minds, Brains and Science – the 1984 Reith Lectures* (BBC, London, 1984), p. 25. It is noteworthy that Searle was subsequently to abandon talk of 'access' (see J. R. Searle, *The Rediscovery of the Mind* (MIT Press, Cambridge, MA., 1992), p. 98).

experience, not to an external observer'.[47] Blakemore maintains that 'Although I assume that other human beings think in much the same way as I do, I have no direct evidence about their conscious minds'.[48] And Crick concurs that 'Strictly speaking, each individual is certain only that he himself is conscious'.[49] So the mental domain is conceived to be 'the inner', to be contrasted with the domain of publicly observable behaviour, 'the outer'. It is not only *privately owned*, but also *epistemically private*; that is, only the subject knows with appropriate certainty what obtains and occurs within it. That is because only the subject has *direct access* to it, and it is only direct access that confers the title of knowledge.

4. Misconceptions about the meaning of psychological predicates

(4) Psychological predicates are names of inner entities (objects, states, events and processes), and their meanings can be grasped independently of any conceptual connection with behavioural criteria. This supposition is rarely articulated, yet it is important, and it wittingly or unwittingly underpins the received neuroscientific conception of the mental.[50] Certainly the supposition that our judgements about other people's mental states or states of consciousness are inductive is not uncommon among neuroscientists. Edelman contends that we know what consciousness is 'for ourselves but can only judge its existence in others by inductive inference'.[51] Others, such as Crick, hold that such inferences are analogical.[52] In so far as neuroscientists have given the question any thought, there is a consensus that the relation between behaviour and the mental state for which it is evidence is non-logical and non-conceptual. Further, as we have seen, each person is assumed to have privileged access to his own experiences, and to be able to speak of them without recourse to his own behaviour. Evidently he must know what the expressions that he uses to signify his experiences mean. It *appears* that they must have a meaning that is *independent of their associated behavioural expression*, since a person does not apply these expressions to himself on the grounds of his behaviour. The most plausible explanation of how names of experiences are endowed with meaning then *appears* to be that *we know what these words mean in virtue of associating them with the experiences we have, and to which we have privileged access*. The neuroscientific conception of the mental is in effect committed to this *semantic* conception, even if most neuroscientists are unaware of this. This commitment is of the first importance. *If* this conception were correct, then the thought that psychological predicates are *logically* bound up with the behavioural criteria for their ascription in the third-person case would be mistaken. *If* it were mistaken, then, to be

---

[47] Libet, 'Neural time-factor', p. 368.
[48] Blakemore, *The Mind Machine* (BBC Books, London, 1988), p. 230.
[49] Crick, *Astonishing Hypothesis*, p. 107.
[50] Damasio argues that 'In the sentence "I see a car coming" the word *see* stands for a particular act of perceptual possession perpetrated by my organism (*sic*) . . . And the word "see" is there, . . . to translate the wordless play unfolding in my mind' (Damasio, Feeling of What Happens, p. 186). Here 'see' is conceived to stand for, be the name of, an inner act. Humphrey explains that he *derives* the psychological concepts which he possesses *from his own experience* (*Consciousness Regained*, pp. 34f.).
[51] Edelman, *Bright Air, Brilliant Fire*, p. 111.
[52] Crick, *Astonishing Hypothesis*, p. 107.

sure, one could not support the accusation that neuroscientists commit a mereological fallacy by reference to the fact that nothing the brain can do satisfies the criteria for the ascription of psychological attributes to a being. For on this different account, the meaning of psychological expressions is given by 'direct' association with the attributes they signify, unmediated by behavioural criteria.

Each of these four theses is misguided, involving far-reaching conceptual confusions:

i.   It is true that there are no experiences that are not someone's experiences (no pains unless someone is suffering, no beliefs without believers). But it does not follow that different people may not have the same pain, belief or experience.

ii.   Introspection is not a quasi-perceptual faculty at all, and it is not the source of knowledge about 'the inner'.

iii. Far from the subject having direct access to the inner, and others having only indirect access, the subject does not have *access* to anything inner at all (he has pains, not access to pains), and others, who observe the manifestations of the inner in behaviour thereby have as direct an access as there can possibly be. Hence too, one can be, and one often is, completely certain that another person is (or is not) conscious, is in pain, sees, hears, believes this or that, is angry or cheerful.

iv.   Finally, psychological terms are not names of inner entities in the sense in which typical physical terms can be loosely characterized as names of outer entities. Moreover, their meanings are not explained by association with 'inner' experience.

We shall show why these ramifying conceptual commitments ((1) − (4) on pp. 85–7 above) are misconceived. To relieve neuroscientific reflection of these misconceptions will be a first step on the road to ridding it of its crypto-Cartesianism and also of its empiricist heritage. This in turn will make it possible to apprehend correctly what neuroscience has achieved in respect of shedding light on the empirical relations between the mental and the neural. We shall start by trying to clear away some misconceptions regarding the commonly invoked dichotomy of what is 'inner' and what is 'outer'.

3.5 The Inner

The conception of the psychological attributes as 'inner' and as 'mental' It is striking that, save in neuroscience or philosophy lectures, no one says that toothache is something 'inner', any more than one says that toothache is something 'mental'. Toothache is in a tooth, not in the mind − although, of course, it is not *in* the tooth as either a cavity is *in* the tooth or an infection is *in* the tooth. Why do we say that it is 'in' the tooth at all? Because it is the tooth that hurts (not the mind), and the sufferer points to the tooth when asked where he has a pain, nurses his cheek, and refrains from biting on the infected tooth. There is no such thing as mental toothache, and the expression 'mental toothache', far from being a pleonasm, is a nonsense. Of course, one would not feel toothache unless the nociceptor nerve terminals in the tooth pulp were excited, and this increased impulse firing was conveyed by the trigeminal nerve to the pons and then to the brain. But this does not imply that there is toothache in the brain, or that the brain feels toothache. Rather, these neural events are proximate causes or concomitants of the person's feeling toothache. It is no coincidence that we speak of *physical pain* (since it has a *bodily* location) and contrast it with *mental suffering*. But mental suffering is not burning or stabbing pains in the mind – there are no such things. Rather, it is anguish or grief, feelings of humiliation or loss of self-respect, etc.

The metaphor of the 'inner' and the 'outer'

Nevertheless, it is true that we are inclined to compare pain with something 'inner' and its behavioural manifestations with something 'outer'. The comparison is not silly, for, to be sure, one does not say that one has toothache on the basis of observing one's behaviour, whereas one does say that another person has toothache when one sees him clutching his swollen jaw and groaning. But, Wittgenstein nicely remarked, 'We must get clearer about how the metaphor of revealing (outside and inside) is actually applied by us; otherwise we shall be tempted to look for an inside behind that which in our metaphor is the inside.'[53] This methodological advice is profound – but it needs clarification.

Revealing and concealing

Someone may have a pain and not reveal it, may see something and not say what he sees, think something and not voice his thoughts. In this sense, one may say that the mental is 'inner', in so far as it is what *can*, in *some* cases, be kept to oneself, concealed, and its manifestations suppressed. But if a person groans in pain, says what he sees or expresses his opinions, then he has 'revealed' what, *in our metaphor* of 'inner' and 'outer', is the inner. If he screams with pain as the dentist prods his tooth, one cannot say, 'Well, that is only behaviour (something "outer") – his pain is still concealed (it is "inner")'. If someone sincerely tells us what he thinks, we cannot say, 'These are only words – he has kept his thoughts to himself'. And if he shows us what he sees, we too can see what he sees – even though we do not look *into* anything. (What he sees is not in his brain, and if we were to scan his brain by the most sophisticated PET, we still would not see what he sees.) Someone may feel ashamed of what he said or did and conceal his shame, but if he blushes with shame, then his shame is revealed, not concealed, by his blush. The 'inner' does not stand *behind* the 'outer', concealed in the brain or mind – but *sometimes* one may keep one's thoughts and feelings to oneself, and *sometimes* one may positively conceal them – suppress their natural manifestations, pretend or lie. But it should be remembered that one may conceal one's thoughts by writing one's diary in code – and there is nothing 'inner' about that.

Observing the inner

So, it is misconceived to claim, as Damasio does, that 'the term *feeling* should be reserved for the private, mental experience of an emotion . . . this means that you cannot observe a feeling in someone else, although you can observe a feeling in yourself when, as a conscious being you perceive your own emotional states'.[54] To feel angry or ashamed, to feel compassion or pity, to feel jealous or envious, is not *to perceive* or *observe* anything. And far from it being impossible to observe a feeling in another person, it is perfectly common and familiar.

---

[53] L. Wittgenstein, 'Notes for lectures on "private experience" and "sense data"', ed. R. Rhees, *Philosophical Review*, 77 (1968), p. 280.
[54] Damasio, *Feeling of What Happens*, p. 42.

When someone, in circumstances of danger, blanches with fear, cries out in terror, trembles and draws back from the danger – his fear is *manifest*. Of course, to observe the manifestations of another person's fear is not to feel the same fear as he (although that too is possible, if we are just as frightened as he and frightened of exactly the same thing). Rather, it is to observe that he is afraid – to see the fear written all over his face, exhibited in his demeanour and behaviour. When someone is insulted and grows red with anger, raises his voice and clenches his teeth, do we not observe that he is angry? We may not feel equally angry, or indeed angry at all, but his anger is perfectly visible, and we may quail before it. There is nothing 'inner' or unobservable about the *manifest* emotions of others – they are exhibited to public view. All that is true is, first, that when we observe the anger or fear of another, *we* do not usually feel anger or fear ourselves; second, *sometimes* a person may feel angry or frightened and not show it.

3.6 Introspection

Privileged access and introspection, as conceived by Humphrey, Johnson-Laird and Weiskrantz

The above remarks on the metaphor of inner and outer may seem trivial and irrelevant. Surely, no one is confused about *that*! The salient point about the notions of inner and outer is surely that each of us has privileged access to the contents of our own consciousness. And is this not what scientists such as Damasio mean when they insist that each person can observe only his own feelings and not the feelings of others? For each person can *introspect* what is in his mind, and no one can introspect what is in the mind of another person. Indeed, some biologists currently argue that the power of scrutinizing the contents of the mind is a crucial *natural* development. Nicholas Humphrey holds that 'a revolutionary advance in the evolution of the mind occurred when, for certain social animals, a new set of heuristic principles was devised to cope with the pressing need to model a special section of reality – the reality comprised by the behaviour of kindred animals. The trick which nature came up with was *introspection* . . . [the] examination of the contents of consciousness.'[55] (But, as we shall show, the ability to reflect on what one thinks or feels is a result of the ability to say what one thinks or feels; hence it is not 'a trick which nature came up with', but a corollary of possessing a developed language.) Cognitive scientists, such as Johnson–Laird, who try to envisage computational analogues of the workings of the mind, conceive of introspection on the model of a parallel-processing device the operating system of which 'has a model of its own operation, which it uses to guide its own processes. This "self-reflective" procedure can be applied to its own output so that the system can construct a model of its own use of such models, and so on, in a series of ever-ascending levels of representation.'[56]

---

[55] Humphrey, *Consciousness Regained*, p. 30. Humphrey's idea is that introspection informs a creature of the contents of its own mind, and, on this basis, it can, by analogy, construct a theory or model of the minds of other animals akin to it.

[56] P. N. Johnson-Laird, *The Computer and the Mind* (Fontana, London, 1988), p. 362.

And neuro-psychologists follow Weiskrantz in explaining the strange phenomenon of blind-sight in terms of a disconnection between a monitoring system and the neural events it allegedly monitors, identifying the hypothesized monitoring system with 'awareness', which is conceived to be a form of privileged access.[57] Accordingly, introspection is conceived to be the operation of a neural monitor – a neural analogue of an imagined form of inner perception.

Introspection is not a form of inner vision or internal sense
The conception of consciousness or introspection as a form of inner vision is misconceived. The analogy between our ability to say what we perceive and our perceptual faculties, on the one hand, and our ability to say what we think, feel, want, etc. and the alleged faculty of introspection, on the other, limps. It does not warrant conceiving of introspection as akin to a perceptual faculty (an 'internal sense'), or of our ability to say what we are thinking, feeling or intending to do as the upshot of any form of perception. The perceptual faculties are faculties the exercise of which is dependent upon the state of the relevant perceptual organ, on the conditions of observation, and on the observational skills of the subject. But introspection involves no perceptual organ – one does not use one's eyes, ears or any other organ in order to be able to say what one thinks or expects, wants or intends. It involves no observation – one does not observe one's thoughts, or descry one's desires or intentions. Hence, too, it involves no observation conditions. So there is no analogue of good or poor eyesight, no 'more light' or 'having a second look from closer'. Nor are there any observational skills which might be greater or lesser, and which might be honed with practice and training. There is no more a *mind's eye* in anything other than a wholly metaphorical sense than there is a mind's ear, nose or tongue. And where we do invoke the metaphor of the mind's eye, we speak of seeing *in* not *with* our mind's eye (see §6.3.1).

What introspection actually is
There is, to be sure, such a thing as introspection, but it is not a form of inner vision or observation. Some people are more skilled at introspection than others, but not because they have a better 'inner eye'. In one sense, the introspective person is he who reflects upon himself and his character, on his emotions and motives, on his attitudes and moods. Introspection, in this sense, is a form of reflexive thought, not a form of perception. It is a route to self-knowledge and self-understanding, albeit one that is beset with the perils of self-deception.

In another sense, introspection is a matter of *attention* to one's moods and emotions, sensations and feelings. So, one may attend to the waxing and waning of one's pains in the course of the day for medical purposes, or to the changes in one's emotions and attitudes towards someone over a period of time. But to attend to one's feelings is not to *perceive* one's feelings; it is rather to take note of them. I may write in my diary that the pain in the morning was not too bad, but that by noon it was becoming so severe that I had to lie down. But, in order to note this, I do not *perceive* my pain (there is no such thing as perceiving one's own pain) – I have it, and register the fact and the description of

---

[57] L. Weiskrantz, 'Neuropsychology and the nature of consciousness', in Blakemore and Greenfield (eds), *Mindwaves*, p. 319.

the pain in my diary. I may note that my passion for Maisy is waning, and that I am now more attracted to Daisy – but to do so, I do not observe my emotions with an inner eye. I feel my passion for Maisy diminishing – but what that means is that, for example, I think about her less frequently, realize that I am no longer eager to see her or to be in her company, dwell less in thought upon her charms than hitherto. But I do not *perceive* my thinkings, realizings and dwellings. My ability to register or report my feelings and emotions involves no faculty of inner vision. That ability is not to be explained in terms of a 'monitoring system', let alone a 'neural monitoring system', but, as we shall argue below, in terms of the linguistic capacities which any normal, mature language-user possesses to a greater or lesser degree.

3.7 Privileged Access: Direct and Indirect

Misconceptions concerning privileged access and direct/indirect access

Perhaps so, one might respond, but nevertheless, it must surely be conceded that a person has a form of *privileged* access to the contents of his own consciousness which no one else has. For another person to find out, come to know, whether I am in pain, what I am thinking, how I am feeling, etc., he must rely on my behaviour, on what I do and say. So he has only *indirect access* to my mental states. Maybe the metaphor embedded in the term 'introspection' is altogether misleading. But it surely cannot be denied that I have *direct access* to my own states of mind, to my thoughts and feelings, and that others do not.

Whether it can *legitimately* be denied or not depends on how it is understood. Taken in one way, it is innocuous; taken in another, it is misguided. What is true is that the grounds justifying others in ascribing psychological attributes to me are the behavioural criteria constituted by my manifestations and expressions of sensation, perception, thought, volition, etc., whereas I avow or aver what I think or feel without any criteria at all. But it does not follow that I have direct access to anything, or that others, who judge that things are thus-and-so with me on the basis of what I do and say, have only indirect access.

What 'access' might be, and why the ability to give expression to 'the inner' is not a matter of access to anything

To have a pain, to feel cheerful or depressed, to think that such-and-such is the case, to want to do so-and-so, to intend to act thus, and to be able to say so is not to *have access* to anything. One has access to a library, for example, if one is permitted to use it; one has access to such-and-such a closed room or garden if one legitimately has a key to it; one has access to the President if one is permitted to see him on request; and one has access to information on the Web if one has a computer with appropriate facilities. But there is nothing comparable to these cases which can be characterized as 'access' to one's pains – what *is* true is that when I have a pain, I can say so immediately, without evidential grounds.

When a baby is in pain, he screams. He cannot yet say 'I have a pain' or 'My stomach aches' – not through lack of *access* to his pain, but because he has not yet learnt to speak. When a small child is cheerful, he bounces around merrily – but he has not yet learnt to express his good cheer with the utterance 'I'm feeling cheerful'. A person who has mastered the use of language can make assertions. He may assert that it is going to rain, or that the government is going to fall, or that it is wrong to hunt foxes. For such assertions he will normally have grounds – for example, that there are rain clouds on the horizon, that the opposition has mustered enough votes to win a motion of no confidence, that cruelty is wicked. But in some cases he may be aware that the grounds he can offer in support of his assertion are insufficient to rule out the possibility that what he asserts is, or may turn out to be, false. In other cases, he may be aware that what he asserts is essentially a matter of opinion. So he will preface his assertion with the words 'I believe' or 'I think' or 'In my opinion'. Such ability to say that one thinks, believes or opines this or that does not turn on one's having *privileged access* to one's thoughts, beliefs and opinions or to one's thinkings, believings and opinings. Rather, in such cases (and there are others, which complicate the tale), one has grounds for an assertion, one is aware that these grounds are less than decisive, and one qualifies one's remarks accordingly. What the person needs in order sincerely to express his belief is not access to his 'mental state of believing',[58] but awareness that his grounds are less than decisive, and fall short of warranting an unqualified assertion, and mastery of the use of the qualifying expressions 'I believe', 'I think' or 'In my opinion'.

Misconceptions of 'indirect access' and indirect evidence

The idea that others have only *indirect access* to or *indirect evidence* for the subject's being in pain, feeling cheerful or depressed, wanting a drink or thinking such-and-such is equally misconceived. We can speak of 'indirect evidence' or of 'knowing indirectly' only where it also *makes sense* to speak of direct evidence and of knowing directly – for to characterize evidence or knowledge as 'indirect' is meant to draw a *contrast*. And the contrast between having direct evidence that A is in pain and having indirect evidence thereof is not between *A's* having a pain and *his* saying so and *our observing* that A has a pain and saying so. For *having a pain* is not a form of knowledge, nor yet a kind of evidence, and the person who groans or says that he has a pain does not say so on the basis of either evidence or observation, for to have a pain, as noted above, is not to *observe* anything. There is no more direct a way of knowing that a person has a pain than seeing him writhe and groan in circumstances of injury or sickness. There is no more direct a way of knowing what another sees than by his showing one what he sees, and no more direct a way of knowing what he thinks than from his sincere confession. Knowing indirectly that another person is in pain might be a matter of noticing a bottle of analgesics by his bedside together with an empty glass of water. Coming to know what another person thinks on the basis of hearsay might be taken to be a case of 'indirect knowledge' – but there is nothing indirect about a confession from the horse's mouth. It is altogether mistaken to suppose that in order to know directly what another person thinks, one would have 'to "get inside" other human beings to inspect the nature of their conscious cogitations'.[59]

---

[58] Among other things, believing is not a mental state. For elaboration of this point, see P. M. S. Hacker 'Malcolm and Searle on "intentional mental states"', *Philosophical Investigations*, 15 (1992), pp. 245–75. For discussion of the concept of a mental state, see §10.2 below.

[59] Cf. Blakemore, *Mind Machine*, p. 231.

The sense in which there is literally any such thing as 'getting inside another human being' is: examining the interior of his body and brain – for there is no such thing (save figuratively) as getting inside his mind. This is not something we cannot do; rather, there is no such thing to do. That there is no such thing is no more a *limitation* than it is a limitation that one cannot checkmate in draughts. So, we *can* 'get inside' another person's *brain*, but no amount of investigation of another person's neural processes by means of PET will allow us to inspect his reasoning or what he is thinking. On the other hand, we *can* and often *do* inspect a person's reasoning and the content of his thinking. We examine the *sincere expression* of his thought and argument. If we want to know what Newton or Kant thought, and wish to examine his reasoning, we read his writings – and there is nothing *indirect* about that.[60]

3.8 Privacy or Subjectivity

Misunderstandings of the notions of 'subjectivity', 'privacy', and 'private ownership' of psychological attributes

One might grant that the terminology of 'direct' and 'indirect' is at best misleading. Perhaps the idiom of 'access' and 'privileged access' is ill-chosen. Nevertheless, it is surely indisputable that the mental has a 'subjective mode of existence'; that 'in consequence of its subjectivity, . . . pain is not equally access-ible to any observer. Its existence . . . is a first-person existence.' Every pain 'must be *somebody's* pain'; 'every conscious state is always *someone's* conscious state'. Pains, we might say, are a kind of logically private entity. No one else can have *my* pain, only a similar one. Another person's pain is another pain. 'And just as I have a special relation to my conscious states, which is not like my relation to other people's conscious states, so they in turn have a special relation to their conscious states, which is not like my relation to their conscious states.'[61]

There is nothing indisputable about these claims. On the contrary, they exhibit further confusion. We must try to separate the wheat from the chaff.

Having the same beliefs or thoughts as another

Would one also wish to say that another person cannot have my beliefs or thoughts? Which belief do I have? Suppose I believe that My Love will win the 3.30. So, the belief I have is: *that My Love will win the 3.30.* Suppose I now tell you the evidence I have for believing what I believe, and you too come to believe that My Love will win the 3.30. So now you have the very same belief as I. This might be conceded, but, it might

---

[60] It would be a further error to suppose that when a person expresses his thoughts, views or opinions, he is *describing* them – as if he could see something invisible to others, which he then describes for their benefit. To say what one thinks is not to describe one's thoughts, but to state or express them. A description of one's thoughts is given by characterizing them as brilliant, confused, insightful or muddled.

[61] J. R. Searle, *The Rediscovery of the Mind* (MIT Press, Cambridge, MA, 1992), pp. 94f. Searle does not use the idiom of 'privacy', but favours 'subjectivity'. Other philosophers and, as we have seen, some neuroscientists favour 'privacy'.

still be objected, pains are altogether different. After all, you can't *feel* my pain! Only I can feel my pain – I stand in an altogether special relationship to my pains.

Having the same pain as another – the criteria of identity for pains

If this means merely that when you have a headache, I do not usually have one, then that is true. If it means that two people cannot have the same headache, then it is false. If we both have a dull throbbing pain in the left temple, then we *do* have the same pain. – Surely not; it is just that they are exactly similar, but they are nevertheless two distinct headaches! That is incorrect. There are two distinct people, with exactly the same headache. For, after all, what headache do you have? A dull throbbing one in the temples? That is precisely the same headache as I have. But surely, your headache is in your head, and mine is in mine. How can they be the same headache if the headaches have a different location? To this there are two replies. First, if one is worried about the problem of distinct location, one's worries should be alleviated by the example of Siamese twins with a pain at the point of juncture. Here one cannot say that the pains have a different location – the twins both indicate the same location. The fact that this does *not* alleviate one's qualms – that is, the fact that one still wishes to say that the twins have different pains (even though they are in the same place) – shows that one's worries do not really turn on the matter of location. Second, we should note that the concept of location of sensation is *not* like that of location of a physical object. For two people to have a pain in the same place is neither for them successively to be in the same place and to have a pain, nor for them to be Siamese twins with a pain at the point of juncture. Rather, it is for corresponding parts of their bodies to hurt in the same manner.

Being had by a subject does not characterize a pain, so who the subject of pain is does not determine the identity of the pain he has

Identity and difference of location, then, is a red herring. One might grant that, yet still insist that different people cannot have exactly the same headache. Surely, one wants to object, *yours is yours, and mine is mine* – how could they be identical? Another person's headache, as we remarked above, is another headache. This is the nub of the confusion. For *being mine* and *being yours* are not identifying characteristics of the headache – these possessive phrases characterize *who has* a headache, not *what* headache is in question. *Being mine* is not an identifying property of the headache from which I am suffering, which might differentiate it from your headache, any more than being the colour of my eyes is an identifying property of the colour which my eyes have. If my eyes are brown and your eyes are brown, we both have eyes of the same colour. (Two red cherries don't have different colours just because the red of the first cherry 'belongs' to the first cherry and the red of the second 'belongs' to the second.)

Having a pain is not owning anything; nor is it standing in a relation to a pain

Having a pain is not owning or possessing anything – any more than having a train to catch is owning or possessing something. Having a pain is *not* standing in any special relation to a pain, since it is not a relation at all – any more than is having a depression, which is no more than a matter of feeling depressed. To have a pain in one's foot is a matter of one's foot hurting.

The criteria of identity of a pain consist in its intensity, location and phenomenological features, and if your pain and mine tally in these respects, then we both have the same

Having a pain compared with having a penny

pain, just as if the colour of this cushion tallies with the colour of that cushion in hue, value and chroma, then the two cushions have the same colour. We are inclined to think otherwise, because we unwittingly construe *having a pain* on the model of *having a penny*. But that is mistaken, for *having a penny* is indeed a case of ownership or possession, and for a person to have a penny is for him to stand in a relationship – namely, of ownership or possession – to the penny. But for a person to have a pain is not for him to stand in a *relation* to a pain, any more than for a cushion to have a red colour is for the cushion to stand in a relation to the colour red.[62]

Sensation nominals are derived from sensation verbs

So, to have a pain is not to have *access* to anything. In particular, it is not to have *privileged* access to something which one *inalienably possesses* and which is, accordingly, *logically private* so that no one else could possess it (but only something like it). To have a pain is to suffer. It is for part of one's body to hurt. If A's left temple aches, throbs intermittently, and is sufficiently severe to stop him from reading, and B's left temple aches in like manner, then we say that A and B have the same headache. Our discourse about sensations and about the sameness and difference of sensations is an *abstraction* from talk of hurtings, achings, itchings, throbbings, etc. Sensation names are useful precisely because they allow us to abstract from A's head's aching and B's head's aching in order to focus upon what is common to these two distinct states of affairs.[63] Different people may indeed have the very same pain (not just a very similar one), for what *counts* as two people having the *same* pain is that the sensation each complains of should have the same phenomenological characteristics (e.g. throbbing, burning, nagging, dull), be located in the same part of the body, and be of the same intensity. This is what is *called* 'having the same pain', and the fact that two people have the same pain can be an important diagnostic mark of their suffering from the same disease.

Of course, it is true that when I have a headache, you need not have one. And it is also true that when I say I have a headache, I do not do so on the basis of perceptual observation of my own behaviour, since I do not have to observe myself clutching my head in order to be able to say that I have a headache – for to have a headache is not to *perceive* anything. However, I do not do so on the basis of 'introspective observation', conceived as 'inner perception', either, since there is no such thing. I just say so – give vocal expression to my pain. Of course, I *feel* a headache, but to feel a headache just *is* to

---

[62] In the jargon of logicians, the distinction between qualitative and numerical identity, which applies to material objects, does not apply to properties, such as colours, or to pains. Two material objects may be qualitatively identical but numerically distinct. Neither colours nor pains admit of this distinction (although in other respects they are categorially very different).

[63] Reflect on the following analogy. Imagine that colour predicates were exclusively verbs, so that we spoke of A's redding and B's blueing, etc. Then we might introduce colour nouns and adjectives as an abstraction from what is common to, for example, A's greening and B's greening: viz. the colour green that they both have. Although the event or process of A's greening is distinct from the event or process of B's greening, the colour A and B both have – viz. green – is the very same colour.

have a headache – that is, for one's head to ache. To feel a pain in one's head is not a form of tactile perception, but a form of sensation. It is categorially quite distinct from feeling a penny in one's pocket (with one's fingers), which *is* a form of tactile perception. To be able to say that one has a headache when one has migraine requires no grounds at all – any more than a groan of pain needs grounds.

3.9 The Meaning of Psychological Predicates and How they are Learnt

Psychological expressions are not assigned a meaning by being linked to experiences, states or processes by association or private ostensive definition

We have suggested that misunderstandings concerning the concepts of *inner* and *outer*, *direct* and *indirect*, *privileged access* and *introspection*, *subjectivity* and *privacy*, collectively support a wholly misguided picture of the mental. These same misconceptions also conspire together to support an equally mistaken idea of the meaning of psychological expressions, the manner in which they are learnt, and what is involved in their use. In particular, they foster the thought that each person knows what the word 'pain', for example, means in virtue of associating the word with the sensations of pain to which he has privileged access; knows what the words 'want', 'believe' and 'intend' mean because he attaches the words to his own inner feelings of desire and his private experiences of believing and intending. In short, the psychological vocabulary is thus conceived to consist of *names* of subjective experiences, mental states or processes, to which each person has private, direct and privileged access. And the words are conceived to be given their meanings by being linked to the experiences, states or processes.

Ostensive definition and the use of samples in such envisaged definitions

Wittgenstein discussed this misconception at length, in what is the most famous battery of philosophical arguments of the twentieth century. Popularly known as 'the private language argument(s)', it is as difficult as it is famous (and controversial). In this context, we can give only a thumbnail sketch of the thrust of Wittgenstein's arguments.[64] The conception of meaning that is in play here is that of naming an object (e.g. an apple) or property (e.g. being red, or scarlet, or magenta) by pointing at an appropriate thing and saying '*That* (fruit) ☞ is an apple' or '*That* (colour) ☞ is red (scarlet, magenta)'. The utterance gives a definition (technically termed 'an ostensive definition', i.e. a definition by pointing) or rule for the use of a word – for example, 'apple' or 'red ("scarlet", "magenta")'. For it says that a fruit which is perceptibly of the same kind as that pointed at is correctly denominated 'an apple', or that any object which is visibly the

---

[64] For a more detailed account, see P. M. S. Hacker, *Insight and Illusion: Themes in the Philosophy of Wittgenstein*, rev. edn (Clarendon Press, Oxford, 1986, and Thoemmes Press, Bristol, 1997), chs 9–10. For an exhaustive anatomization of Wittgenstein's arguments, see P. M. S. Hacker, *Wittgenstein: Meaning and Mind, Volume 3 of an Analytical Commentary on the Philosophical Investigations* (Blackwell, Oxford, 1990).

colour pointed at is correctly said to be red (scarlet or magenta). The object pointed at is a *sample* or *paradigm* for the application of the word defined; that is, it functions as a standard for the correct application of the word. Being a sample, it can (and sometimes does, e.g. in the cases of scarlet or magenta) fulfil its function by being employed as an object of comparison to determine the correct application of the expression defined. This way of assigning meaning to a name, explaining the meaning of a name, and determining the application of a name is perfectly familiar and commonplace, used constantly in teaching children or in explaining to adults the meanings of many common words in our language and in determining the application of, for example, numerous names of shades of colours.

Can psychological expressions be assigned a meaning by private ostensive definition?

The crucial question is whether the meanings of *psychological* expressions can be taught or explained in this, or in an analogous, way. Does anyone learn the meaning of 'pain' in such a way? Given that we all know what 'to see' or 'to hear' mean, did we acquire mastery of the use of these perceptual predicates by associating them in this way with our experiences of seeing and hearing? Did we master the use of 'I think' or 'I want' or 'I intend to' by *naming* a private experience or process which we had? Do we – indeed, could we – give the rules for the use of such words as 'think' or 'believe' in this manner?

Careful reflection shows that we *could not* have mastered the use of these words by naming experiences thus. We *could not* give an operative rule for the use of these words in this form. Indeed, a subjective experience *could not* function as a standard for the correct application of a psychological expression in the manner in which a public sample does. We shall now show why not.

If our psychological expressions were assigned a meaning by private ostensive definition, no one could know what others meant by their psychological vocabulary

It should be noted that if *per impossibile* we had mastered the use of psychological expressions by naming our own experiences in the envisaged manner, and if the nature of the mental is as conceived by neuroscientists, we could never know whether what other people mean by 'pain', 'want', 'see', 'think', 'believe', 'intend', etc. is what we mean by these words. For what a person means by the word 'pain', for example, is allegedly defined by reference to the experience he has (which, on the favoured model is private and cannot be had by others), and he cannot in principle know what other people have when they say that they have a pain (since, on the favoured model, it is inaccessible to anyone else). For all he knows, others may have a quite different feeling, which just happens to be linked with crying and groaning (for, on the favoured model, pain-behaviour is not conceptually linked with pain). But does this make sense? Do we – should we – have any doubts about what others mean when they say that they are in pain? Is it only a *hypothesis* that the person writhing on the ground with a broken leg and crying out 'It hurts, it hurts!' is in pain? Can anyone really think that when a person is seriously injured and lies screaming in a pool of blood, perhaps what he feels is not pain (not what we mean by 'pain') at all, that for all we know it may even be quite pleasant? Nor can one reasonably argue that we *do* know that others have pains just as we do, because we know that they share the same neurophysiology. For, among other objections, that would absurdly imply that prior to the discoveries of neuroscience, scepticism about other minds was rational.

Trying to assign a meaning to a sensation term by means of an inner, private, ostensive definition is incoherent

This, however, is not the worst consequence of the favoured model. For, as Wittgenstein showed, if we think matters through, it will be evident that it is not merely that such an imaginary person would not be able to know whether others mean by 'pain', etc. what he takes himself to mean, but rather that he himself could not have mastered the use of the word 'pain' at all. The envisaged procedure of assigning a meaning to the word 'pain', for example, is incoherent, and the conception of what it is for such a psychological expression to have the meaning it has is likewise confused. Let us see why.

Defining colour words by ostensive definition

We do define, and explain, the meanings of colour words such as 'red' or 'Wellington blue' or 'ultramarine' by reference to samples. We can, and sometimes (e.g. in the latter two cases) do, use the defining samples as objects of comparison to check the correctness of saying of an object that it is, for example, Wellington blue or ultramarine. We consult a colour chart, and compare the colour patch under which is written 'Wellington blue' with the object in question (perhaps a swathe of cloth), and if the object is the colour of the sample, we can correctly say that it is Wellington blue. 'Anything which is *this* ☞ ■ colour', we say, pointing at the sample, 'is Wellington blue.' But if we were to try to define the word 'pain' by reference to a sensation of pain which we feel, could we do likewise? No – for there can be no proper analogue of this procedure in the case of mental predicates.

Four disanalogies between public ostensive definition and the illusory private ostensive definition

First, there is no analogue of *pointing* at a sample. The most one can achieve is concentrating one's attention on a sensation of pain or on the memory of a pain in one's reproductive imagination. But concentrating one's attention is not a kind of pointing.

Secondly, there is no proper analogue of a sample. A sample is essentially something reproducible – for use on subsequent occasions. But in the imaginary case of trying to define a sensation word such as 'pain' by reference to a sensation of pain, the most we can reproduce is a putative memory of the sensation upon which attention was originally concentrated. We have to remember with *which* sensation we originally associated the word 'pain'. And this putative mnemonic reproduction of the original sensation is supposed to function as a sample, the role of which is to constitute a standard for the correct use of the word. But now, we have no criterion of correctness to determine whether the mental image or representation that occurs to us when we try to remember what we mean by 'pain' is a mental image of pain or of something else. (Of course, it seems otherwise, because anyone who *has* mastered the use of the word 'pain' can remember what a pain is, can conjure up a memory of a past pain – but *here* remembering *presupposes* the concept of pain.) *Anything* our memory throws up in association with the word 'pain' will do just as well as anything else, and if *anything* counts as right – that is, as the right memory exemplar – then *nothing* counts as right – that is, there is no such thing as right or wrong. But if so, then the word 'pain' has no correct use at all, and is quite meaningless.

Thirdly, with respect to an expression legitimately defined by means of an ostensive definition involving a sample, one can explain, both to another person and to oneself, what the expression means. In the case of the putative private ostensive definition, *ex hypothesi* one cannot explain to another person what the expression allegedly so defined means. But there is an illusion that one can nevertheless explain to oneself what it means. One simply calls up a mental representation, a memory, of the defining sample, and bethinks oneself that *this* is what the expression means. But this is an illusion, both because there is no genuine analogue of pointing and because there is no analogue of a genuine sample. So one cannot even explain to oneself what an expression allegedly so defined means.

Fourthly, there is no proper analogue of *comparing* a sample with an object to determine whether the object matches the sample and can therefore be said to instantiate the concept defined by reference to the sample. For suppose we have a sensation in our foot, and we want to check whether it can correctly be denominated 'pain'. So we conjure up a mental image (representation) in association with the word 'pain'. How are we supposed to compare the image with the sensation? In the case of the colour sample of Wellington blue and the swathe of cloth, we juxtapose the sample with the cloth and see whether they match. But how do we juxtapose the putative memory sample with the sensation in the foot? Neither can be *perceived* (seen, heard, tasted, smelled or tactilely felt). The sensation can be said to be felt, but, as noted, this use of 'feel' does not signify a form of tactile perception – the pain is *had*, but not perceived. Similarly, the mental image or representation is *had*, but not seen or felt. And one cannot *juxtapose* the recollected image with the felt sensation to see or feel whether they match. (But, of course, anyone who *has* mastered the use of the word 'pain' can say whether he has a pain in his foot or not, without going through any such charade.)

How do we teach a child the rudiments of the use of the psychological vocabulary

A simpler point can be made. We do not teach a child how to use the word 'pain' by getting him to associate the word with a sensation he feels, and to use the memory of that sensation as a standard of correctness for the subsequent use of the word. We do not teach the child the use of doxastic verbs such as 'believe' or 'think' by getting him to associate the words with some inner phenomenon, a special feeling or sensation that he allegedly has whenever he thinks or believes something. Nor do we teach the child how to use the phrase 'I intend to' or 'I am going to' by getting him to identify a special feeling of intention or of tending. (These facts should give us pause, and lead us to examine Wittgenstein's arguments with care.)

Logically different kinds of name

The truth is that psychological terms are not names of psychological properties, acts and activities *in the sense in which* 'red' can be said to be the name of a colour property, 'to wave' can be said to be the name of an act, and 'to dig the garden' can be said to be the name of an activity. To be sure, it is not wrong to say that 'pain' is the name of a sensation, or that 'anger' is the name of an emotion. But this masks deep logical differences between being the name of a colour and being the name of a sensation, or between being the name of an act or activity and being the name of a so-called mental act or mental activity. It suggests a similarity in kind of expression where there are important logical differences, obscuring their profoundly different uses, and occluding the distinctive ways in which they are taught and explained in our common practices. They are not defined by private ostensive definition at all, and the word 'pain', for example, does not stand to the sensation pain as the word 'red' stands to the colour red, just as the word 'believe' does not stand to believing as the word 'run' stand to running. They are words of quite different logical categories, they are used quite differently, and we teach or explain their meaning in a quite different manner. And, on reflection, that should be evident.

First-/third-person asymmetries characterize psychological verbs

Psychological predicates are attached, for example, to personal names, pronouns or definite descriptions. There is an asymmetry between the first-person, present-tense use of these words and the corresponding third-person use. Indeed, this much is recognized even by the received conception, for, on the favoured view, we apply these predicates to ourselves on the basis of introspection or inner perception, whereas we apply them to others on the basis of the non-logical evidence of their behaviour. But this misconstrues the nature of the asymmetry, which is rather that we apply (a subset of) them to ourselves without any 'basis' or evidential grounds at all, and apply them to others on the basis of behavioural criteria – which constitute logically good evidence. This can seem baffling: how can we apply a predicate to ourselves without any criteria of application? Do we apply it *arbitrarily*? That would be absurd. We sincerely say that we are in pain only when we are in pain – and there is nothing arbitrary about that. So, there is more to explain.

To learn the meanings of those psychological predicates that are of concern to us, one must master both their first-person and their third-person uses. For these are different facets of one and the same concept. We have explained that the third-person use involves learning the behavioural criteria that warrant the application of the relevant predicate to another person. But now the first-person use appears to be puzzling. But it is only puzzling because, having rejected the model of name and *nominatum*, we now find ourselves at sea, and sinking. But if we bethink ourselves how we might actually teach the use of these words, how we might explain their use to a learner, how a learner then goes on to use them, and what we count as a correct or an incorrect use, we shall stay afloat and find our bearings.

A child acquires the concept of pain as an extension of natural pain-behaviour

Of course, we do not teach a child the use of 'pain' by getting it to identify a sensation and then to name it. The child learns to substitute pain-utterances for its natural groans and cries. He learns to scream 'Ow' (or, in some countries, 'Aya'); later to say, first, 'Hurts' and then 'It hurts!' or 'Hand hurts!'; and later still to say 'I have a pain'. The *primitive* or *elementary* pain-utterance is learnt as an extension of natural *expressive behaviour*. A child does not scream or groan with pain *arbitrarily*, nor does he learn to give verbal expression to his pain *arbitrarily*. But he no more needs grounds, either 'introspective' or behavioural, for crying out 'It hurts' or 'I have a pain' than he needs grounds for screaming in pain. *Later still*, he will learn to use 'I have a pain' as a cool report (when the pain is not too severe, and the doctor asks how he is feeling). Side by side with this, the child also learns that just as screaming is a way of getting his parent to attend to him, assuage his pain, etc., so, too, saying 'I have a pain' provides the parents (and others) with a reason for attending to him, a ground for sympathy and compassion. Hence too, he learns that when Mother hurts herself and cries out 'Ouch!' or 'I have hurt myself', then that is a ground for the utterance 'Mummy has hurt herself'. So the child simultaneously learns the two complementary facets of the use of 'pain', its expressive (and later also reportive) first-person use and its descriptive third-person use, and the complex manner in which the employment of the word in sentences is integrated into human natural *and* acculturated behaviour.

A child acquires the concept of want-ing as an extension of primitive conative behaviour
Something similar holds in the case of 'want'. *Obviously*, a child does not learn to identify by means of introspec-tion an inner phenomenon to which it has 'access' and then to name it 'wanting'. Rather, the child displays conative behaviour – he *tries* to get things, reaches for a toy that is outside the cot or for some appealing food beyond his reach, and cries or screams in frustration. He learns that this is an efficacious means of getting his parent to give him the object. The parent picks up the object, saying, for example, 'Does Tommy want Teddy? Here it is.' And, in due course, the child learns to say 'Want', and later 'I want Teddy', and so forth. The child's *primitive* or *elementary* use of 'I want' is *as an extension of its natural conative behaviour*. In learning this primitive use of 'I want', the child is learning a new form of conative behaviour – learning to give verbal expression to its wants. Here, 'I want' is an *expression* of wanting, not a description of an inner process or state. The child no more needs to identify an inner process before saying 'I want' than he needs to identify an inner process before striving to reach something. On this primitive foundation are built other, more or less closely related, uses of 'want' and of other conative verbs.

It would be wholly mistaken to think that all the psychological concepts are thus grafted on to natural expressive behaviour. The category of the psychological is not only vague and indeterminate at its boundaries; it is also highly variegated. There are profound *logical* differences between different categories within the domain of the psychological. So we shall give a few more examples to illustrate differences.

The fundamental function of the doxastic vocabulary and the mode of its acquisition
We have already intimated above that the use of doxastic verbs such as 'believe' or 'think' are not learnt as exten-sions of natural doxastic behaviour. Their use already presupposes substantial linguistic skills – in particular, mastery of the use of declarative sentences to make assertions. For 'I think' and 'I believe' (and also 'I know' and 'I doubt whether') are used as prefixes to declarative sentences – they are, the logical grammarian may say, sentence-forming operators on declarative sentences. And, as we have remarked, *one* central use of such expressions is to indicate the character of the grounds that support or warrant the assertion to which they are affixed. So, to master this use, one must already have learnt something about evidential support, grounds for assertion and for doubt. For one says, 'I think . . .', 'I believe . . .', 'As far as I know . . .' or 'Unless I am much mistaken . . .' when one recognizes that one's grounds for the subsequent assertion are insufficient in the circumstances to rule out the possibility of error, or to make it unreasonable to doubt. The detailed story here is long (although not complicated). But this much is clear. One does not learn the use of 'I think' or 'I believe' by identifying an inner state or process of belief within oneself

by means of introspection. Nor is one warranted in prefixing an 'I believe' or an 'I think' by the presence within one of an introspectible state or process of believing or thinking.

How one might teach a child the use of expressions of intention

Different again is the use of expressions of intention. How might a parent teach a child their use? Again, *not* by getting the child to identify an inner phenomenon of intending, and then naming it. There *is* no such inner phenomenon – there is no phenomenology of intending, no distinctive experience called 'intending' – and 'I intend' is neither the name of nor a description of any 'inner experience'. But we might fruitfully think of the *primitive* or *elementary* uses of expressions of intention along the following lines. First, the parent exemplifies for the child the use of the intention-expressing phrase 'I am going to . . .'. To master this, the child need not 'introspect' anything. Rather, he must gather that when one says 'I am going to . . .', then one is expected to go on to. The parent says, for example, 'I am going to give you a bath', and then goes on to give the child a bath. The child must learn that 'I am going to . . .' is used to herald an action, and that when one uses this phrase, one must go on to do the announced action. On this primal foundation rests the more sophisticated use of 'I am going to . . .', in which the projected action may be temporally distant from the expression of intention, as well as the somewhat different use of 'I intend to . . .'. But the nexus with the primal case is maintained. For in all cases, what must be understood by the speaker, and what is understood by the comprehending addressee, is that an expression of intention gives the addressee a (non-inductive) ground for prediction. Hence, if one changes one's mind, or fails to carry out an expressed intention on which the addressee might reasonably have been supposed to have relied in his plans, one is under some obligation to inform him of one's change of plans, or, after the event, to apologize for disappointing legitimate expectations.

Clearly, different psychological concepts are embedded in different ways in human natural and acculturated behaviour. Different concepts subserve very different purposes. And the various concepts are integrated in very different ways into communicative and interpersonal reactive and interactive behaviour. Each concept must be scrutinized in its own right, and generalization is unwarranted. But we hope that we have demonstrated the bankruptcy of the received neo-Cartesian and empiricist conception that pervades neuroscientific reflection, and have indicated the character and some of the advantages of the conception with which they should be replaced.

3.10 Of the Mind and its Nature

The Cartesian misascription of psychological attributes to the mind

Few people are inclined to ascribe psychological predicates to the body. No one says such things as 'My body has a toothache', 'My body sees an apple', 'My body wants to go to New York', or 'My body intends to catch the 3.30'. That is no coincidence, since we have given no sense to such forms of words. But it does not follow that it is correct to apply them to the mind. Descartes did just that, ascribing a wide range of psychological predicates – namely, everything which he subsumed under his idiosyncratic-ally defined category of 'thoughts' – to an immaterial substance, the *res cogitans*, which he held to be intimately, although only causally, related to the body. It is, he held, the mind (thus embodied) which has sensations, perceives (i.e. has the sensible experience as of perceiving an external object), imagines, thinks and doubts, feels emotions, wills and decides. This is misconceived, and it is important to understand the nature of the mis-conceptions. For today, as we have seen above (§3.1), many scientists are prone to ascribe a similar range of psychological predicates to the brain. Some, in the wake of Chomsky and his followers, are even prone to speak of the 'mind/brain', as if the mind and the brain were (or might be discovered to be) one and the same entity. This is no less erroneous than the Cartesian confusions it displaces. Since the concept of mind plays such a signific-ant role in neuroscientific reflection and speculation, it is important to avoid the pitfalls that surround it. So we shall try to clarify our common or garden concept of the mind – putting aside for the moment what philosophers and scientists have made of it.

The mind and its place in English idiom   It is noteworthy that the English term 'mind' is etymo-logically derived from expressions in Indo-Germanic languages (*mynd* (ME), *gimunt* (OHG), *gamunds* (Oteut), *munan* (OE)) that were associated primarily with memory, thought and intention. Current usage, as so often, has not cut itself free of its origins. To hold, keep or bear something in mind is to retain it in memory; to call or bring to mind is to remember or recollect; and for something to be, go or pass out of mind is for it to be forgotten. To speak one's mind, to let someone know one's mind, is to tell that person what one thinks or opines; to turn one's mind to something is to begin thinking about it; to have something on one's mind is to be thinking of or be preoccupied with it; and to be of one mind with another is to agree in judgement. To be minded or to have it in mind to do something is to intend to do it; to have half a mind to do something is to be inclined or tempted to do it; to be in two minds whether to do something is to be undecided; to make up one's mind is to decide, and to change one's mind is to reverse one's decision or judgement.

Of course, these English idioms ramify in further directions. At the most general level, the mind is associated with intellectual faculties: a person is said to have a powerful, agile, subtle or devious mind if he is skilful, quick and ingenious at problem solving, or if his solutions, plans and projects display subtlety or cunning. Hence, too, it is connected with appropriate intellectual virtues and vices: a person has a tenacious, idle, vigorous, judicious or indecisive mind according to the manner in which he grapples with problems requiring reflection and according to the typical upshot of his reflections. A person is of sound mind if he retains his rational faculties, and out of his mind if he thinks, proposes or does things that are irrational. He has lost his mind if he has lost his rational faculties. Other uses fade off in different directions: we speak of people being broad- or narrow-minded, small- or petty-minded, having a dirty mind or a mind like a razor, displaying presence of mind, lacking peace of mind, and so on.

The sense in which talk of the mind is merely a façon de parler   There are some morals to these reminders of linguistic idiom. First, each such use, as is evident from the above examples, is readily paraphrasable into a phrase which does not include the word 'mind', but only a psychological predicate predicable of a human being. In this sense, reference to the mind is eliminable without any loss in the informational content of our sentences. Talk of the mind, one might say, is merely a convenient *façon de parler*, a way of speaking about certain human faculties and their exercise. Of course, that *does not* mean that people do not have minds of their own, which would be true only if they were pathologically indecisive. Nor does it mean that people are mindless, which would be true only if they were stupid and thoughtless. For a creature to have a mind is for it to have a distinctive range of capacities of intellect and will, in particular the conceptual capacities of a language-user which make self-awareness and self-reflection possible.

The mind is not a kind of entity

Second, it is obvious that in these various phrases we are not speaking of one and the same thing: namely, an entity named 'the mind'. When we say that someone changed his mind, that he has a dirty mind, and that he has turned his mind to such-and-such a question, we do not imply that there is one thing, a mind, which has changed, is dirty and has been turned.[65] Indeed, the only *thing* we are speaking of is the person, and from case to case (and phrase to phrase) we are saying very different things *of* the person. To say that our ordinary talk of the mind is a mere *façon de parler* is *not* to say that there are no minds. On the contrary, it is in effect to say that there are, but that they are not kinds of things. The mind, one might say, adapting a phrase which Wittgenstein used in a different context, is not a *nothing*, but it is not a *something* either.

Why the question 'What is a mind?' is misleading

Third, the natural habitat of the English term 'mind' is in such phrases. There can be no guarantee that removed from its habitat it fulfils any genuine role. In particular, the question, which we are all tempted to ask, namely, 'What is the mind?', may be altogether misleading – precisely because the mind is not a kind of thing. Rather, in speaking idiomatically of the mind, we are speaking of a wide range of characteristic human powers and their exercise, and of a range of human character traits.

Three consequences: it makes scant sense to identify the mind with the brain; it is illegitimate to ascribe psychological attributes to the mind rather than to the human being; characteristic descriptions of results of commissurotomy are incoherent

If that is so, and we suggest that it is, then further consequences follow. First, the question of whether the mind is identical with the brain is either a misconceived question or it is to be understood as a question concerning the identity of some or all of these character traits, powers and the instances of their exemplification and exercise with states, events and processes in the brain. Second, it becomes obvious that it is as illegitimate to ascribe most psychological predicates to the mind as it is to ascribe them to the body or the brain. One can, to be sure, say that A's mind is subtle or devious – but that just means that A is subtle or devious in his thoughts, plans and projects. One can say that A's mind is sharp or cunning – but that is just an idiomatic comment on A's theoretical and practical reasoning. On the other hand, it is not my mind that makes up its mind, that has a mind of its own, that is in two minds whether to do this or that, it is I, a human being, a living

---

[65] See B. Rundle, *Mind in Action* (Clarendon Press, Oxford, 1997), p. 26.

animal with intellectual and volitional capacities. And so too, it is not the mind that feels pain, perceives, thinks and desires, makes decisions and forms intentions, but the person, who is a psychophysical unity, not a duality of two conjoined substances, a mind and a body.

Third, it displays profound confusion to suppose that the forms of functional dissociation consequent upon commissurotomy produce two minds, one belonging to the left hemisphere, the other to the right. The *brain* does not *have* a mind, and neither do the two hemispheres of the brain ('I am in two minds whether to . . .' does not mean that each hemisphere of the brain has one). Michael Gazzaniga's descriptions of the experimental data resulting from split-brain operations which he is attempting to explain are conceptually awry. The suggestion that 'mind left dealt with the world differently than mind right seemed to be the major conclusion of studies during this era'[66] is not merely incorrect (as Gazzaniga came to realize); it is incoherent.[67] It is human beings, not their brains, that are said to have minds, and to say that is simply to say that human beings have an array of distinctive capacities. The fact that some of those capacities become dissociated as a result of commissurotomy does not show that the capacities belong to their brains, let alone to the hemispheres of their brains. Even more confused is the supposition that Sperry's investigation of patients who have undergone such operations 'has forever changed the way the mind is viewed as the product of the brain; indeed, two brains, the two hemispheres, each endowed with human thought and emotion, separable, but normally uncannily intertwined . . . Hemispherectomy confirms the humanity of each'.[68]

What needs to be said can be said clearly
It is important to be clear about the nature of the criticisms which we have elaborated, and the intention with which we have elaborated them. Our criticisms do not in any way diminish the importance of the scientific work done by neuroscientists. What we are trying to show is that there are significant conceptual confusions in the descriptions and reasoning of distinguished neuroscientists. These confusions lead them to pose misguided questions, and, as we shall show, sometimes to devise misconceived experiments. They also lead to misrepresentations of the results and implications of experiments. We suggest, and shall, in the sequel, try to substantiate the suggestion, that careful attention to

---

[66] Michael S. Gazzaniga, 'Consciousness and the cerebral hemispheres', in Gazzaniga (ed.), *The New Cognitive Neurosciences*, 4th edn (MIT Press, Cambridge, MA, 1997), p. 1392.

[67] It is equally incoherent to suppose, as Gazzaniga does, that his experiments are describable in the following terms: 'When asked why he [the patient] chose these items [in a matching test], *his left hemisphere replied*, "Oh, that's simple. . . ." Here the left brain, observing the left hand's response, interprets that response according to a context consistent with its sphere of knowledge – one that does not include information about the left hemifield snow scene' (ibid., p. 1393 (our italics)). For it is not hemispheres that reply to anything, it is human beings. Neither brains nor their left halves observe anything, and they do not interpret what they see, since they neither see nor interpret anything. These are functions that human beings perform, and the normal association of functions of sight, cognition and action is sorely disrupted as a result of commissurotomy. For a more detailed examination of the problem of correctly describing the phenomena that follow a commissurotomy, see §14.3 below.

[68] R. W. Doty, 'Two brains, one person', *Brain Research Bulletin*, 50 (1999), p. 423.

conceptual questions can prevent such confusions. What needs to be said can be said clearly, and saying it clearly will benefit, not diminish, the actual achievements of neuroscience.

The conclusions of our investigations in this chapter have a direct bearing on the themes of Part II. We shall try to give an overview of the logical features of some psychological categories that are of concern to cognitive neuroscientists. We shall pay particular attention to the mereological principle and to neuroscientific misconstruals of specific psychological concepts. These conceptual confusions, we shall argue, are anything but trivial verbal matters. They affect and infect the understanding of the results of neuroscientific work.

Part II

Human Faculties and Contemporary Neuroscience: An Analysis

Preliminaries

1 Brain–Body Dualism

Contemporary cognitive neuroscience propounds a form of crypto-Cartesianism

We have argued that contemporary cognitive neuroscience, despite its extraordinary experimental achievements in the twentieth century, continues to work in the shadow of Descartes. For, in spite of their adamant repudiation of Cartesianism, the generation of neuroscientists who succeeded Sherrington's pupils have in effect replaced the Cartesian dualism of mind and body with an analogous dualism of brain and body. Of course, this does not appear to be a form of dualism at all. It does not involve two distinct kinds of Cartesian substance, a material body and an immaterial mind. Both the brain and the body are material, and there appears, at first blush, to be no duality whatsoever, since the brain is, after all, just a part of the body. However, as we have argued, appearances are deceptive.

Like Cartesianism, it commits the mereological fallacy

A cardinal conceptual error of so much current cognitive neuroscience is that it ascribes to the brain attributes that it makes sense to ascribe only to the animal as a whole. In so doing, contemporary neuroscience commits what we called 'a mereological fallacy' – that is, a fallacy of ascribing to a part properties that can be ascribed intelligibly only to the whole of which that part is a part. Strikingly, neuroscience ascribes to the brain much the same range of properties that Cartesians ascribed to the mind. It thus operates with a conceptual scheme that is roughly isomorphic with – that is, has much the same form or structure as – Cartesian dualism, differing primarily with respect to the nature of the subject of psychological attributes. It replaces the immaterial Cartesian mind by the material brain. But it retains the fundamental *logical structure* of dualist psychology.

Like Cartesians, it explains ascription of psychological attributes to human beings by reference to their ascription to the brain

Like Cartesianism, it ascribes psychological attributes to a part of a human being – not, to be sure, to a putative immaterial part, but to a material one. Furthermore, it *explains* the possession of psychological attributes by a human being by reference to the psychological attributes allegedly ascribable to a part of a human being: namely, to the brain. This, as we have suggested, and shall argue further below, is not an error of fact, but a logical or conceptual error. It is not false that the brain thinks, perceives, feels emotions and desires to do things – it is a conceptual confusion. For it makes no sense to ascribe such properties to the brain, any more than it makes sense to ascribe them to a stone (an inanimate physical object) or to a number (which is not a spatio-temporal object at all) – for neither brains nor stones nor numbers are living creatures that behave in ways that logically warrant the ascription to them of psychological attributes.

Like Cartesianism, it conceives of mental states, events and processes as occurring, obtaining or going on in a part of the person

Hence, too, like Cartesianism, contemporary neuroscience conceives of mental events, states and processes as occurring, obtaining or going on *in* a human being – in particular, *in his brain* – rather than conceiving of mental states as states *of the person*, of mental acts or activities as acts and activities *of the human being*, and of mental processes as processes undergone, gone through or engaged in *by a person*. The neuroscientific conception is incoherent, involving a misuse of the concepts of mental event, mental state and mental process. Ascribing mental states to the brain makes no more sense than ascribing them to the kidneys (i.e. to any other part of an animal). Ascribing so-called *content-bearing states* (i.e. states specified by a that-clause, such as 'thinks that . . .', 'remembers that . . .', 'concludes (or infers) that . . .') that are in the relevant respects *analogous* to reasoning, conjecturing, inferring, etc. to subsystems of the brain merely draws a cloud of jargon over an incoherence. If it makes no sense to ascribe 'content-bearing states' to the brain, it certainly makes no sense to ascribe them to parts of the brain. It is not the brain, but the human being, that is in a state of trepidation in view of a forthcoming examination, or in a state of intense concentration while writing an examination. There is *no such thing* as a mental process (such as reciting the alphabet in one's imagination) going on in a part of an animal, no matter whether that part be the kidneys or the brain. And there is no such thing as a part of the brain (the amygdala, hippocampus, prefrontal cortices) being in a state analogous to the 'state of reasoning, conjecturing or inferring', since neither reasoning nor conjecturing nor inferring are states, and there is no such thing as a part of the brain satisfying the criteria that would warrant ascribing to it the attributes of reasoning, conjecturing and inferring, or thinking, remembering and deciding. What go on *in* the brain are neural processes, which need to occur in order for the person, whose brain it is, to be going *through* the relevant mental processes. It is the person, the living human being, who goes through the *mental process* of reciting the alphabet, or Hamlet's 'To be or not to be' soliloquy, in his imagination (these being genuine mental processes); it is the person whom we ask how far he has got in his silent recitation, and when he says that he has reached 'K', or 'it is a consummation devoutly to be wished', he is not reporting on what his brain is doing but on what he himself is doing. It is the person who is in a *mental state* of concentration, excitement or anxiety (these *are* genuine mental states), not his brain or its parts. And it is people who reason and infer from known or assumed premises to conclusions, not their brains, let alone parts of their brains. Nor could there be any state ascribable to part of the brain that is relevantly *analogous* to reasoning, conjecturing or inferring, for the categories of attributes that are intelligibly ascribable to the brain *and* its parts are *categorially* different from the attributes ascribable to human beings. One might just as well ascribe to parts of the brain attributes *relevantly similar* to the state of being married or divorced, in debt or bankrupt.

Neuroscientists retain the logical structure of Cartesian psychology in respect of the explanation of perception, voluntary action, and the perception of secondary qualities

The flaws in the conceptual scheme of current neuroscience are not limited to the mereological fallacy and its immediate consequent confusions. As remarked, neuroscientists *also* retain the *logical structure* of Cartesian psychology. Descartes conceived of human perception as the causation of a 'thought' (in his idiosyncratic use of this term[1]) in the mind of a human being by the impact of light on the retinae, or sound waves on the eardrums, etc. And John Locke, the founding father of British empiricism, conceived of perception as the causation of ideas or representations in the mind by objects relevantly similar to those ideas or representations. So too, many neuroscientists conceive of perception as the causation of (visual, auditory, etc.) images in the brain or mind. Both Cartesian and Lockean dualism, on the one hand, and current neuroscience, on the other, conceive of perception as an attribute of *a part* of a human being, ascribable to the human being only derivatively. Both Cartesianism and Lockean empiricism accept the distinction between primary qualities, such as extension, shape, size and motion, which are conceived to be objective properties of objects, and secondary qualities, such as colour, sound, smell and taste, which are not so conceived. Secondary qualities, as we experience them, were held to be no more than ideas in the mind, which do not resemble anything to be found in extra-mental reality. As they are 'in objects', they are but powers to cause ideas in us. Contemporary neuroscientists by and large take colours, sounds, smells and tastes to be 'mental constructions created in the brain by sensory processing. They do not exist, as such, outside of the brain.'[2] This again differs from Cartesianism only in replacing the mind by the brain. Not only do neuroscientists hold that it is the brain that perceives, feels and thinks, but also that it is the brain that has desires. So it is the brain that wills, and the 'unconscious' acts of will of the brain, like the acts of will of the Cartesian or Lockean mind, are the causes of the bodily movements that are constitutive of voluntary action.[3] Just as Cartesianism and classical British empiricism fostered the idea that human behaviour is to be rendered intelligible in terms of causal interaction between mind and body, the mind being the subject of volitional psychological attributes, so current neuroscience

---

[1] Descartes did not count perceiving an apple as a thought, but its seeming to one that one is perceiving an apple is a Cartesian thought.

[2] Eric R. Kandel, James H. Schwartz and Thomas M. Jessell, *Essentials of Neural Science and Behaviour* (Appleton and Lange, Stamford, CT, 1995), p. 370.

[3] Indeed, some neuroscientists, such as Benjamin Libet, even suppose that they can show by means of EEG and PET that the putative 'conscious' act of will or of decision, which they suppose to be a constituent of voluntary action, occurs *after* the initiation of the movement of which it was thought to be the cause, thus allegedly showing that freedom of the will is either an illusion or that it is limited to restraining the outcome of an 'unconscious' volitional process *initiated by the brain*. This, we shall argue in chapter 8, is a confusion stemming from misconceptions of voluntary action, and of what can be unconscious, as well as from subscription to the misguided Cartesian mythology of acts of will as causes of voluntary movement. Paradoxically, in thinking that they have found a refutation of the Cartesian conception, such scientists actually subscribe to the deepest errors which characterize that misconception, as we shall show.

fosters the idea that human behaviour is to be rendered intelligible in terms of causal interaction between the brain and the body, the brain being the subject of volitional psychological attributes.

2 The Project

The project is the clarification of the conceptual scheme of discourse concerning the faculties of mankind and other sentient animals

In the next five chapters we shall sketch out the conceptual framework for neuroscience. There is nothing new about it. It consists of the familiar array of concepts we have all acquired in the course of mastering the humdrum psychological vocabulary of sensation and perception, cognition and cogitation, imagination and emotion, volition and voluntary action, which we employ in our daily lives. It is new only *for* neuroscience. For we shall argue that the crypto-Cartesianism[4] of contemporary neuroscience is as conceptually incoherent as the Cartesianism from which it is inadvertently derived. It leads to incoherent descriptions of the results of neuroscientific research, and sometimes to the formation of incoherent research programmes. Abandoning the style of thought that is enmeshed in the mereological fallacy in neuroscience, and thereby ceasing to ascribe psychological attributes to the brain, as well as ceasing to misconstrue the concepts of perception and introspection, of mental images and of the will, of consciousness and self-consciousness, will not deprive neuroscientists of any of their hard-won and remarkable achievements. On the contrary, it will enable those achievements to be seen clearly, stripped of the conceptual confusions in which they are currently all too often wrapped. In this sense, it is our view that the conceptual framework we are offering neuroscientists – the ordinary conceptual framework properly elucidated – should be seen as liberating neuroscience from various forms of incoherence and from bogus mysteries which are generated by current conceptual confusions. Elucidating the conceptual scheme that determines the psychological concepts with which neuroscientists actually work, but which they inadvertently misuse, of course, in no way intimates any illegitimacy in neuroscientists' introducing new technical concepts for their purposes.

The relation between neuroscience and empirical psychology

Brain neuroscience aims, among other things, to discover the neural substratum in the brain that endows animals in general, and human beings in particular, with their characteristic powers and abilities. Study of the forms and limits of these powers and abilities belongs primarily to psychology. For one studies powers and abilities by studying their *exercise*; and the study of the exercise and exemplification of human powers and abilities is an investigation into human *behaviour* and *behavioural dispositions* in the varying circumstances of life. The study of behaviour, its circumstance dependence, individual differences and cultural variability, falls within the ambit of experimental psychology.

---

[4] And the Lockean empiricism with which it is crossed in the received account of introspection among neuroscientists.

Study of the neural conditions that endow animals with such powers, and the neural processes that occur when they are exercised, is the task of the neurosciences.[5]

Neuroscientific research, therefore, abuts on the psychological, and clarity regarding the achievements of brain research presupposes clarity regarding the categories of ordinary psychological description – that is, the categories of sensation and perception, cognition and recollection, cogitation and imagination, emotion and volition. To the extent that neuroscientists fail to grasp the contour lines of the relevant categories, they run the risk not only of asking the wrong questions, but also of misinterpreting their own experimental results. These categories of concepts, and the more specific concepts that they subsume, are the spectacles through which psychological phenomena are viewed and understood. If these spectacles are askew, then neuroscientists cannot but see the phenomena awry.

Entanglement in conceptual confusions   It is easy for us today to discern some of the conceptual confusions of the past. We can readily point out that it is conceptually confused to suppose that since the reflected image on the retina of the eye is inverted, we would therefore see the world upside down were the brain not to reinvert the image. It is not difficult to apprehend the fact that it is similarly confused to suppose (as Descartes did) that 'the images from the two eyes' must be reunited somewhere in the brain to form a single image 'so that they do not present to [the soul] two objects instead of one'.[6] It is far less easy to pin down our own conceptual confusions or, indeed, even to become aware of them.

But there is no reason to suppose, and every reason not to suppose, that we are less prone to become entangled in conceptual confusions than were our predecessors. Our confusions may be different from theirs. We know very much more about the functioning of the brain than they did, have far greater knowledge of various forms of brain malfunctioning than they did, and consequently the concepts we use to characterize the data upon which we work are, in many cases, novel, and, in other cases, involve extensions of previous concepts. And if the concepts differ, so too may the conceptual confusions. Furthermore, the fruitful analogies that we can call on in our explanations are often novel. So, in certain respects, our concepts and our explanatory analogies and models have become richer and ramified. But the greater the ramifications, the greater the dangers of conceptual entanglement. Our predecessors could not invoke computer analogies in their investigations of thought and reasoning, or in their study of neural networks. So they could not misuse whatever analogies there may be between human thought and machine computation, or between neural networks and computer hardware. Moreover, our conceptual confusions may be much the same as theirs, only in different guise. Few today are confused, as were the great thinkers of the seventeenth and eighteenth centuries, about *ideas* and *impressions* in the mind. Few of us think that the whole of human experience is a matter of receiving ideas, which can be decomposed into simple, unanalysable ones;

---

[5] Many neuroscientists embrace one form or another of reductionism, and are inclined to think that in the fullness of time, psychology will prove to be reducible to, and eliminable in favour of, neuroscience. We shall address the issue of reductionism in chapter 13.

[6] Descartes, *The Passions of the Soul*, I-32.

and few of us think that the range and limits of human thought are determined by the combinatorial possibilities of simple ideas given in experience. But our contemporary talk of 'mental representations' or of 'qualia' is, we shall argue, little more than the seventeenth- and eighteenth-century confusions recapitulated in modern jargon. Few of us think that the mind is an immaterial substance somehow connected with the brain, but many of us think that the mind is a material substance – indeed, that it is identical with the brain. And the latter claim is no less grievous a confusion than the former.

The purposes of the clarifications

It would be a mammoth task to depict the structure of our main psychological categories in detail. But we shall try to sketch in rough outline the salient conceptual forms. This will be useful for three reasons.

1. To remind us of what we know but overlook

First, it will serve to remind us of the psychological concepts with which we are all familiar, and which neuroscientists invoke in their investigations. It is important to keep them in sharp focus. For the clarity of the questions which neuroscientists try to answer is a function of their clarity concerning the concepts they employ in asking them and the precision with which they deploy them.

2. To keep us within the bounds of sense and to help us avoid their transgression

Secondly, clarity regarding these psychological categories will help to keep us on the safe tracks of what makes sense. The boundary between what does and what does not make sense, what is meaningful and what is actually nonsense – that is, *what transgresses the bounds of sense* – is determined by the concepts we employ. For our concepts fix the limits of what is *logically* possible (which must not be confused with what is *empirically* possible). They do not determine what is actually *true* (that is discovered by experience and experiment), but only what it *makes sense* to say or think. Misuse of our concepts involves transgressing the bounds of sense. Conforming to the correct employment of the relevant concepts, as we have already explained (§3.2), is not a constraint on thought. It does not prevent us from contemplating genuine possibilities, it prevents us from talking nonsense. It excludes logical impossibilities. But a logical impossibility, as we have emphasized, is not a possibility that is impossible – it is a form of words which makes no sense, which says nothing at all, even though it may seem to say something. So cleaving to the correct use of our concepts does not fence us in from paths we might wish to tread – it fences us in only from the void of nonsense.

3. To demonstrate how numerous neuroscientific theories transgress the bounds of sense

Thirdly, our sketches serve as a backcloth against which to illustrate some confusions to which some neuroscientists succumb when they are unclear about the concepts they deploy. We have selected a variety of remarks made and doctrines propounded by leading neuroscientists which we demonstrate to be conceptually awry. These examples make vivid the fact that conceptual hygiene, as it were, is no less important for neuroscientific research than the immense care that goes into the experimental work that these very same neuroscientists do with such remarkable success. For it is crucial to the correct interpretation of that experimental work. We hope that our sketches will alert neuroscientists to the conceptual complexity and diversity of the psychological attributes the neural concomitants of which they investigate. This may help them avoid the conceptual confusions we pinpoint and so give a correct description of the results and implications of their experiments.

All the psychological categories and concepts we shall examine signify attributes of human beings (and, in many cases, of other animals too). The logical grounds for their ascription to a subject, as we have seen (§3.3), are the behaviour of the subject, of *the human being*, not of *his brain*. For *nothing* a brain can do could possibly constitute a ground for ascribing thought, perception, imagination or volition *to the brain*. Rather, we can *correlate* neural events and processes with the human being's thinking or perceiving, imagining or intending, and discover (if we can) what neural states, events and processes are *causally necessary* conditions for the human being to think or perceive, imagine or intend.

Our sketches are intended to be uncontroversial. They are meant to outline distinctions which are familiar and in constant use. But though we are all self-conscious creatures, one thing about which we are rarely self-conscious is our own conceptual apparatus. And some of the distinctions we shall point out, although they are, in our view, patent in the ordinary employment of the concepts involved, are also commonly overlooked in current neuroscientific thought.

3 The Category of the Psychological

On the unhelpfulness of the dichotomy of mental and physical

It is tempting to try to demarcate the domain of ordinary psychological concepts by invoking the contrast between the mental and the physical and identifying the psychological with the mental, on the assumption that the mental and the physical constitute two exhaustive, exclusive domains. But this is mistaken, and the dichotomy is unhelpful. There are many things that are neither physical nor mental. The laws of the land, the laws of physics and of logic, numbers and theorems, statements and rumours, are neither physical nor mental entities. Equally, many things that interest us about ourselves cannot be segregated exclusively into the category of the mental or into that of the physical. We do not conceive of groaning in pain, laughing with joy, taking pleasure in playing tennis, reading attentively, speaking deliberately or writing hastily as something 'mental' and not *also* 'physical'. It is a confusion to suppose, as the behaviourists did, that behaviour is 'bare bodily movement', describable in exclusively physical terms. We characterize behaviour as attentive, deliberate, intentional, thoughtful, careful or reckless, and these descriptions do not mean that bare bodily movements are accompanied by mental events. We describe smiles as kind or amused, ironic or polite, loving or cruel, embarrassed or smirking, and we could not even describe the physical differences between these smiles,[7] which we recognize immediately as *expressions* of kindness, amusement, irony or politeness, etc. And, to be sure, we do not mean that such smiles are *accompanied* by an inner feeling, any more than a kind, amused, ironic or polite remark is a remark accompanied by an inner feeling.

---

[7] Indeed, there often is none, since the differences lie in the context.

So, the classification of human attributes, in particular human powers and dispositions, as either 'physical' or 'mental' is too restrictive. The disposition to put on weight might be deemed a 'physical' disposition (a liability or susceptibility), since when a person puts on weight, his body weighs more. But to have good eyesight or hearing is to be able to exercise the powers of sight and hearing optimally, and this cannot be characterized as a physical capacity, nor yet as a mental one. Irascibility, timidity, recklessness, etc. are dispositions *to behave* – but they are attributes of the person, not of his mind or of his body. They are dispositions of character and temperament – dispositions of a human being. To be irascible is to have a tendency to lose one's temper with little provocation; to be of a sanguine disposition is to be prone to take certain attitudes towards eventualities of life; to be benevolent is to be disposed to manifest goodwill towards others. None of these fit readily into the straitjacket of being either 'physical' or 'mental'. But they can be characterized as 'psychological', inasmuch as they are powers, tendencies and dispositions of sentient beings who have a *psuchē* – in the case of human beings, a rational *psuchē* – that is, powers of intellect and will. The category of the mental, unclear as it is, might profitably be used to demarcate a subcategory of the psychological that concerns certain features of the distinctive powers of the intellect and the will of a living being.

Nagel's misconceptions about the mind and concepts of the mental   Thomas Nagel argues 'that the concept of a mind, or of a mental event or process, fails to plainly leave space for the possibility that what it designates should turn out also to be a physical thing or event or process, as the result of closer scientific investigation – in the way that the concept of blood leaves space for discoveries about its composition. The trouble is that mental concepts don't obviously pick out things or processes that take up room in the spatio-temporal world.' From this he wrongly concludes that 'We do not at present possess the conceptual equipment to understand how subjective and physical features could both be essential aspects of a single entity or process'. [8] But, as we have argued (§3.10), 'the mind' does not designate a *thing* of any kind. A creature that can be said to have a mind does indeed possess a distinctive range of active and passive powers (capacities, abilities, liabilities, susceptibilities, dispositions, tendencies, pronenesses). Powers, to be sure, do not take up space, no matter whether they are such powers as elasticity or fragility (i.e. powers of mere physical things) or such powers as cognition, cogitation, ratiocination, imagination, perception and sensation. These latter are powers of *animate* beings who are *also* physical things. The concepts of such powers, of course, do not leave room for the scientific discovery that the designated powers have a physical composition, any more than the concepts of fragility or elasticity leave such room – for powers are not tangible, space-occupying entities, but *attributes of* space-occupying entities. Powers are not *made* of stuff, as material objects are. (The intoxicative power of whisky is not made of, but is only due to, C_2H_5OH, and the horsepower of a car is not made of cylinders or of steel.) What the concept of a power leaves room for are scientific discoveries concerning the *physical basis* for possession of such powers, no matter whether the powers are simply 'physical' or the distinctive powers of human beings. And, as we shall

---

[8] T. Nagel, 'Conceiving the impossible and the mind–body problem', *Philosophy*, 73 (1998), pp. 339, 342.

argue, we have all the conceptual equipment we need to understand how both 'subjective and physical features' could be 'essential aspects' of a single entity – that is, of a living creature. It is only conceptual confusion that generates the illusion that our concepts are inadequate to the task of explaining how animate beings have the kinds of capacities that characterize them.

The ordinary category of the psychological is vaguely bounded; its concepts are not theoretical

We cannot elucidate the category of the psychological by recourse to the category of the mental or by simply contrasting it with the physical. Nevertheless, there is a rough-and-ready consensus on what count as central cases of characteristics that can uncontroversially be deemed to be psychological. This large range of attributes can be ascribed to human beings, and many of them can also be ascribed to the higher animals – although not all of them, and some of them apply to non-human animals only in an attenuated sense. Although they are used in psychological theory, they are not theoretical concepts, but common or garden ones – no more theoretical than our humdrum concepts of chair and table, book and newspaper, pen and paper.[9] Like all concepts, theoretical and atheoretical alike, they are embedded in a rich web of logical connections of mutual implications, compatibilities and incompatibilities.

Difficulties in surveying psychological concepts

The web of psychological concepts is singularly difficult to survey. For the network is dense, the connections of each psychological expression with others are multiple, and many terms have multiple uses, sometimes appearing in one guise and sometimes in another. So, for example, 'feeling' may sometimes signify a sensation (feeling a pain), sometimes an emotion (feeling angry); it may signify an inclination to act (feeling like going to the cinema), but it may signify a form of perception (feeling a penny in one's pocket); sometimes it is used to signify a form of thought or opinion (feeling that justice must be seen to be done) or to signify an inclination to believe (feeling that the accused is innocent); and sometimes to indicate an overall physical or psychological condition (feeling ill or contented). Similarly, 'thinking' may sometimes be used to indicate belief (thinking that the next train is at 2.30), sometimes an opinion (thinking that justice is more important than liberty); in some uses it signifies something one does or is engaged in (as when one spends an hour thinking about the current state of the nation) which may involve *reasoning* from certain premises to a conclusion supported by them – and this too is thinking; in yet other uses 'thinking' signifies an occurrence (thinking of something, a thought's crossing one's mind), and in others it signifies something meant (as when, in saying that Henry was a great king, one was thinking of Henry II of England). This multiplicity and these kinds of ramifying conceptual connections make generalization perilous. Each concept and each conceptual category has to be scrutinized in its own right, and its manifold connections with adjacent concepts have to be traced out. The delineation of the main conceptual categories that are relevant to our project is the task of the following chapters.

---

[9] This is denied by Paul and Patricia Churchland, who contend that our ordinary psychological vocabulary is part of something they call 'a folk-psychological theory'. For an analysis of the misconceptions involved in this claim, see §§13.2–13.2.4.

4

Sensation and Perception

4.1 Sensation

Bodily feelings distinguished into sensations and feelings of overall bodily condition

Among the manifold powers and abilities that human beings possess we can distinguish the passive power (susceptibility or liability) to have bodily feelings from the perceptual powers of the five senses. Bodily feelings can be roughly distinguished into *sensations*, which are localized feelings such as pains, tingles, tickles or itches, and feelings of overall *bodily condition*, such as feeling well or ill, awake or sleepy, seasick or nauseous, fit or weak. (The latter merge with feelings of overall *psychological condition*, such as feeling tranquil, contented, dissatisfied, bored or interested.) We shall concentrate on sensations (construed narrowly to encompass only localized feelings) rather than on feelings of overall bodily condition, even though the latter are also sometimes misleadingly referred to as 'sensations' (as when we speak of a sensation of well-being). Conceptual unclarities regarding sensations (narrowly construed) are responsible for many confusions among theorists of perception. So clarification of the concept is necessary prior to an examination of perception.

Sensations distinguished from objects of perception; having sensations and feeling sensations

To have or feel a sensation, such as a pain, tingle or itch, is not to perceive anything. Sensations are not perceptible objects of any kind, for objects perceived exist whether perceived or not. By contrast, as is often remarked, sensations cannot 'exist' unfelt. There is nothing odd about this, and to conceive of it as constituting a special 'ontological mode' is to make a metaphysical mystery out of a grammatical molehill.[1] Rather, it is just an obscure way of saying that for a person to have a sensation *is* for that person to feel a sensation, that there is no difference between *having* a sensation and *feeling* a sensation.[2] So, 'feeling' here does not signify a form of

---

[1] See J. R. Searle, *The Rediscovery of the Mind* (MIT Press, Cambridge, MA., 1992), ch. 1.
[2] For a curious anomaly, however, see Norman Malcolm's discussion of distraction of attention from a pain, in D. M. Armstrong and N. Malcolm, *Consciousness and Causality* (Blackwell, Oxford, 1984), pp. 15f. This can be viewed as a singularity (in the mathematical sense) in the grammar of sensation (see below ch. 9, n. 32).

perception, as it does in the sentence 'I felt a penny in my pocket' or 'I felt the cold wind on my cheek'. The penny and the wind exist whether one feels them or not, but the pain in one's tooth and the itch in one's foot can be said to 'exist' only in so far as one feels or has them. The opaque and unfamiliar sentence 'a sensation exists' or 'there is a sensation' means no more than 'someone has a sensation'. Aches, cramps, tickles, itches and tingles are various kinds of sensation. One has a headache only if one's head aches; one has an itch only if some part of one's body itches. So it is no surprise that there is a toothache only if someone's tooth aches; nor is there anything remarkable about there being no such thing as one's tooth aching and one not feeling anything. For if one feels nothing, then one's tooth does not ache. Similarly, one has an itch in one's foot only if one's foot itches; if one feels nothing, then one's foot is not itching and one does not have an itch in one's foot. A sensation, unlike an object perceived, is as it is felt to be. And this too is altogether unmysterious. It is no more than an obscure way of emphasizing the fact that we assign no sense to such forms of words as 'A felt his toothache getting worse, although it wasn't', 'His toothache seemed to hurt more, although in fact it didn't', or 'The pressure on A's foot hurt more, but it didn't hurt *him* more'. And it is evident why we assign no meaning to such sentences.

Sensations and their bodily location

Sensations have a bodily location: it always makes sense to ask 'Where does it hurt (itch, tickle, etc.)?' and the answer specifies some part of the body. Sensations are felt *in* (one's arm or leg, head or toe), but not felt *with* (an organ of perception). It is a confusion to suppose, as John Searle does, that 'the pain-in-the-foot is literally in the physical space of the brain', that 'the brain forms a body image, and pains, like all bodily sensations, are parts of the body image'.[3] Pressure on the brain causes sensations, but these are known as 'headaches'; one does not have a pain in the foot, a toothache or stomach-ache in the brain or 'in the physical space of the brain'. Further, a headache, although it is a pain in the head, is not in the head as the brain is in the head (opening up the head will reveal a brain, but not a pain; one can take a brain, but not a pain, out of a skull). The sentences 'He has a pain and a brain in his head' and 'I have an eyelash and an itch in my eye' are sylleptic (compare: 'I have a penny and a hole in my pocket' – both are located in the pocket, but one can be taken out, whereas the other can only be sewn up). That is why 'What have you got in your mouth?' – 'Thirty-two teeth and a toothache' is a joke. The logical grammar of 'pain in the head' (location of a sensation) is unlike that of 'penny in the box' (location of a material object) and unlike that of 'party in the garden' (location of an event). Of course, one would feel no sensations were the brain not functioning appropriately, but that does not mean that they are felt either in or by the brain.

The subject of pain is the person (or animal) that manifests it, not his mind or brain

The subject (or 'bearer') of pain (i.e. the entity that *has* a pain) is the *person* who manifests *being in pain* in his grimaces, groans or screams, not his mind or his brain.

The subject of itches or tickles is the person who mani-fests having an itch or a tickle in scratching or rubbing the part of his body that itches or

---

[3] Searle, *Rediscovery of the Mind*, p. 63.

tickles (his foot may itch or tickle, but the foot does not *have* an itch or tickle). If a person's tooth aches, it is he who suffers (not his tooth); if his leg hurts, it is the person who is in pain (not his leg). We can see the pain in his face, for although the pain may be in his leg, it is the person who expresses pain in his grimaces, demeanour and groans. We tend the leg, but we console the person.

The criterion of pain location is the behaviour of the subject of pain; logical differences between 'pain in the knee' and 'penny in the box'

The location of pain is given by *the behaviour of the subject of pain*. His pain is located wherever he sincerely says it is. If, when asked where it hurts, he points to his knee and assuages or nurses it, then his knee hurts – not his brain. And if his knee hurts, then he has a pain in his knee. But, of course, to have a pain *in* one's knee is not, in respect of the spatial locative 'in', at all like having a penny *in* a box.[4] The latter use of the locative spatial preposition allows substitution of 'inside' ('the penny is inside the box'). But to have a pain in one's knee does not mean that one has a pain *inside* one's knee – the box *contains* the penny, but the painful knee does not *contain* the pain. If the penny is in the box, it must be smaller than the box, but pains are neither smaller nor larger than, nor yet the same size as, the part of the body that hurts. The penny that is inside the box can also be taken out of it, but the pain in the knee cannot intelligibly be taken out of it – only stopped. If the box is taken to London, then the penny is in London; but if the person goes to London, it does not follow that the pain is in London – it is the person whose knee hurts that is in London, but the pain has not moved. Again, the reason is clear: 'There is a penny in the box' specifies a spatial relation between two independent objects. But the objectual form of 'There is a pain in my knee' is misleading, for it does not specify a relation between two independent objects, a pain and a knee, any more than 'I have a pain' specifies a relation (of ownership) between me and a pain.[5]

Referred pains and phantom pains

So-called referred pains (e.g. sciatica, referred toothache) are not pains which the subject *mistakenly* thinks are where he points and assuages, but rather pains that are felt in places other than the locus

---

[4] There are many different locative uses of 'in' that are non-spatial: e.g. 'It happened in the story', 'We shall meet in September', 'I saw her in my dreams'. There are also many *different* locative uses of 'in' that *are* spatial: e.g. 'penny in the box', 'stain in the shirt', 'flashing lights in (the top left of) my visual field', and 'pain in my leg'. The kinds of substitutions, implications, compatibilities and incompatibilities vary from case to case, even though these uses are all locative (spatial) ones; so, the logical grammar of 'in the leg' varies according to whether what is said to be in the leg is a pain or a pin. Similarly, the logical grammar of 'in my jacket' varies according to whether what is said to be in the jacket is a coin or a crease – for here too there are logical differences in the grammar of the spatial location of the entities in question. The coin may fall out, but the crease can only be ironed out; if the jacket is taken to Paris, then the coin in the jacket will be in Paris too, but the crease in the jacket cannot be said to be in Paris (any more than if there is a hole in the jacket and the jacket is in Paris, it follows that there is a hole in Paris).

[5] In this respect (but not others), 'I have a pain in my knee' is grammatically akin to 'I have a crease in my shirt'. However, whereas 'I have a crease in my shirt' does not imply that I am creased (let alone that I am 'in crease'), 'I have a pain in my knee' does imply that I am in pain. Similarly, if you hurt my leg, you hurt me, but if you crease my shirt, you don't crease me.

of the injury, infection, etc. So-called phantom pains are not pains which *seem* to be in one's amputated limb – if one's limb is in the disposal bin, it is not there that one points when asked where it hurts. Rather, they are pains felt outside the body (in the 'phantom limb'), *where the limb still seems to be* (it feels to the patient just as if the limb is still there). So *the location of the cause of a pain* must be distinguished from *the location of the pain itself*. It is not the character of the pain that enables one to say where it hurts; that is, one's ability to say where it hurts is not dependent on the felt character or phenomenal features of the pain. If I say that I have a pain in my foot (that my foot hurts), that is not because I felt a foot-indicative sensation of pain that informed me, as it were, of the location of the pain. Our normal ability to locate our pains is non-evidential.

Sensations have degrees of intensity, but not of clarity; they have phenomenal qualities, and are linked to inclinations to behave

Sensations have degrees of intensity – they may be excruciatingly painful, or a mere twinge or tickle. One's scalp may be intolerably itchy, or merely mildly irritating. Sensations may wax or wane, becoming more or less intense. Unlike perceptions, they do not have degrees of clarity – one does not have a pain clearly and distinctly as one may hear a cry clearly and distinctly. Sensations have phenomenal qualities, such as burning, stinging, gnawing, piercing, dull or throbbing (pains). They may be caused internally or externally. They are typically linked with felt inclinations to behave – for example, to scratch (an itch), to assuage (a pain), to laugh (when tickled). Sensations may be momentary, as is a twinge, or prolonged, like the pains of childbirth; but they do not persist through periods of loss of consciousness – one does not *feel* pain when one is unconscious. The time of the commencement of a sensation is when the subject feels a sensation, and the criterion for his feeling the sensation is his behaviour and what he says. Hence it is misguided to suppose, as Libet does, that the subject might 'refer the sensation' to an earlier time than that at which it actually occurs.[6]

Sensations belong to the category of the hedonic

Sensations belong to the category of the hedonic: that is, they may be pleasant or unpleasant. Unsurprisingly, we have a richer vocabulary for pains and unpleasant sensations than for pleasant ones. They disturb our well-being and optimal functioning, and their characterization is significant for diagnostic purposes.

Sensations also belong to the category of passivity. Having or feeling a sensation is an undergoing, whether suffered or enjoyed. One can, of course, bring it about that one feels

---

[6] Libet's 'time-on' theory holds: '(1) After a delayed achievement of neural adequacy for awareness, there is an automatic subjective referral of the experience backwards in time, to approximately the delivery time of the stimulus. (2) The initial cortical response (primary evoked potential at S1 cortex), to the fast specific (lemniscal) projection sensory message, serves as the timing signal for this backward referral. The experience would thus be subjectively antedated and would appear to the subject to occur without the substantial neural delay required for its production' (B. Libet, 'Conscious subjective experience vs. unconscious mental functions: a theory of the cerebral processes involved', repr. in his *Neurophysiology of Consciousness* (Birkhäuser, Boston, 1993), p. 328). This is misconceived, since the sensation does not *appear* to the subject to occur before it actually occurs. It occurs when the subject feels it.

Sensations belong to the category of passivity (of undergoings)

a certain sensation, but there are no voluntary sensations, only voluntarily inflicted or produced ones. While people may be more or less skilful at perceiving certain things, they cannot be more or less skilful at feeling sensations, only more or less susceptible to having them. To be more sensitive in this respect is not to be *better* at feeling pains or tickles. Hence there is no such thing as learning to have sharper or more accurate sensations. Indeed, although there are sharp sensations, they are not more discerning ones, and there are no accurate or inaccurate, correct or incorrect, sensations. But one may learn to describe one's sensations better, and enrich one's descriptive vocabulary.

There are tactile illusions, but no illusions of sensation

One must take care not to confuse tactile illusions, which do occur, with supposed illusions of sensation, which do not exist. There are tactile illusions, such as the 'cutaneous rabbit' illusion.[7] Here one has the illusion that one is being touched at equal distances all the way up one's arm, while in fact one is touched, for example, five times at the wrist, twice near the elbow and thrice near the shoulder. But it is not an illusion that one feels a sequence of sensations equally distributed along the length of the arm. It seems to one as if one is being touched at ten different locations. But it does not *seem* to one as if one has ten sequential sensations distributed along the length of one's arm – one really does have such sensations. Similarly, a person who has had his leg amputated and has a phantom pain does not *seem* to have a pain in his foot, for there is no such thing as *seeming to have a pain*. Nor, as we have seen, can one say that he has a pain which *seems to be in his foot* either. A pain is where (and, *pace* Libet, when) the sufferer sincerely indicates it to be. So he actually has a pain where his foot would have been (i.e. in his 'phantom limb').

4.2 Perception

What a perceptual organ is

Of the five senses, four – namely, sight, hearing, taste and smell – involve the use of specific sense-organs. One sees *with* one's eyes, not with one's brain, just as one hears with one's ears, tastes with one's tongue and palate, and smells with one's nose. The expression 'with one's . . .' here indicates the organ that is used in exercising the faculty in question. The sense in which it is used is clarified by drawing attention to the fact that one brings one's eye, not some other part of the body, to, a keyhole in order to see through it; that in order to hear better, one puts a hand behind one's ear and cocks it or brings one's ear closer to the source of the sound; that in order to smell, one sniffs, and brings one's nose closer to the odorous object to smell it better; and in order to taste, one licks the object or bites off a piece of it and chews it in one's mouth. Tactile perception, however, has no special organ. Perceiving something by feeling may involve almost any part of the body, or indeed the body as a whole. One may feel the shape or size of a thing with one's hands, its thickness

---

[7] F. A. Geldard and C. E. Sherrick, 'The cutaneous "rabbit": a perceptual illusion', *Science*, 178 (1972), pp. 178f.

or sharpness with one's fingers, the solidity of the door with one's shoulder, the warmth of a bath towel with one's cheek. One may feel the slipperiness of the ground by walking across it, the viscosity of a liquid by stirring it, the elasticity of an object by pulling it, its movability or immovability by pushing it, and the weight of an object by lifting or carrying it. The brain, however, is not an organ of perception, even though, of course, one cannot see, hear, taste, smell or feel anything unless one's brain is functioning appropriately.

The senses are cognitive faculties The perceptual powers are cognitive faculties, in the sense that by their exercise we can acquire knowledge of objects and their qualities, of events and their characteristics, and of states of affairs that obtain in our environment. Because the senses are cognitive faculties, they are bound up with the endeavour to attain knowledge. And since they are not infallible cognitive faculties, they are conceptually linked with success and failure. One can try to perceive and attempt to discern better. One may decide to look, smell or taste, and do so carefully or carelessly. There may be success, failure and error, unlike in the case of sensation – that is, one may perceive, fail to perceive, or misperceive. The successful upshot of perceptual activities such as looking, feeling for, sniffing or scenting, tasting or sampling, and listening is seeing, feeling, smelling, tasting, or hearing – more generally, recognizing, discerning, detecting or distinguishing perceptibilia. These verbs, like 'perceives that', are sometimes (a little misleadingly) called 'achievement verbs' or 'success verbs', signalling the successful upshot of perception. More soberly, they are 'factive verbs', inasmuch as if one perceives (e.g. sees or hears, recognizes or detects) *that* things are so, then things are in fact as one perceives them to be. If one finds out that things are not as one says one perceives them to be, then one must withdraw one's claim to have perceived that things are thus, and fall back upon the qualified utterances 'It seemed to me just as if . . .', 'I thought . . .' or 'It visually appeared to me . . .', and so forth. Of course, verbs of perception need not take a noun-clause 'that such-and-such' as their grammatical object. They may take names of perceptibilia or of perceptual qualities as their objects. These may be of many categorially different kinds of things and 'non-things' (like holes or gaps).

Unlike the powers of sensation, perceptual abilities can be trained; perception is (loosely) linked to the hedonic Unlike having sensations, one can be more or less skilful at perceiving, one can to some extent be trained in the exercise of one's perceptual capacities and acquire a trained eye or ear and a discriminating palate. Just as the liability to sensation is linked to possible pleasure and pain, the powers of perception are linked to possible pleasure and displeasure. We often take pleasure in seeing, hearing, feeling, smelling or tasting things, and are sometimes disgusted, horrified, or revolted by what we perceive. One distinction between perceptual knowledge acquisition and other forms of acquisition of information is precisely that perceiving can be pleasant or unpleasant.

Perception and voluntariness There is a sense in which the exercise of the sense-faculties is not voluntary. One cannot choose to hear a loud noise in one's vicinity or to see a salient object in one's visual field, to feel the heat in a hot room or to taste the sweetness of the liqueur one has just sipped. One can only block one's ears, close one's eyes, leave the room to escape the heat, and refuse another sip. In another sense, the perceptual faculties can be exercised at will. The sense of sight is bound up with looking for, looking at, watching, scanning, surveying, observing and inspecting, all of which may be voluntary activities. So, too, the sense of hearing is bound up with voluntarily listening *for* a sound or *to* a sequence of sounds. One does not voluntarily feel the heat of the day, but one may voluntarily feel for something in one's pocket, and voluntarily stretch out one's hand to feel the thermal quality or texture of a thing within one's reach.

The criteria for perception lie in behaviour; the brain is neither a perceptual organ nor a subject of perception

Possession of a sense-faculty is manifest in behaviour. The sighted are identified by their exercise of the ability to discriminate visible objects and qualities, by their (illumination-dependent) competence in finding their way around without bumping into or falling over things, by their searching for and finding things by looking, by their following things with their eyes and orienting their head and body appropriately, and by their responses to visual stimuli such as lights, glimmers and flashes. In general, the forms of behaviour that manifest possession of a given perceptual faculty consist in relative efficiency in discrimination, recognition, discernment, pursuit of goals and exploration of the environment, and, in the case of human beings, in corresponding utterances. These kinds of behaviour in response to visibilia, for example, are logical criteria for a creature's seeing things. Neural events in the brain are not – they are inductive correlations with seeing, which presuppose the non-inductive identification of seeing by reference to criterial behaviour. One does not see anything in one's brain or look for something in the bookcase with one's brain. Nor does one see the colour of flowers with or in one's brain, but with one's eyes as one looks at the garden. The brain is neither *an organ of perception* nor *a subject of perception*. The neural events in the brain are not forms of perceiving behaviour, and nothing the brain can do could count as a criterion of its perceiving something in its vicinity. It is the animal that perceives and manifests its perceiving in its behavioural responses to its environment.

Crick errs in ascribing perception to the brain or to one of its hemispheres

Consequently, to speak, as neuroscientists are prone to do, of the right hemisphere of the brain seeing things is at best a misleading *façon de parler*. It is similarly misguided to suggest, as Francis Crick does, that:

> In perception, what the brain learns is usually about the outside world or about other parts of the body. This is why what we see appears to be located outside us, although the neurons that do the seeing are inside the head. To many people this is a strange idea. The 'world' is outside their body yet, in another sense (what they know of it), it is entirely within their head. . . . Of course, if we open up the skull and pick up the signals sent out by a particular neuron, *we* can often tell where that neuron is located, but the brain we are studying does not have this information. This explains why we do not normally know exactly where our perceptions and thoughts are taking place in our heads.[8]

This is at best misleading, since in perception the brain learns nothing – it is the person whose brain it is that perceives and learns something in perceiving. What we see does not

---

[8] F. Crick, *The Astonishing Hypothesis* (Touchstone, London, 1995), pp. 104f.

appear to be located outside us. What we see is *necessarily* located outside our body – unless we are looking at ourselves in a mirror, or at our limbs or thorax (which are neither inside nor outside our body, but part of it). The neurons without which we would not see anything are located in our heads, but, of course, it is not those neurons that see or that 'do' the seeing, any more than the cylinders of a car do 70 mph. There is no sense in which 'the world' is inside anyone's head, and it is a mistake to suggest that what we know of the world is inside our heads. We know that the earth is spherical, but what we know – namely, *that the Earth is spherical* – is not in our heads (or anywhere else). And finally, it is misleading to say that we do not know where in our heads our perceptions take place, since our perceptions do not take place in our heads at all. Neuroscientists apart, we do not know which array of cells is *causally responsible* for our being able to perceive whatever we perceive. Our perception – our perceiving whatever it is we perceive – does not take place in our heads, but takes place wherever we are when we perceive what we perceive. Perceiving is an epistemic relation between a perceiver and an object perceived, and since the objects we perceive are not in our heads but in our environment, the supposition that perceiving takes place in one's head makes no more sense than the supposition that Jack's running faster than Jill takes place in Jack. The questions 'Where did you last hear Beethoven's Ninth?' or 'Where did you see Jack?' can be answered by 'In the Sheldonian theatre' (if one saw Jack at the concert), but not by 'Four inches behind my left eye'.

4.2.1 Perception as the causation of sensations: primary and secondary qualities

It is misconceived to think that all perception involves having sensations

It is important not to conflate perception with sensation. A long tradition in philosophy, as well as in psychology and neuroscience, assumed that perceiving something characteristically involves having sensations. The roots of this conception lie in the seventeenth- and eighteenth-century conception of perception as the causation of ideas or impressions in the mind resultant upon the impact of stimuli on our nerve endings and the consequent excitation of the animal spirits in the nerves. Damage to nerve endings by cutting, burning, etc. causes ideas of pain; the impact of light on the retina or of sound waves on the eardrum causes ideas of colour or of sound. Ideas of pain and ideas of colour and sound were held to stand on the same level – they are all produced by the action of things upon our nerve endings. In so far as neuroscientists today conceive of perception as a matter of the reception of sensations, they are conforming to a venerable (although confused) tradition. We shall revert to this issue after we have clarified the source of the confusion.

Galileo's conception of primary and secondary qualities

A complement to the conception of perceiving as the reception of ideas or impressions was the thought, originating with Galileo and further developed by Descartes, Boyle and Locke, that just as the sensation of pain is a subjective modification of the mind caused by an object's deleterious impact upon our nerve endings and is not the apprehension of a quality of pain in the object, so too the 'sensations' of colour, sound, smell, taste, warmth and cold are merely subjective modifications of the mind, and not the apprehension of objective qualities of perceptibilia. Objects as they are, independently of our perception of them, were thought to have only primary qualities of extension, shape, size, solidity, motion or rest. The secondary qualities of colour, sound, smell, taste and thermal (as well as further tactile) qualities, as they are objectively, are merely powers of objects to cause ideas of colour, sound, etc. *in us*. As we experience them, they are no more than ideas or sensations in our minds. According to this conception, the world as we perceive it is dramatically different from the world as it is in itself. Perceiving an object was conceived of as having an array of partly unrepresentative ideas of the object caused in one's mind as a consequence of the activities of the brain. What we apprehend in perception is not the object itself, but rather the ideas it causes in us. Ideas of primary qualities represent objective qualities of the objects we perceive, but ideas of secondary qualities do not. This conception became embedded in the foundations of the scientific conception of reality and the psychological and neuroscientific conception of perception.

Neuroscientists still cleave to this seventeenth-century doctrine

It is still as firmly entrenched as ever. Kandel, Schwartz and Jessell introduce their discussion of 'The sensory systems' thus:

> We *receive* electromagnetic waves of different frequencies but we *perceive* colors: red, green, orange, blue or yellow. We receive pressure waves but we hear words and music. We come in contact with a myriad of chemical compounds dissolved in air or water but we experience smells and tastes.
>
> Colors, sounds, smells and tastes are mental constructions created in the brain by sensory processing. They do not exist, as such, outside of the brain. Therefore, we can ask the traditional question raised by philosophers: Does a falling tree in the forest make a sound if no one is near enough to hear it? We can say with certainty that while the fall creates pressure waves in the air, it does not create a sound. Sound occurs only when pressure waves from the falling tree reach and are perceived by a living being.
>
> Thus, our perceptions are not direct records of the world around us but are constructed internally according to innate rules and constraints imposed by the capabilities of the nervous system.[9]

This misconception contributes to a systematic distortion of empirical investigations into the neural mechanisms of perception. So, although this is not the place for a detailed examination of the doctrine, some remarks are in order.

The claim that colours, sounds, etc. are essentially subjective is not a physical hypothesis or theory, but a metaphysical one

First, it is important to emphasize that this is not an empirical claim or a scientific hypothesis, let alone a scientific theory that can be or has been confirmed experimentally. It is a *philosophical* or *conceptual* claim, which can be confirmed or disconfirmed only by conceptual investigations

---

[9] Eric R. Kandel, James H. Schwartz and Thomas M. Jessell, *Essentials of Neural Science and Behaviour* (Appleton and Lange, Stamford, CT, 1995), p. 370. Psychologists of perception tend to concur: e.g. I. Rock, 'Colors, tones, tastes and smells are mental constructions, created out of sensory stimulations. As such they do not exist outside of living minds' (*Perception* (Scientific American Books, New York, 1984), p. 4).

and a priori arguments. No scientific experiment could possibly prove that grass, as it is in itself, is not really green, but only appears to us to be so, that sugar is not really sweet, but only seems so, or that ice is not really cold, but merely strikes us thus, etc. All scientific experiment can do is to explain the processes by which we are able to perceive colours, sounds and thermal qualities, and investigate whether other species of animals have the same perceptual, discriminatory powers. It cannot demonstrate that things that we apprehend to be coloured are actually lacking in colour, or that things we apprehend as making sounds do not really do so. What it can demonstrate is that the former objects reflect light of certain wavelengths that affects our eyes and brains in such-and-such ways, as a result of which we see what we call 'their colour'. And it can demonstrate that the latter objects cause sound waves that affect our ears and brain in certain ways which exercise our auditory faculty. Of course, no sound is *heard* unless sound waves reach the ears of a hearer – but it does not follow that there was no sound *to be heard*, that trees fall silently to the earth in the absence of hearers. Scientific discovery in no way demonstrates that grass is not really green or that cellos do not have a rich and mellow sound. It does not establish that there are no colours in the absence of observers or sounds independently of listeners. To establish whether *that* thesis is correct or incorrect turns on a careful conceptual analysis of the *meaning* of secondary quality predicates – that is, how these expressions are taught, learned, and explained, how they are applied, and what follows logically from their application. Whether being coloured is an objective, non-relational property of objects is a matter of meaning. What kinds of things *can* be coloured – that is, what are *intelligible* subjects of colour predicates – is an a priori logico-grammatical question. It needs no science to tell us that it is senseless to ascribe colours to numbers as opposed to numerals, or that what is coloured must be extended. Which of the things that *can* be coloured *are* actually coloured is a contingent matter of fact, to be discovered in experience, not by science but by sight.

The metaphysical doctrine concerning secondary qualities is far more extraordinary and has far more dramatic implications than is commonly realized

Second, it is important not to lose sight of the extraordinary nature of this ancient conception. If it is right, then we are subject to perpetual illusion. The world as it is independently of our perception of it is *profoundly* different from the world as we perceive it to be. If colours, sounds, smells and tastes are 'mental constructions created in the brain by sensory processing', and if they 'do not exist, as such, outside of the brain', then, to be sure, what we perceive when we perceive the golden sunset, blue sea and silvery waves is no more than a mental construct created in the brain, and what we enjoy when we dine is not the taste of the food we eat, but a mental construct in the brain. The world as we experience it is largely a figment of our imagination (or 'fantasia', see §6.3) – that is, of our image-making faculty. Nature, as it really is, independently of our perception of it, 'is a dull affair, soundless, scentless, colourless; merely the hurrying of material'.[10] This is a *metaphysical*, not a physical, conception of reality.

---

[10] A. N. Whitehead, *Science and the Modern World*, Lowell Lectures 1925 (Mentor Books, New York, 1948), p. 56.

The doctrine concerning the subjectivity of secondary qualities is not one which we can or do in practice believe

Third, according to this metaphysical picture, we live in a world of illusion – but none of us, neuroscientists included, *can possibly believe this*. With normal illusions, such as the Müller–Lyer lines or the Ponzo illusion, once they are exposed as illusions, we realize that appearances deceive, and we cease to believe that things are as they appear to be. But not even neuroscientists really believe that their roses are not red, their lawns not green, that the winter snow is not white and coal is not black. Their behaviour satisfies the criteria for believing, not for disbelieving, that objects around them are coloured, noisy, odorous, tasty, warm or cold. They attribute colour to things like anyone else, choose things because of their colour and reject other things because they are the wrong colour. Nor do neuroscientists really think that all the beliefs of human beings concerning the colours of things in their environment are false or nonsensical. They are not in the habit of gainsaying their spouses and friends when they ascribe colours to objects, admire or deplore the colours of things, whereas they do correct false utterances concerning bent sticks in water, Müller–Lyer lines or the Ponzo illusion.

Reasons for doubting the doctrine

The seventeenth-century conception is a powerful one. But although it has won widespread acceptance in the community of scientists, it is not obviously true; indeed, it is eminently disputable. It is not a *scientific* theory at all, and it is not supported by any validating experiment. It is a purely *philosophical* or *conceptual* claim, and accordingly it is supported only by a priori arguments. But those arguments are questionable and contentious. Even though we cannot in this context pursue the matter to the end, we shall raise some objections – sufficient, we hope, to raise doubts and prevent neuroscientists from unthinkingly nailing their colours to this shaky metaphysical mast.

The causal processes involved in visual perception do not show that what is perceived is not a multi-coloured world

That we can see an object to be red only when light is reflected off its surface and on to our retina does not show that the object 'in and of itself' is not really red. It merely shows that a condition for its colour being visible is that it be illuminated. Similarly, that photons reflected off the illuminated object cause changes to protein molecules in the retina, which in turn transmits electrical impulses to the fibres of the optic nerve, does not show that what we see is not really coloured, any more than it shows that we do not see what we see directly. *What* we see is not the *effect* of an object on us. The effect of an object on our nervous system is the stimulation of the cells of the retina, the effect of this on the optic nerve, the consequent excitation of the cells in the hypercolumns of the 'visual' striate cortex – but none of this is perceived either by the brain (which can perceive nothing) or by the person whose brain it is. Rather, *that* we see is a consequence of the action of illuminated or luminous objects on our visual system, and *what* we see are those objects, colour and all. What we thus see, we see 'directly' (to see something 'indirectly' might be to see it through a periscope or in a mirror – not to look at the thing itself in full daylight with one's eyes).

So too, it is confused to suppose that because it is senseless to attribute colour to light waves or sounds to sound waves, therefore *what* we see is not coloured and *what* we hear

The fact that what is received by sense-organs, e.g. light and sound waves, is neither coloured nor noisy does not show that what is perceived is not objectively coloured or noisy

is not noisy – but rather the colour and sound are *in us*, being 'mental constructions created in the brain'. That thought arises from the idea that what we *receive* (as Kandel, Schwartz and Jessell put it), what we are *given*, are electromagnetic waves of certain frequencies (which cannot be said to be coloured) and pressure or sound waves (which are not sounds). So, it is supposed that to perceive a perceptual quality, the quality must either be *transmitted* from object perceived to perceiver (the intromissionist conception favoured by the ancients and medievals) or alternatively *caused in* the perceiver (as was supposed by the seventeenth-century theorists and our contemporaries, such as Kandel and his colleagues). But this is confused. *We* do not receive electromagnetic waves and pressure waves – that is what our eyes and ear-drums are subjected to. And though one might say that they 'receive' them, these stimuli are not *given* in the sense in which data are given, but only in the sense in which a cold is given. They are not data which one can argue *from* and need not argue *to*, but mere neural stimuli. But what *we* are given are perceptions of red, green or blue objects, or perceptions of sounds, speech and music. And it is no more necessary for my perceiving a red object that there be something red in me than it is necessary for me to perceive an explosion that something explode in me. The red colour of the geranium does not have to be *transmitted* to me in order for me to see it. Nor does it have to be *caused in* me. For the red I see when I see the geranium is neither *in* me nor *in* the geranium. It is not *in* anything. But it is an attribute *of* the geranium, not of my perception of the geranium.

Perceiving is not the final link in the chain of micromechanisms

It is a further confusion to suppose that seeing the red geranium is the last link in a causal chain that commences with low-energy light of around 700 nm being reflected off the surface of the flower and terminates with a sensation of a red geranium in the brain, the occurrence of which *is* the seeing. This misconception stems, among other things, from a miscegenous crossing of the scientist's causal explanation of the neurophysiology of perception with the normal description of a creature's perceiving an object. Neuroscientists explain the event of A's seeing the red geranium in terms of a causal transaction between the surface of the red petals and the retina of the observer, and then between the retina of the observer and his optic nerve, and so on to the events in the 'visual' striate cortex. It is tempting, but mistaken, to conceive of the final link in this causal chain to be the perceiving. But such an explanation of A's perceiving G in terms of micromechanisms does not link explanandum and explanans as items in a microphysical causal chain; and the explanandum – that is, A's perceiving G – is not the final link in the chain. Rather, the explanans is the whole chain of microphysical events, which is *constitutive* of A's perceiving G.

Seeing something is not having a 'visual sensation'

A further incoherence is manifest in the idea that the final link in the causal chain is not the perceiving of G, but rather *having a sensation of G*. Accordingly, seeing G is conceived to be having a sensation of G that is caused by G's reflecting light on to A's retina, etc., etc. Having a sensation of G which is differently caused is not *perceiving G*, but is *having a hallucination of G*. But this too is incoherent. 'A saw a red geranium' describes an event which involves A, the geranium and the epistemic relation of seeing, not a different event – namely, the alleged event of A's having a G sensation – that occurred in A's mind or brain. The neural events that are empirically constitutive of seeing a red geranium do not *mediate* between the geranium and a sensation in the 'visual' striate cortex. As we shall see below, the very idea of a 'sensation' of a red geranium is confused. To see an object is not to have a sensation of any kind. The excitation of the retina by the impact of photons and the subsequent excitation of the 'visual' striate cortex, etc. are causally necessary conditions for the person's seeing the red geranium. But seeing the red colour of the flower does not occur in the brain at all – it occurs in the garden or the drawing room; and what is seen is a red geranium, not a sensation of red, which is neither seen nor had.

Neuroscientists are in effect committed to the view that in ascribing colours to objects we are committing a category mistake

It is noteworthy that, strictly speaking, neuroscientists who propound the Galilean/Cartesian conception are not committed to the claim that what we ordinarily think to be coloured objects are not coloured. For objects that we ordinarily think are not coloured – that is, that have no colour – are things that are colourless and transparent, like a pane of glass; they *could* be, and may *become*, coloured. But such neuroscientists are not claiming that in our ordinary colour attributions we are making a *factual* mistake, and attributing colours to things that are actually colourless. Rather, they are in effect claiming that in our ordinary colour attributions, we are making a flagrant *category* mistake. Objects we ordinarily take to be coloured – for example, geraniums (red) and delphiniums (blue) – *could* not be coloured, for colours are 'sensations in the sensorium' (as Newton put it). Such neuroscientists are committed to the view that it is *senseless* to attribute colours to objects in our environment, just as senseless as it is to attribute colours to numbers or smells to propositions. But it is surely bizarre to put the sentence 'Geraniums are red and delphiniums blue' on the same level as 'Two is green and twenty-two violet'. For the first sentence makes sense, but the second is nonsense.

Being red can't be explained in terms of looking red

Of course, it is tempting to try to explain what it is for something to be red in terms of its looking red to a normal observer under normal observation conditions, and to think of looking red as a sensation. But, quite apart from the fact that looking red is not a sensation, that is wrong. For normal observation conditions are precisely those conditions under which coloured things look the colour they actually are, and normal observers are those observers to whom coloured things look the colour they are under normal conditions of observation. Moreover, one cannot explain what it is to *be* red in terms of *looking* red, for the correct explanation of what it is for something to look red is that it should look *thus* ☞ (and here we point at something which *is* red). One can no more teach someone the use of 'looks red' antecedently to 'is red' than one can teach someone the use of 'is probably F' antecedently to teaching him the use of 'is F'. Finally, if 'red' were the name of a sensation in the brain, the concept of red would have to be explained by means of a private ostensive definition, and, as we have seen (§3.9), there is no such thing. Not only could we have no public, shared concept of red, we could not even have a private concept of red.

Neuroscientists need not, and should not, commit themselves to questionable seventeenth-century metaphysical doctrines

We are not suggesting that these considerations settle the a priori question of whether colours (and other secondary qualities) are objective qualities of objects or subjective modifications of our sensibility. The arguments are complex and ramified.[11] What we are suggesting is that cognitive neuroscientists should not adopt a non-scientific, metaphysical doctrine of questionable philosophical ancestry, which is supported by philosophical arguments of questionable validity. This recommendation is by no means trivial, since the seventeenth-century conception of reality, of what is objective and what is subjective, of the nature of perception and its objects, has profoundly affected the ways in which brain scientists currently conceive of their investigations. This particular philosophical doctrine is not necessary for coherent, successful neuroscientific investigation, and neuroscientists' reports of the results of their investigations would benefit, not suffer, from bypassing this contentious conceptual matter.

Secondary qualities (as we perceive them) are not sensations

The metaphysical conception of reality propounded by the founding fathers of modern science and modern philosophy assimilated perceptual qualities such as colours, sounds, smells, tastes and various tactile qualities to sensations. But if the term 'sensation' is intended to include such things as pains, twinges and tickles, then these perceptual qualities cannot be sensations. For they are categorially altogether unlike sensations. Roses, poppies or sunsets may be red, and so have a colour, but they have no sensations; drums and trumpets *make* sounds, but not sensations; and while the cello *has* a melodious sound, it does not have a melodious sensation.

To perceive a secondary quality is not to have a sensation of that quality

Well and good, it might be said; but what is meant is that to perceive a secondary quality just is to have a certain sensation *of* that quality. But this too is misconceived. To see a red apple is not to have any sensations, nor is to hear a sound or to smell a smell. One has and feels sensations *in* a part of one's body, but one normally feels no sensations *in* one's eyes when one sees something, in one's ears when one hears something, or in one's nose when one smells something. There *can* be sensations in perceptual organs. One's eyes may itch, and one's ears may ache – but these sensations are not produced by the exercise of the perceptual faculty. There *can* be sensations in organs of perception produced by their exercise. Looking into a blinding light produces a sensation of being dazzled and sometimes makes one's eyes *hurt*; hearing a very loud noise produces a sensation of being deafened. But far from these sensations being constitutive of perceiving, they are accompaniments of, and impediments to, perceiving.

A colour is neither a sensation nor a property of a sensation

If seeing red were a sensation, and the objects seen could not be said to be red, then the question would arise whether redness is a property of the sensation itself. But it makes no sense to speak of red sensations, since sensations are felt and not seen, and

---

[11] For detailed examination, see P. M. S. Hacker, *Appearance and Reality* (Blackwell, Oxford, 1987), and, more recently, B. Stroud, *The Quest for Reality* (Oxford University Press, Oxford, 2000).

colours are seen and not felt. So the alleged sensation must be a sensation *of* red, not a red sensation. But it is unclear how to construe the concept of a 'sensation *of* red'. Should it be understood on the model of a 'sensation of pain'? That is absurd, for a sensation of pain just is a pain, whereas the putative sensation of red is not 'a red'. Is the sensation of red felt? Surely not, for when one sees a geranium, one does not *feel* a sensation of red in one's brain or anywhere else. Does the visual sensation of red have any characteristic behavioural manifestations akin to the behavioural manifestations of pains, tickles or tingles? No, one does not scratch, rub or otherwise assuage one's head when one sees red geraniums. In short, seeing something red (and seeing it to be red) is a form of perception, not of sensation. The colour seen is a property of what is seen, not of the seeing of it.

4.2.2 Perception as hypothesis formation: Helmholtz

Helmholtz's misconception that all perception involves having sensations

The idea that sensations are essential constituents of any perception was embedded in the source and origin of modern neuroscientific theories of perception: namely, in the work of Hermann von Helmholtz. According to him, physical stimuli (which he calls 'external impressions') are transmitted to the brain, where they *become sensations*.[12] Helmholtz viewed these putative sensations as the raw materials from which perceptions are allegedly synthesized by the unconscious mind. Having appropriate sensations is a prerequisite for perceiving. For the sensations in the brain are combined there to form *conceptions* or *ideas* or *perceptions of objects*.[13]

This is confused. Physical stimuli to nerve endings do not *become* sensations: one can no more *transform* photons or sound waves (the physical stimuli) or neural excitations in the brain (the consequences of the stimulation of the relevant nerve endings) into sensations than one can transform frogs into princes. There are no visual or auditory 'sensations' in the brain. But pressure on the brain can cause sensations – and these are headaches, not sensations of colour, sound, smell or taste. There is no such thing as *combining* sensations so as to form a perception, any more than there is such a thing as combining objects to form a fact. And there is all the difference in the world between a conception and a perception; one can have a conception of X without perceiving X – indeed, even if X is not a perceptible entity – and one can perceive X without having any conception of what one is perceiving.

Helmholtz's conception of perceptions as the conclusions of unconscious inferences was also mistaken. He thought that perceptions are conclusions of unconscious inferences the

---

[12] Hermann von Helmholtz, 'The recent progress of the theory of vision', repr. in translation in R. M. Warren and R. P. Warren (eds), *Helmholtz on Perception* (Wiley, New York, 1968), p. 101. It is noteworthy that Helmholtz admitted to writing under the influence of the reflections of seventeenth-century philosophers. 'In the writings of . . . Locke', he wrote, 'were correctly laid down the most important principles on which the right interpretation of sensible qualities depends' (ibid.). He correctly recognized that this conception is the product of philosophical reflection, not of scientific experimentation.

[13] Ibid., p. 82.

Helmholtz's misconception of percep-
tions as conclusions of inferences

premisses of which are unconscious and (more or less) indescribable sensations and (unconscious) generalizations about the correlation between past sensations and objects perceived. This confused idea is the linchpin of Richard Gregory's theory of perception, and is common among neuroscientists.[14] Like Gregory, Ian Glynn suggests that a variety of illusions (e.g. the Ponzo illusion, Kanizsa's illusion, the Ames' Room illusion) are explicable in Helmholtz's terms.[15] In all these cases, it is claimed, the illusion is explained by reference to the brain's drawing inferences from its past experience to form hypotheses about the objects of its present experience. J. Z. Young held that we can

> regard all seeing as a continual search for the answers to questions posed by the brain. The signals sent from the retina constitute 'messages' conveying these answers. The brain then uses this information to construct a suitable hypothesis about what is there and a programme of action to meet the situation. As a hungry boy looks around, his eyes may send signals that suggest a fruit tree. Signals go back to the eyes to search for food and if the returning messages indicate 'apples' he starts to climb to pick and eat them.[16]

And, as we saw in the previous chapter, Blakemore supposes that the brain 'constructs its hypothesis of perception' on the basis of information given it by the neurons (which he picturesquely describes as 'arguments' (see above, p. 69). So Helmholtz's conception of perceptions as hypotheses of the brain still flourishes in one form or another. But there are compelling objections to it.

To perceive is not to form a
hypothesis

First, to perceive something is not to form a hypothesis, and to form a hypothesis is not to perceive anything. A hypothesis is an unconfirmed proposition or principle put forward as a provisional basis for reasoning or argument, a supposition or conjecture advanced to account for relevant facts. *Seeing geraniums in the garden* is not a proposition or conjecture. The articulate judgement *there are geraniums in the garden* may be called 'a perceptual judgement' if its grounds are perceptual, as opposed to hearsay or evidence (e.g. geranium petals on the carpet). *Seeing that there are geraniums in the garden* might, in a different sense, also be called a perceptual judgement, but it too is not a proposition. It has no grounds, but presupposes the successful exercise of a recognitional ability (viz. the ability to recognize geraniums). It does not follow that a perceptual judgement (in either of these senses) is a hypothesis or a conjecture – and, of course, our normal perceptual judgements are not. (That perceptual judgements, in the first sense, are fallible does not

---

[14] Here we cannot defend the claim that Helmholtz's conception of perception as unconscious inference is thoroughly confused. For detailed criticism, see P. M. S. Hacker, 'Helmholtz's theory of perception', *International Studies in the Philosophy of Science*, 9 (1995), pp. 199–214. For an examination of Gregory's theory, see *idem*, 'Experimental methods and conceptual confusion: an investigation into R. L. Gregory's theory of perception', *Iyyun – The Jerusalem Philosophical Quarterly*, 40 (1991), pp. 289–314.

[15] I. Glynn, *An Anatomy of Thought* (Weidenfeld and Nicolson, London, 1999), pp. 194f.

[16] J. Z. Young, *Programs of the Brain* (Oxford University Press, Oxford, 1978), p. 119.

imply that they are hypotheses.) Moreover, one may perceive something (as opposed to perceiving that something is thus-and-so) without making any judgement, and even without knowing what one has perceived. A perception – that is, a person's perceiving something – is not a hypothesis, but an event or occurrence.

It is human beings, not brains, that form hypotheses

Secondly, as we have pointed out many times, it is human beings, not their brains, that form hypotheses and make inferences. There is no such thing as a brain's putting forward a proposition as a basis for reasoning or argument or acting on the basis of a supposition. So, too, hypotheses are formed on the basis of data. The data consist of information that is thought to provide evidential support for the hypothesis – but the brain does not, and could not, have any information in this sense. This is not because it isn't clever enough, but because it is not the right sort of thing to have information.

A perception cannot (logically) be the conclusion of an inference

Thirdly, a perception – that is, someone's perceiving something – can no more be the conclusion of an inference than winning a race or climbing a wall can be the conclusion of an inference. *That* someone has perceived something may be the conclusion of an inference, if, for example, the premisses are that he has normal eyesight, that he was confronted by something that was both visible and salient, and that there was nothing distracting him. But his perceiving what he perceived cannot be the conclusion of an inference. Given that we know that appropriate conditions obtained, *we* may infer that Jack sees a rose; but Jack himself does not infer that he is seeing a rose when those conditions obtain: he simply sees the rose.

Inferences are not processes

Fourthly, inferences are neither conscious nor unconscious mental processes, since inferences are not processes, but transformations of propositions in accordance with a rule, derivations of propositions from premisses in conformity with a pattern of derivation. But perceiving something involves no transformation of propositions either by the perceiver or by his brain. One must not confuse inferences (conscious or unconscious) with assumptions or suppositions. But, again, the brain neither assumes nor supposes anything – only people do so.

Finally, even if we absurdly suppose that it makes sense for the brain to hypothesize something, it remains wholly unclear how constructing a hypothesis bears on *perceiving something*, an unclarity that is not even papered over by the incoherent assertion that perceptions are conclusions of unconscious inferences. One may form hypotheses about what one sees, but to see is not to form a hypothesis. One may taste something and conjecture what it is that one has tasted, but to taste is one thing, and to conjecture or hypothesize is another.

4.2.3 Visual images and the binding problem

The misconception that what is seen or heard is an image (Sherrington, Damasio, Edelman, Crick)

The classical doctrine of ideas and impressions, conceived as the results of the impact of the material world on our nerve endings, is the source of the thought that perceiving always involves sensations, which are, on Helmholtzian theory, the premisses of unconscious inferences. It is also the source of the equally misguided and far more widespread thought that what is seen (or heard, etc.) when we see (or hear, etc.) something is a *picture* or *image* (visual or auditory). It is not surprising to find a Cartesian like Sherrington averring that 'When I turn my gaze skyward I see the flattened dome of the sky and the sun's brilliant disc and a hundred other visible things underneath it . . . In fact, I perceive a picture of the world around me.'[17] It is perhaps more surprising to find the same representationalist view defended by contemporary neuroscientists. So, for example, Damasio holds that

> When you and I look at an object outside ourselves, we form comparable images in our respective brains. . . . But that does not mean that the image we see is the copy of whatever the object outside is like. Whatever it is like, in absolute terms, we do not know. The image we see is based on changes which occurred in our organisms . . . when the physical structure of the object interacts with the body. . . . The object is real, the interactions are real, and the images are as real as anything can be. And yet, the structure and properties in the image we end up seeing are brain constructions prompted by the object. . . . There is . . . a set of correspondences between physical characteristics of the object and modes of reaction of the organism according to which an internally generated image is constructed.[18]

In a similar vein, Edelman asserts that 'Primary consciousness is the state of being mentally aware of things in the world – of having mental images in the present', and 'As human beings, we experience primary consciousness as a "picture" or a "mental image" of ongoing categorized events'.[19] And Crick avers that

> we can see how the visual parts of the brain take the picture (the visual field) apart, but we do not yet know how the brain puts it all together to provide our highly organized view of the world – that is, what we see. It seems as if the brain needs to impose some global unity on certain activities in its different parts so that the attributes of a single object – its shape, color, movement, location, and so on – are in some way brought together without at the same time confusing them with the attributes of other objects in the visual field.[20]

But *this* is confused. What one perceives by the use of one's perceptual organs is an object or array of objects, sounds and smells, and the properties and relations of items in one's environment. It is a mistake to suppose that what we perceive is always or even commonly, an image, or that to perceive an object is to *have* an image of the object perceived. One does not perceive images or representations of objects, unless one perceives paintings or photographs of objects. To see a red apple is not to see an image of a red apple, and to hear a sonata is not to hear the image or representation of a sonata. Nor is it to *have* an

---

[17] C. S. Sherrington, *Man on his Nature*, quoted in G. Edelman and G. Tononi, *Consciousness: How Matter Becomes Imagination* (Allen Lane, The Penguin Press, London, 2000), p. 1.
[18] A. Damasio, *The Feeling of What Happens* (Heinemann, London, 1999), p. 320.
[19] G. Edelman, *Bright Air, Brilliant Fire – On the Matter of the Mind* (Penguin, Harmondsworth, 1994), pp. 112 and 119.
[20] Crick, *Astonishing Hypothesis*, p. 22.

image in one's mind or brain, although one *can* conjure up images in one's mind and sometimes images cross one's mind independently of one's wish or will. But the mental images we thus conjure up are not visible, either to others or to ourselves – they are 'had', but not seen. And the tunes one rehearses in one's imagination are not heard, either by oneself or by others.

The brain neither takes a picture apart nor assembles one

To assert that 'the visual parts of the brain take the picture apart' is a misdescription. The visual scene is not a picture, although it may contain a picture if one is in an art gallery. The electrochemical reactions of the rods and cones of the retina to the light falling on them cause a multitude of responses in *different* parts of the 'visual' cortex, but that is not correctly characterized as 'taking the picture apart'. Nor does the brain have to 'put it all together' again in order to provide our view of the world. For our 'view of the world' is not a *picture* of the world (or of the visible scene), and the *attributes* of the visibilia in front of us do not have to, and cannot, be 'brought together'. For the colour, shape, location and movement of the blue delphiniums swaying in the breeze cannot be taken apart (there is no such thing as separating these attributes from the objects of which they are attributes), and the colour, shape, location and movement of the delphiniums cannot be brought together in the brain, since these attributes are not to be found in the brain, either together or separately. The fact that different cells in different locations respond severally to colour, shape, location and movement does not imply that these several responses need to be united *in order to form an image*, since no image is or needs to be formed in order to see the object which is visible.[21]

Misconceptions about the binding problem (Kandel, Wurtz, Crick)

It is precisely this confusion that informs neuroscientists' characterization of 'the binding problem'. Eric Kandel and Robert Wurtz, in a discussion interestingly entitled 'Constructing the visual image', explain that 'information about' (i.e. presumably, electro-chemical responses to) form, motion and colour is carried by parallel pathways. This, they aver, creates the binding problem:

> How is information carried by separate pathways brought together into a coherent visual image? . . . How does the brain construct a perceived world from sensory information and how does it bring it into consciousness? . . . what the visual system really does [is] to create a three-dimensional perception of the world which is different from the two-dimensional image projected onto the retina.[22]

This is prima facie confusing, since the brain does not 'construct a perceived world', but enables the animal to see a visible scene. Moreover, the brain does not create a

---

[21] But if neuroscientists swallow the seventeenth-century doctrine of primary and secondary qualities, they will be prone to think that objects in the visual field cannot be coloured. If so, it seems, then something had better be coloured when we see a geranium – if not the geranium itself, then the image or 'picture' of the geranium in the mind or brain! But it is not necessary to swallow this bit of seventeenth-century philosophy in order to investigate the neural nature of perception.

[22] E. R. Kandel and R. Wurtz, 'Constructing the visual image', in Kandel, Schwartz and Jessell (eds), *Principles of Neural Science and Behaviour*, p. 492.

'three-dimensional perception' which is different from the 'two-dimensional image' on the retina. It confers depth vision upon the animal, but the ability visually to discriminate depth is neither different from nor the same as an inverted reflection on the retina (which is incidental to vision anyway) – it is categorially distinct.[23] One might think that this misdescription is altogether irrelevant to the serious business of the binding problem. But it is not. Kandel and Wurtz continue thus:

> How is information about color, motion, depth, and form, which are [*sic*] carried by separate neural pathways, organized into cohesive perceptions? When we see a square purple box we combine into one perception the properties of color (purple), form (square), and dimensions in depth (box). We can equally well combine purple with a round box, a hat or a coat. . . . visual images are typically built up from the inputs of parallel pathways that process different features – movement, depth, form, and color. To express the specific combination of properties in the visual field at any given moment, independent groups of cells must temporarily be brought into *association*. As a result, there must be a mechanism by which the brain momentarily associates the information being processed independently by different cell populations in different cortical regions. This mechanism, as yet unspecified, is called the *binding mechanism*.[24]

Such confused statements of the so-called binding problem are widespread. Francis Crick, discussing the binding problem, points out that at any given moment, any particular object in the visual field is 'represented by' (i.e. causally correlated with) the firing of a set of neurons, which are distributed in different 'visual' areas (for form, colour, motion, etc.). We perceive the object as a unity. *If* one also thinks, as Crick does, that 'One striking feature of our *internal picture of the visual world* is how well organized it is . . . we seldom get things jumbled in space when seeing them under ordinary conditions',[25] or if one thinks, as Kandel and Wurtz do, that what we perceive are visual images, then there is indeed a 'binding problem'. For if perceiving involves an internal picture or image of the external scene, the picture must be constructed, and the image 'built up'. And one might indeed wonder how the brain produces such coherent pictures or images, correctly associating the shape, motion, depth and colour of the perceived object and not 'jumbling them up'.

---

[23] One cannot intelligibly ask whether a reflection resembles the ability visually to discriminate depth or the exercise of this visual ability. Nor is it licit to characterize a reflection, as opposed to the reflective surface, as two-dimensional. What is visible in a mirror is not an image (picture or representation) of something, but the thing itself – reflected in the mirror. (An image, in the sense in which a painting is an image, needs to be luminous or illuminated in order to be seen, but to see an object in a mirror, one must illuminate the object, not the mirror.) So if what is reflected is three-dimensional, then what is visible in the mirror is three-dimensional. So the reflection on the retina of the visible scene is not a two-dimensional image, since, strictly speaking, it is neither an image nor two-dimensional! All of which is neither here nor there, since neither the person nor his brain can see the reflection, and it is not the so-called retinal image (the reflected light) that enables us to see what we see, but the light that is absorbed by the retina.

[24] Kandel and Wurtz, 'Constructing the visual image', p. 502.

[25] Crick, *Astonishing Hypothesis*, p. 232, our emphasis.

The current conception of the binding problem is confused

To be sure, the cells that respond to motion, those that respond to shape, and those that respond to colour had better be active *at (more or less) the same time*, otherwise the person or animal will not see a coloured, moving object of the relevant shape (or the asynchronicity will simply be reflected in a corresponding delay in the perception). And presumably the simultaneous activity of these cell groups had better be connected in some way to the centres that control recognition, movement and co-ordination. That much seems obvious. And indeed the first step towards clarifying the processes involved has been taken by the discoveries of Wolf Singer, Charles Gray and their colleagues of the synchronous 40-Hertz oscillations of neuronal firing in different neurons in the different parts of the brain that are involved in seeing.[26] However, the conception of the binding problem that is current among many neuroscientists is arguably confused.

Confusions about information

The sense in which separate neural pathways carry *information* about colour, shape, movement, etc., is not semantic, but, at best, information-theoretic. In neither sense of 'information' can information be 'organized' into 'cohesive perceptions'. In the semantic sense, information is a set of true propositions, and true propositions cannot be organized into perceptions (i.e. into a person's perceiving something). In the engineering sense, 'information' is a measure of the freedom of choice in the transmission of a signal, and the amount of information is measured by the logarithm to the base 2 of the number of available choices – and this too is not something that can be 'organized' into perceptions. One cannot combine colour, form and dimensions into perceptions, just as one cannot put events into holes – this form of words makes no sense. And, correspondingly, when we see a square, purple box, we do not 'combine' purple, squareness and boxhood – for this too is a nonsensical form of words. It is true that in order to see a coloured, moving object with a given shape, separate groups of neurons must be active simultaneously. But it does not follow that, in the semantic sense of information, the brain must 'associate' various bits of information; nor could it follow, since brains cannot act on the basis of information or associate pieces of information. Whether the brain, in some sense that needs to be clarified, 'associates' information in the information-theoretic sense is a further question. But if it does, that is not because the features of the object perceived have to be 'combined in the brain', for that is a nonsense.

For an animal to see, it is neither necessary nor possible that its brain build up a visual image or internal picture

Above all, to see an object is neither to *see* nor to *construct* an image of an object. The reason why the several neuronal groups must fire simultaneously when a person sees a coloured, three-dimensional object in motion is not because the brain has to build up a visual image or create an internal picture of objects in the visual field. When we see a tree, the brain does

---

[26] C. M. Gray and W. Singer, 'Stimulus-specific neuronal oscillations in orientation columns of cat visual cortex', *Proceedings of the National Academy of Science, USA*, 86 (1989), pp. 1698–1702, and C. M. Gray, P. König, A. K. Engel and W. Singer, 'Oscillatory responses in cat visual cortex exhibit inter-columnar synchronization which reflects global stimulus properties', *Nature*, 338 (1989), pp. 334–7.

not have to (and could not) bind together the trunk, boughs and leaves, or the colour and the shape, or the shape and the movement of the tree. One may see the tree clearly and distinctly or unclearly and indistinctly, and one may be sensitive to its colour and movement, or one may suffer from one or another form of colour-blindness or visual agnosia for movement. Which neuronal groups must simultaneously be active in order to achieve optimal vision, what form that activity may take, and how it is connected with other parts of the brain that are causally implicated in cognition, recognition and action, as well as in co-ordination of sight and movement, are what needs to be investigated by neuroscientists. Since seeing a tree is not seeing an internal picture of a tree, the brain does not have to construct any such picture. It merely has to be functioning normally so that we are able to see clearly and distinctly. It does not have to take a picture apart, since neither the visual scene nor the light array falling upon the retinae are pictures. It does not have to put a picture back together again, since what it enables us to do is to see a tree (not a picture of a tree) in the garden (not in the brain).

Confusions about representations (Barlow) The neuron doctrine in perception fostered the belief that the pathways that are active for a given sensory scene converge and produce activity in a single cell (a pontifical cell or a 'grandmother' cell) or group of cells (cardinal cells), 'whose role is to represent that scene'.[27] The idea was motivated, at least in part, by the thought that if the animal is to see, the brain must combine the information derived from the retinae to produce a representation of the visual scene. Undoubtedly, confusion was generated by the philosophical presuppositions of representationalism. The term 'information' was employed equivocally, as indeed was the term 'representation'. So, when Horace Barlow claims that the hypothesized cardinal cells 'do not represent arbitrary or capricious features in the environment, but features useful for their representative role', and that they can be active in combinations, and 'thus have something of the descriptive power of words',[28] the phrase 'representative role' might mean 'their role as correlates of features of the object perceived'. But in that *causal* sense of 'representation', a representation could not have anything of the descriptive power of words. For the sense in which the excitation of a group of cells represents a certain feature in the visual field is the sense in which a wide ring in a tree trunk represents a year with ample rainfall, and that has nothing whatsoever to do with the *lexical* or *semantic* sense in which a sentence represents the state of affairs it describes, or with the *iconic* sense in which a picture represents what it depicts. Ambiguity is further multiplied when it is suggested that not only does the brain make a representation of the external world, but also that we see a representation of the world:

> The usual way to analyse behaviour is to split what the brain does into two halves: Sensory messages are used to make a representation of the external world, we say, and the brain then uses this representation to decide a course of action that will accomplish its goals. This seems natural because we fool ourselves that we perceive a straightforward

---

[27] See Horace Barlow, 'The neuron doctrine in perception', in M. S. Gazzaniga (ed.), *The New Cognitive Neurosciences*, 4th edn (MIT Press, Cambridge, MA, 1997), p. 421.

[28] Ibid., p. 422.

representation of the world and decide simply according to what that representation shows, but even the most elementary knowledge of the psychology of perception tells us that it is very far from being a straightforward representation. . . . by the time the perceptual representation has been generated, a large proportion of the brain's guesswork has already been done,[29]

This is confused. Neither in the iconic nor in the lexical sense could there be any representations of the external world in the brain. The brain can neither make a decision nor be indecisive; and it cannot engage in guesswork either. Human beings, when they perceive their environment, do not perceive representations of the world, straightforward or otherwise, since to perceive the world (or, more accurately, some part of it) is not to perceive a representation. (To perceive a photograph or painting is to perceive a representation.) And in whatever legitimate sense there is to the supposition that there is a representation of what is seen in the brain, *that* representation is *not* what the owner of the brain sees. The term 'representation' is a weed in the neuroscientific garden, not a tool – and the sooner it is uprooted the better.

4.2.4 Perception as information processing: Marr's theory of vision

Marr's conception of perception as information processing

Helmholtz's conception of perception as a matter of unconscious hypothesis formation was a misconceived intellectualization of sense. An analogue of this nineteenth-century confusion is the late twentieth-century computational conception of perception. In its most sophisticated form, this conception was elaborated by David Marr, who 'adopted a point of view that regards visual perception as a problem in information processing'.[30] The informational input is conceived to be the light array (which he referred to as an 'image') falling upon the retina, and the output is held to be the construction of efficient and useful symbolic descriptions of objects in view. According to Marr, 'vision is the *process* of discovering from images what is present in the world and where it is'.[31] It is the process of transforming the information implicit in an image into an explicit *description* of what is seen.

Marr's conception of the brain as operating on a symbolism to produce descriptions

Marr conceived of the brain as operating a system of symbols that represent features of an image in order to construct descriptions. By a series of computational operations on the symbolism, the brain can, in the final stage of the visual process, produce a description of shapes of objects, their distance, orientation and identity. From the 'image' the brain is alleged to construct a *primal sketch*,

---

[29] Ibid., p. 429.
[30] D. Marr, 'Visual information processing: the structure and creation of visual representations', *Philosophical Transactions of the Royal Society*, B 290 (1980), p. 203.
[31] D. Marr, *Vision, a Computational Investigation into the Human Representation and Processing of Visual Information* (W. H. Freeman, San Francisco, 1980), p. 3.

which describes the light intensity changes in the 'image', out of which it then constructs a *2½-D sketch* which represents the surface orientations in a scene. This is a viewer-centred description of the layout of structures in the world. An image-space processor is then held to operate on the 2½-D sketch and to transform it, with the help of a stored catalogue of 3-D model descriptions, into object-centred co-ordinates of an axis-based structural *3-D description*. Marr's theory is, as he himself granted, an extension of representational theories of the mind,

> according to which the senses are for the most part concerned with telling one what is there. Modern representational theories conceive of the mind as having access to systems of internal representations; mental states are characterized by asserting what the internal representations currently specify, and mental processes by how such internal representations are obtained and how they interact.[32]

This scheme, he concluded, 'affords a comfortable framework for our study of visual perception, and I am content to let it form the point of departure'.

We suggest that it forms an inadequate framework, and that it should not form a point of departure for any serious investigation of animal vision. (This does not, of course, preclude the possibility of there being neural *analogues* of some of the features we build into the machines we design to execute visual tasks *without seeing*.)

Marr's misconceptions about seeing   To see is not to discover anything from an image or light array falling upon the retina. For one cannot, in this sense, discover anything from something one cannot perceive (we do not perceive the light array that falls upon our retinae, what we perceive is whatever that light array enables us to perceive). The light array is not a datum or piece of information from which one might derive or infer anything; and the brain draws no inferences from information, since in the sense in which information provides premises for inferences, the brain has no information and could not understand any information anyway. Not all seeing is discovering (when one reads what one has written, one may discover one's mistakes, but one does not *discover* what one has written; when in conversation, one looks up at one's interlocutor, one does not *discover* that he is there). And although seeing involves neural processes, it is not itself a process (just as although keeping time involves mechanical processes in the movement of an antique clock, telling the time is not itself a process). Observing, watching, scrutinizing may be processes or activities, but seeing, spotting, noticing or glimpsing are not.

Marr's misconceptions about representation and description   Marr claimed that 'if we are capable of knowing what is where in the world, our brains must somehow be capable of *representing* this information'.[33] But, as should already

---

[32] Ibid., p. 5.

[33] Ibid., p. 3. J. P. Frisby similarly argues that 'there must be symbols inside our heads for the things we see . . . It is an inescapable conclusion that there must be a symbolic description in the brain of the outside world, a description cast in symbols which stand for the various aspects of the world of which sight makes us aware. . . . The world we see . . . is so very clearly "out there" that it can come

be evident, there is no such thing as a brain's representing information, in the ordinary sense of this phrase (and it is evident that Marr needs the ordinary sense in order to carry through his argument[34]). Moreover, it is not intelligible to suppose that there can be a *symbolic description* of the visual scene in the brain.[35] A description is a form of words or symbols, a sentence expressing a proposition that specifies an array of features of an object, event or state of affairs. It can be true or false, accurate or inaccurate, detailed or rough-and-ready. Descriptions are contrasted with prescriptions, questions, recommendations and exclamations. A symbolic description may be written down or spoken; it may be encoded for concealment or for transmission. But there is no such thing as a description in the brain. A pattern of neural firing that is a causal response to a stimulus in the visual field is not a description of the stimulus or of anything else. For patterns of neural firing are no

---

as something of a shock to realize that somehow the whole of this world is tucked away inside our skulls as an inner representation which stands for the real outside world' (*Seeing: Illusion, Brain and Mind* (Oxford University Press, Oxford, 1980), pp. 8f.). Similar misconceptions are evident in Crick: '[the brain] must produce a *symbolic description at a higher level*, probably at a series of higher levels . . . what the brain has to build up is a many-levelled interpretation of the visual scene, usually in terms of objects and events and their meaning to us. . . . When something has been symbolized explicitly, this information can easily be made available so that it can be used, either for further processing or for action. In neural terms, "explicit" probably means that nerve cells must be *firing* in a way that symbolizes such information fairly directly. Thus it is plausible that we need an *explicit multi-level, symbolic interpretation* of the visual scene in order to "see" it. It is difficult for most people to accept that what they see is a symbolic interpretation of the world – it all seems so like "the real thing". But in fact we have no direct knowledge of the objects in the world' (Crick, *Astonishing Hypothesis*, p. 33).

[34] It is evident, as we have argued in §3.2, from what Marr says about representations and from the inferences he draws from his ascription of representations to the brain. What Marr meant by 'representation' is *not* merely a causal correlate of something, for according to his view, symbolic notations (such as roman, arabic and binary notations in arithmetic) are representations, we all *use* representations all the time in order to make *descriptions* of things – and these assertions make sense only if Marr is *also* thinking of representations in the semantic sense of the term, and confusing the semantic sense with the causal one.

[35] Simon Ullman explains that 'when we say that a certain device can be viewed as a symbolic system we imply that some (but not all) of the events within the system can be consistently interpreted as having a meaning within a certain domain'. So, 'some of the events inside the brain may have a consistent interpretation in terms of depth, surface orientation, reflectance and the like' ('Tacit assumptions in the computational study of vision', in A. Gorea (ed.), *Representations of Vision, Trends and Tacit Assumptions in Vision Research* (Cambridge University Press, Cambridge, 1991), p. 314.). To be sure, if Ullman wishes to call this 'a symbolic system', there is nothing stopping him. Of course, like Humpty Dumpty's 'there's glory for you', by which he means 'there's a nice knock-down argument', what Ullman means by this phrase is not what it means. But, if he stipulates that this is what *he* means by it, so be it. The moot question is whether, in his reasoning, he remembers that that is all he means, and does not draw inferences that depend upon the customary meaning of the phrase 'a symbolic system'. Marr certainly draws inferences from ascriptions of representations which depend upon the customary meaning of the term.

more symbols than are rings in the trunk of an oak tree, or molecules in a material subjected to carbon dating.

The logical requirements on symbols

For something to be a (semantic) symbol, it must have a *rule-governed use*. There must be a correct and an incorrect way of using it. It must have a grammar determining its intelligible combinatorial possibilities with other symbols, which is elucidated by explanations of meaning, that are used and accepted among a community of speakers. There can be no symbols in the brain, the brain cannot use symbols and cannot *mean* anything *by* a symbol (but, of course, neural events may mean – i.e. be causally correlated with – certain other events, in the sense in which smoke means fire). A symbol is used only if the user means something by it – but brains cannot mean anything. To mean something by a symbol is to intend the symbol to signify such-and-such a thing – but brains can have no intentions.

Marr's misconceptions about the 'output' of the visual system

We shall not probe Marr's ingenious analysis of the requirements for deriving an image from a light array, an analysis that may well be apt for the design of machines that can carry out visual tasks.[36] Our concern is exclusively with the conceptual incoherences in applying this model to animal vision. According to Marr, the output of the computational process is the production of a *description* of visible objects, embodied in an internal representation which is made available as a basis for decisions.[37] But this is confused. The 'output' of the neuro-visual process, in so far as it can be said to have an 'output', is that the creature sees whatever it sees. But to see something is no more to construct or produce a description than it is to construct a hypothesis. Indeed, it is not even *being able* to produce a description (non-human animals can see, but cannot describe anything). Seeing is not describing (and neither is hearing, feeling, smelling or tasting). And the idea that the *brain* might produce a description or 'internal representation' and make it available to the mind, and that this transaction is constitutive of seeing, is doubly incoherent.

The senses are not information-transmitters

It is misleading to say that the senses are concerned with 'telling us what is there'. That is a picturesque figure of speech, but, in the context of Marr's theorizing, it is an injudicious one. For the sense-organs are not information-transmitters. Our eyes do not see things and tell the brain what they see, and the brain does not tell us what the eyes see. We use our sense-organs to find out, observe, apprehend what is in our environment. Our sense-faculties are capacities for apprehending, by the use of our sense-organs, how things are in our environment. The senses are not information-transmitters, although we acquire information by their use. (Radio and television are information-transmitters – and

---

[36] For a detailed critical account, see P. M. S. Hacker, 'Seeing, representing and describing: an examination of David Marr's computational theory of vision', in J. Hyman (ed.), *Investigating Psychology* (Routledge, London, 1991), pp. 119–54.

[37] This characterization is derived from machine vision, since the processor's 'identification' of the object or feature triggers, in a predetermined way, the robotic 'decision'. To be sure, for this to occur, *vision* is not necessary – which is why we use machines rather than workers.

so too is the town crier.) The senses do not transmit 'internal representations' to us, nor do they make symbolic descriptions available to the mind. The study of perception is not an investigation into symbolic representations and their relation to what they are representations of. That is the study of symbol systems, languages, notations, pictures and other (paradigmatically social) artefacts employed by concept-using creatures. To perceive is not to represent anything.

The production of 3-D model descriptions could not possibly explain vision

Marr's theory dispenses with images in the brain or images produced by the brain. Instead he offers us 3-D model descriptions encoded in the brain. But it should be obvious that what this fails to do is precisely to explain *vision*. To say that the mind has 'access' to the 'internal representations' produced by the brain is no less mysterious than the Cartesian claim that the mind has access to an image on the pineal gland. Moreover, it is altogether obscure how the mind's having access to putative neural *descriptions* will enable the person *to see*. And if Marr were to insist (rightly) that it is the person, not the mind, that sees, how is the transition from the presence of an encoded 3-D model description in the brain to the experience of seeing what is before one's eyes to be explained? To be sure, *that* is not an empirical problem, to be solved by further investigations. It is the product of a conceptual confusion, and what it needs is disentangling. For seeing something is the exercise of a power, a use of the visual faculty – not the processing of information in the semantic sense or the production of a description in the brain.

Neuroscientists should avoid three cardinal errors

Some lessons can be learned from these extended reflections on the conceptual character of perception in general, and visual perception in particular. First, neuroscientists need to take great care in using terms such as 'information' and 'information processing'; they should beware of the pitfalls associated with the terms 'representation' and 'internal representation', and cease to refer to neural correlates of features in the visual scene as either 'representations' or 'symbols'. Second, neuroscientists should take care not to commit the mereological fallacy in their endeavour to explain perceptual processes. Not only is it not the brain that perceives, but also it is futile to try to explain perception by reference to alleged cogitative, cognitive or image-making activities of the brain, since there can be none. Third, neuroscientists would do well to bypass the question of whether secondary qualities are or are not objective, and to abandon the misguided idea that seeing something involves having or seeing an image of that thing.

5

The Cognitive Powers

In the previous chapter we examined sensation and perception. Our purpose was to sketch the contour lines of these important psychological categories. Clarifying them, and elucidating the concept of visual perception in particular, has implications for neuroscientific research, much of which is focused upon the *empirical* nature of sensation and perception. A prerequisite for fruitful and illuminating empirical research on the neural foundations of our psychological capacities is clarity concerning the concepts involved. We tried to demonstrate the relevance of the analytic, conceptual task to the pursuit of the scientific one by examining some claims made by eminent neuroscientists who, in our judgement, have paid too little attention to the elucidation of the concepts they invoke. In this chapter, we shall examine the cognitive categories of knowledge and memory – concepts that also figure prominently in neuroscientific discussions.

5.1 Knowledge and its Kinship with Ability

Knowledge is not a state, but bears a kinship to an ability

Perception is a primary source of knowledge, and, as noted, to perceive *that* something is so is to acquire knowledge of how things are in respect of objects of one's possible perception. To know that something is thus-and-so is trivially to be in possession of information. It is tempting to think that to possess information – that is, to know something – is to be in a certain mental state from which overt performances manifesting knowledge flow. But that would be mistaken. For if it were so, then there would be two quite distinct sets of criteria for whether someone knows something: first, criteria for whether the mental state of knowing is present, and second, criteria consisting of the performances manifesting knowledge. But we have only the latter criteria – we do not determine whether someone knows something by reference to any kind of mental state, but only by reference to his evidently learning something (e.g. by being told) and by reference to those actions of his that manifest knowledge. To acquire information is not to change from a 'mental state of ignorance' to a 'mental state of knowing'. To know something to be thus-and-so is ability-like, hence more akin to a power or potentiality than to a state or actuality. To learn that something is so is to come to be able to do a wide range of things (to inform others, to answer certain questions, to correct others, to find, locate, identify, explain things, and so forth). To forget that something is so is not to cease to be in some state, but to cease to be able to do certain things. We ask *why* someone is in a given state, but *how* someone knows. Mental states can be interrupted and later resumed (as when one's intense concentration is interrupted by a telephone conversation and later resumed), and mental states such as intense anxiety or excitement are broken off by sleep. But one cannot interrupt someone in knowing, and one does not cease to know when one falls asleep. To ask someone 'How long have you known such-and-such?' is not like asking 'How long have you been concentrating (agitated, feeling nervous)?', but more like 'Since when have you been in a position to . . . ?', and akin to 'Since when have you been able to . . . ?'[1]

Knowledge makes it possible for one to act on the information known
If we know that things are thus-and-so, then it is possible for us to act on the basis of this information. The information that things are so may provide us with reasons, in the context of our projects, not only for acting, but also for thinking or feeling something or other (e.g. feeling pleased or angry). What one knows is what can occur as a premiss in one's reasoning from truths to the conclusions one may draw. For language-using creatures such as ourselves, to know where, when, who, what, whether or how . . . is, among other things, to be able to answer these questions. Of course, other animals, no less than human beings, know things, although their cognitive powers are less than ours; they can act for reasons, at best, only in an attenuated sense; and they cannot answer questions, but exhibit their knowledge only in their non-linguistic behaviour.

Being able to do something does not entail knowing
Although knowledge can be said to be ability-like, being able to do something is not necessarily to know anything. Indeed, it is not necessarily even knowing how to do anything. (These distinctions, as we shall see in §5.2, have an important bearing on neuroscientists' attempts to distinguish between declarative and non-declarative memory.) To justify these claims, we must clarify the relationship between being able to do something and knowing how to do something. Then we must shed some light on the relationship between knowing how to do something and knowing that something is so.

5.1.1 *Being able to* and *knowing how to*

Innate and acquired abilities; one-way and two-way abilities; active and passive powers
We may distinguish between innate abilities, such as the ability to breathe, to perceive or to move one's limbs, and acquired abilities, such as the ability to walk or talk. We may further distinguish between one-way abilities (or powers) and two-way abilities (or powers). All inanimate abilities are one-way powers, and may be active or passive. The ability of an acid to dissolve a metal is a one-way active power: if the conditions are appropriate, the sulphuric acid will dissolve the zinc. The acid is the active agent, but it has, as it were, no choice in the matter – it cannot refrain from dissolving the metal. The liability or susceptibility of zinc to dissolve in acid is a one-way

---

[1] For further discussion of the categorial characteristics of mental states, see §9.2.

passive power. Some of the abilities of animate creatures are one-way abilities: for example, the ability to see, to hear, or to feel pain. Others are two-way abilities, which the animal can exercise at will or refrain from exercising if it so chooses: for example, the ability to walk or to talk.

Abilities may be acquired through maturation or by learning
Acquired abilities may be gained simply through natural maturation (e.g. the ability of animals to engage in sexual intercourse) or through learning (which may or may not include training or teaching). Not all successful learning results in the possession of knowledge – it may result in the possession of an ability or a skill which does not involve knowing how to do anything. So, a child must learn, and indeed is taught, to be patient, or to be silent, but these do not involve acquisition of knowledge. The successful upshot of such learning is being able to do the relevant things, but not knowing, and hence remembering, the way to do them.

Knowing how to compared with being able to
What then distinguishes knowing how to V from merely being able to V? For us to speak of an animal's knowing how to V, its ability must be a two-way ability, which the animal can exercise or refrain from exercising as it pleases.[2] That is not sufficient, since the ability to walk, for example, is an acquired two-way ability; but, although we have to learn to walk, the upshot of learning to walk is being able to walk, not knowing how to walk. One may lose the ability to walk through paralysis, but one cannot forget (i.e. there is no such thing as forgetting) how to walk, and one cannot later be reminded or remember how to do it. To know how to do something differs from being able to do something inasmuch as knowing how to do something is knowing the way to do it (just as knowing when or where to do something is knowing the time and place to do it). To know the way to do something includes knowing the manner, means and method (where these are appropriate). Exercise of knowledge of the way to do something is plastic, adaptive and circumstance-sensitive. To know the way to do something typically involves knowing that it is done thus, and the 'thus' may, in the case of human beings, be stated or demonstrated.

Knowing how to do something is knowing the way to do it
One can learn how to do something by experience, trial and error, by being trained or taught, by being shown how to do it and, with human beings, by being told how to do it. What one knows how to do is something of which it makes sense to say that one has forgotten how to do it, that one remembers, recollects, or can be reminded how to do it. It also makes sense to say that one made a mistake in trying to do something one knows how to do, that one realized that one was doing it wrongly and that one tried to correct oneself. For to know how to do something is to know the way to do it, and knowing the way to do it implies an ability to distinguish between doing it correctly and doing it incorrectly. Of course, non-human animals cannot state or show how to do something. But an animal's knowledge of the way to do something – for example, a dog's knowing

---

[2] A very helpful discussion of *knowing how* is to be found in A. R. White, *The Nature of Knowledge* (Rowman and Littlefield, Totowa, NJ, 1982), pp. 14–29.

how to get home from a given point – is exhibited in the plasticity of the skill in response to obstructive circumstances, the recognition of error when it occurs, and its rectification in performance.

The relationship between knowing how to and being able to

So, one may be able to do something, although it would be wrong to say that one knows how to do it, and conversely, one may know how to do something but be unable to do it. (i) Being able to do something does not imply knowing how to do it in those cases in which the concept of knowledge (and hence too of remembering and forgetting) is simply inapplicable. It may be inapplicable because knowledge is irrelevant to the kind of ability in question (e.g. to feel the heat of the fire from three feet away – a one-way passive ability – or to walk or to be quiet – two-way abilities which involve no knowledge of a way of doing anything). It may be inapplicable because knowledge is irrelevant (because categorially inappropriate) to the type of possessor of the ability (e.g. a plant's ability to grow in the shade). (ii) Knowing how to do something does not imply being able to do it. For one may know how to do things for which one has lost the physical power or lacks the strength of will. The aged tennis coach may no longer be able to play tennis, but he surely knows how to, and one may know perfectly well how to lose weight, but be unable to.

Knowing how and knowing that: Ryle's error

We distinguish not only between being able to do something and knowing how to do something, but also between knowing how to do something and knowing that something is so. But it is mistaken to suppose, as Gilbert Ryle (who introduced and made much of the latter distinction) did,[3] that *knowing how* is always and essentially different from *knowing that*. *Knowing how* and *knowing that* are not so much two different forms which knowledge may take, as knowledge of two different kinds of thing. To know how to do something, as suggested, is to know the way to do it, and to know the way to do something is often to know, and to be able to say or show, that it is done thus-and-so.

5.1.2 Possessing Knowledge and Containing Knowledge

Knowledge acquisition

Knowledge may be acquired, for example, by active or passive perception, or by reasoning. But it may be given one in the form of the authoritative judgement or testimony of others. Indeed, it should always be borne in mind (but is often forgotten by epistemologists and by psychologists) that much of what a human being knows is not perceptual knowledge but transmitted knowledge, learnt from the written or spoken word of others. Of course, to acquire transmitted knowledge, one must be able to perceive – that is, to see (in order to read) and hear (in order to listen to what is said) – but what is learnt is not what is perceived (one sees the words one reads, but what one learns is the information they convey). Knowledge is not only *given*, in the form of passive perception or of information imparted

---

[3] G. Ryle, *Concept of Mind* (Hutchinson, London, 1949), ch. 2. For criticism of Ryle's distinction, see White, *Nature of Knowledge*, pp. 14–18, 22–8, to which we are indebted.

by others, it may also be *attained* by endeavour – by reasoning, or by discovery or detection, which may be the upshot of seeking, searching for, experimenting or trying to find out how things are. Further, it may also be *received*, without endeavour and independently of being given by others, by recognizing or noticing, becoming aware or conscious of something, or by realization, on the basis of information already possessed, that things are so. As we shall see in chapter 9, the distinction between knowledge attained by endeavour or given one by the word of others, on the one hand, and knowledge received in noticing, recognizing, becoming aware or realizing, on the other, is crucial for a correct grasp of the idea of becoming and then being conscious of something.

Knowledge and the mereological fallacy (LeDoux, Crick, Young, Zeki, Blakemore) — Again, it must be emphasized, it is the human being, not his brain, that knows that things are thus-and-so, knows how to do things, and possesses the abilities constitutive of knowing something. It makes no sense, save as a misleading figure of speech, to say, as LeDoux does, that it is 'possible for your brain to know that something is good or bad before it knows exactly what it is',[4] or for Crick to speak, as we have seen he does, of the brain's learning things about the outside world. It is a confusion to speak, as J. Z. Young does, of the brain's asking and answering questions,[5] and a muddle for Semir Zeki to suppose that the acquisition of knowledge is 'a primordial function of the brain',[6] since it is not the function of the brain at all. It is misguided of Colin Blakemore to write that 'Somehow the brain knows about the properties of the retina and fills in the missing information'.[7] A person who knows where the railway station is, what time the next train is, whether it is likely to be on time, who else might be on it, etc. can answer the corresponding questions. But there is no such thing as the brain knowing when . . . , where . . . , whether . . . , etc., and there is no such thing as the brain's answering such questions. It is not the brain, but the person whose brain it is, that acquires knowledge by perception, reasoning or testimony. A concept-exercising creature that can know things may be knowledgeable or ignorant, learned or untutored, an expert or a charlatan who pretends to know. But brains cannot be said to be knowledgeable, ignorant, learned, untutored, experts or charlatans – only human beings can be such things.

The brain cannot be said to contain knowledge, as books do, or to possess knowledge, as human beings do — It is equally confused to speak, as Young does, of the brain's containing knowledge and information, which is encoded in the brain 'just as knowledge can be recorded in books or computers'.[8] We may say of a book that it contains all the knowledge of a lifetime's work of a scholar, or of a filing cabinet that it contains all the available knowledge, duly card-indexed, about Julius Caesar. This means that the pages of the book or the cards in the filing cabinet have written on them *expressions* of a large number of known truths. In this sense, the brain *contains* no knowledge

---

[4] J. LeDoux, *The Emotional Brain* (Phoenix, London, 1998), p. 69.
[5] J. Z. Young, *Programs of the Brain* (Oxford University Press, Oxford, 1978), pp. 119 and 126.
[6] S. Zeki, 'Abstraction and idealism', *Nature*, 404 (April 2000), p. 547.
[7] C. Blakemore, 'The baffled brain', in R. L. Gregory and E. H. Gombrich (eds), *Illusion in Nature and Art* (Duckworth, London, 1973), p. 38.
[8] Young, *programs of the Brain*, p. 192.

whatsoever. There are no symbols in the brain that by their array express a single proposition, let alone a proposition that is known to be true.[9] Of course, in this sense a human being *contains* no knowledge either. To possess knowledge is not to contain knowledge. A person may possess, for example, a smattering of knowledge about seventeenth-century woodcuts, but he contains none; Hind's history of early woodcuts contains a great deal of such knowledge, but has none. The brain neither possesses nor contains any knowledge. Libraries, books, diaries, and index cards contain information – information that human beings can look up, learn, memorize and add to.

Brains do not contain or possess information

Similar considerations apply, as we saw in the last chapter, to the idea that the brain contains information. A great deal of information is contained in the *Encyclopaedia Britannica*. In that sense, there is none in the brain. Much information can be *derived* from a slice through a tree trunk or from a geological specimen – and so too from PET and fMRI scans of the brain's activities. But this is *not* information which the brain *has*. Nor is it *written in* the brain, let alone in the 'language of the brain',[10] any more than dendrochronological information about the severity of winters in the 1930s is written in the tree trunk in arboreal patois.

Misdescriptions of commissurotomy (Crick, Gazzaniga)

Bearing in mind the lessons derived from examination of the mereological fallacy in neuroscience, it should be immediately obvious that the common neuroscientific descriptions of the results of severing the corpus callosum and anterior commissure are again awry. After such 'split-brain' operations, patients exhibit dramatic forms of malfunctioning. This is commonly explained (e.g. by Crick) by reference to the alleged fact that 'one half of the brain appears to be almost totally ignorant of what the other half saw'. When the patient is asked to explain why he moved his left hand as he did, 'he will invent explanations based on what his left (speaking) hemisphere saw, not what his right hemisphere knew'.[11] As we have seen, Gazzaniga claims that 'the left brain, observing the left hand's response, interprets that response according to a context consistent with its sphere of knowledge'. But if it is senseless to ascribe knowledge to the brain, as opposed to the person, it is equally senseless to ascribe knowledge (or ignorance) to one hemisphere of the brain, let alone to suppose that the other hemisphere sees things. And it is incoherent to suppose that a hemisphere of the brain has a 'sphere of knowledge'. The forms of functional dissociation consequent on commissurotomy can readily be described without transgressing the bounds of sense in this way (see §14.3).

---

[9] The fact that a neural event is *correlated* with a perceived object does *not* imply that the neural event is a *symbol* of the object (or of anything else). There is no such thing as the brain's having, using or containing lexical symbols, i.e. signs with a rule-governed use among a community of speakers and a meaning which is given by customary explanations of meaning. And there is obviously no such thing as a brain's containing or using iconic symbols.

[10] Young, *Programs of the Brain*, passim. For a detailed analysis of Young's misconceived analogy between neural activity and language use, see P. M. S. Hacker, 'Languages, minds and brains', in C. Blakemore and S. Greenfield (eds), *Mindwaves* (Blackwell, Oxford, 1987), pp. 485–505.

[11] F. Crick, *The Astonishing Hypothesis* (Touchstone, London, 1995), p. 170.

5.2 Memory

Memory is a cognitive power of human beings, not of their nervous system (Milner, Squire and Kandel)

The faculty of memory is a cognitive power of human beings. Again, it is at best misleading to speak, as Milner, Squire and Kandel do, of the progress that has been achieved in our understanding of 'how the nervous system learns and remembers'.[12] For it is not the nervous system that learns or remembers anything at all, but the animal. And the achievements that can be hoped for are of understanding the neural processes that make it possible for animals to remember whatever they can remember.

Memory is the faculty for retention of knowledge; what is remembered need not be of the past, but must be something one previously knew or was aware of

Memory is the faculty for the *retention* of knowledge acquired. *Recollecting* is the bringing to mind of knowledge retained. It is logically possible to remember only what one previously *came to know* or *was aware of*. But *what* one remembers need have nothing to do with the past. For, apart from facts about the past that one remembers, one also learns and remembers facts concerning the present (e.g. where one's keys are), concerning the future (e.g. when the next train leaves), as well as general facts (e.g. laws of nature) that hold at all times, and truths of mathematics or logic that are atemporal.

Factual, experiential and objectual memory distinguished

One may distinguish among the forms which memory can take the following three. *Factual memory* is linguistically expressed by sentences in which the verb 'remember' takes as its grammatical object a that–clause: for example, 'I remember that the Battle of Hastings was fought in 1066.' *Experiential memory* is expressed by sentences in which the verb 'remember' is followed by a gerund which specifies a previous perceptual experience of the person: for example, 'I remember seeing . . .' (or 'hearing', 'feeling', etc.), as well as sentences of the form 'I remember *V*'ing . . .' and 'I remember being *V*'d' (where '*V*' is any verb signifying something the agent might do or undergo). Clearly, I may remember *that* I perceived something, did or underwent something, without remembering perceiving it, doing or undergoing it, although I cannot remember perceiving, doing or undergoing something unless I remember *that* I perceived, did or underwent it. So experiential memory implies factual memory, but not vice versa. *Objectual memory* is sometimes expressed by sentences in which the verb 'remember' is followed by a direct object signifying a perceptible thing or quality: for example, 'I remember her (her smile, the house) well', 'I remember the scent of jasmine (the colour of the wall, the taste of rasberries) clearly', where a contrast with mere factual memory is intended (I may remember *that* she had a sweet smile, but not be able to remember *it*; I may remember much *about* the house, but not be able to *visualize it*). *Sometimes* we use such sentences to indicate our ability to conjure up images (visual or auditory) of something previously perceived. Mnemonic imagery, in this sense, although it may be common, is not logically necessary

---

[12] Brenda Milner, Larry R. Squire and Eric R. Kandel, 'Cognitive neuroscience and the study of memory', *Neuron*, 20 (1998), p. 446.

for either factual memory or experiential memory. Moreover, having a mental image of something previously perceived is no more sufficient for remembering the object antecedently perceived than is having a photograph of it, since one must also remember what one's mental image (or photograph) is an image of. Memory of objects or qualities may involve any or all of the above forms.[13]

Remembering how and remembering that

Parallel to the previously discussed distinction between *knowing how* and *knowing that* we must distinguish between remembering how to do something and remembering that something is so. And just as *knowing how* is not always essentially distinct from *knowing that*, so too remembering how to do something is not always essentially distinct from remembering that something is so. For to remember how to do something is to retain one's previously acquired knowledge of the way to do it. Not to have forgotten the way to *V* is to remember that one *V*'s *thus* rather than *thus*. In many kinds of case, this is no different from remembering *that* the way to *V* is to do such-and-such (as is obviously the case in remembering how to open a combination lock, how to integrate, how to address the Pope, or how to spell 'Edinburgh').

5.2.1 Declarative and non-declarative memory

Neuroscientists' conception of non-declarative memory

The above classification bears on a distinction widely invoked by neuroscientists investigating the neural underpinnings of memory. The findings of Neal Cohen and Larry Squire 'suggested a fundamental distinction in the way all of us process and store information about the world'[14]: namely, between *declarative* and *non-declarative memory*.[15] Declarative memory is held to be 'what is ordinarily meant by the term memory'; it is 'propositional', it can be true or false, and it is involved 'in modelling the external world and storing representations about facts and episodes'.[16] Non-declarative memory is held to underlie 'changes in skilled behaviour and the ability to respond appropriately to stimuli through practice, as the result of conditioning or habit learning'. It is held to be involved in priming, in so-called habit memory ('acquired dispositions or tendencies that are specific

---

[13] For more detailed discussion, see N. Malcolm, 'Three forms of memory', in *Knowledge and Certainty* (Prentice-Hall, Inc., Englewood Cliffs, NJ, 1963), pp. 203–21.

[14] Milner, Squire and Kandel, 'Cognitive neuroscience and the study of memory', p. 450.

[15] It is striking that Milner, Squire and Kandel remark that before neuroscientists drew their distinction between declarative and non-declarative memory, 'similar ideas had been proposed by philosophers and psychologists on the basis of intuition and introspection' (ibid., p. 449). The philosopher they cite is indeed Ryle, and they refer explicitly to his distinction between knowing how and knowing that. To be sure, Ryle's distinction was not drawn on the basis of either intuition or introspection, but rather on the basis of grammar. But the neuroscientists seem unaware of the flaws in Ryle's sharp differentiation between the two. Like Ryle, they suppose that knowing how to *V* is the same as being able to *V*. They similarly assume that knowing how is never the same as knowing that. Being unaware of Ryle's mistakes, they repeat them.

[16] Milner, Squire and Kandel, 'Cognitive neuroscience and the study of memory', p. 450.

to a set of stimuli and that guide behaviour'), and in Pavlovian conditioning (both emotional conditioning and eyeblink reaction conditioning). All these different phenomena are deemed to be kinds of memory, because 'performance changes as the result of experience, which justifies the term memory'.[17] Many forms of non-declarative memory, such as habituation, sensitization and classical conditioning, are already, it is held, well developed in invertebrates.

Accordingly, the gill withdrawal reflex in *Aplysia* was found to be modifiable by habituation, dishabituation, sensitization, classical and operant conditioning. Similar investigations were carried out on the tail flick in crayfish, feeding in *Limax*, phototaxis in *Hermissenda*. These were held to show that 'non-declarative memory storage does not depend on specialized memory neurons or systems of neurons whose only function is to *store* rather than process information'.[18] Similar research on *Drosophila* was held to show that they 'can remember to avoid an odour that has been paired with an electric shock', but that accumulation of cAMP 'interferes with their ability to acquire and store new information'.[19]

Misconceptions about 'declarative memory'

Valuable although this research undoubtedly is, most of it is not research on memory in any sense of the word, and the extent to which it bears on actual memory has to be demonstrated. For the conceptual framework is badly confused. We shall comment below on the misconception that we *store* information about the world in our brains. We shall not comment on the misconception that factual memory is involved in 'modelling the external world and storing representations about facts and episodes', save to remind neuroscientists that ordinary people do not go in for 'modelling the external world', unless they are sculptors, and that they 'store representations about facts and episodes' primarily when they stick photographs into the family album. It should, however, be noted that it is misleading to say that declarative memory is 'what is ordinarily meant by the term memory'. It would be more accurate to say that declarative memory is *included* in what is ordinarily meant by the term 'memory', for in the ordinary use of 'memory' we include both *remembering that* and *remembering how* as well as *remembering V'ing* and *remembering O* (i.e. experiential and objectual memory). It is claimed that what is called 'conscious recollection' is central to declarative memory but inapplicable to non-declarative memory.[20] But it is unclear what is meant by 'conscious recollection'. It is possible that the phrase is being used to suggest that whenever one remembers that something is so, one is aware of the past occasion on which one acquired the knowledge in question; or it may mean that whenever one remembers, one is aware that one is remembering. But it is false that whenever one remembers a piece of information previously learnt – for example, that the Battle of Hastings was in 1066 or that $F = ma$ – one remembers the event of learning it.

---

[17] Ibid., p. 450. Were this correct, then limping as a result of injury, or impairment of hearing as a result of over-exposure to noise, would be forms of memory.
[18] Ibid., p. 454.
[19] Ibid., p. 457.
[20] Ibid., p. 451.

And it is also false that whenever one remembers some fact (as when one remembers to turn off the light,[21] or when, having spoken to Jack earlier, one remarks to one's wife that one is going to meet Jack tomorrow), one is aware or conscious of remembering anything. It would be equally confused to suppose that when one exercises one's non-declarative memory, no conscious recollection is ever involved. For *if* non-declarative memory includes remembering how to do something, then one very often remembers how to do something by calling to mind the episode in which one was taught to do it, and one may well, in exercising one's memory of how to do something, be aware of the fact that one is trying to do so. Of course, neither is necessary. But then they are not necessary for declarative factual memory either. These conceptual confusions are easily rectified.

Misconceptions about
non-declarative memory

The confusions about non-declarative memory, however, are deeper. For the habituation, sensitization, desensitization, classical conditioning, etc. of invertebrates, as well as the conditioned eyeblink responses and fear reactions of mammals, are not forms of memory at all. The animal may indeed have come to respond in certain ways to certain kinds of stimuli, and its responses may change – for example, accelerate – as a result of continued exposure to a stimulus. So, one might say that the animal, as a result of experience and habituation, has learnt to react more rapidly or has acquired the ability to react more rapidly. But that does *not* warrant characterizing the animal as remembering anything. For nothing *cognitive* is involved here. Not all learning is acquisition of knowledge, for sometimes it is merely acquisition of non-cognitive abilities. In the case at hand, the animal learnt neither that something is so nor the way to do anything. An accelerated reflex or a conditioned reaction is not a form of *knowledge*. But memory is the *retention of knowledge acquired*, and remembering to *V* is the *use of knowledge retained*. One can indeed condition insects and molluscs to avoid a certain stimulus, but that, by itself, does not show that any knowledge was either acquired or retained. The primitive animals in question cannot be said to have come to know that things are thus-and-so, nor can they be said to have learnt the way to do anything. It is surely misconceived to hold that *Drosophila* 'can remember to avoid an odor that has been paired with an electric shock',[22] for all that has been shown is that *Drosphilas*, as a result of conditioning, learn to avoid (i.e. acquire a disposition to avoid) an odour that has been paired with an electric shock. They can be said to have acquired *a primitive one-way ability*, but that is not sufficient to demonstrate any form of memory whatsoever. Indeed, even in the case of a mouse that is conditioned to fear an electric shock on hearing a tone, there is no reason to take the mouse to have acquired any knowledge. All that has been shown is that conditioning produces a regular, conditioned fear reaction.

Whether the neural phenomena that have been discovered to accompany such forms of conditioned reaction also characterize cases of genuine memory is possible, but it has to

---

[21] To remember to turn off the light is to turn off the light because one knows (has not forgotten) that one must do so. Nothing need cross one's mind when one is doing so, but if asked why one did so, one would explain that it is one's obligation, that one has to do it.

[22] Ibid., p. 457.

Whether the neural accompaniments of conditioned reactions also accompany genuine memory has to be shown

be shown to be so. What is clear is that these studies are not actually studies of memory at all. It is argued that the findings in question 'illustrate that non-declarative memory storage does not depend on specialized neurons or systems of neurons whose only function is to *store* rather than process information'.[23] But this is doubly mistaken. For, first, no form of *memory* is involved in the phenomena investigated. And secondly, there is, as we shall argue below, no form of *storage of information* in the brain.

5.2.2 Storage, retention and memory traces

LeDoux's incorrect supposition that memory must be of the past

Failure to clarify even the basic contours of the concept of memory is responsible for much further unclarity in neuroscientific reflection on this crucial capacity. So it is confused to suggest, for example, as does LeDoux, that 'to remember is to be conscious of some past experience'.[24] For, first, what one remembers need not be anything past – it can be present, future or timeless, although, of course, one must have learnt such facts in the past. Second, what one remembers *need not* be an experience at all, and *is not* when what is remembered is, for example, the date of the Battle of Hastings. Third, to remember the date of Hastings, who Caesar's wife was, or the way home is not to be conscious of 1066, of Calpurnia, or of the way home. Moreover, even when remembering does take the form of experiential memory, to remember *V*'ing – that is, a past experience – is not to be conscious of that past experience; nor is remembering feeling ill last month to be conscious of feeling ill last month. It is merely to know now that one was ill then, and to know it *because* one then felt ill (and not because, having forgotten the episode, one was subsequently told that one previously felt ill).

Mnemonic success, failure, error and delusion distinguished

Just as one can perceive, fail to perceive, misperceive or suffer from hallucinations, so too one can remember, fail to remember, misremember or suffer from mnemonic delusions. If one comes to know that things are so, and does not forget what one learnt, then one can be said to remember that things are so. One may be altogether unable to recollect something one previously knew, and such failure of memory may be a temporary lapse or it may be permanent. If one errs correctably in one's belief concerning something one previously knew, one misremembers. But one may also labour under a mnemonic delusion regarding one's own past experiences (as the Prince Regent did in thinking that he remembered fighting at Waterloo) – in which case what one believes is *so* out of line that it no longer amounts to a correctable *error*, but to a form of derangement. Much more commonly, one may think one remembers *V*'ing, but come to realize that one remembers only *that* one *V*'d – here one confuses experiential with factual memory, typically as a result of hearing the tale of one's *V*'ing repeated numerous times by one's parents.

---

[23] Ibid., p. 454.
[24] LeDoux, *Emotional Brain*, p. 181.

Memory is knowledge retained, not knowledge stored

Memory, as we have emphasized, is knowledge *retained* (including the knowledge that one perceived, did or underwent this or that in the past, which may take the form of factual memory, of experiential memory, and may or may not involve mnemonic imagery). But it is a confusion to suppose, as do Squire and Kandel,[25] that memory is knowledge *stored*, let alone *stored in the brain*. It is confused to claim, as Milner, Squire and Kandel do, that declarative and non-declarative memories 'are stored in different brain areas',[26] for there is no such thing as storing memories in the brain. Rather, the capacity to remember various kinds of things is *causally dependent* on different brain areas and on synaptic modifications in these areas.

The origins of the ideas of memory traces and memory storage (LeDoux)

The notion of storage and the associated idea of memory traces long antedate neuroscience. They began life as metaphors (of wax tablets) in Plato, and as a rudimentary speculative theory in Aristotle, who conceived of memory as the storage of an impression of a percept in the heart, functionally dependent upon the humidity of the tissues. The idea of memory as a 'storehouse of ideas' runs through the empiricist tradition of the seventeenth, eighteenth and nineteenth centuries. Indeed, this conception continues to cause confusion, the metaphor being taken to be what it is merely a metaphor for. So, for example, LeDoux recently listed an array of things one might be said to have learnt and not forgotten, and queries 'What do all of these have in common?', to which he replies, 'They are things I've learned and stored in my brain'.[27] But one may surely be sceptical about the intelligibility of storing the things he cites, such as the smell of banana pudding, the meaning of the words 'halcyon days', and the rules of dominoes, *in the brain*. One can store smells in bottles, write down the meanings of words in dictionaries, and codify the rules of games in documents which can then be stored – but one cannot *store* smells, meanings of words, or rules *in a brain*! Of course, what LeDoux means is that these are things that he can remember – and that is right; where he errs is in the supposition that in order to be able to remember them, he must have stored them in his brain (or anywhere else).

The temptation to think that what is stored in the mind or brain is a representation

It is deeply tempting to insist that while what is stored is obviously not what is remembered (e.g. smells, meanings of words, or rules of games) it is a *representation* of what is remembered. One is inclined to think that the knowledge antecedently acquired *must* be stored in one's mind or brain, in the form of either an image or an *encoded description* representing what is remembered. If it were not, it seems, one would not be able to remember what one remembers – the knowledge would be *unavailable* to one. The classical empiricists tended to think that what is stored is stored in the mind, and the manner in which it is stored is as a mental image or picture that

[25] L. R. Squire and E. R. Kandel, *Memory: From Mind to Molecules* (Scientific American Library, New York, 1999), pp. 211–14.

[26] Milner, Squire and Kandel, 'Cognitive neuroscience and the study of memory', p. 463.

[27] LeDoux, *Emotional Brain*, p. 179.

represents or is a copy of the original experience. Neuroscientists think that what is stored is stored in the brain, and the manner in which it is stored is given by a pattern of synaptic connections with efficacies that lead to the excitation of certain neurons under certain conditions, which excitation represents or encodes the original experience. Gazzaniga, Mangun and Ivry, for example, contend that

> *Encoding* refers to processing information to be stored. The encoding stage has two separate steps: *acquisition* and *consolidation*. Acquisition registers inputs in sensory buffers and sensory analysis stages, while consolidation creates a stronger representation over time. *Storage*, the result of acquisition and consolidation, creates and maintains a permanent record. Finally, *retrieval* utilises stored information to create a conscious representation or to execute a learned behaviour like a motor act.[28]

We shall examine these pervasive ideas in a moment. But simply seeing the analogy between the classical empiricist conception and the current neuroscientific one should be enough to put us on our guard.

James's conception of memory traces in the brain

Unsurprisingly, with the development of neurophysiology, the obscure idea of storing mental images *in the mind*, and the idea that these images are *unconscious* until recalled, fell from favour. In its place, the conception of brain traces became popular. At the end of the nineteenth century James wrote:

> The *retention* of *n* [the previously experienced event which is now remembered], it will be observed, is no mysterious storing up of an 'idea' in an unconscious state. It is not a fact of the mental order at all. It is a purely physical phenomenon, a morphological feature, the presence of these 'paths', namely, in the finest recesses of the brain's tissue. The recall or recollection, on the other hand, is a *psycho-physical* phenomenon, with both a bodily and a mental side. The bodily side is the functional excitement of the tracts and paths in question; the mental side is the conscious vision of the past occurrence, and the belief that we experienced it before.[29]

It should be noted that, according to James (in this passage), the memory trace ('tract' or 'path') is not *a condition* of retaining the knowledge acquired – that is, a condition of being able to do something – it *is* the storage of that knowledge ('The retention . . . is a purely physical phenomenon, a morphological feature'). This, as we shall see, fails to distinguish the retention of the abilities of which knowing something consists from the neural conditions for possession of those abilities, and from the storage of information in inscribed or otherwise recorded form. The background presupposition of James's reasoning is that remembering is repeating a past experience in attenuated form 'in memory' – 'the

---

[28] M. S. Gazzaniga, G. R. Mangun and R. B. Ivry, *Cognitive Neuroscience: The Biology of the Mind* (Norton, New York, 1998), pp. 247f. The equivocation over the word 'representation' is noteworthy.
[29] W. James, *The Principles of Psychology* (Holt, New York 1890), vol. 1, p. 655.

conscious vision of the past occurrence', as he puts it. This is part of the empiricist legacy, according to which to remember is to revive in one's mind a faint copy (an 'idea') of a previous experience (an 'impression'). The possibility of reproducing a facsimile of a past experience thus can be explained, James conjectures, if the original experience left a 'path' or 'tract' – that is, a brain trace – which, if excited again, causes the recurrence of a faint copy of the antecedent experience together with a belief that one has 'experienced it before'.

Köhler's conception of memory traces

The idea was repeated, with modifications, by such distinguished Gestalt psychologists as Koffka and Köhler, and became a commonplace among neuroscientists. The basic picture, which, as we shall see in a moment, informs neuroscientific reflection to this day, was nicely elaborated by Köhler:

> What does recognition mean? It means that a present fact, usually a perceptual one, makes contact with a corresponding one in memory, a trace, a contact which gives the present perception the character of being known or familiar. But memory contains a tremendous number of traces, all of them representations of previous experiences which must have been established by the processes accompanying such earlier experiences. Now, why does the present perceptual experience make contact with the *right* earlier experience? This is an astonishing achievement. Nobody seems to doubt that the *selection* is brought about by the similarity of the present experience and the experience of the corresponding earlier fact. But since this earlier experience is not present at the time, we have to assume that the trace of the earlier experience resembles the present experience, and that it is the similarity of our present experience (or the corresponding cortical process) and that trace which makes the selection possible.[30]

And again:

> All sound theories of memory, of habit, and so forth, must contain hypotheses about memory traces as physiological facts. Such theories must also assume that the characteristics of traces are more or less akin to those of the processes by which they have been established. Otherwise, how could the accuracy of recall be explained, which in a great many cases is quite high.[31]

Anyone holding this conception is committed to the thought that an original experience created a brain trace, which *represents* that experience. Recognition is a feeling of familiarity in response to an object perceived, caused by the excitation of a trace, which is itself caused by the neural stimulus which resembles the original cortical process. Recollection is a matter of *being reminded* of the antecedent experience by a current experience which resembles it in producing a brain trace that corresponds (at least in part) to the trace

[30] W. Köhler, *The Task of Gestalt Psychology* (Princeton University Press, Princeton, 1969), p. 122; quoted in N. Malcolm, *Memory and Mind* (Cornell University Press, Ithaca, NY, 1977), p. 192.
[31] W. Köhler, *Gestalt Psychology* (Liveright, New York, 1947), p. 252; quoted in Malcolm, *Memory and Mind*, p. 192.

already laid down. Recalling something is a causal consequence of the excitation, by a partly corresponding neural stimulus, of the very same trace as was laid down by the original experience. This thought, as we shall see, continues to inform neuroscientific research on memory.

Squire's and Kandel's conception of memory storage and memory traces   Squire and Kandel elaborate the Jamesian conception with the sophistication of late twentieth-century neuroscience. Conscious declarative memory, they claim, 'provides the possibility of re-creating in memory a specific episode from the past'. The 'starting point' is the set of cortical sites that were engaged when one perceived whatever one perceived. The consequent memory 'uniquely depends on the convergence of input from each of these distributed cortical sites into the medial temporal lobe and ultimately into the hippocampus'. This convergence, they claim, 'establishes a flexible representation', so that one can remember the object perceived and the episode of perceiving it. 'The resulting memories are stored as changes in strength at many synapses within a large ensemble of interconnected neurons.' Furthermore, 'the stored information in its specifics is determined by the *location* of the synaptic changes', although, they admit, 'we still know relatively little about how and where memory storage occurs'. Nevertheless, they have no doubts that what they call 'declarative information' is stored in the brain.[32] This stored information enables one to 're-create in memory' a past episode.

Glynn's conception   Ian Glynn has recently articulated part of the present picture thus:

> Since the episodes that give rise to memories involve a variety of perceptions, it seems likely that the laying down of such memories involves nerve cells in the association areas and in secondary or higher order cortical areas concerned with the different senses. . . . It is also likely that recalling memories involves recreating something like the original pattern of activity in those same sets of cells, or at least some of them. . . . Initially then, both the hippocampal zone and the neocortical zone must act together. Eventually, when consolidation is complete, the memories are stored in such a fashion that they are available without the involvement of the hippocampal zone, implying that storage is then wholly in the neocortical zone.[33]

It should be noted that the thought that recollecting involves re-creating a part of the original pattern of neural activity follows both James and Köhler. And presumably the

---

[32] Squire and Kandel, *Memory*, pp. 212f.

[33] I. Glynn, *An Anatomy of Thought* (Weidenfeld and Nicolson, London, 1999), p. 329. Glynn is confused, however, about the subject of learning and remembering. He writes, 'what is clear is that at the cellular and sub-cellular level machinery exists that is capable not only of simple logical operations but also of being modified by previous experience so that its behaviour changes. It is this machinery that forms the basis of the ability of networks of nerve cells to learn and to remember' (ibid., p. 327). Of course, cellular machinery is not capable of logical operations in any literal sense – cells cannot transform propositions in accordance with rules. And it is not networks of nerve cells that remember anything, but human beings, who are able to remember what they remember in virtue of presumed changes to networks of cells in their brain.

motivation for this hypothesis is that it seems to offer the hope of an explanation of the possibility of accurate recollection, on the assumption that recollection is a phenomenon of 're-creating in memory a specific episode from the past' (as Squire and Kandel put it). For the activation of the 'trace', like the movement of a stylus along the grooves of a gramophone record, is conceived to 're-create' the original experience 'in memory' (ideas of memory being thought to be, as the empiricists held, faint copies of the original impressions of which they are ideas).

Bennett's, Gibson's and Robinson's model of associative memory Building on the idea that recalling memories re-creates something like the original pattern of neural excitation, Bennett, Gibson and Robinson constructed a model of the mechanism of the putative associative memory network in the hippocampus. The fundamental idea is as follows: associative memory is construed as the disposition of a set of neurons (which previously fired according to a given pattern in response to a given input) to repeat the firing pattern when just part of the pattern is fed into them. If there are x neurons in the circuit, then these can be joined with connections that have such properties that a very large number of different patterns of inputs can use different overlapping sets of these x neurons, with each of these sets being made to fire when only a subset of the original input to the circuit is presented. This might be called 'a memorizing circuit'. This model is invoked to explain the neural basis for human memory. So, it is claimed,

> Memories are stored at the recurrent collateral synapses using a two-valued Hebbian. . . . The recall of a memory begins with the firing of a set of CA 3 pyramidal neurons that overlap with the memory to be recalled as well as the firing of a set of pyramidal neurons not in the memory to be recalled . . . The CA 3 recurrent potential network is shown to retrieve memories under specific conditions of the setting of the membrane potential of the pyramidal neurons by inhibitory interneurons. . . . The number of memories which can be stored and retrieved without degradation is primarily a function of the number of active neurons when a memory is recalled and the degree of connectivity in the network.[34]

The account provides a formal model of the brain traces envisaged by James and others.

Four questionable ideas However, a number of questionable ideas is involved in the received conception:

1   It is supposed that when we perceive something and remember what we thereby learnt, then something is *stored*.
2   What is stored is a memory, which *represents* the original perceptual experience.
3   The memory is *laid down* in such-and-such parts of the brain, in the form of changes in strength at synapses. So the neurons contain a *representation* of the original experience.
4   Recollection involves re-creating the original pattern of activity in the relevant neurons. In particular, being reminded of something (associative memory) involves having an

---

[34] M. R. Bennett, W. G. Gibson and J. Robinson, 'Dynamics of the CA 3 pyramidal neuron auto-associative memory network in the hippocampus', *Philosophical Transactions of the Royal Society*, **B** 334 (1994) pp. 167f.

experience which bears some similarity to the antecedent experience in which one acquired the information of which one is reminded by the associative experience. For recollecting results from stimulating the original memory trace by a neural input of a part of the original pattern of neural excitation.

These four claims are disputable, and we shall raise some doubts and questions about them.

Retention and storage distinguished

(1)   The thought that to remember is to store something confuses retention with storage. To remember is to retain. But although storage may sometimes imply retention, retention does not imply storage. Memory, being the retention of knowledge acquired, is the retention of an ability to just the extent that knowledge itself is an ability – but it is not the storage of an ability. One may acquire and retain an ability, but that does not imply storage. For there is no such thing as *storing* an ability, even though there is such a thing as retaining the neural structures that are causal conditions for the possession of an ability.

The supposition that if one remembers, then one *must* have stored a representation rests on the idea that unless there were a stored representation, the knowledge in question would not be available to one. How could one remember unless it is 'written down' in encoded form? Encoding, as Gazzaniga, Mangun and Ivry argued (see p. 160), is processing information into a form that will ensure that 'a permanent record' will be maintained. *Retrieval*, which presumably means *remembering*, 'creates a conscious representation' by utilizing the 'stored information'.

Neural storage of semantic representations makes no sense

But that is a confusion. Writing things down is indeed a way of storing information (as long as one remembers how to read). Pictures do remind one of what one has seen (as long as one remembers what the pictures are pictures of). But the idea that in order to remember, there must be a *neural* record stored in the brain is incoherent. For even if there were such a 'record', it would not be *available* to a person in the sense in which his diary or photograph album is available to him – after all, a person cannot see into his own brain, and cannot read Neuralese. Moreover, the idea that there must be a stored memory which is available to a person and is a necessary condition of his being able to remember *presupposes* memory (in two different ways), and cannot explain it. For were such a record available to one, one would have to *remember* how to read it, just as one can make use of one's diary only if one remembers how to read. Similarly, one can use one's photograph album as an *aide-mémoire* only if one remembers what the photographs are photographs of. The idea of a store of knowledge makes sense only if the store is indeed available to one, and one can read or recognize the 'representation' – which is obviously not the case when it is supposed that the relevant information is 'stored' in the brain. The idea of neural storage of *representations* (in the semantic or iconic sense) is incoherent. But a neural representation in the non-semantic, non-iconic sense – that is, a causal correlate – is not a form of storing *information* and does not involve any *encoding*. (A tree does not store information about the annual rainfall in its trunk, and does not encode the rainfall in its growth bands, although *we* can *derive* such information from examination of a slice through its trunk. However, we do not derive any information whatsoever from any neural representations (in the non-semantic sense) that may be in our own brains.)

To remember is not to store any-thing; one cannot store information in one's brain

If one perceives or learns that things are thus-and-so, one has come to know how things are. One may remember *what* one has thus learnt, retain the information one acquired – that is, continue to possess the diffuse abilities constitutive of knowing things to be thus. To 'retain' here simply means that one once knew and has not ceased to know, that one acquired the ability, for example, to answer the question whether . . . or where . . . or when . . . and has not lost it, that it became possible for one to act on the information that things are so, and that it is still possible for one to do so, since one has not forgotten that things are so. Nothing is implied about *storage* of information.[35] To remember that *p* is to *possess* the information that *p*, but it is not to *store* or *contain* the information that *p*. One stores the information that *p* if, for example, one writes it down, and stores the inscription in a filing cabinet or computer, which then contains it (but does not possess it). Indeed, the storage of information does not imply the mnemonic retention of that information – there is much stored in one's filing cabinet, diary or card index which one has long since forgotten. But one *cannot*, save metaphorically, store information in one's head, and one's head, unlike one's diary, contains no information.

Similarly, if one perceives an object, place or person M, and one does not forget M, then one will recognize M if one encounters it or him again. One's remembering M may therefore include, apart from facts about M, also a recognitional ability. But to remember M well, to be able to recognize M (or a picture of M) does not imply that one has stored anything. It implies the acquisition and retention of a recognitional ability. What the neural prerequisites of this are merit investigation.

What is stored is supposed to be a memory, which is a representation of an antecedent perceptual episode

(2)   When neuroscientists invoke the notion of storage, their thought is apparently that (a) what is stored when one remembers something is a memory, (b) this stored item is a representation, and (c) what it represents is the original perceptual episode. This is anything but clear.

A memory is not a representation

First, we speak of 'a memory' and of having 'many happy (or sad) memories' of something or other. Thus used, the expression 'a memory' typically signifies *what is remembered* when one remembers *that such-and-such* or *having such-and-such an experience*. We say such things as 'My memory is that (things are so)', which means much the same as 'As I remember . . . (things are so)', or 'As far as I can remember . . .'. We say 'I have a dim memory of . . . (Euclidean geometry, Toledo, my grandfather)', which means much the same as 'I remember . . . but dimly'. So *a memory* is an item of information (or putative information) that such-and-such or concerning this or that (or that one had such-and-such an experience), previously acquired and not forgotten. In so far as this is what is meant by 'a memory', it is evident that a memory is not a *representation* of what is remembered, any more than a belief is a

---

[35] For a more detailed discussion, see Malcolm, *Memory and Mind*, part 2.

representation of what is believed. But one might say that the *verbal expression* of what is remembered is such a representation.

One cannot store what is remembered, but only a representation of it

Secondly, a memory – that is, what is remembered, namely *that such-and-such* or *having such-and-such an experience* – is not even a candidate for storage. For there is no such thing as storing *that such-and-such*, let alone storing *having an experience*; at most one might store an inscription which expresses what is remembered or a picture which represents what was experienced. But it would be absurd to suppose that what is allegedly stored in the brain is an English (or any other) *sentence or inscription* or an array of *pictures* (like a photograph album).[36]

What is remembered need not be the episode of knowledge acquisition

Thirdly, the idea that what is remembered when one remembers something is necessarily an original perceptual episode is mistaken. As we have noted, what we remember need not be anything past. We have all long since forgotten how we acquired most of the knowledge we possess. In order to be able to remember the myriad facts we know, we need not, and typically do not, recollect the episode on the occasion of which we acquired the information in question. When we learn by reading or by being told, for example, what we typically remember is *what* we read or were told, not the reading or the telling of it. But neuroscientists seem to suppose that *the original episode of knowledge acquisition* must be 'registered' in the brain in the form of a representation. For the excitation of this representation allegedly explains three things. First, it seemingly explains the aetiology of remembering when one is reminded of something previously learnt. The current stimulus, which causes one to remember (i.e. reminds one of what one then remembers), produces a neural correlate which is the same as part of the neural pattern which was laid down by the original episode. That is why it reminds one of the antecedent experience. Secondly, it explains the phenomenon of remembering. For the stimulus excites the very same neural structure which has 'stored the memory', and that excitation

---

[36] Even if remembering involved reproducing mental images of previously perceived scenes, one would still have to *remember* what the images were images of. Antonio Damasio holds that remembering involves not exact reproductions, but rather reconstructions, of images that are approximations to their originals. Remembering, he suggests, takes the form of 'conjur[ing] up, in our mind's eye or ear, approximations of images we previously experienced'. These explicitly recalled mental images 'arise from transient synchronous activation of neural firing patterns largely in the same early sensory cortices where the firing patterns corresponding to perceptual representations once occurred' (*Descartes' Error: Emotion, Reason and the Human Brain* (Papermac, London, 1996), pp. 100f.). To be sure, those of us who are good at producing mental images may visualize objects, scenes and events we wish to remember. But much of what we remember could not be pictured in principle (e.g. that all Xs are F, or that no Xs are F, that if *p* then *q*, that had it been the case that *p* then it might have been the case that *q*, why such-and-such is thus-and-so, A's reason for thinking that *p*, and so on and so forth, through a myriad cases that spell bankruptcy for the imagist theory of memory), and anything we visualize in the course of remembering presupposes memory and cannot explain it, since we must remember what our mental image is an image of. We shall discuss these matters in detail in the next chapter.

causes the person to have a memory experience. Thirdly, it allegedly explains why repetition strengthens or reinforces memory. For changes in strength at synapses increase with repetition.[37] We shall investigate these suppositions in a moment.

The idea of a neural representation is questionable

(3)   Given that what is allegedly 'stored' or 'laid down' in the brain is not (and could not be) a verbal report or pictorial representation of an antecedent experience, it seems that the perceptions that 'give rise to memories' must be *encoded* in the nerve cells and synapses, and that this *neural representation* is what is stored. But this idea too is questionable.

The idea of encoding a perception is questionable

First, perceiving something does indeed lead to neural changes, but it is altogether obscure what might be meant by the suggestion that *a perception* is *encoded*. One can *describe*, in words, what one perceives and one's perceiving of it – and then *encode the descriptions*, assuming that one knows the transformation rules. But there is no such thing as encoding a perception. Nor is there any such thing as *encoding* something in the brain (at any rate, not in the ordinary sense of 'encode') – for there is no such thing as a neural *code*. For a code is a method of encrypting a linguistic expression (or any other form of representation) according to conventional rules.[38]

The idea that a neural configuration can represent a remembered fact is questionable

Secondly, it is unclear what is meant by the claim that a neural configuration may *represent* a memory. Suppose the relevant memory is that one was told that the Battle of Hastings was fought in 1066. What would count as a neural representation of this remembered fact? It is unclear whether, in the requisite sense of 'representation', *anything* could count as a representation, short of *an array of symbols belonging to a language*. Nothing that one might find in the brain could possibly be a representation of the fact that one was told that Hastings was fought in 1066 in the sense in which the English sentence 'I was told that Hastings was fought in 1066' can be said to be such a representation. But, of course, it may well be the case that but for certain neural configurations or strengths of synaptic connections, one would not be able to remember the date of the Battle of Hastings and would not recollect being told it. But it does not follow from that idea that what one remembers must be, as it were, written down in the brain, or that there must be some neural configuration in the brain from which one could in principle read off what is remembered. Nor can it be said that this neural configuration *is* a memory.

It might, however, be supposed that the original perceptual episode must have caused a certain neural configuration in the brain, and the excitation of this pattern is precisely what causes one *to have the experience of remembering* whatever one remembers about the original episode. But even this relatively modest idea is problematic.

---

[37] To recast the idea in the earlier jargon of engrams, the deeper the engram is 'engraved' on the brain, the more readily and vividly the memory it encodes can be invoked.

[38] We have all got used to the metaphorical use of the term 'code' in the phrase 'the genetic code'. It is a metaphor that has been more damaging than illuminating.

The idea that a reactivated neural trace causes a mnemonic experience rests on six questionable assumptions

(4)   The idea that when one remembers something on a given occasion, the brain must reactivate the pattern of neural excitation that was stimulated by the antecedent perceptual experience in which one came to know what one is now recollecting, rests upon a number of questionable assumptions:

i.   Currently remembering something is a (mnemonic) experience variously described as 're-creating in memory' a past episode, 'the conscious vision of a past occurrence', or 'creating a conscious representation'. (In eighteenth-century jargon, it is having a current idea corresponding to an antecedent impression.)

ii.   What is remembered is a past experience or some feature of a past experience.

iii.   Currently remembering is triggered by a reminding experience. The reminding experience in certain respects resembles the past experience which is remembered.

    Correlative to these assumptions, current neuroscientific speculation adds a series of neuroscientific assumptions:

i′.   Currently recollecting something is the re-excitation of a neural firing pattern. It is this which causally explains the person's having the mnemonic experience.

ii′.   The original experience now remembered laid down a neural trace (a neural structure which, when excited, will repeat the pattern of firing generated by the original experience). The reactivation of the memory trace causes a mnemonic experience (the 'conscious memory event'), which 'reproduces in memory' the original perceptual experience or some part thereof. (It is an idea or faint copy of the original impression.)

iii′. The current reminder triggers the brain trace, and hence the mnemonic experience, by a pattern of neural input which is part of the original pattern generated by the past perceptual experience. The similarity between the current memory experience and the original experience of which it is the memory is explained by its being caused by the reactivation of the brain trace or pattern of neural firing, which was laid down by the original perceptual experience.

    This reasoning, though tempting, is flawed. We have already noted that what is remembered need not be anything past. The information acquired in the past need not be about the past, and one typically does not remember the occasion of its acquisition. All that is logically required for remembering in such cases is that one came to know something and that one still knows it (i.e. one has not forgotten the knowledge one acquired).

To remember something need involve no reproductive representation

Now a further two points need to be stressed. First, currently remembering something need involve no reproductive 'representation'. To remember that *p* (e.g. that the Battle of Hastings was fought in 1066, that one did such-and-such last week, that 25^2 = 625), to remember perceiving, doing or undergoing something, to remember M (a person, place, object or event), or to remember how to do something need not involve reproducing a 'representation', either in the form of a mental image or in the form of a sentence spoken aloud or in the imagination. So, for example, to remember the way home need involve no mental imagery, but only the exercise of the ability to go home without losing one's way. To remember how to drive need involve nothing more than exercising the ability to drive. To remember what someone said need involve nothing more than acting or reacting on the grounds of the information conveyed by the utterance. To remember perceiving, doing or undergoing something is not essentially an ability to 're-create' the experience in the imagination. It is, of course, exhibited in recounting the experience; but this is not necessary for currently remembering it. It is, as is evident from the above examples, sufficient that one act (or react) *for the reason* that one previously perceived, was told, did or underwent such-and-such. (And here, the reason is not a *cause*, but a *justification*, which one might adduce in answer to the question of why one did what one did.)

Remembering something is no more an experience than is knowing something

Secondly, remembering what we remember on a given occasion is no more *an experience* than is knowing what we know on a given occasion. This should not be surprising, since to remember that something is so just is to know something previously learnt and not forgotten. Of course, I may suddenly remember something, and this may be accompanied by various experiences (e.g. a feeling of relief, or having a mental image). But remembering something on an occasion (like knowing something) is not essentially a *phenomenon*; that is, it is not akin to a feeling about which one may ask 'What did it feel like?' Rather, there may be various *manifestations* of the fact that I remember something, none of which *is* the remembering. If you cancel this evening's meeting, there are indefinitely many things that I, remembering that the meeting is cancelled, may consequently do. I may go home, go to the cinema, phone any number of friends and arrange to dine together, stay on at the office until late, go to the bookshop to buy a book to read in the evening, and so forth. All these possibilities involve my remembering that the meeting is cancelled. But in none need I 're-create in memory' your cancelling this evening's meeting, or even say to myself that you have done so. All that is necessary is that part of my reason for doing what I do is that you have cancelled the meeting – and that is not an experience.

So remembering need not involve exciting a brain trace in order to re-create a reproductive mnemonic experience

If remembering something need not involve remembering the past episode in which the relevant information was acquired, it clearly need not involve exciting a hypothesized brain trace or pattern of neural firing *in order to re-create* 'in memory' a reproduction of the original episode. And if memory need involve no reproductive mnemonic experience, it is not necessary that the hypothesized brain trace be reactivated in order to produce the relevant experience. Of course, it is tempting to think that if one learnt that *p* (e.g. that the Battle of Hastings was fought in 1066, or that $E = mc^2$) and one remembers this fact, then it must be 'laid down' or 'encoded' in the brain. Otherwise, how could one possibly recollect it? But, as we have seen, no sense has been given to the idea of encoding or representing factual information in the neurons and synapses of the brain.

The neuroscientific conception of the triggering of memory is confused

It is false that whenever one remembers something (e.g. the day of the week, the way home, one's last birthday, the opening bars of Beethoven's Fifth) one's remembering is triggered by a current experience that causes a neural excitation similar to part of the neural excitation that was originally caused by the perceptual event in which one learnt whatever one now remembers. It is not true that whenever one's reason for doing something is a fact one previously learnt, one must have been reminded of that fact by some current experience, let alone by an experience which bears some resemblance to the past experience from which one learnt what one now recollects. Consequently, the demand that the putative brain trace be reactivated by a current experience that generates a part of the original pattern of neural excitation is altogether redundant. It was produced to meet the demands of a *picture* – a picture of what remembering consists in. But that picture is altogether misconceived.

The neuroscientific discoveries of the prerequisites of retention of knowledge do not support the neuroscientific picture of memory

Neuroscientists have discovered that damage to the hippocampus deprives one of the ability to recollect anything subsequently learnt or experienced for longer than 30 seconds. This certainly suggests that retention of certain neural firing patterns and synaptic connections is essential for the possibility of recollection. But it does not follow that 'memories are stored at recurrent collateral synapses', *if* the terms 'memory' and 'store' are being used in the normal sense. For, to repeat, there is no such thing as 'storing' what one remembers – for example, *that the Battle of Hastings was fought in 1066*, or *visiting Florence for the first time* – unless it is inscribed in symbolic form and the inscription is stored. It may be that the retention of certain synaptic connections and the creation of certain recurrent firing patterns are a necessary condition for one to be able to recall something – but that is all. The relevant synaptic connections and firing patterns cannot be said to *represent* 'a memory' or what is remembered. Remembering something is not a matter of retrieving something stored in the hippocampus. Nor is it having a special kind of experience – a mnemonic experience which re-creates 'in memory' some past experience. Memory is the retention of knowledge previously acquired. It is an ability that may be exercised in indefinitely many forms: for example, in *saying* what one remembers, affirming *that* one remembers it when asked, not *saying* anything but *thinking* about what is remembered, neither saying nor thinking anything but acting on what one remembers in any of indefinitely many ways, recognizing something or someone, and so forth. It is very tempting to think that the diverse forms in which remembering something may be manifest are all due to the fact that what is remembered is *recorded* and *stored* in the brain. But that is a nonsense. *What is remembered* when it is remembered that such-and-such is not anything laid down in the brain, but rather something previously learnt or experienced. What neuroscientists must try to discover are the neural conditions of remembering and the neural concomitants of recollecting something.

In short, neuroscientists investigating memory must distinguish between the experience of information acquisition and the information acquired, and hence between remembering the information acquired and remembering the acquiring of it. They must be careful not to slip into the error of thinking that all remembering is remembering a past experience. When they are concerned with remembering a past experience, they must not suppose that remembering need be a form of imaginative reproducing, as opposed to recounting or otherwise acting, and they must not suppose that recounting involves reading off information from a mental image. And they should avoid thinking that remembering something is a kind of experience. So, too, they must distinguish the memory – that is, what is remembered – from the expression of the memory in words, symbols or images, and also distinguish between the verbal expression of a memory and the multiple forms in which the overt remembering may be manifest. The expression of a memory must be distinguished from the neural configurations, whatever they may be, which are conditions for a person's recollecting whatever he recollects. But these configurations are not the memory; nor are they representations, depictions or expressions of what is remembered.

6

The Cogitative Powers

In the previous chapter we sketched the main contour lines of the general cognitive concepts of knowledge and memory. We now turn to a group of related general concepts that similarly signify distinctive powers of human beings: belief, thought and imagination. Although not all instances of believing are cases of thinking, some are — for example, when the verb 'to believe' is used to express an opinion, what one thinks about the matter at hand. Similarly, the subject of the imagination straddles both the cogitative use of the verb 'to imagine' and its employment to signify the exercise of the power to conjure up mental images, which need have no connection with thinking. Nevertheless, the connecting thread warrants subsuming all three, at least for present purposes, under the heading of 'the cogitative powers of human beings'. Here too it is important to realize that these attributes are attributes of human beings, not of their brains. We shall not dwell on belief, which has not been the subject of much neuroscientific research. But we shall investigate thinking, imagining and mental images in some detail.

6.1 Belief

The relation between knowledge and belief

Related to the concept of knowledge are the various concepts concerned with belief and conviction. Believing falls short of knowing, for one can believe something without knowing whether things are as one believes them to be. Knowing entails that things are as they are known to be, whereas believing does not entail that things are as they are believed to be. So 'to believe', unlike 'to know', is not factive. One can know things in detail, well or thoroughly, but one cannot believe things in any of these ways. Hence there are degrees of knowledge (in extent), but no (comparable) degrees of belief: I may know more mathematics, physics or history than you, and I may know Jack better than you do; but I cannot believe more mathematics, physics or history than you do, any more than I can believe Jack better than you do (although I may have more faith in him and his story than you do). We may both believe *that* things are thus-and-so, but you cannot believe that things are so *more* or *better* than I do, and your belief cannot be *greater* than mine. But you may believe that things are thus with greater *conviction* than I, for there are, to be sure, degrees of conviction – that is, one may cleave to a belief more or less firmly or tenaciously.

Belief, unlike knowledge, may be right *or* wrong, correct *or* incorrect, true *or* false. It is right, correct or true if *what one believes* – namely, *that* things are thus-and-so – is right, correct or true; that is, it is right or correct to believe, or true to say, that things are thus-and-so. Belief can be firm or tentative, passionate or dogmatic, which knowledge cannot be. It is firm or tentative if *one believes* firmly or tentatively, and it is passionate or dogmatic if *one believes* passionately or dogmatically (but what one believes is neither firm or tentative, nor passionate or dogmatic). So, it is important not to confuse belief – understood as what is believed – which may be right or wrong, with belief – understood as believing – which may be passionate or dogmatic.[1] What is believed cannot be passionate or dogmatic, and believing what is believed cannot be certain, probable or possible (which what is believed can be, if it is certain, probable or possible that things are thus-and-so). Like knowing, believing is neither an act nor an activity, and it is not a feeling or a mental state either. Unlike knowing, believing is neither an ability nor akin to an ability. Like knowing, and unlike feeling sensations or perceiving things, one does not cease to believe whatever one believes when one falls asleep or otherwise loses consciousness.

The links between belief and related attributes

Belief is linked in various ways with doubt, certainty, conviction and being sure, hence with feeling doubtful, certain, convinced and sure. If one believes something to be so, then one does not doubt that it is so, and one will doubt whatever one apprehends as being improbable if things are as one believes them to be. To be or feel doubtful whether something is so is to feel inclined not to believe that it is so. One can believe something to be so without being certain, sure or convinced that it is; but one cannot be certain, sure or convinced that something is so without knowing or believing that it is. Objective certainty relates to the exclusion of the possibility that things are not as one believes or knows them to be. It is certain that things are thus-and-so if the possibility of their not being so can be ruled out on the basis of the facts about the situation. Subjective certainty (feeling and being certain or sure) relates to the exclusion of doubt. Although there are no degrees of belief, there are degrees of confidence, ranging from feeling sure, certain or completely convinced to feeling uncertain or doubtful.

Belief is an attribute of people, not of brains (Crick)

Like the other psychological attributes, believing such-and-such is ascribable to a person, but not to his brain. Hence it is misleading of Crick to suggest that 'What you see is not what is *really* there; it is what your brain *believes* is there'.[2] There are sceptical and gullible people, but no sceptical and gullible brains. We all know what it is

---

[1] One may believe truly, correctly or rightly that *p*, and one may believe passionately, tentatively or firmly that *p*. But in the former case, the adverbs 'truly', 'correctly' and 'rightly' do not characterize the manner in which one cleaves to one's belief, whereas the adverbs 'passionately', 'tentatively' and 'firmly' do. Rather, one believes truly, correctly or rightly that *p* if it is true, correct or right that *p*.

[2] F. Crick, *The Astonishing Hypothesis* (Touchstone, London, 1995), p. 31.

for a person to believe or not to believe in God, to believe in the Conservative Party or in fairies, to believe a person or his story or to doubt a person's word and be sceptical about his story. But we do not know what a religious, agnostic or atheist *brain* might be. No sense has been given to such a form of words. There is no such thing as a brain that *believes* or does *not believe* in God, for there is no such thing as a brain's believing or not believing something. We can *give* this form of words a sense; we can *stipulate* that an agnostic brain is the brain of a person who is an agnostic – although there is no use for such a stipulation: it is altogether redundant. But we cannot stipulate that an agnostic brain is a brain that is agnostic in its beliefs about God, for brains have no beliefs – that is, there is no such thing as a brain believing or not believing something. Similarly, there are no Conservative or Labour brains, only people who believe in these parties; and the brain can neither believe in fairies nor believe fairy-tales, and it cannot be sceptical about them either. I may believe my friend and his story, but my brain cannot – *logically cannot* – believe my friend or his story.

Why belief could not be a state of the brain

It is noteworthy that believing that something is thus-and-so cannot – logically cannot – be a neural state of one's brain (see also §13.1 below). For if it were, and if 'I believe that such-and-such' were a report on one's believing, then it would be a report on the state of one's brain. But if it were, then since the state of one's brain is entirely independent of whether such-and-such is actually the case, it would make sense to ask the person himself whether such-and-such *is* the case. But if a person has said that he believes that such-and-such, he has already committed himself to the view that it is the case – which he would not have done if all he were doing were reporting on his inner state. He cannot say 'I *believe* that things are thus, but as to the question of whether things *are* thus, I have no idea (or, I have an open mind)'. But if 'I believe that . . .' were a report on the state of his brain, he could intelligibly assert this nonsense.

The use of 'I believe' to qualify an assertion, to indicate the character of the grounds of an assertion, or to take a stand on what is asserted

'I believe that . . .' is typically (but not uniformly) used to express a judgement that things are thus-and-so, together with a rider indicating that one might be wrong, that one's grounds for the assertion that things are thus-and-so do not suffice to rule out the possibility that they are not. It is not a report on how things are with one, either in one's mind or in one's brain. It is commonly akin to saying 'Such-and-such, *to the best of my knowledge*, is the case', or 'Such-and-such, *unless I am much mistaken*, is the case' – which are not even reports on one's mental, let alone on one's neural, state.[3] Slightly differently, it is sometimes used in the same way as 'I gather that things are thus-and-so', which indicates that I do not have first-hand knowledge. But in other contexts – for example, where knowledge is excluded by the very nature of the case – it may be used to express an opinion, and so too to indicate where the speaker stands on the matter at hand.

---

[3] For elaboration of this point, see A. W. Collins, *The Nature of Mental Things* (University of Notre Dame Press, Notre Dame, IN, 1987).

6.2 Thinking

The relation between believing and thinking

Believing and thinking differ, but they do run along parallel tracks for a while. To think that something is so and to believe that something is so may be akin.[4] In certain cases, there is no difference between thinking and believing, or indeed opining, that something is so. However, the concept of thinking also diverges from that of belief. For one can be engaged in thinking, but not in believing; hence one can be interrupted in thinking but not in believing. One can think through, but not believe through, a problem, and think of, as well as think up, a solution. To think of an answer to a question is not to believe of an answer, not even to believe the answer one thought of. One can think, but not believe, aloud or silently, quickly or slowly, efficiently or inefficiently, fruitfully or fruitlessly. One can believe, but not think, a person, rumour or story, as indeed one can believe, but not think, *in* a person, a god or a cause.

The different logical categories to which thinking may belong

Thinking can be something that occurs, as when a thought crosses one's mind, or something one does, as when one thinks of a solution, as well as something one engages in, both as when one thinks through a problem for an hour and as when one engages in an activity with attention, thinking about – that is, concentrating on – what one is doing. Or it may be none of these, as when one thinks, is of the opinion that, something is thus-and-so; or as when one thinks of something *as* something – for example, of the Epilogue to *War and Peace* as a stroke of genius or of Paul Klee as the most inventive artist of the twentieth century – that is how one conceives of it or of him; or as when one thinks – that is, assumes – that the bridge one is walking across is safe.

The varieties of thinking

There are, as indicated above, varieties of thinking. We are all too prone to focus upon one particular variety to the exclusion of others, and to suppose that by studying it we are studying thinking in general. The favoured paradigm is the thinking of *Le Penseur*, sitting quietly, with furrowed brows, sunk in thought. As we shall see in a moment, even this paradigm conceals unexpected diversity in what, in *this* context, is called 'thinking'. But, what is worse, giving undue prominence to this kind of thinking obscures from sight many other things that also constitute thinking. So, first let us shift focus, and bring to mind varieties of thinking that are far removed from the cogitations of the meditator.

(i)   There is the thinking involved in non-meditative activities – the thinking that is constituted by attending to the task at hand. Mechanical tasks can be engaged in without

---

[4] Yet they are not everywhere the same. Having been told that your rose garden is beautiful, I may ask to see it, saying 'I believe it is beautiful'. Having seen it, I would respond by telling you that I *think* (not that I *believe*) that it is beautiful. Here 'believe' would function to indicate hearsay, whereas 'think' functions to express my own opinion, gleaned at first hand. (See B. Rundle, *Mind in Action* (Clarendon Press, Oxford, 1997), pp. 73–80.)

Thinking as attending to a task at hand

attention or concentration. Indeed, when one is engaged in such tasks – for example, polishing the furniture or cleaning the windows – one does so without thought – which does not mean that one is not thinking while polishing or cleaning, for normally one will be thinking of *other* things. It means that the task does not require much attention or care. But the more complex or delicate the task, as when one is mending a watch, conducting a refined experiment, or doing a surgical operation, the more it demands concentrated attention and thought, requiring one constantly to be aware of, and to take into account, possibilities that may obtain and difficulties that may arise. This does not mean that one is talking to oneself about such possibilities while engaged in the activity. It means that one is alert to these possible eventualities and takes precautions against them. By contrast, to engage in such activities *without thought* or *thoughtlessly* is to engage in them mechanically, without due care and attention.

Thinking as intelligently engaging in an activity

(ii)   Related to, but different from, this is the thinking that is engaging in an activity not merely with care and attention, but with *cunning* and *ingenuity*, applying one's *intelligence* swiftly to the changing circumstances in unanticipated ways – so that one does not merely not fall short of performing the task adequately, but rather one performs it intelligently and cleverly, as does the outstanding tennis-player or ingenious chess-master, as well as the skilful debater in the cut and thrust of disputation. Rather differently, the brilliant actor playing Hamlet or the pianist playing the 'Hammerklavier' Sonata manifest the thoughtfulness of their performances, not by swift and intelligent response to changing fortune and circumstance, but by the intelligence, originality and sensitivity of their rendering.

Thinking as intelligent speech

(iii)   There is the thinking involved in intelligent speech. This itself is heterogeneous. To speak without thinking may be to speak without taking into account all the factors relevant to what one is speaking of. It is not to speak without accompanying one's speaking with an inaudible activity. By the same token, to speak with thought is to speak, taking appropriate factors into account in what one says. To be thinking hard as one speaks is not to be doing two things, speaking and thinking hard, but to be doing one thing with concentration. If, as one argues a case in public, one reasons from premises to a certain conclusion, one is thinking, but the thinking is not something distinct from the overt reasoning manifest in one's assertion that *b* follows from *a*, *b* implies that either *c* or *d*, but *c* is incompatible with *a*, hence *d*, and so on. But speaking thoughtfully may also mean thinking *before* one speaks.

Thinking as opining, judging, assuming, supposing, etc.

(iv)   Putting aside the kinds of thinking which involve activities, one may think that such-and-such. This, depending on how one arrived at what one thinks and the kinds of grounds one has for it, may be a belief, an opinion, a judgement, an assumption, a supposition or presupposition, a conclusion or assessment. 'I thought it was safe (solid, robust, secure)', said ruefully after a mishap, need not mean that one reflected and came to a conclusion – it may mean that one *gave* the matter *no* thought – that is, reflection – but took it for granted, assumed or supposed – that is, thought – it to be thus-and-so. But it may mean that one gave the matter due attention, and came to this conclusion – for example, if one says 'I knew such-and-such, *so* I thought (inferred) that it was safe'.

Thinking as associating or recollecting

(v)   To think *of* something may be merely for some object of thought to come to mind randomly, or by association; but it may be a recollection, of which one was either reminded by something or which just crossed one's mind. On the other hand, it may be a *result* – the upshot of thinking what (to do), how (to get to the Opera House from here), where (one left one's keys), who (was at the meeting), when (the Battle of Zama was fought), etc. Here the thinking is a form of searching (for an answer), and what one thinks, when one thinks of whatever it is, is the putative answer that one has arrived at.

Thinking as a manner of conceiving

(vi)   One may think of something *as* something, as when one thinks of an unpleasant experience one is about to undergo as a rite of passage, or of a painting as an allegory, or of a musical phrase as a response to a previous passage. Thinking of something *as* something is *a way of viewing it* or *a manner of conceiving of it*, which may be illuminating and helpful or misguided and confusing.

Thinking and meaning something

(vii)   As we noted previously, there is a thinking which consists in meaning something or other by what one said. This itself may take different forms. 'When (but not while) I said "He is in town", I was thinking of Jack' renders explicit to whom one was *referring*. But 'When (not while) I said "We must take more care", I was thinking that we must check the timetable and look at the map' *elaborates* what one has in mind. Here to refer to one's thinking thus is to refer to a time – namely, the time at which one said what one said – but not to any further act or event over and above the saying that took place at that time. That one was thinking *of* Jack (i.e. that one meant Jack) or that one was thinking *that* we must do so-and-so (i.e. that this is what one meant) is not something that then happened, but is rather a matter of what one would have said or done if certain circumstances had arisen (e.g. if one had been asked who or what one had in mind).

Thinking and reasoned problem solving

Now, to revert to the model of *Le Penseur*'s thinking: this kind of thinking is paradigmatically silent, ratiocinative – that is, reasoned – problem solving. What one thinks about holds one's attention – hence one is 'sunk in thought'. This sort of thinking is something engaged in. It may be done continuously or intermittently. The thinking is the endeavour to find the answer to a question or the solution to a problem by *reasoning*. It can be done methodically, efficiently, swiftly or slowly. Its upshot is the conclusion one arrives at, which may be a discovering of something or a creating of something. The conclusion one then thinks of may be original or pedestrian, correct or incorrect.

But such silent thinking need not be ratiocinative – it can be trying to remember who . . . , when . . . or what . . . (see (v) above), and its successful upshot may be *thinking of* that which one was trying to recollect. This 'thinking of' is not mere associating (as in 'I was thinking of my great Aunt Jemima'), but rather is problem answering – for example, thinking that it was NN who . . . , or that it was such-and-such that . . . .

Thinking, idle rumination and imagining

There are prolonged silent thinkings that are neither ratiocinative problem solving nor attempts to recollect the answer to a question, but more or less idle rumination, as when one thinks about last summer's holiday or daydreams about next summer's holiday. One thinks *of* such-and-such or *about* this-or-that, but one's thinking in these cases cannot be methodical, efficient or successful, inasmuch as it is not directed at a solution or answer *to* anything. It may be random association, pensive recollection, or pleasant anticipation. It may, as we shall see below, be a form of imagining – thinking of and daydreaming about possibilities, of what it would be like to . . . or what would happen if . . . Such rumination may be voluntary, involuntary or compulsive, depending on the agent, the topic and the circumstances.

The implications of the varieties of thinking for neuroscientific study of thinking

We have dwelt at such length on the manifold varieties of thinking for two reasons. First, neuroscientific research on thinking is prone to take one or two examples of thinking to represent the whole variegated field. So, experimenters try to identify the 'locus' of thought in the brain by using such techniques as PET and fMRI, asking the subject whose brain is being scanned to 'think of' something (e.g. to associate a word with another word, or to solve some rudimentary calculation), oblivious to the multiple varieties of thinking, and illegitimately generalizing from the special cases in question to all kinds of thinking. But one may not *assume* that because thinking of a word that goes with 'husband' (viz. 'wife'), or thinking of the answer to an elementary computation, etc. is shown to involve the excitation of such-and-such a region of the brain, therefore *all* kinds of thinking, including the thinking involved in arguing a case aloud, playing the piano with thought, giving a thoughtful rendering of 'To be or not to be', mending a mechanism with intense thought and concentration, daydreaming about next summer's holiday, assuming, supposing or presupposing, opining, believing, and so on, through the whole range which we have just sketched, have a similar neurological basis. This should be obvious from the following considerations.

The polymorphous character of thinking

(a)   Thinking is polymorphous – that is, each of its variants can take many forms – so that what one does when one thinks something on one occasion and in one circumstance may be done on another and yet not count as thinking at all – as saying '1314' may, in one circumstance, count as having thought of the date of the Battle of Bannockburn, but in another may be mechanically counting, or telling the time, or telling someone one's telephone number (which need involve no thought). Equally, the form which thinking takes on one occasion may be quite different from the form which thinking the very same thing takes on another – as when, on one occasion, thinking that one must tell one's friend something may take the form of telling him then and there, whereas on another it may take the form of making a note in one's diary, and on yet another it may take the form of picking up the telephone to give him a call. What counts as thinking, like what counts as rehearsing, obeying, or practising, fighting, farming or playing (which are also polymorphous verbs), depends not only on what is said or done, but on the context or circumstances in which it is said or done, the manner in which it is said or done, the purpose with which it is said or done, and the forms of evaluation (if any) of success or failure appropriate to what is said or done.

That there are different species of a variety of thinking is not to be confused with the polymorphousness of thinking

(b)   Thinking that such-and-such is the case may be any number of *different* things: for example, it may be concluding, assuming, presupposing, recollecting, believing, opining. We might call these 'species' of *thinking that* something is so. Similarly, thinking of something can be associating that thing with something else; it may be referring to – that is, meaning – that thing ('When I said that, I was thinking of Jack'); it may be finding an answer ('I have thought of a solution'); it may be being reminded of something; or it may be daydreaming about something. These might be termed 'species' of *thinking of* something. This multiplicity is not the same as the polymorphousness of thinking, for each member (e.g. concluding or supposing or assuming) of a given species (e.g. of *thinking that*) is a species of a genus (in the sense that concluding, supposing, assuming are all species of thinking that something is thus-and-so), whereas a particular form which thinking that something is so may take is not a species of a common genus, which therefore shares generic features with another form which thinking the very same thing may take.

Awareness of the varieties of thinking should make it evident that thinking is not an attribute of the brain

The second reason for elaborating the varieties of thinking is that, by displaying the manifold varieties of thinking, it should be evident that the subject that thinks is not the brain, but the human being. It is not the brain that concentrates on doing an operation with due care and attention, but the surgeon. It is not the brain that plays a cunning game of tennis or gives a brilliant performance of the 'Hammerklavier' Sonata, but the tennis-player and the pianist. It is the skilled debater, not his brain, who argues intelligently, responds to objections in a flash, displays superb intelligence in his repartee and ingenious reasoning in his arguments. There is no such thing as a bigoted or opinionated brain, for brains do not hold opinions – only human beings do so, and it is not the brain that can be open-minded or prejudiced, any more than the brain's arguments presuppose this or assume that, for brains do not argue. Brains do not conceive of things as this or that, since brains do not conceive of anything, and brains cannot elaborate whom they were thinking of in saying something or what they were thinking of when they said something, since brains do not say anything and cannot mean anything by saying something. Brains cannot reason well or poorly, although the brain processes of people who can reason well no doubt have distinctive features which endow them with this gift.

The brain is not the locus of thoughts (Edelman and Tononi)

Not only is the brain not the subject of thinking, it is not the locus of thoughts either. Contrary to what is often claimed by neuroscientists (who speak, e.g., of 'the human head within which we have no doubt that thoughts occur'[5]), thoughts do not

---

[5] G. M. Edelman and G. Tononi, *Consciousness: How Matter Becomes Imagination* (Allen Lane, The Penguin Press, London, 2000), p. 200.

occur *in* the brain, but in one's study, in the library, or as one walks down the street. The location of *the event of a person's thinking a certain thought* is the place where the person is when that thought occurs to him. *Thoughts* are to be found written down in texts, but not in the heads of human beings. Thoughts may be expressed by human beings, but not by brains. For a thought is just what is expressible by an utterance or other symbolic representation. The fact that human beings may think and not say what they think does not imply that what they then think is said or otherwise expressed inside their brains.

The brain is not the organ of thought and the senses in which it is false that one thinks with one's brain

Nor is it helpful to claim that the brain is the organ of thought, in the sense in which the eye is the organ of sight. For one sees *with* one's eyes (brings one's eyes closer to the object being scrutinized to see better), but one does not, in that sense, think with one's brain. Nor does one think with one's brain in the sense in which one walks with one's legs or, differently, digests food with one's stomach. Of course, there is *a* sense in which one can be said to think with one's brains – we say such things as 'Use your brains!' (which just means 'Think!'), just as we say 'I love her with all my heart' – a metaphorical sense. But neuroscientists should not be misled by metaphor. It is true, to be sure, that without very specific neural activities one could not think – but equally, without very specific neural activities one could not walk or talk either. But no one would say that we walk and talk with our brains. Of course, I may 'wrack my brains', but it is I who think, not my brain. And when I think, I can say what it is that I think. I may be thinking something over, without yet having arrived at a conclusion. But it would be absurd to say, 'My brain is thinking it over, but I don't yet know what conclusion it has reached', let alone 'Wait a minute; when my brain has finished thinking it over, it will tell me what it thinks, and then I'll be able to tell you what I think'.[6]

6.3 Imagination and Mental Images

The imagination and other faculties

The family of concepts constituted by 'imagine' and such cognates as 'imaginary', 'image', 'imaginative' and 'imaginable' is a ramifying one. It is linked, by means of one member or another, with the concepts of thought and conception, memory, perception, illusion, creativity and invention.

Imagination and creativity

The faculty of the imagination is associated with artistic and intellectual creativity, with originality, insight and deviation from stock solutions to problems. A powerful imagination is manifest in the novelty, ingenuity, or insight of the products of great artists, scientists or philosophers, in

---

[6] We shall examine further aspects of the topic of thinking and the expression of thoughts in chapter 12, with particular reference to the questions of whether one thinks in images, words or neither, and whether thoughts are composed of images or words or neither.

their works of art, scientific theories or philosophical writings. We know that they have a remarkable imagination by scrutinizing their work, not by peering into their brain or speculating about what mental events may have accompanied their creative labours.

Imagination and perception   Imagination is connected in various ways with perception, inasmuch as it takes imagination to see or hear certain resemblances, forms of connectedness, or patterns of relationships between diverse visibilia and audibilia. It takes imagination to hear a piece of music as a variation on a theme, for example, or to see 'quotations' in paintings (e.g. Michelangelo's *Isaiah* in Reynold's *Mrs Siddons as the Tragic Muse*), or to 'see' various figures in a Rorschach spot.

Imagination and the power to have mental images   There is a conceptual connection between the imagination and the power to conjure up visual or auditory images, either in memory or in fancy. We speak here of 'seeing' or visualizing things 'in our mind's eye', of talking to ourselves or rehearsing tunes 'in our imagination'. Mental images, which have attracted much attention from cognitive neuroscientists and psychologists concerned with recognition, are a major source of conceptual confusion. For it is deeply tempting to conceive of mental images as species of the genus *image* – that is, as just like physical images, only mental. We shall investigate this misconception below, for, as we shall argue, it is no more illuminating to conceive of mental images thus than to conceive of square roots of negative numbers as just like real numbers only imaginary.

Imagination and supposition   There is a connection between imagining and supposing, guessing and suspecting. This is evident in such sentences as 'He never imagined he could surpass them all', 'The town was further away than he had imagined', and 'One would imagine it impossible that any creature could survive an Arctic winter'. But it is important to note that although the verbs 'imagine', 'suppose', 'guess' and 'suspect' are sometimes interchangeable, they are not always so. And while there is a connection between the verbs, there is no such connection between the cognate nouns. There is a faculty of imagination, but none of supposition, and to suppose something to be so is not, per se, an exercise of the faculty of the imagination, even though one's guesses, suppositions and suspicions may be the product of a rich creative imagination.

Imagination and falsely believing, misremembering, or misperceiving   Imagining sometimes signifies falsely believing, mistaken memory or misperception. We may imagine ourselves halfway to our destination when we have covered barely a quarter of the distance; we may think we have seen a friend in a crowd, only to realize, on closer scrutiny, that we were merely imagining it. Again, falsely believing, misremembering and misperceiving are not conceived of as exercises of the *faculty* of the imagination. The reason for this is evident. The imagination is not a cognitive faculty concerned with truth and falsehood (and thus whose faulty exercise might result in false belief, misremembering or misperceiving), but, as we shall argue, a cogitative one. But the connection between the concept of imagining and what is false is made, on the one hand, via notions of the imaginary or fictitious as that which has no real existence or 'exists only in the imagination', and, on the other hand, via the relationship between imagining and making things up.

Imagination is a cogitative faculty The imagination is a cogitative, not a cognitive, faculty.[7]

To exercise one's imagination is to engage in a form of thinking – to think of something as possible or to think of its possible features. One can imagine entities of a certain kind, events that may or may not happen or have happened, and one can imagine doing certain things or certain people (oneself or others) doing certain things. One can imagine what it would be like if things were thus-and-so, as one can imagine why things are or are not thus-and-so, how something was, is, will be, or ought to be done, where something is or might be. And one can imagine something *as* such-and-such, imagine being such-and-such, as well as imagining being in so-and-so's shoes.

Imagination is the capacity to think of possibilities The imagination is the faculty exercised in imagining. It is the capacity to think of possibilities (which may or may not be actual – for things may, in certain cases, actually be as one imagines them to be).[8] One's imagination may be powerful or weak, rich or poor. When the possibilities stretch beyond the bounds of the plausible, one's imaginings are fanciful, fantastic and incredible. Unsurprisingly, the powers of the imagination are associated with originality, inventiveness and creativity, according to the novelty of the possibilities one thinks up or the richness with which one imagines what it would be like if. . . . One uses one's imagination both in discovering and in creating, in thinking of solutions by way of imagining what would happen if . . . or how something might have occurred, and in thinking what it would look like or be like if. . . . The exercise of the imagination can be active or passive. One can imagine voluntarily and intentionally, and one can be asked or ordered to imagine things. But one may not be able to help imagining things being thus-and-so, as an anxious mother may not be able to help imagining the dreadful things that might have happened to her missing child. Her imaginings are involuntary.

Imagination is a power possessed by human beings, not by their brains It should be obvious that it is not the brain, but the human being, that has a rich or poor imagination, that the brain is not a possible subject of a powerful or weak imagination. It is not the brain that has the power to think up novel, amusing, ingenious or inventive possibilities, but the human being, even though, as is equally obvious, a person who has a rich imagination doubtless owes his imaginative powers *also* to features of his brain. Similarly, it should be evident that it is misconceived to suggest, as Blakemore does, that since there are topographically arranged sensory areas in the brain, therefore 'the brain does contain images of the outside world and it seems likely that these images are of functional value in the brain's task of analysing

---

[7] The most comprehensive philosophical investigation of the imagination is A. R. White's *The Language of Imagination* (Blackwell, Oxford, 1990).

[8] In a qualified and sometimes misleading sense, it is also the capacity to think up impossibilities. Lewis Carroll excelled at thinking up entertaining logical impossibilities, i.e. forms of words which amusingly appear to make sense but which actually do not, just as Escher excelled at imagining logically impossible objects and states of affairs, i.e. pictorial representations that transgress the rules of perspective.

sensory signals'.[9] A topographically arranged sensory area is not an image of anything; there are no images *in* the brain, and the brain does not *have* images.

Mental images are neither necessary nor sufficient for imagining
It is important to note, since it is all too often forgotten, that mental images are neither necessary nor sufficient for exercising the powers of the imagination. Mental images may occur or be invoked in the course of recollecting, anticipating, dreaming and day-dreaming, none of which are or need be imagining. While mental images *may* cross one's mind when one imagines something perceptible, they need not. One can imagine, as Tolstoy did, the Battle of Borodino without conjuring up images – what was necessary was to conjure up descriptions of what it might have been like. One can imagine, as Shakespeare did, the last words of Othello or the parting of Cassius and Brutus – what was necessary was to think up (invent) what they did or said.

Much of what is imaginable is not picturable
Moreover, there is much that we can imagine which *could* not be pictured, mentally or literally, such as what Caesar thought on the eve of the Ides of March, why Harold Godwinson did not tarry in London to raise the fyrd, and so forth. One can imagine that *all* men, *some* men, or *no* men are such-and-such, but nothing in a picture or image can capture what is expressed by 'all', 'some' and 'none'. One can imagine that if Jack were wiser, Jill would be happier; one can imagine what might have happened if Harald Hardrada had not invaded in the summer of 1066, or if the wind in the Channel had not changed at the very time of the Norwegian invasion. One can imagine difficulties facing one's project as well as objections to one's arguments, and so forth. A powerful imagination is not the ability to conjure up vivid mental images, but rather the ability to think of ingenious, unusual, detailed, hitherto undreamt of possibilities. And the imagination is not exercised only, or even primarily, in mere reflection, but in speech and action – in invention, creation, story-telling and problem-solving.

The faculty of imaging (fantasia) is only loosely connected with the cogitative faculty of the imagination
So, conjuring up mental images is not essential for the use of the imagination. Indeed, the association between the cogitative (and creative) faculty of the imagination and the capacity to conjure up images is largely coincidental. It might be advantageous if we were to conceive of these as two distinct faculties, the first being the imagination (as conceived above), the second being fantasia.[10] For to be sure, one may have a remarkably lively capacity for calling up vivid visual and auditory images, for

---

[9] C. Blakemore, 'Understanding images in the brain', in H. Barlow, C. Blakemore and M. Weston-Smith (eds). *Images and Understanding* (Cambridge University Press, Cambridge, 1990), p. 282.
[10] See A. J. P. Kenny, *The Metaphysics of Mind* (Oxford University Press, Oxford, 1989), ch. 8, for a helpful discussion. Kenny has used the terms 'creative imagination' and 'fancy' where we have opted for 'cogitative imagination' and 'fantasia'. 'Cogitative imagination' links this faculty firmly to thinking, which can, but need not, be creative (when the anxious mother imagines all the dreadful things that may have happened to her absent child, she is exercising her imagination, but not being creative). 'Fantasia', not being a term with much current use, seems to us to have an advantage over 'fancy', which has a verbal use as in 'I fancied that . . .', which is equivalent to 'I imagined that . . .' (and not to 'I had an image of . . .').

visualizing things and talking to oneself or rehearsing tunes to oneself 'in the imagination', without being an imaginative person at all. And conversely, one may have a rich and fertile creative imagination without having much ability to conjure up images. There seems little *logical* connection between the two powers. Indeed, there seems a greater connection between the faculty of memory and the faculty of imaging (fantasia) than between the latter and the cogitative imagination. Those who are endowed with vivid mental imagery can typically call up lively images of what they previously saw, vividly picture so-and-so's face or smile, 'relive' past experiences in their imagination. This is an exercise both of memory and of fantasia, as is the ability to repeat poetry or to rehearse a familiar piece of music to oneself in one's imagination or to remember so-and-so's voice when he said such-and-such.

The sources of the neuroscientific interest in mental imagery   The capacity to conjure up mental images, in particular visual images, has attracted much attention from neuroscientists. Part of the reason for their interest in the subject stems from the fact that they think of mental images as mysterious, publicly unobservable entities about which the cognitive scientist can make discoveries, just as the physicist makes discoveries about electrons or mesons. It is certainly true that one can make discoveries about people and their faculty of fantasia, hence about the extent to which people's imaginative or mnemonic abilities depend upon their powers of fantasia. But it is misconceived to suppose that mental images are akin to theoretical entities in physics, or that studying the exercise of fantasia by means of PET or fMRI is akin to studying electrons in a cloud chamber. A further part of neuroscientists' interest in the subject stems from their supposition that recognition is a process of comparing a mental image with a perception. While it is true that *machine recognition* – that is, the ability of a machine to register an object it has been programmed to pick out ('recognize') – involves matching input with electronically stored images, it is a fiction that human recognition similarly involves matching a perception with a mental image.

Posner and Raichle's hypothesis of neural similarities between imaging and perceiving   It is claimed, on the basis of extensive experiments with PET and fMRI, that visualizing something (i.e. conjuring up visual images of it) involves the excitation of much the same neural systems as would the corresponding visual experience. Furthermore, Michael Posner and Marcus Raichle contend that 'when we construct an image, a number of the mental operations resemble those that occur when the stimulus is physically presented. In other words, there are fundamental similarities between perceiving an image and imagining one.'[11]

---

[11] M. I. Posner and M. E. Raichle, *Images of Mind* (Scientific American Library, New York, 1997), p. 89. It is surprising that the primary focus of neuroscientific research has been visual imaging, rather than auditory imaging. Yet talking to oneself 'in the imagination' is at least as common, if not more common, that conjuring up visual images 'in the imagination'. Moreover, it is a field that is less subject to conceptual confusion than that of visual imagination. So, for example, it would be of interest to investigate the relation between the neural systems involved in, say, talking and talking to oneself in the imagination, or between those involved in listening to a piece of music, humming the same piece of music, and rehearsing the music in one's imagination, or between those involved in reading a poem, listening to that poem, reciting the poem from memory, and reciting the poem from memory in one's imagination.

Whether or not much the same neural systems are involved in the exercise of fantasia as in the corresponding perceptual experience is an empirical question of some interest. But before this question can be resolved, the experimental scientist must be clear about the concepts involved. In particular, he must be clear about the differences between seeing and its objects, on the one hand, and between visualizing and its objects, on the other. But many neuroscientists, active in this area, do not give adequate attention to such conceptual matters. Consequently, they fall into confusion.

Posner and Raichle err in suppos-ing that in perception and fantasia alike an image is formed in the mind

So, for example, Posner and Raichle assume that in per-ception and in fantasia alike, 'an image of the scene is formed in the mind. The image formed from actual visual experiences is called "a percept" to distinguish it from an imagined image.'[12] This is mistaken. To perceive my room and the objects in it is not to form an image in the mind of my room and the objects in it. To perceive, as we have seen (§4.2.3), is not to have or to form images, and what is perceived is not an image save in cases in which one perceives pictures. Moreover, to form a mental image of a scene is not to imagine *an image* of that scene. That is something a painter might do when he is trying to visualize the painting he intends to paint. But to form a mental image of a scene is visually to imagine *that scene* (not an image of it).

Furthermore, the idea that there are 'fundamental similarities' between perceiving an image and imagining one is not actually what is meant. The claim is the much more gen-eral one that there are fundamental similarities between perceiving an object O and having a mental image of O, and (perhaps) also between perceiving that things are so and having an image of things being so. What kinds of similarity do neuroscientists have in mind?

The alleged neural similarity between imaging and perceiving (Shepard)

One kind of similarity that is claimed is, as noted above, that similar neural systems are involved. So, Roger Shepard explains that when a person conjures up a mental image of O:

> whatever neural activity is going on in his or her brain overlaps sufficiently with the neural activity that has previously been elicited in that same brain by the physical presence of [O] itself, or of a picture of [O]. Thus, although it is the causal connection of the neural activity with the verbal report that informs us that someone is imagining something, it is the causal connection of that neural activity with a previously encoun-tered external object that defines what is being imagined.[13]

This claim incorporates a conceptual and an empirical component. The conceptual claim is confused, and the empirical claim cannot be correct.

Shepard's claim incorrectly limits fantasia to memory

First, fantasia is here unwarrantedly restricted to its exercise in memory. But one can conjure up mental images of innumerable objects one has never encountered. Having read Plutarch's *Life of Julius Caesar*, one may have mental images of Caesar and of his being

---

[12] Ibid., p. 88.

[13] R. Shepard, 'Postscript on understanding mental images', in Barlow, Blakemore and Weston-Smith (eds), *Images and Understanding*, p. 367.

murdered in the Senate. Having been told all about a certain person one is about to meet (or place or building one is about to visit), one may have a mental image of him and find, when one encounters him, that he is (or is not) as one imagined him to be. Moreover, there is much of which one may have mental images that one could not conceivably perceive, such as mental images of fictional and mythological characters (Lancelot, Pluto) or places (Camelot, Hades), as well as of fictional and mythological events. The exercise of fantasia in the context of creativity, when composing tales or music or painting mythological paintings, cannot be explained in terms of reviving antecedent impressions.

Shepard's incorrect empirical claim concerning the criteria for the exercise of fantasia

Secondly, it is not a causal connection between a neural activity and a verbal expression of what one is imaging that 'informs us' that one is exercising fantasia – it is just the sincere verbal expression. What informs us whether someone has conjured up an image in his mind is what he sincerely says. Any neural concomitants are merely inductive, not criterial, evidence, and these inductive correlations presuppose the non-inductive criterion of human avowals that determine whether a person has an image before his mind. Moreover, it is patently not the causal connection between the neural activity and a previously encountered object that *defines* what is being visualized. For what the mental image I have is an image *of* is determined by what I sincerely *say* it is of, not by its causal antecedents (just as whom I meant by 'John', in my utterance 'John is at home', is determined by whom I sincerely say I meant). It is true that there is an essential connection between having visual imagery and seeing (and between having auditory imagery and hearing).[14] *This* essential connection, however, is not that the images are derived from neural storage that was 'laid down' while seeing (or hearing). Rather, the criterion for whether someone has a visual image of something is *that he says that he has* and *can say how he visualizes what he imagines*. For that he must have mastered the use of our ordinary vocabulary which describes visibilia, including colours and visible shapes. To have mastered such a vocabulary, he must be able to see, for without sight a person cannot, for example, master the use of colour words or describe visual appearances (save derivatively).

Posner and Raichle err in attributing a similarity in the mental operations underlying perception and fantasia

Other similarities, suggested by Posner and Raichle, are between 'the mental operations that underlie perception and image formation'.[15] One similarity they allege is between the operation of scanning the letters in three-letter words and scanning a corresponding mental image.[16] But this is misconceived, since *there*

---

[14] See Kenny, *Metaphysics of Mind*, p. 119.

[15] Posner and Raichle, *Images of Mind*, p. 89.

[16] The experiment involved asking people to read off backwards the spelling of a word before their eyes, and then to do the same for the mental image of a word. In the latter circumstance, people found it easy to spell 'cat' backwards, but not so easy to spell 'catapult' backwards. That they had a mental image of the word before their mind was of no help; and that is not surprising, since they could not *see* it (any more than they can *hear* their voice when they recite their favourite poem in their imagination). One can imagine a page and have a vivid image of it, but one cannot *read* (let alone *misread*) the image of a page of text.

is no such thing as scanning a mental image. One cannot see – that is, there is no such thing as *seeing* – a mental image. I do not *see* the mental images I *have*. There is no such thing as *looking at*, *scrutinizing* or *viewing* a mental image, hence too, no such thing as *scanning* one. Consequently, the conclusion drawn – namely, that 'the image is like a percept for three-letter words, but not for longer ones' – is mistaken, as is the claim that 'only a few items can be imaged at one time'.[17]

6.3.1 The logical features of mental imagery

The logical differences between perception and fantasia have been obscured ever since Galton's psychological questionnaire

The fundamental flaws in the research and in the conclusions drawn from it stem from failure to apprehend the *logical* differences between perceiving an object and having an image of that object, between objects and mental images of objects, and between mental images and physical images. It is noteworthy that these confusions go back to the very inception of research on mental imagery in the 1880s. Francis Galton's famous 'breakfast table' questionnaire[18] queried

(a) whether the brightness of a mental image is comparable to that of the actual scene;

(b) whether one can 'mentally see more than three faces of a die, or more than one hemisphere of a globe at the same instant of time';

(c) whether one's mental images appear to be situated 'within the head, within the eyeball, just in front of the eyes, or at a distance corresponding to reality';

(d) whether one has ever mistaken a mental image for a reality;

(e) whether one can cause one's mental images of people to sit, stand or turn slowly around;

(f) whether one can see one's mental image of a person 'with enough distinctness to enable [one] to sketch it leisurely'.

Most of these questions are nonsensical, and all are based on the misconceived supposition that mental images are private pictures, which one sees with the mind's eye – a supposition still rife among cognitive scientists.[19] But, as we shall argue, mental images are not pictures, let alone private ones; and, *pace* Stephen Kosslyn and Kevin Ochsner, they are

---

[17] Posner and Raichle, *Images of Mind*, pp. 89f.

[18] F. Galton, *Inquiries into Human Faculty and its Development* (Macmillan, London, 1883), pp. 378–80.

[19] e.g. 'Mental imagery is essentially a "private" or "subjective" experience, in the sense that we cannot directly observe other people's mental images' (J. T. E. Richardson, *Imagery* (Psychology Press, Hove, East Sussex, 1999), p. 9). It is true that there is no such thing as *observing* other people's mental images; but there is no such thing as *observing* one's own mental images either. The sense in which one's mental images are private is simply this: that one can have a mental image and not tell others that one has such an image or what it is an image of. If one does not tell anyone, then others will not know.

seen *in* not *with* the mind's eye[20] – which is no eye. To see something *in* the mind's eye is not to *see* it at all – it is visually to imagine or recollect it.

Differences between perception and fantasia, between their objects, and between mental and physical images   We shall spell out a number of differences between perception and fantasia, between objects perceived and mental images of objects, and between physical and mental images. For the concepts are much *more* different than psychologists and cognitive scientists suppose. Fantasia is not a form of private perception at all – one can neither see nor hear one's mental images. A mental image of an object is not related to what it is a mental image of as a picture is related to what it is a picture of. And mental images are not 'just like physical images, only mental' – physical images and mental images are not co-ordinate species of the genus *image*.

Objects of perception contrasted with mental images   (1)   The objects of perception exist whether one perceives them or not, and, being mind-independent, have objective and determinate properties. By contrast, mental images do not exist independently of the exercise of fantasia. They are, as it were, made, not discovered. Their properties can be indeterminate, for a mental (visual) image of an object O may be an image of an O with no particular colour or size, even though any O must have some colour and size. (A mental (visual) image is, in *this* respect (but not all respects), more like a drawing than like an object seen, and visualizing is more like depicting than it is like seeing.)

Galton's confused question   Consequently, Galton's question of whether one can 'mentally see more than three faces of a die or more than one hemisphere of a globe' at a given time is confused, and was doubtless confusing for those who answered his questionnaire. To 'mentally see' – that is, to visualize or to conjure up a mental, visual image, is not to see anything. More correctly phrased, the question is whether one can visually imagine more than three faces of a given die at the same time (or more than one eye of a person imagined in profile). And the answer is that, of course, one can – especially if one is familiar with the paintings and drawings of Picasso. But then, of course, one will not be imagining (visualizing) the relevant objects as they visually appear to a perceiver.

Finke's confused Principle of Spatial Equivalence   Hence too, R. A. Finke's Principle of Spatial Equivalence, that 'The spatial arrangement of the elements of a mental image corresponds to the way objects or their parts are arranged on actual physical surfaces or in an actual physical space'[21] is at best misleading. It

---

[20] S. M. Kosslyn and K. N. Ochsner, 'In search of occipital activation during mental imagery', *Trends in Neuroscience*, 17, no. 7 (1994), pp. 290f. Visual mental imagery, they claim, 'is a quintessentially private event' – intimating that only the subject can see it. They write of the 'internal representations that produce the experience of "seeing with the mind's eye"'. Not only is visualizing or having a mental image of something not a matter of 'seeing *with* the mind's eye', but, as we shall argue, mental images are not 'representations'.

[21] R. A. Finke, *Principles of Mental Imagery* (MIT Press, Cambridge, MA, 1989), p. 61.

depends upon whether one has a surrealist or cubist imagination – and, of course, *on what one is trying to do*. If one asks one's subjects to conjure up images of what they have seen, and to imagine them as they appeared, then that is how they will be imagined. But if one asks a Picasso, a Magritte, an Escher or a Dali to imagine something *ad libitum*, how he imagines it will be very different from ordinary appearances, and the Principle of Spatial Equivalence will have as little validity as a corresponding principle applied to painting.

The contrast in respect of the use of sense organs

(2) One uses one's sense-organs to perceive. These organs are parts of the body, which are under one's voluntary control in a way that affects one's powers of perception and discrimination. One may have good or bad eyes or ears, be more or less good at perceiving, depending on the condition of one's organs of perception. By contrast, there are no organs of fantasia, one cannot improve one's image of O by more careful observation of it, and one's powers of imaging are not dependent on one's organ of imaging, since there is none.

The contrast in respect of observation conditions

(3) Observation conditions for perception can be optimal or sub-optimal; one may have to approach closer, or move closer to the light, to perceive better. By contrast, there are no optimal *observation* conditions for the exercise of fantasia, since fantasia involves no observation. Hence, too, there is no such thing as approaching one's mental images more closely or illuminating them better in order to perceive them more clearly and distinctly, although one may imagine seeing something from closer, in good light, and conjure up an image of a well-illuminated object as it would appear from close to. One needs light in order to see an object, but one often visualizes an object better with one's eyes shut. Whereas dazzling objects blind one temporarily, one's vivid mental image of a dazzling object does not blind or bedazzle one, although one can imagine being bedazzled by such an object.

The contrast in respect of possible error

(4) One can perceive correctly or incorrectly, make mistakes, or overlook features of what one perceives. One can check whether one has done so by looking more closely in better light or asking another. By contrast, one cannot make such mistakes about one's mental images. One cannot 'overlook' features of one's mental images. They have no hidden properties which one might fail to 'discern', no occluded backsides, as it were. Rather, they are as we take them to be and as we sincerely say they are. One cannot notice or fail to notice features of one's mental images, as one can notice or fail to notice features of objects one perceives.

Luria's mnemonist and his confused explanation of his mnemonic mistake

Hence the incoherence of the explanation of a mnemonic error offered by Luria's famous mnemonist (and accepted by Luria): namely, that he imagined placing a bottle of milk in front of a white door, and then, when he subsequently imagined walking down the same street, he *didn't notice* the milk bottle.[22] For what would be the criterion for the milk bottle being there 'unnoticed'? The explanation of the mnemonist's not mentioning a milk bottle is not that he imagined one but did not notice it standing in front of a white door; it is that he failed to include it in the scene he revisualized.

Can one derive information from one's mnemonic images by observation?

Comparable incoherence is to be found in the supposition that one can *discover* things by *reading off*, from one's mnemonic image of an antecedently seen object, visual or spatial information about the object. According to this conception, a mental image is a pictorial representation, akin to a private photograph, from which one can derive information about what it is an image of *by observation*. So, for example, Shepard claimed that in order to answer the question of how many windows there are in his house, he had to picture the house from different sides or from within various rooms and then count the number of windows depicted in these images.[23] It was subsequently suggested by P. R. Meudell that there is a direct linear relationship between the time taken to answer the question and the number of items counted.[24] It is uncontentious that one might try to recollect how many windows there are in one's house by thinking of or imagining each room or each elevation, and counting them up as one proceeds. One may then remember correctly or incorrectly how many windows there are in one's house. What is problematic, however, is the idea that one might *count* (and hence, too, *miscount*) the number of windows *in one's mental image*. Suppose there are in fact fifteen windows in one's house. One conjures up a mental image of the different elevations, and concludes that there are fifteen windows. Is it intelligible that there might have been only fourteen windows in one's mental image, which one miscounted, giving a correct answer to the question 'How many windows are there in your house?' but an incorrect one to the question 'How many windows are there in your mental image of your house?'?

The conceptual limits on counting items in one's mental image

The matter is perhaps clearer in the case of the 'creative' (as opposed to the 'reproductive') imagination. Suppose one conjures up before one's mind's eye a wholly imaginary building, perhaps an imaginary skyscraper with numerous windows. There is no such thing as *counting* how many windows there are in the mental image. For it makes no sense to try to *count* items where there is no such thing as *miscounting*, and no such thing as rectifying a miscount by a *recount*. The upper limit on the *determinate* number of things of

---

[22] A. R. Luria, *The Mind of the Mnemonist* (Penguin, Harmondsworth, 1968). The mnemonist earned his living by performing extraordinary mnemonic feats. His audience would call out names of numerous objects, which the mnemonist was subsequently able to recollect in order. The heuristic device he used was to imagine walking down a familiar street in St Petersburg, and as names of objects were called out, he would imagine placing them at specific places along the street. In order to recollect the objects mentioned in the right order, he would imagine walking down the street again, and visually recollect where he had 'placed them'.

[23] R. Shepard, 'Learning and recall as organisation and search', *Journal of Verbal Learning and Verbal Behaviour*, 5 (1966), pp. 201–3.

[24] P. R. Meudell, 'Retrieval and representations in long-term memory', *Psychonomic Science*, 23 (1971), pp. 295–6.

a given kind in one's mental image is the upper limit of the number of things one can recognize at a glance to be present (this may be called 'the visual number', and it is to be contrasted with 'the inductive number'[25]). One can visualize a battalion of soldiers marching down the Champs Elysées, but there is no such thing as *counting* how many soldiers there are in the mental image of a battalion, since the number is much greater than any visual number.[26] One may visualize an imaginary building, and, in some cases, *calculate* how many windows there are in the imagined elevation – for example, six storeys and five windows to a storey, so there are thirty windows. In this way one may come to *realize* that one was visualizing a house with thirty windows in its front elevation. But one cannot *count* thirty windows in one's mental image of a building in order to *find out* how many there are. (Similarly, one cannot measure, but only imagine measuring, the objects one visualizes, and one cannot weigh, but only imagine weighing them.)

One can mistake hallucinating for perceiving, but not fantasia and its objects for perception and its objects
(5)   One can, in one's own case, mistake hallucinating for perceiving. But there is no such thing as mistaking conjuring up a mental image of something for perceiving that thing. Similarly, although one may, like Macbeth, mistake the hallucination of an object for the object itself, one cannot mistake a mental image of an object for the object thus visualized. Nor can one mistake a mental image for an after-image or a hallucination.

Galton's confused questions
Hence Galton's question of whether one has ever mistaken a mental image for reality is as misguided as the question of whether one's obligations have ever weighed as much as one's shopping bag. There is *no such thing* as mistaking a mental image (as opposed to an after-image or hallucination) for reality. Mental images and what they are images of do not coexist in the same *logical* space (any more than heavy obligations and heavy shopping bags).

Equally, Galton's question as to whether mental images appear to be located 'within the head, within the eyeball, just in front of the eyes, or at a distance corresponding to reality' makes no sense. An hallucinated dagger may appear to Macbeth to be three feet in front of him; an after-image may seem to be a stain on the white wall one is looking at. But a mental image cannot *appear* or *seem* to be located anywhere, although, of course, one may imagine Ariadne at Naxos or at Knossos.

Mental images and physical images contrasted
(6)   We have emphasized that mental (visual) images are not like private pictures that only the subject can see. It is worth elaborating further conceptual differences. As

---

[25] The visual number, of course, depends upon the pattern of the array, and is subject to considerable individual differences.
[26] Of course, one may 'count sheep' in one's imagination in order to try to fall asleep, and count hundreds – but here one is not counting how many sheep there are in one's mental image of a flock of sheep, but rather how many times one imagined a sheep jumping over a stile. And when one wearily reaches 1,000, that does not mean that there are 999 sheep in one's mental image of the field on the other side of the stile.

we have noted, one cannot see one's mental images, but one sees physical pictures. A physical image of an object may be a perceptible likeness of it. But a mental image cannot be a *perceptible* likeness of what it is an image of, since it is not perceptible.

One cannot compare one's mental image, as one can compare a physical image, with what it is an image of. For one cannot juxtapose one's mental image with what it is an image of and look at them both, discerning similarities and dissimilarities. Indeed, one cannot simultaneously perceive something and have an image of it as one perceives it to be.

One cannot copy (there is no such thing as copying) one's mental image of something as one can copy a picture of something. For, first, one cannot copy something that one cannot see. Secondly, a copy reproduces its original. But to reproduce one's mental image of X, if this phrase means anything at all, would be to imagine or visualize X *again*.

Galton's confused question   Galton asked whether, if one has a mental image of a person, one *sees* the mental image with enough distinctness to enable one to sketch it at leisure? The question is confused, for it presupposes that one's mental images are private visibilia. But one might ask whether one can sketch one's mental images. To answer this curious question, one should first clarify what could be *meant* by 'drawing one's mental images'. Certainly, one cannot draw one's mental images as an artist draws (but does not copy) a person or a landscape that is before him. For, as we have pointed out, one cannot see one's mental images, and one cannot compare one's sketch with one's mental image for verisimilitude. One can draw what one imagines, and draw it as one imagines it. But it would be deeply misleading in such cases to say that one is drawing one's mental images. One depicts *what one imagines*, but one does not imagine one's mental images. One imagines what one's mental images are images of. Consequently, a sketch of what one visually imagines does not *resemble*, is not a good *likeness* of, one's mental image – it does not *look like* one's mental image. Rather, it represents *what* one imagined or remembered and how one imagined or remembered it – just as one's words, one's descriptions of what one imagined, do.

Why mental images are not   (7) Neuroscientists and cognitive scientists character-
internal representations   ize mental images as 'internal representations'. Mental imagery is alleged to be 'a form of internal representation in which information about the appearance of physical objects, events, and scenes can be depicted and manipulated'.[27] But if pictures, maps and verbal descriptions are paradigms of representations, then mental images are *not* representations of what one imagines. Anything that can be said to be a representation of something has both representational and non-representational properties.[28] Non-representational properties of paintings are properties of the paint (e.g. the colours of the pigments), of the canvas or panel, of the paint strokes (e.g. the thickness of the impasto) and paint patches (e.g. trapezoidal, rectangular). Representational properties of paintings are the colours, locations and shapes of the objects in the painting (i.e. of the painted trees, the painted house and the painted figures). Non-representational properties of writing are the colours of the ink, the features

---

[27] Richardson, *Imagery*, p. 35.
[28] We owe this point to John Hyman.

of the handwriting, and the legibility. The representational properties are the semantic properties of the words. We can apprehend the representational properties of representations only because we can perceive the non-representational ones. We could not apprehend what is said on the radio if we could not hear the sounds made. We could not read and understand what is written if we could not see the inscription. And we could not admire Rembrandt's portrait of Jan Six if we could not see the paint on the canvas. But mental images, like thoughts, *are all message and no medium*. All their visual attributes are attributes of what they are images of: if one imagines red poppies in a field, the redness is *of* the poppies (not of any pigments), and if one imagines a dancer pirouetting rapidly, the speed is of the imagined dancer, not of the mental image. So mental images have no non-representational properties. So they are not representations.

What a person *says* may represent how he imagines whatever he imagines. What he *depicts* when he draws how he imagined whatever he imagined represents what he imagined. But what he says and what he depicts do not represent what he imagined in virtue of *resembling* his mental imagery, any more than *the verbal expression of his thought resembles his thought*. What makes his sketch a good representation of what he imagined and how he imagined it is not a *resemblance* between the sketch and the mental image. It is not as if the sketch is a good likeness of the mental image. Rather, what makes the sketch a good representation is his sincere assertion that *this* is what he had in mind, *this* is how he imagined it. This avowal does not rest upon an 'inner glance' at his mental image. The sketch is not an 'outer picture' of an 'inner picture'. The mental image is not a representation at all. To make a representation of how one imagines something is to depict it as one imagines it, or to describe how one imagines it. It is *not* to conjure up an image of it. A representation represents whatever it represents in virtue of conventions of representation (semantic, cartographical, emblematic), in virtue of intended perceptible similarities between the items in the picture (the person, building or view in the picture) and the items the picture depicts (Wellington, Salisbury cathedral, the Seine). A mental image is not determined as the image it is by convention, by similarity, or by *representational* intention. It is not a *representation* of what it is a mental image of at all.

The vividness of mental images contrasted with the vividness of other things
(8)   Because neuroscientists and cognitive scientists think of mental images as private pictorial representations, they suppose that having a mental image of an object can be compared with perceiving an object in the dimension of vividness or vivacity. This venerable conception was made prominent by Hume, who thought that perceiving, remembering and imagining were distinguished primarily by descending degrees of vivacity.[29] We saw above that the same conception was evident in

---

[29] Hume, *Treatise of Human Nature*, I, iii, 5. Hence Thomas Reid mocked him: 'Suppose a man strikes his head smartly against the wall, this is an impression; now, he has a faculty by which he can repeat this impression with lesser force, so as not to hurt him: this, by Mr Hume's account, must be memory. He has a faculty by which he can just touch the wall with his head, so that the impression entirely looses its vivacity. This surely must be the imagination' (*Essays on the Intellectual Powers*, Essay III, ch. 7.)

Galton's questionnaire, in which he asked whether 'the brightness of a mental image is comparable to that of the actual scene'. It is equally evident in Betts's questionnaire of 1909, in which he queried whether mental images were

(i)   perfectly clear and as vivid as the actual experience;
(ii)   very clear and comparable in vividness to the actual experience;
(iii)   moderately clear and vivid;
(iv)   not clear or vivid, but recognisable;
(v)   vague and dim;
(vi)   so vague and dim as to be hardly discernible.[30]

And it informs the current 'Vividness of Visual Imagery Questionnaire' devised by D. F. Marks.[31]

The moot question, however, is not whether mental images of objects are as vivid or less vivid than perceiving those objects. We must first investigate what precisely is *meant* by ascribing vividness or vivacity to mental images, as opposed to perceiving and what is perceived. Brief reflection should make it evident that the vividness of one's mental images is more akin to the vividness of a description than to the vividness of the flaming colours of an African sunset, and that one could no more confuse the vividness of a mental image with the vividness of what it is an image of than one could confuse the vividness of a description with the vividness of what it is a description of. Some things are said to be vivid if they are full of life, vigorous and active. In this sense, people, material things and their properties can be said to be vivid ('He was a most vivid and quick-thoughted person', 'The violin is a vivid and volatile instrument', '. . . vivid and awful stenches'). People's feelings are vivid if they are strongly felt, their utterances are vivid if they are strongly or warmly expressed, and their recollections are vivid if they are clear and detailed. Colour and light are vivid if they are bright, brilliant, fresh and lively, and coloured things are accordingly said to be vivid in respect of their colour. A description, a report or a history is vivid if it presents its subject matter in a lively, clear, detailed and striking way.

Consequently, a landscape is said to be vivid in the sunshine if the air is clear and the light is brilliant, if the different shades of green of the trees and sward are bright and distinct, if the red poppies or yellow daffodils stand out brilliantly against the green of the grass, if the blueness of the sky and sea is intense, if the shadows are clear and sharp. *In this sense*, one's mental images cannot be said to be more or less vivid than what they are images of. They are not vivid and vivacious *in this dimension* at all. If a stage designer says to his painter that he had imagined the redness of the backcloth to be more vivid, that does not mean that it was brighter in his imagination, any more than if an explosion was not as loud as one expected it to be, then it must have been louder in one's expectation. If the stage designer says that he imagined the light to shine more brilliantly on the

---

[30] G. H. Betts, 'The distribution and functions of mental imagery', Contributions to Education, no. 26 (Teachers College, Columbia University, New York, 1909), pp. 20–1.
[31] D. F. Marks, 'Visual imagery differences in the recall of pictures', *British Journal of Psychology*, 64 (1973), pp. 17–24.

backcloth, that does not mean that when he imagined it, it bedazzled him. One's mental images can be said to be vivid according as to whether one can give a clear, detailed and lively description of what and how one imagined (or recollected) what one imagined (or recollected), or recognize such a description as accurate if given one, or reproduce in a painting or drawing a clear, detailed and lively representation of what one imagined (or recollected) and how one imagined (or recollected) it, or acknowledge someone else's detailed drawing (e.g. one's stage designer's) as being exactly how one imagined the scene (or set). The brightness of one's mental image of a scene is no more comparable to the brightness of the scene than the liveliness of the description of a party is comparable to the liveliness of the party. So, too, the clarity and vividness of one's mental image of a scene are no more comparable to the clarity and vividness of the landscape bathed in brilliant evening sunshine after rain than are the clarity and vividness of one's description of the landscape. But it is true that one may be able to imagine a person more clearly than one can see him (if the light is bad and he is a long way away). What that means is that one can describe him in more detail and with greater confidence by visualizing him than by looking at the distant figure in the gloom.

Confusions about rotating mental images in mental space

(9) One can often manipulate what one perceives (depending on what it is). If it is small, one can often pick it up, turn it around, and examine it from all sides. One can rotate such an object quickly or slowly, at constant or variable velocity. As noted above, Galton thought that it made sense to speak of 'causing one's mental image to turn round slowly'. The moot question is whether this is intelligible, whether it makes sense to speak of *manipulating* mental images, and of *rotating* them 'in mental space' slowly or fast.

There is such a thing as imagining something rotating slowly (or fast), and such a thing as having a mental image of something rotating thus. But there is no such thing as rotating a mental image of an object, any more than there is such a thing as rotating an image of an object in a painting. If one wants to have a painted picture of the object's backside, *one must paint it*; and if one wants to have a mental image of the backside of the object one is visualizing, one must imagine it – that is, make a mental image of it. One cannot turn one's mental image of an object around and see its backside, any more than one can rotate one of Cézanne's apples in his paintings. What one can do is imagine the object rotating. But to imagine an object rotating is not to rotate an object of any kind.

Galton's confusion

Consequently, Galton's question as to whether one can cause one's mental images of people to sit, stand or turn slowly around is misleading. It mistakenly suggests that one might be able to turn one's mental images slowly around, whereas the only intelligible (and trivial) question that can be asked here is whether one can visualize people turning round slowly (or quickly). One can imagine (visualize) manipulating a person (turning him around, making him sit down), but there is no such thing as manipulating one's mental image of a person. Moreover, to imagine an object rotating is not to manipulate anything – it is not to cause one's mental image to move. (One's mental image has no weight, inertia or momentum.)

Galton's confusion pervades current psychological research on mental imagery. Shepard and J. Metzler presented their subjects with drawings showing perspective views of possible

Shepard and Metzler's recognition experiments

objects that can be constructed by joining together ten identical cubes. Pairs of drawings showed the same object viewed at different orientations, and the subjects were asked to find the matching pairs among half a dozen such drawings. Shepard and Metzler found that the time taken to match two different views of the same object was proportional to the angle between the two views (0° − 180°), and that this did not differ between objects rotated within the plane and those which had to be rotated in depth. This suggested to them that the subjects were 'mentally rotating three-dimensional representations' of one or both objects at a constant rate until they had the same orientation – at which point they could easily be judged to be the same or different by simple matching.[32]

Cooper's and Shepard's recognition experiments; Finke's Principle of Transformational Equivalence

L. A. Cooper and Shepard experimented with a more complex task.[33] Subjects were required to judge whether common alpha-numeric characters were presented in their normal form or as mirror-image reversals. The subjects were instructed to imagine the appropriate character in one of six distinct orientations; the character was then presented either in that orientation or in one of the other five, and they had to judge them the same or different. The results showed that the reaction time again increased with the angular discrepancy between the imagined orientation and the orientation of the presented character. Cooper and Shepard inferred that the subjects rotated their mental images at constant velocity until they were at the same orientation as the presented character. This suggested to Cooper and Shepard that the 'manipulation' of mental images of objects corresponds to the ways in which physical objects can be manipulated. Finke subsequently formulated this as 'the Principle of Transformational Equivalence': imagined transformations and physical transformations exhibit corresponding dynamic characteristics and are governed by the same laws of motion.[34]

Posner's and Raichle's recognition experiments

These research results and the hypotheses that inform them are accepted by such distinguished neuroscientists as Posner and Raichle.[35] Following Cooper and Shepard, they claimed that if one is shown a letter at an angle and asked what letter it is and

---

[32] R. N. Shepard and J. Metzler, 'Mental rotation of three-dimensional objects', *Science*, 171 (1971), pp. 701–3. It might be interesting to conduct the same kind of experiment with respect to matching people's faces photographed at different angles of orientation. It is probable that it takes longer to match a face seen *en face* with one seen in quarter-profile than with one seen in three-quarter-profile, but it is far from evident that this is to be explained in terms of rotating imagined faces. Similarly, it is plausible to suppose that it takes longer to match a young face to a very old one than to a middle-aged one, but this is not because it takes longer to age it in one's imagination. It should be noted, however, that it is a fallacy to suppose that recognition in general essentially involves matching. To 're-cognize' is to know again, not to match something perceived with something stored or recorded.

[33] L. A. Cooper and R. N. Shepard, 'Chronometric studies of the rotation of mental images', in W. G. Chase (ed.), *Visual Information Processing* (Academic Press, New York, 1973), pp. 75–176.

[34] Finke, *Principles of Mental Imagery*, p. 93.

[35] Posner and Raichle, *Images of mind*, p. 35.

whether it is correctly oriented or a mirror image, one's reaction time increases with the angle of rotation in roughly linear fashion, *because* it takes longer to perform the internal rotation than to tell which letter it is. It may well take longer to determine whether the letter is a mirror image or not than to determine which letter it is, but *not because it takes longer to rotate the image of the letter in one's mind*, since there is no such thing as rotating a mental image.

The conceptual confusions underlying the recognition experiments and the interpretation of their results   The fact that the reaction time, in all these experiments, is proportional to the angle of rotation of the figures visualized does *not* suggest that it takes longer to perform a greater rotation at constant velocity 'in mental space' than to perform a lesser rotation, since there is no such thing as rotating a mental image at constant (or variable) velocity – only such a thing as imagining an object rotating at constant (or variable) velocity. What it *does* suggest is that it may take longer *to work out* how a certain figure will appear when rotated thus than to work out how the same or another figure will appear when rotated otherwise. For one needs to exercise one's imagination – that is, one's powers to think of possibilities, to work out where *this* part of the figure will lie in relation to *that* part if the whole figure is rotated by 90°. One needs to *think about* the rotation of a figure, not to rotate an imaginary figure (since there is no such thing). In so thinking, one *may*, but *need not*, imagine a rotating figure. (And it is important to remember that thinking about something does not imply saying anything to oneself.)

One *can* imagine a rotating object. But to imagine an object moving quickly does not mean that anything moved quickly in the imagination. A choreographer may say to his dancers that he imagined a particular *pas de deux* much faster than they danced it, but that does not mean that they danced more quickly in his imagination. If someone insists that by the phrase 'they danced more quickly in my imagination' he just means 'I imagined them dancing more quickly', we can accept that, as long as it is clear that 'they danced more quickly in my imagination' does not imply that they danced more quickly. To imagine something louder does not imply that it was louder in one's imagination, just as to have expected an explosion to be noisier than it was does not imply that it made more noise in one's expectation.

The idea that it *must* take longer to imagine rotating a figure by 90° than to imagine rotating it by 45° is as misconceived as the thought that it must take longer to paint a slow-moving figure than it takes to paint a fast-moving one. There is no obvious reason why it should take one longer to imagine a figure rotating through 90° than to imagine it rotating through 45° – for one is at liberty to imagine the first figure rotating fast and the second more slowly. To assume that it takes longer to match a figure rotated by 90° than to match one rotated by 45° *because* the figure is being rotated at constant velocity adds a further incoherent hypothesis to the misconception. One might with equal cogency hypothesize that the gravitational force in mental space is also constant and that it is equivalent to 1G.

The cognitive scientific research we have been discussing rests on the fundamental misconception that mental images are kinds of things that exist in a private mental space, which can be observed by the subject alone, and which he can move at will. It presupposes that when one imagines something moving quickly or slowly, then there is something that moves quickly or slowly in one's imagination, and further, that if something moves quickly in one's imagination, then there is something that moves quickly. If one fails to grasp the structure of our concepts in this domain, then one may embark on investigations into the 'mental physics' of these putative 'mental objects', and suppose (with Finke) that mental images 'are governed by the same laws of motion' as physical objects. This is an exemplary case of being caught in the trammels of language, enmeshed in the web of grammar.

7

Emotion

7.1 Affections

The emotions are a subclass of affections

The affections can be roughly subdivided into emotions, agitations and moods. These shade off into attitudes that are not emotions, such as liking and disliking, approval and disapproval, on the one hand, and into character traits, such as benevolence, irascibility and vindictiveness, on the other. The emotions are traditionally referred to as 'passions', inasmuch as one is, in an important sense, passive in their reception. They are not actions or, for the most part, even things one does, but things one feels, that one may be in the grip of or full of, that come over one and often overcome one. One can order a person to perform an action; but in so far as one cannot order someone to do something that is not a voluntary action, one cannot literally order someone to love or hate. One can decide and intend to act, but one cannot decide or intend to be angry or to feel jealous. Nor can one try to feel, succeed in feeling, or *get better* at feeling angry, love or pity (only *become* more irascible, loving or compassionate). On the other hand, we do say of a person that he *ought* to feel grateful or *ought not* to feel jealous, that his anger is *warranted* in the circumstances or that he *has reason* to feel resentful, and we blame people for their excessive anger or unreasonable resentment. Although we cannot feel emotions at will or to order, we can cultivate and refine our emotional responses. We can give way to our emotions or bring them under control, we can give expression to them or suppress them. This suggests that the idea that our emotions are not, in any sense, voluntary may be wrong. Indeed, we are sometimes, in some ways and to some degree, responsible, answerable, for our emotions. We shall investigate this matter below.

Affections are feelings, but categorially distinct from feelings that are sensations, tactile perceptions or appetites

Affections are *feelings*. One can be said to feel love or hate (emotions), to feel excited or astonished (agitations), and to feel cheerful or depressed (moods). But the feelings that are affections are categorially distinct from the feelings that are sensations, which, unlike affections, have a bodily location and may inform one about the state of one's body. They are similarly distinct from the feelings that are modes of tactile perception, which, unlike affections, enable one to detect or apprehend features of one's environment. And they are distinct from the feelings that are appetites, such as feeling hungry, thirsty or lustful, and from addictive feelings, such as craving for opiates or alcohol, that are a subcategory of appetites – namely, induced, non-natural, ones. They are similarly distinguishable from feelings that resemble appetites in certain respects, such as feelings of weariness, lassitude or fatigue. These are not traditionally conceived of as appetites, perhaps because hunger, thirst and lust arise independently of action, and lead to action (e.g. food-seeking behaviour), whereas weariness results from action and leads to inaction.

The importance of distinguishing appetites from emotions – Rolls's error

The distinction between affections in general and emotions in particular, on the one hand, and appetites, on the other, is important to observe. Recent work on appetites has been mischaracterized as a result of failure to note the difference. E. T. Rolls's book *The Brain and Emotion* purports to be an investigation into the neural substrate of the emotions. But it takes as its paradigmatic examples of emotions, and as the object of all its experimental research, thirst, hunger and lust. Despite the interest of the results of these investigations, they are not about, and do not obviously have any bearing on, the emotions, for the simple reason that hunger, thirst and lust are appetites, not emotions.

Appetites are blends of sensation and desire

Appetites are blends of sensation and desire that are characteristic of animals. The sensations that are partly constitutive of appetites have a specific localization. The sensation characteristic of hunger is located in the midriff – one could not have a feeling of hunger in one's throat, any more than one could have feelings of thirst in one's midriff. The feelings of hunger in one's belly must be distinguished from mere accompanying sensations such as light-headedness and dizziness that may occur after one has been hungry for a time. The sensation characteristic of thirst is the feeling of a dry throat that is, as it were, blended with a desire for drink. The sensations associated with appetites are forms of unease that dispose one to action to satisfy the appetite. The intensification of the sensations, particularly in the cases of hunger and thirst (as in the case of appetites of addiction), is progressively more and more unpleasant. 'Hunger', as Beaumont and Fletcher remarked, 'is sharper than the sword,' and a 'ravening fellow has a wolf in his belly'; but, as Eliza Cook observed, 'Hunger is bitter, but the worst of human pangs, the most accursed of Want's fell scorpions, is Thirst.'

The desire that is blended with the sensation is characterized by its formal object. Hunger is a desire for food, thirst a desire for drink, and lust is a desire for sexual intercourse. What distinguishes the desires that are partly constitutive of appetites from other kinds of desire is not merely the fact that the former are blended with characteristic sensations, but also that the appetites lack any *specific* object. The child who announces that he is not hungry for the main course, but only for the pudding, is inadvertently making a grammatical joke. The adult who announces that he is very thirsty for a gin and tonic, but not for a cup of tea, is intentionally making one.

The intensity of the desire is typically proportional to the intensity of the sensation. Satisfying an appetite leads to its temporary satiation and so to the disappearance of the sensation. Of course, the glutton may still want food, but no longer because he is hungry, just as the drunkard may want another drink, but not because he is thirsty. Appetites are not constant, but recurrent. They are typically and naturally caused by bodily needs (or, in the case of lust, by hormonally determined drives) consequent upon, for example, deprivation of food, drink or sexual intercourse, although needing food or drink or having a felt urge to have sexual intercourse is not the same as wanting it.

Differences between appetites and emotions

Appetites are therefore unlike emotions. First, emotions are not linked to localized sensations in the same way. Some emotions are associated with sensations (fear, rage), others are not (pride, remorse, envy). One does not have a feeling of pride in one's stomach or in one's chest, and although there are sensations characteristic of occurrent anger, such as throbbing temples and tension, one does not feel anger in one's temples or stomach muscles as one feels hunger in one's belly. Second, emotions have not only formal objects, in the sense that what one fears is what is thought to be frightening or harmful and what one feels remorseful about is a misdemeanour one has committed, they have specific objects, as when one fears tomorrow's examination or feels remorseful about lying to Daisy. Third, the intensity of emotions, as we shall see, is not proportional to the intensity of whatever sensations may occompany their occurrent manifestation. How much I fear heights may be manifest in the lengths I go to avoid them, and how proud I am of my children's achievements cannot be measured by reference to sensations. Fourth, emotions do not display the pattern of occurrence, satiation and recurrence characteristic of appetites, for the obvious reason that they do not have the same kind of physiological and hormonal basis as the appetites. Fifth, the emotions have a cognitive dimension absent from the appetites. The hungry animal wants food, the thirsty animal wants drink, the animal on heat wants sexual intercourse, but no particular knowledge or beliefs are essentially associated with these appetites. By contrast, the frightened animal is afraid of something it knows or thinks is dangerous; a mother is proud of her offspring inasmuch as she believes them to have such-and-such merits; a repentant sinner is remorseful, knowing himself to have done wrong. Finally, many human emotions are exhibited by characteristic facial expressions and manifested in typical tones of voice – as in the case of fear, anger, love and affection. Appetites are not.

Paradigmatic emotions are things such as love, hate, hope, fear, anger, gratitude, resentment, indignation, envy, jealousy, pity, compassion and grief, as well as emotions of self-assessment such as pride, shame, humiliation, regret, remorse and guilt.

Agitations distinguished from emotions

Agitations are short-term affective disturbances, typically caused by something unexpected. They include such temporary states as being and feeling excited, thrilled, shocked, convulsed, amazed, surprised, startled, horrified, revolted, disgusted or delighted. They are caused by what we perceive, learn or realize. Because they are disturbances, caused by unanticipated disruptions, they are not motives for action as emotions may be, but temporarily *inhibit* motivated action. One may behave in certain ways *because* one is excited, thrilled or shocked. But one does not act *out of* excitement, thrill or shock in the sense in which one acts out of love, compassion or gratitude. Agitations are modes of reaction: one cries out *in* horror or amazement, recoils *with* revulsion or disgust, is convulsed *with* laughter or paralysed *with* shock. Occurrently felt emotions, by contrast with longer-standing emotional attitudes, often bear a kinship to agitations in the perturbations of, for example, the throbbing temples of rage, the trembling, sweating and shallow breathing of fear, the tears and cries of grief.

Moods distinguished from emotions
Moods are such things as feeling cheerful, euphoric, contented, irritable, melancholic or depressed; they are states or frames of mind one is in, as when one is in a state of melancholia, or in a jovial or relaxed frame of mind. They may be occurrent states of mind or longer-term dispositional states. One may feel depressed, melancholic, joyful, jovial, irritable or cheerful for an afternoon, or one may be suffering from a long-term depression that lasts for months, as one may be in a cheerful mood for days on end. As a disposition, a mood is a proneness to feel, during one's waking hours, joyful, or depressed, or cheerful, and so forth. Moods are less closely tied to objects than emotions, for one may feel cheerful or depressed without one's mood being directed at any specific object, whereas one cannot feel love without feeling love for someone or something or feel angry without feeling angry with anyone or about anything. Equally, moods are closely linked not to specific patterns of intentional action, let alone to motives, but to manners of behaviour. Cheerfulness, melancholia and depression, unlike love, envy or compassion, do not provide motives for action, but they are exhibited in the manner in which one does whatever one does, in one's demeanour and tone of voice. This is a corollary of the fact that moods colour one's thoughts and pervade one's reflections.

Moods are not emotional states that are frequent or prolonged
It is unwarranted, therefore, to characterize moods, as Damasio does, as emotional states that are frequent or continuous over long periods of time.[1] One may fear war for a long period, but this does not imply that one is in any particular mood, although, to be sure, one's fear of an impending war may contribute to one's melancholic mood. Othello's jealousy was persistent and continuous, but, unlike his consequent depression, it was not a mood. One may be envious of A's success for years, but envy, whether prolonged or not, is no mood. And frequently, to fear things may be to be timorous by nature, but it is not to be in any mood.

The boundaries between emotion, agitation and mood are not sharp. Emotional perturbations (as we shall refer to the typical somatic, expressive and behavioral manifestations of many occurrent emotions) have, as remarked, an affinity with agitations. Emotions may fade into moods, as when terror that abates leaves behind a mood of objectless anxiety. And conversely, a feeling of undirected anxiety may crystallize into a specific fear. The psychological category of the affections displays both conceptual complexity and diversity; the conceptual patterns to be discerned are irregular, and the variations from type to type are considerable. Consequently, most generalizations concerning the concepts within the three subcategories need to be qualified with a 'for the most part' or a 'typically'.

---

[1] A. Damasio, *The Feeling of What Happens* (Heinemann, London, 1999), p. 341.

7.2 The Emotions: A Preliminary Analytical Survey

Emotional character traits distin-guished from emotions as episodic perturbations and as attitudes

One must distinguish between emotional character traits (which are not feelings), emotions as episodic perturbations, and emotions as longer-standing attitudes (both of which are said to be feelings). Many emotion terms have a use as names of character traits: we speak of people as having a compassionate or loving nature, as being of a jealous or envious disposition, or as being irascible, timid or timorous by nature. Ascription of such character traits signifies a proneness to be and to feel compassionate or loving, jealous or envious, angry or timid, given appropriate circumstances; and so too to act *out of* compassion or love, jealousy or envy, *in* anger or *with* timidity.

Episodic emotional perturbation dis-tinguished from emotional attitude – neuroscience typically neglects the latter

The notion of *felt emotion* does not discriminate between an episodic emotional perturbation and a longer-standing emotional attitude. One may feel a wave of pity for poor so-and-so, feel furious with someone who has given offence, feel proud to be given the trophy one is being awarded – here emotion clearly converges on the subcategory of agitations. But equally, one may feel pity for someone for as long as he is in a pickle, feel angry for years with someone (but not furious or enraged – which are perturbational forms of anger), and feel proud for the rest of one's days to have won a trophy.[2] When we speak of a person as 'giving way to his emotions', 'controlling his emotions', 'being overcome with emotion', it is usually emotional perturbations that we have in mind. When we characterize a person as being 'emotional', we do not mean that he feels love or hatred for many people, harbours numerous fears and hopes, etc. Rather, what we have in mind is that he is prone to emotional perturbation, is given to outbursts of feeling, expresses his anger, indignation, love or hate freely, and perhaps to excess, and tends to allow his emotions to affect his judgement deleteriously. It is important, however, not to let this aspect of the emotions occlude others, or to think that research on emotional perturbation alone can provide an adequate account of the emotions in question. Neuroscientific work, much influenced by the misconceived James–Lange theory of the emotions, has systematically, but unwittingly, screened out the attitudinal, as well as the motivational, cogitative and fantasy aspects of the emotions.

---

[2] It is perhaps tempting to suppose that the term 'feeling' (as in 'feeling angry, afraid, proud') is confined to emotional perturbations, while 'being' (as in 'being angry, afraid, proud') earmarks the emotional attitude. But that would be a mistake. *For the most part*, 'feeling angry' and 'being angry' are intersubstitutable. By and large, there is little, if any, difference between *feeling* afraid of the impending war and *being* afraid of it, between feeling proud to have won the trophy and being proud to have won it. Respect and admiration, for example, involve no agitation, yet are nevertheless said to be felt, and there seems to be no difference between respecting and admiring someone and feeling respect and admiration for him. Where there is a nuanced difference in usage here, it is not to distinguish between emotional perturbation and emotional attitude.

The standing emotional attitude is no less an aspect of our complex notion of an emotion than the correlative emotional perturbation. One's judgement may be clouded by one's emotional distress and agitation, as when one feels overwhelmed with grief, engulfed with rage, or in the grip of fear. But it may be equally distorted by one's long-standing resentments, envies or jealousies. Love of another person is an emotion which, on the one hand, may be felt as an emotional perturbation – the wave of tenderness, the melting heart, the trembling hands, the blushes and so forth that may come over a young Romeo in the presence of his Juliet, and, on the other hand, as a standing attitude, exhibited, for example, in the mature conjugal love of Pierre and Natasha in the Epilogue of *War and Peace*. The standing attitude is not a disposition to the corresponding episodes of emotional perturbation, but a lasting concern for the object of love, a standing motive for action beneficial to or protective of the person loved, a knowledge of and desire for shared experience, and a persistent colouring of thought, imagination and wish. The standing emotional attitude of love of, say, Pierre for Natasha is indeed linked to emotional perturbations, but not those of the melting heart, the joyful flushing, trembling hands and confused speech of youthful passion. Rather, it is linked to those perturbations that characterize *concern* for those one loves – *anxiety* about their welfare, *joy* in their achievement, *longing* to be reunited after absence, and so forth. (And one should not forget that one may love not only people (parents, spouse, children, friends), but also activities (conducting an orchestra, gardening, fighting battles), objects, places, views and landscapes (flowers, trees, the sea, one's home, one's city), works of art (paintings, musical compositions), and ideals (honour, liberty) – many of which are wholly unsuited to some of the occurrent perturbations of love.) Again, the hatred that Edmond Dantès bears his treacherous erstwhile friends is manifest far less in emotional outbursts than in the iron determination of his will for revenge, in the cast of his thought and fantasy, and in his motives and reasons for action over many years. The envy that moves Cousine Bette need not sweep over her every morning, but it informs her life in a multitude of ways. The love, hate or envy lie in the manner in which the object of one's emotion matters to one and the reasons for which it is important for one – one cannot at the same time feel an emotion which is directed at a given object and also feel indifferent about that object. Hence, too, it lies in the motives that move one to action; for someone who feels these emotions will normally act *out of* love, hate or envy. One's emotions are then evident in the reasons that weigh with one in one's deliberations, in the desires one harbours, and in the thoughts that cross one's mind in connection with the objects of one's feelings. One's emotions are inseparable from one's fantasy life and imagination, one's wishes and longings. So, for example, one dwells on one's hopes and fears, fantasizes about the fulfilment of one's wishes with respect to the objects of one's love or pride, and worries obsessively about the objects of one's anxieties.

Emotion cannot be measured simply by the frequency and intensity of perturbations

As noted above, one cannot measure a person's emotion simply by the frequency or intensity of the emotional perturbations he feels. A person's fear, for example, may be manifest above all in the lengths he will go to avoid situations which strike terror in his heart. The strength of its motivating force does not lend itself to quantification in the sense in which the rise in pulse, breathing, or perspiration rate does. Rather, its strength is evaluated by reference to the extent to which the emotion determines behaviour over time, and the kind of behaviour it determines. Moreover, although fear is a ubiquitous aspect of the animal, and hence too human, condition, it is a poor representative. For there are many emotions which typically involve little, if any, emotional perturbation or disturbance; for example, humility, respect, admiration, contempt and gratitude. Indeed, not *all* instances of fear need involve fearful agitation, not because the fear is slight, but because of the character of the *object* of fear. What one is afraid of may preclude any particular, or at least any intense, fearful perturbation. Fear of imminent physical danger, harm or injury typically *will*. But fear of rain during the garden party one has planned for tomorrow, fear of a rise in the rate of inflation next month or of global warming over the next decades will not – even though the ensuing motivation may be powerful, and the effect on the agent's mood may be substantial. Similarly, the depth of a person's remorse may be exhibited not in a syndrome of sensations and perturbations that he feels, but rather in his strenuous endeavours to make amends for his past action and in his obsessive thoughts about his sin. The strength of a person's love for another is not to be evaluated only by the degree of his agitation in the presence of his beloved, but also by his concern for her welfare and by the sacrifices he is willing to make for her sake. The former without the latter may be more indicative of infatuation and desire than love.

Ambiguity of 'duration of emotion'

Consequently, the idea of the duration of an emotion is likewise equivocal. For it may refer to the duration of the perturbation of an emotional episode, or to the duration of a thought-infusing, fantasy-inducing, motivating emotional attitude which, in many different ways, may inform a person's life over a prolonged period of time.

Because of the conceptual complexity and diversity of emotions, there is no single conceptual prototype

Any experimental investigation of the emotions must take into account the complexity of the concept of an emotion and the conceptual diversity of the various emotions to which human beings are susceptible. There is no single paradigm of an emotion which can serve, as it were, as a conceptual prototype. Some emotions, when felt in appropriate circumstances and with respect to a certain range of objects, are closely associated with a pattern of sensations and characteristic facial expressions, as in the case of fear of physical harm, grief or anger. Others, such as hope, remorse or compassion, are not. Some emotions are exhibited in forms of agitation involving characteristic reactive behaviour, as in the case of terror (crying out, trembling, turning white) or grief (weeping, wailing). Others, such as pride, respect or compassion are not. Some emotions are closely associated with relatively specific forms of action or inclinations to act, as in the case of fear of imminent danger (inclination to avoid or flee) or pity (inclination to help). Others, such as regret or hope, are not. So one should not take a single emotion, such as fear (let alone episodes of conditioned fear), restricted to a single object (e.g. pain), as a representative paradigm and generalize from that one kind of case. Conditioning rats to fear an electric shock (cf. LeDoux's important research) is a poor foundation for insight into human emotion and its neurophysiological conditions and accompaniments.

The differences between human and animal emotion are important for neuroscience

Since so much experimental work is done on non-human animals, it is important to be aware of the differences between human emotions, on the one hand, and the emotions of non-language-using animals, on the other.

We share many emotions with other animals – for example, curiosity, fear and anger. But the scope of possible objects of human curiosity, fear or anger vastly outstrips that of mere animal curiosity, fear and anger. The cognitive and appraisive aspects of human emotions reach far wider than those of animal emotions. Of course, the monkey that screams in fear of a snake knows snakes to be harmful. The lion that snarls in anger at the cub that is pestering it apprehends the cub as annoying. The pet cat that purrs with delight as its food is being prepared knows that it is about to be given its meal. But the cognitive capacities of animals are strictly limited by their lack of language. Many of the kinds of beliefs that enter into an account of human emotion are not beliefs that could possibly be ascribed to an animal. Emotions, we have suggested, are ways in which we manifest what is important to us. But human beings characteristically reflect on what matters to them, whereas non-language-using animals merely manifest what they care about (their territory, possession of the prey they have killed, their dominance in their group, etc.) in their behaviour. Hence the motivating power of an emotion in a non-language-using animal is both very restricted and importantly different from the motivating force of emotions among human beings. For human beings act for reasons, whereas animals at the most do so in a limited and attenuated sense. Human emotions colour thoughts and fantasies, but non-language-using animals do not dwell in thought upon the objects of their emotions and do not fantasize about the fulfilment of their hopes and fears – they lack the conceptual equipment which makes such thoughts and fantasies possible. Finally, there are many emotions, such as feelings of guilt, awe, remorse and moral indignation, which it is not logically possible for non-language-using animals to have. For such emotions presuppose mastery of a language and possession of appropriate concepts. An awareness of the limitations on animal emotion and its objects should provide a brake on unwarranted generalization in which conclusions derived from experiments on animals are extended without more ado to human beings. So neuroscientific research that focuses upon conditioned fear in rats screens out most of what is distinctive of human fears, in particular, and emotions in general. Even if this is the correct point from which to begin one's endeavours to understand the neurological underpinings of human emotion, it is not at all obviously a point from which sweeping generalizations can be drawn – just as the calls of a wild animal are a poor basis for generalizing about the nature of human speech.

Object and cause of emotion distinguished

Emotions generally have objects. If one is afraid, one is afraid *of* someone or something, or *that* something has happened or is going to happen; if one feels remorse, guilt or regret, it is *for* doing something; if one feels envy, it is envy *of* another *for* his good fortune. Evidently, there is more than one sense of 'object of an emotion' at work here, and it is important, as we shall see, to distinguish them. The object of an emotion must be distinguished from its cause – what *makes* one jealous is not the same as what one is jealous *of*; your indignant tirade may make me feel ashamed, but what I am ashamed of is my own misbehaviour; a change in the fortunes of war may make one feel hopeful, but what one hopes for is final victory.

Emotions linked to knowledge and belief

Emotions are also linked in complex ways to knowledge and belief. One cannot feel envious unless one knows or believes that another has enjoyed good fortune, feel jealous unless one knows or believes that a person one loves is showing favours to another, or feel fear of something unless one apprehends it as a threat to an interest one has. In this way the emotions essentially involve an appraisal or evaluation of their objects relative to the concerns of the agent. Knowledge or belief are equally involved in a human being's rationale for his emotion – that is, in the specific reasons he has for feeling what he feels.

Somatic accompaniments and beha-
vioural manifestations of emotions
Some emotions have characteristic somatic accompaniments, sensations and physiological reactions that occur on occasions in which the emotion – for example, fear, anger or grief – is felt as a perturbation. Some emotional perturbations have characteristic behavioural manifestations. Some of these are expressive *reactions* of facial grimace, gesture and bodily demeanour. Others are voluntary expressive (as opposed to instrumental) *actions*; they are typically done not intentionally, for a purpose, or for the sake of a goal, and to the extent that they are, to that extent they are not purely expressive. Expressive manifestations of emotional perturbations include the *manner* of acting, even when the action *is* instrumental: when one is angry, one may slam the door rather than shut it quietly; when one is excited, one may raise one's voice; and one's hands may shake with fear during a viva voce. But standing emotional attitudes may also be exhibited in facial expression, mode of action, and demeanour – as is evident in the reciprocal behaviour of people who love each other, or the manner of behaviour of a person in the presence of another whom he admires and respects or fears and hates.

Emotions linked to volition,
motivation, rationality and fantasy
Emotions commonly involve desire or aversion, and hence are linked to volition and motivation. Emotions are linked to reasonableness and irrationality inasmuch as there can be reasons for an emotion, and the emotions commonly involve reasons for action for the the agent. Emotions are linked to the imagination or fantasy, inasmuch as an emotion and its objects may inform one's thoughts, occupy one's daydreams, and preoccupy one during one's sleepless nights.

7.2.1 Neuroscientists' confusions

LeDoux's misconceptions
We shall explore a small part of this densely woven conceptual web in a moment. But it should already be evident that the conception of emotion shared by eminent neuroscientists is flawed, partly as a consequence of an inadequate grasp of the concept of an emotion. So, for example, LeDoux summarizes the conclusions of his major book on the subject with the following observation:

> Emotional feelings result when we become consciously aware that an emotion system of the brain is active. Any organism that has consciousness has feelings. However, feelings will be different in a brain that can classify the world linguistically and categorize experiences in words than in a brain that cannot. The difference between fear, anxiety, terror, apprehension, and the like would not be possible without language. At the same time, none of these words would have any point if it were not for the existence of an underlying emotion system that generates brain states and bodily expressions to which these words apply. Emotions evolved not as conscious feelings, linguistically differentiated or not, but as brain states and bodily responses. The brain states and bodily responses

are the fundamental facts of an emotion, and the conscious feelings are the frills that have added icing to the emotional cake.[3]

But this is confused, and does not provide insight into either the nature of or the empirical conditions for feeling any given emotion.

The causal conditions for feeling an emotion are distinguished from both the cause and the object of the emotion

(i)   An emotion may indeed 'result' in response to a cause. Unquestionably the appropriate functioning of the brain is a *causal condition* of feeling emotions. Damage to the ventromedial prefrontal cortices, for example, or to the somatosensory cortices in the right hemisphere severely compromises normal emotional responsiveness. But it would be misguided to assimilate the causal conditions for the possibility of feeling an emotion to the cause of a specific emotion on a given occasion. So, for example, what one is frightened *by* (e.g. the sound of a shot) is the cause of one's fear – not the condition of one's brain that makes fear possible. Furthermore, the object of an emotion need not be the same as (although it may sometimes coincide with) the cause of an emotion. What one is frightened *by* – namely, the sound of a shot – need not be the same as what one is frightened *of* – namely, being killed – just as what *makes* Othello jealous (Iago's fabrications) need not be what he is jealous *of* (Desdemona's supposed love for Cassio). When one feels an emotion, one is *not* 'consciously aware that an emotion system of the brain is active'. For one feels emotion without knowing anything at all about the activities of the brain, any more than one need know the cause (as opposed to the object) of one's emotion. To feel love, jealousy or envy, and to be 'consciously aware' that one so feels, is not to be aware of an emotion system of the brain that is a causal condition for being able to have such an emotion. Rather, it is to feel love for so-and-so (jealous or envious of so-and-so) and to *realize* that one does.

The differences between animal and human emotion are not due to our brain's classifying things, but to our possession of a language

(ii)   We have already noted that the felt emotions of a non-language-using animal are far narrower in range and in object than the emotions of a human being. I can, but my dog cannot, now hope for a good dinner on Christmas day; I can, but my dog cannot, fear the ravages of war; and while my dog may be apprehensive after having done something it associates with punishment, it cannot feel regret or remorse. These differences between human and animal emotions obtain not because our brain 'classifies the world linguistically and categorizes experiences in words' (for this is not something brains can do), but because we (not our brains) have mastered a language, and that has enlarged the horizon of our thought and feeling alike.

Because animals have not mastered a language, they cannot have characteristic human emotions

(iii)   It is mistaken to suppose that 'the difference between fear, anxiety, terror, apprehension and the like would not be possible without language'. These feelings are not dependent on mastery of a language. A cat may

---

[3] J. LeDoux, *The Emotional Brain*, (Phoenix, London, 1998), p. 302.

feel anxious when it perceives a large dog, even though the cat is safely up a tree; a dog may exhibit fear when it is threatened with punishment; and a rabbit pursued by a fox may feel terror. But it is perfectly true that many emotions that human beings feel are not possible for non-human animals. Only a language-user can fear bankruptcy, feel anxious about inflation, feel terror of ghosts, and feel apprehensive about the state of the nation. These are emotions of a type which non-human animals can feel, but with objects which lie beyond their cognitive horizon. Similarly, only a language-user can feel remorse for his lies or treachery, feel awe at the sublime or contempt for the despicable. These are emotions of a type which non-human animals cannot feel.

Emotions are neither brain states nor somatic reactions

(iv)   Emotions cannot be said to have evolved *as* 'brain states and bodily responses'. Rather, brains evolved in such a way as to make it possible for animals to respond affectively to objects of their concern. Emotions evolved as animals' responses to features of the environment apprehended as affecting in one way or another the good of the animal. Neither brain states (which are essential for feeling an emotion) nor somatic responses (which may characterize an emotional perturbation) are emotions. They lack the intentionality, or 'directedness towards an object', which is constitutive of most emotions. One cannot individuate an emotion by reference to either brain states or somatic reactions independently of the circumstances of their occurrence and the knowledge or beliefs, as well as the desires or wishes, of the creature.

Emotions and somatic responses

(v)   Emotion words do not apply to brain states at all, but to creatures, who feel emotions and exhibit them in their behaviour. Emotion words are not names of bodily responses that characterize emotional perturbation. Brain states are 'the fundamental facts of an emotion' only in the sense that they are essential for the animal to feel the emotion it feels, as indeed they are also essential for the animal to breathe or move, to perceive and to respond to what is perceived. Bodily responses are not 'the fundamental facts of an emotion' in any illuminating sense. My acrophobia may be manifest in my avoidance of heights, not in my sensations when I climb heights – since I carefully avoid climbing them precisely because of my fear (once may have been quite enough). Anger at the Ruritanian National Party need not be manifest in going red in the face and shouting (such behaviour being unseemly), but in terminating one's subscription to the party. And love of honour in a knight errant was manifest not in *perturbations of love*, but in what he counted as a reason for action, in the lengths he was willing to go to preserve his honour, in his admiration for honourable men and their deeds, and in the *perturbations of indignation* at what he viewed as dishonourable in others. The bodily responses of fear of physical harm – for example, increased pulse rate, perspiration and trembling – can all be exhibited without any fear whatsoever, as when one trembles with excitement on entering a hot room expecting a delightful surprise. What make those responses fear responses are the circumstances in which they are exhibited, and the beliefs, desires and thoughts of the agent. The 'fundamental facts of an emotion', in the case of human beings, are the agent's awareness of, or beliefs about, an appropriate object of emotion in the circumstances, the character of his concern for the object of his emotion (why it matters to him), and the consequent reasons for action he may have, the motivation afforded the agent by the relevant appraisal or evaluation, the behaviour or behavioural disposition thus connected with the object of the emotion, and the associated thoughts, fancies and wishes. That a creature *feels* fear when it apprehends danger, or anger when it perceives encroachment upon its territory; that a human being *feels* hope that a certain desideratum will eventuate, *feels* filial, conjugal or parental love, *feels* pride at the completion of a difficult and worthy task, remorse for a sin, or embarrassment at a gaff, are not the 'icing [on] the emotional cake' but the flour from which the cake is made. It is precisely in the context of the recognition of an appropriate object of an emotion, of concern for it, and of a form of behaviour or inclination to behave appropriate to that object (given the agent's goals and beliefs) that somatic accompaniments, voluntary actions and involuntary reactions of an agent can be characterized *as* manifestations of that emotion.

LeDoux is mistaken to think that a creature can have an emotion without feeling it

(vi)   It is a mistake to distinguish between having an emotion and feeling an emotion, and to suppose that animals that are conscious can both have and feel emotions, whereas animals lacking consciousness may have an emotion – that is, appropriate brain states and bodily responses – even though they do not feel emotions. Emotions, we have noted, are not brain states or bodily responses. They are neither objects of perception nor sensations that are felt. To *feel* frightened just is to *be* frightened, just as *feeling* angry is not distinct from *being* angry. One cannot be afraid or angry on an occasion and not feel afraid or angry. It is a further confusion to suppose that there are animals that can have emotions but that are not conscious (as opposed to self-conscious) creatures (a distinction that we shall examine in chapter 12).

Damasio on the emotions

Comparable confusion is evident in the writings of another distinguished neuroscientist. Antonio Damasio's work on patients suffering from emotionally incapacitating brain damage is rightly renowned, and his insistence on a link between the capacity for rational decision making and consequent rational action in pursuit of goals, on the one hand, and the capacity for feeling emotions, on the other, is bold and thought-provoking. However, his speculations on the emotions are, in our view, vitiated by conceptual confusion.

The influence of James on Damasio

Damasio's conception of the emotions is much influenced by William James, who held that emotions are essentially the feelings of somatic disturbances consequent on the perception of an 'exciting fact'. An emotion, according to James, is not the somatic change itself, but the agent's perception or apprehension of it. The changes are indefinitely numerous and subtle, and the entire body is a 'sounding board' for such excitations. Every one of these bodily changes is allegedly felt as soon as it occurs. One cannot abstract from an emotion 'all the feelings of its bodily symptoms' and find anything left behind other than a cold and neutral state of intellectual perception.[4] Damasio contends that James, 'well ahead of both his time and ours, . . . seized upon the mechanism essential to the

---

[4] William James, *The Principles of Psychology* (Molt, New York, 1890), vol. 2, pp. 449–51. For a brief critical discussion of James's confusions, see A. J. P. Kenny, *Action, Emotion and the Will* (Routledge and Kegan Paul, London, 1963), pp. 39–41.

understanding of emotion and feeling'.[5] Damasio himself sees 'the essence of emotion as the collection of changes in body state that are induced in myriad organs by nerve cell terminals, under the control of a dedicated brain system, which is responding to the content of thoughts relative to a particular entity or event'.[6] The somatic changes are held to be caused by thoughts. Damasio's conception of thoughts is firmly rooted in the eighteenth-century empiricist tradition. Thoughts, he claims, consist of mental images (which may be visual or auditory, etc., and may be of items in the world or of words or symbols that signify such items).[7] The images constituting thoughts are comparable to the images of which perception allegedly consists, differing from them in being fainter or less lively. In this respect Damasio self-consciously but misguidedly follows in the footsteps of David Hume.[8] Damasio apparently holds the view that if thought were not exhibited to us in the form of images of things and images of words signifying things, then we would not be able to say what we think.[9]

Damasio's conception of emotion

Damasio, unlike James (but like LeDoux), distinguishes *an emotion* – that is, 'a collection of changes in body state connected to particular mental images that have activated a specific brain system' – from the *feeling of an emotion*. '*The essence of feeling an emotion is the experience of such changes in juxtaposition to the mental images that initiated the cycle.* In other words, a feeling depends on the juxtaposition of an image of the body proper to an image of something else, such as the visual image of a face or the auditory image of a melody.'[10] So, an emotion is a bodily response to a mental image, and the feeling of an emotion is a cognitive response to that bodily condition, a cognitive response 'in connection to the object that excited it, the realization of the nexus between object and emotional body state'.[11] Feelings of emotion,

---

[5] Antonio R. Damasio, *Descartes' Error: Emotion, Reason and the Human Brain* (Papermac, London, 1996), p. 129. He remarks that James's insights on the human mind have been rivalled only by Shakespeare's and Freud's. This praise, in our view, would be more properly directed towards William's brother Henry.

[6] Ibid., p. 139.

[7] Ibid., pp. 107f.

[8] Ibid., p. 108. Hume's account is in *A Treatise of Human Nature*, I. i. 1.

[9] He writes: 'Most of the words we use in our inner speech, before speaking or writing a sentence, exist as auditory or visual images in our consciousness. If they did not become images, however fleetingly, they would not be anything we could know' (*Descartes' Error*, p. 106). He fails to see that one *could not* find out what one thinks by mere attention to whatever mental images cross one's mind when one thinks. A mental image may, as it were, illustrate a thought, as a picture may illustrate a text. But it is the thought that makes the mental image the image of what it depicts, just as it is the text of the book that makes the illustration an illustration of the story. Without the text the picture of Lancelot in full armour could depict any knight whatsoever, illustrate how to sit in the saddle, or how *not* to sit in the saddle, illustrate armour of a given period, or depict the kind of horse used by knights in armour, and so on. And what applies to the relation of picture to text applies similarly to the relation of mental image and thought.

[10] Ibid., p. 145.

[11] Ibid., p. 132.

Damasio avers, '*are just as cognitive as any other perceptual image*, and just as dependent on cerebral-cortex processing as any other image'. However,

> feelings are about something different. But what makes them different is that they are first and foremost about the body, they offer us *the cognition of our visceral and musculoskeletal state* as it becomes affected by preorganized mechanisms and by the cognitive structures we have developed under their influence. Feelings let us *mind the body* . . . Feelings offer us a glimpse, of what goes on in our flesh, as a momentary image of that flesh is juxtaposed to the images of other objects and situations; in so doing, feelings modify our comprehensive notion of those other objects and situations. By dint of juxtaposition, body images give other images a *quality* of goodness or badness, of pleasure or pain.[12]

Damasio's somatic marker hypothesis   Accordingly, Damasio proposes what he calls 'the somatic marker hypothesis'. The hypothesis is that somatic responses to 'images' (i.e. perceptions and thoughts) serve to increase the accuracy and efficiency of decision processes, screening out a range of alternatives and allowing the agent to choose from among fewer.[13] 'When a negative somatic marker is juxtaposed to a particular future outcome the combination functions as an alarm bell. When a positive somatic marker is juxtaposed instead, it becomes a beacon of incentive.'[14] So somatic markers, constituted by the somatic response to situations confronting us, assist deliberation by highlighting some options and eliminating them. These somatic responses which we allegedly use for decision making 'probably were created in our brains during the process of education and socialization, by connecting specific classes of stimuli with specific classes of somatic state'.[15] Culturally inculcated 'gut reactions' provide the basis for rational decision making.[16] This leads Damasio to conjecture that the decision-making and executive deficiencies in patients suffering from lesions in the prefrontal cortices is to be explained in terms of a lack of somatic markers to guide them.

This conception, we suggest, involves conceptual confusion.

---

[12] Ibid., p. 159.

[13] Ibid., p. 173.

[14] Ibid., p. 174.

[15] Ibid., p. 177.

[16] Damasio's theory is to a large degree a stimulus–response theory, operating at the neural, rather than at the behavioural, level. He writes:

> Somatic markers are thus acquired by experience, under the control of an internal preference system and under the influence of an external set of circumstances which include not only entities and events with which the organism must interact, but also social conventions and ethical rules.
>
> The neural basis for the internal preference system consists of mostly innate regulatory dispositions, posed to ensure survival of the organism. Achieving survival coincides with the ultimate reduction of unpleasant body states and the attaining of homeostatic ones, i.e. functionally balanced biological states. The internal preference system is inherently biased to avoid pain, seek potential pleasure, and is probably pretuned for achieving these goals in social situations.' (Ibid., p. 179)

Damasio's confusions: An emotion is not a somatic change caused by a thought. Four objections

(i)   An emotion is not an ensemble of somatic changes caused by a 'thought' about (i.e. mental image of) an object or event. First, even if a given emotional perturbation does involve a range of somatic changes, what makes the sensations sensations of fear as opposed to anger, and what makes the blushes blushes of shame rather than of embarrassment or of love, is not the 'thought' or mental image, *if any*, that causes them, but the circumstances and the object of the emotion. One might indeed argue that what connects the sensations with the circumstances and object of the emotion is that, had the object of the emotion not been apprehended in the manner in which it was, the sensations would not have occurred – and perhaps this is part of what Damasio had in mind. Nevertheless, it is not the somatic changes or their apprehension that constitutes the emotion.

Secondly, if emotions were essentially ensembles of somatic changes caused by thoughts (mental images) – that is, if that is what the term 'emotion' means – then learning the meaning of emotion words, and hence learning how to use them, would be a matter of learning the names of complexes of bodily changes with specific causes (akin to learning the meaning of an expression like 'giddiness' or 'seasickness'). But we do not learn the use of emotion words by learning sensation names or names of overall bodily condition, but rather by learning what are appropriate objects of the relevant emotions – for example, of fear (what is dangerous or threatening), of anger (what is annoying, offensive or in some way wrong), of pride (worthy achievement or possessions), of guilt (one's own moral misdemeanours), and so forth, and learning how to use these terms ('afraid', 'angry', etc.) in the expression of one's feelings towards the appropriate objects and in the description of the feelings (but not the sensations) of others.

Thirdly, if emotions were ensembles of somatic changes caused by mental images, then one could not have good reasons for feeling a certain emotion, and would not be answerable for one's emotions in the manner in which we are. For although there may *be* a reason (i.e. an explanation) as to why one has a headache, or why one's breathing rate or heartbeat rises, one cannot *have* a reason (i.e. a ground or warrant) for such things. Given appropriate circumstances, we can say that someone ought to, and has good reason to, feel proud or ashamed, but we cannot say (save in what is merely a predictive sense) that his pulse rate ought to rise, or that his psychogalvanic reflex reactions ought to change.

Fourthly, one can feel an emotion E without any E-type perturbation. One can love a person, an object (place, artefact or work of art) or a value without undergoing any somatic changes of love when one thinks about the parents, wife or children one loves, or about Venice, Chartres Cathedral or Beethoven's late quartets, let alone about liberty, justice or honour. There need be no somatic changes accompanying the thought that the rate of inflation is likely to rise – but one may well fear that it will. One's pulses need not race in order for one to hope that tomorrow's picnic will be a success. If A did one a major favour in one's youth, one may remain grateful for the rest of one's days – but one need not break out in a sweat whenever one thinks of A and the favour done. One may be proud for the whole of one's subsequent life to have won an Oxford Blue, but there are no somatic changes characteristic of pride in something – or of many other types of emotion and many other emotions with certain kinds of object.

Of course, to insist on these points is not to deny that there is an essential link between *certain* emotions and emotions directed to *specific objects*, on the one hand, and types of emotional agitation involving somatic changes, on the other. At the very least, the emotional agitation may be *characteristic* of that emotion, or of that emotion with that type of object, given appropriate circumstances. It is merely to insist that the emotion is not the somatic changes that might be caused by the thought of the object of such an emotion.

Damasio's confusions: any somatic changes need not be caused by mental images

(ii)   It is, as we have already argued (§4.2.3), a mistake to suppose that perceiving an object or perceiving that things are thus-and-so involves having images of anything. It is equally misguided to suppose that in order to think something or think of something, it is either necessary or sufficient to have an image of anything, let alone an image of what one thinks or thinks of or of words that would, if uttered, express what one thinks or refer to what one thinks of. This should be evident from the schematic analysis of thinking in the previous chapter. Moreover, as we shall argue in §12.5, it is mistaken to suppose that one thinks *in* images, or that in order to speak with thought, one must first say to oneself in one's imagination what one is going to say out loud. One can talk to oneself in the imagination (which involves auditory images) without thinking (as when one counts sheep in the imagination or recites a mantra in order to *prevent* oneself from thinking), and one can think without talking to oneself in the imagination (as when one speaks thoughtfully to another, engages in an activity with thought and concentration, etc.).

Since neither thinking nor perceiving need involve images, the somatic changes that *may* be part of a given emotional agitation and which *may* (but need not) be caused by a thought (in the proper sense of the term) or by perceiving something need not be caused by mental images.

Damasio is mistaken in his distinction between having and feeling an emotion

(iii)   While there is a difference between feeling an emotion (e.g. feeling jealous) and realizing what emotion one feels (e.g. that it is jealousy), there is, by and large, as previously noted, no significant difference between having an emotion and feeling an emotion (being jealous and feeling jealous), any more than there is a difference between having a pain and feeling a pain. Where there is a subtle difference, it is not between the occurrence of somatic changes and the apprehension of such changes in association with mental imagery. Damasio's stipulated distinction between emotion and feeling an emotion has nothing to recommend it, since an emotion is not an ensemble of somatic changes, and feeling an emotion is not the experience of such changes in juxtaposition to mental images that caused them.

An emotion is not a cognitive response to a bodily condition caused by mental images

(iv)   It is mistaken to suppose that feeling an emotion is a cognitive response to a bodily condition caused by mental images. If, when frightened by a noise at night, I feel frightened that there is a thief in the house, and my pulses race, my (felt) fear is not a response to my racing pulse. What I was frightened *by* was the noise (not an image of a noise), what I was frightened *of* was a burglar's having broken in (which may or may not have been the case). I may or may not notice my racing pulses – but whether I do or do not, my fear of a burglary is not a response to them.

Emotions are not about the somatic changes that accompany them

(v) Feelings of emotion are not *about the body* at all. What they are 'about' is the object of the emotion, in one or another sense of the term (see below). What a person is proud about (or of) may be his achievements, his lineage, his children, his possessions, etc. – but not any somatic changes that may occur when he thinks of them. What a person feels guilty about are his sins or wrongdoings, not any bodily perturbations that may or may not occur when he thinks about them. What a person feels angry about is perhaps the annoying behaviour of another, but not (normally) his somatic responses to it.

Emotional response is independent of knowledge of the cause of the emotion

(vi) An emotional response need not be cognitively linked to the cause of the emotion or the cause of the somatic changes that may accompany an emotional perturbation. We are often ignorant of the causes of our emotional feelings. I may not know what caused me to feel love for Maisy, to hate injustice, to feel fear of death – but what I must know, what *is* 'cognitively linked' to these feelings, is what their objects are. If the connection of a feeling of emotion to what it is 'about' – that is, its object – were a causal one, then unless such causal knowledge were non-inductive, knowing what one is frightened of, angry with or about, proud or ashamed of, would be a hypothesis. But I don't discover the object of my feelings by tracing the causes of the perturbations (if any) that I feel.

Emotions are not ways of discovering somatic facts, but somatic facts may inform one about one's emotions

(vii) One's 'feelings of emotion', one's love or hate, fear or hope, pride or shame, are not ways of finding out facts about 'our visceral and musculoskeletal state'. Indeed, one's emotions do not inform one of either the state of one's body or the state of the world around one. But one's emotional perturbations may inform one of one's emotional attitudes. A pang of jealousy may indicate that I am in the process of falling in love with Maisy; a blush of embarrassment may bring home to me that I am ashamed of having lied; my tears of grief may make me realize how much I loved Daisy. Far from one's emotions informing one about the state of one's body, the state of one's body informs one about one's emotions. Feeling grief does not inform me of the state of my lachrymal glands, but my hot tears may show me just how much I grieve for so-and-so. Feeling fear on a given occasion does not inform me of the condition of my heart, but my thumping heart may show me how frightened I am. Feeling embarrassed does not inform me of the state of my facial arteries, but my blushes may indicate to me that I am more embarrassed than I would have imagined.

The somatic marker hypothesis is misconceived

(viii) Damasio's somatic marker hypothesis is misconceived. The emotions are not somatic images that tell one what is good and bad. Bodily reactions are not ersatz guides to what to do, and do not inform us about good and evil. If one is indignant at a perceived injustice, what tells one that the object of one's indignation is an evil is not that one feels flushed in association with the thought of the act in question. On the contrary, one is indignant at A's action because it is unjust, not because one flushes in anger when one hears of it. And one knows it to be unjust because it rides roughshod over someone's rights, not because one flushes in anger. Indeed, the flush is only a flush of anger in so far as one is thus indignant. And one will feel indignant only to the extent that one cares about the protection of the rights of human beings (or of *this* human being).

It is the capacity to care that con- One might conjecture that although Damasio may be
nects the emotions with rationality perfectly correct in associating the capacity for rationality
in pursuit of goals in practical reasoning and in pursuit of goals with the
ability to feel emotions, the linkage lies in a common feature underlying both. Since the emotions do not let us 'mind the body', and since feeling the somatic reactions to circumstances is not a litmus test for good and evil, or for the beneficial and the harmful, it is implausible to suppose that what is wrong with patients who have suffered damage to the ventromedial sector of the prefrontal cortex is that their somatic responses are awry or uninformative for them (which would be, as it were, a Pavlovian deficiency). But what might be investigated is whether the brain damage in the kinds of patient that Damasio studied affects the capacity to care or to persist in caring about goals and objectives. For such a deficiency would affect both the patients' emotions and their ability to pursue goals over time. One feels no emotions about things concerning which one is indifferent, and one does not pursue goals efficiently unless one cares, for one reason or another, about achieving them.

So, clarification of the concept of emotion is relevant to neuroscientific investigation (and so is clarification of the related concepts of mood and agitation). Unclarity about these concepts is likely to generate incoherence in experimental investigation and confusion in the interpretation of experimental results. We shall try to shed some light on the matter by examining several issues already raised: the multivalent notion of the object of an emotion, and the distinction between object and cause; the connection of emotion to knowledge, belief, appraisal and concern or care; the somatic accompaniments and behavioural expression of an emotion; and the connection of emotion with motivated action.

7.2.2 Analysis of the emotions

Different senses of 'object' of an The concept of the object of an emotion needs clarifica-
emotion tion. For one must distinguish between different senses
of 'object' in this context. If one asks what the object of someone's love, fear or anger is, one might specify the person or thing one loves, fears or is angry with. The teacher, one would then suggest, is the object of one's fear, not his wrath; the man who won the lottery is the object of one's envy, not his winning the lottery; the benefactor, not the benefit, is the object of one's gratitude; and Jack, with whom Jill is flirting, is the object of one's jealousy, not her flirting with him. This is one sense of the term 'object of an emotion' (which may be singled out as the *object accusative* of an emotion verb). The object of our emotion, in this sense, is the referent of an

appropriate referring expression. If one feels an emotion E with respect to a certain object, thus understood, then the object of the emotion may or may not exist, but the agent must, at any rate, believe that it does. In this sense of 'object', not every emotion need have an object, and some emotions cannot have one (e.g. hope).

Equally, one may fear disaster, hope for victory, feel pride, shame, regret or remorse for having done something, or feel resentful or indignant that A has acted unfairly, feel envious of B's success. Believing that one has done something untoward, one may feel guilt, regret or remorse, even if one's belief is false, just as Othello may be jealous of Desdemona's love for Cassio, even though she does not love Cassio. In this sense of 'object of emotion', the object is singled out by a *nominalization accusative* – that is, an abstract noun (e.g. 'disaster', 'victory', 'Desdemona's love') or a noun-clause (e.g. of the form 'that such-and-such is, was or will be the case'), and it does not follow from the fact that one hopes for victory or fears that one will be defeated that one will be victorious or that one will be defeated.[17]

What the formal character of the object of an emotion is

Many emotions are partly defined by reference to the *formal* character of their objects. One cannot feel remorse for having done something one knows not to be wrong, for remorse is essentially directed at one's own past offences. One cannot hope for something that one knows has happened or cannot happen, for hope is essentially directed towards a desired eventuality the occurrence of which is in doubt. One cannot feel indignation or resentment, but only shame, regret or remorse, at what one has done or thinks one has done oneself, for indignation and resentment are essentially directed at the actual or supposed misdeeds of others. To fear something is to apprehend the object of one's fear as dangerous or as a threat, and accordingly to feel apprehensive. One cannot envy another unless one sees that person as possessing a good that one wishes to have oneself. So, if a person feels a certain emotion with respect to a certain object, then, for many emotions, he must hold the object of his emotion to satisfy the relevant formal requirements if it is indeed the case that he feels the emotion in question.

The connection between emotion and evaluation

Consideration of the concept of the formal object of an emotion makes it clear that emotions commonly involve an appraisal or evaluation. The manifestation of an emotion exhibits an appraisal of people, things and events relative to one's concerns (and one's concerns may stretch far beyond one's personal welfare and illfare). Pride, shame, embarrassment, feelings of guilt and humiliation are obviously emotions of self-appraisal. But an element of appraisal is generally involved in emotions: fear involves the appraisal of a situation as threatening or dangerous; hope involves the evaluation of a possible situation as desirable;

---

[17] This still leaves many further grammatical constructions. One may love *playing tennis*, hate *war*, fear *dying*, and it is not obvious that these can be recast in the form of a that-clause. To love playing tennis is not to love that one plays tennis (one should be wary of mangling grammar), to hate war is not the same as hating *that* anything, and to fear dying is not the same as fearing that one will die. These difficulties need to be resolved, but they merely confirm our point: viz. that the term 'object of an emotion' masks the logical diversity of the kinds of things that can be specified in answers to the question 'What (or whom) do you E?' or 'What are you E of (or at, etc.)?'.

anger involves the appraisal of an act, event or agent as (in some way or other) wrong; envy an evaluation of another person's circumstances as desirable for oneself, and so forth.

Only what one cares about (posit-ively or negatively) can be an object of one's emotion

The object of one's emotion (in one sense or the other) is something of consequence for one. That which one loves or hates, fears or hopes for, feels proud or ashamed of, is something or someone that, in some way, matters to one (positively or negatively). One is anything but indifferent to the people and things one loves or hates. The objects of one's hopes or fears are things which signify, things which one knows or believes affect one's interests or concerns. What one is proud or ashamed of is (very roughly) something the possession or performance of which one believes enhances or diminishes one's worth – and that is something we naturally care about. One cannot feel angry, resentful or indignant about something towards which one is altogether indifferent, any more than one can feel remorse for doing something that does not matter to one or guilt for doing something which does not rate. One would not be moved to act out of pity or compassion if one did not care for the object of one's feelings, and one would not be impelled to act out of pride or shame if one did not care for one's self-esteem or for the esteem of others. When things cease to matter, one ceases to feel anything about them. One's emotions are the various forms which one's concern may take. In manifesting our emotions, we show what we care about. The objects of our emotions and the intensity of our feelings about them reveal what sort of person we are – hence the non-contingent connection of the emotions with character traits.

The link between emotion and knowledge or belief

Emotions are linked in complex ways to what the agent knows or believes. For in so far as an emotion must have a proper object in order to qualify as the emotion it is, the agent must take the object of his emotion to satisfy the formal characteristics which deter-mine the object as appropriate. If he fears A or A's action, he must know or believe that A or A's action is a threat. If an agent feels pity or compassion for another, he must know or believe that person to have suffered a misfortune. If he feels regret, remorse or guilt, he must know or believe that he has done something unfortunate, wrong or untoward; and if he feels envious of another, he must know or believe the other to be better off in some way than himself. In addition, the agent must, for many emotions, have an array of further beliefs regarding the object of his emotion (in either sense of the term), beliefs which he holds to *warrant* the ascription to the object of the appropriate formal characteristics. For the formal characteristics are shared by all objects of a given emotion; whatever A regrets is something he wishes he had not done or had not had to do, but the reasons which make *V*'ing regrettable will typically be very different from the reasons that make *X*'ing regret-table. What a person fears is something he believes to threaten his interests, but his reasons for fearing tomorrow's exams (viz. his knowledge that he is ill-prepared and may fail) provide quite different grounds for seeing what he fears as threatening his interests from his reasons for fearing heights (viz. his belief that he may fall and injure himself). To the extent that his reasons are cogent, they *may* also provide a justification for his emotion.[18]

---

[18] But they may not: one might argue that envy, jealousy and hatred, for example, are rendered intelligible by the relevant reasons, but that they are not justified.

This cognitive component in emotions has important ramifications. First, a person cannot ordinarily feel a certain emotion and fail to know what the object of that emotion is. He cannot feel grateful and yet know neither to whom he is grateful nor what he is grateful for; he cannot feel ashamed and yet not know what he is ashamed of doing; he cannot feel pity, yet know neither for whom nor for what. In *limiting cases*, one may feel objectless fear (i.e. *Angst*), or irrational guilt which lacks an object, or longing without there being anything determinate for which one longs; but these are necessarily exceptions to the rule.

The connection of the emotions with reasons, justification and reasonableness

Secondly, even though emotions belong to the category of the passions – that is, they are not actions one performs or things one does – nevertheless there can be, and usually are, reasons for feeling as one does. If one fears A, it is because one knows or believes that A threatens an interest one has. One will normally have reasons for thinking that this is so, reasons one may adduce to explain or justify one's fear. If one feels resentful of A's behaviour, it is because one believes that it has unfairly harmed one's interests, and one will normally have reasons for so believing. Hence one's emotions can be reasonable or unreasonable, justified or unjustified, depending upon one's reasons and the emotion (its intensity and objects) for which they are reasons. So, despite the fact that one cannot feel an emotion at will, it makes sense to say of someone that he *ought* to feel proud or ashamed of himself because of what he did, or that he *should not* feel resentful of A since A could not help doing what he did. If a person's emotional reaction to a circumstance is not warranted, either at all or to the degree to which he feels it, we criticize him for the unreasonableness of his emotional response. It is unreasonable, we may say, to be jealous about something as trivial as *that*; or, while conceding that A's spouse's behaviour *is* an intelligible ground for jealousy, we may criticize A for the intensity of his jealousy – that is, for his excessive reaction.[19] A person may feel an emotion as a result of a false belief. Normally discovery of the falsity of the belief eliminates the emotion. If one finds out that the belief one has that warrants one's jealousy is false, one will normally cease to feel jealous. If the grounds for one's fear evaporate, the fear will normally evaporate with it. Conversely, things being thus-and-so may be a reason for feeling a given emotion – and those who come to know or to believe that things are so, and *who care*, will normally feel that emotion. They have a reason for so feeling. The reasonableness of emotions lies in such forms of sensitivity to reasons, and it is here that the responsibility a person has for his emotions resides. The emotions we feel are reasonable to the extent that they are directed towards an object that warrants the feeling, and to the extent that the intensity of the emotion felt is proportional to its object.[20] Of course,

---

[19] Of course, we may also criticize a person for his excessive *display* of his emotion, for his failure to exercise appropriate self-control.

[20] Phobias are pathological cases. They are fears that persist despite known lack of warrant. They are, in this sense, insensitive to reason. An acrophobe's fear is not diminished by the knowledge that there is no danger of falling, and an arachnophobe's fear does not wane on being informed that the spider he has seen is harmless. Other emotions, such as hatred (e.g. in the case of racial prejudice), can equally be pathological. But the form of pathology differs, inasmuch as the emotion does not persist despite the disappearance of the associated beliefs, but rather the beliefs persist despite refutation.

knowledge of the facts that constitute a reason for feeling such-and-such an emotion does not necessitate any such feeling. But if one does not respond appropriately to the tragic or joyful circumstance, one is deficient in sensibility, and lacks the feeling proper to the circumstance – which is a mark of *not caring* about things which, in general, we think we should care about.

Emotions tend to cloud judgement
Like agitations, some perturbational emotions involve heightened arousal – for example, fear, rage, indignation. Not all forms of arousal are prone to affect one's capacity for rational judgement and action deleteriously. Agitations such as delight or surprise do not usually do so, and interest, close attention and concentration typically do the opposite. But such heightened forms of emotional perturbation typically cloud one's judgement and lead to irrational or unreasonable action. So, for example, it is ill-advised to make serious decisions when one is enraged, and mastery of one's fear is a prerequisite for rational decisions at times of danger, for one cannot think clearly when in a panic. But it is equally evident that one's standing emotional attitudes may affect one's judgement deleteriously – not through judgement-clouding perturbation, but through judgement-distorting bias. Overfond parents commonly misjudge their children; a person in love, it is said, is as competent to choose a spouse as a blind man is to choose a painting; and the jealous spouse loses all sense of evidential support. Hence it is no coincidence that, as Aristotle emphasized, mastery of one's passions is a prerequisite for a virtuous life, and that an excess of uncontrolled sensibility leads to a deficiency of good sense (Jane Austen).

The connection of the emotions with valuations
Thirdly, as is evident from the previous point, human emotions characteristically involve moral and ideological beliefs and valuations. Our emotions are characteristically aroused by what is just or unjust, fair or unfair, kind or cruel; by what is thought to be appropriate for oneself and for others, given one's social status and the standing of others. The proper objects of pride and shame, guilt and remorse, and much love and hate are commonly determined by the values of one's society or social group. Many human emotions are driven by moral, social, political and religious beliefs and commitments. These in turn may or may not be defensible, and the extent to which they are affects the reasonableness of the associated emotion.

Object and cause of an emotion again
As we have seen, the object of an emotion should not be confused with its cause. What one is frightened *by* is the cause of one's fear, what one is frightened *of* is its object. These can coincide in certain cases, as when one is both frightened *by* and frightened *of* a peal of thunder and a bolt of lightening, but in other cases they cannot. For when the object of fear, hope or excitement lies in the future (and may or may not eventuate), or if it is non-existent (as when one is afraid of ghosts or of Satan), what one is afraid *of*, hopes *for*, or is excited *about*, cannot be the cause of the emotion. What causes an emotion may be what sparks it off, which may be a sudden thought, a casual remark, or a reminder. But equally, the explanation of why one feels as one does may lie in one's natural dispositions. For when A fears such-and-such an outcome and B is hopeful that things will turn out well, the explanation of A's fear may be his pessimistic nature, whereas B's equanimity may be explained by his sanguine temperament. One may feel an emotion

without knowing the cause of one's feeling (as in the case of forgotten or repressed childhood trauma). But one cannot feel an emotion and not know what the object of one's feeling is, save in aberrant cases of objectless emotions. So, when we say of a person that he felt a certain emotion *because* such-and-such, it may be unclear whether the explanation offered by the because-clause specifies the object of the emotion or its cause. This can be clarified by reference to the further question of whether it is a necessary condition for the truth of the statement that the person should know or believe that such-and-such. If it is not, then what was specified was the cause of his feeling the emotion. If it is, then it was the object of the emotion.

Two kinds of somatic accompaniment of an emotion; three kinds of behavioural expression of an emotion

The somatic accompaniments of an emotional agitation can be divided into two categories; the subjective felt sensations and the objective physiological characteristics. The subjective somatic accompaniments consist in the sensations that commonly characterize a given emotional perturbation – for example, the sensation of beating pulses and thumping heart, feelings of tension, the 'butterflies in the stomach', the felt dry throat, that characterize fear, hope and excitement. The objective somatic accompaniments are the physiological changes that typically characterize the emotional perturbation, the neural excitation in the brain, visceral activities and glandular secretions, the psychogalvanic reflex, and so forth. The behavioural expressions of an emotion can be differentiated into those non-voluntary forms of behaviour that are not actions (blushing, sweating); the forms of behaviour that are actions, which may be voluntary, involuntary or partly voluntary[21] (smiles, scowls, grimaces, cries, groans, moans, bodily demeanour, expressive gestures, and such actions as jumping for joy or from fright, scratching one's head in puzzlement, punching the air in triumph); and the forms of behaviour that are modes or manners of acting (tone of voice, manner of gesture). Expressive behaviour, even if it is voluntary, is characteristically non-instrumental. Some forms of expressive behaviour can be exhibited for a purpose, but to that extent its authentic expressive character is diminished.

Emotions, contrary to what Damasio claims, are commonly perceptible

So, contrary to what Damasio claims, there need be nothing 'hidden' about the emotions of others. It is mistaken to say that 'you cannot observe a feeling in someone else'.[22] It is equally mistaken to think that 'you can observe a feeling in yourself'. We are prone to confuse the fact that we often do not show our feelings, and indeed sometimes make an effort to conceal them, with the misguided idea that the emotions are in some deep sense 'private' and 'hidden'. But this is confused. We can often see delight and rage in a person's face, joy, anguish or horror in their eyes, contempt or amusement in their smile. We can hear the love and tenderness, the grief and sorrow, the anger and contempt,

---

[21] An action is involuntary if it is not done at will, but is of a kind which *can* be done at will (smiling involuntarily as opposed to voluntarily). An action is partly voluntary if it cannot be initiated at will, but can be suppressed at will (weeping). The matter will be further discussed in chapter 8.

[22] Damasio, *Feeling of What Happens*, p. 42, quoted above, p. 89.

in a person's voice. We can observe the tears of joy or grief, the cries of terror, joy or amazement, and the blushes of embarrassment or shame. On the other hand, to feel an emotion oneself – for example, to feel proud or ashamed – is not to observe anything.

Somatic accompaniments of an emotion do not suffice to identify the emotion or to warrant its ascription   It is important to realize that neither the subjective nor the objective somatic accompaniments of an emotion *by themselves* are sufficient conditions for the identification and ascription of a given emotion. For one's bodily state, subjectively experienced in terms of sensations or objectively determined in physiological terms, is not an emotion. It is only part of the syndrome of an episode of an emotional perturbation *in appropriate circumstances, given the appropriate knowledge, beliefs and concerns of the agent*. Similarly, the behavioural reactions and actions that manifest an emotion do so *only given the appropriate subjective context of their manifestation*. One's hands may tremble with fatigue, one may sweat because it is hot, and one's throat may be dry because one is thirsty – and not because one is afraid. One may shed tears (because one is peeling onions), one may groan (with pain), and one's eyes may be dull (with fatigue) – not because one is grieving. Whether these reactions are manifestations of one emotion or another, or have nothing to do with an emotion, depends upon the circumstances and on what the agent knows or believes of the circumstances in which he finds himself and upon what he cares about.

Connection of emotion and volition   The connection of emotions with volition is equally constitutive of many (but not all) emotions. Fear of harm is bound up, other things being equal, with a desire to avoid what is harmful (and the wish or hope that no harm will ensue), remorse with a desire to make amends, love of a person with a desire to protect or further their welfare, shame with the desire to conceal what is shameful. It is important, however, not to confuse a desire with a motive. A desire can furnish a motive. However, a desire for X is not a motive for obtaining X, although it may be a motive for doing Y, if doing Y is a means of obtaining X.

Emotion and motive   Nevertheless, it is no coincidence, but constitutive of our concept of emotion that many emotion terms also specify motives for action. We often act out of love or fear, jealousy or compassion. The citation of such motives is one form that explanations of human actions may take. Such explanations of action do not allude to causes, however, but to characteristic patterns of action for the sake of a goal. If one acts from a certain motive, it is not the motive that *makes* one act, as a man with a gun may make one act by threatening one. Despite the etymology, motives are not ethereal pushes, any more than goals are ethereal pulls. Nor are the emotions that motivate us neural or somatic causes that make us act. Many emotion words also signify motives precisely because emotions typically imply or intimate forms of care and goals for the sake of which an action might be done – for example, the elimination or avoidance of an undesirable state of affairs, the preservation or achievement of a desirable state of affairs. To shake or cry out with fear is not to act with a motive; but to act out of, and be motivated by, fear is (roughly) to act, apprehending one's present situation as threatening, with the goal of eliminating or avoiding the threat. To act out of love is (roughly) to apprehend the object of one's love as lacking a good or as being threatened with a harm, and to act for the sake of providing the good or eliminating the harm. To act out of gratitude to A is to act with the knowledge that A has previously benefited one, and with the intention of benefiting A *because* he has previously benefited one (and if one also acts in order to *show* one's gratitude, then one further intends that A (or others) should recognize one's intention). In short, many emotions are also motives for action, not because they are causes of action, but because they indicate a form of concern and structure of belief that informs common patterns of explanation of human action. Explaining a human action by saying that it was done out of a motivating emotion, such as fear, love, envy or compassion, is to cite not a factor in an explanation (such as a reason, a cause, a desire, a habit or a tendency), but an explanatory pattern.[23]

---

[23] For a more elaborate account of motives, see Kenny, *Action, Emotion and the Will*, ch. 4, and A. R. White, *The Philosophy of Mind* (Random House, New York, 1967), ch. 6.

8

Volition and Voluntary Movement

8.1 Volition

Concepts of volition and forms of explanation of action

The conceptual field subsumed under the category of volition is wide. A multitude of conceptual pathways run through it, criss-crossing in bewildering ways. Since matters of volition are primarily concerned with action, each of the concepts within this domain is linked in more or less direct ways with explanations of human action. And the forms of explanation are manifold, often differing profoundly in their logical character. So we have the wide range of concepts of volition and the will: felt inclinations; felt desires; wanting in all its confusing conceptual complexity; purpose, goal and aim; decision and reasons for acting; intention; and so forth. Hence, too, we have the various volitional categories of action, such as the voluntary, involuntary and non-voluntary; the intentional, the unintentional, the deliberate or impulsive, the attentive and the careless, rash or negligent; and so forth. And we have the manifold forms of explanation of human behaviour in terms of reasons and motives, intentions and purposes, and of habits, tendencies or inclinations, as well as in terms of dispositions and character traits. To survey this would be a lengthy task indeed. We shall be concerned only with sketching some of the contours of the concepts of voluntary and intentional action. Our secondary aim is to show neuroscientists that voluntary human action is not behaviour caused by acts of will, volitions, wants, intentions or decisions.

Voluntary, involuntary and not voluntary acts

Among the things that human beings do, we can distinguish the acts we perform (or fail to perform, i.e. our omissions, abstainings and refrainings) from the doings that are not acts, such as slipping or falling, falling asleep or sleeping. Among our acts we can distinguish those that are voluntary from those that are not voluntary. Acts (or omissions) which are not voluntary may in turn be not voluntary because they are involuntary – that is, acts which could be performed voluntarily, but were not, as when one smiles or blinks involuntarily. They may be not voluntary because they were neither voluntary nor involuntary, as when one unknowingly or unintentionally acts – for example, mistakenly takes the wrong glass, unknowingly treads on an insect, or mispronounces a name. And they may be not voluntary because they were done under duress or because one was obliged by circumstances to perform them (e.g. to take the low road because the high road was blocked).

Intentional, unintentional and not intentional acts

Our voluntary acts may be intentional, unintentional or not intentional. Intentional acts are voluntary, unless they are performed under duress or because one is obliged by circumstances to perform them. Our normal acts and activities, such as eating, drinking, walking and talking, are typically voluntary and intentional. But many of our acts are voluntary without necessarily being intentional: for example, drumming with one's fingers, whistling while one works, running one's hand through one's hair, smiling, frowning, scowling, and the innumerable expressive gestures one makes with one's hands while one talks, as well as many of one's movements when one is engaged in habitual actions, such as dressing or brushing one's hair or teeth. Similarly, the foreseen but unintended consequences of our actions are voluntary without being intentional, as when we knowingly crush the blades of grass when we walk intentionally across the lawn.

The marks of voluntary acts or movements

Voluntary acts typically involve making physical movements. (Those that do not include the category of mental acts which one can do at will, such as calculating in one's head, and, in certain cases, acts of omission, such as abstaining or refraining from doing something. We shall say no more about these.) In virtue of what features is a human act or movement a voluntary, as opposed to an involuntary, act or movement? Clearly, among the marks of voluntary acts is that they are of a kind that one can *try* to perform, *decide* or *intend* to perform, can perform *on request* or *to order*; they can be done with or without *care*, and one can often *learn* to perform them (as one may learn to thread a needle). When one performs a voluntary act, one knows and can say what one is doing, and one is not *surprised* at one's doing what one does. For when one acts voluntarily, one exercises a two-way power to do or refrain from doing, knowing that it is within one's choice. By contrast, one's involuntary movements may occur when one does not want them to and may surprise one. How does one prove that one *can* do something voluntarily? By doing it. One says to another, 'Ask me to do so-and-so, and I'll show you that I can.' And how does one *know* that one has done it voluntarily (and not by accident or involuntarily)? *Not* by a special feeling. It is true that raising one's arm voluntarily does not feel the same as one's arm rising by itself (as when one presses one's arm against the wall for a minute and then stands back and lets one's arm rise). But one does not know that one has raised one's arm voluntarily by any special feeling. If it were a special feeling that informed one that one has made a voluntary movement, one might forget *which* feeling was the right feeling to indicate voluntariness, and therefore make a mistake about whether one had acted voluntarily or not. But that, in non-pathological cases, would be absurd. Rather, one does not know any *how*; one *can say* that one's act or movement was voluntary, and that is a mark of voluntariness.

A fully voluntary movement is the exercise of a two-way power; it is behaviour that is under one's control

Can one put any order into this welter of detail? A necessary condition for a movement to be voluntary is that it involve the exercise of a two-way power to do or refrain from doing. Behaviour is voluntary if one can engage in it at will. In this sense, it is behaviour which one can *control* directly – that is, not by doing something else that causes it or stops it (hence not as one can control one's heartbeat by jumping up and down to increase it or by lying down to reduce it). A fully voluntary movement is one which the agent controls in its inception, continuation and termination. Hence blinking is only partly voluntary, since one can blink at will, but cannot control its 'continuation' or termination, and sneezing is only partly voluntary, inasmuch as one can inhibit it but not initiate it directly.

Voluntary movement is not move-ment caused by a volition or act of will

A voluntary movement is *not* a movement caused by a volition or act of will, or by a want, intention or decision, although what we do because we want to do it, intend to do it, or have decided to do it is also something we do voluntarily (unless it is done under duress or because we are obliged to do it by circum-stances). This point is difficult to grasp, and neuroscientists often suppose, as Descartes and the empiricists (e.g. Hobbes, Locke, Hume and Bentham) did, that voluntary action is movement caused by inner acts of volition. So further explanation is needed.

What an act of will and will-power are

It is misguided to suppose that voluntary and intentional actions are bodily movements caused by antecedent acts of willing to move. There are such things as acts of will. They are acts performed with great effort to overcome one's reluctance or difficulties in acting, typically in adverse circumstances. They are not mental acts called 'willing', which cause bodily movements. There is such a thing as will-power, but it is not a mental equivalent of muscle power. Rather, it is determination and persistence in pursuit of one's goals in the face of difficulties. There is such a thing as strength of will, but it is not a matter of causally efficacious mental acts of willing, but rather a matter of tenacity in sticking to one's purpose.

The incoherent consequences of sup-posing willing to be an event or act

If willing were some mental happening that antecedes and is the cause of voluntary action, then, it seems, it would have to be either a mental act or an event. If it were an act, then it would have to be voluntary. For if willing were an involuntary act, then the consequent behaviour would not be voluntary either. (If one involuntarily knocks over a vase, causing the vase to break, then one does not break the vase voluntarily.) If willing were voluntary, however, it too would have to have been caused by an antecedent volition, for, on this account, that is what it is for an act of any kind to be voluntary. But that leads to a vicious regress. On the other hand, if the willing were merely an event that happens when it happens, then the behaviour it causes would not be voluntarily performed at all – any more than if a feeling caused one to sneeze, one would be sneezing voluntarily.

Why acts of will conceived as causes of voluntary acts are fictions

Furthermore, if willing were an antecedent happening of each and every voluntary act, which it causes, then, given that we know whether we acted voluntarily or not, we should have to be able to establish the occurrence of such willings (and be able describe their character and duration). And we should have to be able to establish that these happenings are the causes of the subsequent behaviour. But:

(a) We have no idea what these mythical events of willing might be. We have seen that they cannot be inner acts. Equally obviously, as we just noted, they cannot be feelings either. For were willing a feeling, then it would simply be something that happens when it happens, and its causal consequences would not be voluntary actions at all, but movements caused by feelings.

(b) We do not know how to identify these acts of willing. But surely, we would have to identify them, to be sure that we did whatever we did voluntarily. And presumably, we might also misidentify them, and mistakenly think that we did something voluntarily which was actually *not* caused by any act of willing. Yet we do know (i.e. we can say), without any such identifications, let alone misidentifications, when we act voluntarily, and when involuntarily.

(c) We have certainly not identified such inner acts and established a causal relation between them and subsequent bodily movements, on the basis of which we now confidently assert that voluntary acts are acts caused by mental occurrences of willing. Rather, we simply have a *picture* of what free, voluntary action *must* be – a picture which rests on neither evidence nor argument.

(d) It would surely be absurd to suppose that before each voluntary act there is a separate act of willing. Each of the words of the previous sentence was voluntarily (and intentionally) written down, and each letter in each word was intentionally inscribed. But it is absurd to suppose that in writing them a separate act of willing occurred for each letter and word.

(e) It is typically easy enough to identify and distinguish the voluntary and involuntary acts of others. But we do not distinguish these by finding out whether their movements were caused by mental acts of willing, which neither we nor they can identify. When we ascribe responsibility for an action to another person, we do not do so on the basis of identifying an act of will which he has performed and which has caused his bodily movement.

Wanting, intending and deciding are not causes of actions or movements

Of course, we commonly act *because* we want to, intend to or have decided to act, either for its own sake or for the sake of some further goal. But it is mistaken to think that this 'because' is causal. For if it were, then once the want has occurred, the intention been formed, or the decision taken, then we could remain passive, sit back, and let nature take its course. For the action would occur without our taking any initiative. If I want (have decided, intend) to turn the light on at six o'clock, then when I hear the clock chime 6.00, I should not have to turn the light on in order to fulfil my purpose. I could just let the want (intention or decision) cause my arm to rise and turn the light on. I could say, 'And now it is six o'clock, just look and see my arm rise!' – but that is precisely what does *not* happen and what one *cannot* say. Moreover, wants and intentions cannot fulfil the role of acts of will, since they are not acts of *any* kind. Willing, if it is anything, must be something we do, not a want or a desire that besets us or that we happen to have. And although making a decision can be termed 'a mental act', it is not a cause of behaviour, but a terminus to a state of indecision. Once we have decided, we have formed an intention, and we know what we are going to do. But we have yet to do it – the decision cannot cause us to perform the voluntary action upon which we have resolved.

To say that someone did something because he wanted to does not introduce a causal explanation of his action by reference to a mental act or event. But it may serve to *exclude*

Saying that someone did something because they wanted to is not to give a causal explanation

certain kinds of causal explanation; for example, it excludes involuntary action, so if something was done because the agent wanted to do it, then it was not a mere twitch or an involuntary start. Rather, saying that he did it because he wanted to characterizes his behaviour as action, hence as something for which it *makes sense* to ask for reasons (even though it may not have been done for a reason), as opposed to an involuntary twitch, for which a mere causal explanation is appropriate. Of course, that is perfectly compatible with the existence of a causal explanation of the muscular contractions involved in his action. There are other possibilities too. One may say, 'I am leaving the room because I want to, not because you told me to'. This characterizes my action as voluntary and intentional, while excluding one kind of explanation in terms of the specified reason – that is, that you told me to leave. Again, when one acts with a further intent, then 'Because I wanted to do so-and-so' or 'Because I wanted to bring that about' serves to introduce the goal aimed at (e.g. 'I raised my arm because I wanted (to get) the book'). Here one could just as well have said, 'I raised my arm *in order to* get the book'. Specifying what I wanted gives my *reason* for acting, not the cause of the movement of my arm as I raise it voluntarily. If we know what a person wants (aims at) and what his relevant beliefs are, we can often predict his *actions*, but not because his wants (in conjunction with his beliefs) cause the relevant *movements*. Indeed, typically we cannot predict *how* – that is, by what movements – he will execute his intentions, whereas we can predict his actions. If one knows a chess-player, one can often predict his moves, but what enables one to predict his moves will not enable one to predict his movements.[1]

8.2 Libet's Theory of Voluntary Movement

Libet's discoveries and consequent theory

This fragmentary sketch of a small part of the field of volitional concepts suffices to enable us to see what is awry in a well-known neuroscientific theory of voluntary action. Benjamin Libet has argued that neuroscientific research shows that all voluntary actions are initiated by the brain independently of any conscious acts of volition. 'The brain "decides" to initiate or, at least, to prepare to initiate the act before there is any reportable conscious awareness that such a decision has taken place.'[2] Libet argues that the neurons in the supplementary motor cortex that are related to a particular physical movement of a hand start firing 500 ms before the impulses arrive at the muscles involved

---

[1] See J. Gosling, *Weakness of the Will* (Routledge, London, 1990), p. 183. For more detail on the manifold forms of these familiar non-causal explanations of human behaviour, see A. J. P. Kenny, *Will, Freedom and Power* (Blackwell, Oxford, 1975); B. Rundle, *Mind in Action* (Clarendon Press, Oxford, 1997); A. R. White, *The Philosophy of Mind* (Random House, New York, 1967), ch. 6. For elaboration of Wittgenstein's ideas on the subject, see P. M. S. Hacker, *Wittgenstein: Mind and Will* (Blackwell, Oxford, 1996), essays VII and VIII.

[2] B. Libet, 'Unconscious cerebral initiative and the role of conscious will in voluntary action', in *Neurophysiology of Consciousness* (Birkhäuser, Boston, 1993), p. 276.

in making the movement. However, the feeling of intention, want or urge to move the hand, as reported by the subjects, occurred only 150 ms before the movement was executed. From this he concludes

(a) that the performance of even a freely voluntary act is initiated unconsciously, some 350 msec before the individual is consciously aware of wanting to move, but also (b) that conscious control of whether the act will actually be performed is still possible during the remaining 150 to 200 msec before activating the muscles. This would appear to preserve the possibility for at least a controlling role for conscious free choice or will.[3]

It is important to understand that, according to Libet, an act is voluntary if, in addition to 'arising endogenously', without externally imposed restrictions or compulsions, 'subjects *feel* introspectively that they are performing the act on their own initiative and that they are free to start or not to start the act as they wish'.[4] In the experiment the subjects were 'to choose to perform this act at any time the desire, urge, decision, and will should arise in them. (They were also free *not* to act out any given urge or initial decision to act . . .).' The subjects were asked to move their hand if they pleased, and to note the exact time when they *felt* an urge, desire, wish or intention to move, which, as the experiment showed, succeeded the neural initiation of movement by 300 ms. The premiss of the experiment, as Libet observes, is that this 'subjective event [feeling an urge or desire to move] is only accessible introspectively to the subject himself', and 'each subject was instructed to "watch for" and report the earliest appearance of the awareness in question'.[5]

Confused presuppositions of Libet's experiment

This experiment is based on confused presuppositions. It is neither necessary nor sufficient for an act to be voluntary that it be preceded by a feeling of desiring, wishing, wanting or intending to perform it or by an urge to do it.

Feelings of volition are not necessary for voluntary movement

It is not necessary, inasmuch as an agent is not held, and does not hold himself, to have moved involuntarily if he moved without feeling an urge to move or feeling a desire to move. When one moves voluntarily – for example, picks up one's pen in order to write a note or gets up in order to answer the doorbell – one feels no urges, desires or intentions, and that is not because one does not notice them! Of course, one can *say* whether one moved voluntarily or involuntarily, but not on the grounds that one felt an urge, desire or intention just before moving.

Feelings of volition are not sufficient for voluntary movement

Neither is it sufficient for a movement to count as voluntary, inasmuch as feeling an urge, for example, to sneeze just before one sneezes does not make the sneeze voluntary. Indeed, although normal human beings can voluntarily *inhibit* a sneeze, they

[3] B. Libet, 'Epilogue: I. Some implications of "time-on theory"', in *Neurophysiology of Consciousness*, pp. 389f.
[4] Libet, 'Unconscious cerebral initiative', p. 270.
[5] Ibid., p. 274.

cannot sneeze at will at all. Strikingly, Libet's theory would in effect assimilate all human voluntary action to the status of inhibited sneezes or sneezes which one did not choose to inhibit. For, in his view, all human movements are initiated by the brain before any awareness of a desire to move, and all that is left for voluntary control is the inhibiting or permitting of the movement that is already under way.

Movement caused by a felt urge is not voluntary

There is such a thing as feeling an urge to do something, and also as being aware of a desire to do something. But a movement that is *caused* by an urge or felt desire is precisely *not* a voluntary action. If an urge to sneeze, to vomit, to cough, etc. *causes* one to behave accordingly, then one has sneezed, vomited or coughed *involuntarily*. One may feel an intense desire to drink, eat or move one's hand, and, other things being equal, one will go on to drink, eat or move one's hand. But the desire is not the cause of one's doing so. Rather, one drinks *in order to* assuage one's thirst, eats *for a reason* – namely, that one is hungry – and moves one's hand *on purpose*, one's purpose being, for example, to cease touching something repulsive. So too, one may feel an urge to do something, and act *because* one feels an urge, but this 'because' is not causal. The urge one feels to have another piece of cake does not *make* one's hand move irresistibly towards the plate any more than feeling inclined to go to the cinema tonight will, by 7 p.m., cause one's legs to move.

Libet's question presupposed a misconception of voluntary action

If one asks one's subjects to move their hand voluntarily within the next minute, but to take care to note when they feel an urge, an intention or a desire to move it, one's very question subjects them to a tempting (but mistaken) philosophical picture of the nature of action and its causal genesis. Indeed, one of the most interesting (inadvertent) results of these experiments is that people, when asked to report such bizarre things as 'a feeling of intention to move one's hand', will find such a feeling to report, even though it is more than a little doubtful whether there is any such thing as 'a feeling of intention'. Equally, when asked to note when they feel an urge to move, they come up with such a feeling, even though moving one's hand voluntarily does not require and does not normally involve any such feeling.[6] The feeling reported is not what makes their movement voluntary, and any absence of feeling would not make it involuntary. The fact that the neurons in the supplementary motor cortex fire 350 ms before the feeling is allegedly apprehended does not show that the brain 'unconsciously decided' to move before the agent did. It merely shows that the neuronal processes that activate the muscles began before the time at which the agent reported a 'feeling of desire' or 'feeling an urge to move' to have occurred. But, to repeat, a voluntary movement is not a movement caused by a felt urge, any more than to refrain voluntarily from moving is to feel an urge *not* to move which *prevents* one from moving.

---

[6] This, in our view, has important methodological implications for the design of such experiments. What it shows, among other things, is that conceptual confusions on the part of the experimenter are not likely to be weeded out by the subjects upon whom the experiment is made. The latter are likely to succumb to the very same confusions, or at any rate to be sufficiently intimidated by the experimenter to go along with his forms of description.

We should also remember that a large range of acts are decided on in advance. Reflecting on whether to V this evening, next week or next month, we weigh the reasons for and against V'ing, and decide to V (or not to V). So, when the time approaches (assuming that we have not forgotten and do not change our mind), we V. But to V thus intentionally, in accordance with our antecedent plans and intentions, could not require that we 'feel an intention' (there being no such thing as a feeling of intention), and does not require that we 'feel a desire'. We simply act in order to fulfil our plans, and the relevant movements we make are accordingly voluntary and intentional.

A second example of misconceived questions in an experiment   Another example of how research on voluntary movement can go awry due to conceptual confusion is to be found in some recent work by C. D. Frith and his colleagues.[7]
Taking from William James their definition of 'willed action' as 'action performed when we consciously pay attention to its selection', they reasoned that 'a deliberate selection is subjectively experienced as willed and occurs when we have a choice of action'. Such 'spontaneous or self-generated actions are not specified by an external trigger stimulus, but are internally driven' by contrast with 'automatic acts where the appropriate response is fully specified by an external stimulus'. Hence, in their view, if a subject is asked to move a finger which is touched by the experimenter, the subject's movement is not 'willed', but is 'automatic'; whereas if the subject is told to move one of two different fingers when one or the other is touched, the movement is 'willed', inasmuch as the subject has 'a choice of action'. To be sure, all such talk of 'willed action' is likely to be confused, and the confusion is bound to be multiplied by James's misconception of voluntary actions and by his incoherent ideo-motor theory.[8] But, disregarding that, it should be obvious that moving a finger that one was requested to move is no less voluntary an act than is moving one or another of two fingers on request.

8.3 Taking Stock

The concepts surveyed here and in the last four chapters partly define what it is to be a human being   The concepts which we have surveyed in this chapter and the four previous ones fulfil manifold functions in human life, and are used to draw a multitude of fine distinctions. They lie at the heart of our experience, and are indeed partly constitutive of, and define, our experience. For it is because we are concept-using creatures that we can have the wide range of experiences that we do have, many of which are foreclosed to other animals who lack the rich array of concepts available to language-users such as ourselves. For we can know or believe, think or imagine, fear or hope, want or intend, a multitude of things which other animals cannot.

---

[7] C. D. Frith, K. Friston, P. F. Liddle and R. S. J. Frackowiak, 'Willed action and the prefrontal cortex in man: a study with PET', *Proceedings of the Royal Society*, B 244 (1991), pp. 241–6.
[8] For Wittgenstein's detailed criticisms of James's account of volition, see P. M. S. Hacker, *Wittgenstein: Mind and Will* (Blackwell, Oxford, 1996), pp. 565–8.

It should not be surprising to find that the conceptual field is as complex and subtle as the form of life which it informs – *our* form of life. For the concepts in question are partly definitive of what it is to be a human being, and their employment in the expression and description of our experience is partly constitutive of the life of language-using creatures such as ourselves.

They are not theoretical concepts   The latter point is of paramount importance. The concepts we have been dealing with are not *theoretical concepts* of a science of any kind, although they are rightly invoked and employed in psychology and in brain neuroscience.[9] Our avowals of love or fear, anger or regret, are not theoretical statements of *any* kind. Cyrano, pouring out his heart to Rosanne below her balcony, was not theorizing about his own behaviour, but expressing his love; Lear, fulminating at the ingratitude and perfidy of humanity, was not an amateur theorist conjecturally applying emotion terms to himself in accordance with a popular theory of human nature, but venting his rage. It is a disastrous confusion, fostered by the eliminative materialists,[10] to represent these concepts as part of something called 'folk psychology', which is held to be a defective, primitive theory of human behaviour. Of course, these concepts are used not only in the overt expression of emotion, but also in the description of the states of mind and character traits of other people, and in the explanation of human conduct. But it is an equally dire confusion to suppose that all explanation is theoretical. Explanation of human behaviour by reference to emotions and motives, knowledge and belief, thought and imagination, is neither theoretical nor part of a science.

The point of our conceptual sketches   The descriptions we have given are only sketches. The conceptual complexity is greater than we have indicated. A detailed treatment would require a very long book indeed. Nevertheless, our sketches will suffice, we hope, to serve the purpose for which they are designed. They are meant to remind neuroscientists of the familiar concepts which they themselves constantly invoke in designing experiments and describing their results. The sketches of the conceptual articulations involved in the various categories of concepts provide guidelines as to what does and what does not make sense. We hope that neuroscientists will find it useful to consult these sketches (which are, we believe, more accurate guides to the concepts involved than those of William James). The examples we have examined are intended to alert neuroscientists to the numerous pitfalls that open if insufficient attention is paid to conceptual clarity. As we remarked at the beginning of chapter 4, the conceptual framework for neuroscience is our familiar psychological conceptual scheme. But though familiar, the explicit description of its forms and structure is far from familiar, and most neuroscientists, in many of their writings, flout them. In flouting them, they have not produced a *different* conceptual scheme, but only incoherences in their employment of the existing one. We shall discuss this point in more detail in chapter 14.

---

[9] Obviously one cannot characterize a theoretical concept as a concept that occurs in any statement of a theory.

[10] We have in mind the conception fostered by Paul and Patricia Churchland in their various writings. We examine these in chapter 13.

The crypto-Cartesianism of current neuroscientific reflection

A further point to which we have recurrently drawn attention is the extent to which current neuroscientific thought is covertly Cartesian. We have, of course, acknowledged that contemporary neuroscientists, unlike the first two generations of twentieth-century neuroscientists such as Sherrington, Adrian, Eccles and Penfield, are overtly anti-Cartesian. Their anti-Cartesianism consists in their correct rejection of the two-substance dualism of mind (understood as an immaterial substance) and body, interacting, if not in the pineal gland, then in the 'liaison brain' or 'the highest brain mechanism'. Their covert Cartesianism, as we have tried to make clear, consists in the first place in their allocating to the brain a multitude of the psychological functions that dualism allocated to the mind. This involves committing the mereological fallacy in neuroscience that was discussed in chapter 3. It also involves retaining the *logical structure* or *forms* of Cartesian explanations of characteristic human psychological functions. We shall briefly give a recapitulative overview of this point.

Cartesianism in the form of explanation of perception

First, in the case of perception, most neuroscientists accept not only the distinction between primary and secondary qualities adopted by Galileo, Descartes and Locke, but also a form of representationalism characteristic of Cartesianism and Lockean empiricism alike (see chapter 4). For they entertain the thought that what we perceive are images or representations of an 'external world' that are caused (in the mind or the brain) by the stimulation of sense-organs.

Cartesianism in the form of explanation of memory

Secondly, the neuroscientific research on memory is understandably committed to the view that memories are stored in the brain. The picture underlying this conception is trace theory that dates back to Aristotle. But it is of some interest, in the present context, to note the similarities (and differences) with Cartesian theory. For Descartes thought that the functions that Aristotle and the scholastics ascribed to the 'sensitive soul', including the memory or 'storage' of sensory impressions or images, can be fully explained in purely mechanical, corporeal terms. In his *Treatise on Man* he wrote:

> I should like you to consider . . . all the functions I have ascribed to this machine [the body] – such as the digestion of food, the beating of the heart and arteries . . . the reception by the external sense organs of light, sounds, smells, tastes, heat and other such qualities, the imprinting of the ideas of these qualities in the organ of 'common' sense and the imagination, *the retention or stamping of these ideas in the memory* . . . I should like you to consider that these functions follow from the mere arrangement of the machine's organs every bit as naturally as the movements of a clock or other automaton follow from the arrangement of its counter-weights and wheels. In order to explain these functions, then, it is not necessary to conceive of this machine as having any vegetative or sensitive soul or other principle of movement and life, apart from its blood and its [animal] spirits. (AT XI, 202, our italics)

Quaint physiology apart, there is little in this conception of the 'corporeal memory' that a contemporary neuroscientist would wish to gainsay. Disagreement would break out, however, with respect to Descartes's conception of 'intellectual memory', unique to human beings, who possess a mind (or 'rational soul'), and who accordingly store concepts in the mind. Rejection of the Cartesian conception of the intellectual memory as lacking any corporeal foundation is one thing. Retention of the structural features of the Cartesian conception of the corporeal memory is another, however, and it is arguably the retention of one thing too many. For, as we have argued in chapter 5, the conceptions of memory storage and memory traces that are here involved are not coherent. Memory is indeed an ability, but not an ability to reproduce copies of antecedent impressions, images or ideas.

Cartesianism in the conception of mental images as inner pictures

Thirdly, the conception of mental images as private, inner pictures that only the subject can see is the received conception among neuroscientists. Mental images are commonly thought to be copies of antecedent impressions. These images are supposed to be such as can be scanned, examined and turned around, and their features, like the features of a picture, may be discerned or overlooked (see chapter 6). Again, this conception recapitulates the errors of Descartes. In his *Conversation with Burman*, Descartes claimed that

> When external objects act on my senses, they print on them an idea, or rather a figure, of themselves; and when the mind attends to these images imprinted on the pineal gland in this way, it is said to have sensory perception. When, on the other hand, the images in the gland are not imprinted by external objects, but by the mind itself, which fashions and shapes them in the brain in the absence of external objects, we have imagination. The difference between sense-perception and imagination is thus really just this, that in sense-perception the images are imprinted by external objects which are actually present, whilst in imagination the images are imprinted by the mind without any external objects. (AT V, 162)

For here too the images of the imagination are conceived to be just like external pictures, only 'internal'. This is a part of the Cartesian legacy that, as we have argued, neuroscience should jettison.

Cartesianism in the conception of the emotions

Fourthly, although, as we observed in chapter 7, the primary conceptual influence upon contemporary neuroscientific investigations of the emotions is the flawed James–Lange theory, it is noteworthy that the Jamesian conception of the emotions itself is of Cartesian ancestry. As we have seen, LeDoux claims that 'the brain states and bodily responses are the fundamental facts of an emotion', the conscious feelings being 'added frills' (see §7.2.1). Damasio holds that an emotion is 'a collection of changes in a body state connected to particular mental images that have activated a specific brain system', and that a feeling of an emotion is 'the experience of such changes in juxtaposition to the mental images that initiated the cycle' that offer us the 'cognition of our visceral and musculoskeletal state' as it responds to perception or imagination. In this conception they are repeating some of the errors of the Cartesian conception of the passions of the soul as being 'perceptions, sentiments or emotions of the soul, which are referred particularly to the soul itself, and which are caused, maintained and strengthened by some movement of the [animal] spirits'.[11] In general, the passions, according to Descartes, are generated immediately by turbulence in the heart, blood and animal spirits[12] that produces a mental event – the experienced emotion – in the soul. The proximate physical cause of the feeling of emotion may itself be caused by the perception of a certain (fearful, attractive, etc.) external object. Like Descartes, contemporary neuroscientists characteristically fail to distinguish the causes of an emotion from its object.

Cartesianism in the form of explanation of voluntary action

Fifthly, the conception of voluntary action that characterizes current neuroscientific research is inspired by very much the same picture of voluntariness as informed Cartesian (and British empiricist) reflection. According to Descartes, volitions are actions of the soul. A subclass of these terminate in our bodies, 'as when our merely willing to walk has the consequence that our legs move and we walk'.[13] 'The activity of the soul consists entirely in the fact that simply by willing something it brings it about that the little gland to which it is closely joined moves in the manner required to produce the effect corresponding to this volition.' Hence, 'when we want to walk or move our body in some other way, this volition makes the gland drive the spirits to the muscles which serve to bring about this effect'.[14] As we have seen above, Libet conceives of a voluntary action as a bodily movement caused by an antecedent volition. His purported discovery is that the volition itself is an act of *the brain*, performed before the human being is aware of any desire to move his limbs in accordance with that volition. Here he simply ascribes to the brain the volitional acts which Descartes ascribed to the mind. But the deep misconception that voluntary action is movement caused by an act of volition remains intact. And, as we have seen, it is this that needs to be eradicated.

The crypto-Cartesianism of contemporary neuroscientific reflections on the essential psychological functions of humankind has, we hope, been amply demonstrated in this and the previous four chapters. However, it is even more deeply entrenched in contemporary neuroscientific and cognitive-scientific reflections on the nature of consciousness. It is to this theme that we turn in Part III.

---

[11] Descartes, *Passions of the Soul*, I-27.

[12] Ibid., I-46.

[13] Ibid., I-18.

[14] Ibid., I-41, 43.

Part III

Consciousness and Contemporary
Neuroscience: An Analysis

9

Intransitive and Transitive Consciousness

9.1 Consciousness and the Brain

The importance of distinguishing conceptual from empirical problems about consciousness

Problems concerning consciousness and its nature have been at the centre of neuroscientific, philosophical and cognitive scientific investigations for the last two decades. Leading neuroscientists have gone so far as to suggest that 'Perhaps the greatest unresolved problem . . . in all of biology, resides in the analysis of consciousness'.[1] There are, no doubt, many problems concerning consciousness. Some are empirical problems amenable to scientific investigation. Others are conceptual problems, which can be tackled only by means of conceptual analysis. Distinguishing the two kinds of problem is important, for when a conceptual problem is confused or conflated with an empirical one, it is bound to appear singularly intractable – as indeed it is, for it is intractable to empirical methods of investigation. Equally, when an empirical problem is investigated without adequate conceptual clarity, misconceived questions are bound to be asked, and misguided research is likely to ensue. For, to the extent that the concepts are unclear, to that extent the questions themselves will be unclear. In the following discussion (chapters 9–12), we shall try to shed some light on the concept of consciousness, and to show that clarity concerning the conceptual structures involved in discourse about consciousness has important bearing on the current neuroscientific debate.

Ascribing consciousness to the brain is a mereological mistake

Neuroscientists are prone to ascribe consciousness to the brain. Gerald Edelman and Guilio Tononi claim that 'consciousness arises as a particular kind of brain process'; indeed, it is a 'special kind of physical process that arises in the structure and dynamics of certain brains'.[2] Ian Glynn agrees with John Searle (see below) that mental phenomena 'are themselves features of the brain'.[3] Susan Greenfield contends that consciousness 'is an

---

[1] T. D. Albright, T. M. Jessel, E. R. Kandel and M. I. Posner, 'Neural science: a century of progress and the mysteries that remain', review supplement to *Cell*, 100 (2000) and *Neuron*, 25 (2000) p. S40.
[2] G. M. Edelman and G. Tononi, *Consciousness: How Matter Becomes Imagination* (Allen Lane, London, 2000), pp. xii and 14.
[3] I. Glynn, *An Anatomy of Thought* (Weidenfeld and Nicolson, London, 1999), p. 396.

emergent property of non-specialized groups of neurons that are continuously variable with respect to an epicentre'.[4] Rudolfo Llinás holds that consciousness (or 'mindedness' as he puts it) is a functional state of the brain, one 'of several global physiological computational states that the brain can generate',[5] and Michael Gazzaniga asserts that consciousness 'is a property of a neural network'.[6]

Many philosophers with an interest in neuroscience concur. John Searle contends that 'My present state of consciousness is a feature of my brain'.[7] In a similar vein, Colin McGinn claims that 'The brain has *some* property which confers consciousness upon it', and wonders what could make the brain 'uniquely the organ of consciousness'.[8] This conception is a particular instance of what we have called 'the mereological fallacy in neuroscience', inasmuch as it involves ascribing to the brain – that is, to a part of an animal – an attribute which it makes sense to ascribe only to the animal as a whole.

Neuroscientists and philosophers hold that we are largely ignorant about the nature of consciousness
Many scientists, as well as philosophers, argue that at the moment we are almost completely in the dark about the nature of consciousness. Stuart Sutherland, in a much-quoted remark, wrote that 'Consciousness is a fascinating but elusive phenomenon; it is impossible to specify what it is, what it does, or why it evolved'.[9] Cognitive scientists, such as Phillip Johnson-Laird, aver that 'no one knows what consciousness is, or whether it serves any purpose',[10] and others, such as David Chalmers, go on to proclaim extravagantly that our ignorance about consciousness may be 'the largest outstanding obstacle [to] a scientific understanding of the universe'.[11]

The alleged ignorance is commonly explained by reference to a misconceived notion of privacy
How is this alleged ignorance of the nature of consciousness to be explained? Daniel Dennett, a leading philosopher and advocate for cognitive science, suggests that while science has revealed the secrets of magnetism, photosynthesis, digestion and reproduction, it has so far failed to penetrate the nature of consciousness, for the following reason:

> particular cases of magnetism or photosynthesis or digestion are in principle equally accessible to any observer with the right apparatus, but any particular case of consciousness

[4] S. Greenfield, 'How might the brain generate consciousness', in S. Rose (ed.), *From Brains to Consciousness?* (Penguin Books, Harmondsworth, 1998), p. 214.
[5] R. Llinás, '"Mindedness" as a functional state of the brain', in C. Blakemore and S. Greenfield (eds), *Mindwaves* (Blackwell, Oxford, 1987), p. 339.
[6] Michael S. Gazzaniga, 'Consciousness and the cerebral hemispheres', repr. in Gazzaniga (ed.), *The New Cognitive Neurosciences*, 4th edn (MIT Press, Cambridge, MA, 1997), p. 1396.
[7] J. R. Searle, *Minds, Brains and Science – the 1984 Reith Lectures* (BBC Publications, London, 1984), p. 25.
[8] C. McGinn, 'Could a machine be conscious?', in Blakemore and Greenfield (eds), *Mindwaves*, pp. 281, 285.
[9] Stuart Sutherland, *Dictionary of Psychology* (Macmillan, London, 1989).
[10] P. N. Johnson-Laird, *The Computer and the Mind* (Fontana Press, London, 1988), p. 353.
[11] D. J. Chalmers, *The Conscious Mind* (Oxford University Press, Oxford, 1996), p. xi.

seems to have a favoured or privileged observer, whose access to the phenomenon is entirely unlike, and better than, anyone else's, no matter what apparatus they have. For this reason and others, not only have we so far no good theory of consciousness, we lack even a clear and uncontroversial pre-theoretical description of the presumed phenomenon.[12]

Searle too argued that the brain's 'conscious aspects are accessible to me in a way that they are not accessible to you. And your present state of consciousness is a feature of your brain and its conscious aspects are accessible to you in a way that they are not accessible to me.'[13] In much the same vein, Richard Gregory, an eminent psychologist, suggests that 'Consciousness is difficult to discuss because it is uniquely private: so we do not have analogies from our shared concepts of the physical world at all adequate to describe our experience of it'.[14] And we have already seen (§3.4) that neuroscientists, such as Damasio, Edelman and Tononi, hold that consciousness is an 'entirely private, first-person phenomenon', and that 'privateness' is 'one of those fundamental aspects of conscious experience that are common to all of its manifestations'. On this widely shared conception, our alleged ignorance is explained by reference to the thought that each person has privileged access to his own consciousness, but not to the consciousness of others. So consciousness is not a publicly observable, but a privately observable, phenomenon and, in this respect, unlike the phenomena typically studied by the sciences. For the sciences, it is often held, investigate inter-subjectively verifiable phenomena. This alleged difference is held by some to constitute a methodological difficulty.[15]

It should be evident from our previous discussion in chapter 3 that this conception of privacy is confused. It conflates the conceptual truths that there is no such thing as being conscious that is not a case of *someone's* being conscious, and that some states of consciousness can sometimes be suppressed or concealed, with the conceptual confusions that a person's consciousness is in some deeper sense *private* and *accessible* only to the subject, so that *only the subject can know truths about it directly.*

Neuroscientists and philosophers hold that consciousness is mysterious

Ignorance is one thing, mystery another. Not only do scientists and philosophers confess to lamentable ignorance, they also commonly allege that consciousness is profoundly *mysterious*. Crick and Koch remark that consciousness is 'the most mysterious aspect' of the mind/brain problem.[16] 'Consciousness', Glynn observes, 'has always been a

---

[12] D. Dennett, 'Consciousness', in R. L. Gregory (ed.), *The Oxford Companion to the Mind* (Oxford University Press, Oxford, 1989), p. 160.

[13] Searle, *Minds, Brains and Science*, p. 25.

[14] R. L. Gregory, *Mind in Science* (Penguin Books, Harmondsworth, 1984), p. 480.

[15] Consciousness has a 'subjective' or 'first-person ontology': J. R. Searle, 'The future of philosophy', *Philosophical Transactions of the Royal Society*, B 354 (1999), p. 2074.

[16] F. Crick and C. Koch, 'Mind and brain', *Scientific American*, 267 (Sept. 1992), p. 111. Interestingly, Crick writes elsewhere of 'our strange feeling of being conscious' (*Of Molecules and Men* (University of Washington Press, Seattle, 1966)). But is being conscious a *feeling*? Is being conscious *of* something or other a *feeling*? And is there anything *strange* about it? What would it be like if this 'strange feeling' went away? Would one lose consciousness, i.e. become *unconscious*?

mystery.'[17] Psychologists concur: consciousness, Frisby maintains, 'remains a great mystery, despite considerable advances in our knowledge of perceptual mechanisms'.[18] And philosophers and cognitive scientists agree: Dennett holds that consciousness is 'the most mysterious feature of our minds',[19] and Chalmers asserts that 'Conscious experience is at once the most familiar thing in the world and the most mysterious'.[20]

What a mystery is; the difference between the mysterious and the sublime

One should be wary when told that something is a deep mystery. There are many subjects about which scientists are ignorant, and many empirical questions to which they do not know the answers. There are some subjects about which they are not merely ignorant, but do not have any clear idea, and perhaps not even a vague idea, how to answer the questions that baffle them. These subjects and questions may be dignified by the name of 'mysteries', although, to be sure, one should be careful not to confuse such 'mysteries' – that is, forms of ignorance – with what is wonderful or awesome. For there is much that is wonderful, such as the beauty and fecundity of nature, the impressiveness of great works of art, which is not in the least mysterious, and the wonder need have nothing to do with ignorance. Similarly, that which strikes awe in our hearts, such as great heroism or self-sacrifice, or sublime mountain peaks and raging storms, is typically *not* that of which we are ignorant.

The difference between empirical mysteries and conceptual mystifications

Not only must one avoid assimilating what is puzzling and baffling due to ignorance to what is wonderful or awesome, but one must also take care not to confuse forms of puzzlement about nature consequent on our *ignorance* with mystifications consequent upon *conceptual entanglement*. One may be too hasty in declaring something to be a 'mystery'. For, in some cases, we do not merely have no clear idea how to discover the truth about a certain subject, we have thoroughly confused ideas. Such confusion may involve not empirical ignorance and misunderstanding, or inadequate theory and theoretical understanding, of intractable phenomena, but *conceptual* confusion. Conceptual confusion is not the same as error of fact. The latter involves false belief, but the former involves *incoherence*. It is an error of fact to suppose, as Kepler did, that there are only five planets in the solar system or, as Descartes did, that the pineal gland is the organ in the brain in which signals from the two eyes or the two ears are brought together. But it is a conceptual confusion to suppose that the mind is a kind of entity (either an immaterial substance, as Descartes thought, or the brain, as many suppose today) or that the brain thinks, perceives or calculates (as many neuroscientists suppose), or that self-consciousness is consciousness of a self or an 'I' (see chapter 12). Conceptual confusion consists in transgressing the bounds of sense, and the result of transgressing the bounds of sense is *nonsense* – that is, a form of words which has no sense.

Some kinds of nonsense are patent: for example, 'Is has good' or 'The number 3 fell in love with the number 2 and they got married in world three'. But the forms of nonsense

[17] Glynn, *Anatomy of Thought*, p. 193.

[18] J. P. Frisby, *Seeing: Illusion, Brain and Mind* (Oxford University Press, Oxford, 1980), p. 11.

[19] Dennett, 'Consciousness', p. 160.

[20] Chalmers, *Conscious Mind*, p. 3.

Projecting conceptual confusions on to phenomena and then thinking that there is a mystery in the nature of things

that it is the task of philosophy to disclose are *latent* non-sense. In particular, the conceptual confusions that bedevil us in our reflections on the mind and the brain *appear* to make perfectly good sense. It is all too easy to mistake conceptual confusion for empirical ignorance. When we do so, we mistakenly suppose that what we need is simply more information and a better theory that will explain the phenomenon that bewilders us. But what we need is more *clarity*, not so much about the phenomenon as about the concepts we deploy in articulating our lack of understanding. We are all too prone to project the knots we have inadvertently tied in our own understanding on to the phenomena, and to imagine that *the phenomena are singularly mysterious* and intractable to human understanding. Some have even declared that the nature of consciousness is a mystery which is in principle beyond the powers of the human mind to fathom. But he is a poor navigator in conceptual waters, who, when *he* is at sea, declares the land to be unattainable. To think thus is to take the mystification consequent upon our conceptual confusions for an intractable mystery in the nature of things.

It is largely conceptual confusions about consciousness that generate the sense of mystery

We shall argue that the widespread sense of profound mystery about the nature of consciousness stems largely from conceptual confusions rather than factual ignorance. That there are conscious creatures at all is wonderful –

and it is meet that we should preserve a sense of wonder at the existence of life in general, and conscious forms of life in particular. There is, to be sure, much that we do not know about the neurological basis of consciousness in its various forms. But the various pronouncements of neuroscientists, scientists and philosophers make it clear that their sense of *mystery* does not stem from factual ignorance alone, but, as we shall try to demonstrate, from conceptual entanglement. *That* is remediable, by clarification of our concepts and the elimination of the mystification produced by conceptual confusions. And what is left, when clarity has been attained, is ignorance of fact, on the one hand, and a proper sense of wonder at the marvels and contingencies of nature, on the other.

The subject of human consciousness is the person, not the brain

To begin at the beginning, we should remind ourselves of some simple conceptual truths which we outlined in the preceding discussion. It is not the brain that is conscious or unconscious, but the person whose brain it is. It is not the lecturer's brain that is conscious *of* anything, but the lecturer, who becomes and is conscious of the ticking of the clock or of the interest or boredom of his audience. The brain is not the organ of consciousness. One sees with one's eyes and hears with one's ears, but one is not conscious with one's brain. There is nothing uniquely private about consciousness. There is nothing private or unobservable about a patient's regaining consciousness after an operation; nor is there anything private about the patient becoming conscious of the nurse tiptoeing about the room – *that* he has become conscious of her is evident in his smile of recognition, and *what* he has become conscious of is in full view to any observer. A person who *is* conscious does not thereby have *access* to anything, and it is a confusion to suppose that we can *uniquely observe* our own consciousness.

There is nothing inadequate about the concepts we ordinarily deploy to talk about consciousness, although there are indeed abnormal phenomena which lack any common

The apparent mysteries of con-
sciousness do not stem from any
inadequacy in our language

or garden nomenclature and for which psychology has found it useful to introduce technical terminology (e.g. 'epileptic automatism'). And there is no difficulty of principle in describing the 'presumed phenomenon' of consciousness. The phenomenon, or rather phenomena, are not *presumed* at all – it is not a *presumption* that human beings and many kinds of animals are conscious creatures, are commonly conscious *of* features in their environment, and are subjects of experience – that is, suffer pain, perceive things, feel angry, pleased or frightened. Nor is it a presumption that human beings, *unlike mere animals*, are self-conscious creatures in the sense that they have the capacity to reflect on and be conscious of their own mental states, thoughts and desires, their motives for action, their likings and dislikings, their traits and dispositions, and their history. These phenomena are readily describable. But one must be clear *what* phenomena are correctly characterized as 'phenomena of consciousness'. Finally, in so far as the question of what consciousness is *for* makes sense, there is no difficulty in answering it. But unclarity about our concepts is a seedbed for a misplaced sense of mystery.

The role of this chapter is to clarify the ordinary concept of consciousness. Its range of application is far narrower than that intended by neuroscientists' and cognitive scientists' use of the term 'consciousness' and its cognates. For they are prone to apply the term to the whole range of human waking experience (and beyond). In the next chapter we shall examine some of the reasons for this extension of the terms 'conscious' and 'consciousness'.

A first step towards clarity is to distinguish *transitive* from *intransitive* consciousness. Transitive consciousness is a matter of being conscious *of* something or other, or of being conscious *that* something or other is thus or otherwise. Intransitive consciousness, by contrast, has no object. It is a matter of being conscious or awake, as opposed to being unconscious or asleep.

9.2 Intransitive Consciousness

Intransitive consciousness contrasted
with sleep or unconsciousness

Intransitive consciousness is something that a person or animal may lose (on fainting or being anaesthetized) and subsequently recover (when regaining consciousness). 'To be conscious' differs from 'to be awake', if at all, in so far as predicating the latter of a creature implies that it was previously asleep, rather than unconscious. 'Is A awake?' is more appropriate at home, 'Is A conscious?' and 'Has A recovered consciousness?' belong typically in a hospital. To be unconscious differs from being asleep. It may be caused by fever, anaesthetics, alcohol, etc. It is a state in which a person is not only incapable of perceiving his environment, but also insensible to stimuli, even though parts of his body may react without the person feeling anything. A sleeping person, unlike someone in a coma, dead drunk, or anaesthetized, can be woken by being shaken, by noise, light, heat or cold. He may respond to certain stimuli without awaking – for example, kick off a heavy blanket as the bed warms up. The range of responses of the sleeping is much greater than that of the unconscious, but in neither case do we attribute any perceptual awareness – the sleeper does not *feel* hot when he kicks off the blanket, and he does not *see* the light that wakens him, although it is the light stimulus that causes him to awaken.[21] The transition from unconsciousness to sleep is typically imperceptible (though neurally differentiable), since it is a transition from absence of potentialities to their presence.

Borderline cases   Being unconscious and being asleep, being conscious and being awake, admit of borderline cases. Ordinary language is rich in non-technical terms for such cases. One can be almost unconscious, semi-conscious, barely conscious, dazed or groggy, half-asleep or not fully awake, stupefied, benumbed, etc. There are abnormal conditions to which neither 'conscious' nor 'unconscious' or 'asleep' apply. Some of these are signified by familiar terms – for example, 'delirium', 'hypnotic trance', 'somnambulism' – while others are designated by technical terms of abnormal psychology – for example, 'fugue', 'epileptic automatism'.

Discovering and explaining the neurological states and processes associated with all these conditions is a task for neuroscience and pharmacology. But the fact that people and other diurnal animals are awake or conscious for most of the day, rather than asleep or unconscious, is neither amazing nor mysterious. The question 'What is consciousness for?', if it were directed at this target, would patently be silly. If we are trying to pinpoint areas of scientific ignorance, it is sleep and its necessity, rather than being conscious or awake, that is puzzling and demands explanation.

The subject of intransitive consciousness   Only of creatures that *can* be conscious does it make sense to say that they are *un*conscious, just as only creatures that can be said to be awake can also be said to be asleep. Only of a living being, in particular a sentient creature, can one say that it is conscious *or* unconscious. Hence it is senseless to say this of a machine or a tree – a computer that is switched off is not unconscious and it does not regain consciousness when it is switched on again, and a tree is only figuratively said to awaken in the spring from its winter slumbers.[22] Consequently, intransitive consciousness and unconsciousness are not

---

[21] Of course, one might say that he 'subliminally' feels hot, sees light, hears sounds, or even that he feels, sees and hears, but is not conscious of doing so or of what he thus feels, hears and sees. But these are merely different (more or less misleading) ways of describing the same phenomena, in which the ordinary criteria for perceiving and feeling sensations are partially satisfied *and* the ordinary criteria for not perceiving and not feeling sensations are also partially satisfied.

[22] Consequently, Searle's remark (*The Mysteries of Consciousness* (Granta Books, London, 1997), p. 209): 'I can't prove that this chair is not conscious. If by some miracle all chairs suddenly became conscious, there is no argument that could disprove it' is confused. For there is no such thing as a chair's being either conscious or unconscious. We have assigned no meaning to the phrase 'a conscious chair', hence too none to the phrase 'an unconscious chair'. To be sure, one can no more *prove* that this chair is not conscious than one can prove that the number three is not green or not in love with the number two. But if Searle is suggesting that one cannot prove that this chair is not conscious because of *epistemological* reasons, because one does not *have access* to another being's consciousness or lack of consciousness, then that is misconceived. For 'This chair is conscious' is a senseless form of words and describes no state of affairs which one might prove to obtain or not to obtain. Moreover, if 'by a miracle' (which transgresses the bounds of sense) all chairs became conscious, as in fairy-tales, one would not need to *prove* it, one would *see* it – as the chairs woke from their slumbers, yawned, smiled and started talking to each other. But in such fairy-tales, the chair *has a face*!

properties or features of the brain. They are predicable only of sentient creatures, and, like other psychological terms, they are predicable only of the creature as a whole, not of its parts. If neuroscientists speak of the brain and its parts as being conscious, what they say makes sense only in so far as this is a synecdochical or metonymical use of words. Then it simply signifies a state or activity of the brain or its parts that is systematically correlated with, and has been found to be a condition of, the creature's being conscious. When a person who has been under an anaesthetic stirs, groans and opens his eyes, we say that he has regained consciousness, that he is awake. But we do not say that his brain is awake. For it is not his brain that sits up in bed and asks for a drink, looks around and gets out of bed. The criteria for attributing consciousness to a being – that is, for saying of a creature that it is awake – consist in its behavioural responses to its environment, its perceptual and affective reactions and goal-directed actions. In this primary, literal use, it makes no sense to attribute consciousness to the brain, for the brain can neither perceive nor fail to perceive objects in the environment; only the living animal can do that (although a condition of its so perceiving is that appropriate parts of its brain are functioning normally, and its failures to perceive may be due to malfunctioning of those parts of its brain). The brain can neither be pleased nor displeased by what is seen, and can neither manifest feelings by expression, gesture or action, nor conceal them by keeping poker-faced.

In what sense the brain is the cause of intransitive consciousness

It has been argued that 'the brain causes consciousness'.[23] We have claimed that it is not the brain that is conscious (or unconscious), but the human being whose brain it is. Can it be said that the brain causes a person to be (intransitively) conscious? It depends on what is meant. Of course, if there is such-and-such neural malfunctioning in the brain, the person will not be conscious, but unconscious (or suffering from akinetic mutism, epileptic fugue, etc.). Equally, when a person awakens or regains consciousness, the intralaminar nuclei trigger cortical activity, but for which he would not awaken or regain consciousness. On the other hand, the answer to the question 'What is the cause of A's awakening?' is *not* 'Why, his brain, of course'. Rather, the brain events, triggered by the intralaminar nuclei, are viewed as causal conditions of awakening and/or of being awake, the 'precipitating cause' being such an event as a loud noise, being shaken by the shoulder, etc. (This is parallel to the fact that we do not normally identify the cause of a fire with the presence of oxygen in the air, even though in the absence of oxygen there would be no fire.)

There is nothing intrinsically private about intransitive consciousness

There is nothing essentially private about intransitive consciousness. That another person has regained consciousness or awoken is normally fully visible in his behaviour. We can ordinarily see *that* a person is conscious (also what he is conscious *of*, and very often also what *state of consciousness* he is *in* – of which more below). It is true that someone may pretend to be unconscious, and take us in – but no one can pretend to be conscious. People may dissimulate and veil their feelings or conceal their current state of consciousness – that is, what state of mind they are in. But what *can* be thus suppressed or concealed is also what *can* be manifest or revealed. It may not be evident whether

---

[23] Searle, *Minds, Brains and Science*, pp. 18–22.

someone was or was not conscious of something, just as it may not be evident whether someone noticed something. But it also may be obvious that he did – wholly evident in the changes in his behaviour.

The first-person case   Of course, that *I* am conscious is not something that is evident to me on the grounds of any behavioural criteria. But nor is it evident by introspection or privileged access of any kind. If it *seems* as if any particular case of consciousness has 'a favoured or privileged observer, whose access to the phenomenon is entirely unlike, and better than, anyone else's',[24] then it wrongly seems so. That one is conscious is not a piece of information which one might lack and acquire by having access to it by some means or other. I may become, and so be, conscious of your regaining consciousness, but I cannot become, and be, conscious of my regaining consciousness. My own (intransitive) consciousness is not an object of possible experience for me, but a precondition for any experience.[25]

The peculiar use of 'I am   Consequently, there are not, and could not be, any *conscious'*   grounds or evidence for claiming to be conscious. To say 'I am conscious' is not to make a claim, and there can be no *grounds* for saying this. One cannot mistakenly or falsely claim that one is conscious, as one may mistakenly or falsely claim that another person is conscious. If someone said in his sleep 'I am conscious', we would not accuse him of making a false claim, any more than if he said 'I am asleep', we would say 'He is quite right'.[26] It cannot *seem* to one that one is conscious. For one cannot say, 'It seems to me that I am conscious, but I may be wrong', or 'It seems to him that he is conscious, so he is probably right'. Hence it is misguided to claim that 'If it consciously seems to me that I am conscious, then I am conscious',[27] and even more confused to try to describe 'those features of my life *and the nature of my acquaintance with them* that I would cite as my "grounds" for claiming that I *am* – and do not merely *seem to be* – conscious'.[28] There is *a* use for the sentence 'I am conscious', but it is not to express an item of indubitable, privileged knowledge or to convey to others one's private observations or to report one's current experience. It is rather akin to a signal. As I recover consciousness after an anaesthetic, I might say to a nurse, whom I notice tiptoeing around the room, 'I am conscious'. I do not say this after 'observing my own consciousness', but after observing that she thinks I am still

---

[24] Dennett, 'Consciousness', p.160.

[25] It might be objected that since one dreams when one is asleep, one can have experiences even though one is not conscious. But to dream is not to have any experiences, although it may involve dreaming that one has experiences (if one dreams about oneself, and dreams that one perceives, does and undergoes various things). However, to dream that one is watching a football match, enjoying a party, etc. is not to have any experience at all – it is only to dream that one is having such experiences.

[26] L. Wittgenstein, *Zettel*, ed. G. E. M. Anscombe and G. H. von Wright, tr. G. E. M. Anscombe (Blackwell, Oxford, 1967), §396.

[27] Searle, *Mysteries of Consciousness*, p. 122.

[28] D. Dennett, 'Towards a cognitive theory of consciousness', repr. in his *Brainstorms* (Harvester Press, Brighton, 1981), p. 173.

unconscious. I might just as well say 'Hello' or ask what time it is.[29] For these utterances, no less than 'I am conscious', show that I have regained consciousness. The latter, however, also asserts what its utterance shows.

9.3 Transitive Consciousness and its Forms

Dispositional and occurrent transitive consciousness distinguished; being conscious of and being aware of distinguished

Transitive consciousness may be dispositional or occurrent.[30] When we say of a person that he is conscious of his ignorance or expertise, or conscious of his superior or inferior social status, we are typically speaking of a *disposition* or *tendency* he has to be conscious, from occasion to occasion, of these things. Hence, too, when we speak of a person as being class-conscious, money-conscious or safety-conscious, we are indicating a proneness to be conscious of his or others' social background, of financial considerations, or of matters pertaining to safety. *Occurrent* consciousness, by contrast, is a matter of currently being conscious of something or conscious that something is thus-and-so.[31] We cannot, in this sense, be conscious of many things at the same time, since we cannot have our attention held by many things at once or have our mind occupied by many different things at the same time. Nor can we remain conscious of what no longer holds our attention or occupies our thoughts. In this respect, being conscious of something differs from *being aware* of something. For whereas one ceases to be conscious of something that ceases to engage one's attention or to occupy one's thoughts, one remains aware of things of which one has been informed, as long as one does not forget the information in question and adverts to it reasonably frequently. So whatever one is conscious of, one is also aware of, but one may be aware of things of which one is not conscious. The following discussion is concerned primarily with occurrent transitive consciousness.

Intransitive consciousness is a condition for the various forms of occurrent transitive consciousness – that is, for being conscious *of* something at a given time, for a time. Borderline cases of intransitive consciousness yield borderline cases of transitive consciousness. One may be vaguely or half-conscious of something when one is half-asleep or semi-conscious.

---

[29] L. Wittgenstein, *Philosophical Investigations*, ed. G. E. M. Anscombe and R. Rhees, tr. G. E. M. Anscombe (Blackwell, Oxford, 1953), §416.

[30] The following discussion is much indebted to A. R. White, *Attention* (Blackwell, Oxford, 1964), ch. 4.

[31] To be conscious of something is not, we note in passing, a mere matter of 'having a thought about it or a sensation of it' (D. M. Rosenthal, 'Thinking that one thinks', in M. Davies and G. W. Humphreys (eds), *Consciousness* (Blackwell, Oxford, 1993), p. 198). One does not, *pace* Rosenthal, become conscious of a chair by thinking that one must repair the old armchair in the attic, any more than one can become conscious of Caesar by thinking about him. Nor, as we shall argue below, is merely perceiving an object thereby a matter of being conscious of what one perceives.

Being conscious of *and being conscious* that

Being conscious *of* something and being conscious *that* something is so are sometimes equivalent, just as perceiving something and perceiving that something is so are sometimes equivalent. To be conscious of one's ignorance is to be conscious that one is ignorant, to be conscious of the boredom of one's audience is to be conscious that one's audience is bored, and to be conscious of a movement in the bushes is to be conscious that something moved in the bushes. But although being conscious of Jack implies that Jack is present (otherwise one could not be (perceptually) conscious of him), to be conscious of Jack, standing in the corner, is not the same as being conscious that Jack is standing in the corner. The phrase 'conscious *of* so-and-so' (where 'so-and-so' is the name or description of a material object or person) specifies what object has caught and held one's attention. The phrase 'conscious that such-and-such is the case' emphasizes the state of affairs or fact that occupies one's mind and weighs with one. So, for example, one may become conscious of Jack, standing in the corner of the room, if he catches and holds one's attention. But one cannot continue to be conscious of him if he leaves the room. By contrast, having become conscious of a friend's embarrassment as manifest in his behaviour, one may remain conscious of the fact that he was embarrassed long after one has ceased to be perceptually conscious of his embarrassment, and indeed long after he has ceased to be embarrassed, if, for example, the thought of his embarrassment occupies one subsequently.

Becoming and being conscious of; noticing and being conscious of

Becoming conscious of something is the beginning of being and remaining conscious of it. What we become conscious of typically pre-exists our becoming conscious of it. What we are and, for a while, remain conscious of must be something that persists or is continuous. That which is momentary is what we may *notice*, rather than what we may become and remain conscious of. So, we may notice, but not become and remain conscious of, a flash or a bang, and we may, in the course of a conversation, become and be conscious of, but cannot notice, our own ignorance or feelings of doubt.

Transitive consciousness admits of a variety of types of object, and may take different forms. The following classification is rough-and-ready, but will perhaps serve to bring some preliminary order into a highly variegated field.

Perceptual consciousness One may be conscious of perceptibilia, as when one becomes conscious of the ticking of a clock or the flashing of a light, of an X in the corner or of Y's strange colour. So, too, we may become conscious of the smell of burning, or be conscious of the scent of lilies-of-the-valley which pervades the room. While listening to a piece of music, we may become conscious of the muted *leitmotif* or of the periodic inversion of a theme. And while listening to a friend, we may realize that he is agitated or depressed, and so become conscious of his state of mind.

Perceiving something and being conscious of something distinguished

To become and to be conscious of such things is not an alternative to perceiving them. Nor is what one is thus conscious of anything other than what is visually, auditorily, olfactorily, etc. perceived. However, to be conscious of something one perceives is not the same as perceiving it *simpliciter*, any more than to perceive something is the same as to notice what one perceives. Only those things which we perceive and realize we perceive are things of which we are conscious. If we perceive a shadow in the bushes and think it is a cat, we are not conscious of the shadow, *a fortiori* not conscious of a cat. Furthermore, as we shall argue below, we are perceptually conscious only of what catches and holds our attention.

Somatic consciousness   One is conscious of one's sensations: for example, of the pain in one's tooth, the tickling sensation in one's foot, or the itch in the small of one's back. Sensations, although they are not objects, *a fortiori* not objects perceived, do catch and hold our attention. Furthermore, one can be conscious of the waxing and waning of their intensity, as when one becomes conscious of the increasing severity of one's headache, or, with relief, one becomes conscious of the waning of one's feeling of nausea. One may, of course, be conscious of a pain, without being aware of the fact that it is sciatica. This does not imply that one has an unconscious sciatic pain; rather, it implies that one has, and is conscious of, a pain, but does not realize that it is a sciatic pain.

Kinaesthetic consciousness   A different form of somatic consciousness is kinaesthetic. One may become conscious of one's cramped position, of one's mouth being open, or of the orientation of one's body if one realizes that things are thus. Similarly, one may be conscious of the movements of one's limbs or fingers. This may, but *need not*, involve kinaesthetic sensations, and one's knowledge of the disposition or movement of one's body or limbs is not *inferred* from any kinaesthetic sensation. It is true that anaesthetizing a limb, neural injury to a limb or brain damage deprives one of one's normal ability to describe its position or movement (without looking). But this does not show that one's judgement that one's limb is oriented thus or is moving thus rests on, or is derived from, the evidence provided by kinaesthetic sensations. The case is similar to one's ability to detect the direction from which a sound is coming. This ability may well depend on the fact that the sound waves do not reach both ears simultaneously or that they affect one ear differently from the other. But one does not hear, feel or otherwise sense the different effect of the sound waves on one ear as opposed to the other, and so does not *infer* the direction of the sound from any perceived difference between the ears. Rather, one's knowledge of the direction of a sound rests on no *evidence* at all. One's ability to make such immediate, non-evidential judgements causally depends on the fact that each ear is differently affected by the sound waves. Similarly, our ability to say how our limbs and body are disposed or how our limbs are moving no doubt depends on our limbs not being anaesthetized and on our nerves functioning normally, but it is not typically *derived* from evidence provided by kinaesthetic sensations, even though there may be some such sensations.

Apart from feeling sensations and feeling one's limbs move, one also feels one's overall bodily condition, as when one feels sleepy or wide awake, exhausted or refreshed, ill or well, and of these too one may become and be conscious. These may be accompanied by an array of more or less diffuse sensations, but the overall condition of which one is conscious is not identical with whatever sensations, if any, may accompany it.

Affective consciousness   We feel not only sensations and our overall bodily condition, but also emotions and moods. We feel excited or frightened, overjoyed or angry, happy or sad, and we may be in a good mood, if we are cheerful and contented, or in a foul one, if we feel irritable or depressed. These too are objects of transitive consciousness. One may become conscious of one's current emotion, as when one becomes conscious of one's increasing irritation as old Snodgrass drones on interminably, of one's feeling of jealousy as one watches Daisy flirting, or of one's rising excitement as the time of some eagerly anticipated event draws nigh. Similarly, one may, but need not, become and be conscious of one's mood and of its changes. One may become conscious of the deepening of one's depression, and one may be conscious of feeling unusually cheerful. One may be in an irritable mood, but it may take a couple of outbursts of bad temper before one realizes and becomes conscious of one's current state of mind. Affective consciousness typically takes the form of realization, not of captured attention. For to feel jealous without being conscious of the fact that one is jealous is, for example, to feel irritated by Daisy's flirting with Jack, to wish that she would stop, to think that the attention she is giving him is disloyal to one, etc., without realizing that to respond thus *is* to feel jealous. To realize that one is feeling jealous is not to have one's attention caught by one's jealousy (which is not an object or event that can catch one's attention). Rather, it is for it to dawn on one that what one feels constitutes jealousy. Having realized that one is jealous, one may then be conscious of being jealous if the fact that one is so weighs on one and occupies one's thoughts.

Consciousness of one's motives The emotions are related to motives (§7.2.2), for in many (but not all) cases, that which we feel when we feel a certain emotion may also be what, metaphorically speaking, moves us to action. So we may feel jealous and act out of jealousy, feel vengeful and act out of revenge, feel compassion and act out of compassion. People often act from certain motives without knowing that they do. One may be moved by jealousy or vindictiveness, without realizing that one is, as one may act out of pity or revenge without acknowledging to oneself or to others that one does. This may be the result of lack of reflection or of self-deception. But one may reflect on why one is doing what one is doing, and one may realize one's true motive. Hence one may become conscious of one's motivation. It should be noted that failure to be conscious of one's motive is *not* the same as having what psychoanalysts term 'an unconscious motive'.

Reflective consciousness Consciousness of one's motives in action has affinities with other forms of consciousness, which we shall call 'reflective'. These constitute a mixed bag. They all involve realization of facts and reflection on things being as one realizes they are, and may be either self- or other-directed, or neither. Unlike somatic and perceptual consciousness and consciousness of one's actions (see below), reflective consciousness is not confined to what is present. So, one may be conscious of an honour recently done one or of one's rashness or chronic indecision, *if such facts currently occupy one's mind, or knowingly colour what does occupy one's mind*. Similarly, one may be dispositionally or occurrently conscious of the circumstances of one's birth, marriage or election to office, if the relevant facts tend to, or currently do, occupy one's thoughts. And one may be conscious of one's own or of another's social class, or of one's own or of another's skills or lack of skills. So, one may be acutely conscious of one's ignorance while speaking to an expert, and also conscious of *his* erudition and skill as one listens to his reply. This does not merely involve knowing that something is so, but further, it requires that what one knows should impress one. The knowledge must then weigh with or on one, affecting one's reactions and actions. One may be conscious of the lateness of the hour if one knows it is late and that fact occupies one's thoughts and affects one's behaviour.

Consciousness of one's actions   Distinct again is the consciousness of one's actions, which may take two forms. It may be *agential*, as when one consciously does something – for example, cracks a carefully planned joke in the course of a lecture, or consciously repeats what one said in last week's lecture. Here the agent knows what he is doing, and is attending to the doing of it. He is acting intentionally, and his knowledge of what he is doing, or, at least, of what he is trying to do, is not derived from observation, as knowledge of what another person is doing commonly is. The agent is acting in the execution of his intention, and is occupied and absorbed in carrying it out, as is emphasized by the common conjunction 'consciously and deliberately'. Agential consciousness is not a matter of having one's attention caught and held by something, but rather of giving one's attention to what one is intentionally doing. By contrast, one may be conscious of what one is doing, not *qua* agent, but *qua* spectator. Here what one becomes and is conscious of is something which one is typically not doing intentionally at all. So, when one realizes to one's dismay that one is repeating last week's lecture, or boring one's audience, one may become embarrassingly conscious of the fact. One realizes that this is what one is doing, and the fact that one is so doing occupies one's thoughts and colours one's reactions.

Self-consciousness   Self-consciousness, in the ordinary sense of the term, may take different forms. (i) In one sense, it concerns one's awareness of others observing one, the consequence of which is that one's behaviour is affected – one becomes embarrassed or intimidated, etc.[32] (ii) In a further sense, it is a matter of the deliberation and thought which one customarily give to one's creative work – in this sense we contrast the intuitive and spontaneous artist with the highly self-conscious, deliberative one. (iii) In yet another sense, it signifies a tendency to introspective reflection on one's own motives, attitudes and reactions. It is in this sense that one says that Proust was a highly self-conscious person. These uses, however, must not be confused with the philosophical use of the expression 'self-consciousness', according to which human beings are unique in nature in being self-conscious creatures. This notion of self-consciousness is not a matter of being conscious of something called 'a self' (see chapter 12), but rather of a person's capacity to think about, reflect on, report and be conscious of his own mental states, beliefs, desires and motives, his skills, tendencies, attitudes and character traits, as well as his past life and experiences. So it is exemplified or actualized by the third form of self-consciousness just mentioned.

This rough classification of forms of transitive consciousness is neither exhaustive nor exclusive. Its primary purpose is to alert us to the diversity of, and conceptual heterogeneity of, transitive consciousness.

---

[32] Curiously, the German equivalent, *Selbstbewusstsein*, signifies not embarrassed awareness of others observing one, but self-confidence or self-assertiveness.

9.4 Transitive Consciousness: A Partial Analysis

The parameters of the analysis   Transitive consciousness lies at the confluence of the concepts of *knowledge, realization* (i.e. one specific form that acquisition of knowledge may take), *receptivity* (as opposed to achievement) of knowledge, and *attention* caught and held, or given. The various categories or kinds of transitive consciousness that we have distinguished are differently related to these. We shall sketch some of the connecting links and some of the conceptual differences between these loose categories. Our purpose is threefold. First, to emphasize the conceptual diversity within the field of transitive consciousness. Secondly, to emphasize that the various categories are not related in any simple way. They are not members of a common genus distinguished by specific differentia. Indeed, it is more illuminating to view them as centres of variation. Thirdly, to forestall unwarranted generalization.

We must first make some conceptual connections and classifications. First, 'to become (or be) conscious of (or that)' is polymorphous. Second, 'to become (and to be) conscious of (or that)' are, depending upon their complement, either factive or existence-implying verbs – one cannot be conscious of something's being thus-and-so unless it is *in fact* thus-and-so, and one cannot be conscious of X unless X *exists*. Transitive consciousness is a form of *knowledge*. Third, what is distinctive about the knowledge which becoming conscious of something involves is that it is knowledge *received*, as opposed to *achieved* or *attained*. There are means and methods of attaining knowledge, but no means and methods of becoming conscious of (or noticing, realizing, or becoming aware of) something. Becoming consciousness of something, like becoming aware, realizing and noticing, is generally a *form of receptivity*.[33] Fourth, some forms of transitive consciousness are attentional – a matter of having one's attention *caught and held* by something's being thus-and-so. Others (e.g. agential consciousness of one's actions) are a matter of focusing one's attention on what one is doing. Other forms of transitive consciousness are not so much attentional as a matter of knowledge currently *occupying one's thoughts and feelings*, and/or *weighing with one in one's deliberations and actions*, or *knowingly colouring one's thoughts, feelings and reactions*.

The polymorphous character of transitive consciousness   'To become conscious of' and 'to be conscious of' are polymorphous verbs. In this respect they are like 'working', 'obeying an order', 'practising', 'rehearsing', 'fighting' and, as we have previously seen, 'thinking'. What counts as working or rehearsing, for example, will vary from context to context and occasion to occasion, and what one does on one occasion may be done on another occasion and yet not then count as working or rehearsing at all. The various instances of a polymorphous activity may be forms which the polymorph may take, but are not species of a genus. So, what counts as becoming or being conscious of X depends on what X is. To be told that someone is conscious of something does not tell one what form his

---

[33] See White, *Attention*, ch. 4.

consciousness takes, any more than being told that someone is practising tells one whether he is declaiming, singing, playing the piano or hitting golf balls. Becoming or being conscious of the ticking of a clock takes a quite different form (viz. hearing) from becoming or being conscious of the colour of Daisy's eyes (viz. seeing), as rehearsing a dance takes a quite different form (viz. dancing) from rehearsing a song (viz. singing). What one does on becoming conscious of X may, on another occasion, be done even though one cannot be said to have become conscious (or *not* to have become conscious) of X, as what one does on rehearsing a song may be done on another occasion without rehearsing – namely, when actually performing. So, for example, I may go over to greet Daisy, having become conscious of her in the corner of the room; but I may equally go over to greet her on seeing her immediately I entered the room – and in this case, I did not *become conscious* of her. Immediately to see someone familiar before one is neither to become conscious of them nor to recognize them, although, to be sure, one does not *fail* to recognize them either and one is *neither* conscious *nor* unconscious of their presence.[34]

The different forms of transitive consciousness

Transitive consciousness therefore takes diverse forms. Perceptual consciousness may take the form of seeing, hearing, smelling, tasting or tactilely feeling something. What one is perceptually conscious of is not something over and above some of the things one perceives. Somatic consciousness takes the form of feeling (sensing, rather than tactilely feeling), and what one is somatically conscious of is nothing different from what one (non-tactilely) feels or has. Similarly, what one is affectively conscious of is nothing other than the current emotion and mood which one feels (although it should be noted that to feel cheerful or angry, depressed or excited, is *logically* unlike feeling a pain or a tickle). *Becoming* reflectively conscious of something – for example, when one becomes conscious of one's ignorance or of another's erudition, of the lateness of the hour or of one's chronic indecision – typically takes the form of knowledge consequent upon realization. *Being* reflectively conscious of something is not a matter of captured attention at all. That *of which* one is currently thus conscious occupies one's thoughts, weighs with one and/or knowingly colours one's deliberations, reactions and actions.

There is no special faculty or organ of transitive consciousness

So, first, there is no special faculty of transitive consciousness, although one's perceptual faculties are engaged whenever one is perceptually conscious of something. Similarly, there is no organ of transitive consciousness. Sometimes becoming and being conscious of something involves the use of an organ, as in the case of perceptual

---

[34] It would be absurd to say that when one has breakfast each morning with one's wife, one recognizes her, let alone that one recognizes her afresh each time one raises one's head and looks at her. *Of course*, that does not mean that one *fails* to recognize her. What it does mean is that it requires a *special context* for it to make sense to speak of recognizing the familiar. Similarly, one cannot be said to be either conscious or not conscious of one's wife as one sits chatting to her, for, again, a special context is required for these expressions to be brought into play – as we shall argue below.

consciousness. Sometimes it does not, as in the cases of somatic, affective and reflective consciousness. Of course, one cannot be transitively conscious of something unless one's brain is functioning normally in appropriate respects.

There is no one thing that needs investigating for the neuroscience of transitive consciousness

Secondly, if neuroscientists are interested in transitive consciousness, *there is no one thing that they can investigate*, for transitive consciousness takes many different forms. What would have to be studied are the neural correlates of the various forms of perception, sensation, affective feeling and mood, as well as reflection – *not*, to be sure, in all their aspects, but only in those that are pertinent to being, in one form or another, conscious of something. The moot question is: What marks out transitive consciousness? What is distinctive of perceptual consciousness as opposed perception in general? What is characteristic of somatic consciousness over and above sensation? What are the marks of affective and reflective consciousness, as opposed to the general phenomena of feeling emotions and moods, or of thinking about this or that? We need to get a firmer grip on the logical character of transitive consciousness.

The connection between transitive consciousness and knowledge   Grammarians classify such verbs as 'know', 'remember', 'realize', 'perceive', as factive verbs (see §4.2). When they occur in the form 'A knows that such-and-such is the case' or 'A remembers doing so-and-so', the truth of the proposition expressed or intimated by the complement is implied. If A knows, remembers, realizes or perceives *that things are thus-and-so*, then it is, *in fact*, the case that things are thus-and-so. Some factive verbs (but not all) may also occur with a direct object rather than a clausal complement: for example, 'A knows (perceives) B'. So used, the sentence implies the existence of the object of the verb. If A knows or perceives B, then B must exist.

The factivity of transitive consciousness

'To become conscious of (or that)' and 'to be conscious of (or that)' are factive, or existence-implying – that is, one cannot logically become conscious or be conscious of something that is not the case or is not there. One cannot become and then be conscious of things being thus-and-so (or that things are thus-and-so) unless they *are* thus-and-so. One cannot be conscious of the honour done one, of the hostility of the audience, of the increasing pain in one's back, or of the absurdity of one's thoughts, unless one *is* being honoured, the audience *is* hostile, one's backache *is* getting worse, and one's thoughts *are* absurd. Similarly, if one becomes and then is conscious of a rabbit in the quadrangle, then there must *be* a rabbit in the quadrangle. If there is none, then one *thought* one spotted or noticed a rabbit, and one was mistaken – it was a hare, or a mere shadow. So one was *not* conscious of a rabbit, since there was no rabbit to be conscious of. If one *is* conscious of it, one also knows it to be there.

Consciousness and knowledge

The factivity of transitive consciousness is unsurprising, given the etymological connection of 'conscious' with cognitive verbs, for cognitive verbs are paradigms of factive verbs. 'To be conscious of' is derived from *scio* ('I know') compounded with *cum* ('with') to yield *conscio*, which may mean 'I know together with' or 'I share (with someone) the knowledge that'; or, when the prefix *cum* functions merely as an intensifier, it may mean 'I know well' or 'I do know'.[35] Transitive consciousness is *essentially connected with knowledge*. So, to be conscious of a movement in the bushes is to know that there is a movement in the bushes, to be conscious of one's ignorance is to know that one is ignorant, and to become conscious of the folly of one's thoughts is to realize, and so come to know, that one's thoughts are foolish. Similarly, to be conscious of Jack, standing in the corner of the room, is to know that Jack is present, and to be conscious of a noise entails knowing that there was a noise.

Of course, we know much of which we are not conscious. We are not conscious of the bulk of the myriad facts that we have learnt or come to know. There is much that we know, but which we may need to be reminded of, but there is nothing of which we are already conscious which we need to be reminded of. Whatever one has learnt or come to know and has not irretrievably forgotten, one knows, but one is conscious of those objects of transitive consciousness *that occupy one's mind*. One may learn or come to know many things by being informed, by discovering or finding out that things are so. But one cannot become conscious of something by being informed that things are so – only made aware that they are so. (And to be aware that things are so is not the same as being conscious that they are so. You need not tell me things of which I am already aware, although you may have to remind me of them; but you need not remind me of that of which I am already conscious.) One can be good at learning, discovering, detecting or finding out certain things, but one cannot be good at becoming or being conscious of things. This *logical* point is manifest in the general acceptability of the question 'How do you know?' and the unintelligibility of 'How are you conscious of the F-ness of X?' as opposed to 'What made you conscious of the F-ness of X?' or 'How did you become conscious of the F-ness of X?'.

---

[35] The English 'conscious', 'conscious of' and its nominal, 'consciousness', emerged only in the seventeenth century. Cognates of the verb 'conscio' are the noun 'conscientia' and the adjective 'conscius'. These share the ambiguity of the verb. For 'conscientia' may signify a sharing of knowledge or knowledge, awareness or apprehension as such, and even just mind or thought. Signifying *being privy to what another knows*, it naturally evolved a reflexive use: 'conscious to oneself', i.e. the knowing of something secret about oneself. As 'conscience' acquired the more specialized sense of an internal witness, and later of an internal lawgiver, 'conscious' evolved in a different direction. Its overt reflexive form 'to oneself' and its necessary association with privity disappears, although the ghost of the latter persists in talk of a person's being conscious of his own sensations and feelings. Consciousness *of* something acquired a far wider domain, involving no sense of *secret* or *privileged* knowledge. I may be conscious of something, e.g. the ticking of a clock, the scent of roses or the lateness of the hour, of which others too are conscious. The objects of consciousness are no longer confined to secret items of knowledge, let alone to one's own good and evil deeds, but incorporate a wide range of items (though not all) that may occupy a person's mind. Being self-conscious, in the sense of 'preoccupied with', 'excessively attentive to' oneself and one's qualities, or, differently, 'apt to apprehend or imagine that one is the object of others' observation' come on the scene in the eighteenth century. Being conscious, as opposed to unconscious or insensate, emerges only in the nineteenth century. And being 'class-', 'money-' or 'colour-' conscious are twentieth-century additions to our vocabulary. See C. S. Lewis, *Studies in Words* (Cambridge University Press, Cambridge, 1960), ch. 8.

Becoming conscious of something is a form of reception of knowledge   What then distinguishes the knowledge that is acquired by becoming conscious of something from other forms of knowledge acquisition? Becoming conscious of something is an occurrence – as are becoming aware of, noticing and realizing something. Unlike learning, finding out or discovering, becoming conscious, becoming aware, etc. are not things we do, let alone actions we perform. One cannot voluntarily, intentionally, deliberately or on purpose become conscious of the flashing lights, notice X, or realize that X is Y. Consequently, one cannot resolve, refuse or try to become conscious of something, or to notice or realize something. Nor can one do so skilfully or clumsily. One cannot ask for a person's reason for becoming conscious of something, or for noticing or realizing something. Rather, one may ask what *made* him conscious of it.

The family of verbs of cognitive receptivity   To *be* conscious of something is typically the upshot of *becoming* conscious of it. 'To become conscious of' belongs to a small family of cognitive verbs, together with 'to become aware of', 'to realize' and 'to notice'. Like the different family of cognitive verbs which has 'detect', 'discover', 'solve', 'ascertain', 'find out' and 'discern' among its members, they signify the acquisition of knowledge. What distinguishes the former family from the latter is that its members involve *reception* of knowledge as opposed to *achievement* of knowledge. One may try to find out, detect, discover, by various means or methods, and if one succeeds, then one achieves knowledge. But one does not try to become conscious of or aware of something, or to notice or realize something – rather, knowledge is, as it were, thrust upon one. One may be trained and become skilful in the means and methods of knowledge acquisition, but one cannot be trained and skilful in the means and methods of becoming conscious of things, since there are none.

Attention, reflection, deliberation and the object of consciousness   What is distinctive of some forms of transitive consciousness is that one's attention is *caught* and *held* by that of which one is conscious. A different kind of attentional consciousness is agential consciousness of one's own actions, when one's attention is wholly *given* to what one is 'consciously and deliberately' doing. In the case of other forms of transitive consciousness, as we have seen, what one is conscious of *occupies one's mind* and may *weigh with one* in one's deliberations, and/or *knowingly colour one's behaviour and reactions*. (The concept of transitive consciousness is thus non-uniform, and the distinctions we have drawn may be said to mark 'centres of variation' within this conceptual field.)

Not everything we perceive is an object of our transitive consciousness   Obviously, whatever one is perceptually conscious of is something perceived. But not everything one perceives is something of which one is conscious.

First, much that we perceive we may not even notice, let alone attend to – so we cannot be said to be conscious of it.

Secondly, if we perceive an X (e.g. a cat in the bushes), but do not realize that it is an X and take it to be a Y (e.g. a shadow), we cannot be said to be conscious of an X (e.g. of a cat), since we do not know that there is a cat in the bushes.

Thirdly, even if we notice something fleetingly, it does not follow that we are conscious of that thing, for to be perceptually conscious of something, it must catch *and hold* our attention. So, one may notice the brilliant colours of the roses as one rushes by to catch a bus, but one need not thereby become or remain conscious of their colour.

Fourthly, when we are intentionally giving our attention to something and to its features, as when we are scrutinizing a painting or conversing with a person, we cannot be said to be conscious (or not conscious) of what thus engages our attention, unless our attention is riveted to that thing. For what we can become and be conscious of is what *catches* our attention, not what we *intentionally* attend to. This requires further explanation.

Intentional attention precludes perceptual consciousness and its negation

If I carefully examine the surface of a painting, looking for signs of deterioration, I may become conscious of a faint crack in the panel, but not of the surface of the painting which I am scrutinizing. If I am attentively conversing with Daisy, I may become and then be conscious of her lack of interest, but not of her, even though I perceive her and perceive that she is present. Of course, it would be equally awry to say that one is not conscious of the surface of the painting or of Daisy. For that would wrongly suggest inattention or ignorance of the object of one's concern. In such cases, it may be what disrupts, partially disturbs or distracts our attention, such as the ticking of a clock in the background or the smell of dinner wafting in from the kitchen, that is what we might become and be conscious of. Alternatively, what we may become and then be conscious of are *features* of the object of our attention to which we were *not* attending, but which catch and hold our attention: for example, the colour of Daisy's eyes or her boredom, the faint crack in the panel, or the small wormhole in its corner.

The reasons for this are evident:

(a) If our attention is *intentionally* focused, what we are attending to is not something in relation to which we are *passively receptive*.

(b) Those features of an object to which we are intentionally giving our attention are not features of which we *become* conscious; rather, it is *other* features which bring about a *shift* in our attention that we can be said to become and then be conscious of.

(c) What *does* obtrude itself upon us, impress itself on us independently of our wish or will, is often precisely that which we are not purposefully occupied with at all: namely, distracting features which demand our attention, like the ticking of a clock or the smell of dinner. Much of what we become and then are perceptually conscious of are objects of *peripheral perception*, which, in one way or another, *catch and hold our attention*.

However, in cases in which a person's attention is riveted to something, typically but not only to something he is doing with intense concentration, we say that 'he was conscious of nothing other than . . .' to mark the exclusive focus of his attention. Here the emphasis shifts from one's attention being *caught* to one's attention being irresistibly *held*, hence from reception of knowledge to riveting of attention (which may be the result of intentional concentration).

Somatic consciousness and attention

Somatic consciousness of sensations is again a matter of having one's attention caught and held. Since having a pain is not a form of perception, to be conscious of a pain is not a case of perceptual consciousness. For the most part, there is no difference between feeling a pain and being conscious of a pain. If a sensation is intense, it cannot but catch one's attention. The more intense it is, the more it thrusts itself upon our attention. If it is momentary, like a sudden twinge, one cannot but be aware of it. If it is persistent, one cannot but be conscious of it. The more intense the sensation, the more difficult it is to attend to anything else or, indeed, to think of anything else. It is no coincidence that we speak of being 'in the grip' of pain. The less intense a sensation, the easier it is for us to have our attention *distracted* from it or to *forget* it. (Note that to forget our aches and pains (or our troubles) when a visitor comes to entertain us at our sickbed is not a lapse of memory, but a distraction of attention.)

Affective consciousness and realization

Affective consciousness, as noted above, is also concerned with feelings, but in a different sense of the term. Its objects include *emotions*, such as feeling anger, pity, compassion, fear, pride or shame and the corresponding motives; *agitations*, such as feeling startled, shocked or amazed; *moods*, such as feeling irritable, cheerful, depressed, bored, anxious or happy; and *attitudes*, such as feeling pleased, interested or indifferent. Here too, one may become conscious of such feelings and be conscious of feeling them, as well as realize and become conscious of one's motives. Some of these cases involve sensations, which one cannot have without being aware of, or conscious of, them. In some cases, one may have a certain pattern of sensations without realizing that they amount to or are part of the larger syndrome of feeling thus-and-so. Once one does realize this, one may be conscious of feeling bored or jealous or anxious. But many involve no distinctive sensations, or indeed none at all. One may become conscious of one's boredom if one becomes aware that one's attention is wandering. One may then remain conscious of being bored if the feeling of boredom occupies one. One may become conscious of one's embarrassment when one apprehends that others have noted one's gaffe and the thought disturbs one accordingly, and one realizes and remains aware of this fact. One may become conscious that one is acting out of jealousy if one bethinks oneself, reflects on one's reasons, and realizes that they fall into such-and-such a pattern.

Reflective consciousness

We introduced the notion of reflective consciousness to allow for cases of being conscious of a range of things that are neither objects of current perception or sensation, nor emotions, agitations or moods that are currently felt. The rather heterogeneous collection of items involve reflection on, and realization of, facts, which may be about oneself or others or neither, and may concern the past as well as the present. The knowledge that concerns us here is knowledge that occupies one's thoughts, weighs with one in one's deliberations, colours one's reactions and affects one's actions. Conscious of your recent bereavement, I tailor my remarks about so-and-so to avoid inflicting pain; conscious of my ignorance, I choose my words with extra care and display diffidence; conscious of the lateness of the hour, I glance anxiously at my watch and wonder whether I can still catch the last bus; and so on. In general, consciousness of facts such as these, as well as such cases as being conscious of an honour done one, of the significance of an occasion, or of the gravity of a situation, is a matter of bearing in mind the knowledge one possesses and of its affecting one in various ways.

Agential consciousness of one's own action is, like perceptual consciousness, attention-involving. But while the characteristic feature of becoming and then being perceptually conscious of something is that one's attention is caught and held (and not intentionally bestowed), 'consciously and deliberately' doing something involves the intentional focusing of one's attention upon one's action or activity.

The conceptual complexity and heterogeneity of transitive consciousness, as well as its polymorphous character, suggest that there is no a priori reason for supposing that transitive consciousness can be correlated with any single neurological array of events or processes, and some reason for thinking that it is improbable that there be any such uniform correlation.

10

Conscious Experience, Mental States and Qualia

10.1 Extending the Concept of Consciousness

Puzzlement about consciousness is not especially concerned with transitive consciousness

The investigation thus far has, we hope, shed some light on difficult conceptual terrain. The sketches we have given are incomplete, but they suffice to demonstrate the conceptual diversity of the forms of transitive consciousness. However, many neuroscientists (and philosophers) will rightly object that *this sense* of 'consciousness' was never what captured their attention. The distinction between transitive and intransitive consciousness is evident enough, and the differentiation of the forms of transitive consciousness may be of some interest. But those who characterize 'the problem of consciousness' as the leading problem of neuroscience are not puzzled about the different forms of transitive consciousness.

The puzzlement is generated by the very idea of experience or 'the realm of consciousness'

Puzzlement is generated by the thought that a merely *physical* description of the world would omit *experience*. To be sure, the behaviour of animate bodies would be included in it. Experiences, however, are not behaviour. They are something that underlies behaviour, something essentially subjective. The behaviour that exhibits sorrow, hope, joy, fear, affection, etc. is merely the outer husk of the *inner* psychological reality with which each subject is intimately acquainted. It is this 'realm of consciousness' which is mysterious – and it encompasses much more than the forms of transitive consciousness delineated in the previous chapter.

The current extension of consciousness to 'experience' is crypto-Cartesian

This extension of the concept of consciousness to encompass the whole range of what its proponents call 'experience' runs parallel to the Cartesian identification of 'thoughts' with consciousness, for Descartes held that sensation, perceptual experience, imagination, cogitation, affection and volition constitute the domain of consciousness.[1]

---

[1] See Descartes, *Principles of Philosophy*, I–9: 'By the noun *thought* I understand everything which takes place in us so that we are conscious of it (*nobis consciis*), in so far as it is an object of awareness' (see also Reply to the Second Objections (AT VII, 161) and letter to Mersenne, 27th April 1637 (AT I, 366)). For discussion, see A. J. P. Kenny, 'Cartesian privacy', in *The Anatomy of the Soul* (Blackwell, Oxford, 1973), pp. 113–28.

This parallel is yet another facet of the crypto-Cartesianism that characterizes contemporary neuroscience and cognitive science, as well as some philosophy of mind. We shall investigate what motivates this extension of the ordinary concept of consciousness, and how the notion of 'experience' is (mis)construed.

The puzzlement over how physical (neural) events can produce consciousness is essentially Cartesian

Why should the fact that human beings (and other creatures too) enjoy experiences of a wide variety be thought to constitute a mystery? Why should it be the central problem of brain neuroscience? It is striking (and perhaps it should be disturbing) that the most fundamental reason is philosophical, indeed Cartesian. Seen *from one particular perspective*, it can appear deeply puzzling how causal transactions in the material world can give rise to anything as *categorially distinct from matter* as experience. How can the impact of radiation upon the cones and rods of the retinal generate the *experience* of (consciously) seeing something? How can events in the cortex 'give rise' to *conscious mental states*? The particular perspective in question is, of course, the Cartesian one, according to which the world consists of two categorially distinct domains, the material (essentially characterized in terms of extension) and the mental (essentially characterized in terms of consciousness). But that perspective, it should now be evident, is neither necessary (it was no part of the Aristotelian conception (see §1.1)) nor unproblematic (see §1.2 and the Preliminaries to Part II).

These Cartesian problems drag other apparent puzzles in their wake. Why should the impact of radiation of a certain kind produce just the experience it produces? Why should light of such-and-such a wavelength result in our having the experience of seeing red, rather than seeing blue or green, or indeed a qualitatively altogether different experience, such as hearing a sound? If conscious experience is the upshot of such neural excitation, what is it for? Why could there not be creatures whose nervous system responds as ours does, and who behave as we do, but without conscious experience (thus understood)? It is here, in questions such as these, that the puzzles and mysteries lie – or so it is thought. We shall come back to them in chapter 11.

Neuroscientists and philosophers extend the domain of consciousness

So, what interests neuroscientists in their reflections on the nature of consciousness are *conscious mental states* or *conscious experience*. Benjamin Libet, writing in the *Encyclopaedia of Neuroscience*, characterizes consciousness as 'subjective awareness and experience, whether it be sensory experiences of our environment, external and internal, or subjective experience of our feelings and thoughts, or simply awareness of our own existing self and presence in the world. Our own subjective inner life, including sensory experiences, feelings, thoughts, volitional choices, and decisions, is what really matters to us as human beings.'[2] Similarly, B. J. Baars observes that 'Coming back to consciousness in the morning, we humans report a rich and varied array of experiences: colors and sounds, feelings and smells, images and dreams, the rich pageant of everyday reality. . . . Our brains begin a whole new mode of functioning. In this broad sense, the centrality of consciousness

---

[2] B. Libet, 'Consciousness: conscious, subjective experience', in *Encyclopaedia of Neuroscience*, vol. i, (ed.) George Adelman (Birkhäuser, Boston, 1987), pp. 271f.

is pretty much beyond doubt.'[3] Crick, reflecting on how to approach consciousness 'in a scientific manner', resolved to concentrate on 'visual awareness', by which he evidently meant the visual experience of seeing something.[4] Edelman similarly characterizes 'primary consciousness' as 'the state of being mentally aware of things in the world'.[5] In short, the concern is with *forms of sentience in general*, especially with perceptual (and in particular visual) experience – not specifically with intransitive consciousness or with the various forms of transitive consciousness.

Philosophers similarly extend the concept of consciousness to encompass all perceptual experience and more. So, for example, Searle identifies consciousness with 'our ordinary states of sentience and awareness when we are awake, as well as our states of dreaming when we are asleep', incorporating all 'inner, qualitative, subjective states such as our pains and joys, memories and perceptions, thoughts and feelings, moods, regrets, and hungers'.[6] And Chalmers contends that 'What is central to consciousness, at least in the most interesting sense, is *experience*'. This ranges 'from vivid color sensations to experiences of the faintest background aromas; from hard-edged pains to the elusive experience of thoughts on the tip of one's tongue; from mundane sounds and smells to the encompassing grandeur of musical experience; from the triviality of a nagging itch to the weight of a deep existential angst'.[7]

The idea that whenever we perceive something we are conscious of it is, we have argued, unwarranted. Transitive consciousness is polymorphous, and encompasses both less (in certain respects) and more (in other respects) than the range of perceptual experience. Similarly, it is mistaken to suppose that whenever one is in a certain mental state, one must also be transitively conscious of so being. One may be jealous without realizing it, and be irritable without being conscious of being so. But neuroscientists, cognitive scientists and philosophers are inclined to equate consciousness with sentience in general, or indeed to extend it dramatically to almost the whole range of the mental. Our first task is to investigate this extension. Subsequently, we shall probe one of its roots: namely, the conception of qualia that is currently embraced by many neuroscientists and philosophers.

10.2 Conscious Experience and Conscious Mental States

The ambiguity of 'conscious experiences' and 'conscious states'

The extension of the concept of consciousness involves the use of the phrases 'conscious experiences' and 'conscious states'. Taken one way, the phrases signify experiences and states *of which one is conscious*. Understood thus, they are (or should be) concerned with a subcategory of transitive consciousness. For there is no doubt that one *can* be

---

[3] B. J. Baars, *In the Theater of Consciousness* (Oxford University Press, New York, 1997), p. 14 (see also p. 3).

[4] F. Crick, *The Astonishing Hypothesis* (Tonchstone, London, 1995), p. 21.

[5] G. Edelman, *Bright Air, Brilliant Fire – On the Matter of the Mind* (Penguin, Harmondsworth, 1994), p. 112.

[6] J. R. Searle, *The Mystery of Consciousness* (Granta Books, London, 1997), pp. xii–xiii.

[7] D. J. Chalmers, *The Conscious Mind* (Oxford University Press, Oxford, 1996), pp. 3f.

conscious of various experiences one is undergoing or of various states one is in, if one's attention is caught and held by them (e.g. pain), or if one realizes that things are thus with one (e.g. that one is jealous) and the fact that things are thus occupies one's mind and knowingly affects one's thoughts, reactions and actions. However, this is not how the matter is generally understood. One might equally understand the terms 'conscious experience' and 'conscious states' respectively to signify experiences had, enjoyed or undergone, and mental states one is in, *while conscious.*

A conscious experience is not an experience that is conscious

Irrespective of whether we take the expression 'conscious experience' one way or the other, we must avoid the error of supposing that a conscious experience is an experience which has the property of being conscious.[8] It is the person who has the experience who is conscious, and who may be conscious of a certain experience – for example, of his rising anger or of feelings of jealousy. If I realize that I am losing my temper, and so become conscious of my rising anger, it is no more my anger that has become conscious than, if I become conscious of the ticking of a clock, it is the clock or its ticking that has become conscious. That of which one becomes conscious is an object, not a subject, of consciousness. And an experience had while conscious does not have the property of being conscious, and, indeed, need not be one of which one is transitively conscious, and is not if it neither catches and holds one's attention nor occupies one's thoughts or knowingly weighs with one in one's deliberations. Of course, that does not imply that it is an 'unconscious experience'; nor does it imply that one cannot *say* that one is experiencing such-and-such. One does not have to be occupied with the fact that one is in a cheerful or anxious state of mind in order to be able to say that one is feeling cheerful or anxious; nor does one have to be reflecting on the fact that one is watching, looking at, observing something or other, in order to be able to say that one is doing so.

Dreams apart, all experiences are had while conscious; problems over the extent of 'experience'

If we put aside the contentious issue of whether dreaming is to be called 'an experience', the phrase 'conscious experience', understood as an experience had while conscious, is normally pleonastic. For if dreaming is misconceived as an experience, then *all* experiences are normally enjoyed or undergone *while conscious.* It is, however, a moot point what exactly is encompassed by the ill-defined term 'experience'.[9]

---

[8] As is argued, for example, by Rosenthal: 'we explain *the property of a mental state's being conscious* in terms of our being conscious of that state' (D. M. Rosenthal, 'Thinking that one thinks', in M. Davies and G. W. Humphreys (eds), *Consciousness* (Blackwell, Oxford, 1993), pp. 198f., our italics). But a conscious mental state is no more a mental state that *has the property of being conscious* than a passionate belief is a belief that has the property of being passionate. Evidently what Rosenthal meant was that we explain the *phrase* 'conscious mental state' in terms of our being conscious of the relevant state.

[9] It is noteworthy that in ordinary discourse 'an experience' normally signifies something noteworthy one did or underwent, as when one had a wonderful experience yesterday – one was given a surprise party by all one's friends, or as when one had a most unpleasant experience – one had to tell a friend that his wife had died. Rather differently, we also say of a person that he has had wide or extensive experience, of life in general, or of politics or of any other department of practice or study. These uses or aspects of usage are irrelevant to the current debate, and we shall disregard them.

Perceiving, in its various modalities and multiple forms, can indeed be characterized as 'experience'; so too may sensations and overall bodily feelings, occurrently felt moods and emotions, and doubtless much else that a person may have, enjoy or undergo, including activities and adventures. But it is obvious that 'experience' does not encompass the whole domain of the psychological. Is thinking an experience? If I *think* that it is about 2.30 p.m., is that an experience? How long did it last? As long as it took to say 'I think it is 2.30'? If I think (opine) that freedom is more important than justice (or vice versa), is that an experience? And if two people think the same thing, does it follow that they have had the same experience? If I *believe* that the Battle of Agincourt was fought in 1416, is that an experience? And if you correct me, and I come to believe that it was fought in 1415, is the change in my belief an experience? And is your *remembering* the date an experience? If I *intend* to have lunch at 12.30, is my so intending an experience? Is my *knowing* that lunch is at 12.30 an experience? And if I *decide* to skip lunch, have I had an experience? If I say something, and *mean* what I say, is my meaning what I say an experience I underwent? If I say 'Napoleon was a fool', and mean Napoleon III, is *my meaning him* an experience I had? We must be careful not to stretch the term 'experience' beyond its already generous and exceedingly vague boundaries. It is evident that there is a wide range of psychological predicates which cannot be classified as 'predicates of experience', and so a wide range of psychological attributes which are not experiences.

Consciousness and perceptual experience

One might plausibly extend the term 'consciousness' to the range of *perceptual experience* by arguing, as some philosophers have done, that the various modes of perception are forms of consciousness of objects. So seeing is visual awareness or consciousness of visibilia, hearing is auditory awareness or consciousness of audibilia, and so forth. It is, of course, true that transitive perceptual consciousness takes the various forms of the perceptual modalities. However, as we have argued (§9.4), not every object we see or hear is an object of which we are conscious, for not everything we see or hear catches and holds our attention. Some of the things we see or hear are things to which we *intentionally* give our attention, and, other things being equal, of these we cannot be said to be either conscious or not conscious. Sometimes we see or hear things – for example, a shadow in the bushes or a backfiring car – and take them to be something else – for example, a cat in the bushes or a rifle shot – and accordingly cannot be said to be conscious of what we see or hear, since we do not know that there is – a shadow in the bushes or a backfiring car in the vicinity – for we mistakenly take ourselves to have seen a cat or heard a rifle shot. *A fortiori*, we cannot be said to be conscious *that* a cat moved in the bushes (or *of* the movement of a cat in the bushes) or conscious *that* there was a rifle shot (or *of* a rifle shot). So this extension of the concept of consciousness to the whole range of perceptual experience, though perfectly understandable, masks distinctions which are nicely discriminated by means of our ordinary concept of transitive perceptual consciousness. For some purposes, this may not matter, and in some contexts, it is unobjectionable. For other purposes and in other contexts it does matter. In particular, if we wish to have a firm grasp of the concept of consciousness which we employ in our actual discourse, it is ill-advised to extend it thus. For by so doing, we screen out what is distinctive about the notion (and hence too the phenomena) of transitive consciousness.

Consciousness and mental states　　Much the same applies to the expression 'conscious mental state'. Like many other categorial terms in the domain of the psychological, such as 'mental process', 'mental activity', 'mental event', the term 'mental state' is vague. We must first distinguish between *dispositional* and *occurrent* mental states. When we speak of someone's being in a prolonged state of depression or neurotic anxiety, which may persist for weeks or months, we are speaking of the person's *disposition* to feel depressed or anxious during his waking hours. Of course, a person may become and then be conscious of the fact that he is in a prolonged state of depression, as he may become and then be conscious of any other disposition of temper or character trait he has, if he realizes that he is in such a dispositional state and this fact recurrently occupies his thought for a time or weighs with him in his deliberations. By contrast, when we speak of finding someone in a state of acute anxiety, when we say that the good news made us feel cheerful for the rest of the day, or that we felt angry when insulted and seethed with anger until an apology was given, we are speaking of *occurrent* mental states. These obtain during our waking life, and can be called '*conscious* mental states'. This does not mean that one is necessarily (transitively) conscious *of* them – one may feel jealous for a while on seeing Daisy flirting, without realizing that one is so, as one may be bored or be in an irritable mood for a while without being conscious of the fact. What it does mean is that these are mental states that one is in *while conscious*, and so too, they are states *of which* one may *become* conscious, if one realizes that one is in such a state, and if the fact that one is occupies one's thoughts, and so forth.

Clarifying the concept of a mental state　　Mental states, in this sense, are typically states one is *in*, which last for a while. At any given time during which they obtain, one can, so to say, 'spot check' whether they still obtain, and one can determine, sometimes precisely, sometimes roughly, when they commenced and when they terminated. They can be interrupted by distraction or shift of attention and later resumed. They have degrees of intensity, and they may wax and wane. They do not persist through periods of sleep or loss of consciousness. So I may be in a state of intense concentration, which began when I started to write and ended when I finished. It may have been interrupted by a telephone call and later resumed, perhaps with lesser intensity. I may be in an anxious or cheerful state of mind all day, feeling worried or buoyant. But I do not continue to *feel* either anxious or cheerful when I am asleep, and sleeping is not an *interruption* of such a conscious mental state. Although we do not speak of 'being *in a state* of pain', it is reasonable to conceive of being in pain as a mental state. Unlike a twinge or stab of pain, being in pain has genuine duration,[10] degrees

---

[10] 'Genuine duration' is a term of art introduced by Wittgenstein to distinguish the kind of duration which occurrent mental states have, as opposed to the duration of dispositions and abilities or potentialities (see *Zettel*, (ed.) G. E. M. Anscombe and G. H. von Wright, tr. G. E. M. Anscombe (Blackwell, Oxford, 1967), §§46–7, 82, 281, and *Remarks on the Philosophy of Psychology* vol. 2, (ed.) G. H. von Wright and H. Nyman, tr. C. G. Luckhardt and M. A. E. Aue (Blackwell, Oxford, 1980), §45).

of intensity which wax and wane, and, if not too severe, one's attention can be distracted from one's pain. One can spot check whether it continues to obtain at any given time. Mercifully, one does not continue to feel pain when asleep or unconscious; and we *do* speak of being *in* pain, as we speak of being *in* a state of anxiety or *in* a cheerful state of mind. One can say 'I felt depressed when I went to bed, and I felt depressed when I awoke', but not 'And I felt depressed the entire time I was asleep too'.

Beyond these vague boundaries, the concept of a (conscious) mental state gradually loses its grip; it is unclear whether to characterize watching, looking, observing, scrutinizing as mental states, for unlike mental states they bear a kinship to activities. Yet, for all that, they are not activities either. It is quite clear that spotting, glimpsing, detecting, discerning are not mental states, any more than are noticing or realizing – they lack the necessary duration. For states must obtain *for a while*, and one cannot ask *how long* someone was spotting, detecting or noticing something, nor can one *interrupt* someone's realizing or glimpsing something. Some psychological expressions have a dual use, sometimes to signify a mental state and sometimes not. So, for example, we may be in a state of excited expectation, as we wait impatiently for an eagerly anticipated event. But to expect the rate of inflation to decline next year is not to be in a mental state of any kind, either occurrent or dispositional; it is merely to have a belief about the future. And it is clear that knowing, thinking that something is so, opining, believing, remembering, intending to do something, are not mental states. They have duration, but not 'genuine duration'. There is no such thing as being in a state of knowing or believing that something is so. One cannot be interrupted in knowing or in believing something, and one does not cease to know or believe when one falls asleep, as one ceases to feel cheerful, anxious or depressed as one sleeps.

The extended concept of consciousness is broader than that of conscious mental states

So, if one does extend the notion of consciousness to encompass all occurrent mental states, which one enjoys or suffers *while* one is conscious, but of which one need not *be* transitively conscious, one has not thereby extended it to the whole range of the psychological, for what are still excluded are momentary *occurrences* which are not *states* (e.g. a stab of pain, the flashing of a thought across one's mind, noticing or realizing something, spotting or glimpsing something), as well as knowing, believing, supposing, remembering (i.e. not having forgotten), which have a closer kinship with powers and abilities than with mental states. Equally excluded are intending, deciding and meaning something. And so too are the host of dispositions and tendencies of mind, affection and will that characterize human beings. For these too are not mental states characterized by 'genuine duration'. Moreover, as in the case of 'conscious experience', one will have screened out what is distinctive about transitive consciousness in its manifold forms.

These extensions of the concept of consciousness do not characterize everything that might be conceived to be 'mental' or 'psychological', and it remains unclear why the concept of consciousness thus conceived should appear to be so deeply problematic. So we must probe deeper, as we shall indeed do in §10.3.1. But first we must ward off a confusion regarding 'unconscious activities of the brain'.

10.2.1 Confusions regarding unconscious belief and unconscious activities of the brain

A bogus distinction between conscious and unconscious mental states

It might be claimed that the distinction we have drawn between occurrent and dispositional mental states, and the distinction between mental states such as being elated, excited, cheerful, chronically depressed or anxious, on the one hand, and items which are neither occurrent nor dispositional mental states, such as knowing, believing, opining, intending, on the other, is a confusion. What is needed, it might be said, is the distinction between *conscious* mental states and mental states that are *unconscious*. So, for example, Searle contends that 'the belief that the Eiffel Tower is in Paris is a genuine mental state, even though it happens to be a mental state that most of the time is not present to consciousness'.[11] A conscious belief state, therefore, is manifest when one's belief is 'present to consciousness'. So almost all one's beliefs are normally unconscious, no matter whether one is awake or asleep. They are only conscious if one is currently thinking or 'occurrently believing', for example, that the Eiffel Tower is in Paris. So one is literally in uncountably many different unconscious mental states at any given time, as many as the uncountably many different beliefs (memories, intentions, items of knowledge) one has.[12] But this is misconceived, not only because believing is not a mental state of any kind, but also because the concept of an unconscious belief is misconstrued.

The ambiguity of 'belief'

We must distinguish between believing and what is believed, both of which are confusingly called 'beliefs' (§6.1). If a person has a passionate or tentative belief that *p*, then he passionately or tentatively *believes* that *p*, but *what he believes* (also called 'a belief'), namely *that p*, is neither passionate nor tentative. On the other hand, if his belief is certain, doubtful, probable or possible, then it is certain, doubtful, probable or possible that *p*, but his believing what he believes need be neither certain or doubtful, nor probable or possible. We must be careful not to confuse the ascription of predicates to a person's believing with the ascription of predicates to what he believes.

Unconscious belief incorrectly construed

Bearing this distinction in mind, what is supposed to be a mental state? Clearly the believing, not what is believed, since the belief *that the Eiffel Tower is in Paris* is obviously no mental state, even if the believing might (wrongly) be thought to be. Now, what is supposed to be 'present to consciousness' when a belief is conscious, and unconscious – that is, 'not present to consciousness' – when it is not? Evidently it is not the believing, for then what one would be conscious of would be *that* one believes whatever one believes,

---

[11] J. R. Searle, *The Rediscovery of the Mind*, (MIT Press, Cambridge, MA, 1992), p. 154.

[12] Uncountably many, not merely because there are practical difficulties in counting a person's beliefs, but because there are no clear principles of countability. When I believe that the roses in your garden are red, is that one belief or many? For do I not also believe that the roses in your garden are not green, not blue, not yellow or orange, etc.? And when I believe that the carpet is 12 feet long, do I not also believe that it is not 10 or 11 and not 13, or 14, etc. *ad infinitum*, feet long?

not *what* one believes – for example, *that the Eiffel Tower is in Paris*. But, according to Searle, the belief that *p* is conscious when the thought that *p* crosses one's mind, or when one bears it in mind that *p*. Although there is here an important distinction, it is not between a conscious and an unconscious belief, but the distinction between bearing in mind or thinking about something one believes to be thus–and–so and not bearing it in mind or thinking about it. I believe that Hannibal should have besieged Rome after Cannae, that no one poet wrote both the *Iliad* and the *Odyssey*, and myriad other things too. I rarely think about most of what I believe, but that does not make it *unconscious*, any more than my knowledge that the Battle of Bannockburn was fought in 1314, Agincourt in 1415, and my knowledge of a myriad other things too, is unconscious knowledge.

Unconscious belief correctly construed

An unconscious belief, correctly construed, is something I believe, believing which colours my emotional reactions and informs my actions, but which I am *unwilling to acknowledge*, either to myself or to others, *as* something which I believe. Nevertheless, that I so believe *explains* my aberrant behaviour (my neuroses) – or so it is conjectured. Only in special circumstances – for example, in the course of psychotherapy – do I come to recognize that I unconsciously believed this or that about myself, my childhood or my parents. And my recognition, under analysis, that I so believe is held to be confirmation of the explanatory hypothesis. It is this that is called 'an unconscious belief'. But there is nothing unconscious about my myriad beliefs (i.e. *what* I believe), about which I am not thinking. Nor is any one of the myriad things I know – for example, that Hastings was fought in 1066 – 'unconscious knowledge' just because I am not thinking about that known fact, any more than my intention to take a holiday in Naples this summer is an unconscious intention just because I do not continuously think about what I so intend.

A confusion about 'occurrently believing'

Furthermore, while I may now believe that *p* and later cease to believe that *p*, it would be misleading to speak of my *occurrently* believing something as opposed to my currently believing something. To believe is not an act or activity that one may be engaged in, and there is no answer to the question 'What are you doing?' which runs 'I am believing that *p*'. Nor is there a well-formed question 'What are you now believing?' (as opposed to 'What do you now believe?'). The fact that I am now thinking about Hannibal's invasion of Italy, and reflecting that he should have besieged Rome after Cannae, does not imply that I am now 'consciously believing' that he should have done so, whereas normally I am in an unconscious state of so believing. To think about something which I believe is not to believe it 'consciously', let alone to 'be believing' it 'consciously'; and not to think about something I believe is not to believe it or 'be believing' it 'unconsciously'.

Misusing the term 'mental state'

Finally, while the concept of a mental state is indeed vague and elastic, there is no reason to stretch it to the point at which it becomes legitimate to talk of being in tens of thousands of (unconscious) mental states at the same time. There is nothing to be gained by adopting this novel form of speech, and our common notion of a mental state is thereby blurred and rendered obscure to no purpose. In the licit use of the expression, one can no more be in, suffer or enjoy indefinitely many mental states at a given time than one can attend to, or be occupied with, tens of thousands of things at a given time.

Activities of the brain are neither unconscious nor conscious
There is another misuse of the term 'unconscious' that is common among psychologists and neuroscientists. They are prone to talk of the activities of the brain as being 'unconscious'. So, for example, it is said that 'much of the brain's work is done unconsciously, by innumerable small bits of specialized brain tissue', and that 'the great bulk of these tissues are unconscious'; that when reading the phrase 'visual focus', we are not conscious that the word 'focus' in this phrase is a noun, but the phrase would be incomprehensible if the brain 'did not label "focus" as a noun *unconsciously*'; and similarly, that when we read or, more generally, engage in highly practised 'automatized' skills, 'we do much more work unconsciously than consciously'.[13] But this is confused.

The tissues of the brain, like the brain itself, are neither conscious nor unconscious, neither awake nor asleep. The 'work' done by the brain is not done consciously and deliberately, but nor is it done unconsciously and without deliberation. For the brain cannot do anything consciously *or* unconsciously, since it is not a conscious creature with the capacity to be conscious or to be conscious *of anything*, let alone with the capacity of doing anything either with or without *deliberation and attention*. Rather, unless we are in a laboratory under a visible scan, *we* cannot perceive activities of our brain, any more than we can perceive the back of our heads or the far side of the moon. And since normally we cannot perceive the activities of our own brain, we cannot become and then be conscious of them; but this does not mean that they are unconscious activities, either of ourselves or of our brains. The fact that we are not conscious of the activities of our brains does not imply that *we* are engaged in them unconsciously; but nor does it imply that the brain is engaged in these activities unconsciously. For only a creature that can do something *consciously* can also be said to do something *unconsciously*.

It is true that when we read the phrase 'visual focus', we do not reflect on the fact that it is a noun – we take it for granted that it is, and read it *as* a noun. This does not mean that our brain unconsciously *labels* 'focus' as a noun, for the brain does not label anything, either as a noun or as anything else. We *know* that 'focus', in this occurrence, is a noun; but knowing is not an activity we engage in. We do not have to parse the phrase in order to understand it. But this does not mean that we parse it 'unconsciously'. More generally, many of our skills can be practised without thought, but this does not mean that the thought that would be necessary for a beginner now goes on 'unconsciously'; it means that it no longer goes on at all. It does not have to go on, precisely because we have now acquired the relevant skill. (Someone who has learnt to touch-type no longer needs to look at the keyboard, but this does not imply that he looks at it unconsciously or that he has to work out where the keys are unconsciously.) A small child may need to spell out each letter as he laboriously reads, an adult can scan a sentence at a time. The adult has an ability the child lacks: namely, to take in a sentence as a whole. He would presumably not have that ability unless certain synaptic connections in the brain were in place and certain

---

[13] Baars, *Theater of Consciousness*, pp. 4, 6, 17.

brain events were taking place when the ability is exercised. But this does not imply that either he or his brain spells out each letter or word unconsciously.

10.3 Qualia

Qualia conceived of as the qualitative character of experience – the philosophers' conception

The temptation to extend the concept of consciousness to encompass the whole domain of 'experience' was greatly strengthened by philosophers' misconceived introduction of the notion of qualia. Unfortunately, neuroscientists picked up this aberrant idea and the misconceptions associated with it. The term 'qualia' was introduced to signify the alleged 'qualitative character of experience'. Every experience, it is claimed, has a distinctive qualitative character. Qualia, Ned Block holds, 'include the ways it feels to see, hear and smell, the way it feels to have a pain; more generally, what it's like to have mental states. Qualia are experiential properties of sensations, feelings, perceptions and . . . thoughts and desires as well.'[14] Similarly, Searle argues that 'Every conscious state has a certain qualitative feel to it, and you can see this if you consider examples. The experience of tasting beer is very different from hearing Beethoven's Ninth Symphony, and both of those have a different qualitative character from smelling a rose or seeing a sunset. These examples illustrate the different qualitative features of conscious experiences.'[15] Like Block, Searle holds that thinking has a special qualitative feel to it: 'There is something it is like to think that two plus two equals four. There is no way to describe it except by saying that it is the character of thinking consciously "two plus two equals four".'[16] The subject matter of an investigation of consciousness, Chalmers suggests, 'is best characterized as "the subjective quality of experience"'. A mental state is conscious, he claims, 'if it has a *qualitative feel* – an associated quality of experience. These qualitative feels are also known as phenomenal qualities, or *qualia* for short. The problem of explaining these phenomenal qualities is just the problem of explaining consciousness.'[17] He too takes the view that thinking is an experience with a qualitative content: 'When I think of a lion, for instance, there seems to be a whiff of leonine quality to my phenomenology: what it is like to think of a lion is subtly different from what it is like to think of the Eiffel tower.'[18]

Neuroscientists follow the philosophers

Neuroscientists have gone along with the notion of qualia. Ian Glynn contends that 'Although qualia are most obviously associated with sensations and perceptions, they are also found in other mental states, such as beliefs, desires, hopes, and fears, during conscious episodes of these states'.[19] Damasio states that 'Qualia are the simple sensory qualities to be

---

[14] Ned Block, 'Qualia', in S. Guttenplan (ed.), *Blackwell Companion to the Philosophy of Mind* (Blackwell, Oxford, 1994), p. 514.
[15] J. R. Searle, 'Consciousness', *Annual Reviews*, 23(2000), p. 560.
[16] Ibid., p. 561.
[17] Chalmers, *Conscious Mind*, p. 4.
[18] Ibid., p. 10.
[19] I. Glynn, *An Anatomy of Thought* (Weidenfeld and Nicolson, London, 1999), p. 392.

found in the blueness of the sky or the tone of a sound produced by a cello, and the fundamental components of the images [of which perception allegedly consists] are thus made up of qualia'.[20] Edelman and Tononi hold that 'each differentiable conscious experience represents a different quale, whether it is primarily a sensation, an image, a thought, or even a mood', and go on to claim that 'the problem of qualia' is 'perhaps the most daunting problem of consciousness'.[21]

Explaining the qualitative character of experience in terms of there being something it is like to have it

The subjective or qualitative feel of a conscious experience is in turn characterized in terms of there being *something it is like* for an organism to have the experience. What it is like *is* the subjective character of the experience. 'An experience or other mental entity is "phenomenally conscious"', the *Routledge Encyclopaedia of Philosophy* tells us, 'just in case there is something it is like for one to have it.'[22] 'Conscious states are qualitative', Searle explains, 'in the sense that for any conscious state . . . there is something that it qualitatively feels like to be in that state.'[23] The idea, and the mesmerizing turn of phrase 'there is something which it is like', derive from a paper by the philosopher Thomas Nagel entitled 'What is it like to be a bat?'. Nagel argued that 'the fact that an organism has conscious experience *at all* means, basically, that there is something it is like to *be* that organism. . . . fundamentally an organism has conscious mental states if and only if there is something it is like to *be* that organism – something it is like *for* the organism'.[24] This – that is, what it is like for the organism – is the subjective character or quality of experience.

Nagel's explanation of consciousness in terms of there being something it is like . . .

If we take for granted that we understand the phrase 'there is something which it is like' thus used, then it seems that Nagel's idea gives us a handle on the concept of a conscious creature and on the concept of a conscious experience:

(1)   *A creature is conscious or has conscious experience if and only if there is something which it is like for the creature to be the creature it is.*

(2)   *An experience is a conscious experience if and only if there is something which it is like for the subject of the experience to have it.*

So, there is something which it is like for a bat to be a bat (although, Nagel claims, we cannot imagine *what* it is like), and there is something which it is like for us to be human beings (and, he claims, we all know what it is like for us to be us).

---

[20] A. Damasio, *The Feeling of What Happens* (Heinemann, London, 1999), p. 9. Note that there is here an unargued assumption that colour and sound are not properties of objects but of sense impressions.

[21] G. M. Edelman and G. Tononi, *Consciousness: How Matter Becomes Imagination* (Allen Lane, The Penguin Press, London, 2000), p. 157.

[22] E. Lomand, 'Consciousness', in *Routledge Encyclopaedia of Philosophy* (Routledge, London, 1998), vol. 2, p. 581.

[23] Searle, *Mystery of Consciousness*, p. xiv.

[24] T. Nagel, 'What is it like to be a bat?', repr. in his *Mortal Questions* (Cambridge University Press, Cambridge, 1979), p. 166.

It is important to note that the phrase 'there is something *which it is like* for a subject to have experience E' does *not* indicate *a comparison*. Nagel does not claim that to have a given conscious experience *resembles* something (e.g. some other experience), but rather that there is something which it is like *for the subject* to have it; that is, 'what it is like' is intended to signify 'how it is for the subject himself'.[25] It is striking, however, that Nagel never tells us, with regard to even one experience, what it is like for anyone to have it. He claims that the qualitative character of the experiences of other species may be beyond our ability to conceive. Indeed, the same may be true of the experiences of other human beings. 'The subjective character of the experience of a person deaf and blind from birth is not accessible to me, for example, nor is mine to him.' But we know what it is like to be us, 'and while we do not possess the vocabulary to describe it adequately, its subjective character is highly specific, and in some respects describable in terms that can be understood only by creatures like us'.[26]

Philosophers and neuroscientists concur   Philosophers and neuroscientists have gone along with this idea. It seems to them to capture the essential nature of conscious beings and conscious experience. Thus Davies and Humphreys contend that, 'while there is nothing that it is like to be a brick, or an ink-jet printer, there is, presumably, something it is like to be a bat, or a dolphin, and there is certainly something it is like to be a human being. A system – whether a creature or artefact – is conscious just in case there is something it is like to be that system.'[27] Edelman and Tononi agree that 'We know what it is like to be us, but we would like to explain why we are conscious at all, why there is "something" it is like to be us – to explain how subjective experiential qualities are generated'.[28] And Glynn holds that with respect to our experiences – for example, of smelling freshly ground coffee, hearing an oboe playing, or seeing the blue of the sky – 'we know what it is like to have these experiences only by having them or by having had them. . . . Just as it feels like something to smell freshly ground coffee, so it can feel like something (at least intermittently) to believe that . . . , or to desire that . . . , or to fear that. . . .'[29]

Qualia, then, are conceived to be the qualitative characteristics of 'mental states' or of 'experiences', the latter pair of categories being construed to include not only perception, sensation and affection, but also desire, thought and belief. For every 'conscious experience' or 'conscious mental state', there is something which it is like for the subject to have it or to be in it. This something is a quale – a 'qualitative feel'. 'The problem of explaining these phenomenal qualities', Chalmers declares, 'is just the problem of explaining consciousness.'[30]

---

[25] Ibid., p. 170n.
[26] Ibid., p. 170.
[27] Davies and Humphreys (eds), *Consciousness*, p. 9.
[28] Edelman and Tononi, *Consciousness*, p. 11.
[29] Glynn, *Anatomy of Thought*, p. 392.
[30] Chalmers, *Conscious Mind*, p. 4.

10.3.1 'How it feels' to have an experience

The primary rationale for extending the ordinary concept of consciousness One reason given for extending the concept of consciousness beyond its legitimate conservative boundaries was that what is distinctive, remarkable, indeed mysterious, about experiences is *that there is something which it is like to have them*. An experience, it is argued, *is* a *conscious* experience just in case there is something which it is like for the subject of the experience to have it. Consciousness, thus conceived, is *defined* in terms of *the qualitative feel of experience*. There is a specific way it feels to see, hear and smell, to have a pain, or indeed 'to have mental states' (Block); every conscious state has a certain *qualitative feel* to it (Searle), and each differentiable conscious experience represents a different quale (Edelman and Tononi). This qualitative feel, unique to every distinguishable experience, is *what it is like for the subject of the experience to have the experience*. Or so it is held.

Our suspicions should be aroused by the odd phrases used to invoke something with which we are all supposed to be utterly familiar. We shall examine 'ways of feeling' first, and there being 'something which it is like' subsequently.

Is there always a way it feels to have a 'conscious experience'? Is there really *a specific way* it feels to see, hear or smell? One might indeed ask a person who has had his sight, hearing or sense of smell restored, 'How does it feel to see (hear, smell) again?' One might expect the person to reply 'It is wonderful', or perhaps 'It feels very strange'. The question concerns the person's attitude towards his exercise of his restored perceptual capacity – so, he finds it wonderful to be able to see again, or strange to hear again after so many years of deafness. In these cases, there is indeed a way it feels to see or hear again: namely, wonderful or strange. But if we were to ask a normal person how it feels to see the table, chair, desk, carpet, etc., he would wonder what we were after. There is nothing distinctive about seeing these mundane objects. Of course, seeing the table differs from seeing the chair, desk, carpet, etc., but the difference does not consist in the fact that seeing the desk *feels different* from seeing the chair. Seeing an ordinary table or chair does not evoke *any* emotional or attitudinal reaction whatsoever in normal circumstances. The experiences differ only in so far as their objects differ.

One may say, clumsily, that there is a way it feels to have a pain. That is just a convoluted way of saying that there is an answer to the (rather silly) question 'How does it feel to have a pain?' – for example, that it is very unpleasant, or, in some cases, dreadful. So, one may say that there is a way it feels to have a migraine: namely, very unpleasant. This is innocuous, but lends no weight to the general claim that for every differentiable experience, there is a specific way it feels to have it. Pains are an exception, since they, by definition, have a negative hedonic tone. Pains are sensations which are intrinsically disagreeable. Perceiving, however, is not a matter of having sensations. And perceiving in its various modalities and with its indefinitely numerous possible objects can often be, but typically is not, the subject of any affective or attitudinal quality (e.g. pleasant, enjoyable, horrible) at all, let alone a different one for each object in each perceptual modality. And for a vast range of things that can be called 'experiences', there isn't 'a way it feels' to have them; that is, there is no answer to the question 'How does it feel to . . .?'

One cannot but agree with Searle that the experience of tasting beer is very different from hearing Beethoven's Ninth, and that both are different from smelling a rose or seeing a sunset, for perceptual experiences are essentially identified or specified by their modality – that is, sight, hearing, taste, smell and tactile perception – and by their objects – that is, by what they are experiences of. But to say that the several experiences have a unique, distinctive *feel* is a different and altogether more questionable claim. It is more questionable in so far as it is obscure what is *meant*. Of course, all four experiences that Searle cites are, for many people, normally enjoyable. And it is perfectly correct that the identity of the pleasure or enjoyment is dependent upon the object of the pleasure. One cannot derive the pleasure of drinking beer from listening to Beethoven's Ninth, or the pleasure of seeing a sunset from smelling a rose. That is a logical, not an empirical, truth; that is, it is not that, as a matter of fact, the qualitative 'feel' distinctive of seeing a sunset differs from the 'feel' distinctive of smelling a rose – after all, both may be very pleasant. Rather, as a matter of logic, the pleasure of seeing a sunset differs from the pleasure of smelling a rose, for the identity of the pleasure depends upon what it is that pleases. It does not follow that every experience has a different *qualitative character* – that is, that there is a specific 'feel' to each and every experience. For, first, most experiences have, in this sense, no qualitative character at all – they are neither agreeable nor disagreeable, neither pleasant nor unpleasant, etc. Walking down the street, we may see dozens of different objects. Seeing a lamp-post is a different experience from seeing a post-box – did it have a different 'feel' to it? No; and it didn't have the same 'feel' to it either, for seeing the two objects evoked no response – no 'qualitative feeling' whatsoever was associated with seeing either of them. Second, different experiences which *do* have a qualitative 'feel' – that is, which can, for example, be characterized hedonically – may have the very same 'feel'. What differentiates them is not the way they feel, inasmuch as the question 'What did it feel like to *V*?' (where '*V*' specifies some appropriate experience) may have exactly the same answer – for the different experiences may be equally enjoyable or disagreeable, interesting or boring.

The qualitative character of experiences correctly construed

Both having a pain (being in pain) and perceiving whatever one perceives can be called 'experiences'. So can being in a certain emotional state. And so, of course, can engaging in an indefinite variety of activities. Experiences, we may say, are possible subjects of attitudinal predicates; that is, they may be agreeable or disagreeable, interesting or boring, wonderful or dreadful. It is such attributes that might be termed 'the qualitative characters of experiences', not the experiences themselves. So one cannot intelligibly say that seeing red or seeing *Guernica*, hearing a sound or hearing *Tosca*, are 'qualia'. Consequently, when Damasio speaks of the blueness of the sky as being a quale, he is shifting the sense of the term 'quale' – since if the colour of an object is a quale, then qualia are not the qualitative characteristics of experiences at all, but the qualities of objects of experience (or, if one holds colours not to be qualities of objects, then constituents of the contents of perceptual experiences). Similarly, when Edelman and Tononi claim that each differentiable conscious experience represents a different quale, whether it is a sensation, an image, a mood or a thought, they are shifting the sense of the term 'quale'. For it patently does not mean 'the qualitative character of an experience' in the sense we have been investigating. What it does, or is supposed to, mean is something we shall examine shortly (§10.3.4).

It should be noted that to say that an experience is a subject of an attitudinal predicate is a potentially misleading *façon de parler*. For to say that an experience (e.g. seeing, watching, glimpsing, hearing, tasting this or that, but also walking, talking, dancing, playing games, mountain climbing, fighting battles, painting pictures) had a given qualitative feel to it (e.g. that it was agreeable, delightful, charming, disagreeable, revolting, disgusting) is just to say that the subject of the experience – that is, the person who saw, heard, tasted, walked, talked, danced, etc. – found it agreeable, delightful, charming, etc. So, the qualitative character of an experience E – that is, how it feels to have that experience – is the subject's affective attitude (what it was like for him) to experiencing E.

To avoid falling into confusion here, we must distinguish four points:

(1)   Many experiences are essentially individuated – that is, picked out – by specifying what they are experiences of.

(2)   Every experience is a *possible* subject of positive and negative attitudinal predicates: for example, predicates of pleasure, interest or attraction. It does not follow, and it is false, that every experience is an *actual* subject of a positive or negative attitudinal predicate.

(3)   Distinct experiences, each of which is the subject of an attitudinal attribute, may not be distinguishable by reference to how it feels for the person to have them. Roses have a different smell from lilac. Smelling roses is a different experience from smelling lilac. One cannot get the pleasure of smelling roses from smelling lilac. But the experiences may well be equally agreeable. So, if asked how it feels to smell roses and how it feels to smell lilac, the answer may well be the same: namely, 'Delightful'. If that answer specifies the way it felt, then it is obviously false that every distinct experience can be uniquely individuated by its distinctive qualitative character, or quale. We must not confuse the qualitative character of the experience with the qualitative character of the object of the experience. It is the latter, not the former, that individuates the experience.

(4)   Even if we stretch the concept of experience to include thinking that something is so or thinking of something, what essentially differentiates thinking one thing rather than another is not how it feels or what it feels like to think whatever one thinks. Thinking that $2 + 2 = 4$ differs from thinking that $25 \times 25 = 625$, and both differ from thinking that the Democrats will win the next election.[31] They differ inasmuch as they are essentially specified or individuated by their objects. One can think *that* something is thus-and-so or think *of* something or other without any accompanying affective attitude whatsoever – so there need be no 'way it feels' to think thus. A leonine whiff may accompany thinking of lions, of Richard Coeur de Lion, or of Lyons Corner House, but, contrary to Chalmers, to specify the associated whiff is not to characterize *how it feels* to think of such items, let alone uniquely to individuate the thinking. That one associates thinking of one of these with a leonine whiff is no answer to the (curious) question 'How does it feel to think of lions (Richard Coeur de Lion, Lyons Corner House)?', and certainly does not distinguish one's thinking of lions as opposed to thinking of Lyons's or Richard I.

---

[31]   Cf. Searle, *Mysteries of Consciousness*, p. 201.

10.3.2 Of there being *something which it is like . . .*

Clarifying the question 'What is it like to V?'

We shall now turn to the thornier issue of *there being something which it is like* to have a given experience, something it is like *for the subject* of the experience. We can ask a person A, 'What is it like (for you) to *V*?', where '*V*' is a verb that specifies an experience. Here 'What is it like?' is a request *not* for a comparison but for a characterization (i.e. we want to know not what Ving *resembles*, but what is its *felt character*). If A answers, 'It is quite agreeable (disagreeable, pleasant, unpleasant, charming, repulsive, delightful, disgusting, fascinating, boring) to V,' then we can say (rather clumsily):

'There is something which it *is* for A to *V*.'

For evidently *V*'ing is quite agreeable; that is, A finds it quite agreeable to *V*. What we *cannot* say is:

(1)　'There is something which it is like to *V*.'

Let alone

(2)　'There is something it is like for A to *V*.'

(1) is apt only for cases of comparison. If to *V* is, in certain respects, like to *W*, then indeed there is something it is like to *V*: namely, to *W*. (But it should be noted that the less cumbersome form would be: '*V*'ing is like *W*'ing; so there is something which *V*'ing is like, namely *W*'ing'.) (2), however, is a miscegenous crossing of the form of a judgement of similarity with the form of a request for an affective attitudinal characterization of an experience.[32] For when A answers the question 'What was it like for you to *V*?' by saying 'It was wonderful (awe-inspiring, exciting, fascinating)', one *cannot* go on to say: 'For A to *V* is like . . .', and then specify the qualitative character or subjective hedonic tone of A's *V*'ing, for that would (a) be ungrammatical gibberish and (b) duly tidied up, would not specify that for A to *V* was *like* something but rather that it *was* something (viz. wonderful, etc.).

Why one cannot circumscribe conscious experience in terms of there being something it is like to have it

So, it is misconceived to suppose that one can circumscribe, let alone define, *conscious experience* in terms of there being something which it is like for a subject to have it. It does not matter whether 'conscious experience' is understood as 'experience had while conscious' or as 'experience of which one is

---

[32] In technical terms, the existential generalization of a judgement of similarity ('To *V* is like to *W*' or '*V*'ing is like *W*'ing') retains the expression 'like' ('There is something it is like to *V*' or 'There is something which *V*'ing is like'). By contrast, the existential generalization of an answer to the question 'What was it like for you to *V*?' does not ('There was something that it *was* for me to *V*'). It is obvious why: the answer to that question is 'For me to *V* was . . .', not 'For me to *V* was like . . .'.

conscious'. The very expression 'There is something it is like for a person to have it' is malconstructed. The question from which it is derived 'What is (or was) it like for you (or for A) to *V*?' is a perfectly licit request for specification of one's affective attitude at the time to the experience undergone, a specification of 'how it is (or was) for one'. If there is an answer, then there is something which it *is* (or *was*) for you (or A) to *V* – namely, . . . (and here comes a specification of the attitudinal attribute). But for a vast range of experiences, one has *no* affective attitude at all. And even for the limited range of being transitively conscious of something or other, it would be quite wrong to suppose that there is always or even usually an answer to the question 'What was it like for you to be conscious of . . . ?'.

A meagre truth

What is trivially true, and indeed the only truth to emerge from all this confusion, is that only conscious, sentient creatures are subjects of experience and can have affective attitudes to their experiences, can find them pleasant or unpleasant, interesting or boring, and so forth. But to find experience E to be F (pleasant, unpleasant, etc.) is not a mark of experiences as such, or of those experiences had while conscious, or of experiences of which one is conscious, let alone of transitive consciousness in general (which encompasses far more than experiences).

One cannot characterize a conscious creature by reference to there being something it is like to be it

It is equally misconceived to suppose that one can characterize what it is to be a conscious creature by means of the formula 'there is something which it is like to be' that creature, something it is like *for* the organism. To be sure, we can ask 'What is it like to be an X?', where the expression 'X' is a role name (e.g. 'soldier', 'sailor', 'tinker', 'tailor'), or 'What is it like to be a *V*'er?', where the expression '*V*'er' is a nominal formed from a verb (e.g. 'winner', 'murderer', 'driver') or similar phrasal nominal (e.g. 'old-aged pensioner'). Such questions are answered by itemizing features of the role, of what one has to do and undergo, and of its pros and cons, or of the standard features of the experiences of a *V*'er. It is a striking and distinctive property of such questions that they require a specification of the qualitative character – in particular, of the pros and cons – of being an X. Indeed, it is precisely because of this that such forms of words have been chosen to explain the peculiar nature of consciousness.

Typically, there is no need to specify the subject class of the general question 'What is it like to be an X (or to be F)?'. For the context will normally make it evident. 'What is it like to be a doctor?' is restricted to adult human beings; 'What is it like to be pregnant?' is confined to women. But sometimes the question concerns a subclass of the class of possible Xs, as in 'What is it like *for a woman* (as opposed to a man) to be a soldier?' or 'What is it like *for a teenager* (as opposed to an older person) to be the winner at Wimbledon?' And sometimes the question is personal, as in 'What was it like *for you* to be a soldier in the Second World War?' This question typically demands a statement of one's impressions, of the difficulties encountered, the nature of the experiences undergone, the satisfactions derived, etc. Where there is an appropriately framed answer, then one can go on to say, 'There is something which it is to be an X (or, a *V*'er), namely (say) very exciting but dangerous'; 'There is something it is for a Y to be an X, namely . . .'; and 'There was something it was for me to be a *V*'er, namely . . .'.

As in the previously examined case of 'What is it like to *V*?', so too here the 'like' drops out in the reply, and hence too in the generalized form 'There is something which it is to be an X'.

Logical constraints on 'What is it like for . . . to be . . . ?'

But such questions are not the same as the question of what it is like for a human being to be a human being (or for a bat to be a bat), or for me to be me. For the latter have the general form 'What is it like for an X to be an X?', not 'What is it like for a Y to be an X?' Is this a difference that makes a difference? Reflecting upon the indisputably licit forms of the question, three features stand out. First, the subject term 'Y' differs from the object term 'X'. Second, where the subject class is specified by the phrase 'for a Y', then a principle of contrast is involved. We ask what it is like *for a Y* to be an X when there is a contrast between Ys being Xs and some other class being Xs. We want to know what it is like for a Y, *as opposed to a Z*, to be an X. So, one can ask what it is like for a woman to be a soldier. We might wish to find out what is distinctive about the career of a woman, as opposed to a man, in the army. Similarly, in the personalized version of the question, when we ask 'What is it like for you to be an X?', we are asking for *your* particular and perhaps idiosyncratic impressions of being an X, as opposed to the impressions of someone else. Third, the question 'What is it like for a Y to be an X?' involves a second principle of contrast: namely, with regard to X. For we want to know what it is like, or what it is like for Y, to be an X as opposed to something else Y might be or have been.

The problematic cases with which we are concerned, the cases which supposedly shed light upon the nature of consciousness, are not like this. They reiterate the subject term in the object position. But the question 'What is it like for a soldier to be a soldier?' is surely awry. It is not akin to 'What is it like for a soldier to be a sailor?' or 'What is it like for a woman to be a doctor?', where there are obvious principles of contrast. One cannot ask 'What is it like for a doctor to be a doctor, *as opposed to* someone else who is not a doctor being a doctor?', for that makes no sense. (Someone who is *not* a doctor cannot also *be* a doctor, although he may *become* one.) The interpolated phrase 'for a doctor' is illicit here, and adds nothing to the question 'What is it like to be a doctor?'. A question of this form, as we have seen, asks for a description of the role, the rights and duties, hardships and satisfactions, the typical episodes and experiences of a person who is an X. Of course, if the addressee is an X, then the question might reasonably be understood as a more personal one, converging on 'What is it like for *you* to be an X?' – that is, a request for personal impressions and attitudes.

Problems with the question 'What is it like for a human being to be a human being?'

The question 'What is it like for a human being to be a human being?' (or, indeed, 'What is it like for a bat to be a bat?') falls foul of the same objection of illegitimate reiteration. The interpolated phrase 'for a human being' cannot play the role which a phrase in that position is meant to play. But there is perhaps another source of unease. Proteus, avatars and gods apart, a human being (unlike a soldier or a sailor who can abandon his vocation) cannot cease to be a human being without ceasing to exist. Nor can anything other than a human being be a human being. So neither principle of contrast is satisfied. One cannot ask 'What is it like for a human being, as opposed to another creature, to be a human being?', for, mythology apart, nothing other than a human being can be a human being. Nor can one ask 'What is it like for a human being to be a human being, as opposed to being something else?', since there is no other creature a human being might be. (Similarly, there is nothing other than a bat which might be a bat, and there is no other creature a bat might be, other than a bat.) So, if any sense can be made of the question 'What is it like for a human being to be a human being?', it collapses into the question 'What is it like to be a human being?'. This question is curious. One might take it to mean: 'What is human life like?' That is a nebulous question indeed. It might be answered variously: for example, 'Nasty, brutish and short', or 'Full of hope and fear'. Similarly, 'What is it like to be a bat?', if it means anything, can be no more than a request to describe the life of a bat in a comparable manner. There seems no difficulty of principle in doing that, but there is no reason to suppose that it sheds any light on the nature of consciousness. But it is true that the question can be asked only of conscious creatures who take pleasure in certain things, fear other things, find interest in things, and so forth.

Similar arguments apply to the claim that there is something which it is like for us to be us or for me to be me, and that we all know what it is like. It makes no sense to ask what it is like for me to be me, for no one else could be me, and I could be no one other than myself. 'I am me', apart from being ungrammatical, says nothing (what could it be intended to say – to affirm an instance of the identity of a thing with itself?).[33] So 'There is something which it is like for me to be me' likewise says nothing. Not only do I not know what it is like for me to be me, there is nothing to know. The claim that there is something it is like for me to be a human being is equally questionable. For the question 'What is it like for you to be a human being?' presupposes that I might be, or have been, something other than a human being, something that might be contrasted with my being a human being – and there is no such thing.

Incoherences that ensue   So, let us take stock:

(i)   The sentences 'There is something which it is like to be a human being', 'There is something which it is like to be a bat', and 'There is something which it is like to be me', as presented by the protagonists in this case, are one and all awry.

(ii)   The question 'What is it like for an X to be an X?' is illicit because of the reiterated term, and, if 'X' is a name of a kind of animal (like 'human being' or 'bat'), doubly at fault. The most that can be made of it is to interpret it as equivalent to 'What is it like to be an X?', and to interpret that question as an inquiry into the characteristic attitudinal features of the life of an X. Such questions can be answered, and one need not be an X or similar to an X in order to answer them. One merely has to be well informed about the lives of Xs.

(iii)   The questions 'What is it like for me to be me?' and 'What is it like for me to be a human being?' are equally illicit.

---

[33] When Shakespeare's Richard III mutters with relief 'Richard is himself again', he does not mean that he had not been identical with himself but that now, mercifully, he is again!

If this is correct, then it is wrong for Nagel to suggest that 'we know what it is like [for us] to be us', that there is something 'precise that it is like [for us] to be us', and that 'while we do not possess the vocabulary to describe it adequately, its subjective character is highly specific'. It is mistaken of Edelman and Tononi to assert that we all 'know what it is like to be us', and confused of them to suppose that 'there is "something" it is like to be us'. And it is a confusion to think, as Searle does, that for any conscious state, 'there is something that it qualitatively feels like to be in that state'.

10.3.3 The qualitative character of experience

Experiences are specified by what they are of, but not by reference to how they feel

The attempt to capture the essential nature of consciousness or of what it is to be a conscious creature by means of the notion of there being something which it is like to experience this or that or to be the creature one is has failed. Similarly, the notion that every conscious experience has a special 'feel' – that is, that there is a unique way it feels for a person to have any experience – has likewise proved misguided. Nevertheless, it may well be thought that less than justice is being done to those who seek to characterize experience in terms of its qualitative character. We have argued that it is licit to ask how it feels to have a certain experience or what it is like to have such-and-such an experience, and that these are actually questions concerning the subject's current attitudinal response to the experience he is undergoing. But, one may reply, this is *not* what was meant at all. So what was meant by the introduction of qualia? And is it coherent?

Qualia and the distinctive character of each experience

It will have been noted that the employment of the term of art 'quale' is unstable. The notion of a quale equivocates between signifying whatever it is like for a person to have experience E and experience E itself. In view of our previous analysis, we must set aside the misbegotten phrases 'there is something which it is like' and 'there is something which it feels'. If we wish to get to the bottom of the concern with qualia, we must concentrate on the idea that every experience has a unique and distinctive character. Seeing red is different from seeing blue, and seeing a colour differs from hearing a sound or tasting a taste. So, too, feeling angry is different from feeling jealous, and both differ from feeling love or affection. We noted that some writers attempt to extend the idea of qualia to thinking thoughts, holding (perfectly correctly) that thinking that $2 + 2 = 4$ differs from thinking that $25 \times 25 = 625$, and conceiving of the difference (quite wrongly) as a matter of a difference in the qualitative character of the 'experience' of thinking. It is such differences that theorists have in mind when they misleadingly insist upon the unique qualitative character of conscious experience.

Taken one way, this is both correct and innocuous. *Of course*, seeing red differs from seeing blue, and feeling love differs from feeling hatred. *Of course*, thinking that $2 + 2 = 4$ differs from thinking that $25 \times 25 = 625$. Taken another way, it is confused. For the difference between seeing red and seeing blue does not lie in the way it feels or in what it is like for a person to see the two colours. Yet these experiences *do* differ, and a normal human being who has such an experience knows perfectly well that the experience of seeing red differs from the experience of seeing blue, and is not likely to confuse the two. And whether or not thinking is correctly conceived to be an experience, someone to whom the thought that 2 + 2 = 4 occurs is hardly likely to confuse it with the thought that 25 × 25 = 625. So must not the difference between the experiences or between thinking the various thoughts reside in some quality of the experiences? And whatever this qualitative characteristic may be, it must be something that is apprehended by the subject of the experience, for it is this subjective apprehension that explains how the subject can differentiate the experiences he has. Or so it seems.

10.3.4 *Thises* and *thuses*

Indexical reference to the distinct-ive character of each experience We noted above that although many philosophers and neuroscientists are taken with the notion of qualia, and accordingly insist that every experience has a unique qual-itative character, none of them actually tells us, with respect to even one experience, what its specific character is. But it is striking that it is natural to try to refer to the specific quality of a given experience by means of an indexical expression, such as 'this' or 'that'. So we find David Chalmers asking 'Why do conscious experiences have their specific character?', and in particular, 'Why is seeing red like *this*, rather than like *that*?'.[34] And it seems evident that the 'like *this*' and the 'like *that*' are intended to be ways of referring to the specific qualities that experiences are alleged to have.

The logical constraints on such indexical reference So, human beings with normal visual capacities can see red (green, blue, etc.) objects in their environment. See-ing a red object, we are told, has a particular 'subjective feel'. What is this 'subjective feel'? Well, seeing red is like *this*, seeing green is like *this*, seeing blue is like *this* – that is, *this* is the way I see red, *this* is how I see red. It is interesting, and striking, that Wittgenstein anticipated this confusion more than fifty years ago. He wrote:

> The *content* of experience. One would like to say 'I see red *thus*', 'I hear the note that you strike *thus*', 'I feel sorrow *thus*', or even '*This* is what one feels when one is sad, *this* when one is glad', etc. One would like to people a world, analogous to the physical one, with these *thuses* and *thises*. But this makes sense only where there is a picture of *what is experienced*, to which one can point as one makes these statements.[35]

His point is simple: it makes no sense to say 'I see red *thus*' unless one can go on to say *how* I see red. We labour under an illusion that when we see a red apple, we can, as it were, *attend to our seeing*, and say to ourselves '*This* is how I see the red colour of the apple' and mean something intelligible, at least to ourselves, in saying this. But nothing meaning-ful is said, either to ourselves or to others, by saying '*this*' or '*thus*' unless there *is* a *this* or a *thus* to which we can point – that is, unless there is a *this* or a *thus* in terms of which we

[34] Chalmers, *Conscious Mind*, p. 5.
[35] Wittgenstein, *Remarks on the Philosophy of Psychology*, vol. 1, §896.

can cash the sentence '*This* is how I see red', or 'I see red *thus*'. It makes perfectly good sense to say, 'I see the colour of the apple *thus* ☞ ■', pointing to a sample of red. Here the sample pointed at is what Wittgenstein, in the above passage, means by 'a picture' – that is, something that can represent, both for oneself *and for others*, how one sees the colour of the apple. But it is an illusion that one can, as it were, point *inwardly* (and for oneself alone) to the experience one is currently enjoying, saying 'I see red *thus*', and thereby say anything meaningful – one might just as well say 'This is this' (see §3.9). It is 'as when travelling in a car and feeling in a hurry I instinctively press against something in front of me as though I could push the car from inside'.[36]

Incoherences that ensue when the logical constraints are disregarded

If one thinks of perceptual experiences as *thises* and *thuses*, it is tempting to go on to ask, as Chalmers does, 'Why do conscious experiences have their specific character?' – in particular, 'Why is seeing red like *this*, rather than like *that*? ... Why ... do we experience the reddish sensation that we do, rather than some entirely different kind of sensation, like the sound of a trumpet?'[37] But now it should be obvious that the question 'Why is seeing red like seeing *this* ☞ ■ [pointing to *a red sample*]?' is misguided. First, seeing red does not *resemble* seeing *this* ☞ ■ colour; it *is* seeing this colour. Second, the only cogent answer to the confused question 'Why is seeing red like seeing *this*?' is that seeing *this* ☞ ■ colour *is* seeing red, since this colour is what we call 'red'.

Equally, the question 'Why, when one looks at red roses, does one not have the experience of seeing blue?' is a muddle. For the only possible answer (assuming normal vision and normal observation conditions) is trivial: namely, 'Because they *are* red, not blue.' What else would a normally sighted person expect to see when he looks at red roses in normal light? The concept of a normally sighted person is defined in part in terms of the ability to discriminate coloured objects. The visual system of normal human beings gives a person the capacity to discriminate between different colours, and normal human beings can distinguish between red and blue objects. We can investigate what features of our brains endow us with this capacity and what neural deficiencies deprive the colour-blind of it, and that is precisely what neuroscientists investigating colour vision do. There is no further question as to why when one looks at a red object in normal light one sees a red object.

Even more misconceived is the question 'Why does one then have a reddish sensation rather than the sensation of the sound of a trumpet?'[38] The eye and the rest of the visual system evolved as a light-sensitive system endowing the animal with powers of *visual* discrimination. There is no such thing as *seeing* sounds with one's eyes. So there can be no puzzle as to why, when one looks at a red rose, one does not *see* the sound of a trumpet. Nor is it puzzling that, when one looks at a red rose, one does not, at the same time, *hear* the sound of a trumpet – given that no one blew a trumpet, and hence that there was no trumpet to hear.

---

[36] L. Wittgenstein, *The Blue and Brown Books* (Blackwell, Oxford, 1958), p. 71.

[37] Chalmers, *Conscious Mind*, p. 5.

[38] Note that Chalmers is here using the term 'sensation' to refer to perceptions rather than to sensations. Seeing red, strictly speaking, involves no sensations whatsoever.

Crick's puzzlement   Neuroscientists become similarly enmired in this morass.
                                Crick, for example, characterizes the problem of qualia
as 'how to explain the redness of red or the painfulness of pain', and observes that 'this is
a very thorny issue', since the redness of the red that I perceive cannot be precisely
communicated to another human being, at least in the normal course of events.[39] But it is
less than obvious what is meant by 'explaining the redness of red'. Are we puzzled why
red *things* are red? One can ask why post-boxes in Britain are red – it is to make them
salient. One can ask why blood is red – the haemoglobin, which contains iron, makes it
red. These are no puzzles, and this, surely, is not what Crick means. But it is altogether
unclear what he *does* mean, or, indeed, whether any intelligible question has been raised.
Crick's puzzlement appears to be rooted in a pair of misconceived ideas. First, he appears
to think that what I perceive cannot be communicated to another person. Secondly, he
seems to think that colours are not properties of coloured things, but affections of the
mind (so the redness I perceive is not a property of the poppies I am looking at, but rather
the effect of those poppies on my sensibility – which cannot be compared with their
effects on another person's sensibility). We shall revert to these misconceptions in the next
section.

What the qualitative character of   So, what remains of the 'qualitative character of experi-
an experience might be   ence'? We must distinguish. With respect to any experi-
                                            ence we can ask what it was. The answer will specify the
character of the experience – for example, whether it was feeling a twinge or a tickle,
seeing a red rose or hearing the sound of music, feeling angry with A or jealous of B,
playing cricket or going to the opera. We can also ask with respect to an experience what
it was like to undergo it, and the answer, if there is one, will specify whether one found
it enjoyable or unpleasant, interesting or boring, frightening or exciting, etc. None of this
is mysterious, surprising or baffling.

However, a false sense of mystery is engendered by the thought that the 'qualitative
character of experiences' is incommunicable or only imperfectly communicable, that it is
indescribable or only describable by reference to other experiences. It is to this ramifying
confusion that we now turn.

10.3.5 Of the communicability and describability of qualia

The indescribability and incom-   Whether the character of our experience is communic-
municability theses   able and, if so, to what degree are matters of dispute. We
                                          noted previously that Nagel holds that we do not possess
a vocabulary adequate to describe the qualitative character of experience, as he conceives
it. It is, he suggests, describable only in some respects, and such a description can be
understood only by creatures like us. Edelman contends that 'qualia constitute the collection
of personal or subjective experiences, feelings, and sensations that accompany awareness.
They are phenomenal states . . . For example, the "redness" of a red object is a quale.'

---

[39] Crick, *Astonishing Hypothesis*, pp. 9f.

Qualia, he holds, 'are experienced directly only by single individuals', and this gives rise to a methodological difficulty. For, 'What is directly experienced as qualia by one individual cannot be fully shared by another individual as an observer.' But, he suggests, the difficulty can be overcome if we '*assume* that, just as in ourselves, qualia exist in other conscious human beings'.[40] Glynn argues that

> When we smell freshly ground coffee, or hear an oboe playing, or see the intense blue of a Mediterranean sky, or have a toothache, we are having experiences that it is impossible to describe except by pointing to similar experiences on other occasions. We can know what it is like to have these experiences only by having them or having had them. There are all sorts of other things we may be told about these experiences – what in the outside world is causing us to have them; what can be deduced about us or the outside world from the fact that we are having them; what effect they are having or likely to have on our behaviour; what is going on in our brains while we are having them – but none of these things tells us about the subjective qualities of the experiences; what it is like for us to have them.[41]

Human beings with normal chromatic vision see red (green, blue, etc.) things in their environment. They can, in decent lighting, distinguish those things that are red from those that are differently coloured. If they suffer from colour-blindness in its various forms, then their discriminatory powers are deficient. But there are standard tests for colour-blindness. So we can establish, with a relatively high degree of precision, whether another person sees red, green or blue objects as normally sighted people do. Whence then the illusion that so-called qualia are incommunicable or only defectively communicable?

One source of the incommunicability thesis

One source of the illusion is that I cannot show you my seeing. But what is that supposed to mean? You can certainly see *that* I see something. – Yes, it might be replied, but you cannot see *what* I see. But that is wrong, at any rate if we both have reasonably good eyesight and are observing the same thing under optimal conditions, for then I can see exactly what you see. – All right, one might respond, but at any rate, you cannot do my seeing *for me*! But what does that mean? I can certainly see something, look at something, instead of you, and report back to you what I see. – Yes, but for all that, you cannot *do* my seeing. But that is confused. For you cannot *do* your seeing either. *Seeing* is not something *done*. You may see something, and I may or may not see what you see. All that is true is (a) that it does not follow from the fact that you see such-and-such that I too see such-and-such. Hence, (b) that the event of your seeing such-and-such is a distinct event from the event of my seeing such-and-such, even if I do see what you see. And, (c) the fact that you see it in a certain way does not imply that I do, for what you see clearly, I may see indistinctly, and what strikes you as threatening may seem to me to be altogether innocuous. But there is nothing mysterious or incommunicable about that.

---

[40] Edelman, *Bright Air, Brilliant Fire*, pp. 114f.
[41] Glynn, *Anatomy of Thought*, p. 392.

A second source of the incom-
municability thesis

A second source of the confusion is one we have already tried to clarify (§§3.6–3.9). It is the thought that experiences are privately owned and privately accessible. If that were true, then it would indeed be the case that one person could not know, or could not know for certain, whether and what experience another person had. For experiences, or qualia, thus conceived would indeed be strange, ethereal (mental) *objects*, which no one else can perceive, like beetles in a box which only I am allowed to look into – only here the box is the mind, and the beetles are qualia. But, as we have argued, it is a mistake to suppose that experiences are, in this sense, private. I do not own or *possess* my experiences. I *have* experiences – that is, I see and hear things, I am cheerful or depressed, etc. – and another person may have the same experiences. I do not *perceive* my experiences, although I may sometimes be conscious *of* having a particular experience, if I realize its character and the thought of having it occupies my mind. And experiences are not kinds of *objects*. If I see a red apple, the only object involved is a red apple, not my experience of seeing a red apple; and what I see is the apple, not my seeing of it. It is true that while I may enjoy looking at a Rembrandt painting, you, looking at the same painting, may find it dull and boring. In that sense, the qualitative character of my experience may differ from yours, even though it is of the same object, and perceived with equal clarity. But, of course, it is also possible that you will find it equally interesting and enjoyable.

The idea that the character of experi-
ence is indescribable is a third source
of the incommunicabililty thesis

A third source of confusion is the idea that the character of experience is indescribable. The roots of this confusion are multiple. First, we must distinguish between describing the relevant experience and describing the object of the experience. Secondly, we must distinguish describing the object of the experience and describing the properties or qualities of the object of the experience. Hence too, thirdly, we must distinguish between describing the experience and describing the qualities of the experience.

Describing a perceptual experience

There is no difficulty whatsoever in describing an experience of smelling freshly ground coffee, of hearing an oboe being played, or of seeing the Mediterranean summer sky. The first is rather pleasant, at least to most coffee drinkers; the second may be absolutely wonderful, if the player is first-rate and the piece played sublime, but may be excruciating if the player is a beginner or the piece mediocre; and the last may be intoxicating and enthralling (if one is a van Gogh at Arles, as it were) or something altogether unremarkable (if one is a standard average dweller on the coast of the Mediterranean). The properties of experiences such as these, or at least those properties that interest us, are primarily their positive and negative hedonic features. This is unproblematic, and evidently it is not this that is meant by those who claim that qualia are indescribable.

Describing the objects of such
experiences

Similarly, there need be no difficulty of principle in describing the objects of experiences, if these are construed as the coffee one smells, the oboe playing one hears, or the Mediterranean sky one sees. The coffee is, as Glynn says, freshly ground, has an aroma of freshly roasted coffee, is dark brown or mocca-coloured, is finely or coarsely ground. The oboe playing may be skilful, the trills handled with panache, the modulation subtle and refined, etc. And the Mediterranean sky is a deep blue, the light clear and brilliant. This too is unproblematic, and, equally, it is not this that is meant.

The idea that the qualities of objects of experience are indescribable

So what is meant? One thing that might be meant is that one cannot describe the *qualities* of the objects of experience, the particular aroma of coffee, the mellifluous sounds of the oboe, and the blue colour of the Mediterranean sky. Here there are difficulties; but the difficulties stem from conceptual confusion.

We are indeed tempted to say that the aroma of coffee, the sound of an oboe, or the blueness of the Mediterranean sky are indescribable. We know what they are like, we think, but our vocabulary is inadequate to describe them. This is surely confused; for if our vocabulary is inadequate, it is open to us to introduce a more refined vocabulary. And we must have some conception of a description which a more subtle language would provide – that is, we must think that the aroma *is* in principle describable, only not in our inadequate language. But it is *not* evident that this is what a defender of this 'ineffability' thesis has in mind. So let us broach the matter slowly.

Describing the aroma of coffee

First, is it even true that we cannot describe the aroma of coffee? After all, we can say that the aroma of the coffee is fresh, rich and delicious, that it is the aroma of freshly roasted coffee. Is this not a description of the aroma of coffee? Of course, it is. And, moreover, it is *not* a description given by 'pointing to similar experiences' of smelling the aroma of coffee on other occasions. The defender of the ineffability thesis will doubtless respond that this is not what he meant, that such a form of words does not describe the essential thing – which cannot be put into words.

The appearance of the indescribability of qualities is due to non-conformity with the paradigm for the description of substances

His inclination to say *this* has nothing to do with the poverty of our language, but with a *paradigm of description*, which such descriptions of aroma do not satisfy. The claim that the aroma of coffee is indescribable amounts to the claim that one *form* of description is inapplicable to this kind of case, and to the *rejection* of the form of description which *does* apply to this kind of case. So someone who insists that the aroma of coffee is indescribable refuses to count what *is* describable about the aroma of coffee – that is, what it *does* make sense to call 'a description of the aroma' – *as* a description, or as a description of the kind he craves. But the form of description which he craves is inapplicable in principle to the characterization of qualities of objects, such as their smells, colours or tastes. This point is not easy to see, and requires careful explanation.

What is the paradigm of description, presupposed by the ineffability claim, which leads one to reject as inadequate the descriptions of the aroma which *can* be given? It is the description of a material object by specification of its properties or qualities. We describe a table as being circular, made of mahogany, three feet in diameter, etc., just as we describe a cup of coffee as being black, hot and bitter. To describe a material object is to give its properties or qualities. But when asked to describe the *properties* or *qualities*, rather than *the object* that has these properties or is qualified by these qualities, this paradigm of description does not apply.

The moot question is: What do we call 'the description of a property or quality'? We might compare the description of the cup of coffee, as black, hot and bitter, with the description of the aroma of the coffee of which it was made, as fresh, rich and well roasted, as we might compare the description of a rose, as well shaped, sweet scented and red, with the description of its red colour, as dark and matt. This is a perfectly decent analogy, but only an analogy. For being dark and matt do not stand to being red as being red stands to a rose. For being matt red or being dark red can also be said simply to be two different complex properties or qualities which coloured things may have – and if one thinks thus, one may be inclined to think that saying that the red colour is dark and matt is *not* to describe the red colour. For the red colour in question is not an object or substance with the properties of being matt and dark, which properties may change without the object ceasing to exist – it is simply a dark matt red. Similarly, having a rich, freshly roasted aroma can be said simply to be a complex quality of the coffee – and if one does wish to say this, then one may be inclined to think that saying that the aroma is rich and fresh is *not* to describe the aroma.

The alleged indescribability amounts to no more than an objection to a convention

To be sure, one cannot force an analogy on someone who has set their face against it. But it is evident that the claim that the aroma of coffee, the sound of an oboe, or the colour of the Mediterranean sky are indescribable simply means that there is no such thing as describing properties or qualities *in the manner of a favoured paradigm*: namely, the paradigm of describing a material object by specifying its properties. Even if we are willing to heed such qualms, it is evident that the 'indescribability' is neither a mystery nor a token of the limitations of language, but a matter of a *convention*, regarding what we should *call* 'a description' of a quality. If someone wants to insist that one cannot describe qualities, then we may grant that there is no such thing as describing a quality after the manner of describing an object by specifying its qualities. But we must realize that such a person has not uncovered a mysterious limitation on our descriptive powers. They are merely objecting to a convention.

The alleged indescribability of the subjective qualities of an experience

All this, it may be said, is beside the point. What is said to be indescribable or only describable by pointing to (or, more accurately, pointing out) similar experiences is neither the object of the experience nor the qualities of the object of experience, but *the subjective qualities of the experience itself.* But this is patently wrong. For one can describe the experience of smelling the aroma of coffee or the stench of rotten eggs – the former is pleasant, the latter is horrible. One can describe the experience of looking at the Mediterranean summer skies or the experience of listening to Mozart's Oboe Concerto; the former may be wonderfully peaceful, one wants to drink in, as it were, the deep blue, it calms the soul and washes away the worries that plague one; and the latter may be enthralling, moving one to tears of joy and exhilaration.

But this too, it will be said, is not what is meant. It *feels like something* to smell freshly ground coffee, to hear an oboe playing, and so too, Glynn asserts, it feels like something to believe something or to desire something – and *that* cannot be described. But this, as we have already seen, is confused.

A description is no substitute for an experience; the impression of a description differs from the impression of an experience

Of course, it may be replied, but what is really meant by saying that a description cannot capture what it feels like to experience such-and-such is that a description is no substitute for the experience. After all, do we not say that one must experience love or grief to know what they are really like? One must hear Beethoven's Ninth and see Michelangelo's Sistine Chapel to know what they are really like. It is, of course, true that we say such things. The moot question is: what do we mean? Of course a description is no substitute for what it describes. A description of a humble cup of coffee or of a chair is no substitute for a cup of coffee or a chair – but this does not imply that one cannot describe them. A description *can* tell one what the object of an experience is like – that is, what properties it has that will, for example, enable one to recognize it (that is what descriptions do). But, one may concede, the *impression* made by a description may be altogether *unlike* the impression made by what it describes. A description of the Sistine Chapel, no matter how refined, will not, and should not be expected to, impress one in the way in which seeing the Sistine Chapel will impress one. But that is just a form of the triviality that a description is no substitute for the experience of seeing Michelangelo's great fresco. A description of love or grief, even the most detailed and refined one, by a Tolstoy, Proust or Henry James, will not affect one in the same way as feeling love or grief oneself. But that does not betoken any limitation on our powers of description or on what descriptions can convey.

Further confusion engendered by the misconception of secondary qualities

There are still further confusions lurking here. One may think, as many scientists do, that the aroma of coffee, the sound of an oboe, or the colour of the Mediterranean sky are *in the mind*. Impressed by Galileo, Descartes, Locke and Boyle, one may be brought to think that *brains* have a 'special trick that enable[s] them to add to the cosmic scheme of things: colour, sound, pain, pleasure, and all the other facets of mental experience'.[42] If one thinks thus, then deep problems do indeed ensue. For then, to be sure, there *is* no aroma in the coffee shop, no mellifluous sounds of an oboe in the concert hall, and the myriad objects one perceives are not coloured. Smells, sounds and colours are then conceived to be essentially mental – 'ideas' or 'impressions' in the mind. *Then* their description and communicability become highly problematic. For the meaning of colour words, names of sounds and smells, could not be explained by reference to public samples that are perceptible by all with the appropriate faculties. They would have to be explained by reference to private mental samples – and that is not an option. *But there is no good reason to think thus, or to recapitulate the confusions of seventeenth-century metaphysics* (see §4.2.1).

The confused idea that one cannot know what it is like to have a given experience unless one has had it

An intimately related confusion is the thought that one cannot know what it is like to have an experience of a given kind unless one has had that experience oneself. This confuses the conditions that have to be satisfied in

---

[42] Roger Sperry, quoted by Baars, *Theater of Consciousness*, p. 11.

order for a person to possess *the concept* of such-and-such an experience with knowing
what it is like to enjoy or suffer a given kind of experience.

It is obviously false that in order to grasp the concept of jealousy, say, of envy or
vengefulness, one must have felt jealous, envious or vengeful. Anyone who has read
Proust will find jealousy described in refined detail, and will have no difficulty in understanding what jealousy is or what it is like to feel jealous. And anyone who has read
Balzac's *La Cousine Bette* will know a great deal about the nature of vengefulness and
vindictiveness, and what it is like to be in the grip of such a passion. One need not have
experienced such passions in order to grasp the relevant concepts, and if one has read such
novels, one will be able to describe what it is like to be moved by such passions (not what
it *resembles*, but what the salient characteristics are).

The confused idea that mastery of   By contrast, someone who is blind is not able to grasp,
colour concepts involves defining   or fully grasp, colour concepts, just as someone who is
them by reference to experiences   deaf is not able to grasp, or fully grasp, concepts of sounds.
                                             The explanation of this, however, is *not* that one must
see coloured things or hear the notes of the octave and then, when one (allegedly) knows
what it is like to have the visual or auditory experience, *define* colour concepts or sound
concepts *by reference to one's experience*. That would imply that concepts of perceptual
qualities are ostensively defined by reference to 'private experiences'. And this in turn would
mean that words such as 'red' or 'green', etc., and 'F-sharp' or 'B-flat', etc., are defined by
reference to *private samples* of colour or of notes. It would mean that the word 'red', as I
use and understand it, is defined by reference to a *this*, which only I have – that is, by
reference to a *mental* sample, which cannot be shown to anyone else.

The correct idea that colour concepts   But, as we have argued in chapter 3, this makes no sense.
are defined by reference to public   For there is, and can be, no such thing as a *private sample*
samples   by reference to which an expression in a language is
                                             defined and which functions as a standard for the correct
use of a word. Not only could other speakers of the language not know what the word,
as used by the speaker, means; the speaker himself could not know what he means by it
either. And, indeed, it would mean nothing at all. Rather, concepts of perceptual qualities,
such as colour, sound, smell and taste concepts, are defined by reference to *public* samples.
'Red' (or 'scarlet', 'maroon', 'magenta', etc.), one may explain to someone who does not
know what one of these colour names mean, is *this* ☞ ■ colour (pointing at a public
sample of the colour). And the sample may then be used as a standard for the correct
application of the word thus ostensively defined. For anything which is *this* ☞ ■ colour
can rightly be said to be red (or scarlet, maroon, magenta, etc.). The defining sample is a
public one, not a private experience. But only a person with normal colour vision can see
and discriminate the sample, and so *use* the public sample as a standard for the correct use
of the colour name thus defined. He does not have to 'know what it is like' to see red, or
scarlet, or maroon – he has to be able to see and discriminate red, scarlet or maroon
things. He has to be *able* to see, and *actually* see, the sample pointed at, and to be able to
use it as a standard of correct application for the defined colour word. He has to be able
to *do* something which only people with normal colour vision can do. Does he also have
to know what seeing red is *like*? It is now unclear what the question means. He certainly

must know what seeing red *is* – that is, what this phrase signifies: namely, that seeing red is seeing *this* ☞ ■ colour (and here he must point to the public sample). Whether it is pleasant or indifferent is irrelevant. And whether it is like something else is equally irrelevant.

Only someone who can see colours can master colour concepts, but they are defined not by reference to his experience but by reference to its object

So, one must not confuse the truth that only someone who can see colours can fully master the use of colour words with the falsehood that colour words are defined by reference to private and incommunicable experiences. Moreover, one must not extrapolate from the case of concepts of perceptual qualities, which *are* defined by public ostensive definition, to concepts of sensation. For, as we have seen (§3.9), sensation words such as 'pain' are defined neither by reference to public samples nor by reference to private ones. For they are not defined ostensively at all. Rather, they are learnt as extensions of natural behaviour – i.e. the natural behaviour in response to pain (tickles, itches, etc.) – and *these* concepts, as we have explained, are Janus-faced. For they are used in the first-person case without any criteria, and in the third-person case on the basis of public behavioural criteria. So they are, *logically*, altogether *unlike* concepts of perceptual qualities. But, like concepts of perceptual qualities, and indeed like all other concepts, they are not defined by reference to *private experiences* or *qualia*. Nor may one assume that concepts of emotions and moods, or epistemic concepts such as knowing or believing, are defined by reference to samples – for such an assumption would be mistaken. One does not have to 'know what it is like' to know or believe something in order to master the use of the verbs 'to know' and 'to believe' (and, indeed, it is not even clear what this 'knowing what it is like' to know or to believe *means*).

Neuroscientific theory cannot bypass the philosophical problem

One final point: the thought that experience is imperfectly communicable, but that *neuroscience* may discover that different people *do* see red 'in the same way' (Crick) is mistaken. It is mistaken not merely because we *can* establish whether different people see the same without the aid of neuroscientific researches, but also because if we could not, we would not be able to do so *with* the aid of neuroscience either. For in order to establish the requisite neuroscientific correlations between perceptual experiences and neural events and processes, we must *already* have established what people perceive, *a fortiori* whether different people perceive the same thing in the same way. Any differences in the neural events will show simply that there is diversity in the neural events in different people corresponding to their exposure to the same stimulus. It will not show that they see things differently. Moreover, given that we can and do establish that different people enjoy or suffer the same experience, differences in the underlying neural processes would not show that, despite their sincere avowals to the contrary, they do not really have the same experience. To think otherwise would be to suppose that someone might sincerely avow pain, groan and scream, but, nevertheless, that a brain scan might show that the person was not in pain at all. But that is absurd. All that would thus be shown is that a neuroscientific theory, which assumes neural uniformity across different individuals, is false. For the criterial (logically good) evidence for being in pain, which is required for the non-inductive identification of the pain of others, is presupposed by inductive evidence correlating pain with neural states and events, and accordingly overrides it.

We have not tackled, and we have not tried to tackle, all the conceptual puzzles and confusions surrounding the notion of qualia. What we have done is to unravel a few of the issues that baffle and confuse neuroscientists (and others), and to argue that the very concept of a quale is a misbegotten progeny of conceptual confusions. We suggest that the problems of so-called qualia are not problems with which neuroscience need concern itself. The manifold puzzles about qualia, which stem from conceptual entanglements, can be left to philosophers. Philosophers may (and should) disentangle the confusions; but they may become (and many of them already are) enmeshed in the net of language. Neuroscientists, on the other hand, may safely by pass these puzzles and confusions, as long as they do not fall victim to the illusions of 'private ownership' of, and 'privileged access' to, experience, of an incommunicable or imperfectly communicable 'qualitative feel' of experience, or of there being something which it is like to have any given experience.

11

Puzzles about Consciousness

11.1 A Budget of Puzzles

On the question of how neural events can give rise to the 'world of consciousness'?

We pointed out in the previous chapter that the distinctions between intransitive and transitive consciousness and between the various forms of transitive consciousness that are embedded in our language are bypassed by current neuroscientists and philosophers bent upon investigating the nature of consciousness. Puzzled primarily by the philosophical question of the relationship between neural events and cogitative, cognitive, affective and volitional phenomena and functions, both neuroscientists and philosophers are prone to extend the concept of consciousness far beyond its ordinary use. In particular, consciousness is equated with experience in general. Moreover, that nebulous term is itself extended well beyond its normal range of application. Neuroscientists and philosophers are concerned above all with a 'realm of consciousness' conceived to be associated with the behaviour of animate bodies. Mere behaviour belongs to the physical world. But conscious experience and conscious mental states appear to be categorially quite distinct. How then can events in the physical world – that is, neural events – give rise to the 'world of consciousness'?

The 'world of consciousness' was characterized in terms of qualia

Naturally enough, it seemed incumbent upon philosophers and neuroscientists who are concerned with such questions to circumscribe the phenomena of consciousness thus conceived. We noted that many of them did so by invoking the idea of the 'qualitative character of experience', which was itself explained in terms of the thought that experiences all have a distinctive 'qualitative feel' and the idea that 'there is something which it is like' to have a given experience. We argued that although one can ask of an experience of any kind how it felt to undergo it or what it was like to have it, the supposition that there is always an answer is mistaken. Moreover, the received conception of there being something which it is like to have a given experience is rooted in a confusion. Numerous psychological attributes, such as knowing, believing, supposing and thinking (in some of its forms), are not forms of *experience* at all. Finally, we examined the idea that each subject of experience is immediately acquainted with his own experiences, which he can indicate to himself by a *this* or a *thus* which points to the qualitative character of the experience, even though he can communicate what he experiences only imperfectly or perhaps not at all. But this line of argument too proved to be futile.

Undermining the notion of qualia does not resolve the Cartesian puzzlement

Undermining the notion of qualia, however, does not by itself resolve the problems that bewilder neuroscientists and others. The perceived difficulty in accommodating facts about subjectivity in our conception of an objective physical world that is investigated by science still needs to be addressed. The Cartesian puzzle of how physical, neural events can give rise to facts concerning consciousness remains pressing. Even if consciousness is *mis*conceived in terms of qualia, the puzzlement recurrently expressed by scientists over the question of what consciousness is *for* requires scrutiny. This chapter will address these and other questions which, we shall argue, are imposed upon us by misconceptions of one kind or another. Once those misconceptions are eradicated, the puzzlement evaporates. The questions either dissolve or have familiar, and sometimes trivial, answers.

11.2 On Reconciling Consciousness or Subjectivity with our Conception of an Objective Reality

Puzzlement over how consciousness can exist in a physical world

Philosophers and cognitive scientists commonly express bafflement at the very existence of consciousness. Searle observes that 'It is just a plain fact about the world that it contains . . . conscious mental states and events, but it is hard to see how mere physical systems could have consciousness. How could such a thing occur? How, for example, could this grey and white gook inside my skull be conscious?'[1] Indeed, he suggests elsewhere, 'Given our concept as to what reality must be like and what it would be like to find out about that reality, it seems inconceivable to us that there should be anything irreducibly subjective in the universe. Yet we all know that subjectivity exists.'[2] Chalmers argues that while consciousness 'is central to a subjective viewpoint, . . . from an objective viewpoint it is utterly unexpected'. The 'objective viewpoint' is that of physics – and it gives an account of the world in terms of the interaction of particles, fields and waves in a spatio-temporal manifold. From this viewpoint, consciousness 'is utterly unexpected'; indeed, 'consciousness is *surprising*. If all we knew about were the facts of physics, and even the facts about dynamics and information processing in complex systems, there would be no compelling reason to postulate the existence of conscious experience. If it were not for our direct evidence in the first-person case, the hypothesis would seem unwarranted – almost mystical, perhaps. Yet we know, directly, that there is conscious experience. The question is, how do we reconcile it with everything else we know?'[3]

---

[1] J. R. Searle, *Minds, Brains and Science – the 1984 Reith Lectures* (BBC, London, 1984), p. 15.
[2] J. R. Searle, *The Rediscovery of the Mind* (MIT Press, Cambridge, MA, 1992), p. 99.
[3] D. J. Chalmers, *The Conscious Mind* (Oxford University Press, Oxford, 1996), pp. 4f.

Misconceptions about the conceptual nature of consciousness are at the root of the puzzlement

It is, we have argued, mistaken to think that experiences are owned by the subject of experience, or to suppose that two people cannot have the same experience (§3.8). It is equally mistaken to suppose that the subject of experi-ence has access or privileged access to his own experience (§3.7). There is, we argued, nothing intrinsically private about experience. It is true that I may not disclose what I experience – I may not show that I have a slight pain, not reveal that I can see such-and-such, not confess that I overheard this or that, and I may suppress my anger or sadness. But that does not make these experiences intrinsically private. And if I do manifest my pain and emotions, do show what I see or hear, then others may know perfectly well what experiences I have enjoyed or undergone.

These remarks are no more than reminders of points established earlier. They are necessary in order to combat the *picture* of consciousness and of so-called conscious experience, conscious mental states or qualia, that is implicit in the neo-Cartesianism blended with neoclassical empiricism that is unwittingly embraced by many contemporary neuroscientists and cognitive scientists, as well as philosophers. For the contrary assumptions collect-ively support a profoundly misleading picture. According to this picture, consciousness or conscious experience is a special domain of phenomena. It is altogether distinct from, though mysteriously dependent on, the physical realm. The physical realm is popu-lated by public physical objects, with physical properties (especially the primary qualities emphasized by Galileo, Descartes, Boyle and Locke, but also more up-to-date ones, such as electrical charge or magnetic field). It is equally accessible to all competent perceivers. It is the realm of the *objective*. By contrast, the domain of consciousness is essentially private to each subject of experience. So it is a realm of the *subjective*.[4] And there are as many such 'realms' as there are subjects of experience. Each such 'realm' is populated by *qualia* – which are altogether distinct from physical objects. Each subject of experi-ence inalienably possesses his qualia, and has access only to his own qualia. He cannot show his qualia to another, and he cannot know whether the qualia of others are similar to his.

Misconstruals of the notion of subjectivity

The idea of a realm of subjectivity, thus construed, demands close scrutiny. For while it is true and innocu-ous to think that each subject of experience enjoys or undergoes experiences, feels emotions and thinks thoughts, has beliefs and knowledge, which he may keep to himself, and so can be described as having, as we sometimes say, an 'inner life', it is far from obvious that this platitude leads us to the idea of a realm of subjectivity. Searle characterizes 'subjectivity' by reference to the fact that every con-scious state or experience is always *someone's* state or experience (it 'belongs' to a *subject* of experience), that each person has a *special relation* to his own conscious states, that a person's consciousness of how things are in the world is always *from his own point of view*, and it has a *subjective, qualitative feel* to it. Another person's 'subjectivity', he claims, is not observable, for all that we can observe is his behaviour. Subjectivity, he contends,

---

[4] Searle, *Rediscovery of the Mind*, pp. 93–100.

is problematic in so far as it is difficult to fit into our overall conception of reality as consisting of an *objective* world.

One may indeed grant that there is no such thing as an experience that is not someone's experience (a pain that is not someone's pain, etc.). But there is nothing odd or anomalous about that. There are no dances danced without dancers, or songs sung without singers. But there is no puzzle or difficulty in fitting dances or songs into our conception of an objective world. So too there are no perceivings or perceptions without perceivers – and it is easy to see why. For the nominals 'a perceiving' or 'a perception' are simply convenient derivatives from the verb 'to perceive'. If A perceives an object O, then there was a perceiving of an O by A, and A had a perception of O. But these nominals introduce no new entities other than those already presented by the simpler sentence 'A perceives O'; they merely introduce convenient *façons de parler*, abstractions from the familiar phenomena. This does not mean that there are not really any perceptions (or that pains, tickles or twinges do not really exist, or that there are no hopes or fears). It means that there are, but that they are not 'entities' or kinds of things. When A is or feels angry with B, it is convenient to speak of A's anger. Obviously there is no anger that is not someone's anger. But there is nothing strange or mysterious about this which could generate puzzlement about how to accommodate such 'facts about subjectivity' into a realist conception of an objective world. There is no such thing as a smile that is not someone's smile or a sneeze that is not someone's sneeze. But there is nothing subjective about smiles and sneezes, save in the innocuous sense that for there to be a smile or for a sneeze to have occurred, someone must have smiled or sneezed.

Having an experience does not imply 'standing in a relation' to an experience

One should surely deny that having a certain experience – for example, having a pain or seeing a red apple ('having a visual experience of a red apple') – involves standing in a *special relation* to an experience, since 'having' here does not signify a relation, and the experience a person has is not a relatum (§3.8). Pain is a sensation, but sensations are not kinds of objects to which one may stand in a certain relation. To have a headache is not to stand in a relation to any kind of object – it is just for one's head to ache. 'To see an apple' may cumbersomely be rephrased as 'to have the visual experience of an apple'. To see an apple may be to stand in a certain relation to an apple, but it is not to stand in any kind of relation to the seeing of an apple. Similarly, to have the visual experience of an apple is not to stand in a relation to a visual experience. By parity of reasoning it is also misconceived to suppose, as Searle does, that each person stands in a special relation to his own conscious states.

Misconstruals of the notion of 'a point of view'

One may grant that when a person sees something, he always does so from a particular point or position in space. But one should surely deny that it follows that whatever he sees or, more generally, experiences, he sees or experiences from *his* unique *point of view*. For, first, anyone else can see what he sees from the same position in space if he vacates it. And other people may hear the same sounds or smell the same smells if they are standing next to him. And second, this is a misuse of the term 'point of view'. I don't feel pain from *my*, or indeed from *any*, point of view, and I do not perceive what I perceive from *my point of view*, but from a position in space. I may *pass judgement* or *give an opinion* from a political, or economic or moral point of view, or from *my* point of view – that is, from the point of view of my interests, preferences or concerns. A judgement passed from the 'point of view' of my preferences can rightly be said to be subjective; perhaps, too, a judgement passed from the 'point of view' of my interests. But there is nothing subjective about a judgement made from a political, economic or moral point of view. Moreover, innumerable judgements that one makes – for example, that the Second World War broke out in September 1939, that force is the product of mass and acceleration, that lions are carnivorous – are not made from *any* particular point of view at all.

Misconceptions about the observability of the experiences of others

The idea that we cannot observe another person's 'subjectivity', but only their behaviour, is mistaken (§3.5). For we can and do observe other people perceiving things, observe their emotions and moods, and observe that they are in pain. Of course, it is true that to observe that another is in pain is not to have the pain he has; to observe his joy or anger – that is, to observe that he is joyful or angry – is not to feel joyous or angry; and one may observe another person perceiving something without perceiving what he is perceiving. It is tempting to reply that, for all that, we cannot perceive his perception, or feel his feeling. But that is confused. For in one sense we can: we can perceive him perceiving what he perceives and often perceive exactly the same things he perceives; we can feel the same pain as he and be in the same mood as he is. In another (non)sense, we are inclined to say that we cannot 'feel his pain' or 'perceive his perceptions'. But if 'feeling his pain' does not mean the same as 'feeling the same pain as he', it means nothing. And if 'perceiving his perceptions' does not mean either 'perceiving that he perceives' or 'perceiving what he perceives', it too means nothing. After all, it is not as if *he* perceives his perceptions and we do not – he does not *perceive* them either, he *has* perceptions; and if we perceive what he perceives, with equal clarity and distinctness, we have the same perceptions.

These misconceptions generate puzzlement about the place of consciousness in a physical world

If one conceives of 'conscious experience' or 'conscious mental states' as a domain of subjectivity, consisting of qualia, essentially private and accessible only to the subject, known immediately by introspection, incommunicable or only imperfectly communicable, then the fact that there is any such thing as conscious experience will indeed seem puzzling (see §9.1). Experience thus conceived seems to be what characterizes conscious beings – it is 'the realm of consciousness'. For if we think thus, we shall want to understand how something as bizarre as qualia can possibly exist in a physical world. We shall indeed query, 'How can physical bodies in a physical world contain such a phenomenon as consciousness?'[5] Qualia, experiences with their own peculiar qualitative character, seem to emerge from physical events, seem to be produced by the excitation of neurons. But how can the excitation of neurons produce such a realm of consciousness? And one might wonder whether 'consciousness is merely a

---

[5] D. Dennett, 'Consciousness', in R. L. Gregory (ed.), *The Oxford Companion to the Mind* (Oxford University Press, Oxford, 1989), p. 160.

passive concomitant of the possession of a sufficiently elaborate control system and does *not*, in itself, actually "do" *anything*.[6] If one starts from such misbegotten assumptions, then there is no question but that the really deep problems lie here. But *these* problems arise out of conceptual confusions; and they are to be resolved by disentangling the knots that we have inadvertently tied in our understanding.

It is misleading to assert that the world 'contains' conscious states or events

It is misleading to assert that it is a plain fact about the world that 'it contains ... conscious states and events'. The world may be said to 'contain' sentient creatures, including human beings, who are conscious (or unconscious), and who, when conscious, enjoy a wide variety of experiences, may be in various mental states, and are conscious of various things. That is indeed a plain fact. Of course, we want to know how this came about. That is a scientific question about the origins of life – to which we now have promising answers – and a question in evolutionary biology concerning the evolution of life forms that possess such perceptual, affective, cognitive and other capacities that warrant ascribing experiences in general to them, as well as intransitive and transitive consciousness – to which we also have reasonably good answers. But it is confused to query how physical bodies in a physical world can *contain* consciousness, or how *mere physical systems* could have consciousness.

Sentient creatures do not 'contain' consciousness

For, first, sentient creatures who are conscious beings do not *contain* consciousness, they *are* conscious (or unconscious), and conscious *of* various things. They feel pain, perceive objects in their environment, feel fear or anger, take pleasure in various activities and conditions, desire things and pursue what they want. They have various active and passive powers, including the passive power of having their attention caught and held by something they perceive: that is, the power to become and then be conscious of something they perceive. If they are language-using, self-conscious creatures, they have the power to realize or recognize how things are with them, and to bear that fact in mind, to be preoccupied with it – that is, to be conscious that things are thus-and-so with them.

Sentient creatures are not 'mere physical systems'

Second, sentient beings are not *mere physical systems*. The atmosphere (weather system) might be said to be a 'mere physical system', a volcano can be said to be a mere physical system, and so too might a pocket calculator or a computer. But animals and human beings are not mere physical systems, but living, sentient 'systems'. Sentient beings are precisely what we *contrast* with mere physical systems. And it is obvious why we do so, for they have capacities that mere physical systems lack, capacities to acquire knowledge of their environment by the use of their sense-organs, to feel pleasure and pain, to adopt goals and pursue them in the light of their knowledge.

The question of how the brain can be conscious is misconceived

And third, the question of how the brain ('this grey and white gook inside my skull') can be conscious is misplaced. For, as we have argued, it cannot. It is the living being whose brain it is that can be said to be conscious or unconscious.

---

[6] R. Penrose, *The Emperor's New Mind*, rev. edn (Oxford University Press, Oxford, 1999), pp. 523f.

The question of how mere physical systems can be conscious is misconceived

So, it is not *hard* to see 'how mere physical systems could be conscious'; it is altogether *logically impossible*. For a 'mere physical system' is precisely that of which it makes no sense to say 'it is conscious or unconscious'.[7] And the question 'How can animate beings be conscious or unconscious?' is presumably a rather vague and poorly formed question in biological science concerning the development of sentient forms of life of sufficient complexity to be characterized as possessing developed perceptual, cognitive, affective and volitional powers. There is not one question here, but many, to most of which we have incomplete but fairly good answers.

The question of whether consciousness is physical is misleading

Equally misleading is the question of whether consciousness is 'physical' or 'merely a concomitant of physical systems'. This question too was addressed by Wittgenstein:

> It seems paradoxical to us that we should make such a medley, mixing physical states and states of consciousness up together in a *single* report: 'He suffered great torments and tossed about restlessly'. It is quite usual; so why do we find it paradoxical? Because we want to say that the sentence deals with both tangibles and intangibles at once. – But does it worry you if I say: 'These three struts give the building stability'? Are three and stability tangible?[8]

If we think of the 'physical' as a domain of material things, extended in space, public and tangible, and of the mental as a domain of subjectivity, identical with or consisting of qualia, which are private, accessible only to their subject or 'owner', intangible, have an incommunicable or only partly communicable subjective 'feel', then we are bound to be puzzled. For we seem to be concerned with two different 'orders of being'. When in the grip of this picture, innumerable mundane sentences suddenly seem paradoxical, mixing up two different 'ontological realms'. It then seems puzzling that what tosses about – that is, something 'physical' – can be the very same thing that suffers torments. For is *suffering torments* something physical, or merely a concomitant of a 'physical system'? But when we speak of three struts giving a building stability, we do not feel any paradox, even though *stability* and *three* are no more 'tangible' than *suffering torment*.

The paradox is a bogus one, produced by the misguided picture that dominates our reflections. Clearly, being conscious (as opposed to unconscious), being conscious of something and being in a certain state of consciousness (a mental state enjoyed or suffered while conscious), are not *tangible* as are such properties as the shape, size, roughness or smoothness, warmth or cold of medium-sized dry goods. Nor are they 'mere concomitants of physical systems', for it is deeply misleading to refer to sentient beings as 'physical systems'.

---

[7] We may safely leave speculation about androids to writers of science fiction. Our concepts are not tailored to deal with such imaginary cases, and there is no reason to suppose that reflection on such flights of fancy will shed any useful light on our current concepts, any more than reflections on Mickey Mouse can shed light on our concept of a mouse.

[8] L. Wittgenstein, *Philosophical Investigations*, ed. G. E. M. Anscombe and R. Rhees, tr. G. E. M. Anscombe (Blackwell, Oxford, 1953), §421.

Sentient creatures are also, not mere, physical systems

Although sentient beings are *also* 'physical systems', they are not *mere* 'physical systems', but 'biological systems' – or, more lucidly, living beings, with powers of sensation, perception, cognition, affection, desire and, above all, action. They are self-moving creatures with goals and purposes of their own, which they pursue in the light of what they perceive and know. Their consciousness, intransitive and transitive, their conscious states and experiences are not *concomitants* of their bodies. So the question 'Is consciousness physical or merely a concomitant of physical systems?' is a misguided question, offering us a pair of bogus alternatives, *both* of which should be rejected. We must, in our reflections on these vexed questions, always bear in mind that being conscious, being conscious of something, and being in a given state of consciousness are predicable of living beings that behave in certain distinctive ways. It is those forms of behaviour in circumstances of life that warrant the ascription to them of the rich variety of attributes characteristic of sentient life forms.

The 'inconceivability' of irreducible subjectivity depends on misconceptions

Is it really the case that, given our conception of what reality must be like, it seems inconceivable that there should be 'anything irreducibly subjective' in the universe? Only if we have a distorted conception of what reality must be like and an equally distorted conception of so-called subjectivity. If by 'subjectivity' we mean consciousness, understood as identical with or consisting of qualia, then it does not only *seem* inconceivable, it *is* inconceivable. For this conception of consciousness, of experience and of qualia, is, we have argued, incoherent. There is, and could be, no such thing. For qualia, thus conceived, are no more than empiricist impressions and ideas in modern garb, Wittgensteinian 'private objects' the conception of which makes no sense.

The illusion of the incompatibility of consciousness and physics depends on misconceptions

Equally, if our conception of 'reality' is distorted, it may seem inconceivable that there be any such thing as consciousness – that is, as conscious beings. If we think that physics is the ultimate arbiter on what exists, and that what physics reveals is that nothing exists other than physical particles, fields and waves, then, to be sure, we are confused both about physics and about what physics reveals. And if we confusedly think thus, it will be equally inconceivable that there be any such things as Gothic cathedrals or Baroque palaces, flourishing economies in the Western world and collapsing economies in Africa, democratic institutions and societies as well as non-democratic institutions and societies, legal systems and law courts – or, indeed, laws which may be just or unjust. It will be inconceivable that there are numbers and mathematical theorems, symphonies and sonatas and their performances, or novels, poems and paintings. And, to be sure, it will be inconceivable that sentient creatures and human beings exist. Do we *really* find it inconceivable or *apparently* inconceivable that such things exist? Does physics even *suggest* that they do not, or cannot? Do *physicists* claim that there are no such things, or that the existence of such things conflicts with the facts they have discovered about the physical constitution of reality?

Physics investigates the physical features of physical phenomena. It does not, and need not, concern itself with non-physical features of physical phenomena, although it may contribute to the understanding of the physical basis that makes the possession of such features possible. *A fortiori*, it can have little if anything to contribute to the understanding of non-physical features of non-physical phenomena. So it does not concern itself with the biological features of forms of life, which are studied by the biological sciences (which are not a branch of physics), or with psychological features of sentient forms of life, which are studied by the science of psychology (which is not a branch of physics either). And it can have nothing to contribute to the understanding of social features of social beings and their social organizations, or of logical, mathematical and aesthetic features of the intellectual and aesthetic creations of humankind, including numbers, theorems, propositions and works of art. But physics does not suggest that such items and their properties are not *real*, or that there are not really any such things. Nor does it suggest or even intimate that their existence is surprising.[9] Of course, sentient beings, including humans, are *also* physical beings – they are space-occupying physical things, and they consist of matter. Their properties and powers ultimately depend on, but are not reducible to, the physical and microphysical processes that characterize their physical constitution (see §13.1). But their biological, psychological, social and cultural properties are of no concern to physics. Moreover, *these* features *also* depend on factors that are not the subject matter of physics or of physical explanations at all.

The idea that consciousness is un-expected from an 'objective' view-point is confused, for three reasons

Is consciousness, then, surprising? Is it unexpected? Or rather, is it, as Chalmers avers, surprising and unexpected from 'the objective viewpoint' of physics? If all we knew were the facts of physics, would it be surprising and unexpected, an unwarranted hypothesis, perhaps even mystical? The question betrays conceptual confusion.

First, the true propositions or theories of physics are no *more* objective than those of other sciences, or indeed than any other propositions or theories that are true – no matter whether they are true propositions of biology, psychology, sociology, economics or history, or indeed *any* true propositions. Of course, physics does not concern itself with matters of psychology or the social and cultural sciences or disciplines. But that does not lend its truths greater objectivity than those of other departments of knowledge.

Hence, secondly, the 'viewpoint' of physics is irrelevant to the 'viewpoint' of psychology or history or law or economics. Is the rise in the rate of inflation in Britain in the 1970s surprising from the viewpoint of physics? Is the existence of common law in the British legal system unanticipated from the perspective of physics? Is Hannibal's failure to take Rome unexpected from the viewpoint of physics? The questions make scant sense.

Thirdly, the question 'If we knew only the facts of physics, would there be any reason to postulate the existence of conscious experience?' is misconceived. If *who* knew only the facts of physics? Could *any* being know *only* the facts of physics – and not facts about perception and its objects, about knowledge and its evidential grounds, about how to conduct experiments and to construct machines, about how to measure and calculate, not to mention facts about themselves, their family and other people, facts about the social world they inhabit, about their autobiography and about the biographies of others.

---

[9] For an old, but highly readable, and equally highly relevant, discussion of these confusions, see G. Ryle, *Dilemmas* (Cambridge University Press, Cambridge, 1954), ch. 5.

Irreducibility of consciousness to physics does not imply that it is surprising

This cannot be what is meant. So what *is* meant? Is it perhaps that facts about 'consciousness' – that is, about sentient beings, their experiences and mental states – are not *derivable* from facts of physics? Is it that statements about living beings and their lives, about their experiences, thoughts, beliefs, emotions and actions, are not *reducible* to facts of physics? *That* is true enough – the programme of the logical reduction of all empirical statements to statements of physics (which was briefly dreamt of by members of the Vienna Circle in the 1930s) went bankrupt decades ago (for a discussion of reductionism, see chapter 13 below). And that statements of psychology which presuppose, or involve reference to, consciousness are neither reducible to, nor derivable from, statements of physics is *no reason whatsoever* for finding the myriad facts appertaining to consciousness either surprising or unexpected. (Nor, we may remind ourselves, is it true that we know of 'the existence of consciousness' in virtue of 'our direct evidence in the first-person case'. I neither have nor need any evidence for my being conscious whenever I am.)

Consequently, if we see things aright, and shed the heavy load of conceptual confusions that bedevil debates about consciousness, there is no problem of reconciling 'subjectivity' or 'conscious experience', *correctly understood*, with physics, or with our conception (now, we hope, put back on the rails) of 'what reality must be like', let alone with 'everything else we know'.

11.3 On the Question of how Physical Processes can give rise to Conscious Experience

Scientists' puzzlement: Huxley and Tyndalls, Glynn and Humphrey

This puzzlement over the very existence of consciousness and the alleged difficulty of reconciling the facts of 'subjectivity' with our conception of reality as objective is exacerbated by scientists' venerable bafflement as to how physical, neural processes could 'give rise to' conscious experience. In the nineteenth century T. H. Huxley famously observed: 'How it is that anything so remarkable as a state of consciousness comes about as a result of irritating nervous tissue, is just as unaccountable as the appearance of Djin when Aladdin rubbed his lamp.'[10] John Tyndall remarked in astonishment that 'The passage from the physics of the brain to the corresponding facts of consciousness is unthinkable. Granted that a definite thought and a definite molecular action in the brain occur simultaneously, we do not possess the intellectual organ, nor apparently any rudiment of the organ, which would enable us to pass, by a process of reasoning, from one to the other.'[11] Scientists are mesmerized by the same idea to this day: Humphrey observes that 'The gulf between brain states, as described by physiologists, and mind states, as described by conscious human beings, is practically – and some would argue, logically

---

[10] T. H. Huxley, *Lessons in Elementary Psychology* (1866), p. 210.

[11] J. Tyndall, *Fragments of Science*, 5 edn, p. 420, quoted by W. James, *The Principles of Psychology* (Hoet, New York, 1890), vol. 1, p. 147.

– unbridgeable.'[12] And Glynn holds that 'we haven't much more idea why consciousness should emerge from events in the brain than Thomas Henry Huxley had' when he wrote the above-quoted passage.[13]

Misconceptions about consciousness make its evolutionary emergence puzzling

If one thinks of consciousness as a private realm of qualia and of qualitative conscious experiences, one is bound to be puzzled at its evolutionary emergence. For if we conceive of consciousness thus, it seems to be an all-or-nothing affair. Either a being has qualia or it does not. The conscious lives of some lowly beings may be impoverished relative to others, the range of their 'subjectivity' may be thin, but either they have some qualia or they do not. If one thinks of conscious experiences as a matter of having 'images of objects in the brain' in one or other sensory modality, or of having 'a movie in the brain', as Damasio puts it, then either a creature has images in the brain or it does not. It may then seem that 'consciousness arose as a phenotypic property at some point in the evolution of species. Before then it did not exist. This assumption implies that the acquisition of consciousness either conferred evolutionary fitness directly on the individuals having it, or provided a basis for other traits that enhanced fitness.'[14]

The puzzlement lies in the picture

Thinking thus, we are mesmerized by a picture. Of course, we shall want to say that consciousness, experience, emerges only when phenomena in the physical world have evolved a certain degree of complexity. For we do not ascribe consciousness to plants, or experience to amoebas. A very complex biological substratum, a highly evolved nervous system, is a characteristic feature of conscious beings. But our picture of consciousness as a realm of subjectivity, populated by qualia, leads us into confusion. For now the evolutionary emergence of consciousness may suddenly seem altogether mysterious. How can something so unlike mere matter and its properties *emerge* from what is just a more complex arrangement of material particles? How could 'subjectivity' spring into existence through nothing more than an increase in the complexity of the nervous system? How could the 'realm of consciousness' be created? But this is the wrong way to think about the matter. We need to jettison the picture.

Grounds for the attribution of consciousness

We attribute consciousness to a creature on the grounds of its behaviour in the circumstances of its life, not on the grounds of its possessing private qualia or movies-in-the-brain. In so doing, we may be concerned merely with intransitive consciousness, or with transitive consciousness in one of its many forms. The behaviour that warrants the attribution of one form of consciousness differs from that which warrants attribution of another, although, to be sure, any attribution of transitive consciousness presupposes that the creature is intransitively conscious to some degree. We may, in our ascription of consciousness to a creature, be concerned primarily with the attribution to it of the

---

[12] N. Humphrey, 'The inner eye of consciousness', in C. Blakemore and S. Greenfield (eds), *Mindwaves* (Blackwell, Oxford, 1987), p. 379.

[13] I. Glynn, *An Anatomy of Thought* (Weidenfeld and Nicolson, London, 1999), p. 396.

[14] G. Edelman, *Bright Air, Brilliant Fire – On the Matter of the Mind* (Penguin, Harmondsworth, 1994), p. 113.

capacity for experiences within a certain range: for example, sensation, perception, desire and emotion. The actualization of such capacities is exhibited by an animal in its behaviour, and the criteria for ascribing to an animal sensations, the perceiving of this or that feature in its environment, emotions or desires are its behavioural responses to the circumstances in which it finds itself.

The evolutionary emergence of consciousness

Consciousness, to be sure, does not 'emerge', like an ethereal halo or astral body, from inanimate matter or, indeed, from animate matter. It is ascribable to living animals. But there is no sharp divide in nature between creatures to which it makes sense and creatures to which it makes no sense to ascribe consciousness or experience in one or other of their many forms. Rather, as the biological constitution of living creatures becomes more complex, as their nervous systems, perceptual organs and brains become more evolved, more and more forms of apprehension of, and response and reaction to, their environment become possible. The neural structures, which it is the task of neuroscientists to investigate, make it possible for a creature to have and to exhibit higher forms of sentience and purposiveness. There is no point on the evolutionary scale at which images in the brain, movies-in-the-mind or subjectivity emerge – for these are fictions. But nor is there any *point* on the scale at which one can say, *now* such-and-such a genotype produces consciousness. Rather, there is a gradual evolution of more and more complex forms of sensitivity to the environment and more and more complex forms of response. Unless in the grip of philosophical misconceptions, we can have no hesitation whatsoever in attributing sensation, perception, emotion, desire and purpose (of varying degrees and forms) to the higher animals, no matter whether fish, reptile, bird or mammal. With lower forms of life, the rich range of concepts of experience have an increasingly infirm grip. That is not due to our ignorance, nor does it betoken a defect in the concepts we deploy. It is, rather, because there is no sharp dividing line between the very primitive forms of sentience displayed by molluscs and prawns, etc., and the more evolved forms exhibited by fish and reptiles. But there is nothing mysterious here, nor is there any profound puzzle – although there is much that we do not yet know.

It is an illusion that it is mysterious that physical events affect consciousness

Nevertheless, is it not mysterious how mere physical processes can give rise to conscious experience? Is it not mysterious that states of consciousness result from the mere irritation of nervous tissue? Is not the passage from 'the physics of the brain to the corresponding facts of consciousness' unthinkable? Again, we suggest, the impression that something mysterious is afoot is generated by looking at the phenomena askew. The idea of an 'unbridgeable gulf' between consciousness and brain processes is an illusion produced as a consequence of conceptual confusion that is characteristic of philosophical reflection (no matter whether by philosophers or neuroscientists). When we are told that someone drank a bottle of whisky and lost consciousness, we do not feel that something mysterious or miraculous has occurred. It does not strike us that the influence of alcohol involves crossing an unbridgeable gulf. And when a neuroscientist suggests that loss of consciousness through intoxication is accompanied by such-and-such changes in activity in the prefrontal cortex, we have learnt something that is of interest, but we do not think that anything *deeply mysterious* has been explained. Nor, during a brain operation, when the primary visual cortex is stimulated at a site and we consequently see a bright light flashing in the upper left of our visual field, do we feel that something *miraculous* has taken place. Here we should indeed say that this phenomenon of seeming to see a flashing light is produced by stimulation of the brain. Strange it may be, for we do not normally have our brain stimulated thus, but we should not feel that we had experienced anything miraculous or mysterious.[15]

Similarly, it is a kind of illusion, produced by conceptual confusion, to suppose that it is uncanny that states of conscious should be produced 'as a result of irritating nervous tissue'. It is not mysterious that when light is reflected off a red apple into our eyes, we see a red apple. But it may *seem* puzzling or even mysterious *when we redescribe the phenomenon*. For we say, rightly, that when light of such-and-such wavelength, reflected off the apple, strikes our eyes, exciting the rods and cones of the retinae, with the consequent conduction of impulses along the optic nerve to the thalamus and thence to the cortex, then an experience of seeing a red apple occurs. How can neural events suddenly be transformed into an *experience*, which has a 'qualitative feel', and is uniquely 'accessible' to its subject? How could such a thing happen? Is not this 'passage from the physics of the brain to the corresponding facts of consciousness' *unthinkable*?

The sense that we are confronted by something *deeply mysterious* stems from our confusion. For to say that photons excite the light-sensitive cells of the retina is just to redescribe in physical and neural terms what occurs when light enters the eye, and there is nothing mysterious about the idea that in order to see, light is necessary, and that light from the object seen must reach the eye. The neuroscientific description of the subsequent neural events in the retina and the optic nerve, and the transmission of impulses to the 'visual' striate cortex is a fine example of the achievements of neuroscience in the last decades. The complexity of the mechanisms is striking, and the organization of the cells of the 'visual' striate cortex is remarkable – but, *so far*, not at all mysterious.

A source of confusion   Neuroscientists had not expected that one could map features of the visual field – for example, the location and orientation of the lines and corners of the visible object – on to the excitation of specific cells of the striate cortex. That is indeed surprising. But what generates an impression that there is something *mysterious* going on is the idea that at some stage after the cells of the 'visual' striate cortex have been excited, there occurs *in the brain* an altogether new phenomenon: namely, a visual experience, a quale or a visual image.[16] How, we may then wonder, can such neural events produce something so categorially distinct from nerve excitation as a quale or an image in the brain? Where, we may then wonder, does the quale or the visual image occur? And if it occurs somewhere in the brain, how is it that *we* see it? But, of course, no such thing occurs at all. To see a red apple on the table before one is not to see an image of a red apple; nor is it a matter of the brain seeing a red apple.

---

[15] See Wittgenstein, *Philosophical Investigations*, §412.

[16] As Damasio remarks, 'There is a mystery, however, regarding *how* images emerge from neural patterns. How a neural pattern *becomes* an image is a problem that neurobiology has not yet resolved' (*The Feeling of What Happens* (Heinemann, London, 1999), p. 322). It would indeed be a mystery; and not one which neurobiology would ever be likely to resolve.

When one sees a red apple, there is no image of the red apple in the brain or anywhere else. One sees an image of a red apple on a table when one looks at a Cézanne still life. One *has* an image of a red apple when one vividly imagines a red apple, but one does not *see* the image one *has*. And the brain neither sees anything nor has images of anything.

So, when light is reflected off a red apple on to the retinae of a normal human being in normal circumstances, he sees the apple before him. The upshot of the immensely complex sequence of neural events that occur is not that an image or quale miraculously springs into existence, either in the brain or anywhere else. It is, rather, that the person sees the apple. For the neuroscientific description is a description of the neural events that make it *possible* for a human being to see an object in public space, and that *must* (causally) actually occur if he is to see what he sees.

A further source of confusion   We can, if we so please, say that the upshot of the neural events is *a visual experience of a red apple*. But we must not be confused by our own description. Otherwise it may seem that we have described an extraordinary transformation of matter into mind, of physical events into mental events – and how could something as physical as the firing of neurons be transformed into something as categorially different as *a visual experience* (and, to be sure, mystification ensues if one thinks of a visual experience as a quale). But in truth, to say that the upshot of such-and-such neural events is a visual experience is just a potentially confusing way of saying that the upshot of these neural events in the brain of a normal human being is that *he sees the object* that reflected light on to his retinae. No new entity has sprung into existence, and no unbridgeable gulf between brain processes and consciousness has mysteriously been crossed.

Seeing an object is not a kind of object – a quale, which the person sees or has access to – that has come into being. Rather, neuroscientists have partially explained the neural processes that take place in the brain of a human being when a person sees something. This explanation is a remarkable scientific achievement indeed, but it has neither disclosed nor fathomed anything mysterious. It would be mysterious if *no* neural processes were required for an animal to see what it sees. It would be baffling if we had discovered somewhere in the brain, as Descartes supposed that we would, an optical image of what is visible, for then we would wonder how this image enabled the person to see what he sees, since he patently cannot see a little image in his brain, any more than he can see the inverted, reflected image on his retina. It would be puzzling if, *per impossibile*, neuroscientists had discovered that the upshot of the neural events they have traced were that the brain sees an image. For then we would wonder how something that lacks eyes and cannot respond to what is seen with appropriate behaviour could see, or be said to see, an image. And if neuroscientists had, *per impossibile*, discovered that the brain *has* an image, we would still be altogether ignorant about how *the human being* sees whatever he sees. But all of these absurd suppositions stem from conceptual entanglement, not from scientific discoveries. The truly impressive discoveries in visual theory explain the neural processes requisite for *an animal* to see, not for a brain to see. And the explanations do not bridge or purport to bridge any gulf between brain processes and consciousness, for the existence of a *gulf* is an illusion.

Tyndall's bafflement   Is the passage from 'the physics of the brain' to the corresponding 'facts of consciousness' really *unthinkable*, as Tyndall averred? Not at all. Neuroscience has established good inductive correlations between such 'facts of consciousness' as seeing various features in one's visual field and such facts about the brain as the firing of cells in the hypercolumns of the 'visual' striate cortex. These inductive correlations are now embedded in a theory (as yet incomplete) concerning the neural processes that underpin vision. On the basis of this theory, we can now infer from the fact that such-and-such neural events are taking place in the brain of a normal creature with standard visual capacities that it is now seeing such-and-such features in its visual field. This 'passage' from 'the physics of the brain' to 'facts of consciousness' is not *unthinkable*; it is a straightforward inductive inference. Of course, if Tyndall meant that had we known facts about neural events in the striate cortex *without* having correlated them with items in the visual field (line orientations, edges, etc.), then we would not have been able to infer the latter from the former, then that is perfectly correct, but not in the least mysterious. Since such reasoning is inductive, and presupposes inductive correlations, it is hardly surprising that we could not make such inferences prior to establishing the relevant correlations.

11.4 Of the Evolutionary Value of Consciousness

Puzzlement over what consciousness is for

Bewilderment over how there can be any such thing as conscious experience in a physical world, how physical events could 'give rise' to consciousness, and why consciousness should 'emerge' from the brain, leads to yet further puzzlement about what consciousness is *for*. Thus Chalmers queries, 'Why does conscious experience exist?'[17] This teleological question engages scientists as well. So, Horace Barlow raises the question, 'What is the selective advantage conferred on the human race, or any other species, by consciousness? Is it just an epiphenomenon of our brain mechanism – the whining of the neural gears, the clicking of the neural circuitry? Or can one identify a more important role for it in the survival and future of our species?'[18] And Roger Penrose, echoing exactly the same question, points out that the question assumes that consciousness 'actually "does something" – and, moreover, that what it does is helpful to the creature possessing it, so that an otherwise equivalent creature, but without consciousness, would behave in some less effective way'. On the other hand, he notes that consciousness might be thought to be merely epiphenomenal, a passive concomitant of the possession of a sufficiently elaborate control system.[19]

Barlow's answer to the question 'What is consciousness for?'

Various answers have been essayed. Barlow suggests that 'consciousness links the individual to the community within which he lives, a link that is crucial to all that is

---

[17] Chalmers, *Conscious Mind*, p. 5. It is not altogether clear whether he has in mind the teleological question, or merely the question, already mooted, as to how it is physically (neurologically) possible for animals to enjoy 'conscious experience'.

[18] H. Barlow, 'The biological role of consciousness', in Blakemore and Greenfield (eds), *Mindwaves*, p. 361.

[19] Penrose, *Emperor's New Mind*, pp. 523f.

human. Normal perception, learning and memory are thought to be involved . . . but the individual's need for consciousness and its impossibility without social experience means that consciousness itself is what forces an individual to interact with the community.'[20] This he explains as follows:

> Let us suppose that consciousness in the infant is awakened by the first mutual communication with another person – perhaps the first smile that is returned . . . To enlarge this experience and bring it partly under his control the infant brain must build a model of what it is interacting with, that is a model of the mother and her brain which will tell the infant when smiles will be returned, and when other responses and interactions will occur. . . . Thus the content and validity of introspection can be enlarged, but only by social experience leading to the incorporation of models of other people's minds. On this view the crucial feature of consciousness is that it *requires* a remembered partner for its introspections: consciousness is taught, awakened and maintained by interactions with other modelled minds, and its characteristics in any individual depend to some extent upon these other minds.[21]

Humphrey's answer to the question 'What is consciousness for?'

In a similar vein, Humphrey suggests that consciousness has evolved as a biological adaptation for doing introspective psychology. 'The advantage to an animal of being conscious lies in the purely private use it makes of conscious experience as a means of developing a conceptual framework which helps it to model another animal's behaviour.'[22] This, he explains, suggests that 'Somewhere along the evolutionary path that led from fish to chimpanzees a change occurred in the nervous system which transformed an animal which simply "behaved" into an animal which at the same time informed its mind of the reasons for its behaviour. My guess is that this change involved the evolution of a new brain – a "conscious brain" parallel to the older "executive brain".'[23] The 'inner eye of consciousness', as Humphrey calls it, 'provides us with an extraordinarily effective tool for understanding – by analogy – the minds of others like ourselves.'[24]

Penrose's answer

Penrose, by contrast, holds that

> the selective advantage of consciousness is that it enables its possessor to form some kind of non-algorithmic judgement of how to behave in a given situation. Perhaps one could refer to such judgements as 'inspired guesswork'; it is of some value to examine some outstanding examples of inspirational ideas, as recorded by Poincaré and Mozart, for example. Here the inspirational ideas appear to be thrown up by the *un*conscious mind, but it is the *conscious judgements* that are needed to assess the value of the ideas themselves. These judgements have a remarkable globality about them; a vast area seems to be surveyable in an instant – say, an entire mathematical topic, or a symphony. Such

---

[20] Barlow, 'Biological role of consciousness', p. 361.

[21] Ibid., p. 373.

[22] N. Humphrey, *Consciousness Regained* (Oxford University Press, Oxford, 1984), p. 35.

[23] Ibid., p. 37.

[24] Humphrey, 'Inner eye of consciousness', pp. 380f.

globality is also a feature of much of our conscious thinking at a (seemingly) much more mundane level, such as deciding what to have for dinner or appreciating a visual scene.[25]

So, Penrose contends, 'consciousness is needed in order to handle situations where we have to form new judgements, and where the rules have not been laid down beforehand. . . . The judgements themselves, . . . are the manifestations of the action of *consciousness*.'[26] And 'the hallmark of consciousness is a non-algorithmic forming of judgements'.[27]

All the answers rest on misconceptions about the nature of consciousness

It should be clear that all these answers, which draw attention to crucial abilities of creatures such as ourselves, are nevertheless confused. For they do not answer the question that they purport to answer: namely, 'What is consciousness for?' or 'What is the evolutionary advantage of consciousness?' And the reason why they fail to address the question is because they misunderstand what consciousness is; that is, they misconstrue the concept of consciousness, no matter whether understood narrowly as intransitive and transitive

---

[25] R. Penrose, 'Précis of *The Emperor's New Mind*: concerning computers, minds and the laws of physics', *Behavioural and Brain Sciences*, 13 (1990), p. 653. The reference to Mozart, elaborated in Penrose's *Emperor's New Mind*, p. 547, is to a notorious letter dated 1789 to a certain Baron von P. in which Mozart describes his methods of composition, writing that his mind seizes the entire composition 'as a glance of my eye a beautiful picture or a handsome youth. It does not come to me successively, with various parts worked out in detail, as they will later on, but in its entirety that my imagination lets me hear it'. Penrose quotes the letter from J. Hadamard's *The Psychology of Invention in the Mathematical Field* (Princeton University Press, Princeton, 1945), p. 16. The letter, however, is a notorious forgery (see E. Anderson, *Letters of Mozart* (Macmillan, London, 1966), p. xvii). That is unimportant in the present context. What *is* important is what people *mean* when they say, quite justifiably, of a highly complex solution to a problem 'I saw the answer in a flash'. For even if Mozart had said that the whole composition came to him in a flash, he certainly did not mean that he *heard* the whole piece in his imagination in a flash. So there is no reason to think that the solution to the puzzle of how he could have grasped so much, and something that is temporarily extended, *in a flash* will come from gerrymandering *time* in accordance with a putative theory of 'correct quantum gravity', as Penrose suggests. To conceive a solution to a complex problem, in musical composition or in any other domain, 'in a flash' is no more mysterious (although no less remarkable) than being able to make a note of a complex thought by jotting down a few words or a diagram, which constitute, for the author, the epitome of his thought. What makes the jotting into an epitome of a thought is the use its author subsequently makes of it. The sudden flash of inspiration is the dawning of a capacity, not the high-speed articulation of a thought. It is more akin to suddenly being able to do something than to doing something suddenly. The solution one sees in a flash is more of a pointer than a product. What we have here is a form of knowing that one *can* do something, not a mysterious form of doing something at an impossibly high speed. Of course, whether one is *right* to think that one 'has the solution', i.e. that one knows how to prove the theorem or complete the symphony, remains to be seen. For we sometimes *think* we have seen the solution in a flash, only to discover, when we try to work it out, that we were wrong. Naturally enough, it is the occasions on which we really did see the solution in a flash that are recollected and recorded; the occasions on which we wrongly thought we did are quietly forgotten.

[26] Penrose, *Emperor's New Mind*, p. 531.

[27] Ibid., p. 533.

consciousness or broadly as 'conscious experience' or 'conscious mental states'. Correctly understood, we shall argue, the answers to the question are obvious – and much more mundane than those suggested by these eminent scientists.

The misconceptions are evident in the thought that consciousness might be epiphenomenal, and that 'zombies' are logically possible

Misunderstanding is already evident in raising the questions of whether consciousness might not be 'just an epiphenomenon of our brain mechanism – the whining of neural gears', and whether 'an otherwise equivalent creature, without consciousness' might behave in a less effective way than a conscious creature such as ourselves. It is sometimes thought that it makes sense to suppose that there might be creatures who behave exactly as we do, but who are not conscious, not conscious of anything, and who do not have any perceptual – or indeed, any other form of – experience. They conduct their lives just as we do; they respond to visibilia and audibilia just like normal human beings, they act (apparently) in pursuit of goals, manifest (apparent) determination, intention and purpose, speak and discourse just as we do. Nevertheless, it is supposed, they lack 'subjectivity' – there is, as it were, darkness where there should be 'light', or 'life', or 'experience'. They are just 'zombies'.[28]

Were consciousness just a matter of having qualia, then it might indeed be epiphenomenal

If one thinks that being conscious is a matter of having qualia – that is, private mental objects accessible only to their owner, etc. – then the thought that consciousness might be epiphenomenal is unavoidable, and the question of whether consciousness has any evolutionary value is pressing. *But there are no such things as qualia thus conceived.* And it is not intelligible that a living creature manifest perceptual, cognitive, affective and conative powers in its behaviour *and not be conscious.* For these endlessly rich forms of behaviour and speech in the circumstances of life are the *logical criteria* for a creature's being conscious (as opposed to being unconscious or asleep), being conscious *of* various things in their immediate environment, for perceiving, feeling emotions, wanting things and acting intentionally in order to get them. If a creature regularly behaves just as we do in the normal circumstances of life, then it is conscious, just as we are.

Were 'zombies' logically possible, the question of whether other people are zombies or conscious beings would arise

It is worth bearing in mind that if we do think that there might be zombies who behave just as we do only lack consciousness, then we cannot but wonder whether all our fellow human beings may not be such creatures. To

---

[28] See Searle, *Rediscovery of the Mind*, ch. 3, and *idem, The Mystery of Consciousness* (Granta Books, London, 1997), pp. 106–8, 146–8. The picture we have of conscious beings, on the one hand, and of zombies, on the other, is of conscious beings as creatures with a bubble emerging from the head, with images inside the bubble (as in comics), and of 'zombies' as identical creatures with a bubble coming out of their heads likewise, but the bubble being uniformly black inside. There is nothing wrong with the picture – it is an iconographic picture of a conscious being and of a non-conscious one – just as there is nothing wrong with a picture of Love and Death as a putto with a bow and arrow accompanied by an old man with a scythe. The moot question is what one does with the picture – how one interprets it.

suggest that we know they are not, because they have the same biological constitution as we do, that they have brains just like our own, and 'we know that the structure and function of the brain are causally sufficient to cause consciousness',[29] is, *inter alia*, to suggest that prior to the neurophysiological discoveries about the role and function of the brain, no one could be sure that other human beings (not to mention other animals) were conscious beings. And that, surely, is absurd. It is not a *hypothesis* that other human beings are conscious; it is not an *inference*, based on one's 'knowledge of one's own consciousness', let alone on one's 'consciousness of one's consciousness'. We see others lose and regain consciousness; we see them as they become conscious of this or that and notice that they are conscious of such-and-such. We see them perceiving their environment, observe them listening to conversations, music or noise. 'Look into someone else's face, and see consciousness in it, and a particular shade of consciousness. You see on it, in it, joy, indifference, interest, excitement, torpor, and so on. The light in other people's faces. Do you look into *yourself* in order to recognize the fury in *his* face? It is there as clearly as in your own breast.'[30]

'What is the evolutionary advantage of consciousness?': different questions distinguished

So, what is the evolutionary advantage of consciousness? Different questions must be distinguished. One may investigate the evolutionary advantage of a minute primitive change to an organism that led, by means of natural selection, to the emergence of an ability or trait that its remote descendants exhibit in a developed form. These are questions in evolutionary biology. Clearly no mysteries attach to the evolution of primal light-, sound- or smell-sensitive organs in primitive creatures. At the early stages of development there is no question of consciousness, merely varying degrees of primitive sensitivity to light, sound and smell. But from these primal forms, eyes, ears and noses evolved. The creatures endowed with such primitive sense-organs, who therefore possessed primitive sense-faculties, were taking the early steps on the route to the evolution of creatures that can be said to be conscious (or unconscious), and to have the capacities for somatic and perceptual transitive conscious. No conceptual puzzles or mysteries are involved in such questions in evolutionary biology, and the advantages which light, sound and smell sensitivity confer on an organism are patent.

The advantages to a developed being of forms of transitive consciousness are patent

Clearly, neuroscientists who raise the question of what the evolutionary advantage of consciousness is are not concerned with this question. Perhaps they should be, since it may be that had they attended to this question, their puzzlement would never have arisen. Be that as it may, their question evidently concerns the advantages of consciousness to an evolved being. What functions in the life of animals such as ourselves does consciousness fulfil? If this were a question about intransitive consciousness, it would, as we have already remarked, be silly. If it is a question about transitive perceptual consciousness, the answer is obvious. A large part of

---

[29] Searle, *Mystery of Consciousness*, p. 147.

[30] L. Wittgenstein, *Zettel*, ed. G. E. M. Anscombe and von G. H. Wright, tr. G. E. M. Anscombe (Blackwell, Oxford, 1967), §220.

transitive perceptual consciousness concerns peripheral perception – that is, the passive power to have one's attention caught by things and events on the periphery of one's perceptual field. Its evolutionary advantage is patent – an animal in the jungle who lacked such a power would not survive for long. As for somatic consciousness, clearly the question of what the evolutionary value of consciousness of pain is does not differ from the question of what the evolutionary value of pain is. For, other things being equal, there is no difference between having a pain and being conscious of a pain. The sensation of pain just is something that catches and holds one's attention.[31] And the answer to the question of the evolutionary value of pain in general is patent. As for other forms of transitive consciousness, such as affective and reflective consciousness, they presuppose mastery of a language. For to realize and become conscious of the fact that one is angry or depressed, excited or cheerful, requires possession of the concepts of anger, depression, excitement or cheerfulness. So, in so far as it makes sense to speak of an evolutionary value of such forms of transitive consciousness, their value is merely an aspect of the evident evolutionary value of the capacity to acquire and to master a language. (Of course, we need not suppose that *every* form of transitive consciousness must have an evolutionary advantage, any more than we should suppose that every kind of pain is of evolutionary advantage.)

The question of the evolutionary advantage of 'conscious experience' is either naive or confused

But it is evident that this is not what exercises those who raise the question of evolutionary advantage. Some of them are concerned with 'conscious experience'. But that is either naive or confused. It is naive if the question is: 'What is the evolutionary advantage of having experiences while conscious?', for that question amounts to asking what advantage is conferred on an organism by sensibility – that is, by having eyes and ears, nose, palate and a sensitive body, and hence by the faculties of sight, hearing, smell, taste and feeling. The answer is too obvious to be worth rehearsing. The question only appears to be serious because we labour under the Cartesian illusion that an animal might have the very same visual, auditory, gustatory, etc., responsive repertoire of behaviour as we and other higher animals do, but without being conscious at all (and, indeed, Descartes held all 'mere brutes' to be non-conscious creatures). We conceive of conscious experience as a matter of possessing qualia – and *then* it is easy to imagine that it makes sense to suppose that an animal might react to visibilia, audibilia, smells, tastes and tactile qualities as sentient beings do, but without having any qualia. But, as we have argued, the picture that bewitches us is incoherent, and we need to abandon it. When we see things aright, the problem evaporates.

Reply to Barlow

The speculations of scientists rehearsed above do emphasize important human powers (some of which are shared,

---

[31] Of course, one's attention may sometimes be distracted – and then there is a curious singularity in our concept of pain. For we do not want to say that the pain continued unfelt, since an unfelt pain is tantamount to no pain. But nor do we want to say that the pain ceased – since we are not aware of the cessation of pain (if we were, we should say so, but then it would no longer be a case of mere distraction of attention). So, we say, *ex post facto*, that our attention was distracted from the pain, and let the matter rest. It is, so to speak, a singularity (in the mathematical sense of the term), but it is one with which we happily live.

to a greater or lesser degree by other animals). They all presuppose consciousness (taken both narrowly and widely), but they cannot sensibly be proffered as explanations of the 'evolutionary advantages of consciousness'. The idea that consciousness is needed in order that neonate brains should be able to build models of mother and her brain, and to incorporate models of other people's minds, is incoherent. Not only does this supposition misconceive the nature of consciousness, it ascribes to the brain powers that it makes no sense to attribute to it. For only human beings – not brains (or non-language-using creatures) – can *construct models* of anything, and use models to *predict events*. Furthermore, human babies are not in the business of constructing models of any kind – to do that, they must first master a language, and then learn a great deal of science. That a human baby, or for that matter a kitten, puppy or fledgling, reacts in certain standard ways to its parent, ways that are determined within hours of birth by various processes of 'imprinting', is an innate propensity, the evolutionary value of which is well understood. But there is no reason whatsoever to suppose that the neonate, let alone its *brain*, engages in any activity that can be dignified by the name of 'model building'. The innate neural propensities (about which we know virtually nothing) are the product of evolution and natural selection, but they do not involve building models of mother and her brain, let alone of other people's (or cats', dogs' or birds') minds. Wonderful, to be sure, these propensities are. A fledgling penguin, a flamingo, or a new-born seal can identify its mother's call amidst the hubbub of hundreds of thousands of similar calls – and that is truly remarkable. But it involves no model building by either the neonate or its brain. If we think otherwise, we need to reflect further on what is meant by 'a model' and what is involved in *using* a model in order to make predictions.

Reply to Humphrey Similarly incoherent is the idea that consciousness has evolved to enable animals to *develop a conceptual framework* that helps it *to model another animal's behaviour*. Only language-using creatures have anything that can be dignified by the name of a 'conceptual framework'. For a 'conceptual framework' is a web of logically connected concepts, the use of which is rule-governed, and the rules for the use of which are given by explanations of meaning. And that requires a language and highly complex linguistic abilities.[32] It is equally misguided to think that the evolution of consciousness was marked by a change in the brain that transformed an animal from one that 'simply "behaved"' into one that at the same time informed its mind of the reasons for its behaviour. For, first, the only animals that 'simply behave', and do not see or hear, smell or taste, are fairly lowly forms of life. But conscious beings, sentient

---

[32] Some philosophers conceive of concept possession as a linguistic capacity, i.e. the capacity to use words intelligently in accord with their meaning, and of concepts as abstractions from uses of words. Thus understood, it makes no sense to ascribe concept possession to mere animals. Other philosophers associate the notion of concept possession in its most primitive form with possession of mere recognitional capacities, and accordingly ascribe primitive forms of concept possession to animals that exhibit appropriate recognitional capacities in their behaviour. For present purposes it is not necessary to adjudicate the controversy, since in neither case does it make sense to ascribe to a non-language-using animal possession of a conceptual framework. We shall revert to this matter in the next chapter.

creatures with cognitive, affective and volitional powers, emerged in evolutionary development long before any animal could 'inform its mind of the reasons for its behaviour'.
Second, it is unclear what, if anything, is meant by an animal's 'informing its mind' about
anything. And third, the only creature that can both act for reasons and be aware of its
reasons for doing what it does, is man. And that ability, as we shall argue in the next
chapter, is essentially dependent upon the mastery of a language.

There is no doubt that only animals with complex brains and nervous systems, that have
developed perceptual powers and moderately well-developed affective ones, can evolve
complex forms of bonding and hence too the forms of social relations characteristic of
higher animals. But the emergence of sentient life surely long antecedes the emergence of
social animals, and indeed, animals dependent on parent–neonate bonding. There is no
reason to suppose, and many reasons not to suppose, that forms of fully sentient marine
life, not to mention dinosaurs, engaged in building models of their mother and her brain
in order to facilitate social interaction (in which they did not engage), or in developing a
conceptual framework (which they could not possibly have) to help them model another
animal's behaviour and to inform their minds (which they lacked) of the reasons for their
own behaviour (which was not done for reasons).

Reply to Penrose   Finally, Penrose's suggestion that the evolutionary advant-
                            age conferred by possession of consciousness concerns
the nonalgorithmic forming of judgements is, we suggest, greatly over-intellectualized. It
seems to us very unclear which, among the multitude of judgements that human beings
make, are correctly described as algorithmic and which as non-algorithmic. No doubt
non-conscious beings do not make judgements of any kind – neither algorithmic nor non-
algorithmic. But the idea that *the hallmark* of consciousness is non-algorithmic forming of
judgements cannot be right. For both intransitive and transitive consciousness, as well as
sensation, perception, affection and desire, emerged in evolutionary development long
before any creature was in the position to make *judgements* of *any* kind.

11.5 The Problem of Awareness

'The problem of awareness' accord-   A problem that has occasioned puzzlement among neuro-
ing to Johnson-Laird and Blakemore   scientists and cognitive scientists is sometimes characterized
                                          as 'the problem of awareness': namely, how are we to
account for the distinction between what one can and what one cannot be aware of?
Johnson-Laird remarks: 'There are some things that readily enter consciousness, whereas
others evidently cannot enter it. You can be aware of the contents of perception, that, for
example, you are reading words on this page, but you cannot be aware of the process of
perception – of the intricate chain of events that convert the retinal image into an
informative representation of the world.'[33] Blakemore similarly queries

---

[33] P. N. Johnson-Laird, 'How could consciousness arise from computations of the brain?', in
C. Blakemore and S. Greenfield (eds), *Mindwaves* (Blackwell, Oxford, 1987), p. 248. It should be
noted that there *is* no chain of events that *converts the retinal image into an informative representation of
the world*. To see an object is not to have a *representation* of anything.

Why does the inner eye see so little? It gives us only a tiny glimpse, and distorted at that, of the world within. Much of what our brains do is entirely hidden from consciousness. When you recognise a friend, you have not the slightest impression that billions of nerve cells have digested signals from your eyes and distilled them into the wisdom of perception . . . Most of the actions of the human mind are beyond the gaze of the inner eye of consciousness.[34]

Puzzled in this way, one might indeed think that 'There may be good evolutionary reasons why that should be so: if you see a tiger, it is best to take avoiding action, without reflecting on the process of perception. If the process were introspectible, it would evidently be slower since it could not depend on events happening in parallel and you might stop to check whether the tiger was illusory.'[35]

The problem is bogus, and the solution offered, misconceived

Put thus, the problem is a bogus one, and the solution misconceived. The neural events and processes that are causal conditions for one to perceive and that take place when one perceives something are not themselves perceptible to the perceiving agent. It is no more puzzling that he cannot be conscious of them than it is puzzling that he cannot be perceptually conscious now of yesterday's sunset, or perceptually conscious of features of the backside of the moon. It is a logical, not a causal, truth that one cannot be perceptually conscious of what is not perceptible to one. The *neural* processes that underlie perception are not 'the process of perception'. Seeing, glimpsing, spotting, discerning, noticing Daisy in the street or that she is in the room are not processes – for as soon as one sees Daisy, one has seen her, and as soon as one glimpses, spots, discerns or notices her, one has done so. Processes go on, can be interrupted before completed, and it makes sense to ask how far through the process one has got. But one cannot intelligibly be said to be half-way through the process of noticing someone, or three-quarters of the way through the process of glimpsing him or her. One can, to be sure, interrupt the *neural process* that needs to occur in order for one to spot, glimpse, discern or notice something or other; but if this happens, then the person or animal will *not* have spotted, glimpsed, discerned or noticed what they might otherwise have done. Not being processes, these perceptual achievements are obviously not processes of which one might become and then be conscious. On the other hand, in so far as watching, scrutinizing or gazing at something can be said to be processes, they are ones of which one may indeed become, and then be conscious of being, engaged in, if one realizes or is struck by the fact that one is so doing. But, of course, becoming conscious of the fact that one is gazing at Daisy is not to become conscious of a neural process, even though there are neural processes taking place, without which one could not be gazing at Daisy.

There is no such thing as an intro-spectible neural process for evolution to exclude

It is surely true that 'if you see a tiger, it is best to take rapid avoiding action', but not for evolutionary reasons pertaining to neural parallel processing. For it is mistaken

---

[34] C. Blakemore, *The Mind Machine* (BBC Publications, London, 1988), p. 14. See also Penrose: 'not all of the activity of the brain is directly accessible to consciousness' (*Emperor's New Mind*, p. 527).
[35] Johnson-Laird, 'How could consciousness arise', p. 248.

to suggest that 'if the process were introspectible, it would evidently be slower since it could not depend on events happening in parallel and you might stop to check whether the tiger was illusory'. There is no such thing as 'an introspectible (inwardly perceptible) neural process'. For introspection, as we have argued (§3.6), is not a form of perception (an 'inner perception'), but a form of reflection on one's feelings, motives, reasons, etc. In appropriate circumstances, it is perfectly possible to check whether what one apparently sees (the seemingly bent stick in water, or Macbeth's dagger) is illusory or a hallucination. And one's neural processes are not possible objects of perception, unless one is undergoing a brain scan and can see the scanner.

Brain activities are necessarily, not biologically, 'excluded from consciousness'   Finally, it is wrong that *much* of what our brains do is 'hidden from consciousness', for, neurological experiments apart (when the neuroscientist, scrutinizing a scanner, may be perceptually conscious of neural events), *all* of what our brains do is 'hidden from consciousness'. For our own brain states and events are not within our perceptual field, and they are not states of consciousness that might catch and hold our attention or occupy our thoughts, unlike our sensations, moods and emotions. It is equally confused to suggest that 'most of the actions of the human mind' are not within the domain of possible objects of consciousness. It is true, of course, that many of our feelings, moods, emotions, etc. do not catch our attention, and do not occupy our mind in reflection. And it is also true that there are unconscious feelings and passions. But what is unconscious can become conscious, and what does not catch our attention or occupy our thoughts is, in such cases, precisely what could become an object of consciousness.

11.6 Other Minds and Other Animals

Neuroscientists' conception of knowledge of other people's minds   The final problem we shall examine is not recognized by neuroscientists *as* a puzzle. On the contrary, it is a matter on which there is widespread consensus. Scientists generally agree that one knows that one is conscious and what state of conscious one is enjoying with complete certainty. But when it comes to our knowledge of the conscious states or experiences of other people, matters are more problematic. And concerning other animals and whether they are or are not conscious creatures, scepticism seems more difficult to rebut. According to Crick,

> Strictly speaking, each individual is certain only that he himself is conscious. For example, I know I am conscious. Because your appearance and your behaviour seem to me to be rather similar to mine, and in particular because you assure me that you are indeed conscious, I infer with a high degree of certainty that you too are conscious.[36]

Edelman similarly contends that qualia 'are experienced directly only by single individuals', and holds that this gives rise to a methodological difficulty. For, 'What is directly

---

[36] F. Crick, *The Astonishing Hypothesis* (Touchstone, London, 1995), p. 107.

experienced as qualia by one individual cannot be fully shared by another individual as an observer.' But, he suggests, the difficulty can be overcome if we '*assume* that, just as in ourselves, qualia exist in other conscious human beings'.[37] Inconsistently, he also contends that we know what consciousness is 'for ourselves but can only judge its existence in others by inductive inference'.[38] So, on the matter of our knowledge of 'the consciousness' of others, it is held that it is less certain than knowledge of 'our own consciousness', and that it is either an assumption, or rests upon an analogical or an inductive inference.

Scientists' conception of the probability of animal consciousness

Scientists are prone to be more hesitant with regard to other animals. Crick remarks, 'I am less certain that a monkey is conscious than that I am or you are, but I can reasonably assume that a monkey is not a total automaton.'[39] Similarly, Weiskrantz holds that 'In the absence of any verbal discourse with animals, and with the persistent lack of any criteria by which to make a judgement, we are thrown back on various deeply held intuitions and arguments derived from analogy with humans.'[40] And Baars suggests that 'Animals are very probably conscious', although, he writes, 'My sense is that the scientific community has now swung decisively in its favor [i.e. in favour of ascribing consciousness to animals].'[41] So: that animals are also conscious beings is only probable, and the judgement that they are is either an assumption, or rests on an analogical inference or on an intuition.

Their picture is Cartesian

The thought that I know, with complete certainty, that I am conscious, that I *infer*, with a lesser degree of certainty, or *assume*, that you are conscious (because you behave in similar ways to me, and above all, because you *tell me* that you are) and that I am uncertain whether monkeys are conscious, although I can reasonably *assume* that they are, is almost pure Cartesianism. Indeed, it differs from Cartesianism only in *assuming* that non-human animals are conscious; for Descartes thought that we could safely assume that they are not.[42] But this is misconceived.

---

[37] Edelman, *Bright Air, Brilliant Fire*, pp. 114f.

[38] Ibid., p. 111.

[39] Crick, *Astonishing Hypothesis*, p. 109.

[40] L. Weiskrantz, *Consciousness Lost and Found* (Oxford University Press, Oxford, 1997), pp. 77f.

[41] B. J. Baars, *In the Theater of Consciousness* (Oxford University Press, New York, 1997), pp. 32, 33.

[42] He did not think that it could be *proved* that animals are not conscious beings, but he did think that there were better reasons for supposing them not to be conscious than for supposing them to be so. In a letter to Henry More (5 Feb. 1649) he wrote, 'But though I regard it as established that we cannot prove there is any thought in animals, I do not think it is thereby proved that there is not, since the human mind does not reach into their hearts.' It is interesting that Crick thinks that the main grounds of our knowledge that other human beings are conscious is that they *tell us that they are*, i.e. can use language (and so inform us of something they know with certainty), and Weiskrantz holds that it is the absence of 'verbal discourse' with animals that throws us back on to analogical arguments and deeply held intuitions to support the assumption that animals are conscious beings. Descartes explained to More that the main reason for thinking that animals lack thought or consciousness is that 'it has never been observed that any brute animal reached the stage of using real speech, that is to say, of indicating by word or sign something pertaining to pure thought and not to natural impulse. Such speech is the only certain sign of thought hidden in a body.'

These scientists' conceptions are rooted in misconstruals of the concepts of behaviour and consciousness

Such views are rooted in the misguided conception of behaviour, on the one hand, and of consciousness, on the other, which is rife among neuroscientists (and philosophers from whom they draw encouragement). If we conceive of 'conscious experience' as private, as accessible only to its subject, directly known only by means of introspection, as constituted by qualia, and so forth, and if, in addition, we think of behaviour as bare bodily movement caused by neural events, then it is inevitable that we should think of the conscious experience of other people and of other animals in the received way. But it is evident that we should not conceive of matters thus.

That human beings are conscious creatures is a conceptual truth

It is a contingent truth that human beings and other higher animals exist. But that human beings and the higher animals are conscious creatures is not a contingent, but a conceptual, truth – just as it is a conceptual truth that material objects are three-dimensional space occupants that consist of matter of one kind or another. That I, here and now, am conscious, is indeed a contingent empirical truth, since I might have been asleep or unconscious (e.g. had I fallen asleep or been anaesthetized ten minutes ago and not yet awakened). But it is mistaken to represent this humble fact as an item of indubitable knowledge, or as something that I know on the basis of introspection, in virtue of observing my own consciousness or in virtue of being conscious of my consciousness.

The epistemological and logical peculiarities of 'I am conscious'

For, as we have argued (§9.2), there is no such thing as *observing, perceiving,* or *being conscious of* my own consciousness. One has, and can have, no grounds or evidence for claiming to be conscious. Indeed, one cannot *claim* to be conscious. One cannot say 'He claims to be conscious, but he is mistaken'; and to say to the nurse who is tiptoeing around the room 'I am conscious' is not to make a claim. Nor can it *seem* to one that one is conscious, for 'It seems to him that he is conscious, but he is mistaken' is nonsense. 'I am conscious' looks like, and is intended to be, an empirical assertion. But it has no intelligible negation that could be used assertorically ('I am not conscious'). To be sure, it admits of no doubt, but precisely because of that, it is not something that can be said to be certain. For an empirical proposition can be said to be certain only if one is in a position to exclude any possible doubt, but if there is *logically* no possibility of doubt, there is nothing for certainty to exclude. 'I am conscious' does not express something of which one might be ignorant, but, by the same token, it does not say anything that one can be said to know – for to ascribe knowledge to a person is to preclude possible ignorance, and here there is no possible ignorance to exclude. Invoked, in Cartesian fashion, to express an item of absolutely certain knowledge, it might be said not to be a proposition at all, or to be a degenerate proposition (in the sense in which a point is a degenerate case of a conic section). Of course, as we have seen, it has a respectable use, not to express an item of indubitable knowledge or to make a claim, but, for example, to signal to another person (e.g. the nurse) that one has regained consciousness after an operation.

To be sure, I can tell another person that I am conscious *of* something or other – for example, of the hostility of my audience or of the lateness of the hour. This is not only informative but, as we have seen, it is also an implicit knowledge claim. For if the audience is friendly and not hostile, then I was not conscious of their hostility – for to be thus conscious of something, as we have seen, is to know that things are as one is conscious of them as being. The knowledge, in which transitive perceptual consciousness consists, is knowledge received by way of having one's attention caught and held by something one perceives. One is not 'conscious of one's consciousness', but conscious of things being thus-and-so. And one knows that they are thus-and-so inasmuch as one perceives them to be so (§9.4).

Knowledge that others are conscious is typically direct, not inferred

The thought that I *infer* that other people around me are conscious on the basis of inductive or analogical inference, that I infer that they are conscious on the basis of their bare bodily movements, or that I *assume* that they are conscious, because they behave as I do when I am conscious, is equally misconceived. I can *see*, without any inference, that they are conscious. I can see that they are looking at this, that they are attending to that, that they are in pain or enjoying themselves; I can see the delight or grief on their faces, their excitement or boredom, their joy or anger.

Of course, I would *justify* my assertion that someone is in pain or enjoying himself, is delighted or grieving, by reference to his behaviour. If I were asked how I know that he is in pain, I should reply 'I saw him writhing in pain', and if asked how I know that he is enjoying himself, I should say 'I saw him joining in the fun with gusto'. But, first, the fact that I would *justify* my judgement thus does not show that I *inferred* it from the justifying evidence. For I do not reason: 'He is bleeding and groaning, there is a terrible grimace on his face; therefore he is, in all probability, in pain.' Nor is my judgement arrived at by means of an 'unconscious inference'. Rather, I recognize immediately and without any inference that the man is in agony.

The behaviour that justifies judgements about others' mental states is not 'bare bodily movement'

Secondly, the behaviour by reference to which one would justify such judgements does not consist of 'bare bodily movements', as the behaviourists suggested, but of groans of pain, chortles of delight, tears of grief. We describe such behaviour in terms of the rich vocabulary of psychology, and would be hard put to describe it in terms of bare movements. (Try describing the difference between a smile of contempt, of amusement, of embarrassment, a cruel or kind smile, etc. in terms of the muscular movements. But none of us has any difficulty in recognizing such smiles in context.) There is nothing odd or unusual about this. We have the ability to recognize a pattern of behaviour in certain circumstances *in psychological terms* – that is, *as* a groan of pain, a laugh of joy, a sigh of relief. There is nothing more odd about this capacity than there is about our general capacity to recognize faces immediately and non-inferentially. And, indeed, our ability to recognize behaviour as pain-behaviour or as behaviour of joy or affection is intimately related to our general capacity for facial recognition. For it involves, among other things, a sensitivity to, and recognitional capacity for, facial expression. Both powers have an evident evolutionary pay-off.

Judgements about others' states of mind do not rest on inductive or analogical inference

Thirdly, our judgements about others cannot rest on inductive inference. For inductive inference presupposes non-inductive identification of the relata antecedently found to be systematically correlated. It is because phenomenon

A has always been found to be correlated with phenomenon B that one is now warranted in inferring from the occurrence of an instance of A the occurrence of an instance of B. But I obviously cannot identify another person's pain or joy, anxiety or good cheer, *independently of his behaviour*, and find that such-and-such behaviour is well correlated with his pain or joy, etc. Rather, I am supposed to have noted that when *I* am in pain (etc.), then I always behave thus-and-so, and then to reason that since others behave likewise in circumstances of injury, they too are very likely in pain (etc.). But that presupposes (i) that I *identify* my pain, and then correlate it with my behaviour, and (ii) that I extrapolate from my own case. However, that is incoherent.

In avowing and reporting my own pain, neither identification nor criteria of identity are involved

For, first, I do not *identify* my pain (if I did, I might *misidentify* it – and that makes no sense). I employ *no* criteria of identity in sincerely avowing that I have a pain – I just have a pain and say so. But my ability to avow that I am in pain without any criterion of identity presupposes my mastery of the common, public, concept of pain, including the behavioural (non-inductive) criteria that justify ascribing pain to others. These are, as we have argued, two sides of one and the same conceptual coin. So not only do I not extrapolate from my own case when I ascribe pain to others, but rather, for there to *be* any 'my own case' (i.e. for me to be able to employ the concept of pain in saying that I am in pain or in thinking that since I am in pain I had better take an aspirin), I must possess the *concept* of pain. And to possess the concept of pain, I must already know under what circumstances I am warranted in ascribing pain to others – that is, I must know the criteria for ascribing pain to others; – namely, their pain-behaviour in appropriate circumstances. But these behavioural criteria are not inductive evidence, but *logically* good evidence – which is partly *constitutive* of the concept of pain. So I have no need for *inductive* evidence in order to be able to ascribe pain to others. And if I did need inductive evidence, I could not have it, since I would not possess the concept of pain at all, and would not even be in a position to say that *I* am in pain whenever I am.

An analogical inference would pre-suppose identification in my own case

Secondly, were I required to extrapolate from my own case, what could warrant such an irresponsible extrapolation from one single case? So the putative inference cannot be inductive. Nor could it be an *analogical* inference? Do I infer that others are having a certain experience from their behaviour by *analogy* with my own case? This would, of course, make such alleged inferences much weaker than inductive ones. But, again, the supposition is not coherent. For just as with the putative inductive inference, the supposition of an analogical inference presupposes that in my own case I identify my own pain (or joy, depression, excitement, etc.) by using the concept of pain (joy, depression, excitement, etc.) *independently of its nexus with the public criteria that warrant its ascription to others*. But this means that I would have to have a criterion of identity to warrant its application to myself. But I have none. And the only way in which I could have one would be if I had a private mental sample of pain (joy, depression, excitement, etc.) against which to check the application of the concept to myself. But that, as we have argued (§3.9), is wholly incoherent, for there can be no such thing as a private mental sample which functions as a standard for the correct application of a word.

It is not an assumption that other people are conscious

Is it then an *assumption* that others are conscious beings, that they have experiences as I do? No, that too makes no sense. Were it an assumption that they are conscious, then it might be mistaken (as one might assume, and be mistaken, that a patient is conscious when he stirs after an anaesthetic and mutters something). But could *anything* count as showing that we are *mistaken* to take our fellow human beings, behaving as they normally do in the stream of life, to be conscious? When we see another person sorely injured and screaming in pain, do we *assume* that they are in pain? Is it a *hypothesis*? What more would we want, and what more could we have, to *confirm* this alleged assumption or hypothesis? *More* screams of agony?

The thought that we know that other human beings are conscious, and that they have 'conscious experience' and are in 'conscious mental states', on the basis of an inference, inductive or analogical, or on the basis of an assumption, betrays the extent to which we are mesmerized by a misconceived picture, and manifests the manner in which we can become entangled in the network of concepts which, in our daily lives, we employ unproblematically.

Reaction and response to others precedes thought

We should remind ourselves of some platitudes. We *react* to the manifest 'experiences' of others, to their manifest anger and grief, their pain and joy, their amusement and excitement, *instinctively* – long before we are in a position to draw *inferences* from their behaviour, to make *analogical inferences* from our own case, or to make sophisticated *assumptions*. A small child responds with fear to a display of parental anger, smiles with delight in reaction to its mother's loving smiles and gentle laughter, displays immediate unthinking anxiety in response to its mother's tears. These natural, instinctive reactions are the foundations upon which the gradual acquisition of psychological concepts rests. And mastery of the use of these concepts in the first-person case (which involves no evidence and no criteria of identity) is not detachable from the mastery of their use in the third-person case (which involves recognition of the behavioural criteria, which constitute *logically* good evidence for their ascription to others). The idea that the neonate, or its brain, has to 'construct' a model of its mother's mind (or brain) in order for it to 'predict' its mother's responses and behaviour is an absurdity which is part and parcel of a gross over-intellectualization of human behaviour, of human empathetic and instinctive responses, and of the roots of language.

It is neither an assumption nor a hypothesis that other animals are conscious beings

What applies to ascription of consciousness and conscious experience to other human beings applies no less to parallel ascriptions to the higher animals. It is not 'a reasonable assumption' or merely 'very probable' that monkeys, behaving as waking monkeys do, are conscious. After all, they are not asleep or unconscious. Do they not visibly see things? Are they not playful or angry? Do they not want things and try to get them? Indeed, are they not *conscious of* things in their vicinity (the food being brought to them at feeding time) and *not conscious of* other things (of another monkey creeping up behind them to snatch their banana)? This is no *assumption*, and there is nothing uncertain about it. Nor do we need the scientific community to swing decisively in favour of any such assumption in order to know perfectly well, as we do, that such animals are conscious beings. We can see the pleasure a dog takes in playing with a stick in the park with its master, as we can see its joy when it rushes to its returning master, wagging its tail and barking with excitement. So, too, we know perfectly well that the purring cat enjoys being stroked, and it is no less obvious that it is angry and threatening when it spits and raises its fur.

Knowledge that other animals are conscious is not analogical

Our knowledge that the higher animals are conscious beings is not based on an *analogy* with us, any more than our knowledge that human babies are conscious beings, feel pain, perceive, are angry or pleased at this or that, is actually mere belief based on a shaky analogical argument from our own case. Human babies and animals alike satisfy the behavioural criteria for having sensations, for seeing and hearing, for feeling anger, fear and distress. It is visible that they are conscious and enjoy or suffer perceptual and affective experience. We see that they do, and can justify our ascriptions of such experiences to them by reference to the behavioural criteria which they exemplify – not on the basis of an analogy with our own case.

12

Self-Consciousness

12.1 Self-Consciousness and the Self

Self-consciousness in the philosophical sense

We have examined many conceptual features of consciousness, variously understood. But we have deferred thus far any investigation of the idea of self-consciousness. This thorny topic has preoccupied psychologists, cognitive scientists and neuroscientists for well over a century. It has an even longer philosophical pedigree. The concern is with what we previously called *the philosophical sense* of 'self-consciousness', as distinct from the common or garden variety pertaining to embarrassment and from the deliberative sense in which we say of an artist or author that he is a highly self-conscious, reflective craftsman. It is related to the sense of 'self-consciousness' in which we ascribe self-consciousness to an introspective person – that is, to a person who tends to reflect on his motives or reasons, on his likes and dislikes, on his character traits and his relationships with others. Such a person is prone frequently to exercise a power which normal users of a developed language necessarily possess, but exercise relatively infrequently. To say that human beings are self-conscious creatures is not to suggest that we are all constitutionally introspective in the manner of a Proust. Rather, it is to say that we have the ability (mostly to a much lesser degree and with far less skill and refinement than Proust) so to reflect, as well as the more common ability, of which the former is a special case, to take into account, in our reasoning and behaviour, facts about ourselves, our experiences, past and present, and our character traits and dispositions. For we, unlike other animals, can be aware of the fact that we are feeling cheerful or depressed, that we are ignorant or well informed about some subject, that we have certain beliefs or doubts, that we have certain character traits and dispositions, that we have done and undergone various things in the past. Such facts about ourselves, of which we are cognizant, may weigh with us in our deliberations and occupy us in our reflections; they may be *our reasons* for acting, feeling or thinking thus-and-so here and now. They may be premises in our reasoning and our justifications for our actions and reactions. This is partly constitutive of our being self-conscious creatures.

Self-consciousness and 'the self'

Deep conceptual confusions bedevil the debate about the nature of self-consciousness. For philosophers and non-philosophers alike are prone to construe self-consciousness as consciousness of something they call a 'self', an 'I' or an 'Ego'. This entity is supposedly possessed by each person who is said to *have* a self – I have *my* self, and you have *your* self. My self is thought to be something 'in me', of which I can become aware or of which I am allegedly constantly aware. But when philosophers and psychologists have tried to pin down this curious entity, they have found it singularly elusive. And recent efforts by neuroscientists to shed light on the matter have been equally unsuccessful – or so we shall argue. This is not surprising, for, as we shall show, the 'self' or the 'I' (thus conceived) is a fiction generated by conceptual confusions. There is indeed such a thing as self-consciousness in the philosophical sense of the term, but it is not consciousness of a 'self'. It is a distinctively human capacity for reflexive thought and knowledge, wholly dependent upon possession of a language.

Before examining recent scientific reflections on this vexed subject, a brief survey of the roots of the philosophical tradition is appropriate. For many of the confusions of neuroscientists, cognitive scientists and psychologists recapitulate the errors of past philosophers.

12.2 Historical Stage Setting: Descartes, Locke, Hume and James

The Cartesian ego as an immaterial substance

From Descartes onwards, philosophers have been much concerned with trying to elucidate the nature of the subject of experience. Descartes argued correctly that a thought cannot exist without a thinking thing – a substance (a persistent entity that is the bearer of attributes) in which to inhere. Awareness of his own thoughts, he claimed, proved his existence as a substance, which is named or signified by the word 'I'. But what this 'I' is must be investigated, since 'I must be on my guard against carelessly taking something else to be this "I" and so making a mistake in the very item of knowledge that I maintain is the most certain and evident of all'.[1] For while he could, he thought, doubt whether the material world exists, and hence too whether his body exists, 'I cannot doubt whether I exist', for in order for doubting to occur, there must be some thing that is doing the doubting. And he concluded that 'this "I" – that is the soul by which I am what I am – is entirely distinct from the body'.[2] It is, he held, an immaterial thinking substance, intimately conjoined with, but distinct from, the body.

The ungrammaticality of 'the "I"'

We should note immediately that the phrase '*this* "I"' is as ungrammatical as 'this "he" (this "she" or "it")', or 'this "now" (this "here" or "there")'. A similar grammatical aberration is produced in speaking, as so many do, of '*the* "I"' (compare 'the "he"', 'the "you"', 'the "she"' or 'the "it"'). And matters are only apparently improved by switching to Latin, and speaking of 'the Ego'.

Three difficulties for the Cartesian doctrine

The idea that 'the "I"' is an immaterial substance presents insuperable problems. We shall briefly mention three salient ones.

---

[1] Descartes, 'Second Meditation', in *Meditations on First Philosophy*, AT VII, 175f.
[2] Descartes, *Discourse on Method*, AT VI, 33.

The first-person pronoun is not referentially ambiguous

First, it implausibly suggests that the first-person pronoun in ordinary usage is systematically ambiguous, sometimes referring 'correctly' to the immaterial substance that I allegedly am (e.g. in the sentence 'I am thinking of Daisy'), and sometimes confusingly to my body (e.g. in 'I am 6 foot tall', which is, on this account, more accurately or explicitly stated by 'My body is 6 foot tall'). Hence, in such sentences of ordinary language as 'I intentionally lay down', there must be an implicit double reference which requires disambiguation: namely, that the spiritual substance (the 'I') intended that its body lie down, and consequently that the material substance that is its body lay down. By parity of reasoning, and equally implausibly, all verbs that apply to human beings must be, or be analysable into, either verbs that apply to mere material bodies (e.g. verbs of motion) or verbs that apply only to the mind.

The intelligibility of interaction is questionable

Secondly, the interaction between the immaterial substance and the body with which it is conjoined presented insoluble difficulties (some of which were already raised by Aristotle in his criticisms of Platonic dualism). For Descartes was not able to give any account of how an immaterial thinking substance could causally interact with – in particular, produce or direct motion in – the material body. He held that the point of contact between the two substances was the pineal gland in the brain, which, as we have noted (§1.2), he wrongly thought to be suspended in the animal spirits within the anterior ventricle. But the problem of the intelligibility of causal interaction between an immaterial substance and the material body is not resolved by the explanation that the immaterial substance interacts with only one part of the material body.

There are no adequate criteria of identity for immaterial substances

Thirdly, Descartes provided no criteria for identifying a particular spiritual substance and differentiating it from other spiritual substances of the same general kind, or for re-identifying that particular spiritual substance as the same again on a subsequent occasion. So there could be no way to establish that there is one spiritual substance 'in me', as opposed to a thousand different ones all thinking exactly the same thoughts; or that there is one continuous spiritual substance 'in me', as opposed to a different spiritual substance each morning to whom the previous one had passed on all its memories (as one billiard ball passes on its momentum to the next one in line which it hits).

The Cartesian route to the Ego was epistemological

The Cartesian route to 'the "I"' or 'the Ego' was epistemological – that is, by way of considerations pertaining to knowledge, doubt and certainty. For the proof of the existence of 'the "I"' turned on the distinction between what can and what cannot be doubted, and the proof that I am essentially a thinking thing, a *res cogitans*, turned on the idea that I can know for certain that I think, but cannot know for certain that I have a body.

The Lockean route to 'the self' was psychological

A generation later John Locke took a different route to an equally deep misconception of the nature of the subject of experience. Locke's route to 'the self' was psychological rather than epistemological. For his conception of the self arose not from reflections upon what can be known indubitably (viz. one's own thoughts and one's existence as a thinking thing) but from reflection upon introspection, misconceived as a form of perception. He argued that it is 'impossible for anyone to perceive without perceiving that he does perceive. When we see, hear, smell, taste, feel, meditate or will anything, we know that we do so . . . by this everyone is to himself that which he calls *self*.'[3] It is our consciousness of our own experiences that 'makes everyone to be what he calls *self*, and thereby distinguishes himself from all other thinking things'.[4] Indeed, 'it is by the consciousness it has of its present Thoughts and Actions, that it is *self* to it *self* now, and so will be the same *self* as far as the same consciousness can extend to actions past or to come'.[5] It is note-worthy that this use of 'self' as a noun, apparently signifying a persistent entity of a certain kind, was an innovation in philosophy, and, as we shall argue below, an aberration. Unlike Descartes, Locke did not think that a 'self' is a *thinking substance*, but only that it is 'annexed' to a substance (material or immaterial), which may change without the 'self' changing. For if I 'have the same consciousness' that I did such-and-such in the past as that I am writing now,

> I could no more doubt that I . . . was the same self, place that *self* in what Substance you please, than that I that write this am the same *my self* now whilst I write (whether I consist of all the same Substance, material or immaterial, or no) that I was Yesterday. For as to the point of being the same *self*, it matters not whether this present *self* be made up of the same or other *Substances*.[6]

The Humean challenge

Hume challenged the Lockean idea that one is intro-spectively aware of a 'self'. In what is one of the most famous passages in the whole of philosophy, he wrote:

> When I enter most intimately into what I call *myself*, I always stumble on some particular perception or other, of heat or cold, light or shade, love or hatred, pain or pleasure. I never catch *myself* at any time without a perception, and can never observe anything but the perception . . . If anyone upon serious and unprejudic'd reflexion, thinks he has a different notion of *himself* I must confess I can reason no longer with him. . . . He may, perhaps, perceive something simple and continu'd, which he calls *himself*; tho' I am certain there is no such principle in me.[7]

It is noteworthy that Hume's search for a 'self' within himself was no more a genuine search than is a search for the East Pole. For one can search for something only in so far as one has a conception of what would count as finding it (even if one does not succeed). One can search for Eldorado, where the streets are paved with gold, but neither for the East Pole, nor, by means of what one (mis)conceives to be introspection, for a 'self'. For we have no idea what would count as thus coming across a self.

James on 'the self'

Descartes's conception of the self as an immaterial sub-stance is now rightly rejected by most philosophers, and

---

[3] Locke, *An Essay Concerning Human Understanding*, II. xxvii. 9.
[4] Ibid.
[5] Ibid., II. xxvii. 10.
[6] Ibid., II. xxvii. 16.
[7] Hume, *Treatise of Human Nature*, I. iv. 6.

finds little favour with most scientists. But his misconceived talk of 'the "I"' has not been rejected. Locke's psychological, introspective route to 'the self', and his confused talk of 'the self', despite Hume's criticisms, remained, and still remain, popular. So, for example, William James, at the end of the nineteenth century, mindful of Hume's strictures, nevertheless argued that when we reflectively 'think of subjectivity as such, . . . *think of ourselves as thinkers*', then we find, within the stream of consciousness,

> a *certain portion of the stream abstracted from the rest* is so identified in an altogether peculiar degree, and is felt by all men as a sort of innermost citadel within the circle, of sanctuary within the citadel, constituted by the subjective life as a whole. Compared with this element of the stream, the other parts, even of the subjective life, seem transient external possessions, of which each in turn can be disowned, whilst that which disowns them remains.[8]

He called this 'the self of all the other selves', and tried to investigate what it consists in. It is, he claimed, 'the *active* element in consciousness'; 'it presides over the perception of sensations, and by giving or withholding its assent it influences the movements they tend to arouse', 'it is the source of effort and attention, and the place from which appear to emanate the fiats of the will'. This central part of the Self, he claimed, is *felt*. 'It is something with which we have direct sensible acquaintance, and which is as fully present at any moment of consciousness in which it *is* present, as in a whole lifetime of such moments. . . . when it is found, it is *felt*.' What, then, is this *feeling* of the self? The result of James's introspective investigation was that '*the "Self of selves", when carefully examined, is found to consist mainly of the collection of . . . peculiar motions in the head or between the head and the throat*'.[9] This should have been viewed as a *reductio ad absurdum* of an 'inner' search for a 'self', but it was not – and the search continues among neuroscientists.[10]

---

[8] W. James, *The Principles of Psychology* (Holt, New York, 1890), vol. i, p. 297.

[9] Ibid., p. 301. Interestingly, Wundt, whom James quotes (p. 303n.), reached very similar conclusions in his *Physiologische Psychologie*. In his view, 'the images of feelings we get from our own body, and the representations of our own movements, distinguish themselves from all others by forming a *permanent* group. . . . This permanent sense, moreover, has this peculiarity, that we are aware of our power at any moment voluntarily to arouse any of its ingredients. . . . So we come to conceive this permanent mass of feeling as immediately or remotely subject to our will, and call it the *consciousness of ourself*. This self-consciousness is, at the outset, thoroughly sensational, . . . only gradually [does] its subjection to our will attain predominance. . . . This consciousness, contracted down to the process of apperception, we call our Ego.'

[10] It is disturbing to find an eminent cognitive neuroscientist such as Baars suggesting that 'James's thinking is fully up to date, and it is embarrassing but true that much of the time he is still ahead of the scientific community' (B. J. Baars, *In the Theater of Consciousness* (Oxford University Press, New York, 1997), p. 16.). Similarly, Edelman remarks approvingly that James's 'thoughts on consciousness – that it is a process not a substance; that it is personal and reflects intentionality – shape much of our modern view of the subject' (G. Edelman, *Bright Air, Brilliant Fire – on the Matter of the Mind*, (Penguin, Harmondsworth, 1994), p. 216). We agree that it is embarrassing but true that James's misconceptions shape much of the modern neuroscientific view of consciousness. Interestingly, Wittgenstein held James's writings to be a rich source for philosophical confusions about psychology

The confusions survive in the reflections of neuroscientists

That this centuries-long debate involved profound confusions would be of interest primarily to historians of ideas and philosophers but for the fact that similar confusions are currently to be found among the reflections on the nature of self-consciousness by neuroscientists and others who engage with the problems of consciousness.

12.3 Current Scientific and Neuroscientific Reflections on the Nature of Self-Consciousness

Other animals are conscious, but human beings are self-conscious

Scientists and neuroscientists who are currently investigating the nature of consciousness and its underlying neural conditions are unavoidably forced to consider the nature of self-consciousness. For, despite occasional demurs, there can be no good reason for thinking that animals are not conscious beings, or that they do not enjoy states of consciousness, or that they cannot be transitively conscious of things. They have sensations, feel thirst and hunger, and have perceptual and affective experiences. Most of the experimental work on the neural underpinnings of perceptual experience is done on animals other than humans; so much of what we know about the neural basis of perception, and of consciousness broadly conceived, is derived from work on animals. This makes it all the more ironic that so many scientists think that it is only *probable* that animals are conscious. For if so, then it is also only *probable* that the neural underpinnings of consciousness are as these scientists take themselves to have discovered them to be – by their research on animals. Nevertheless, most people, including scientists, are rightly inclined to argue that there is something distinctive about human experience. Mere animals are *conscious* creatures, but humans are *self-conscious* beings. They not only see and hear, feel pleasure and pain, are cheerful or depressed, may think of this or that, but they are or may also be conscious of so doing or being. They can reflect on the fact that they are enjoying something, can think about their emotions and dispositions, can be aware of the fact that they are taking pleasure in this or that and reflect on it. So neuroscientists distinguish between 'core consciousness' and 'extended consciousness'[11] (the latter being what 'provides an organism with an elaborate sense of self'), or between 'primary consciousness' and 'higher-order consciousness'[12] (the latter being what enables human

---

(MS 124, p. 291; MS number in the von Wright catalogue: G. H. von Wright, *Wittgenstein* (Blackwell, Oxford, 1982). James, Wittgenstein wrote in his notebook, claimed that psychology is a science, yet hardly discusses any scientific questions. His moves are just so many attempts to free himself from the metaphysical spider's web in which he is caught. 'He cannot yet walk, or fly at all', Wittgenstein remarked, 'he only wriggles' (MS 165, pp. 150f.). This was no bombast: for details of his devastating criticisms of James's conceptions, see P. M. S. Hacker, *idem*, *Wittgenstein: Meaning and Mind* (Blackwell, Oxford, 1990), and *Wittgenstein: Mind and Will* (Blackwell, Oxford, 1996), in the indexes, under 'James'.

[11] A. Damasio, *The Feeling of What Happens* (Heinemann, London, 1999), p. 16.
[12] Edelman, *Bright Air, Brilliant Fire*, p. 124.

beings 'to construct a socially-based selfhood, to model the world in terms of the past and the future').

Damasio's conception of self-consciousness

Damasio holds that the neurobiology of consciousness faces two fundamental general problems: 'the problem of how the movie-in-the-brain is generated, and the problem of how the brain also generates the sense that there is an owner and observer for that movie'.[13] Extended consciousness, as he calls it, 'provides the organism with an elaborate sense of self'. Analogously to Locke, Damasio believes that besides the 'images of what we perceive externally', there is also 'this other presence that signifies you, as observer of the things imaged, potential actor on the things imaged. There is a presence of you in a particular relationship with some object. If there were no such presence, how would your thoughts belong to you?' And, like James, he holds that the self is a feeling: 'the simplest form of such a presence is also an image, actually the kind of image that constitutes a feeling. In that perspective, the presence of you is the feeling of what happens when your being is modified by the acts of apprehending something. The presence never quits, from the moment of awakening to the moment sleep begins. The presence must be there or there is no you.'[14]

Humphrey's conception of self-consciousness

A less Jamesian, perhaps more Lockean, view is defended by Humphrey. When he reflects on his own behaviour, he suggests,

I become aware not only of external facts about my actions, but of a conscious presence, 'I', which 'wills' those actions. This 'I' has *reasons* for the things it wills. The reasons are kinds of 'feeling' – 'sensations', 'emotions', 'memories', 'desires'. 'I' want to eat because 'I' am hungry, 'I' intend to go to bed because 'I' am tired . . . when I come to the task of modelling the behaviour of another man, I naturally assume that he operates on the same principles as I do. I assume that within him too there is a conscious 'I', and that his 'I' has feelings.[15]

Blakemore's conception of 'the "I" ' in him

A very different line of attack is assayed by other scientists. Blakemore holds that the brain is a model-building machine, but that most of its modelling goes on without our knowledge.

One model, however, often comes into the view of the conscious mind. That is the model of the mind itself. The very act of being conscious, particularly self-conscious, implies that the brain has the capacity to construct a model of the person to whom the brain belongs, and to fit this mental puppet into the theatre of the mind – a world of other people, sharing the same kinds of minds and intentions. . . . [This is] . . . the domain of self-awareness.[16]

[13] Damasio, *Feeling of What Happens*, p. 11.
[14] Ibid., p. 10.
[15] N. Humphrey, *Consciousness Regained* (Oxford University Press, Oxford, 1984), p. 33.
[16] C. Blakemore, *The Mind Machine* (BBC Publications, London, 1988), p. 249.

Rejecting Cartesianism, Blakemore believes 'that the "I" in me is the operation of a mind, which is itself the operation of a brain, constructed solely by genes and environment. I find that notion just as wonderful as, and in many ways more satisfying than, the empty illusion of a spiritual self.'[17]

Blakemore's conception of self-consciousness

It is unclear what Blakemore means by the claim that the mind possesses, or occasionally has in view, *a model* of itself. It is equally unclear what he means by claiming differently in the next sentence that the brain constructs a model not of the mind but *of the person* to whom the brain belongs and that it 'fits this mental puppet into the theatre of the mind'. Does he, like Descartes, think that a person *is* a mind? However, it is clear that Blakemore thinks that the reflexivity involved in self-consciousness implies that the agent has in mind (or 'in his mind') a model of himself. It remains unclear what is meant here by 'a model', but it seems evident that in order for a person to be able to think 'I am too idle, I must work harder', 'I used to be more tolerant', 'I have a tendency to give up too easily', or 'My thoughts are confused', he needs no mental puppets in mental theatres, but only mastery of the first-person pronoun, and of other linguistic devices involved in self-ascriptive predications (of, for example, thought, experience (both present and past), character traits and abilities, of motives, attitudes and dispositions).

Johnson-Laird's conception of self-consciousness

The idea that the mind or brain (or 'mind/brain') constructs models or representations has been popular since the writings of the Cambridge psychologist Kenneth Craik and the great mathematician Alan Turing in the middle of the last century. It is in that tradition that Johnson-Laird contends that 'self-reflection . . . requires access to a particular mental representation – a representation that to some extent enables a processing system to understand itself'. So, on the unclear assumption that the mind is a 'processing system', 'our self-reflection . . . depends . . . on a *mental model* . . . What makes a model a *model* is that it can be used by an interpretative system.' Thinking of this in computational terms has, he admits, a 'whiff of paradox' about it, for

> one of the operating system's options is to use its model of itself in tackling a problem, and this option in turn must be included in the model too. The circle is not vicious, but leads to a special mode of processing that is crucial for self-reflection and self-awareness. It consists in the operating system calling for the construction of a model of its own operations, which it uses to guide its processes. This 'self-reflective' procedure can be applied to its own output so that the system can construct a model of its own use of such models, and so on, in a series of ever-ascending levels of representation.[18]

All this, to be sure, is not fact but abstract speculation – an extended metaphor derived from computer science, the extension of which to human psychology is wholly unclear. However, Johnson-Laird contends that as a hypothesis about the nature of human self-consciousness, it is corroborated by observations about conscious experience. 'You do

---

[17] Ibid., p. 272.
[18] P. N. Johnson-Laird, *The Computer and the Mind* (Fontana, London, 1988), p. 361.

indeed have a capacity to reflect upon what you are doing – at a higher level than actual performance – and as a result of this reflection to modify your performance.'[19]

Doubts about the brain's constructing models that make self-reflection possible

We agree that any normal human being can do so. But we deny that this gives any confirmation whatsoever to the hypothesis that either the mind or the brain constructs a model of its own operations, which makes self-reflection possible. In order for a person, a living human being, to reflect on his own thoughts, or on his own state of mind, he does not need a 'model' of his mind, but only normal mastery of a language and normal human capacities. Reflexive thought requires mastery of the linguistic devices of first-person predications, but not models designed for the use of an 'interpretative system'.

12.4 The Illusion of a 'Self'

The self as identical with me, as something I have, and as something in me

The 'self', as understood in the philosophical tradition emanating from Descartes and Locke, and as conceived by some contemporary neuroscientists, is supposed to be the permanent subject of successive states of consciousness and conscious experiences. If there were no self, then, Damasio observes, how could my thoughts and conscious experiences *belong* to me? However, the self that I am is not supposed to be identical with the flesh-and-blood human being with which all my friends are acquainted. It is instead an entity with which only *I* am directly acquainted, an entity of which I am aware in introspection. I am supposed to be identical with my self. As long as my self continues to exist, I continue to exist, and if my self ceases to exist, I cease to exist. If there were no such 'presence', no self, then, Damasio claims, there would be no me. However, a self is also supposed to be something that I *have*. For such writers speak of *my* self, of *your* self, and of the selves *of* other people. But it is unclear how I can be identical with something that I have. For if *I* have *it*, who is the owner of this self? And what is the relation between the self and its owner? On the other hand, the self is also supposed to be something that is *in* me. For the self, Humphrey suggests, is a conscious presence within me, and he assumes that 'within' other people too there is a conscious 'I'. And Blakemore holds that there is an 'I' within *him*. But it is equally unclear how I can be identical with something that is *within* me, for that would be tantamount to claiming that a whole is identical with some constituent part of itself. For since the pronoun 'me' is nothing more than a form of the pronoun 'I', the contention that I am identical with something that is in me amounts to the claim that I am not identical with myself, but with some part of myself.

The incoherence of this notion of a 'self'

This notion of a 'self' is an aberration. There is no such thing as a 'self' construed thus, and the putative concept of a 'self' thus construed is incoherent. One source of

[19] Ibid., p. 362.

the confusion stems from inserting a space in the reflexive pronouns 'myself', 'yourself', 'ourselves' to yield the aberrant expressions 'my self', 'your self' and 'our selves'. Having opened up an illicit space, we then fall into it. For now it seems as if we have discovered a mysterious object, a self, whose nature must be investigated. So we proceed to ask what this self is. But the question 'What sort of entity is a self?' makes no sense. It is as if, noting that we can do things for Jack's sake or for Jill's sake and that we can ask others to do things for our own sake, we were to go on to ask: 'What is a *sake*?' That is patently absurd, even though the space between the possessive nominal and the word 'sake' *is* licit. It is even more inexcusable in the case of 'myself' or 'yourself', where English spelling excludes a space. To speak of myself is not to speak of a self which I have, but simply to speak of the human being that I am. To say that I was thinking of myself is not to say that I was thinking of my *self*, but that I was thinking of me, *this* human being, familiar to all my friends.

The first-person pronoun does not refer to a self or Ego

It is similarly misconceived to imagine that the first-person pronoun is the name of some entity *within* me, or *owned* by me, with which I am directly and intimately acquainted. If one thinks thus, one will be prone, as so many are, to speak of this entity as 'an "I"' and to suggest that each person has one of these things. It should be striking that those who succumb to these temptations surround the pronoun with quotation marks – being dimly aware that there is something awry. The quotation marks are the silent tribute that ungrammaticality pays to grammar. As we noted above, talk of 'the Ego' only *appears* to be grammatically more correct than talk of 'the "I"'. But the pronoun 'I' is not a *name* of anything, any more than is 'he' or 'it'. It is a *pro*noun, and the noun for which it goes proxy is, for example, a proper name – for example, 'Jack', the proper name of a *human being*, not of some mysterious entity *within* a human being. When I introduce myself by saying 'I am Jack', I am not referring to my Ego and saying that my Ego is Jack. The role of the first-person pronoun is not to refer to a self or Ego. When I announce that I am going to London, I am not making observations about a mysterious inner entity which is about to depart for London, and when I say that I have a headache, I am not saying that my Ego has a headache, but that I do. And if I, Jack, say so, others are now in a position to say that Jack is going to London or has a headache, not that Jack's Ego or self is going to London or has a headache. When I say 'I was in London yesterday' I am, to be sure, speaking of myself, but not of my self.[20]

The illusion of an inner entity

Having conjured a pseudo-entity into existence, we are then tempted to try to identify and characterize it. And since we misguidedly think that it is *in* us, we are prone to think that introspection, conceived as a form of 'inner sense', will disclose its nature. Hence, like James, Wundt and

---

[20] If someone were nevertheless to insist that while talking thus with the vulgar, we must think with the learned, and that our ordinary ways of talking are merely a confused shorthand for speaking of the real self 'within', we should challenge him, as we challenge Descartes. We must ask him to explain what a 'self' is, what the criteria are for identifying a specific self and distinguishing it from other such objects, and also what the criteria are for identifying one of these objects as the same again on a subsequent encounter, and so forth (see above §12.2).

Damasio, we may think that this 'I' or 'self' is special feeling, with which each person is intimately acquainted, a conscious 'presence', as both Damasio and Humphrey suppose, or an 'operation of the mind', which is itself an 'operation of the brain', as Blakemore supposes. But this is an illusion, produced, *inter alia*, by grammatical confusion. And the subject of experience, properly conceived, is not an entity denominated 'the "I"' or 'the self', but the living human being.

The subject of experience is not an owner of experience or a 'self', but a human being

It is perfectly correct to claim that there can be no experience without a subject, that there are no thoughts which are not someone's thoughts, no pains which are not someone's pains. But, first, the *subject* of thought and experience is not the *owner* of thought and experience. And second, the subject of thought and experience is the human being, the living animal – not a 'self' or an 'I'. We are inclined to think otherwise, since in order to assert that we are thinking a certain thought or having a certain experience, we do not first have to check to see *who* is thinking the thought or having the experience – and we do not have to see what we say before we can find out what we think or to observe our behaviour to find out that we are in pain. That is perfectly true, but it does not show that the subject of thought or experience is anything other than the human being who gives it expression, or *would* give it expression if he felt so inclined. What it does show, as already noted, is that there is an important asymmetry between first- and third-person utterances or avowals of thought and experience. A person's avowals and averrals of thought or experience are, we have argued (§§3.3 and 3.9), criterionless. But that is possible only in so far as the speaker has mastered the relevant concepts of thought and experience, and hence has mastered their other-ascription. So he must grasp the kinds of criterial grounds which warrant their ascription to others, and normally be able to adduce such grounds in justification of his ascription, if he is asked how he knows that another person has thought such-and-such or had a certain experience.

Sources of the illusion

This asymmetry is the source of multiple confusions. For, looked at askew, it can seem as if *I* have 'access' to my own thoughts and experiences in a manner in which no one else does. For others have to observe me and my behaviour, but I do not have to observe what I do and say. And if we think of conscious experience as being identical with, or consisting of, qualia (§10.3), then it will also appear that the conscious experience to which I have privileged access is a private domain of essentially private objects. But now it will seem absurd to suppose that the subject that has access to such a 'realm of experience' is the flesh-and-blood human being. It will appear as if the subject of experience is an elusive entity *within* each human being, an entity with an 'inner eye' to observe what goes on within this private realm, and with an 'inner ear' to hear the auditory images that occur. But we have seen that this is a fiction, or group of fictions, generated by conceptual confusions (§§3.4–3.9). To say that I have a pain, it is not necessary, indeed it is not possible, that I should *perceive* the pain. All that is necessary is that I should have a pain, grasp the concept of pain, and give expression to the fact that I am in pain by means of the extension of natural pain-behaviour that is constituted by the utterance 'I have a pain'. Similarly, to be able to say that I think that such-and-such is the case, I do not have to perceive my own thoughts. Indeed, there is no such thing as *perceiving* my own thoughts. Rather, I have to think that such-and-such is the case, and be able to express *what* I think – not to perceive anything. I must also have learnt to affix an 'I think that' to a sentence of the form 'such-and-such is the case' in order, for example, to qualify the blunt assertion, to indicate that what follows the 'I think that' is an opinion, or a judgement based on evidence that does not suffice to rule out contrary judgements. And the first-person pronoun in such first-person utterances is not the name of, and does not refer to, an elusive inner subject of thought and experience.

Respectable uses of 'self'   It should, however, be stressed that although the philosophical conception of 'the self' is confused, there are perfectly respectable uses of the term 'self'. We speak perfectly innocuously of 'my former self' – that is, of myself as I previously was – and also of 'my better self' – that is, of the better aspects of my nature – and of 'my true self' – that is, of my most fundamental and abiding characteristics. Similarly, we talk of a person being 'quite his old self again', when he has recovered from an illness or some temporary aberration of personality. And there is nothing awry about saying of a generous and altruistic person that he is selfless, or that there is 'less of self in him' than in most people. The objections to talk of 'the self' are directed exclusively at the philosophical conception of 'a self', conceived as the 'inner subject' and 'owner' of experience in the Cartesian and Lockean tradition, which still plays havoc with us in neuroscientific, cognitive-scientific and psychological reflection.

12.5 The Horizon of Thought, Will and Affection

Self-consciousness and mastery of a language   Self-consciousness, then, is not consciousness of a self. How should we understand the notion? We shall argue, in §12.6, that self-consciousness is an ability which is available only to creatures that possess rich linguistic abilities. It is a consequence of the possession of sophisticated linguistic powers to use proper names and pronouns, as well as psychological predicates and predicates of action, in both the first- and third-person cases and in the various tenses, and hence a consequence of the possession of the relevant concepts which are typically applied to oneself without any criteria and applied to others on the basis of behavioural criteria. A language-using creature that has mastered these linguistic techniques is a self-conscious creature, who has the ability to be transitively conscious of its own mental states and condition, who can think and reflect on how things are with it, who can not only act but also become and be conscious of itself as so acting. And it will also have the ability to reflect on its own past, on its character traits and dispositions, on its preferences, motives and reasons for action. But to make this clear, we must first explore further some of the complex connections between thought and language. For some scientists find it altogether unbelievable that self-consciousness should be essentially a linguistic ability, and the reasons for their incredulity turn on misunderstandings of the complicated conceptual relationships between thought and language.

Psychological attributes that presuppose mastery of a language   Intransitive and perceptual transitive consciousness, we have argued, are not peculiar to human beings. Nor are some of the forms of so-called conscious experience and conscious mental states, as long as these are rightly conceived to be experiences one has, and mental states one is in, while conscious. A non-human animal can perceive objects in its environment, can feel pains and itches, no less than we. It makes perfectly good sense to say of a dog that it thinks something or other, as long as what it is said to think is something that can be manifest in its behavioural repertoire. A dog may now think that it is going to be taken for walk – if it hears its leash being taken off the peg, it rushes excitedly to the door, wagging its tail and barking excitedly. But it cannot now think that it is going to be taken for a walk next Wednesday. A dog may now expect its master, if it hears and recognizes its master's footsteps, but it cannot now expect its master to return home next Sunday. It may remember where it left a bone inasmuch as it can go and dig it up, but it makes no sense to ascribe to a dog a recollection of *when* (on what day of the week, on what date of the month) it left the bone wherever it left it. It may be angry or frightened, but it cannot reflect on its anger and fear or on the reasons for being angry or afraid. For such capacities presuppose possession of a language.

The limits of thought and knowledge

The limits of thought and knowledge are the limits of the possible expression of thought and knowledge. It makes sense to ascribe to a creature only such knowledge, memory, thought or belief as it can in principle express in its behaviour. For it is the behaviour of a creature that constitutes the criterion for such ascriptions. Hence the horizon of possible cognitive achievements of a creature is determined by the limits of its behavioural repertoire. But nothing in the behavioural repertoire of a dog could constitute criteria for ascribing to it knowledge or belief involving determinate temporal reference. It is *linguistic* behaviour, involving the use of a tensed language and of devices for temporal reference, that constitutes the primary criteria for ascribing to a creature knowledge, memory, thought and belief involving such reference to the past or the future.[21] Similarly, nothing in the behavioural repertoire of a dog could constitute criteria for ascribing to it pride in its courage or shame of its cowardice, for to be proud of one's courage or ashamed of one's cowardice requires possession of the concepts of such virtues and vices. It is the *possibility* of such linguistic manifestations of knowledge, memory, thought and belief which makes *intelligible* the ascription of such cognitive achievements and reflexive attitudes even when they are *not* exhibited. Of course, an animal may exhibit in its behaviour the primitive roots of such emotions of self-assessment as pride or shame – it may manifest pleasure in its victory, distress in its failure, or discomfort at being observed to fail.

Possession of a language extends the intellect

The possession of a language extends the intellect, makes it possible to think not only that things here and now are thus-and-so, but also that things, of an indefinite variety, are severally thus-and-so at indefinitely many other times and places. It is the availability

---

[21] Of course, animals and human beings alike possess 'biological clocks', and accordingly respond to the passing of time. But we can, and other animals cannot, now remember that we did such-and-such *last Wednesday*, think that since *yesterday was Tuesday* today *must be Wednesday*, can now expect Jack to arrive *before* Jill, now want to visit Rome *in 2010*, and so forth.

to a creature of devices of generalization that makes it intelligible to ascribe to it knowledge, belief or conjecture of a universal kind: for example, that *all* men are mortal, that *no* men live *for ever*, that *everyone* can be fooled *some* of the time. It is mastery of the use of general concept words, of count nouns, concrete mass nouns and numerals that renders accessible to a creature thought which goes beyond mere recognition, and knowledge, as opposed to mere recognition, of number and quantity. And it is the availability, in a creature's linguistic repertoire, of logical devices signifying negation ('not'), conjunction ('and'), disjunction ('or') and implication ('if . . . then . . .') that makes possible reasoning, and hence renders intelligible the ascription to it of reasoning, that goes beyond the most rudimentary.

The limits of animal thought

To be sure, we do ascribe to the higher animals rudimentary forms of thinking. Some may even be willing to explain an animal's behaviour by attributing to it a reason for thinking as it does (the dog's reason for thinking it is going to be taken for a walk, they may say, was the rattle of its leash, which it heard). But one cannot go far down that road. For even if one is willing to say that the animal had a reason for thinking such-and-such, a large part of the essential role of reasons for thinking or believing cannot be fulfilled in the case of non-language-using creatures. For a non-human animal cannot deploy thoughts as premises in a *reasoned inference*, cannot *justify* its thinking by reference to a reason, cannot *explain* to itself or to others its *errors*, as we can explain ours, by reference to the reasons it thought it had, for it cannot have *thought it had reasons*; and it cannot *reason from* one thought to another – even if one insists on saying that it had a reason for its action.

Possession of a language extends the will

The possession of a language extends the will no less than the intellect. Like us, animals have wants and act in pursuit of the objects of their desires. But the horizon of their desires is as limited as the horizon of their cognitive powers. Our cat may want food now, but cannot now want fish next Sunday. Our dog may want to be taken for a walk now, but cannot now want to be taken for a walk next Christmas day. Animals have purposes, pursue goals, and choose among different possible ways of achieving their goals. But the trajectory of their desires reaches no farther than their behavioural repertoire can express, and the objects of their desires are constrained by their limited, non-linguistic recognitional capacities. They can choose between patent alternatives, but not deliberate. There are reasons why an animal acts as it does; but, as we have seen, only in the most tenuous sense can we say that they *have* reasons for acting as they do, and it is doubtful whether we can make sense of ascribing to an animal (as opposed to ourselves) reasons for doing something that it did not do. Only a language-using creature can reason and deliberate, weigh the conflicting claims of the facts that it knows in the light of its desires, goals and values, and come to a decision in the light of reasons. In so far as non-human animals can be said to decide, such animal decision is not a matter of calling a halt to a process of reasoning, of weighing the pros and cons of a course of action and coming to a reasoned conclusion. It is only a matter of terminating a state of indecision.

Possession of a language extends the affections

What applies to the will applies equally to attitudes and affections. Non-human animals can like and dislike things, they can be pleased with things, take pleasure in activities, feel fear and anger. But a wide range of emotions, which are infused with thought and cognition, are beyond the powers of such animals. We can, whereas other animals cannot, feel a sense of moral duty. We can, but other animals cannot, feel remorse; for to be capable of feeling remorse, one must have the concepts of good and evil, must be able to recognize that one has done something morally wrong and be capable of regretting that one has done so, wishing that one had not, and be willing to make amends. We can, but other animals cannot, feel excited at the prospect of next week's hunting party, feel angry at the insult inflicted on us last week, and feel pleased that all our offspring are healthy. Possession of a language broadens the range of possible emotional responses no less than it widens the horizon of thought and will. It makes possible not only reflection on the world we encounter around us, but also on our own responses, cognitive and affective, to what we thus find.

12.5.1 Thought and language

Damasio, Edelman and Tononi on the priority of thought over language

The consciousness of animals other than ourselves obviously does not presuppose possession of a language. And the rudimentary forms of thinking that can be ascribed to the higher animals does not require mastery of a language. Distinctively human forms of thought, will and affection do. However, there is much unclarity on this matter in the writings of scientists. Damasio observes that 'the idea that self and consciousness would emerge *after* language, and would be a direct construction of language, is not likely to be correct. Language gives us names for things. If self and consciousness were born de novo from language, they would constitute the sole instance of words without an underlying concept.'[22] This idea is supported by the claim that

> Language, that is, words and sentences – is a translation of something else, a conversion from non-linguistic images which stand for entities, events, relationships and inferences. If language operates for the self and for consciousness in the same way as it operates for everything else, that is, by symbolizing in words and sentences what exists first in non-verbal form, then there must be a non-verbal self and a non-verbal knowing for which the words 'I' or 'me' or the phrase 'I know' are the appropriate translations in any language.[23]

A similar conception of the priority of concepts over their linguistic expression is articulated by Edelman and Tononi, who claim that 'concepts are not, in the first instance, sentential. That is, concepts are not propositions in a language (the common usage of this term); rather, they are constructs the brain develops by mapping its responses prior to language. . . . Concepts, in our view, precede language, which develops by epigenetic means to further enhance our conceptual and emotional exchanges.'[24]

---

[22] Damasio, *Feeling of What Happens*, p. 108.

[23] Ibid., p. 107.

[24] G. M. Edelman and G. Tononi, *Consciousness: How Matter Becomes Imagination* (Allen Lane, The Penguin Press, London, 2000), pp. 215f.

Penrose's conception of the dispens-
ability of language for thought

Matters are rendered even more opaque by Penrose's idea that ordinary human language is not necessary for characteristic human thought or consciousness. To confirm this view, Penrose quotes extensively from remarks by eminent scientists such as Einstein, Galton and Hadamard. Einstein wrote that 'The words or the language, as they are written or spoken, do not seem to play any role in my mechanism of thought. The psychical entities which seem to serve as elements of thought are certain signs and more or less clear images which can be "voluntarily" reproduced and combined.' Galton recorded that

> It is a serious drawback to me in writing, and still more in explaining myself, that I do not think as easily in words as otherwise. It often happens that after being hard at work, and having arrived at results that are perfectly clear and satisfactory to myself, when I try to express them in language I feel that I must begin by putting myself upon quite another intellectual plane. I have to translate my thoughts into a language that does not run very evenly with them. I therefore have to waste a vast deal of time in seeking appropriate words and phrases.

And Hadamard remarked that 'I insist that words are totally absent from my mind when I really think'. Penrose adds to these observations:

> Almost all my mathematical thinking is done visually and in terms of non-verbal concepts, although the thoughts are quite often accompanied by inane and almost useless verbal commentary . . . the difficulty that these thinkers have had with translating their thoughts into words is something that I frequently experience myself. Often the reason is that there simply are not the words available to express the concepts that are required. In fact, I often calculate using specially designed diagrams which constitute a shorthand for certain types of algebraic expression . . . This is not to say that I do not sometimes think in words, it is just that I find words almost useless for *mathematical* thinking.[25]

There are multiple confusions
embedded in these conceptions

Consciousness, we have argued, certainly does not 'emerge after language'. 'Self', however, *does* 'emerge after language', but only in the sense that the conceptual confusion that gives rise to the myth of a 'self' is rooted in misunderstandings of our language and its conceptual structures. However, as we shall show, it is a dire mistake to suppose that language is a *translation* of non-linguistic thought.[26] It is equally erroneous to think that words in general stand for, or are names of, ideas or images in the mind (as the empiricists imagined[27]) or for concepts. Of course, concepts are not propositions in a language – a misconception which has nothing to do with common usage: we speak

---

[25] R. Penrose, *The Emperor's New Mind*, rev. edn (Oxford University Press, Oxford, 1999), pp. 548f.
[26] The error is of venerable ancestry: 'the general use of speech, is to transfer our mental discourse, into verbal; or the train of our thoughts, into a train of words' (Hobbes, *Leviathan*, ch. IV).
[27] An equally venerable confusion: 'words in their primary and immediate signification stand for nothing but the ideas in the mind of him that uses them' (Locke, *An Essay Concerning Human Understanding*, III. ii. 2).

of the concept of a horse, but not of the concept (but only of the proposition) that your horse is in the stable ready for a ride. Neither, however, are they constructs the brain develops by mapping its own responses prior to language. The confusions here are manifold.

Knowing what a word means has nothing to do with having a mental image

First, to know what a word means is to be able to use it correctly. The criteria for whether a person knows what a word means are not that the right mental image springs into his mind whenever he uses it or whenever he hears it being used. If it were, then we would never know whether another person understands the words we use without asking him what mental images he has when he hears them. Moreover, if we had to ask him what mental image he associates with 'W', and if his answer is to be both decisive and intelligible to us, he must understand our question as we do, and we must understand his answer as he does. But if understanding were always a matter of imagist association, this could never be established – which is absurd.

Associated imagery is irrelevant to understanding

Secondly, if someone associates a different mental image with the word 'W' than we do, it would follow, on the imagist theory, that he does not understand it, or that he understands it differently. But if the image that comes to your mind on hearing the word 'perambulate' is of a pram, it does not follow that you don't understand the word or know what it means. As long as you use it correctly – that is, use it to mean the same as 'to walk' – and as long as when asked what it means you answer 'It means "to walk"', then you do know what it means, no matter what images, if any, you associate with it. Moreover, if the image that occurs to you in association with the word is an image of a man walking, how would you know whether 'perambulate' means 'walk' or 'man' or 'man walking' or 'man walking quickly (or slowly)'?

The imagist conception provides no criterion of correctness for a mental image to ensure understanding

Hence, finally, it is altogether obscure what *is* the 'right' mental image that is to be associated with any given word. If I am unsure what a word means, I do not conjure up images in my mind, I look it up in a dictionary. The dictionary spells out what the word means not by listing the images that are to be associated with it, but by specifying other equivalent words or phrases – it gives us a rule for the use of the word. So, the verb 'to perambulate' may be used in place of the verb 'to walk', and, *mutatis mutandis*, is correctly used wherever 'to walk' is correctly used. No picture or image of a person walking is necessary as a guide or standard for the correct use of the verb 'to walk'. In short, mental images are irrelevant to word meaning, and equally irrelevant to whether a speaker understands the words he uses or hears.

Concept possession is mastery of the use of an expression

The idea that words stand for underlying concepts which first exist in non-verbal form, that concepts precede language, is equally misconceived. Concepts are not mental images. To have a concept is not to have, or have a disposition to have, a mental image. Nor are they constructs the brain develops by mapping its own responses. *A concept is an abstraction from the use of a word.* The words 'snow', 'neige' and 'Schnee' differ, but are used in relevant respects in the same way. They occupy the same place in the web of words, admitting (in the relevant respects) the same combinatorial possibilities, and having the same logical powers (implications, compatibilities and incompatibilities). So these different words in different languages express one and the same concept. Hence English, French and German speakers, who have severally mastered the use of the word for snow in their language, share a common concept of snow. *To have a concept is to have mastered the use of a word (or phrase).* So concept possession is a complex ability or array of interconnected abilities. As with other skills, one may have a greater or lesser grasp of a certain concept, a partial but incomplete mastery of its use. Someone who possesses a given concept has the ability to apply it correctly, and may occasionally misapply it. He may on an occasion replace a concept by another related one, or substitute one concept for another more apt one. Sometimes he may extend a concept beyond its usual confines. For certain kinds of concepts (though not all), someone who possesses a concept C will have the ability to recognize cases that fall under it, to discriminate things that are C from those that are not. If being C implies being D and not being E, then a criterion for not having mastered the concept of C will be ascribing it to an object while denying that the object is D or affirming that it is E. So someone who affirms that an object is red but denies that it is coloured and affirms that it is non-extended can, other things being equal, be said not to have understood or mastered the concept of being red. In short, full mastery of a concept involves grasp of its logical implications, compatibilities and incompatibilities.

Words are not sentences (although there can be one-word sentences such as 'Jump!'), and concepts are not propositions. (*Contra* Edelman and Tononi, it is not part of the 'common usage' of the term 'concept' that concepts are 'propositions in a language'.) Words are used in the formation of sentences whereby acts of speech are performed, sentences being the minimal unit of verbal communication. One cannot *say* anything, except by means of a sentence. Just as the role of words is to contribute to the meaning of the declarative, imperative or interrogative sentences we use, so too the role of the concepts which they express is to contribute to the propositions, orders or questions, etc. that are asserted, given or asked by means of sentences in use.

A mere recognitional capacity is insufficient for concept possession

A common objection to this linguistic construal of concept possession is that it implies that non-human animals cannot be said to have concepts. But, it is objected, to possess a concept C is to have the ability to recognize or discriminate things which are C from those which are not. And animals certainly possess recognitional and discriminatory powers. To this one may reply that a mere recognitional and discriminatory capacity does not suffice for the possession of a concept. To have mastered the concept of, say, red is not only to be able to recognize and discriminate things which are red from those which are not; it is also to have grasped the logical form of the concept – that is, its combinatorial possibilities and impossibilities, its compatibilities and incompatibilities with other concepts. A normal human being who has mastered the concept of red must know that red is a colour (i.e. that if anything is red then it is coloured), that it makes sense to ascribe the property of being red to extended objects, but not to sounds, smells or tastes. He must know that if something is red all over, then it cannot at the same time be green (or blue, or yellow, etc.) all over. He must know that red is darker than pink (i.e. that if an object A is red, and another object B is pink, then A is darker than B), and that it is more similar to orange than it is to yellow (so if A is red, B orange and C yellow, then A is more similar in colour to B than to C). And so on. For, to the extent that he does not grasp these conceptual connections, to that extent his mastery of the concept is deficient. In short, he must grasp the logical articulations of the concept. And this is just another way of saying that he must have mastered the rule-governed use of the word that expresses the concept. Thus understood, non-language-using animals do not possess concepts, even though they obviously have a multitude of recognitional capacities. Of course, concept possession is a complex ability or cluster of interrelated abilities, and a recognitional capacity is, for some concepts, a component of the cluster. Is it not sufficient, by itself, for the ascription of a concept to a creature? This is a matter calling for a decision, not for a discovery. We may, if we please, thin down the concept of concept possession so that possession of appropriate recognitional abilities suffices for the ascription of the possession of the relevant concept. But it is difficult to see that there is anything that speaks for this scaling down. It involves the relative detachment of the concept of concept possession from the wide range of interrelated abilities involved in mastery of the use of a word. Moreover, it involves detaching the concept of a concept from its connections with the concepts of application and misapplication, use and abuse, extension, replacement and substitution. There is little reason to do this, given that we can already say all we wish about the relevant animal powers by the use of the term 'recognitional ability'.

Words do not 'stand for' or 'label' concepts Concepts change, and may become more (or less) refined in so far as the uses of words change, becoming more (or less) refined. New concepts are introduced or explained by explanations of meanings of new terms (or of assignments or refinements of meanings of old terms), the explanations of meaning functioning as rules for the correct use of the terms thus explained. And, of course, the explanations of the meanings of the new expressions are couched in terms of old, familiar concepts. It is at best misleading, and altogether unilluminating, to claim that words *stand for* concepts. It is thoroughly confused to suggest that words are labels for underlying concepts that must first exist in non-verbal form.

Speaking is not translating wordless thoughts into language If speaking were *translating* from wordless thoughts, then it would have to be possible for one to check one's wordless thought to make sure that one had translated it correctly, as one can check a German sentence to make sure that one has translated it rightly. But is there any such thing as checking a wordless thought to ensure that the constituents of the thought are captured by the words into which it is translated? Do thoughts have constituents? The only sense one can make of that supposition is that the 'constituents' of a thought are a shadow of (an abstraction from) the constituents of the verbal expression of the thought. If the constituents of a thought *were* images, could there be a method for *translating* images into words, as opposed to describing or specifying images? And if one were to describe or specify the images (if any) that cross one's mind while one is thinking that such-and-such is the case, would one thereby have expressed the thought that such-and-such is the case? One can no more translate 'wordless thoughts' into words than one can *translate* the furniture in the room into words.

We are disposed to think otherwise because we are misled by the idea that we think *in* a medium, just as we speak *in* one language or another, if not in English, then in German,

One source of the confusion is the idea that one thinks in a medium

and if not in German, then in French. And, of course, we do say such things as 'My German is now so good that I even think in German'. So it seems that we always think *in* something. And if we don't think *in* a language, we must think *in* something else – for example, in images. But this is a muddle. We must investigate the very questions 'Does one think in a language?' and 'Is language necessary for thinking?'

What is it to think 'in a language'?

We know what it is to speak in one language or another. What is it to think *in* a language? When I speak with thought in English, am I at the same time thinking in English *in addition* to speaking? Obviously not. To speak with thought is not speak and to accompany one's speech with another covert activity, any more than to sing with expression is to accompany one's singing with a second activity of expressing. It is to sing expressively; and to speak with thought is to speak with understanding, thoughtfully, reflectively, to have adequate reasons for what one says (and to have reasons for what one says is not to accompany one's saying with any concurrent activity). To speak with thought – that is, non-mechanically – is not to speak *and* do something else as well. One can imagine people who can think only aloud (as there are people who can read only aloud), but no one would imagine that when such people speak with thought, they say everything twice!

What speaking with thought is

To say something with thought is, minimally, to say it with understanding, as opposed to simply parroting – but the understanding with which one then says something is not an accompaniment of thought, but the ability to explain what one said. To assert *thoughtfully* that things are thus–and–so is to assert things to be so on the basis of all the relevant considerations (taking all the relevant factors into account), or to assert it as a step in one's reasoning (e.g. as a ground for a subsequent inference). What characterizes speaking *without* thought – that is, mechanically, unthinkingly, thoughtlessly, without understanding, etc. (all of which are different) – is not the absence of an accompaniment. Indeed, it is sometimes (though not always) the presence of an accompaniment which explains one's lack of thought – for example, a violent headache or the distraction of one's attention ('I'm so sorry, I wasn't thinking when I said that, my mind was on the music'). Lack of thought in speech, in one sense, may be manifest in the mechanical, monotonic mode of speech and the lack of expression in voice and face. In another sense, it is marked by the inappropriateness or ineptness of what is said. In neither case is the lack of thought a matter of the absence of an inner process accessible only to oneself. Lack of thought is characterized, for example, by one's inability to explain or justify what one said, by the groundlessness of what one said (given that grounds are needed), by one's reluctance to stick by one's assertion, or by the tactlessness and insensitivity of what one said.

So, one can speak with or without thought; but to speak with thought is not to accompany one's speech with some other, covert process, and to speak without thought is not for an accompaniment to be missing. Of course, one can think without speaking. Does that mean that one does what one does when one speaks with thought, only without the speaking? Obviously not. If one were asked, first, to say something with thought, and then, secondly, just to do what one did when one said it with thought only without saying anything, one would not know what to do. It would be like reading something with understanding, and then being asked to do what one did in reading the passage with understanding – only without reading anything. It is useful here to conceive of 'speaking with thought' adverbially – that is, as akin to running *in haste*, or walking *with vigour* – hence *not* as a *pair* of activities simultaneously engaged in. So, the concept of thinking without speaking requires separate scrutiny.

Does one not think *in* a medium? Does one not think either in English or in some other language? Or, if not in language, then in images, or diagrams, or formulae?

Talking to oneself in the imagination is neither necessary nor sufficient for thinking

One can talk to oneself in one's imagination in English or German. But, first, talking to oneself 'inwardly' need involve no thinking. Reciting the multiplication tables to oneself in one's imagination, or going over one's speech to make sure that one knows it by heart, or 'counting sheep' in order to *stop* oneself from thinking and to enable one to fall asleep, are not forms of thinking. Secondly, one can think without talking to oneself in the imagination at all. One can come to the conclusion that *p* on the basis of evidence *e*, or see that what follows from *a* and *b* is that *c*, without saying anything to oneself; all that is necessary is that one thenceforth be willing, other things being equal, to assert that *p* on the basis of the evidence *e*, or to assert that *c* for the reason that *a* and *b*, or be willing to act for the reason that *p* and be able to cite the fact that *p* as one's reason for doing what one does.

On the use of 'to be able to think in . . .'

We may be inclined to think otherwise because we are over-impressed, or wrongly impressed, by the fact that we say such things as 'I can speak in German, but I cannot think in German'. In so saying, one signifies that before one can say something in German, one must, by and large, first decide what one wants to say (and be *able* to say it in English), and then struggle to find the right German words. It does not follow that it makes sense to say *of a native English speaker* that he thinks *in* English, unless that just means that when he talks to himself in his imagination, what he thus says to himself is in English. Of course, one also says of an Englishman that he speaks German so well that he even *thinks* in German. But that, if it does not mean that he speaks to himself in his imagination in German, just means that he does *not* first think of what he wants to say and then pause to try to think of the German words.

Hunting for the right word – a misleading analogy

We are doubtless also deceived by the analogy between an English speaker hunting for the right German word in order to say such-and-such and an English speaker hunting for the right word in English to express his thought. But the analogy *is* deceptive. For in the first case, he *can* say, in English, what he thinks; but in the second, he cannot. This is not because he has thought *in images* and has not found the right translation, so that, so to speak, he knows what he thinks and is now looking for the correct words to express his (subjectively) wholly perspicuous thought. 'The word is on the tip of my tongue' means much the same as 'The right word escapes me for the moment, but it will come to me shortly, I hope'. Similarly, 'I know exactly what I want to say, but I can't think of the words' is either nonsense, or it means no more than 'Give me another moment for the thought to crystallize and then I'll tell you what I think'. So, too, when *someone else* finds the right words – the words *I* was looking for to express my thought – the rightness of their words does not consist in their being a correct *translation* of my thought or in their correctly *matching* my wordless thought. Rather, it consists in their matching the phenom- enon which is the subject of the thought in a way which strikes me as appropriate, and which I was trying to capture myself.

On so-called non-linguistic thought – Einstein, Galton, Hadamard and Penrose

What, then, of the observations of Einstein, Galton, Hadamard and Penrose? Far from insisting that they think in language, they all insist that they do not. Einstein insisted that the elements of his thought were 'certain signs and more or less clear images'; Penrose asserts that he thinks 'visually' in terms of 'specially designed diagrams' which are a shorthand for algebraic expressions. Galton stated that he had to translate his thoughts into language. Does this not show that one thinks *in* images, and then translates one's thoughts into language? It does not. What it shows is that the description of what goes on in one's mind while one is thinking is typically a description neither of one's thinking nor of what one is thinking. What one is thinking is not what is present to the imagination while thinking, save in cases in which what one says to oneself is what one is thinking. And a description of what passes through one's mind while thinking is not a description of one's thinking.

Mental images may be heuristic devices, but they are not thoughts or expressions of thoughts

Of course, some people may invoke mental images as heuristic devices to aid them in thinking, just as others may scribble diagrams or fragmentary symbols on a piece of paper. Neither the occurrence of the images nor the writing of the scribbles are the thinking. Nor are the images or scribbles expressions of the thought. The mental image one conjures up *may be* a mental image of what one is thinking *about*, but it cannot be *what* one is thinking (viz. *that p*). Mental images may be aids to thought, often essential aids to thought – but a description of the succession of these images, including images of diagrams and/or algebraic symbols, would not be a description either of the person's *thinking* (which may be described as swift, insightful, and impressive, or slow, clumsy and ineffective) or a statement of *what* he was thinking. And there is no such thing as *translating* these images into language.

There is no mystery about not thinking 'in words', but it is con- fused to suppose that one's thought needs 'translating' into words

Galton's insistence that he did not think *in* words is perfectly in order and unsurprising. What it means is that when thinking his way through a problem, he did not talk to himself in his imagination. When he reached a conclusion, he knew that he had solved his problem and knew that he could spell out the solution, even though he had not done so. That is no more mysterious than knowing what one is going to say before one says it, which one normally does – it would be truly mysterious if one never knew what one was going to say before one said it! But knowing what one is going to say does not mean saying it to oneself before one says it out loud. Nor does it imply thinking what one is going to say *in* a non-linguistic medium of thought. Where Galton is altogether mis- leading is in his assertion that he had to *translate* his 'wordless thoughts' into language. For knowing a solution to a problem, and saying what the solution is, is not translating anything. It is actualizing an ability – namely, the ability to give the right answer to the problem.

Confusions about words and concepts

Similarly, Penrose is misleading not in asserting that he does not think 'in words', but in claiming that 'there are not the words available to express the concepts that are required'. For mathematical symbols express concepts, have a rule-governed use, no less than words. The words 'cat', 'chat', and 'Katze' are symbols in three different languages, all of which express one and the same concept; the arithmetical symbols '+', '=', and 'i' are universally accepted symbols in the 'language of arithmetic' expressing the concepts of the addition function, of equality and of the square root of minus 1. There are words to express mathematical concepts. It would be extremely laborious, however, to use those words rather than the mathematical symbols, and quite impossible to make complex calculations without these symbols. No doubt, when Penrose finds a mathematical solution to a problem, words do not play any significant role in what goes on in his mind. Mathematical symbols and imagined diagrams may play a heuristic role. But when he has solved a mathematical problem, he can write down the solution in mathematical symbols, and these express concepts, mathematical concepts, no less than do words of natural language.

Reformulating the question

So, is language necessary for thought? The question is too crude, and needs to be broken down into a sequence of questions.

Can non-human animals think?

First, can creatures who have not mastered a language think? We have already answered this question. Rudimentary thought can be ascribed to non-human animals, but only to the extent that what they are said to think can be manifest in their behavioural repertoire.

The question of whether one has to think 'in' language is misleading

Secondly, in order to think, does one have to think *in language*? We have suggested that this question is misleading. One may talk to oneself in one's imagination while one is thinking, or one may not. One may silently rehearse one's thoughts in an internal monologue, or one may not. But talking to oneself in the imagination is not the same as thinking and need involve no thought. And if one does not say what one thinks to oneself in the imagination when thinking, it does not follow that one must be thinking *in* some non-linguistic medium, such as images. The very phrase 'thinking *in* language' leads us astray, for it is apt to be construed on the model of 'speaking in English' or 'speaking in German'. One need not think *in* anything (in *this* sense), for one need not talk to oneself when one is thinking, and even if one does talk to oneself *while* thinking, what one says to oneself may not be what one is thinking at all (as Penrose rightly points out).

The question of whether one can think 'in images' is misleading

Thirdly, *can* one think *in images*? This question too is misleading. Although images may cross one's mind while one is thinking, and although one may use images heuristically, neither the images nor their descriptions are expressions of the thought. Further, the process of images passing through the mind is no more the process of thinking than the succession of heuristic scribbles on a piece of paper are the process of thinking. In so far as thinking (reasoning) can be said to be a process, it is a process of reasoning *from* such-and-such premises *to* a certain conclusion. The train of thought is laid out in the explicit statement of the inferences, not in the description of the images, symbols or diagrams that crossed one's mind while one was thinking or that one used as heuristic devices to help one think one's way through to the solution. Having an image of X before one's mind, is not thinking *in images* in the sense in which one speaks *in English*. The words one utters when one speaks are the *expression* of one's thought. The images one conjures up while thinking are *not* the expression of one's thought but an aid to thought or an accompaniment of thinking.

The limits of possible thought are the limits of the possible expression of thought

Finally, must one have mastered a language in order to be able to think anything beyond the rudimentary thinking of an animal? That is indeed what we are suggesting.

For, to repeat, the limits of possible thought are the limits of the possible expression of thought. A thinker can think only what he *can* (but need not) express (or what he *would have been able* to express, had he not lost the power of speech which he previously had). An Einstein need not talk to himself while he is thinking. Nor need anyone else. But he can think only what he *can* express (or recognize as being expressed) – in words, symbols, diagrams or formulae.

12.6 Self-Consciousness

Consciousness contrasted with self-consciousness

A non-human animal can feel sensations, perceive things, feel emotions, want things, and act in pursuit of what it wants. It can know a variety of things, and, in a rudimentary sense, it may think or believe various things. It is, as we are, either conscious or unconscious; it enjoys perceptual, affective and volitional (conscious) experiences; and it can become and be conscious of various things inasmuch as its attention may be caught and held by items it perceives. Nevertheless, it is not a self-conscious creature. It can perceive, but it cannot think about or reflect on the fact that it is perceiving whatever it perceives. It can be angry, frightened, jealous, affectionate, excited; it has likes and dislikes, and can take pleasure in a range of activities. But it cannot realize, and so become conscious of the fact, that it is frightened or jealous, or that it is excited or taking pleasure in its activities. Hence, too, the fact that it is feeling anxious or terrified cannot occupy it and weigh with it in deliberation and intentional action, even though its actions are affected by what it is feeling. Even more obviously, the fact that it has, for example, an irascible or affectionate disposition cannot be something of which it may become and then be conscious. Nor can it *reflect on* its past experience, even though its past experience may affect its current behaviour and reactions.

Self-consciousness is not consciousness of a self; it presupposes conceptual skills

That an animal is not a self-conscious being is not to be explained by reference to the idea that it lacks 'a self', or that it has 'a self' but is not conscious of its 'self'. For, as we have argued, there is no such thing as 'a self' conceived as the inner owner of experience, and the fact that we are self-conscious beings does not consist in our having and being conscious of 'a self' either. What an animal lacks, and what we have, is mastery of a language. So, we agree, roughly, with Edelman, who insists that what he calls 'higher-order consciousness', by contrast with 'primary consciousness', requires a language. But this is not because a language is necessary inasmuch as 'A conceptual model of selfhood must be built, as well as a model of the past'.[28] Nor because 'animals, having only primary consciousness also have qualia, [but] cannot report them explicitly either to a human observer or to themselves, for they lack conceptual selves'.[29] But rather, because in order for the fact that one is enjoying an experience of a certain kind to strike one, in order for one to be able to think about it, and in order for it to weigh with one in one's deliberations, one must possess the concept of the relevant experience. To realize, and so become conscious of the fact, that one is jealous, angry or afraid, and for that fact to occupy one's thoughts and to constitute a reason for one to do or think something or other, one must possess the concepts of jealousy, anger or fear. Similarly, for one to be conscious of one's ignorance or erudition, of one's vanity or pride, one must possess the concepts of these characteristics. And for one's past to weigh with one in one's reflections, one must be able to think about it – and that presupposes mastery of language. Human beings, but not other animals, have an autobiography. And human beings, but not other animals, may have a sense of history, may be – and typically are – conscious of themselves as historical beings, as belonging to a society or social group with a certain history.

Self-consciousness requires mastery of personal pronouns

Self-consciousness, we have argued, does not involve consciousness of a self. But it does involve mastery of the use of personal pronouns in general, and of the use of the first-person pronoun in particular. To master the use of 'I' does not require that one notice an inner object which one had not noticed hitherto, which the pronoun 'I' names. For there is no inner object called 'the "I"' or 'the Ego', and the first-person pronoun is not a name. To learn the use of the first-person pronoun, one does not have to learn to identify an object of *any* kind, either inner or outer. The characteristic use of 'I' admits of no misidentification or misrecognition.[30] But that is not because it always involves an unerring identification and recognition of oneself (let alone of one's self). It is rather because *no* identification or recognition is involved at all. But mastery of the use of the first-person pronoun by a child in the course of normal human development does involve, and goes hand in hand with, mastery of the use of other personal pronouns and person-referring expressions. As we argued above, the transition from inchoate cries of pain to 'Hurts!', 'It hurts!', and then to 'I have a pain' is bound up with understanding the question 'Does it hurt?', and hence too with learning the use of the interrogative 'Does Mummy have a pain?', and so with mastering the use of the declarative sentence 'She has a pain'. For in learning to give verbal expression to his own pain, the child also learns to describe others as being in pain – for the first-person and third-person pain-predications are two sides of one and the same linguistic coin. One cannot be said to possess the

---

[28] Edelman, *Bright Air, Brilliant Fire*, p. 131.

[29] Ibid., p. 135.

[30] There is a possibility of misidentification in rather special cases: e.g. when looking at an old photograph, one may point at a figure, and say 'I was quite a pretty baby', and one may be wrong, inasmuch as the photo is not of oneself. This *is* a case of misidentification – but it does not affect the above argument.

concept of pain unless one has mastered both its criterionless use in the first-person case and its criterially based use in third-person ascriptions of pain (see §3.9). Similarly, one cannot be said to have mastered the use of 'I . . .', unless one has grasped that saying 'I am . . .' is a ground for others to say *of* me 'You are . . .' or 'He is . . .'. The first-person pronoun is *one* piece in a complex game in which the other personal pronouns and person-referring expressions are other essential pieces. Like the king in chess, it is the pivotal piece for each player; but without the other pieces, one cannot play the game.

The mastery of perceptual predicates   The pattern that we are invoking in explaining mastery of the first-person pronoun can be applied similarly to first-person perceptual utterances, such as 'I see . . .' or 'I hear . . .', etc. The learning child must first have mastered the use of appropriate descriptive terms to describe what he perceives – for example, 'Teddy is on the floor', 'Rover is barking', and so forth. To learn to prefix an 'I see . . .' or an 'I hear . . .' to such descriptions is again not to learn to identify some other object named by 'I'. Rather, the child must have learnt that seeing can be cited as one way of finding out that things are thus-and-so (e.g. that Teddy is on the floor, that the ball is red, that the sun is round), as hearing can be cited as the way to find out other things. And this he will obviously learn as his parents ask him 'Can you see where Teddy is?', 'Can you hear Rover barking?', and so forth.

The conditions that warrant prefixing an 'I see . . .' or an 'I hear . . .', the child will learn, are no different from the conditions for asserting *what* one sees or hears by using ones eyes or ears respectively. The prefix indicates to another *how* one is or came to be in the position to assert what follows: that is, how one knows (or thinks one knows) that things are as one describes them as being. But in gradually mastering the use of the first-person pronoun in such contexts, the child must, and unavoidably will be taught to, master the use of the second- and third-person pronouns in these contexts as well. He will learn to ask 'Can you see?' and 'Did you hear?, and to report 'Mummy didn't see it' and 'Daddy didn't hear' when he sees that his mother failed to notice something or that his father was not listening. The possibility of the various forms of self-consciousness is therefore acquired *together with*, and not *antecedently to*, the mastery of the linguistic apparatus for describing the experiences of *others*. Hence the idea that the child first learns to ascribe experiences to himself, and only then to ascribe experience to others, on the basis of analogy with his own case or on the basis of his construction of a *theory* about 'other minds', is utterly misconceived.

Self-consciousness is bound up with socialization, but not with model building   It is misleading to characterize such processes of mastering the linguistic techniques that are presupposed by self-consciousness as 'building a conceptual model of selfhood' or 'constructing a socially based selfhood', as Edelman suggests. But it is obvious that the possibility of self-consciousness is bound up with rich and complex forms of infantile socialization. The young child responds to parental emotion instinctively; he reacts, without thought or inference, to his parents' loving caresses, to their anger, to their approval and disapproval, to their smiles and their tears. The idea that in order to do *that*, the child (or his brain) must 'construct a model' of his parents' minds, which model will enable him to predict their behaviour, is surely as preposterous as the idea that the fledgling, kitten or puppy constructs a model of its parents' minds.

Model building is an activity that *presupposes* sophisticated conceptual abilities, and we cannot invoke it to explain their acquisition. Furthermore, it is literally unintelligible to ascribe it to the brain, *if* 'model building' has its normal meaning in the context of such ascriptions. Self-consciousness is not a 'construct' of any kind, but an ability. It is not evident what 'selfhood' is supposed to be. But if what one has in mind here is the emergence of the child's conception of himself, and ability to *think of* himself, *as* a child, as the son of such-and-such parents, as (to put it briefly) the subject of such-and-such predicates, then, to be sure, the child's 'selfhood', or, more perspicuously, the child's sense of himself as a child of whom such-and-such is true, emerges with his socialization and his growing linguistic skills. It is inseparable from his mastery of the first-person *and* other-personal pronouns, of the criterionless use of psychological predicates in the first-person case *and* of their criterial use in the third-person case, and from the very large range of other linguistic skills he must already have mastered before he has reached that stage of linguistic maturation.

The capacities of self-consciousness   A creature that has thus mastered a language is a self-conscious creature. It not only 'has conscious experience' (and is conscious or unconscious, and may be conscious of this or that), but also has the ability to give articulate expression to its thoughts and experiences. It can not only perceive, it can say that it perceives; not only feel, but also say what it feels. It can think, and *not* say what it thinks, precisely because it *can* say what it thinks. Furthermore, it can not only think and give articulate expression to its thoughts and experiences; it can think *of itself* as having those thoughts and experiences. It is precisely because it can give articulate verbal expression to its thoughts and experiences as *its* thoughts and experiences, that it can also *reflect on* its thoughts and on the fact that it is thinking such thoughts. It can *think about* its experiences and about the fact that it is having such-and-such experiences – even though it may not give any overt articulate expression to its reflexive thoughts and ruminations. In short, we not only perceive, feel, want and think whatever we do; but we can say that we do. And inasmuch as we can say what we can thus say, we can also think about our condition and about ourselves as being in that condition without saying anything. This ability is constitutive of self-consciousness, and it is a prerogative of language-using creatures.

The scope of the powers of self-consciousness   It would be a mistake to suppose that the powers of self-consciousness are restricted, in respect of their objects, to one's current thoughts, mental states and experiences. A self-conscious creature such as a human being can be conscious of his own motives, and *that* he is acting for such-and-such motives may occupy his thoughts and weigh with him. Often one becomes conscious of one's motive in action by realizing that what moves one are such-and-such reasons, and that these reasons fall into the pattern of a certain motive – for example, charity, love, jealousy, vindictiveness, ambition, revenge, fear. As we have seen (§7.2.2), the pattern, to which we commonly give a motive name, consists of a backward-looking reason for action – for example, some past or present fact that is undesirable in a certain way – and a forward-looking reason for action specifying a future state of affairs that removes or compensates in some way for the undesirable state of affairs. To act out of love for Mother is (roughly) to conceive of Mother's condition as lacking in some way, to view a future state of affairs that can be brought about by a certain action as beneficial to Mother, and to do that action with the intention of benefiting Mother for her sake. To act out of revenge is (roughly) to believe that, for example, Jack harmed an interest one had, to view a certain action as harming Jack, and to perform that action with intention of harming Jack because he harmed an interest one had. Clearly, one can act out of a certain motive without having a concept of that motive. But one cannot realize, and so become conscious of, one's motive in acting unless one has a concept of the relevant motive. Having realized one's motive, one may be pleasantly or shamefully conscious of the fact that one is acting out of such a motive. So, too, one may be unclear as regards one's true motive in action, and one's lack of clarity may weigh on one and occupy one's thoughts – and this too is something possible only for a self-conscious being.

Self-knowledge   Self-knowledge involves knowledge of one's own character traits, dispositions and skills (or lack of skills). What these are, one may come to know in various ways: for example, by being told by others, or by realizing that one's past behaviour amounts to being timid, idle, vindictive, fastidious or boorish. One does not come to know one's traits and dispositions, however, by being perceptually or 'introspectively' conscious of them. For one's character traits, dispositions and skills are not objects that one can perceive, let alone 'introspect' (misconstrued as apprehension by 'inner sense'), and become conscious of. But knowing that one has them, one may be conscious of them – that is, conscious of the fact that one is thus-and-so. And if one is conscious of them, they occupy one's mind and weigh with one in one's deliberations. This too is only possible for a language-using, self-conscious creature. For in order to be conscious of my ignorance or erudition, my prowess or incompetence, my vanity or ambition, my forgetfulness or weakness of will, I must possess concepts of the relevant characteristics, the self-ascription of which is involved in my being conscious of myself as possessing them.

Having an autobiography and   Self-conscious beings such as ourselves know, and maybe
sense of identity   conscious of, not only their current thoughts and experiences, motives and traits, etc., but also their past history. As remarked above, human beings have, and animals do not have, an autobiography (and, to a greater or lesser degree, an awareness of history). Hence what a person knows or believes about his past (and the past of his society, social group or family) is something of which he will be dispositionally conscious, and of which he may become occurrently conscious (see §9.3) when such facts or putative facts occupy him in thought, deliberation or fantasy. Such facts or beliefs make up a large part of his sense of himself (but not of his self). For they are partly constitutive of a person's sense of identity *as* a person of such-and-such a kind, with such-and-such allegiances, commitments, obligations and rights.

Self-consciousness is not explained   It should now be evident how misconceived is the idea
by reference to self-scanning devices   that self-consciousness is, or *must* involve, a neural self-
in the brain   scanning or self-monitoring device in the brain. Whether the neural networks of the brain contain anything remotely resembling a self-scanning device that might be built into a computer, we do not know, and nor does anyone else. But even if they do, why should we suppose that this would clarify the nature of self-consciousness? It is clear enough that the suggestion that it

would is predicated upon a conception of self-consciousness as a form of introspective scanning of the contents *of the mind*. If one thinks thus, then one might *also* think that to make self-consciousness possible, there must be a correlative self-scanning device in the brain.[31] But this is doubly misconceived.

First, as we have argued, self-consciousness is not a matter of scanning anything in 'inner sense' (i.e. by introspection, wrongly conceived (see §3.6)). Secondly, even if (*per impossibile*) it were, it is obscure how a neural self-scanning device could contribute anything to the possibility of self-consciousness. A neural self-scanning structure in the brain would no more be conscious of brain events than a computer program, which incorporates as a subroutine a 'description' of another program, is conscious of that other program. A self-referential component in a program cannot make *a computer* conscious of anything, let alone of itself. Aiming a video camera at a mirror, as Penrose observes, does not make it conscious of itself.[32] So even if the brain *does* contain some analogue of a self-scanning device, the results of its 'self-scanning' *could not* be something it can communicate to the person whose brain it is. And if it could, the person in question would not be able to understand it, unless he were a 'super-neuroscientist'. For the most that a *neural* self-scanning device could reveal would be *complex neural structures*.

It may be that a person would not be able to do some of the things he can do, and would not be capable of the various forms of self-consciousness, unless complex, self-scanning neural networks were operating. But if that is so, it is not because self-conscious reflexive thought involves scanning anything. There is no special reason to suppose that a person's ability to think about himself, about his current perceptual experiences or his past ones, about his current emotions or motives for action or his past ones, or about his character traits and dispositions, is dependent upon a neural self-scanning device that scans something that *is*, or *is systematically related to*, what the person is conscious of.

Linguistic skills provide the key to understanding the nature of self-consciousness

It is, to be sure, remarkable that there are any self-conscious creatures at all. Certainly, we would not be the kinds of creatures we are, were we not self-conscious beings. To be fully human *is* to be self-conscious – that is, to have the ability to engage in the manifold forms of reflexive thought and reflection. It is therefore also the ability to take facts concerning one's own beliefs or knowledge, experiences and dispositions, emotions and motives, past history and social relations, as reasons for thinking thus-and-so, grounds for feeling such-and-such (including feelings of moral fulfilment, or of remorse or guilt), and as reasons for action. But the key to the understanding of self-consciousness, its nature and possibility, lies not in neural self-scanning mechanisms in the brain, but in *the normal human mastery of language*. And the key to the understanding of its neural foundations lies in an understanding of the neural conditions for the possession and exercise of linguistic abilities and of the neural conditions for the possibility of the forms of thinking that are a consequence of the possibility of speaking. These may, or may not, involve neural self-scanning devices.

---

[31] This is strikingly evident in Weiskranz's explanations of blind-sight; see below §14.3.1.

[32] Penrose, *Emperor's New Mind*, p. 530.

Part IV

On Method

13

Reductionism

13.1 Ontological and Explanatory Reductionism

Ontological and explanatory reductionism distinguished: Crick

Many brain-neuroscientists have an implicit belief in reductionism. Few try to articulate what exactly they mean by this term of art. Among those who do, the most lucid statement of the common conception of reductionism with respect to cognitive neuroscience that we have found is given by Francis Crick in his book *The Astonishing Hypothesis*. Indeed, one reductionist thesis that Crick defends is also what he holds to be the eponymous 'astonishing hypothesis': namely, that '"You", your joys and your sorrows, your memories and your ambitions, your sense of personal identity and free will, are in fact no more than the behaviour of a vast assembly of nerve cells and their associated molecules.'[1] It does not, Crick avers, 'come easily to believe that I am the detailed behaviour of a set of nerve cells', but in fact it is so. This conception appears to be a form of *ontological reductionism*, inasmuch as it holds that one kind of entity is, despite appearances to the contrary, actually no more than a structure of other kinds of entity. Side by side with the ontological reductionism, Crick also defends a form of *explanatory reductionism*: 'The scientific belief is that our minds – the behaviour of our brains – can be explained by the interactions of nerve cells (and other cells) and the molecules associated with them.' The reductionist approach, Crick explains, is that

> a complex system can be explained by the behaviour of its parts and their interactions with each other. For a system with many levels of activity, this process may have to be repeated more than once – that is, the behaviour of a particular part may have to be explained by the properties of *its* parts and their interactions. For example, to understand

---

[1] F. Crick, *The Astonishing Hypothesis* (Touchstone, London, 1995), p. 3. It is surprising that Crick should find his materialist hypothesis 'astonishing', since it was already propounded in Epicurean atomist form in the first century BC by Lucretius in his great poem *De Rerum Natura*. In somewhat different forms, it was defended by Gassendi and Hobbes in the seventeenth century, and by La Mettrie, Diderot and d'Holbach in the eighteenth. So, if it is astonishing, that is certainly not because of its novelty.

the brain we may need to know the many interactions of nerve cells with each other; in addition, the behaviour of each nerve cell may need explanation in terms of the ions and molecules of which it is composed.[2]

Reductionism, Crick holds, is 'the main theoretical method that has driven the development of physics, chemistry and molecular biology. It is largely responsible for the spectacular developments of modern science. It is the only way to proceed until and unless we are confronted with strong experimental evidence that demands we modify our attitude.'[3]

The consequences that are sometimes derived: Blakemore

Colin Blakemore propounded a similar form of reductionism, with a more epiphenomenalist emphasis, in his BBC lectures *The Mind Machine*.

> All our actions are products of our brains . . . We *feel* ourselves, usually, to be in control of our actions, but that feeling is itself a product of the brain, whose machinery has been designed, on the basis of its functional utility, by means of natural selection.
>
> We are machines, but machines so wonderfully sophisticated that no one should count it an insult to be called such a machine. . . .
>
> The *sense* of will is an invention of the brain. Like so much of what the brain does, the feeling of choice is a mental model – a plausible account of how we act, which tells us no more about how decisions are really taken in the brain than our perception of the world tells us about the computations involved in deriving it.[4]

Such assertions as these – namely, that human beings are machines, or that the behaviour of a human being is no more than the behaviour of their nerve cells, or that decisions are taken in and (apparently) by the brain – are not science but metaphysics. Whether such venerable metaphysical pictures are rendered any more plausible by modern science than they were in antiquity by Democritus, Epicurus or Lucretius more than 2,000 years ago is of some interest. Precisely because the various forms of ontological and explanatory

---

[2] Ibid., p. 7.

[3] Ibid., p. 8.

[4] C. Blakemore, *The Mind Machine* (BBC Publications, London, 1988), pp. 270–2. To be sure, in the sense in which all our actions are products of our brains, so too is all our knowledge (including our knowledge of neuroscience). And just as the fact that the normal functioning of the brain is a necessary condition of knowing anything does not show that we do not know anything, so too the fact that normal functioning of the brain is a necessary condition of acting does not show that we do not act. We normally feel, i.e. think, that we are in control of our actions, and so indeed we are – the fact that this feeling is 'a product of the brain' does not show it to be false. The 'sense of will' is not an invention of the brain, since brains do not invent anything, and the feeling of choice is not a 'mental model', since it is not a model. That we often act because we choose so to act is not a 'plausible account of how we act', since it is not an account of *how* we act at all. As argued in chapter 3, no *decisions* are taken in the brain, and our perception of the world is not *derived* from any computations made by the brain. For perceptions are not *derived* from anything, and the brain does not *compute* anything. Are we machines? Only if there are 'machines' that can feel pain and take pleasure in their activities, that have desires and purposes of their own, that are capable of thought and action, that can deliberate on courses of action and decide what to do on the basis of reasons, and that are responsible for what they do.

reductionism are metaphysical theses concerning the logic of existential attributions and the logical structures of explanation, they are not open to scientific confirmation or disconfirmation. If they are to be confirmed or confuted, then it will be by analytical argument.

Classical reductionism and unified science

In order to evaluate such reductionist claims, it is necessary first to clarify what reductionism is and what forms it may take. In the broadest sense, reductionism is the commitment to a single unifying explanation of a type of phenomenon. In this sense, Marxism advocates a reductive explanation of history, and psychoanalysis defends a reductive explanation of human behaviour. More specifically, reductionism in science is a commitment to the complete explanation of the nature and behaviour of entities of a given type in terms of the nature and behaviour of their constituents. The ideal of 'unified science', advocated by the Vienna Circle positivists[5] in the 1920s and 1930s and adopted by the later logical empiricists in the 1950s, was committed to what has been called 'classical reductionism'.[6] This conception held that the objects of which the world consists can be classified into hierarchies such that the objects at each level of classification are composed of objects comprising a lower level. The lowest level was conceived to be constituted by the elementary particles investigated by fundamental physics. Above this, in successive levels, are atoms, molecules, cells, multicellular organisms and social groups. Investigating each level is the task of a given science (or sciences) the purpose of which is to discover the laws that describe the behaviour of entities of the kind in question. The reductivist programme is to derive the laws of any given level from the different laws describing the behaviour of entities at the lower level. *Derivational reduction*, thus conceived, requires, in addition to the laws at the reduced and reducing levels, bridge principles identifying the kinds of objects at the reduced level with specific structures of objects comprising the reducing level.[7]

Scientific reductionism and metaphysical materialism

Reductionism, in its classical form, was a bold and sweeping thesis about ontology and about the logical character of scientific explanation. It was an eminently *philosophical* thesis, driven by two primary considerations. The first was the apparently successful reduction, in a few domains of science, of fragments of one science to elements of another. So, for example, the interactions between stuffs of various kinds is successfully explained in terms of the atomic and valency theories of chemistry. The second was a deep commitment to *metaphysical materialism*, which is an ontological doctrine typically propounded in opposition to Cartesian dualism. In its simplest and warranted form, it

---

[5] See the English translation of the Manifesto of the Circle of 1929: *The Scientific Conception of the World: The Vienna Circle* (Reidel, Dordrecht, 1973), §2. Rudolf Carnap's hand is evident in the characterization of the reductive 'constitutive system' envisaged (see esp. p. 11).

[6] The terminology is derived from John Dupré, *The Disorder of Things: The Metaphysical Foundations of the Disunity of Science* (Harvard University Press, Boston, MA, 1993), to whose discussion of reductionism in chapters 4–7 we are much indebted.

[7] The classical formulation of such classical reductionism is given by P. Oppenheim and H. Putnam in their paper 'The unity of science as a working hypothesis', in H. Feigl et al. (eds), *Minnesota Studies in the Philosophy of Science*, vol. 2 (University of Minnesota Press, Minneapolis, 1958). The flaws in this conception are well discussed by Dupré.

amounts to a denial that there are mental or spiritual substances. In its simplest and crudest form, it involves the claim that everything that exists is material. In this form, it claims that the mind is the brain (hence the proliferation in recent years, in the wake of Noam Chomsky, of the misconceived phrase 'the mind/brain'). In less simple and crude form, it is the claim that mental states, events and processes are in fact neural states, events and processes, that mental attributes are in fact identical with neural ones.

Ontological materialism   Ontological materialism has little to be said for it. Denial that there are mental or spiritual substances does not imply that the only things that exist are material objects (and material stuffs). For evidently laws and legal systems, numbers and theorems, games and plays, are neither material objects nor stuffs. Indeed, the colours, lengths and weights *of* material objects, not to mention their capacities and dispositions, are not themselves material things, although it makes perfectly good sense to speak of there being such properties as colours, lengths and weights, and such dispositions as solubility and elasticity. More importantly, wars, revolutions and cultures, performances of plays, birthday parties and funerals, are not material objects – but there are such things, they occur, happen, or exist at a time or for a time.

One might modify the claim: everything there is, one might suggest, is made of, or consists of, matter. But this is just as misconceived, since laws and legal systems, numbers and theorems, games and plays, political parties, a society and its culture, inflation and economic growth, are not *made* of matter and do not consist of matter. Moreover, denial that there are immaterial substances does not imply that the only thing relevant to the explanation of the properties and/or behaviour of things that do exist – indeed, *even of material things that exist* – is the matter of which they are made. Organs and artefacts are explained primarily by reference to their function, not merely by reference to their material constitution. The behaviour of sentient creatures in general is explained partly in terms of their goals, and of human beings in particular also in terms of reasons and motives, not in terms of the material of which they consist. Even more obviously, the explanation of events and processes such as Hannibal's victory at Cannae, or the decline of the Roman Empire, the Industrial Revolution, or the rise of Romanticism has nothing to do with the matter of which the explananda are made, since they are not made of anything.

So, the materialist might venture a much more modest claim: everything that is made of anything is made of matter. Certainly we should concede that minds are not *made of* immaterial substance[8] – but then, if the argument of §3.10 was correct, minds are not made of anything, and all talk of the mind is a mere *façon de parler* for talk of specific human capacities of thought, memory and will and of the exercise of those capacities.[9] Legal

---

[8] Of course, Descartes never claimed they were. He held that they *are* immaterial substances, not that they are *made of* 'immaterial stuff'.

[9] To be sure, if that argument was correct, then Crick's claim that our minds are 'the behaviour of our brains' is no more coherent than the idea that our sakes are the behaviour of our friends who do things for our sake. Nor, more circumspectly, is making up my mind, changing my mind, or being in two minds whether to *V* the behaviour of my brain, even though the possibility of my making up my mind, changing my mind and being in two minds whether to *V* is possible only if my brain is functioning normally in appropriate respects.

systems consist of laws and not of matter; poems consist of stanzas, not of ink; and revolutions consist of human actions and events. The materialist might grant that this is what laws, and poems, and revolutions *consist* of, but deny that they are *made* of anything. We can concede this too. But even if it is true that everything that is made of anything is made of matter, this thesis goes no way to sustain any form of ontological reduction according to which all 'entities' are reducible to material entities. Nor does it support any form of explanatory reduction according to which the properties and behaviour of everything that exists are to be explained in terms of the properties and behaviour of its constituent matter.

Human beings are not ontologically reducible to their nervous systems

That everything that is made of anything is made of matter does not show that human beings are ontologically reducible to their nervous systems, let alone that their minds are their brains. Human beings are composed of various parts – their organs – and they are made of certain quantities of chemical elements; but they are not identical with what they are made of or with a privileged organ from among those of which they are composed – namely, the brain. We are human beings, and we do not live in our skulls, but in our dwellings. The attributes that we possess (e.g. our physical attributes – height, weight, looks – and our personal relations, our social standing, our economic position, our personal history) are not attributes of our brains, any more than the attributes of our brains are our attributes. It is plainly false that we are 'no more than the behaviour of a vast assembly of nerve cells (and other cells) and the molecules associated with them'. What is tautologically true is that we do not consist of any more cells than the vast assembly of nerve and other cells of which we – living human beings – actually consist. But we are no more *just* a collection of cells (nerve cells or otherwise) than a painting is *just* a collection of pigments or brush strokes, a novel just a collection of words, or a society just a collection of people – although what more there is to a painting than mere pigments is not more pigments, what more there is to a novel than mere words is not more words, and what more there is to a society than mere people is not more people.

This might be granted by the neuroscientific reductionist. He might argue, as Crick does, that:

> Much of the behaviour of the brain is 'emergent', i.e. behaviour does not exist in its separate parts, such as the individual neurons . . . It is the intricate interaction of many of them together that can do such marvellous things. . . . while the whole may not be the simple sum of its parts, its behaviour can, at least in principle, be *understood* from the nature and behaviour of its parts, *plus* the knowledge of how all these parts interact.[10]

But this is confused. For while much of the behaviour *of the brain* may be emergent, explicable by reference to the interactions of its parts, the behaviour *of a human being* is

---

[10] Crick, *Astonishing Hypothesis*, p. 11.

not an emergent or supervenient property of their brain. Emergent or supervenient properties are properties of a complex system that are such that a *complete* knowledge of the relations between elements of the system (knowledge unavailable to us) suffices (for a god, as it were) for deriving the emergent properties of the system as a whole. Perhaps there is some sense in which knowledge of neural events is adequate to derive a description of the movements of 'the system' as a whole (given that 'the system' is the human being and not merely his brain) – for example, the movements of a person's hand (assuming that nothing extraneous moves it or makes it move). It is less than obvious whether neural knowledge can discriminate between the event of a person's hand's moving and the action of a person's moving his hand, and so distinguish between the supervenience of an event (the moving of the hand) and of an action (the person's moving his hand). But even if that were possible, no amount of neural knowledge would suffice to discriminate between writing one's name, copying one's name, practising one's signature, forging a name, writing an autograph, signing a cheque, witnessing a will, signing a death warrant, and so forth. For the differences between these are circumstance-dependent, functions not only of the individual's intentions, but also of the social and legal conventions that must obtain to make the having of such intentions and the performance of such actions possible.

It is perfectly true, as Crick says, that 'it does not come easily to believe that I am just the detailed behaviour of a set of nerve cells' – and this is just as well. I am not *the behaviour* of the nerve and other cells of which I consist, since I am not the behaviour of anything – not even of myself. I am a human being, an animal of a certain kind with very distinctive kinds of capacities. My *history* is my behaviour in the socio-historical context of my life, what I did (and also what befell me) over time; but whether my history is reducible to the history of my nerve cells and other cells is a different question that we must now confront.

Three objections to identifying psychological attributes with neural states   One form of explanatory reductionism in the domain of the mental is the thesis, embraced by Crick, that all our behaviour and our mental states (events, processes, powers) can be fully explained in terms of neural processes. The claim that all human behaviour is 'ultimately' or 'theoretically' explicable in neural terms is open to a multitude of objections. The first array of objections severally turn on the question of the intelligibility of identifying psychological attributes with neural states or events.

(i)   It is one thing to hold that a person would not believe, hope, fear, think, want, etc. whatever he does but for the fact that his brain is, in appropriate respects, functioning normally. It is quite another to hold that there are general bridge principles identifying a person's believing what he believes, etc., with a specific kind of neural state or condition. The former claim is an important platitude. The latter is misconceived. For there is no reason to suppose that two people may not, for example, believe the very same thing, yet the relevant (as yet unknown) neural structures in each person's brain be different. The criteria of identity for mental states, events and processes differ from the criteria of identity for neural states, events and processes.[11] This should be obvious from a further consideration. State X may be said to be identical with state Y only if whenever A is in state X, A is also in state Y. But then believing something cannot, in principle, be identical with a neural state, since the subject of believing is the person A, and the subject of an appropriate neural state is A's brain, and A is not identical with his own brain.

(ii)   If believing, hoping, wanting, etc. were identical with certain neural states, then the location of the mental state M or of the mental event E that consists in the agent's becoming M would be the location of the corresponding neural states or events (whatever they might be). But the question 'Where do you believe that it will rain?' is answered by giving the location of the predicted rain, not by indicating a location in one's skull, and the question 'Where do you believe that $E = mc^2$?' is meaningless. Similarly, 'Where did you acquire the belief that p?' can be answered by 'In the library' or 'When I was walking on the heath with Jack', but not by 'In my brain, of course'.

(iii)   As we suggested in §6.1, for many psychological attributes it makes *no sense* to suppose that they are identical with neural states or conditions, inasmuch as a neural state or condition could not conceivably have the logical consequences of such attributes. So, for example, if believing that p were identical with some (as yet unknown) configuration of neurons in the brain, then if a person avows or avers that he believes that p, he would actually (unbeknownst to him) be making a statement about the state of his brain (just as a person who makes a statement about Hesperus is also making a statement about Phosphorus, since, whether he knows it or not, they are one and the same heavenly body). But if this were so, then it would make sense for a person to say 'I believe that p, but as to whether it is the case that p, that is, as far as I am concerned, an open question (or: that is something on which I take no stand)'. Indeed, he could coherently say 'I believe that Jack is in town [i.e. my brain is in the neural state that is identical with my believing thus], but he is not in town' – for, to be sure, there is no contradiction in asserting that a certain neural configuration obtains in my brain and denying that Jack is in town. But it is incoherent to assert 'I believe that Jack is in town, but he is not in town', and to say that one believes that such-and-such is the case *is* to take a stand on whether it is the case, which it would not be if an avowal or averral of belief were a statement about a neural configuration in one's brain. To say 'I believe that p' is typically a hedged assertion that p, not a reference to, let alone a description of, a neural configuration in one's brain. And one cannot coherently make a hedged assertion that p and at the same time deny that p. Equally, a neural pattern in one's brain cannot have the logical

[11] See A. J. P. Kenny, 'Language and mind', repr. in *The Legacy of Wittgenstein* (Blackwell, Oxford, 1984), p. 142. This difference, as Kenny points out, is paralleled by a comparable difference in computers: there is no one–one correlation between software structures and hardware structures. The electronic events that occur in one computer or pocket calculator that is computing the square root of 123456789 need bear no resemblance to the electronic events in another computer or calculator that is doing the same. Similarly, if one detaches the hardware from the input keys and output display, then no matter what electronic events take place inside it, they would not constitute computing the square root of 123456789.

consequences of believing something: namely, being either right or wrong about what one believes. For there is no such thing as a neural configuration's being right or wrong about the truth of a proposition.[12] Similarly, if believing were a neural configuration, it would make sense to say 'I am in a state of believing that it will rain, which is actually a state of my brain, and my state is trustworthy, so I trust it', or 'I believe it will rain, and since my brain states are reliable, I suppose it will rain'.[13] But this too makes no sense.

So, if there is no sense to literally *identifying* neural states and configurations with psychological attributes, there cannot be general bridge principles linking the reducing entities (neural configurations) with the entities that are to be reduced (psychological attributes). But if there can be no bridge principles, then there is no hope for any form of reduction that will allow one to derive the laws governing phenomena at the higher level of psychology from the laws governing phenomena at the neural level. So this form of derivational reductionism is chimerical.

There are no psychological laws of human action to reduce to neural laws — Not only are there no bridge principles allowing any form of ontological reduction of psychological attributes to neural configurations, but it is far from evident that there is anything that can be dignified by the name of *psychological laws* of human action, that might be reduced to, and so explained by reference to, whatever neurological laws might be discovered. For, as far as explaining human action is concerned, it is clear enough that although there are many different kinds of explanation of why people act as they do, or why a certain person acted as they did, they are not *nomological* explanations (i.e. they are not explanations that refer to a natural *law* of human behaviour).

There are, to be sure, explanations of a person's action that explain it by identifying it as an instance of a general pattern. So, we may explain why A does *V* by reference to the fact that it is a habit, or that A has a tendency to *V* in such moments as these, or that it is a custom in A's community to *V* in such circumstances and A is a conventional sort of person, or that A is in such-and-such a predicament and people with A's kind of person-ality traits tend to *V* in such circumstances. But these explanations do not specify anything that could possibly be deemed a strict *law*; nor do they explain the behaviour by deducing it from a law and a set of initial conditions. Instead, they identify it as an instance of one or another kind of rough regularity of the person's behaviour, which may admit of many exceptions. We may explain why A did *V* by reference to numerous different kinds of factor, in accordance with different kinds of explanatory schemata. To be sure, some actions may be explained by reference to causal factors. It is important to note, however, that this form of explanation need not be nomological either – there is nothing obviously nomological in explaining that A cried out because the sudden noise startled him. But the more typical explanations we require take the form of citing the agent's reason for doing

---

[12] See Arthur Collins, *The Nature of Mental Things* (University of Notre Dame Press, Notre Dame, IN, 1987), ch. 2; and *idem*, 'Could our beliefs be representations in our brains?', *Journal of Philosophy*, 76 (1979), pp. 225–43.

[13] L. Wittgenstein, *Remarks on the Philosophy of Psychology*, vol. 1, ed. G. E. M. Anscombe and G. H. von Wright, tr. G. E. M. Anscombe (Blackwell, Oxford, 1980), §§481–3.

what he did, or of citing his motive, and these are neither causal nor nomological explanation of human behaviour.[14]

Explanation of action by redescription

We constantly ask for explanations of why someone did or is doing something, and we are typically given answers that satisfy us. We want to know why A raised his arm – and we may be told that he was waving to B, or that he was hailing a taxi, or that he was reaching for a book, or that he was stretching his arm because it was stiff. We want to know why A is playing the piano, and we may be told that he is practising, or that he is performing, or that he is tuning the piano. We ask why A handed a coin to B, and we may be told that he was giving B a birthday present, or that he was bribing B, or that he was giving B a loan, or repaying a debt, or showing B an antique coin. Such explanations explain by characterizing an action that is puzzling in different terms, that may, in the context, fully resolve the bafflement. Given the explanation, one now knows *what* A was doing *in* or *by* *V*'ing – and that may suffice. What is germane to our current concerns is the fact that such explanations are non-reductive. They refer to various factors, and presuppose knowledge of social practices and conventions. But it would be absurd to suppose that they might be improved upon by any form of reductive neural explanation of concurrent brain events, or indeed that such an addendum would deepen our understanding of what A was doing and why he was doing it. To understand what is going on when A hands B a small round metal disc, we need to know what money is and why it is used; and if A was bribing B (or repaying a debt, or making a loan), we need to know a fair amount about socio-economic arrangements in human society. Neuroscientific reduction has nothing to contribute to such forms of explanation.

Explanation of action in terms of an agent's reasons

However, having characterized the action of A's handing a coin to B as bribing, lending, repaying a debt, making a gift, or showing a collector's piece, we may still want to know why A is doing one of these things. This is normally a demand for an explanation in terms of the agent's reasons for doing what he is doing or for his motives in doing what he is doing. For present purposes we can disregard motive explanations; we may fruitfully think of reasons as facts that can be cited in a piece of practical reasoning, and that therefore can be cited in explanation or justification of what one does. So, A's reason for handing B a coin may be that A had borrowed that sum of money from B last week, and promised to return it today. Or, A's reason for giving B the coin may be that B agreed to *V* on condition that he was paid this sum of money (and A wanted B to *V*). Or, A's reason for giving B the coin may be that B asked for a loan, or that young B is A's nephew and that A is giving B money to enable him to buy himself a present, or that B is a waiter and A is giving him a tip. And so on. The factors cited in these explanations

---

[14] The logical analysis of action done for reasons and action done from a motive is controversial. For arguments which deny that these forms of explanation are causal, see A. J. P. Kenny, *Will, Freedom and Power* (Blackwell, Oxford, 1975), ch. 6; G. H. von Wright, 'Of human freedom', repr. in *In the Shadow of Descartes* (Kluwer, Dordrecht, 1998); B. Rundle, *Mind in Action* (Clarendon Press, Oxford, 1997), chs. 7–8; A. R. White, *The Philosophy of Mind* (Random House, New York, 1967), ch. 6.

again make reference to a multitude of familiar but complex moral, social and legal conventions. These explanations do not work by explaining the behaviour of wholes in terms of the properties and behaviour of their parts. Rather, they work by explaining the behaviour of human beings by reference to the context in which they find themselves and to the reasoning they go through or would go through if asked why they did what they did. Citing reasons may involve reference to all manner of human goods that constitute goals of action, as well as social norms that permit, prohibit or make possible various forms of human conduct. Indeed, we should note that some kinds of explanation of why someone was *unable* to do something (and perhaps too why someone else *was* able to do it) refer to legal norms which empower people to act or which do not grant powers to certain people to do things that others can do. (No amount of neuroscience can explain why Henry VIII could not divorce Catherine of Aragon without papal permission, or why Edward VIII could not marry Mrs Simpson without abdicating.)

Explanatory reducibility of reasoned action to neuroscience is an illusion

If ontological reduction is a non-starter, and if there are no interesting psychological *laws* of human actions that are done for reasons, then the prospects for the reduction of received explanations of human behaviour to neuroscientific explanations are bleak. For there are neither bridge principles in terms of which to identify items at the psychological level of explanation (viz. beliefs, hopes, fears, intentions, reasons, motives) with aggregates of entities at the neural level of explanation, nor laws at the psychological level of explanation that might be derived from more fundamental laws at the neural level. But that should not be in the least surprising. It is perfectly intelligible that our knowledge of the gross observable reactions of water with various chemicals should be deepened by an understanding of the atomic and subatomic constitution of water (and other chemicals) – which will explain things that we can observe, but do not understand, about the behaviour of water. But is it really intelligible to suppose that the conduct of individual human beings in the circumstances of their lives will always be rendered clearer by neuroscience? We call on Jack only to find him out. We ask where he is, and are told he has gone to town. We want to know why, and are told that it is his wife's birthday, that he booked tickets for *Tosca* weeks ago, and that he has taken her to her favourite opera. Would a neuroscientific story *deepen* our understanding of the situation and the events? In what way does it need deepening? Does anything remain puzzling once the mundane explanation has been given? Could neuroscience explain why birthdays are celebrated, why *Tosca* is worth going to, and why a husband might think it appropriate to get tickets to the opera for his wife's birthday treat?

Neuroscience can explain the neural conditions of the possibility of the possession and exercise of human powers

Neuroscientific explanations can typically explain how it is possible for creatures with such-and-such a brain to do the kinds of things they do. They can explain what neural connections must obtain and what neural activities must take place in order for it to be possible for the animal to possess and exercise the powers it naturally possesses. In the case of human beings in particular, neuroscience may aspire to explain the neural conditions for the possibility of the mastery of a language, the possession of which is itself a condition of the possibility of rationality in both thought and action. However, neuroscience cannot displace or undermine the explanatory force of the *good reasons* we sincerely give for our behaviour, or invalidate the *justifications* we give for *rational* behaviour. The rationality of behaviour that is motivated by good reasons is not given a deeper explanation by specifying the neural facts that make it possible for creatures such as us to act for such reasons. When we apprehend the propriety, adequacy or goodness of the reasons for which a person acted, then we fully understand why he did what he did.

Neuroscience can contribute to explanations of irrational action

What neuroscience can do, however, is contribute to the explanation of irrational or partly irrational action. It may be able to explain why a person is more prone than normal to certain mental states – for example, of depression, which makes him more liable to act for a certain kind of a reason than someone who is not thus depressed. This can play an important role in explaining human behaviour in certain circumstances. But it is also important to note that such an explanation need not *supersede* the reasons the depressed person might give for committing suicide, for example. That he is depressive, perhaps pathologically depressive, does not imply that his reasons for killing himself are mere rationalizations, which play no role in rendering his behaviour intelligible. The neuroscientific explanation may complement the explanation the agent offers in terms of reasons, without rendering those reasons irrelevant.

Neuroscience can explain forms of incapacitation

Furthermore, neuroscience can explain – indeed, specializes in explaining – how gross pathological deficiencies in the exercise of normal human capacities result from damage to the brain. So it can brilliantly explain why patients *cannot* behave as normal humans can in a multitude of different ways. In particular, it may explain why such patients are, in one way or another, incapable of acting rationally in certain respects.

Neuroscience cannot explain normal human behaviour

The remarkable neuroscientific successes in explaining certain kinds of psychological pronenesses and liabilities of temperament, and in explaining pathological behaviour and deficiencies, do not demonstrate that neuroscience can or should ever aspire to explain normal human behaviour (as opposed to explaining the neural conditions of its possibility). What neuroscience can do is to explain, for normal human beings, how it is possible for them to be open to reason. But it cannot explain the rationale of human actions in the particular case, or elucidate what makes a certain reason a good reason. It can identify necessary conditions for the exercise of human capacities. But it does not follow that it is, or ever will be, in the position to specify a set of neural conditions that are sufficient conditions for characteristic human action in the circumstances of life. To explain typical human behaviour, one must operate at the higher, irreducible level of normal descriptions of human actions and their various forms of explanation and justification in terms of reasons and motives (as well as causes). These descriptions will cite multitudinous factors: past and prospective events that in given circumstances may constitute the agent's reasons for action; the agent's desires, intentions, goals and purposes; his tendencies, habits and customs; and the moral and social norms to which he conforms.

Our common or garden explanations of human conduct focus upon what it is that human beings do – typically identified in terms of *action* rather than *movement* (as noted in §8.1, we want to understand a person's moves, not his movements). Such identifications are highly context- and circumstance-dependent. Having clarified what it was that a person did or was doing in a given circumstance, it may still not be obvious *why* he acted as he did. This in turn may be explained by reference to his intentions, goals and purposes, his reasons or motives, his habits, customs and inclinations – in the context of human social, moral and legal life. Neuroscientific explanation is not in competition (let alone in conflict) with these kinds of explanation; but neither does it reduce these forms of explanation to neuroscientific ones.

13.2 Reduction by Elimination

Eliminative reductionism

Derivational reductionism looks singularly unpromising.[15]
But over the last twenty years there has been a more radical suggestion. Conceiving of our common or garden explanations of human conduct as parts of what they contemptuously refer to as 'folk psychology', some American philosophers, most notably Steven Stitch and Paul and Patricia Churchland, have suggested that this 'theory' of human behaviour is destined to be eliminated by a future neuroscientific theory. So they in effect advocate the *eliminative reduction* of psychological explanation of human behaviour to a future neuroscientific theory that will explain all human conduct. They accept the fact that the 'entities' that are involved in psychological explanation (reasons, motives, beliefs, desires, etc.) are *not* reducible to neuroscientific structures. But that, they aver, is because such 'entities' are mere fictions. The psychological level of explanation that intervenes between behaviour and neuroscientific theory is bogus, and requires elimination. All human behaviour will be fully explained by neuroscience without recourse to the primitive terms of psychology – either of the 'folk' variety or of the experimental sort.

What 'folk psychology' is supposed to be

Folk psychology, the eliminativists claim, incorporates the ordinary conceptual framework that we all use 'in order to comprehend, predict, explain and manipulate the behaviour of humans'. This framework 'includes concepts such as *belief, desire, pain, pleasure, love, hate, joy, fear, suspicion, memory, recognition, anger, sympathy, intention*, and so forth'. Accordingly, it constitutes our conception of what a person is. But eliminativists hold that folk psychology is much more than a mere array of concepts. It is also a *theory* about human behaviour. For 'the relevant framework is speculative, systematic, and corrigible, . . . it embodies generalized information, and . . . it permits explanation and prediction in the fashion of any theoretical framework'.[16] Being a theory, it propounds causal, explanatory laws (e.g. a person who incurs severe bodily damage will suffer pain; a

[15] The following section is a much shortened version of P. M. S. Hacker, 'Eliminative materialism', in S. Schroeder (ed.), *Wittgenstein and Contemporary Philosophy of Mind* (Routledge, London, 2001), pp. 60–84.
[16] P. M. Churchland, 'Folk psychology', in S. Guttenplan (ed.), *A Companion to the Philosophy of Mind* (Blackwell, Oxford, 1994), p. 308.

person who suffers pain will wince; a person denied food for any length of time will feel hungry), and it warrants predictions (e.g. people who desire that p, and believe that V'ing will bring it about that p, and have no overriding desires or preferred strategies, will generally try to V).

Three alleged failings of 'folk psychology'

'Folk psychology', thus conceived, is held to be a theory that belongs together with 'folk astronomy', 'folk physics', 'folk thermodynamics', 'folk biology', and so forth. The latter are held to be rudimentary or crude theories that have, over the last four centuries, been replaced by serious scientific theories. Folk psychology is destined for a similar fate. For it stands accused on three counts. (i) Explanatory, predictive and manipulative failures: folk psychology does not explain what sleep is or why we need it, how learning transforms us from infant to educated adult, the grounds of intelligence, how memory works, what mental illness is, or how it is to be cured. (ii) It has not progressed significantly in the last 2,500 years, has not shown the expansion and developmental fertility expected of a successful theory. (iii) It cannot be smoothly integrated into the emerging synthesis of the physical, chemical, biological and neuro-computational sciences. In particular, it is admitted, there is little prospect of a smooth theoretical reduction of the concepts, entities and laws of folk psychology to the more basic concepts, entities and laws of the advanced sciences of neurobiology, chemistry and physics.[17]

The alleged vacuity of its concepts suggests that folk psychology requires elimination

The first two counts suggest that folk psychology should be replaced by the science of experimental psychology, just as, according to the eliminativists, physical astronomy replaced folk astronomy, thermodynamics replaced folk thermodynamics, and biology replaced folk biology. But this is not what the eliminativists have in mind. In their view, the concepts of folk psychology are vacuous – comparable to the concepts of phlogiston, caloric, crystalline heavenly spheres and *élan vital*. So folk psychology must be *eliminated*. For, 'once folk psychology is held at arm's length and evaluated for theoretical strength in the way that any theory is evaluated, the more folkishly inept, soft and narrow it seems to be'.[18] Its concepts are as vacuous as *phlogiston, caloric, witch* and other similarly empty concepts that have been discarded with the progress of science. Hence, too, empirical psychology, which employs much the same array of vacuous concepts, will likewise be eliminated by the march of neuroscience. The crude laws of folk psychology and the alleged laws of experimental psychology will be replaced by precise laws of a future neuroscientific psychology.

13.2.1 Are our ordinary psychological concepts theoretical?

Why it is thought that our ordinary psychological concepts are theoretical

Our common explanations of human behaviour invoke a rich array of psychological concepts. But why should anyone suppose that they involve any *theory* of human

---

[17] Ibid., pp. 310f.

[18] P. S. Churchland, *Neurophilosophy: Toward a Unified Science of the Mind/Brain* (MIT Press, Cambridge, MA, 1986), p. 395.

behaviour? One reason given is that all judgement involves the application of concepts, that every concept is a node in a network of contrasting concepts, and that a concept's meaning is fixed by its position in the network. But any network of concepts is a speculative assumption or theory, minimally a theory as to the classes into which nature divides herself and the relations between them.[19] Learning the ordinary psychological vocabulary involves learning appropriate generalizations that specify conditions of correct application. Psychological terms are implicitly defined by such generalizations, and they are part of the theory of folk psychology. And our ordinary psychological explanations of human conduct include generalizations, which is a characteristic feature of theory.

Logical relationships do not imply theoreticity

This is a misconception. It is correct that concepts are interrelated by way of implication, compatibility and incompatibility. But this does not imply that all concepts are theoretical. That something is red all over implies that it is not blue, green, yellow, etc. all over, that it is darker than any pink object, and more like an orange object in respect of colour than like a yellow one. These propositions are not theoretical but conceptual or grammatical truths that are partly constitutive of the meaning of the word 'red'. That a piece in chess is the king implies that it is the piece that can be checked, that it moves one square at a time, that it can castle, etc. These propositions do not imply that 'chess king' is a theoretical concept, although, of course, they partially define what a chess king is.

The holistic character of language does not imply theoreticity

Every concept is indeed embedded in a ramifying network of concepts. This does not signify theoreticity, but the normative and holistic character of language. It shows that an expression is to be used in accordance with the rules that determine its meaning. And it shows that an expression has a meaning only as an expression in a language, in co-ordination with a host of further expressions with which it is conceptually or grammatically related by rules stipulating compatibilities, incompatibilities and implications. But it would be absurd to claim that *all* concepts are theoretical. For that would render vacuous the claim that a given concept – for example, of a meson or a quark – is theoretical, by contrast with, say, the concepts of a tree, a game of cricket or a table.

A conceptual network does not imply theoreticity

It is mistaken to suppose that a network of concepts is 'a speculative assumption or theory', let alone a theory as to the classes into which nature divides herself. Nature does not 'divide herself' into anything. Our concepts have various purposes. In so far as the purpose of a set of concepts is the scientifically and theoretically fruitful classification of natural phenomena, the concepts we introduce may be more or less useful relative to that purpose. But it is we who classify things thus, not nature. And *how* we classify things is determined not by nature but by our theoretical interests. Even scientific classification does not yield absolute, precise, purpose-independent categories, determined by the natural order of things. In biology, morphological criteria often quarrel with evolutionary criteria, and neither uniformly deliver determinate answers – assigning organisms to species, for example, is no less purpose-relative, variable and partly arbitrary than common or garden

---

[19] P. M. Churchland, *Matter and Consciousness*, rev. edn (MIT Press, Cambridge, MA, 1988), p. 80.

classification. There are many different ways of classifying the products of evolutionary processes, and whether one way or another is the most fruitful depends upon the specific purposes we have and on the peculiarities of the organisms in question.

Not all classification is done for purposes of theory
However, classifying for the purpose of scientific theory is only one kind of classificatory purpose. Our various classifications of artefacts (tools and weapons, clothing and buildings, paintings and sculptures), of their merits and demerits, and of the skills needed to make them are by and large not for scientific purposes at all. But even natural, as opposed to artefactual, objects may be classified for purposes other than scientific ones. They may be classified relative to the varieties of purposes and interests that we have in them. (The concept of a tree is one that finds no place in systematic botanical classification, but is a highly useful one for a multitude of other human purposes.)

A vocabulary is not a theory
Finally, a vocabulary is not a theory. The specialized vocabularies of the arts and crafts of our culture, of games and of rituals, of property and possession, of morality and law, are not theories of anything. English contains no theory, although by now it contains a host of theoretical terms that have accrued over the past few centuries as the theoretical sciences have evolved. A language is not a theory of anything, although it may provide the resources for the articulation of indefinitely many theories, including mutually contradictory ones. The Ptolomaic, Copernican and Keplerian theories of the solar system are all formulable in English and are mutually incompatible, but that does not make English an inconsistent language.

That observation is concept-laden does not imply that it is theory-laden
Of course, all articulate judgement involves the application of concepts. Articulate observation is concept-laden. But it does not follow that it is therefore theory-laden. There must be a contrast between what is theoretical and what is not if the term 'theoretical' is to have any content. A scientist's description of particle decay in a cloud chamber will be theory-laden, involving the use of non-observational theoretical terms. But a description of a garden as tidy, with daffodils and tulips in bloom, is not. Neither is the description of a person as *wondering* whether to go to the theatre tonight, as *thinking* that it would be *enjoyable*, and *deciding* to get tickets.

Acquiring concepts is not the same as learning a theory
In chapters 4–8 we surveyed a range of fundamental psychological concepts. We noted, in many cases, the various ways in which these concepts might be acquired. Some, we suggested, are grafted onto prelinguistic natural expressive behaviour (e.g. 'hurts', 'want'), while others (e.g. 'know', 'believe') are grafted onto pre-existent linguistic behaviour. What should be evident is that in acquiring such concepts a child is not learning a theory of anything; he is learning forms of human *behaviour*. In learning to replace his cries of pain with 'It hurts' and 'I have a pain', in learning to replace his cries of frustrated endeavour to get something with an 'I want', in learning to herald an action with an 'I am going to', the child is not learning a *folk theory* of human conduct; he is learning *human conduct*, learning to give expression to his pain and to express his desires and intentions. He is learning the Janus-faced use of psychological terms – their expressive (and later reportive) use in the first-person present and their descriptive use in the third

person. And in learning the rudimentary use of 'I know', 'I believe', and 'I think', the child is not learning a theory about his own inner states, but a language-game which presupposes a grasp of the difference between a well-founded assertion and one that is not adequately founded, or between expressing one's own judgement and expressing a derived one.

The uses of psychological predicates learnt by a child are not theoretical
The uses of psychological predicates that the child learns are far removed from theoretical concerns. First-person expressions of sensation, desire, intention, etc. are not hypotheses about one's own mental states. Ascriptions of psychological attributes to other people are not hypotheses about the existence of inner states in accordance with a common-sense theory. For thinking, believing, hoping and fearing that *p* are not inner states of a person hidden behind his behaviour. His behaviour, including his avowals of thought, belief, hope and fear, is not inductive evidence, let alone evidence for postulating the existence of unobserved entities. It is no theory that an utterance of the form 'I *V* that *p*' (where '*V*' is a verb such as 'think', 'believe', 'fear', etc.) is a criterion for the speaker's *V*'ing. It is, rather, as we have seen in §3.3, a rule for the use of the verb that is partly constitutive of its meaning.

Psychological concepts are not concepts of theoretical entities
Psychological concepts are not concepts of imperceptible entities, like genes or viruses, or concepts of theoretical entities, like mesons or quarks. They are not concepts of 'entities' at all. Our concepts of beliefs, thoughts, hopes, fears, expectations, etc. are not concepts of kinds of things, but abstractions from believings, thinkings, hopings, fearings and expectings. In one sense, what many of these verbs signify is often perfectly observable. For it is a conceptual confusion to suppose that the evidence for someone's suffering, joy or grief, for his believing or thinking, fearing or hoping, consists of 'bare bodily behaviour', of mere physical movements. On the contrary, we can typically see another's rage (when he is raging), see the grief or anguish visible upon his face and in his demeanour (when he is grieving or in anguish). One can hear a person's thoughts when he tells them to one, and read them if he writes them down. One needs no theory, folkish or otherwise, to hear or read the expressed thoughts of another. The fact that we need not reveal our thoughts, that we can sometimes suppress any manifestation of feelings, and that we can sometimes pretend, lie and deceive does not make psychological predicates theoretical.

13.2.2   Are everyday generalizations about human psychology laws of a theory?

The alleged theoretical doctrines of 'folk psychology'
Eliminativists contend that folk psychology incorporates not merely a large array of theoretical concepts, but also a large body of theoretical doctrine. They hold that the rudimentary, allegedly causal laws of folk psychology are used to explain and predict human behaviour in the standard 'covering-law' fashion. But this is confused.

Three types of generalization
We must distinguish various kinds of proposition here. First, propositions such as (1) 'People who suffer a sharp pain tend to wince' or (2) 'Angry people tend to get impatient' do not state causal laws.

Wincing is a logical criterion for being in pain – it is a form of pain-behaviour. That people commonly wince when in pain is not a discovery resulting from correlating people's winces with their being in pain, since we identify people's being in pain by reference to (among other things) their wincings. Similarly, although it is true that angry people tend to be impatient, this generalization is not a causal law, but a characterization of one form which anger may take. The anger is not a cause of the impatience; rather, it manifests itself in impatience. Moreover, to explain A's impatience by reference to his anger is no more to give a nomological explanation than is explaining someone's weeping by reference to their grief. It is not like explaining someone's white hair by reference to their age.

Second, propositions such as (3) 'People who want it to be the case that p and who believe that V'ing will bring it about that p, and have no overriding reason not to V, will generally V or try to V' and (4) 'People who believe that p, doubt whatever they apprehend as being incompatible with p' are likewise not simple causal generalizations. Rather, they are generalizations that rest on conceptual connections and are partly constitutive of the meanings of their constituent terms. If someone claims to want to bring it about that p, believes that V'ing will bring it about that p, and has no reason not to V, and yet does *not* V, then there is a reason for thinking that he does not really want to bring it about that p. If one knows or believes that if it is true that q, then it is false that p, and if one knows that p, then of course, one will not normally believe that q. But that is no empirical generalization. For not doubting that q here would be a logical criterion for one's *not* knowing that p, or of one's not knowing that if q then not p, or of not grasping the inference rule, and hence of not understanding the conditional. To grasp such truths as (3) and (4) is not to know or believe any psychological laws or empirical generalizations, but rather to have grasped the concepts of knowledge, belief, doubt and want.

Third, propositions such as (5) 'A person denied food for any length of time will feel hungry' and (6) 'Injury usually causes pain' are equally dubious candidates for causal laws allegedly discovered by the bogus 'folk theory' of human psychology. For injury is a circumstance in which pain-behaviour is a criterion of pain, and deprivation of food is a circumstance in which desire for food is a manifestation of hunger (rather than greed, for example). Injury is not merely causally, but also conceptually, linked with pain, as food deprivation is not merely causally, but also conceptually, linked with hunger.

Genuine examples of 'folk psychology'

Finally, one can indeed give examples of something that might be deemed 'folk psychology'. They are propositions such as (7) 'Spare the rod and spoil the child' or (8) 'Once bitten, twice shy'. These can hardly be taken to be theoretical statements, and whatever psychological terms occur in such statements are not implicitly defined by such generalizations.

Psychological explanation and prediction does not conform to the covering-law model

It is, of course, true that we explain and predict people's behaviour by reference to their thoughts, beliefs, wants, intentions, likings and dislikings. But it is mistaken to suppose that such explanations and predictions generally, or even typically, conform to the subsumption-theoretic covering-law model. On the contrary, they typically rely on principles of practical reasoning. That people generally do what they take themselves to have good reason to do, that they try to execute their intentions, that they tend to pursue what they see as desirable, are not causal generalizations. Even when appropriate generalizations and predictions do conform to the covering-law model, they are not in any sense proto-scientific laws. 'He hasn't eaten for hours, so he must be hungry' is no more theoretical or proto-scientific than 'It is starting to rain, so the laundry will get wet'.

We must obviously concede that our common or garden explanations are sometimes mistaken. Our self-understanding may be defective, and we sometimes deceive ourselves, so the explanations we offer of our own behaviour can be wrong. They may be correctable by others. But this does not suggest that our ordinary psychological concepts are obsolete and need to be replaced; it only shows what should be obvious: namely, that one is not always the final authority on one's own emotions and motives. Equally obviously, we can err in the explanations we give of the behaviour of others, and sometimes their behaviour and motivation may be altogether opaque. But this does not indicate deficiency of theory, let alone that the positing of unobservable entities such as beliefs and desires is unwarranted or ineffectual.[20] For ascribing knowledge, belief, desires or intention to others is not *positing* anything, and knowledge, belief, desire and intention are not theoretical entities of any kind. What it does indicate is that the logical criteria for the ascription of psychological attributes to others are, as we argued in §3.3, defeasible. It shows that human beings are fallible, and also that there is a degree of indeterminacy about the mental (e.g. about motivation, or about the authenticity of emotion). Various aspects of human behaviour can undeniably be clarified by empirical psychological research. This augments our understanding, but it *supplements* and does not *displace* our ordinary explanations of human behaviour. And the same applies to neuroscientific insights into the causes of a wide variety of behavioural deficiencies.

13.2.3 Eliminating all that is human

The three reasons for elimination rebutted

As we saw above (§13.2), eliminativists offer three reasons why folk psychology should be eliminatively reduced in favour of future neuroscience. The first was its explanatory and predictive failures in, for example, not explaining what sleep is, how learning is effected, the grounds of intelligence, or what mental illness is, and how it is to be cured. But since our normal psychological vocabulary is not theoretical and our normal observations, explanations and generalizations are not laws of a theory of any kind, the objection falls flat. Empirical psychology should and does offer theories and explanations of why we need sleep, what the basis of differential IQ is, what different kinds of mental illnesses there are, and how they can be cured. But it is as absurd to castigate our ordinary conceptual framework for failing to deliver such goods as it would be to blame our common or garden vocabulary of sticks and stones, chairs and tables (and attendant

---

[20] Cf. P. M. Churchland, *Scientific Realism and the Plasticity of the Mind* (Cambridge University Press, Cambridge, 1979), p. 91.

humdrum generalizations), for failing to come up with theories of matter and laws of mechanics.

The second reason was that so called folk psychology has not progressed over the last 2,500 years. Progress might indeed be argued to be the form of science. But since our psychological language is not a theoretical, scientific language, the accusation of 'lack of progress' is misguided. For it is less than clear what, in this context, 'progress' might mean. One may argue that the empirical science of psychology has indeed progressed – that much knowledge has been attained and that old theories have been refuted and replaced by more adequate theories. But this has no bearing on our common psychological vocabulary, for, as has been argued, a vocabulary and the network of logical relations between its constituents are no theory, and the explanations we give of our own behaviour and of the behaviour of others are not theoretical. One might indeed argue that the English psychological vocabulary (like the English aesthetic vocabulary) has been enriched over the past thousand years, but that would be ill-characterized as a form of scientific progress.

The third reason was that ordinary explanations of behaviour cannot be integrated into 'the emerging synthesis of the physical, chemical, biological and neuro-computational sciences'.[21] Since there can be no bridge principles linking psychological explanations with neuroscientific ones, and since there are no strict psychological laws, the question of the derivational reduction of ordinary psychological explanations to neuroscientific ones cannot arise. However, this gives no support to eliminative reduction. Rather, it indicates the absurdity of any form of reduction of the psychological, no matter whether derivational or eliminative.

That all knowledge and genuine understanding are scientific is a primitive modern belief

Underlying these three considerations is a primitive modern belief, characteristic of our times, that all knowledge and all genuine understanding are scientific. As Richard Dawkins succinctly puts it: 'Science is the only way we know to understand the real world.'[22] 'Science', in such declarations of faith, is physical science – in particular, microbiology, chemistry and, ultimately, physics. For, it is argued, 'in the dimension of describing and explaining the world, science is the measure of all things, of what is that it is and of what is not that it is not'.[23]

There is no such thing as 'explaining the world'

But, first, there is no such thing as 'explaining the world', only different ways of explaining different phenomena in the world. The theories of the various natural sciences do not, and do not purport to, describe and explain everything describable and explicable. Law, economics and sociology describe and explain legal, economic and sociological phenomena no less than physics describes and explains physical phenomena and chemistry describes and explains chemical phenomena. Within their proper domains, the social

---

[21] P. M. Churchland, 'Folk psychology', p. 311.
[22] R. Dawkins, 'Thoughts for the millennium: Richard Dawkins', in *Microsoft Encarta Encyclopaedia 2000* (Microsoft Corporation, 1993–9).
[23] W. Sellars, 'Empiricism and philosophy of mind', in his *Science, Perception and Reality* (Routledge and Kegan Paul, London, 1963), p. 173.

sciences are no less a measure of what is and what is not. And history, which is neither a natural nor a social science, is a measure of what was that it was and of what was not that it was not. Moreover, there is no prospect whatsoever that legal, economic, sociological and historical phenomena should be explained by, let alone be reducible to, any natural or biological science. It is grotesque to suggest that these subjects are all pseudo-sciences or mere fables, enmeshed in a vacuous and obsolete vocabulary. Is it being suggested that our ideas of how to explain the fall of the Roman Empire, the rise of Protestantism, the outbreak of the French Revolution, the causes of the First World War, are all *fictions*?

Science is not the measure of all things

Secondly, it is absurd to suppose that science, no matter whether social or natural, is the primary measure of what does and what does not exist. One needs no science to discover or come to know that there is a tree in the garden or that there are no trees in one's room. Nor does one need any science to explain that one went to Paris because one promised a friend to be there. Not everything that can be known can be known by mere observation, but nothing at all could be known without mere observation – and the ability to learn facts about the world around us is a prerogative of any human being, antecedent to science and the acquisition of scientific knowledge. *It is simply false to suggest that all observation is theory-laden.*

There are forms of explanation and understanding that are neither scient-ific nor theoretical

Thirdly, it is wrong-headed to suppose that the only forms of understanding are scientific, and that the only respectable forms of explanation of empirical phenomena are theoretical. It is wrong to suppose that philosophical understanding and philosophical explanation of conceptual error and confusion are mod-elled on scientific modes of understanding natural phenomena. It is no less mistaken to suppose that historical understanding is modelled on the understanding that characterizes physics, chemistry or neuroscience. Only dogmatism can lead one to suppose that either there is no such thing as understanding aesthetic phenomena – understanding works of literature, music, painting, sculpture and architecture – or that such understanding apes the understanding that scientists hope to achieve of physical or chemical phenomena. And we are all indebted to the understanding of human nature that is displayed in the works of such simple folk as Tolstoy and Dostoevsky, Proust and Henry James.

Abandoning theories and aban-doning concepts

Scientific theories are replaced in the course of scientific progress – Ptolomaic astronomy by Newtonian physics, and that in turn by relativity theory; caloric theory by thermodynamics. Sometimes concepts are jettisoned as vacuous (e.g. phlogiston, caloric, *élan vital*) and replaced by more fruitful ones. But fundamental changes in astronomy did not lead to the abandonment of the concepts of sun, moon and stars, any more than changes in chemical theory led to the abandonment of the concepts of burning and rusting, or of heat and cold, or changes in the life sciences led to jettisoning the concepts of a living creature, a dead creature and an inanimate thing. As we have seen, the eliminativists construe our psychological concepts as proto-scientific concepts on the same level as phlogiston, caloric or *élan vital*. But this is mistaken. Unlike such concepts, our normal psychological concepts are not postulates of *any* theory, but constitutive elements of the human form of life. Phlogiston was postulated to explain combustion, caloric to explain the transfer of heat, and *élan vital* to explain life. In due course it became clear that there are no such things – the concepts are vacuous and the explanations mistaken. But, as we have argued, our psychological concepts are not in the least like this.

Our ordinary psychological concepts are neither theoretical nor empty
Our psychological concepts are not theoretical concepts devised for scientific purposes, though it is true that the psychological and neuropsychological sciences use them, just as chemistry uses the concepts of water and iron, and biology uses such concepts as *cat* and *dog*. They are used, *among other things*, to describe the phenomena that are the subject matter of empirical psychology (but they are *also* used to exhibit or manifest these phenomena, to give them articulate expression). It may well be that there are technical concepts in current empirical psychology that will be abandoned by future psychology. But this does not show that there are no beliefs and thoughts, perceptions and sensations, desires and intentions. Nothing answers to the concepts of phlogiston, caloric or *élan vital*. But it cannot be said that nothing answers to our ordinary psychological concepts. There are criteria for the application of these terms, and these criteria are satisfied daily, innumerable times, in the life of every normal human being. It is only when the logic of these expressions is misconstrued, as it is by the eliminativists, and wrongly taken to signify theoretical, unobservable entities, that it can confusingly seem as if it might be that nothing answers to these concepts.

On misconstruing the role of our psychological vocabulary
Eliminativists construe our ordinary psychological vocabulary as being used 'in order to comprehend, predict, explain and manipulate the behaviour of humans'. It is true that we understand ourselves in these terms. We do predict human behaviour by reference to desires, intentions, purposes and goals. We explain why people do the things they do by reference to motives, character traits, beliefs and commitments. And we sometimes (sometimes immorally) manipulate others, making use of our knowledge of their beliefs, likings and dislikings, hopes and fears (although to advise, persuade or suggest is not, as such, to manipulate). But, first, this does not imply that our psychological vocabulary is a theory of anything. Secondly, it would be absurd to try to specify *the* function or functions of our psychological vocabulary. Its functions are as diverse as those of human speech, and its ramifications as extensive as the phenomena of human life itself. This should not be surprising, since these expressions, both in the diversity of their use and in their signification, are partly constitutive of human life. This 'conceptual framework' does not merely constitute our 'conception of what a person is' – it also makes us the kind of beings that we are.

Our psychological language is partly constitutive of psychological phenomena
Without language, we are but naked apes. Without the language of psychological expressions, we are not self-conscious creatures. Without self-consciousness, we are not moral beings. For what makes us human is what flows from possession of a rich language. And our psychological language is not merely a descriptive instrument for the characterization of what we observe around us. It is partly *constitutive* of the phenomena that it is *also* used to describe, precisely because the first-person, present-tense use of psychological verbs is typically a criterion for others to say

'He believes (wants, intends, etc.)'. The use of these phrases in the first-person present tense is characteristically to *express* a belief, want or intention. The paradigmatic expressions of distinctively human intentions and desires, thoughts and beliefs, loves and hates, are verbal. They are not descriptions of the inner, but manifestations of it. And for a wide range of psychological attributes and their objects, what is thereby manifest is something that is possible only for a creature that has mastered the use of the psychological vocabulary in all its multiplicity and diversity, the use of which is partly constitutive of what it is to be human.

13.2.4 Sawing off the branch on which one sits

The assumption, claim and conclusion of eliminativism are misguided

The fundamental assumption of the eliminativist – namely, that our ordinary psychological vocabulary is theoretical – is false. So too is the eliminativist claim that our ordinary explanations of human conduct are theoretical. And their conclusion that our ordinary modes of describing and explaining ourselves and others are obsolete science destined to be replaced by millennial neuro- and computational science is confused. But their confusions run even deeper than this.

The allegation that 'folk psychology' has failed to explain psychological phenomena is confused

First, among the reasons for faulting what is deemed to be 'folk psychology' are the allegations that it has failed to explain the nature of learning (i.e. acquiring knowledge, well-confirmed beliefs and reasoned opinions), that it has not explained how memory works, or the nature of mental illness (e.g. manic depression, anxiety neurosis, paranoia) or how to cure it. But, if the eliminativists are right, there are no such illnesses. For there is no such thing as being chronically depressed or irrationally exuberant, no such thing as feeling anxious or fearful, and no one ever believes that others are out to harm them. There is nothing to explain about memory, any more than there is anything to explain about the workings of caloric – since the two concepts are equally vacuous. And there can be no such thing as learning theory, since there is no such thing as knowing, believing or opining. So there is nothing, in this dimension of problems, that our ordinary conceptual scheme has failed to do, which, according to the eliminativist, needs to be done.

The eliminativist conception of explanation is internally incoherent

Secondly, the eliminativists look to the advances of neuroscience and computer science to *explain* various phenomena, including phenomena pertaining to memory, learning, consciousness and so on. But *explanation* is internally, conceptually, related to *understanding*, as well as to *coming to know*, to well-founded *belief*, and to reasoned *opinion*. But all these terms are on the Index as far as eliminativism is concerned. Hence it is altogether opaque what they can mean by 'explain', if the concept of explanation is severed from its connections with these epistemic concepts of so-called folk psychology.

If the concepts of psychology are vacuous, there can be nothing for psychology to explain

Thirdly, the eliminativists are concerned with the alleged faults of proto-psychology. They contend not only that 'folk psychology' fails to explain what, in their view, it should explain, but further, that its characterization of the putative explananda is wholly misconceived. For the concepts it deploys are vacuous. What a true science of psychology needs is a new vocabulary, derived from neuroscience and computer science. But there can be no science of psychology if there are no creatures with minds – with intellectual capacities for knowledge, belief, thought and opinion, as well as volitional capacities to act for reasons, and out of motives, and affective capacities to feel emotions, to suffer pain and take pleasure in things. If the concepts of what is so misguidedly deemed to be 'folk psychology' are vacuous, then the subject matter of genuine psychology does not exist – just as there can be no scientific study of witchcraft if there are no witches, or of ghosts if there are no ghosts.

The eliminativist in effect saws off the branch on which he is seated

Finally, the very statement of the eliminativists' claims presupposes the non-vacuous use of the concepts which the eliminativist contends are vacuous. For the mere use of language in making assertions and asking questions presupposes the applicability of such concepts as intention, meaning something by what one says, knowledge and belief, having reasons and being able to give reasons, understanding and explaining. Does the eliminativist *believe* what he says – or does he *not* believe what he says, as the cooling of water in a jug does *not* involve the transfer of caloric? Or does he neither believe nor not believe? Does he *intend* to *convince* his readers of the truth of his words? Or does he *not* so intend, as the oxidation of iron does *not* involve any phlogiston? Is his utterance *intentional*? Or *unintentional*? If it is not intentional, nor yet unintentional, neither accidental nor inadvertent, is it an *utterance* at all? If he neither *means* what he says nor *means anything* by what he says, has he actually *said* anything at all? Does he expect us to be *persuaded* by his arguments? Does he *have reasons* for saying what he says, or is he speaking without reason? Does he have reasons *for what he says*, or are his contentions unfounded dogmatism? Obviously, he claims to be offering many different reasons for his strange theory. But can a being have reasons for certain claims, and yet neither believe nor fail to believe that these reasons support the claims? And so on. The eliminativist saws off the branch upon which he is perched. For if what he claims were true, his utterances could not be taken to be assertions or claims, and his supporting arguments could not be taken to be reasons for believing what he says.

Eliminative materialism is not a serious option, since it is not a serious possibility for the study of human nature and behaviour to jettison the concepts that define its subject matter and the use of which in discourse is partly constitutive of its subjects. Not only could students of human nature not abandon these concepts yet continue to study the explanation of human behaviour, but further, if it could be shown that they had no application to a certain creature, it would thereby be shown that the creature was not a person, nor even a human being.

14

Methodological Reflections

Vindication by practice antecedes defence of the method

We have thus far abstained from any detailed methodological reflections. Such matters are often passion provoking, and, if conducted in the absence of examples of the use of the methodology and of the results of its application, are bound to be indecisive and unconvincing save to the converted. Philosophy, at the beginning of the twenty-first century, is riven with disagreements over the nature, methods and limits of the subject. We have not, in this book, tried to defend our methodology in the face of alternative approaches to the philosophy of psychology.[1] Rather, we have *practised* analytic philosophy of mind of the kind pioneered by Wittgenstein and further developed by many other analytic philosophers. Believing that methods are vindicated by their products, we have preferred to apply the methods of connective analysis[2] to the conceptual problems that characterize neuroscience at the point where it abuts on psychology. Having shown what can be achieved by such methods of conceptual elucidation, we can now turn to methodological questions and objections.

First objection: apparent error is in fact linguistic innovation warranted by new neuroscientific theory

The first matter we shall address is one which has already been mooted. In §3.2 we touched upon three methodological qualms. Now we shall investigate a deeper methodological objection. For it is commonly held that the kinds of errors that we have detected in the writings of neuroscientists are no more than linguistic innovations warranted by *advanced theory*. Philosophy, it is claimed, has no licence to criticize the linguistic innovations of scientists, whose *theories* determine whether it does or does not make sense to ascribe psychological attributes to the brain. Conceptual analysis, of the kind exemplified in this book, is, it is argued, merely a form of pernicious conceptual conservatism that stands in the way of creative science.

---

[1] Our differences with the approaches of Daniel Dennett and John Searle, however, are surveyed in the two appendices.

[2] 'Connective analysis' (or 'connective elucidation') is a term of art introduced by P. F. Strawson in *Analysis and Metaphysics* (Oxford University Press, Oxford, 1992), ch. 2. It is a convenient term to refer to the methods of conceptual investigation cultivated by Wittgenstein and many other analytic philosophers in the middle of the twentieth century.

Second objection: apparent errors are just figurative uses of language by neuroscientists due to inadequacies of the English language

A rather different criticism, more diffident and less ebulliently self-confident, also needs to be rebutted. It is Blakemore's claim that the assertions of many neuroscientists, in which we have detected various forms of violation of the mereological principle, are no more than *figurative* or *metaphorical* uses of language, or even *poetic licence*. For, it is argued, ordinary language does not equip the neuroscientist with an adequate vocabulary with which to articulate his ideas. He knows perfectly well what he thinks, but lacks the verbal equipment to say what he means save in these ways.

Tactics to be pursued in the following discussion

We shall then take some examples from the writings of eminent neuroscientists, who commit the kinds of errors against which we have been arguing, and show, first, that (as should by now be obvious) far from their misuses of expressions being mere *façons de parler*, they are conceptual confusions integral to the theoretical explanations being advanced; and secondly, that there is no difficulty whatsoever in stating all that has been discovered without any logical errors and without recourse to metaphor or poetic licence. All that is lost thereby is an incoherent theoretical explanation. It is not deficiencies in the English language that are responsible for the obfuscations and incoherences that are to be found in the writings of so many cognitive neuroscientists – it is, rather, deficiencies of understanding, inadequate grasp of the concepts and conceptual connections in terms of which those neuroscientists describe their discoveries and endeavour to explain their implications for the understanding of human psychology.

Finally, in view of the widespread misunderstandings among neuroscientists of what philosophy should or should not do, we attempt to clarify the nature of the contribution that philosophy can make to neuroscience.

14.1 Linguistic Inertia and Conceptual Innovation

Recapitulation

Throughout our investigation we have laid much emphasis on how psychological expressions are used. And we have shown, from case to case, how certain neuroscientists (as well as psychologists and cognitive scientists) misuse our ordinary psychological vocabulary, misconstruing the meanings of numerous psychological expressions. Indeed, we have, from the beginning of our analytical discussions, laid emphasis on the error of ascribing to the brain attributes which it makes sense to ascribe only to living persons (and some non-human animals) as a whole. We called this error 'the mereological fallacy in neuroscience', and we drew attention to how widespread it is among neuroscientists, who ascribe psychological predicates to the brain in order to explain the psychological attributes of human beings. We argued that such predications *make no sense*, that *there is no such thing* as the brain's thinking or reasoning, feeling pain or perceiving something, imagining or wanting things.

The kind of approach that we have adopted is not novel. With some qualifications, it can be said to go back as far as Socrates's Way of Words and Aristotle's frequent appeals to *ta legomena* ('what is said'). In the twentieth century, it was brilliantly developed

Churchland's four objections to the
examination of use as a key to the
determination of sense

by those who took the 'linguistic turn' initiated by
Wittgenstein, and it was cultivated by numerous analytic
philosophers quite irrespective of whether they were followers of Wittgenstein. What was common to those who
took the linguistic turn was the belief, as Paul Grice put it, 'that a careful examination of
the detailed features of ordinary discourse is required as a foundation for philosophical
thinking'.[3] This approach, with its insistence that the examination of the ways in which
words are used is a *sine qua non* for the elucidation of concepts, and hence indispensable for
the solution, resolution or dissolution of conceptual problems, has been subjected to
criticism by cognitive scientists and by philosophers influenced by Quine.[4] Their qualms
are well represented by the criticisms of Patricia Churchland, who objects to the scrutiny
of usage in order to clarify what does and what does not make sense. We have argued that
the idea that certain mental states might be identical with brain states is incoherent – that
it does not make sense, for example, to identify a stomach-ache with a state of the brain,
or to identify believing that it is going to rain with a neural state. But, Churchland objects,
'whether a hypothesis makes sense to someone will not be independent of his background
beliefs and assumptions. So what makes no sense to a dualist may make perfectly good
sense to a physicalist.'[5]

Secondly, she adds,

whether something is conceivable or imaginable is not independent of one's belief
network and one's capacity to imagine. It was easy for Galileo to conceive of the Earth

---

[3] H. P. Grice, 'Reply to Richards', in R. E. Grandy and R. Warner (eds), *Philosophical Grounds of
Rationality* (Clarendon Press, Oxford, 1986), p. 51. Indeed, he went further, to 'proclaim it as my
belief that linguistic botanizing is indispensable, at a certain stage, in a philosophical enquiry, and
that it is lamentable that this has been forgotten, or has never been learnt' (ibid., p. 57).
[4] Quine and his followers suppose that all 'conceptualization' is theory-ridden. So as soon as
language is used, theory is involved. (Accordingly, 'Mummy, I want a glass of water' is part of the
child's 'theory of the world', and the response 'Be quiet, dear, it is time to go to sleep' is part of the
mother's 'theory of the world'.) They suggest that there is no distinction between conceptual truths
(e.g. that red is a colour, or that nothing can be red and green all over, or that red is more like
orange than it is like yellow) and empirical truths (e.g. that this carpet is red, or that this carpet is
more like an Afghan than a Shiraz) – and, by implication, no difference between norms of representation (which is what most conceptual truths are) and statements of fact. Hence, too, they think
that philosophy is continuous with science, and a part of the same enterprise as (they ascribe to)
science: viz. the construction of theories about 'the world'. Nothing, in our view, could be further
from the truth. This is not the place to argue the matter. But, we suggest, our analyses of conceptual
structures throughout this book vindicate our approach. For a detailed comparison of the conflicting
views of Quine and Wittgenstein, and for criticisms of Quine's conception of philosophy and its
methods, see P. M. S. Hacker, *Wittgenstein's Place in Twentieth-Century Analytic Philosophy* (Blackwell,
Oxford, 1996), ch. 7. For more comprehensive criticism of Quine, see H.-J. Glock, *Quine and
Davidson on Language, Thought and Reality* (Cambridge University Press, Cambridge, 2003).
[5] P. S. Churchland, *Neurophilosophy: Toward a Unified Science of the Mind/Brain* (MIT Press, Cambridge, MA, 1986), p. 272.

as one planet among others moving around the sun, but his detractors found it outrageous and inconceivable.... Similarly, whether it is or is not part of the concept of mental states that no physical state *could* characterize the essential nature of the mental property denoted ... will depend on whether it is believed to be possible that mental states are brain states. For those who have a framework within which it *is* possible, · *their* concepts of mental states and mental properties, and their intuitions, will run quite the opposite of [others]. Which means that the intuitions one has about certain concepts cannot decide anything about the actual empirical nature of what those concepts are believed to apply to.[6]

Thirdly, Churchland confronts the accusation that the mereological fallacy is rife among neuroscientists and cognitive scientists with the remark that

the suggestion that the brain remembers or has knowledge or uses linguistic symbols is sometimes pilloried as a mere conceptual error that consists in taking categories appropriate to one domain and applying them to a different, inappropriate domain. But one person's category error is another person's deep theory about the nature of the universe.... The important thing for getting at the truth about brains is not whether in customary usage ordinary humans-in-the-street do say that persons remember but do not say that brains remember; rather it is whether we ought to say that brains remember – whether given the empirical facts, it is a reasonable hypothesis that brains remember.[7]

Finally, she argues, criticism of the new neuroscientific usage displays a form of linguistic inertia that is altogether unwarranted:

Since in the normal course of scientific progress the meanings of words undergo change as a result of theory change, then when a hypothesis is advanced that would result in meaning change, this is not *of itself* an objection to the hypothesis.... Hence, what to ancient ears sounded like an odd thing to say comes to seem entirely ordinary and correct. This is because the ancient ears are informed by ancient theory....
... The assumption that a new theory's adequacy is compromised if its terms fail to preserve synonymy with the terms of the old theory is perniciously conservative. For it implies that preservation of the status quo should override considerations of empirical adequacy.[8]

Many neuroscientists may find these objections congenial. The preoccupation with 'mere words' may seem to them to be footling, and irrelevant to the onward march of science. But if it so seems, it seems wrongly. We are what we are because we are masters of a rich, sophisticated language. We have achieved what we have achieved by way of understanding the world and ourselves because of 'mere words' – for these are the instruments of thought and reasoning. It behoves us to be aware of our instruments and to ensure that they are clean.

---

[6] Ibid., p. 273.
[7] Ibid., pp. 273f.
[8] Ibid., p. 274.

Whether a hypothesis makes sense depends on whether its constituent terms are used correctly

To Churchland's objections we reply as follows: first, whether a putative hypothesis makes sense depends upon the meanings – that is, the correct uses – of the words that formulate it. The meanings of words are determined by their rule-governed use, and they are given by what are accepted as correct explanations of meaning by the community of speakers. For explanations of meaning function as rules or standards for the correct use of the expressions concerned. The ordinary use of an expression is no *more* the ordinary use of the 'human-in-the-street' than it is the ordinary use of the professor in his study or the neuroscientist in his laboratory. It is the standard use, which can be contrasted with figurative or metaphorical or secondary uses. It should be noted that the terms which have concerned us throughout this study, and the terms that problematically concern cognitive neuroscientists in their investigations into the neural basis of sensation, perception, thought, imagination, memory, voluntary movement, etc. are non-technical terms. (Of course, they are supplemented by a host of technical and quasi-technical terms, but the dispute does not turn on those.)

The ordinary use of technical and of non-technical terms

The ordinary use of a non-technical expression (e.g. 'mind', 'body', 'to perceive', 'to think', 'to remember') may be contrasted with the ordinary use of technical terms (e.g. 'hippocampus', 'amygdala', 'prefrontal cortex', 'epileptic automatism'). Technical terms in turn may be theoretical terms or non-theoretical terms. Most of the technical terms of neuro-anatomy are not theoretical. By contrast, many of the technical terms invoked in neurophysiology are (although, of course, some of them are theoretical terms of other sciences, such as physics and physical chemistry). Technical terms, both theoretical and non-theoretical, are used in the formulation of scientific hypotheses. However, whether a hypothesis makes sense must be settled in advance of determining its truth or its evidential support. Otherwise we would not know what it is we are supposed to establish to be the case, for which we have to seek confirming evidence. Whether a certain sentence formulates an intelligible hypothesis will, of course, depend upon its constituent technical and non-technical expressions and their mode of combination in the sentence. The meanings of these expressions, whether technical or non-technical, is independent of the beliefs of the hypothesizer.

Churchland's first objection rebutted: questions of sense antecede questions of truth

To turn to Churchland's first worry, the idea that 'what makes no sense to a dualist may make perfectly good sense to a physicalist' is doubly misconceived. Dualism and physicalism are not scientific theories of any kind. No experiments can determine whether the mind is or is not an immaterial substance, and Descartes's arguments in support of his form of dualism did not adduce experimental evidence to support his claims. Similarly, no *experimentum crucis* can prove that believing that it will rain tomorrow is a state of the believer's brain, or that wanting to go to Naples is identical with a certain brain state. Dualism and physicalism are philosophical, metaphysical doctrines. They invoke the normal vocabulary of the mental. These expressions – for example, 'to hope', 'to fear', 'to know', 'to remember', 'to believe', 'to think', 'to perceive', 'to have a toothache' – are not theoretical terms of any science. What meaning they have is not determined by metaphysical doctrines, but by their ordinary use. The question is not whether these expressions make sense *to* a dualist or a physicalist, but rather, whether the dualist's or physicalist's use of these common or garden expressions *makes sense*. The issue is not whether a certain doctrine propounded by a dualist or a physicalist – for example, that the mind is a spiritual substance or that the mind is identical with the brain – makes sense *to him*, but only whether it makes sense. For the question of whether a doctrine makes sense *to* a person is roughly equivalent to the question of whether it *seems* plausible to him. But the question of whether an assertion or apparent hypothesis makes sense is not a person-relative one, nor is it a question about apparent plausibility. It is a question concerning the meaning and well-formedness of a sentence or sentences, a question that antecedes truth and falsehood. And in order for such a putative empirical hypothesis as that the brain thinks and infers (or that the brain is contingently identical with the mind) to be *either* true *or* false, it must make sense – it must be possible to specify what would *count* as its being true, and also what would count as confirming or disconfirming it.

Churchland's second objection rebutted: conceivability and imaginability are not criteria for making sense

Churchland's second objection was that what is conceivable or imaginable is not independent of one's beliefs, one's capacity to imagine things, and one's intuitions. Whether it is a feature of the concept of a mental state that it excludes a mental state's being identical with a state of the brain depends, she argued, on whether one has a 'framework' within which it is possible. But this is mistaken for more reasons than one.

Neither conceivability nor imaginability are criteria for whether a form of words makes sense or is nonsensical, and the determination of the boundaries between sense and nonsense is not fixed by conceivability or imaginability. It is true that Galileo found it easy to conceive of the Earth 'as one planet among others moving around the sun', and that 'his detractors found it outrageous and inconceivable'. But what they found outrageous was Galileo's suggesting what he suggested – which flew in the face of received doctrine and religious dogma – and what they found 'inconceivable' was that God would have created the abode of humanity anywhere other than in the centre of the cosmos. They did not find the idea that the Earth is a planet circling the sun literally inconceivable – they could conceive it perfectly well. They *understood* exactly what Galileo was asserting. They did not think it was a meaningless concatenation of words; on the contrary, they thought it was patently false. They did not object that it makes no more sense to suppose the Earth to move than it does for the number three to turn green with envy. Rather, they objected that if the Earth moves, how can it be that there is no wind, or that objects thrown vertically upwards do not land hundreds of feet away, or that no stellar parallax was observable.[9] These are empirical, not semantic, objections. (By contrast, the relevant criticisms of cognitive neuroscience are all criticisms that cast doubt upon the *sense* of certain cognitive neuroscientific assertions, not upon their truth.) Furthermore, what is and what is not logically possible has nothing to do with anyone's 'intuitions' (hunches,

---

[9] Stellar parallax was not observable until the eighteenth century, when much more powerful telescopes than Galileo had became available.

conjectures or guesses) about concepts. It has to do only with the correct use of words, with the rules for their use and with the explanations of what they mean. Of course, concepts determine nothing about the empirical nature of what they signify – that is something that needs to be discovered in experience. What makes sense and what is nonsense is up to the rules of language, including the explanations of meaning that provide standards for the correct use of words. What is true or false is up to the world.

To adopt a new framework is to change the rules and therewith the meanings

However, given that what does and does not make sense is determined by the rules of language, then surely we can change the rules as we think fit? So it may seem that we can 'adopt a framework' in which it *does* make sense to say that believing is a state of the brain, or that the brain thinks and draws inferences. But this is misguided. There is no such thing as 'adopting a framework' in which nonsense makes sense – *without changing the rules of the game*. It makes no sense to speak of its being five o'clock on the sun, or of something being both red all over and green all over simultaneously – for we have given no meaning to these forms of words. We can *give* them a meaning, and 'adopt a new framework' in which it makes sense to speak thus – *if we lay down coherent new rules for the use of these expressions*. But the words will not then mean what they do now, and we shall have given a new meaning to 'five o'clock' or to 'on the sun', and to 'red', or 'green', or 'all over', or 'simultaneously'. Of course, were we to do this, then what we say would *not* conflict with anyone's previous beliefs – for we should be speaking of something different.

Neuroscientists are not trying to introduce new terms in place of the existing psychological vocabulary

Our criticisms of the mereological fallacy in neuroscience do not preclude neuroscientists from using the verbs 'to think', 'to believe', 'to perceive', 'to remember' in new ways according to conditions other than the received conditions of their use, as long as they can explain what these new uses mean. They can, if they so wish, redefine 'thinking', 'believing', 'perceiving', 'remembering', and *give* a meaning to the phrases 'My brain thought that it was better to keep silent', 'Your brain believes that it is Tuesday tomorrow', 'His brain perceived that she was smiling', or 'Her brain remembered to go home'. Our point was that they have not done so. Nor is there any evidence that they want to do so, for they are trying to discover the neural basis for *thinking, believing, perceiving* and *remembering* – and not for *something else*. But if they did wish to give such phrases a meaning, more work would be needed than merely adding an asterisk to an existing expression (e.g. 'representation*' (see §3.2)) and specifying that the brain has the things signified. New formation rules would have to be stipulated, the conditions for the correct application of these innovative phrases would need to be specified, and the logical consequences of their application would have to be spelled out. Of course, if this were done, the constituent words of these phrases would no longer have the same meaning as they have now. So neuroscientists would not be investigating the neural conditions of thinking, believing, perceiving and remembering at all, but rather those of something else, which is as yet undefined and undetermined. But this is patently not what neuroscientists wish to do.

Churchland confronts the accusation of committing what we have called 'the mereological fallacy in neuroscience' by claiming that 'one person's category error is another person's

Churchland's objection to the accusation of committing the mereological fallacy rebutted

deep theory about the nature of the universe'. What is important, in her view, is not whether people say that brains remember, but whether we ought to say that they do – 'whether . . . it is a reasonable hypothesis that brains remember'. But this is confused. For if a sentence '*s*' contains a category error in one person's idiolect and expresses a deep theory in another person's idiolect, then '*s*' has a quite different meaning in the two idiolects. And whether it is a reasonable hypothesis that brains remember can only be determined once it is clear what is to be *called* 'the brain's remembering'. If that is undetermined, then there is no hypothesis to consider at all, any more than it is a hypothesis that it is now five o'clock on the sun. For the sense of a hypothesis must be settled in advance of determining whether the hypothesis is true or false, reasonable or unreasonable. If a hypothesis makes sense, then we can have recourse to the facts to establish whether it is reasonable or not – but we can no more have recourse to such facts to establish whether a sentence makes sense than we can have recourse to the facts to establish whether a mathematical proposition is a theorem. Empirical facts cannot determine the truth of a mathematical theorem, and facts about the brain cannot determine whether a form of words, such as 'the brain remembers', makes sense either.

Churchland's fourth objection concerning changes of word meaning in new theory rebutted

Churchland's fourth objection was that the meanings of words may change with change of theory, and that this is no objection to the new theory. What is said in terms of the new theory may sound strange to those unfamiliar with the new usage, but it is (or may be) perfectly correct for all that. With this we agree. If it were the case that neuroscientists coherently redefined the terms 'perceive', 'think', 'imagine', 'remember', etc., and if the terms thus redefined were theoretical terms within a complex theory, then accusations of committing the mereological fallacy might lapse. We should then have to find out what neuroscientists mean by these homonyms, and see what is meant by asserting that the brain perceives, thinks, believes or remembers. But, to repeat, neuroscientists have not done so. They are concerned with explaining the neural foundations of our capacity for perception, thought, imagination and memory, and the latter expressions are not theoretical terms in an advanced science, but common or garden terms of daily discourse about ourselves.

Why it cannot be said that neuroscientists are unconsciously changing the meanings of terms

It might be argued that neuroscientists are not consciously, overtly, changing the meanings of our psychological vocabulary, but rather that they are in the process of unwittingly or even unconsciously redefining these terms, gradually and imperceptibly changing their meanings. So, although it makes no sense to speak of the brain's perceiving, thinking, imagining or remembering if these expressions have their old meaning, it does make sense to the extent that they are taking on a new meaning. But this too is confused.

What gradual change of meaning is

First, although the meaning of such psychological expressions may change gradually, the gradual change does not consist in minute and unnoticeable changes of meaning which, over time, accumulate. Rather, it consists in a few speakers using a given psychological term in a way that is importantly different from its received use, and explaining what they mean by it in a given sentence in novel ways. What is gradual is the increase in the number of people who adopt the new usage, not the accretion of a new meaning. But there is nothing 'gradual' about the change in the meaning of a psychological word 'W' when it is given a new use. How could there be? After all, the new use will allow for combinatorial possibilities in syntax which the previous use ruled out as senseless – for example, to attach such verbs as 'think', 'infer', 'guess' to the subject term 'the brain'. But there can be no 'gradual transition' from not predicating one of these verbs of the brain to predicating it of the brain, any more than there can be a gradual transition from talking of $\sqrt{1}$ to talking of $\sqrt{-1}$.

Two sources of conceptual confusions among neuroscientists: from the Cartesian tradition and from AI

Secondly, if such changes are afoot, then the new usage, which is gradually and imperceptibly *being adopted* by more and more neuroscientists, should be explicable. It must be possible for neuroscientists who adopt the new usage to say what they mean by it. But there is no such gradual change going on in neuroscience in this respect. The vast majority of neuroscientists *already* speak and write this way, and none of them offer any explanations of what they mean by ascribing psychological attributes to the brain. Conceptual confusions are built into the received forms of cognitive neuroscientific modes of description. These confusions have at least two primary sources. (i) They are inherited from the Cartesian tradition, ascribing to the brain the very same psychological predicates that Descartes ascribed to the mind. (ii) They are derived from discourse about computers in which psychological predicates are (mis)applied to machines, and in which talk of 'information processing' is apt.[10] The confusions that result from this second source are part of the legacy of the so-called cognitive (computationalist) revolution, which, as Jerome Bruner admits, so unfortunately overtook psychology in the second half of the twentieth century.[11]

14.2 The 'Poverty of English' Argument

Blakemore's objection to the mereological principle rebutted

In §3.2 we mentioned Colin Blakemore's remark that Wittgenstein's statement of what we have called 'the mereological principle' seems trivial or even just plain wrong. Blakemore claimed that the confusions to which we have been objecting are merely metaphors, involving poetic licence and due to an inadequate vocabulary. In his view, neuroscientists do not fall into any 'conceptual blunders' of the kind we have suggested. But we showed that in the very statement of his case, Blakemore himself

---

[10] We shall not here defend the view that the application of cognitive predicates to machines is either figurative or misconceived. For a detailed discussion, see P. M. S. Hacker, *Wittgenstein: Meaning and Mind* (Blackwell, Oxford, 1990), in the essay entitled 'Men, minds and machines'.

[11] It is most striking that Bruner, one of the founding fathers of the cognitive revolution that occurred in psychology in the mid-twentieth century, was subsequently to 'decry . . . the Cognitive Revolution for abandoning "meaning making" as its central concern, opting for "information processing" and computation instead' (J. Bruner, *Acts of Meaning* (Harvard University Press, Cambridge, MA, 1990), p. 137).

committed precisely the kind of conceptual blunder that we have in mind. For he asserted that the metaphorical (or figurative) 'maps' in the brain – that is, the mappings of features presented in the visual field on to the firing of cells in the cortex – 'play an essential part in the representation and interpretation of the world by the brain, just as the maps of an atlas do for the reader of them'. For, we pointed out, the brain cannot intelligibly be said to *interpret* the world (or anything in it), and the relationship between the brain and the mappings of features of the animal's sensory fields on to various areas of the cortex is precisely *not* analogous to the relationship between a reader and an atlas.

Neuroscientists' application of psy-chological predicates to the brain can-not be justified by reference to the poverty of English

In so far as neuroscientists began applying psychological predicates to the brain in a metaphorical or figurative sense, there is ample evidence to show that they became enmeshed in their own metaphors. However, Blakemore went on to claim that the alleged neuroscientific recourse to metaphor and figurative speech, even to 'poetic licence', is due to the fact that neuro-scientists lack an adequate language in terms of which to non-metaphorically articulate their discoveries and give expression to their thoughts concerning the relationship between the brain and human psychological attributes. We shall say nothing about the suggestion that neuroscientific attributions of psychological attributes to the brain are simply poetic licence. But the claim that the vocabulary of English (or indeed of any other developed natural language) is inadequate for the purposes of neuroscience is worth exploring. Science, Blakemore contends, 'runs out of words'.

> One of the most profoundly enigmatic aspects of science is that it often has to use everyday language to formulate questions and concepts concerning a world beyond everyday experience. It is true that some areas of intellectual effort (such as mathematics, logic and music) have devised new systems of notation because everyday language has proved inadequate as a medium of communication of questions and ideas in these disciplines. But most areas of science stumble along, using ordinary language to 'bootstrap' themselves up to new concepts. Nowhere is the problem of language greater than in brain research, but the difficulty is not so much a deep conceptual confusion as an inadequacy of vocabulary and notation.[12]

There is nothing particularly surprising about investigating things that are unobservable to the naked eye. If that is what 'a world beyond everyday experience' signifies, then there is nothing especially enigmatic about investigating such things and using natural language to describe what is discovered, although it is true that some such things are enigmatic. There is no reason why science, in investigating such things, should feel itself restricted to the vocabulary of 'everyday language', if 'everyday language' signifies the vocabulary that refers to things that are part of the everyday experience of ordinary human beings. Physics has not been in the slightest bit hampered in its investigations of the microcosm or in its investigations of the macrocosm by the limitations of everyday language – it has very

---

[12] C. Blakemore, 'Understanding images in the brain', in H. Barlow, C. Blakemore and M. Weston-Smith (eds), *Images and Understanding* (Cambridge University Press, Cambridge, 1990), p. 283.

successfully introduced a rich technical vocabulary. So have chemistry and biology. And so too, of course, has neuroscience. One can hardly claim that such terms as 'parahippocampal and perirhinal cortices', 'the dentate gyrus', 'cAMP-PKA-MAPK-CREB pathway' or 'vesicle exocytosis' are what Blakemore calls 'everyday language', or used for the description of everyday experience.

There is no 'problem of language' in brain research, only conceptual confusions

When technical terminology is needed, there is rarely any difficulty in inventing it and introducing it by means of appropriate explanations. There is no reason whatso-ever to suppose that 'the problem of language' is greatest in brain research – indeed, there is no reason to suppose that there is *any* 'problem of language' in brain research. There is no reason to suppose that there is any inadequacy in the vocabulary of neuroscientists due to the limitations of English – and if there were, there is no reason why they should not introduce whatever novel terms they need into English, thus enriching the language. Blakemore queries rhetorically whether it is 'really a greater conceptual confusion for brain researchers to call the distribution of activity in the visual cortex a "map" than it is for him to call a kneeling-chair "a chair"'. The answer is, of course, that it is not. What is a conceptual confusion is to argue that the 'map' plays an 'essential part in the *representation* and *interpretation* of the world by the brain, *just as the maps of an atlas do for the reader of them*' (our italics). There is no conceptual confusion in calling the lower reaches of a mountain its 'foot' – but there would be if one went looking for its shoe.

The problems upon which we have focused throughout this book are indeed con-ceptual confusions. To resolve them, what is needed is not a novel vocabulary but clarity about the use of the existing vocabulary, which is perfectly adequate. In the next section we shall give some examples of writings by neuroscientists which do involve grievous conceptual incoherences, and we shall show that what has been discovered can be described very readily without any of these incoherences. The fault does not lie with any poverty of the English language, but rather with the misstatements and misunderstandings of these neuroscientists.

14.3 From Nonsense to Sense: The Proper Description of the Results of Commissurotomy

The descriptions given by neuroscientists

It has become customary for neuroscientists to discuss the deficiencies that result from commissurotomy in terms that involve treating each hemisphere of the brain as if it were a possible subject of psychological attributes. The fascinating work on this subject has been done largely by Roger Sperry, Michael Gazzaniga and their respective colleagues. Francis Crick explains some of the results of their work thus:

> For most right-handed people only the left hemisphere can speak or communicate through writing. It also rules most of the capacity to deal with language, although the right hemisphere may understand spoken words to a limited extent and probably deals

with the music of speech. When the callosum is cut, the left hemisphere sees only the right half of the visual field; the right hemisphere, the left half. Each hand is controlled by the opposite hemisphere, although the other hemisphere can produce some of the coarser movements of the hand and arm. Except under special conditions, both hemispheres can hear what is being said. . . .

. . . the patient is made to fix his gaze upon a screen onto which an image is flashed to one or the other side of his fixation point. This ensures that the visual information will reach only one of the two hemispheres . . .

When a picture is flashed into the patient's left (speaking) hemisphere, he can describe it the way a normal person can. This ability is not limited to speech. When asked, the patient can also point to objects with his right hand (largely controlled by the left hemisphere) without speaking. His right hand can also identify objects by touch even though he is prevented from seeing them.

If, however, a picture is flashed into the *right* (non-speaking) hemisphere, the results are quite different. The left hand (largely controlled by this non-speaking hemisphere) can point to and identify unseen objects by touch, as the right hand could do previously. But when the patient is asked to explain why his left hand behaved in that particular way, he will invent explanations on the basis of what his left (speaking) hemisphere saw, not on what his right hemisphere knew. The experimenter can see that these explanations are false, since he knows what was really flashed into the non-speaking hemisphere to produce behaviour. This is a good example of what is called 'confabulation'.

In short, one half of the brain appears to be almost totally ignorant of what the other half saw.[13]

According to Crick's description, the left hemisphere of the brain can speak and communicate by writing; after the callosum is cut, it can see only the right side of the visual field. It can hear what is said. It can learn, know or be ignorant of things. The right hemisphere can understand words only to a limited extent. After the callosum is cut, it can see only the left half of the visual field. It can hear what is said, and it can learn, know or be ignorant of things. In a normal person, 'the detailed visual awareness in the right hemisphere can easily be transferred to the left hemisphere so that the person can describe it in words. When the corpus callosum is fully cut, this information cannot cross to the speaking hemisphere.'[14]

Misdescription of commissurotomy is not confined to popular writing

It might be thought that this misdescription of the phenomena is a corollary of producing a popular book for a lay public who are incapable of understanding the more technical matters well understood by neuroscientists. But this is not so. Roger Sperry, who pioneered the research on split-brain patients and invented the standard tests to determine the hemispheric allocation of functions, wrote of the right (non-dominant) hemisphere that it is 'a conscious system in its own right, perceiving, thinking, remembering, reasoning, willing, and emoting, all at a characteristically human level, and that both

[13] F. Crick, *The Astonishing Hypothesis* (Touchstone, London, 1995), pp. 169f.
[14] Ibid., p. 171.

the left and the right hemisphere may be conscious simultaneously in different, even in mutually conflicting, mental experiences that run along in parallel'.[15]

George Wolford, Michael Miller and Michael Gazzaniga, writing in the *Journal of Neuroscience*, indulge in the same forms of misdescription:

> Gazzaniga and Metcalfe et al. have hypothesized the existence of an interpreter that plays the role of trying to make sense out of the information that it confronts, in other words, generating causal hypotheses. Using split-brain patients, Gazzaniga (1995)[16] provided evidence that this interpreter is located in the left hemisphere in most individuals. The simultaneous concept test provides an example of the function of the interpreter. In this task, a split-brain patient is shown a picture exclusively to the left hemisphere (e.g. a chicken) and another picture exclusively to the right hemisphere (e.g. a snow scene). The patient is then given an array of pictures and asked to point to a picture associated with the present pictures. In the above example, the left hemisphere chose a chicken claw and the right hemisphere chose a shovel. When asked to explain the choices, the patient responded, 'Oh, that's simple. The chicken claw goes with the chicken, and you need a shovel to clean out the chicken shed.' The right hemisphere is unable to produce speech, so it cannot explain its selection. The left hemisphere is unaware of the picture that the right hemisphere is responding to (i.e. of the snow scene), so it must generate its own interpretation of why the left hand pointed to a shovel. The left hemisphere, observing the actions of the left hand and the right brain, interprets those actions within the context of what it knows (i.e. a chicken claw) and generates an explanation for the shovel that is consistent with its knowledge.[17]

It might be thought that the conceptual errors in this discussion are likely to confuse only the lay reader, that the neuroscientists are perfectly clear about what they mean, even if they do not express themselves very well, due to the 'poverty' of the English language.

---

[15] Roger Sperry, 'Lateral specialization in the surgically separated hemispheres', in F. O. Schmitt and F. G. Worden (eds), *The Neurosciences Third Study Programme* (MIT Press, Cambridge, MA, 1974), p. 11.

[16] The reference is to Michael Gazzaniga, 'Principles of human brain organization derived from split-brain studies', *Neuron*, 14 (1995), pp. 217–28. Here too we find the mereological fallacy in neuroscience running amok. 'Right hemispheres', Gazzaniga writes, 'that reveal language capacities are able to make judgments of grammaticality. Thus even though they cannot use syntax to disambiguate stimuli or to guide comprehension judgments, they can recognize that one set of utterances is grammatical while another is not' (p. 225). So, too, 'the left brain, observing the left hand's response, interprets that response into a context consistent with its sphere of knowledge . . . The left hemisphere, . . . with its capacity for making inferences and interpretations, was more strongly influenced by the expectations for actions common to a scene and falsely recognized pictures consistent with the observed scene . . . It also possesses a uniquely human capacity to interpret behaviour and to construct theories about the relationships between perceived events and feelings' (pp. 225–7). It is patent that neither here nor in the above quotations are the authors employing a mere *façon de parler*.

[17] George Wolford, Michael B. Miller, and Michael Gazzaniga, 'The left hemisphere's role in hypothesis formation', *Journal of Neuroscience*, 20 (2000), RC 64 (1–4), p. 2.

We think that on internal evidence alone, this is more than improbable. But even if Sperry, Gazzaniga, Crick and their colleagues are not confused, it is surely true that they cause profound confusion to other neuroscientists. Thus, to take but one example, to which we have already referred (§3.10), Robert Doty writes in *Brain Research Bulletin*:

> With the guiding genius of Sperry, studies on the ensuing series of patients has forever changed the way the mind is viewed as a product of the brain; indeed, two brains, the two hemispheres, each endowed with human thought and emotion, separable, but normally uncannily intertwined via the dense network of callosal fibres, negotiating the interplay between them. Hemispherectomy confirms the humanity of each . . . Recognition of the fact that the two human hemispheres are, potentially, two separable mental entities will reverberate at all levels of society across the coming centuries, redefining the nature of humanity, and humanity's relation with nature.[18]

It should be obvious that the hemispheres of the brain can neither see nor hear. They cannot speak or write, let alone interpret anything or make inferences from information. They cannot be said to be either aware or unaware of anything; they cannot intelligibly be said to recognize or misrecognize anything. They do not make choices or judgements of grammaticality, and they are neither knowledgeable nor ignorant. To be sure, they are neither 'mental entities', nor do they possess humanity. *And there is no need whatsoever to talk in this confused way.*

Correct characterization of the discoveries derived from commissurotomies
What has been discovered by experiments on split-brain patients is a very strange *dissociation of functions that are normally intimately associated* and a consequent *confabulation-generating confusion*, which are manifest primarily (but not exclusively) under experimental conditions when the visual stimulus is controlled by the experimenter. When a patient fixes his gaze upon a screen, and an image is flashed to the left side of his fixation point so that the stimulus of the light array affects only his right hemisphere, then, as a result of the commissurotomy, the patient, unlike a normal person, cannot say what is thus visually presented to him. But he can point with his left hand to objects that correspond to the images on the screen. However, if the patient is then asked why he pointed to the object in question with his left hand, he will offer a rationalization which is based upon the nature of the object on the right side of the screen, although it is evident that he pointed to the object because of what was visually presented to him on the left side of the screen. However, none of these phenomena demand transgression of the mereological principle. The simultaneous concept test, properly described, generates no necessity to explain the phenomenon in terms of the right hemisphere's inability to produce speech, and a consequent inability to explain its own selection, and the left hemisphere's being unaware of the picture to which the right hemisphere is responding, and so generating its own interpretation of why the left hand pointed to the shovel. How, then, should the phenomenon be described?

---

[18] R. W. Doty, 'Two brains, one person', *Brain Research Bulletin*, 50 (1999), p. 423.

Dissociation of functions following commissurotomy

A patient is shown a picture of a chicken, the reflected light from which affects only his left hemisphere, and a snow scene, the light from which affects only his right hemisphere. The patient is asked to point with his right hand to a picture associated with what is on the screen, and he points to a chicken claw. But if asked to point with his left hand, he points to a shovel. If asked why he associated these two objects with what is on the screen, the patient replies that the claw goes with the chicken and the shovel is needed to clean out the chicken shed, apparently completely oblivious to the fact that a snow scene was also within his visual field, and that he had in fact matched the snow scene with the shovel. This functional dissociation and associated confabulation is explained by reference to the fact that the light stimulus from the snow scene affected the right hemisphere, the severance of which from the left hemisphere deprived the patient of the ability to describe or be visually aware of what was presented to him on the left of his visual field, although, remarkably, he was, by pointing, able to associate correctly what was there (viz. the snow scene) with a shovel. Nevertheless, he did not know *why* he made that association (not being aware of the snow scene presented to him), and confabulated a tale to explain why he had done so (a confabulation comparable to those produced by subjects to explain their post-hypnotically suggested behaviour). This, in turn, is (crudely) explicable by reference to the fact that the visual stimulation of the right hemisphere is disconnected from the left hemisphere, so that the patient is deprived of his normal cognitive capacity to be visually aware of what is presented to him and to recognize and describe familiar objects that are thus presented. It does not, however, deprive him of the ability to associate what was visually presented to him on the screen with an appropriate object (viz. a shovel) – but without knowing why he is doing so.[19]

Hemispheres of the brain are not the bearers of psychological attributes

Neither hemisphere selects anything – it is the human being who selects things. Neither hemisphere is either aware or unaware of anything; nor does it know anything – only living animals can be said to know or be aware of things, and brains are not living animals. So, too, neither hemisphere generates interpretations of, or explains, anything. It is human beings that interpret and explain things. It is senseless to speak of the right hemisphere observing the actions of the left hand, for neither hemisphere can observe or fail to observe anything at all – for hemispheres of the brain are not observers, they cannot scrutinize, look or glance at things, put their eyes to the keyhole, put on glasses, or make use of binoculars to see better. They surely cannot observe the actions of the left hand, since the left hand performs no actions. The left hand may move or be moved, but only the person whose hand it is performs actions.

The explanation of the strange dissociation of functions that are normally intimately interwoven is *not* that one hemisphere cannot see what the other hemisphere sees;

---

[19] Note that the two, normally co-ordinate, criteria that provide grounds for saying that a person sees something, viz. what he says and what he does, are in conflict here. So one can neither say that he saw the snow scene nor that he did not see it. This is a striking similarity with cases of so-called blind-sight (see J. Hyman, 'Visual experience and blindsight', in J. Hyman, *Investigating Psychology: Sciences of the Mind after Wittgenstein* (Routledge, London, 1991), pp. 166–200. See 14.3.1 below.

Explanation of the dissociation of functions following commissurotomy

nor is it that one hemisphere does not know what the other hemisphere knows, since neither hemisphere sees or knows anything. Nor is the explanation that one hemisphere is given to interpreting observed actions, and that the other hemisphere is interpretationally impotent. Rather, as is evident from the discoveries made by Sperry and Gazzaniga and his colleagues, the general form of the explanation is that severing the corpus callosum deprives human beings of the capacity to exercise normally co-ordinated functions. And that in turn is to be explained in terms of the disconnection of neural groups that are causally implicated in the exercise of the relevant capacities. It is, of course, not that visual awareness cannot be transferred to the left hemisphere for the person to describe it in words – for 'visual awareness' is not something that can be found in one hemisphere, let alone transferred to another. Nor is it the case that 'information cannot cross to the speaking hemisphere', since there is no *information* in a hemisphere of the brain (not even in the thin sense in which one might say that there is information in a telephone cable while someone is talking), and there is no way in which information might cross from one hemisphere to another (the corpus callosum is not a telephone cable, and the hemispheres, *pace* Doty, are not speakers). Rather, the transmission of neural signals across the corpus callosum, which is a necessary condition of *the person* knowing, and being able to say, what is visually presented to him (under the experimental conditions in question), has been prevented by the commissurotomy. Nevertheless, he is still able to respond to what is visually presented to him by pointing to associated objects, even though he does not know why he thus points, and confabulates a tale to explain it. In short, everything that Sperry and Gazzaniga and his colleagues have discovered *can* be adequately described without transgressing the mereological principle and without recourse to metaphor or figurative speech, let alone to poetic licence. There is no need to blame English for any deficiencies in the description of the phenomena.

14.3.1 The case of blind-sight: misdescription and illusory explanation

The phenomenon of blind-sight has attracted attention among cognitive neuroscientists and psychologists. The name was coined by Lawrence Weiskrantz to signify the curious capacities of a subject whose right occipital lobe had been surgically removed. By ordinary clinical tests, he was found to be blind in most of the left half of his visual field. When asked to fix his gaze upon the centre of a hemisphere on which small points of light were flashed, he averred that he could see nothing within the scotoma (the area of blindness within his visual field). Nevertheless, when faced with forced choices regarding signals within the scotoma, he scored correctly in more than 90 per cent of the cases. Subsequent investigations showed that some blind-sight patients could, under similar conditions, discriminate line orientations, simple patterns, and onset or cessation of movement. The patients thought that they were merely guessing, and were surprised to find that they could achieve the scores they did despite not being aware of anything at all within the scotoma. It seemed, on the one hand, that the patients were evidently blind within a part of their visual field, and, on the other hand, they could evidently see things within it (even though they didn't know this). Hence the paradoxical name 'blind-sight'.[20]

The phenomenon, exhaustively investigated by Weiskrantz, appeared to reveal deep features of our normal visual capacities and of 'conscious experience'. For here was a case in which, it seemed, much could be learned from a *dissociation of dysfunctions*: namely, between visual discrimination and the 'commentary' offered by the subject on their discrimination. The 'commentary', in the simplest human case, is the verbal avowal of whether one can see anything. But, since blind-sight appears to obtain among non-language-using animals too, the concept of commentary is widened, and equated with *monitoring* (see below).

What does blind-sight reveal, and how is it to be explained? Weiskrantz held that it confirms a distinction drawn over a century ago by Luciani in relation to the results of experimental extirpation of the visual cortex in monkeys. Luciani argued that such monkeys were deprived of 'visual perception', but retained 'visual sensation'.[21] This, Weiskrantz wrote, 'must be right'.[22] The discovery of blind-sight in humans seemed to demonstrate that, contrary to received opinion, Luciani's distinction 'between mental and sensorial processing' applied to humans too.

Weiskrantz argued that the explanation of blind-sight is that normal vision involves both reacting to visual stimuli and 'monitoring' or being 'aware of' the sensorial process. Monitoring, he claimed, is a 'form of privileged access',[23] an awareness of private visual sensations. Its upshot is visual perception – which is a form of 'conscious experience'. The monitoring system 'constitutes consciousness', and indeed 'creates conscious experience'.[24] In the case of blind-sight, the patient has visual sensations, but because the monitoring system is *disconnected*, he does not have visual perceptions or conscious visual experiences. This appeared to show that such a monitoring system is what enables the normal-sighted 'consciously' to see, or, more generally, to be conscious of any experience whatsoever.

The meticulous experimental work is impressive. But the *conceptual* apparatus which Weiskrantz invokes to describe the phenomena is defective. Consequently, for purely conceptual reasons, the explanation ventured and the conclusions drawn are questionable. As in the case of commissurotomy, the phenomena can be described without becoming entangled in conceptual confusion.

---

[20] The following discussion is much indebted to Hyman, 'Visual experience and blindsight'.

[21] L. Luciani, 'On the sensorial localisations in the cortex cerebri', *Brain*, 7 (1884), pp. 145–60. Luciani, *unlike* Weiskrantz, associates visual sensations with seeing *simpliciter*, and visual perceptions not with monitoring the occurrence of visual sensations, but with perceptual judgement. On his view, after the extirpation, the monkeys do regain their power to see, but lack powers of judgement and discernment.

[22] L. Weiskrantz, 'Varieties of residual experience', *Quarterly Journal of Experimental Psychology*, 32 (1980), p. 369.

[23] L. Weiskrantz, *Blindsight* (Oxford University Press, Oxford, 1986), p. 169.

[24] L. Weiskrantz, 'Neuropsychology and the nature of consciousness', in C. Blakemore and S. Greenfield (eds), *Mindwaves* (Blackwel, Oxford, 1987), p. 317.

As should be obvious in view of our discussion of sensation and perception (§§4.1 and 4.2), Luciani's distinction between visual sensation and visual perception is incoherent. There is no such thing as a visual sensation (save perhaps for a sensation of glare felt in the eyes that disrupts rather than constitutes vision). For sensations are felt and not seen; there is no such thing as an unfelt sensation; sensations have a bodily location, degrees of intensity, and phenomenal qualities. But it makes no sense to ask *where* a person feels a visual sensation of a red apple, or *what* it feels like. So the capacity retained by blind-sighted patients cannot be described by saying that they have visual sensations but no visual perceptions.[25]

The idea of a 'monitoring system' is a variant of the conception of introspection, understood as a faculty of 'inner sense' – a form of inner perception or apprehension of private objects to which the subject has 'privileged access', and of which he is 'immediately aware'. As we have argued, this conception is incoherent (§§3.6–3.7). Introspection is a capacity for reflection about oneself, one's history and experiences, attitudes and motives, not for perception of events on a private stage. Seeing ('visual experience') is not a private event, accessible only to the subject, and saying that one sees is not a report on a private experience. The role of 'I can see . . .' is to introduce a report on public visibilia that the subject discerns, or to justify such a report by citing the cognitive faculty that was exercised, or to report on the degree of clarity and distinctness of the discernment.

Weiskrantz conceives of a monitoring system sometimes as (i) a psychological phenomenon of consciousness of a private process that he takes to be presupposed for the possibility of commenting on one's visual experience, and sometimes as (ii) a neural monitor of a neural process the disconnection of which might explain blind-sight. On the one hand, the monitoring system is conceived to constitute transitive consciousness of visual sensation (and the subjective experience), and its disconnection is the dissociative clinical syndrome characteristic of blind-sight. On the other, monitoring 'is not part of the serial information-processing chain itself'; rather, it can monitor 'what is going on' – this being 'the kind of neural organization one is looking for to explain awareness'.[26] But the only reason for supposing the latter to exist is that it appears to be a neural correlate (a neural scanning mechanism) homologous with the incoherent conception of introspection (as a psychological scanning activity).

The sources of the confusion are the misguided suppositions that experience is private, that its subject can report verbally to the experimenter on it in virtue of privileged access to it, the latter being a psychological capacity on which all 'conscious experience' depends. Once such assumptions are shed, we must also shed the description of blind-sight patients as people who have sensory experiences of visible objects within the scotoma but who are unable to apprehend that they do. Hence, too, we must reject as unfounded the supposition that the explanation of the phenomenon of blind-sight is the detachment of a neural

---

[25] Moreover, as Hyman observes ('Visual experience and blindsight', p. 191), Luciani's grounds for describing monkeys as deficient in visual perception lay in their agnosic behaviour, and had nothing to do with any dissociation of discriminative capacity and so-called consciousness of seeing.

[26] Weiskrantz, 'Neuropsychology and the nature of consciousness', p. 316.

monitor the normal scanning operation of which enables animals to be conscious of their experiences, and visually to perceive as well as to have visual sensations. The 'neural monitor' is no more than a fanciful expedient designed to explain away the paradox of blind-sight. But, as Hyman has argued, it is never phenomena that are paradoxical, but their description. The blind-sighted patient does not behave in an absurd or contradictory manner. But in describing their behaviour, we resort to paradoxical descriptions such as 'blind-sight' or 'unconscious awareness'.

The reason why we are tempted to such paradoxical descriptions, Hyman argues, is that we demand an answer to the question of whether the blind-sighted can or cannot see items within the scotoma. But that is precisely the question that cannot be answered. For the normal convergence of indices of sight – namely, appropriate affective response, behavioural reaction, reoriented movement, verbal description, answers to appropriate questions, etc. – is subtly disrupted. But such convergences constitute the framework within which verbs of vision are taught and used, and their use challenged and confirmed or infirmed. They constitute part of the background conditions for the use and usefulness of these expressions. Disruption of such constancy is what characterizes blind-sight and also what generates the paradoxical descriptions offered. For, under the very special experimental conditions (the blind-sighted can see perfectly adequately under normal conditions of eye movement), *some* of the criteria for seeing are satisfied (judgements about visibilia under forced choice), and *some* of the criteria for lack of vision are satisfied (the patient's avowal that he can see nothing). The consequence of this conflict of criteria is that one can neither say that the patient sees objects within the scotoma nor say that he does not. *That* is not paradoxical – it merely indicates the inapplicability of a concept under special circumstance. There is no difficulty in describing the phenomenon. What is unwarranted is to misdescribe it in terms of Luciani's distinction between visual sensation and visual perception, and to endeavour to explain a conceptual singularity by postulating a neural monitoring mechanism as a correlate of a bogus conception of introspection and privileged access.

14.4 Philosophy and Neuroscience

Unclarities about the relationship between neuroscience and philosophy

The relationship between cognitive neuroscience and philosophy is unclear to many neuroscientists. Such neuroscientists commonly castigate philosophy for its alleged failings, and are apparently unaware of the extent to which much of the framework of thought within which they operate, and which they triumphantly proclaim, is the (questionable) heritage of seventeenth-century metaphysics. Some of them, as we have seen, do indeed refer to a leading philosopher – namely, William James – as an authority, but appear to be oblivious to the grave flaws that inform James's work.

On the one hand, neuroscientists are aware of the fact that the problems with which they are struggling are not unrelated to reflections of philosophers on the nature of the mind and mental phenomena. On the other hand, they are indignant that philosophy has discovered nothing about the functioning of the brain. Rightly proud of the remarkable achievements of neuroscience in the last century, they are inclined to think that they can solve the problems with which philosophers have been struggling for centuries. When it comes to the problems of the nature of the mind and its relation to the brain, or the relation between the mind and the brain, on the one hand, and human behaviour on the other, it is, many of them think, time for philosophy to step aside and let science have its turn.

Four accusations brought against philosophy by neuroscientists

Against the background of such preconceptions, it is hardly surprising that many neuroscientists display a contemptuous attitude towards philosophy. Their complaints are various. First, it is sometimes suggested that philosophy is simply irrelevant to the concerns of neuroscience. Ian Glynn writes: 'Most of my scientific and medical colleagues tend to be dismissive of philosophy. Their attitude, of course, reflects a realistic assessment of the likely relevance of philosophy to their immediate preoccupations.'[27]

Secondly, the methods of philosophy are commonly deplored by neuroscientists. Edelman suggests that the a priori methods of philosophy render its investigations into the nature of the mind worthless: 'One of the temptations of having a mind is to try to use it alone to solve the mystery of its own nature. Philosophers have attempted this since time immemorial. . . . As a general method to explore the matter of mind, it just won't do.'[28]

Thirdly, cognitive neuroscientists see themselves as being concerned with the very same problems as philosophers of mind. Edelman and Tononi suggest 'that consciousness can be considered a scientific subject and that it is not the sole province of philosophy'.[29] Crick similarly insists on breaking down any trade union demarcation disputes: 'the study of consciousness is a scientific problem. Science is not separated from it by some insurmountable barrier. If there is any lesson to be learned from this book it is that we can now see ways of approaching the problem experimentally. There is no justification for the view that only philosophers can deal with it.'[30] However, given their dissatisfaction with the methods of philosophy, neuroscientists tend to think that philosophy is utterly misguided in its pursuit of the common goal. Crick believes that 'it is hopeless to try to solve the problems of consciousness by general philosophical arguments; what is needed are suggestions for new experiments that might throw light on these problems'.[31] And Edelman observes that 'there is no end of hypotheses about consciousness, particularly by philosophers. But most of these are not what we might call principled scientific theories, based on observables and related to the functions of the brain and the body.'[32]

---

[27] I. Glynn, *An Anatomy of Thought* (Weidenfeld and Nicolson, London, 1999), p. 367.

[28] G. Edelman, *Bright Air, Brilliant Fire – On the Matter of the Mind* (Penguin, Harmondswerth, 1994), p. 31.

[29] C. M. Edelman and G. Tononi, *Consciousness: How Matter Becomes Imagination* (Allen Lane, The Penguin Press, London, 2000), p. 3. Since philosophy has a multitude of 'provinces', presumably what they mean is that it is not the province of philosophy alone.

[30] Crick, *Astonishing Hypothesis*, p. 258.

[31] Crick, ibid., p. 19.

[32] Edelman, *Bright Air, Brilliant Fire*, p. 112.

Fourthly, disappointment is sometimes expressed regarding the achievements of philosophy. Crick remarks that 'Philosophers have had such a poor record over the last two thousand years that they would do better to show a certain modesty rather than the lofty superiority that they usually display'.[33] Similarly, Edelman observes that, 'Given the record of the past history of the philosophy of mind and of psychology, the continued avoidance of the biological underpinnings of such a programme is not likely to enhance our understanding of how the mind emerged and how it functions'.[34]

One conclusion drawn from the alleged faults of philosophy: junior partnership
The conclusion is that philosophers may indeed join this great enterprise, but only as very junior partners. 'I hope', Crick remarks, 'that philosophers will learn enough about the brain to suggest ideas about how it works, but they must also learn how to abandon their pet theories when the scientific evidence goes against them or they will only expose themselves to ridicule.'[35] With this proviso, one may, as Edelman suggests, anticipate that 'a new scientific view of the mind based on biology may help give philosophy a new lease on life. . . . It is certainly worth asking whether a biologically based theory of the mind would invigorate these areas of thought and perhaps even give philosophy a new turn.'[36] Neuroscientists may even go so far as to prescribe the future of philosophy. 'Given how information and consciousness have arisen in nature, one should go one step further [than naturalizing epistemology by grounding it in psychology] and say that epistemology should be grounded in biology, specifically in neuroscience.'[37]

A second conclusion drawn: the obsolescence of philosophy
At least one distinguished neuroscientist actually believes that philosophy itself is obsolete, and that the great problems of philosophy will be solved by neuroscience. Semir Zeki laments 'the poverty of the results' which philosophy's grand manner of formulating problems has achieved 'in terms of understanding our brains and their mental constitution'.[38] The study of 'the brain's capacity to acquire knowledge, to abstract and to construct ideals' is 'a philosophical burden which neurobiology has to shoulder'.[39] Among the 'most prominent problems', which Zeki hopes neurobiology will tackle, 'are the nature of knowledge itself and the relationship between knowledge and belief, given the exquisite capacity of the human brain . . . to acquire knowledge'. In his view, 'the problems that neurobiology will face in the future are those lasting truths and ultimate values which philosophy . . . has so unsuccessfully tackled in the past'.[40] The abstract concepts of honour and justice, Zeki avers, 'are problems which neurobiology has not yet addressed, although

---

[33] Crick, *Astonishing Hypothesis*, p. 258. The context of his remark is his discussion of the investigation of consciousness.
[34] Edelman, *Bright Air, Brilliant Fire*, p. 41.
[35] Crick, *Astonishing Hypothesis*, p. 258.
[36] Edelman, *Bright Air, Brilliant Fire*, p. 159.
[37] Edelman and Tonini, *Consciousness*, p. 207.
[38] S. Zeki, 'Splendours and miseries of the brain', *Philosophical Transactions of the Royal Society* B **354** (1999), pp. 2053–65.
[39] By 'ideals' Zeki apparently means ideas or concepts.
[40] Ibid., p. 2054.

it will be surprising if it does not do so within the coming century'. Neurobiology, he claims, has provided some answers to such philosophical questions as 'Do colours exist in the material world?' and 'Can colours be considered to be the properties of objects?' It has shown that 'bodies have no colour', and that colour 'is a property of the brain'. or (alternatively) that colour 'is really the interpretation that the brain gives to that physical property of objects (their reflectance), an interpretation that allows it to acquire knowledge rapidly about the property of reflectance'.[41] These unfortunate remarks, as we shall show, are informed by misunderstandings of the nature of philosophical problems, ignorance about the methods of solving, resolving or dissolving them, as well as misconceptions about the province of neuroscience and its limits.

14.4.1 What philosophy can and what it cannot do

A task of analytical philosophy: identifying transgressions of the bounds of sense

Analytical philosophy is above all a conceptual investigation. Its primary constructive task is to clarify our form of representation in order to resolve philosophical problems and disentangle conceptual confusions.[42] So it is concerned not with matters of fact, but with matters of meaning. Its province is not the domain of empirical truth or falsehood, but the domain of sense and nonsense. It investigates and describes the bounds of sense: that is, the limits of what can coherently be thought and said. Its destructive task is the criticism of transgressions of the bounds of sense. Such transgressions may occur in the formulation of problems or in the proposing of solutions to problems. The problems formulated may be philosophical problems about the a priori nature of things, or scientific problems about the empirical characteristics of things and their explanation. The solutions proposed may be philosophical clarifications, on the one hand, or empirical discoveries and scientific theories, on the other. Both may inadvertently transgress the bounds of sense. The result of so doing is one form or another of nonsense – that is, forms of words that lack any sense. They will typically *appear* to make sense – and disentangling the knotted threads of misunderstanding is no easy task. In some cases, it may take centuries of endeavour.

---

[41] Ibid., p. 2056.

[42] Of course, many other activities have been subsumed under the venerable name of 'philosophy'. Our remarks apply to the kind of philosophy and philosophical methods exemplified in this book. These are, we believe, the kinds of methods appropriate to the field under investigation. The above characterization of analytical philosophy would have to be modified for the domain of values which is the concern of moral, legal and political philosophy.

We are aware of the fact that many philosophers who conceive of themselves as analytic philosophers repudiate the methods of connective analysis that we advocate and practise. We have no wish to enter the fray over what does, and what does not, merit the epithet 'analytic philosophy'. Methods should be judged by their products. Our methods should be judged by the light they shed upon the concepts and conceptual structures we have tried to illuminate and by the extent to which they facilitate the identification of transgressions of the bounds of sense, misconceived questions, and illegitimate inferences drawn from misdescriptions.

Philosophical clarification   We give articulate expression to our thought and know-
                                        ledge about the world by means of sentences of our
language. The sentences we use to describe our experience and the objects of our experience are made up of words combined in rule-governed ways. We use such sentences to
make statements concerning our experience and its objects, and such statements stand
in relations of implication, compatibility or incompatibility. Clarification of the forms of
licit combination of expressions and detection of subtly *illicit* forms of combination, the
description of the implications, compatibilities and incompatibilities of statements made by
the use of well-formed intelligible sentences are part of the task of philosophy. Such
clarifications are typically undertaken with a particular array of conceptual problems,
puzzles or confusions in view. The clarifications offered in this book, for example, are
tailored to conceptual problems in cognitive neuroscience distinctive of the end of the
twentieth century and of the beginning of the twenty-first. Although they partially overlap
with, they also differ from, the problems that would have had to be discussed at the end
of the nineteenth century to eradicate, for example, the extensive conceptual confusions of
William James. Although the methods of elucidation would be the same, the arrangement of the material would be different. Even though there may be similarities between
successive confusions, each generation's puzzlement is distinctive, moulded by the preconceptions, preoccupations and sometimes the technologies of the day.[43] Consequently,
the task of philosophical clarification is not a finite one, since there is no end to the conceptual confusions into which humankind may fall, and each confusion is a new case for
treatment.

Connective analysis in philosophy   One primary method of dissolving conceptual puzzle-
                                         ment is the careful examination and description of the
use of words – of what competent speakers, using words correctly, do and do not say. For
it is by this means that light can be shed upon the problematic concepts that are one
source of the troubles. They are elucidated by connective analysis, which traces, as far as
is necessary for the purposes of clarification and for the solution or dissolution of the
problems and puzzles at hand, the ramifying logico-grammatical web of connections
between the problematic concept and adjacent ones. This we have tried to exemplify in
chapters 4–8, where, with respect to a small range of pivotal psychological categories
– namely, sensation, perception, knowledge, belief, memory, thought, imagination and
imaging, emotion, mood and volition – we delineated a part of the complex patterns of
interlocking concepts. Our sketches elucidated these concepts by examining and describing the use of the relevant words, although our interest in words was not lexicographical,
but conceptual. Our logico-grammatical investigations were motivated by a concern for
the logical character of the concepts expressed by the words the use of which was

---

[43] A major source of current conceptual confusion in all the sciences concerned directly or indirectly
with human cognitive powers are the misleading analogies between the operations of the mind and
the operations of computers, and between the operations of the brain and the information processing of the computer. The previous model, that of a central telephone exchange, suggested a less
persuasive and mesmerizing analogy, and was correspondingly less pernicious.

investigated. For the network of concepts is exhibited in the web of words. The connective-analytic exercise of chapters 4–8 should have made clear some of the profound differences between philosophical and scientific investigation.

There are no theories or hypotheses in philosophy, for there can be no theories about logical possibilities

In the sense in which there are theories and hypotheses in science, there can be none in philosophy. For the sciences construct theories in order to explain, and formulate hypotheses in order to predict phenomena. Scientific theories must be testable in experience. They may be true (or false); but equally, they may be only approximations to the truth. Philosophy, by contrast, clarifies what does and does not make sense. Determinations of sense antecede experience, and are presupposed by true and false judgements alike. There can be no theories in philosophy from which one can derive hypotheses about events or in terms of which one can explain why things happen as they do. *That is not the task of the subject* – its business, one might say, is with logical possibilities, not with empirical actualities. And its role is not to *explain* logical possibilities by means of testable hypotheses – for there can be no such things. It is, rather, to describe or specify what makes sense (for that is the same as what is logically possible), to elucidate, for any given problematic fragment of a language, what combinations of words are significant and can be used, within or without science, to say something true or false. Its results cannot be approximations, in the sense in which scientific hypotheses may be approximations to the truth, since a mere approximation to sense is one or another form of nonsense. Its critical and destructive task is to describe or specify widely used forms of words that *seem to make sense*, but on closer scrutiny can be shown not to do so. This will show that the concepts invoked are misconstrued, and that conceptual compatibilities and incompatibilities are misunderstood. Part of the critical task is to explain in detail the sources of the conceptual misconstruals and misunderstandings, and the reasons for the conceptual confusions and incoherences.

On the folly of being dismissive about studying 'mere words'

It is, of course, tempting to be dismissive about 'mere words', and to contrast the apparent superficiality of a concern with mere words with the significance of a concern with facts. But that is foolish. For facts can be stated only by the use of words. Scientific thought is possible only because of the availability of words by means of which it can be articulated. The 'mere words' and their rule-governed connections constitute our form of representation or conceptual scheme. The investigation of the structure and limits of our conceptual scheme, though altogether different from, is no less important than the facts and theories which we formulate by its use. It would be absurd to be dismissive about the spectacles by means of which we view the world on the grounds that they are merely glass and that only lens grinders should be interested in that (as if only lexicographers should be interested in mere words). It would be even more absurd to disregard flaws in the lenses as unimportant, on the grounds that one is not interested in lenses and their defects, but only in what one can see.

On the non-triviality of conceptual problems

Conceptual problems are anything but trivial. They are problems that result from misinterpreting the forms of our language, using words in ways that appear to make sense, but do not. The appearance of sense can be as persuasive as a perceptual illusion (e.g. the Müller–Lyer lines), and it can be as difficult to shake oneself free of it as it is to realize that a certain perceptual appearance *is* an illusion. Very often we are positively *attracted* to the misguided form of words (it is evidently appealing to talk of 'the "I"' (or 'the Ego') – although no one ever speaks of 'the "you"' (or 'the "tu"')). Indeed, it may be exceedingly difficult to *abandon* a misleading form of words (e.g. 'the brain infers', 'the brain believes', 'the brain stores information') once it has come to dominate one's thought. The roots of conceptual illusion reach deep, as deep as the forms of our thought. For the conceptual illusions stem from entanglement *in* the forms of our thought.

On the relevance of philosophy to cognitive neuroscience

So, a realistic assessment of the likely relevance of philosophy to the preoccupations of Ian Glynn's scientific colleagues should be anything but dismissive. Cognitive neuroscience is sorely afflicted with various kinds of conceptual confusions, some of which we have tried to point out in the course of our discussions. Conceptual clarification is needed both for the identification and clear formulation of problems and for the description of the discoveries made and the realistic assessment of their significance. Cognitive neuroscience operates across a categorial 'divide' between the psychological and the neural (which is a particular case of the physical). There is nothing mysterious about this 'divide'. It is constituted by the logico-grammatical differences between the characteristic concepts that belong to neuroscience and the concepts of psychology, on the one hand, and their respective conceptual connections and articulations, on the other. These differences, as we have shown throughout this book, are deep and ramified, and the conceptual connections are subtle and complex. Since cognitive neuroscience has perforce constantly to cross this logical divide, to move from descriptions of the structures and processes of neural phenomena to descriptions of psychological phenomena, it unavoidably runs into difficulties. These difficulties are not empirical, but conceptual. They cannot be solved by scientific experiments, but only by a priori conceptual investigations and philosophical arguments.

On the confusion of deploring the a priori methods of philosophy

For neuroscientists such as Edelman to deplore the methods of philosophers as hopelessly a priori is as misguided as it would be for physicists to deplore the methods of mathematicians as a priori. Mathematics is *concept formation* by means of a priori proof – for a mathematical proof forms a novel conceptual connection articulated by the theorem proved. Philosophy is *concept elucidation* by means of the description of the rule-governed use of words. Such descriptions antecede experience, and are presupposed by the use of the relevant words in making *any* true or false empirical claim. Clarifications of the concepts of *perception*, or *memory*, or *imaging* and *the imagination* antecede any empirical theories about the neural underpinnings of these capacities. For the concepts are already presupposed in the formulation of the theories. The neuroscientists' confusions stem in part from failure to distinguish a priori, conceptual questions from empirical, scientific ones. Philosophy can investigate the nature of the mind only in the sense that it can clarify the concept of a mind and its ramifying logico-grammatical connections with related concepts. So it can illuminate the relationships between the concept of a mind and the concepts of a person, of a sentient creature, of the body and of the brain. *This* is the province of philosophy. Neuroscience can investigate the nature of the mind only in the sense that it can discover the neural underpinnings of our psychological and behavioural capacities and their exercise. The philosophical and the neuroscientific enterprises are quite different. Moreover, the second enterprise presupposes the first, inasmuch as unclarity or confusion with respect to the concept of the mind and related psychological concepts will contaminate the description and understanding of the neuroscientific problems and solutions.

The neuroscientific enterprise is quite different from the philosophical one
It is important to realize that, contrary to the assertions of Edelman, Tononi and Crick, cognitive neuroscientists are *not* concerned with the very same problems as philosophers of mind. Despite the averrals of some philosophers, the philosophical enterprise and the neuroscientific enterprise are not the same. The philosophical and neuroscientific investigations of consciousness, for example, are *complementary*, but not *identical*. It is true that consciousness *also* poses scientific problems, that an intellectual interest in the nature of consciousness is common to both philosophy and neuroscience. But the meaning of 'the nature of consciousness' differs from case to case. Philosophy is concerned with elucidating the defining features of consciousness (its a priori nature). Part of its task is to clarify the concept of consciousness and its connections with adjacent concepts – with attention and perception, thought and preoccupation. A further part of its task is to dissolve conceptual confusions concerning consciousness – confusions about qualia, about the ineffable and incommunicable 'redness of red', about there being 'something which it is like to be conscious', and so forth. Neuroscience, presupposing the concept of consciousness as given, has the task of investigating the empirical nature of consciousness, in particular of discovering the neural conditions of intransitive and transitive consciousness. Philosophy can contribute nothing to the scientific theories about the neural basis of consciousness in any of its forms, just as neuroscience can contribute nothing to the clarification of the concept of consciousness. Philosophical argument can solve no experimental problems. But the 'new experiments that might throw light on [the] problems of consciousness' envisaged by Crick can shed no light whatsoever on the *concept* of consciousness. The two activities are, or should be, complementary – not competitive or mutually exclusive. In so far as philosophers offer 'hypotheses about consciousness', as Edelman suggests, they are overstepping their mark. For it is not the business of philosophy to offer hypotheses about anything – its task is to describe the bounds of sense, and there can be nothing hypothetical about that. Philosophical analyses of the concept of being conscious of something and the family of closely related concepts (e.g. being aware of something, noticing, recognizing or realizing something) are not *hypotheses*, and are certainly not 'principled scientific theories based on observables' – any more than mathematical theorems are principled scientific theories based on observables.

It is not the task of philosophy to propose theories for neuroscientists
Consequently, Crick's hope that philosophers might learn enough about the brain to suggest ideas about how it works is risible (and perhaps intended to be). Philosophers are not neuroscientists *manqués*, and it is as probable that philosophers (in their professional capacity) will be able to suggest ideas about how the brain works as it is

probable that pure mathematicians will be able to suggest ideas about the laws of physics.[44] On the other hand, the supposition that scientific evidence may contravene a philosophical analysis of a concept is equally risible. Philosophers very often err in the accounts they offer of a given conceptual field – but the error, like an error in pure mathematics, is an a priori one, identifiable independently of experience and experiment. Philosophers should not find themselves having to abandon pet theories about the nature of consciousness in the face of scientific evidence. They should have no pet theories, since they should not be propounding empirical theories that are subject to empirical confirmation and disconfirmation in the first place. Their business is with concepts, not with empirical judgements; it is with the forms of thought, not with its content; it is with what is logically possible, not with what is empirically actual; with what does and does not make sense, not with what is and what is not true.

On the nature of progress in philosophy by contrast with science The disappointment (e.g. of Crick, Edelman and Zeki) concerning the achievements of philosophy over the past 2,000 years is based upon misunderstandings about the nature of the subject. Certainly philosophy has made no progress in contributing to our knowledge about the world – nor should it. Its task is to clarify the conceptual scheme in terms of which our knowledge is articulated. Its achievements are its contribution to our reflective understanding of the logical structure of our thought and knowledge about the world. It cannot contribute to knowledge about the brain, and it should not be expected to. Philosophers are not closet scientists, and their methods are not designed to discover new empirical truths.

But is it true that there has been no progress in philosophy over the last 2,000 years? It only appears so if one harbours false hopes through a misconceived assimilation of philosophy to a science, and misconceptions over what counts as progress in philosophy. Then one may crave philosophical theories on the model of scientific theories, and entertain misguided hopes for better and more ambitious theories (and it is true that some philosophers have deluded themselves thus). Progress in science consists in the devising and confirmation of ever more powerful theories. But, as we have suggested, there are no theories in philosophy in the sense in which there are theories in science, and philosophy should not propose empirical hypotheses as science does. It does not follow that there is no progress in philosophy, if the conception of progress in this domain is correctly understood. Forms of reasoning are distinguished (e.g. deductive reasoning is distinguished from inductive reasoning, theoretical from practical reasoning), and the logical principles that are constitutive of them are rendered explicit, and sometimes regimented and codified (as in the case of deductive logic). Categorial concepts that characterize a given domain of thought are clarified. Strands in the web of our conceptual scheme are traced, conceptual connections are made explicit, conceptual affinities and differences are articulated.

---

[44] This does not imply that individual philosophers may not acquire expertise in neuroscience and contribute to advances in that subject. A number of great philosophers, including Descartes, have indeed made major contributions to empirical science (but it is much more difficult to think of any scientist who has made a major contribution to philosophy).

Confusions and misconceptions are revealed for what they are. Some of these then sink permanently from sight, and the achievement of their eradication is duly forgotten. Others reappear in fresh guise with each new generation – for the temptations to misconstrue certain features of our conceptual scheme are perennial (qualia are Wittgensteinian 'private objects' in modern clothing, and internal representations are the direct descendants of ideas and impressions). But curing a generation of a sickness of the understanding is a worthy achievement, even if it is likely that the intellectual disease will break out again in a mutated form and afflict a subsequent generation.

What philosophy can contribute to neuroscience

So, what philosophy can contribute to neuroscience is conceptual clarification. We have, throughout this book, tried to show how this can be done. Philosophy can point out when the bounds of sense are transgressed – as we have done with respect to the mereological fallacy in neuroscience. It can make clear when the conceptual framework which informs a neuroscientist's research has been twisted or distorted. So, it can clarify – as we have done – what is awry with the thought that perception involves seeing or having images or that perception is the hypothesis formation of the brain. It can warn – as we have tried to do – against the confusion of supposing that memory is the re-enactment of past experience or is always of the past. It can elucidate why conditioned reactions are not forms of memory and why it is confused to think that memories can be *stored* in the brain. It can show – as we have shown – why the study of emotional perturbations is not the same as the study of emotions, why emotions are not somatic responses to mental images, and why feelings of emotions are not the awareness of somatic changes that inform us about our visceral and musculoskeletal state. It can explain – as we have explained – why mental images are not ethereal pictures and why they cannot be rotated in mental space. And so on. Far from being irrelevant to the goals of neuroscience, the conceptual clarifications of philosophical analysis are indispensable for their achievement.

14.4.2 What neuroscience can and what it cannot do

Why neuroscience cannot contribute to the solution of philosophical problems

It is perfectly correct, as Crick urges, that it is hopeless to try to solve empirical problems concerning the nature of consciousness by general philosophical arguments. But, equally, it is hopeless to try to solve conceptual problems concerning the nature of consciousness by empirical methods. PET and fMRI can scan brains, but not concepts and their articulations. Neuroscience can investigate synaptic connections but not conceptual ones.

It is not altogether clear what Edelman means by 'a biologically based theory of the mind'. But if neuroscientists produce something that can be so denominated, it cannot be expected to give philosophy 'a new lease on life'. For, in the first place, philosophy has not lost its old lease, which is unlikely to run out as long as mankind continues to think and human beings, including scientists, continue to err for purely conceptual reasons. And in the second place, a new neuroscientific theory of anything cannot give philosophy a new lease or turn, but only a new array of conceptual puzzles to resolve and knots to disentangle. Neuroscientific discoveries (e.g. blind-sight) may pose *new* conceptual

problems – they may provide grist for philosophical mills, but not solutions for philosophical problems.

Why epistemology could not be
grounded in neuroscience

The suggestion that epistemology should be grounded in neuroscience can be proposed only by someone with an infirm grasp of what epistemology is. It is, after all, not an empirical enquiry into how, as a matter of fact, human beings can and do acquire whatever knowledge they have – that is learning theory, which is a branch of psychology. Rather, epistemology is an a priori enquiry into the web of epistemic concepts that is formed by the connections, compatibilities and incompatibilities between the concepts of knowledge, belief, conviction, suspicion, supposition, conjecture, doubt, certainty, memory, evidence and self-evidence, truth and falsehood, probability, reasons and reasoning, etc. The relevant connections are *logical* or *conceptual* – and neuroscientific investigations can shed no light upon the *normative* connections of logic (construing 'logic' broadly). Epistemology is also concerned with the logical character of *justifications* of knowledge claims, of confirmation and disconfirmation, of the differences between deductive and inductive support, of what counts as evident and what stands in need of evidence, and so forth. This too is not an empirical investigation. It could not possibly be furthered by the discovery of facts about the brain.

Why neuroscience cannot investigate
the conceptual nature of knowledge:
Zeki's confusions

It could not be the task of neuroscience to investigate the conceptual nature of knowledge, and its relation to belief. If it were to 'shoulder this burden', as Zeki proposes, it would have to investigate why one can know how but cannot believe how; why one asks 'How do you know?' and 'Why do you believe?', but not 'Why do you know?' or 'How do you believe?'; why one can know whether or better but cannot believe whether or better; why knowing that *p* and believing that *p* are not related in the way that knowing NN and believing NN are related; why 'He believes that *p*, but it is false that *p*' is in order, but 'I believe that *p*, but it is false that *p*' is a kind of nonsense; and so on. Could knowledge of the functioning of the brain conceivably shed light on these logico-grammatical questions? Zeki appears to believe that these problems fall within the province of neuroscience because of 'the exquisite capacity of the human brain . . . to acquire knowledge'. But, as should by now be evident, the brain has no capacity to acquire knowledge at all – it is human beings who have that capacity. It is, to be sure, correct that we would not have any such capacity but for the kind of brain we have. And it is true that neuroscience has the task of studying the brain, and hopes to come to understand its structure and functioning, which endow us with this capacity. But that is no reason for supposing that neuroscience can answer conceptual questions concerning the relationship between knowledge and belief.

Nor can neuroscience resolve the
status of secondary qualities

It is equally confused to suppose that neuroscience has provided answers to such philosophical questions as 'Do colours exist in the material world?' and 'Can colours be considered to be the properties of objects?' The answers which Zeki supposes to have been given by neuroscience were already given in essence by Galileo, Descartes, Boyle and Locke in the seventeenth century. The answers that Zeki takes neuroscience to offer are just as questionable as the seventeenth-century metaphysics which anticipated them.

Zeki's confusions   The claim that neuroscience has shown that objects have no colours is evidently confused, at least if taken at face value. For, literally understood, this would imply that all objects are colourless – like transparent, colourless window panes. What is, or should be, meant is that it is *meaningless* to ascribe colours to material objects – that material objects *could not* be coloured. But how could neuroscience show that something is *logically* impossible? In particular, how could it show that no extended spatial object could have a colour? The suggestion that colours are properties of the brain is evidently confused, for, of course, Zeki does not mean that the brain is grey to white in colour, and that nothing else has any colour at all. What he must mean is that the fact that most material objects appear to us to have a colour is due to the functioning of our brains. But all that neuroscience can do is discover the mechanisms that enable us to apprehend the colours of things – and that in no way shows things not to be coloured, let alone that it is logically impossible that they have a colour.

Zeki's other claim – that colour is 'the interpretation that the brain gives to that physical property of objects (their reflectance), an interpretation that allows it to acquire knowledge rapidly about the property of reflectance' – is equally confused. For the brain can neither interpret, nor acquire knowledge of, anything – *a fortiori* not of the reflectance properties of things. The person whose brain it is may acquire knowledge of the colours of the things he sees as a result of processes in his brain, but it does not follow that he acquires any knowledge about the reflectance properties of those objects. For, unless he knows some physics, he is unlikely to know anything about reflectance properties and light wavelengths. But this does not show that the colours he takes himself to see are not actually the colours of objects. After all, if that were so – that is, if colours were not objective properties of objects – then he would not be able to see anything in his environment at all, since what has no colour (*a fortiori* what can have no colour) is not visible. Of course, that colours are not objective properties of objects is exactly what Galileo, Descartes, Boyle and Locke argued. According to their representationalist metaphysics, what we really visually perceive are merely ideas in our minds, from which we draw problematic inferences about the imperceptible world in which we presume we live. But is *that* what twenty-first-century neuroscience has to contribute to philosophy? Such metaphysical doctrines have been with philosophy for 350 years, and whether or not they are defensible, the one thing that should be clear is that they are not empirical questions that could conceivably be settled by neuroscientific investigations.

No factual discovery can resolve a conceptual question   No neuroscientific discoveries can solve *any* of the conceptual problems that are the proper province of philosophy, any more than the empirical discoveries of physicists can prove mathematical theorems. For the description of any discovery in cognitive neuroscience *presupposes* the relevant psychological concepts.[45] Factual discoveries cannot determine what makes sense. They determine what is true – which *presupposes* what makes sense.

---

[45] Of course, this does not imply that individual neuroscientists may not acquire expertise in philosophical analysis and contribute to conceptual clarification.

Neuroscience has a multitude of great tasks. It aims to achieve an understanding of the neural conditions that endow us with the distinctive human capacities we possess. Its investigations into sensation, perception, memory, affection and volition are already shedding light on these subjects. Achievement in cognitive neuroscience is gradually enlarging our understanding of why we are as we are, why we possess the powers we possess, what determines their empirical limitations, and what goes on in our brains when we exercise them. Neuroscientific advances also hold out the hope that in respect of certain fearful afflictions, hitherto conceived to be beyond our powers to treat, it may, after all, be possible to ameliorate the human condition.

14.5 Why it Matters

On the question of how it will
affect the next experiment

We can imagine a scientist reading our analytical discussions with some bafflement. He might be mildly interested in some of our connective analyses, yet nevertheless puzzled at what seems to be endless logic chopping. 'Does all this really matter?', he might query when he has read our opening discussions. 'After all', he might continue, 'how is this going to affect the next experiment?' We hope that any reader who has followed us thus far will not be tempted to ask this question. For it displays incomprehension.

Whether our analytic reflections do or do not affect the next experiment is *not* our concern. They may or may not — that depends on what experiment is in view, and what the neuroscientist's presuppositions are. It should be obvious, from our foregoing discussions, that, if our arguments are cogent, some experiments might best be abandoned (see, for example, our discussion of voluntary movements in §8.2). Others would need to be redesigned (see, for example, our discussion of mental imagery in §6.3.1). Most may well be unaffected, although the questions addressed might need to be rephrased, and the results might need to be described in quite different ways than hitherto (see, e.g., §14.3).

Our concern is with
understanding the last experiment

Our concern has not been with the design of the next experiment, but rather with the *understanding* of the last experiment. More generally, conceptual investigations contribute primarily to understanding what is known, and to clarity in the formulation of questions concerning what is not known. It would not matter in the least if our reflections have *no* effect on the next experiment. But they do have considerable effect on the interpretation of the results of previous experiments. And they surely have something to contribute to the asking of questions, to the formulation of questions, and to distinguishing between significant and confused questions. (If we are right, then questions about 'the binding problem', understood as the problem of how the brain forms images, are largely expressions of confusion (see §4.2.3), and much of the debate about mental imagery is misconceived (see §§6.3 and 6.3.1).)

Does it matter? If understanding
matters, then it matters

Does all this apparent logic chopping, all this detailed discussion of words and their use, *matter*? Does neuroscience really *need* this sort of thing? If the moving spirit behind the neuroscientific endeavour is the desire to understand neural phenomena and their relation to psychological capacities and their exercise, then it matters greatly. For, irrespective of the brilliance of the neuroscientists' experiments and the refinement of their techniques, if there is conceptual confusion about their questions or conceptual error in the descriptions of the results of their investigations, then they will not have understood what they set out to understand.

Most contemporary neuroscientists working in the domain of cognitive neuroscience agree that Sir John Eccles's advocacy of a form of dualism (see §2.3) was a mistake – and it is a *conceptual confusion* that lies at the heart of Eccles's error. We have tried to demonstrate, by reference to a variety of theories of distinguished contemporary cognitive neuroscientists, that conceptual error, far from being eradicated by a superficial rejection of various forms of Cartesian dualism, is widespread. It affects and infects the cogency of the questions addressed, the character of the experiments devised to answer them, the intelligibility of the descriptions of the results of these experiments, and the coherence of the conclusions derived from them. And this surely matters both to the understanding of what current neuroscientists *have* achieved, and to the further progress of cognitive neuroscience.

Why it matters to the educated public

It also matters greatly to the educated public. For, irrespective of whether certain neuroscientists are confused, there is no question but that the forms of description they employ confuse the lay public. Neuroscientists are understandably eager to communicate the knowledge they have attained over the past decades about the functioning of the brain and to share with the educated public some of the excitement they feel about their subject. That is evident from the flood of books written by numerous distinguished members of the profession. But by speaking about the brain thinking and reasoning, about one hemisphere knowing something and not informing the other, about the brain making decisions without the person knowing, about rotating mental images in mental space, and so forth, neuroscientists are fostering a form of mystification and cultivating a neuromythology that are altogether deplorable. For, first, this does anything but engender the understanding on behalf of the lay public that is aimed at. Secondly, the lay public will look to neuroscience for answers to pseudo-questions that it should not ask and that neuroscience cannot answer. Once the public become disillusioned, they will ignore the important genuine questions which neuroscience *can* both ask and answer. And this surely matters.

On the need for conceptual clarity

We have, throughout this book, tried to show that clarity concerning conceptual structures is as important for cognitive neuroscience as clarity about experimental methods. Neuroscience's great contributions to our understanding of the biological roots of human capacities and their exercise are illuminated, not hindered, by such clarification. For only when the long shadows cast by conceptual confusions are chased away can the achievements of neuroscience be seen aright.

Appendices

Appendix 1

Daniel Dennett

Daniel Dennett has written extensively on cognitive science and philosophy of mind. His first book, *Content and Consciousness* (1969), laid the foundations for, and determined the direction of, his endeavours for the next thirty years. He has investigated two themes: intentionality and consciousness. In his next book, a volume of essays entitled *Brainstorms* (1978), he pursued both themes further. But the two subjects were handled separately in his best-known works: *The Intentional Stance* (1987), a volume of essays on intentionality, and *Consciousness Explained* (1992), a full-length treatment of consciousness that presupposes and builds on his account of intentionality. A more recent volume, *Kinds of Minds* (1996) brings both themes together again.

Dennett studied philosophy at Harvard, where he was taught by W. V. O. Quine, and at Oxford, where he was taught by Gilbert Ryle. He acknowledges a debt to both his teachers. Quine's influence is indeed evident, but Ryle seems to have influenced him either merely negatively (in respect of his criticism of Cartesianism) or through misinterpretation.[1] Dennett avers a deep agreement with both his philosophical mentors over the nature of philosophy.[2] This is surprising, since they have diametrically opposed conceptions of the subject, Ryle believing that philosophy is *sui generis*, and radically distinct from science, Quine believing that it is continuous with science. Dennett writes that his 'debt to Wittgenstein is large and outstanding'.[3] However, Dennett's accounts of intentionality and consciousness are very far indeed from anything Wittgenstein would have countenanced.

---

[1] Dennett, like many American philosophers, labours under the illusion that Ryle was a logical behaviourist (see 'Three kinds of intentional psychology', repr. in *The Intentional Stance* (MIT Press, Cambridge, MA., 1987), p. 45; subsequent references in the text to this paper are flagged 'TK'). Despite a few incautious statements that veer in a behaviourist direction, Ryle was certainly *not* a logical behaviourist (see G. Ryle, *The Concept of Mind* (Hutchinson, London, 1949), pp. 327–30, and *idem*, 'Adverbial verbs and verbs of thinking', repr. in his volume of essays *On Thinking* (Blackwell, Oxford, 1979), p. 17).

[2] Dennett, 'Dennett, Daniel C.', in S. Guttenplan (ed.), *A Companion to the Philosophy of Mind* (Blackwell, Oxford, 1994), p. 237.

[3] D. Dennett, *Consciousness Explained* (Penguin, Harmondsworth, 1993), p. 463. Subsequent references in the text to this volume will be flagged 'CE'.

Like Quine, Dennett thinks that 'philosophy is allied with, and indeed continuous with, the physical sciences'.[4] Hence he deems himself a 'philosophical naturalist', taking philosophical problems to be soluble 'through a combination of scientific enquiry and the adjustment of our conceptual prejudices in light of empirical evidence'.[5] Accordingly, his aim in his investigations of intentionality and consciousness is 'to create, defend, and confirm (or disconfirm) theories that are directly about the phenomena'.[6] As a graduate student at Oxford, Dennett decided that he 'had to figure out how the brain could possibly accomplish the mind's work . . . how the mechanical responses of "stupid" neurons could be knit into a fabric of activity that actually discriminated meanings'. He took his task to be 'sketching the outlines of a physical structure that could be seen to accomplish the puzzling legerdemain of the mind'.[7] These are great ambitions – indeed, ambitions that are arguably beyond the province of philosophy and the competence of philosophers. We shall see to what extent Dennett deems himself to have achieved them.

Dennett's books are widely read both by educated laymen and by cognitive neuroscientists eager to discover what light philosophers can shed upon their problems. It has been written of him that he 'has played a central role in changing the way we understand the nature of philosophical problems, the nature of philosophy, and the relationship between philosophy and natural science'. His ability to integrate philosophy, psychology and the study of artificial intelligence has, it is said, 'set the tone and direction for contemporary philosophy of mind'. Even those who disagree with him, it is claimed, 'now follow him in acknowledging the role of empirical research in the solution of traditional philosophical problems'.[8]

Precisely because we disagree with so much of what Dennett has written, and because he is so widely read by neuroscientists, it is important that we make clear why we disagree with him on general methodology, on the account he gives of what he calls 'the intentional stance', and on his 'theory of consciousness'. It should be evident that, like Ryle and Wittgenstein, we do not think that empirical research can solve any philosophical problems, any more than it can solve problems in mathematics. So we part company with Dennett right at the beginning, inasmuch as we repudiate the Quinean naturalism that he adopts. We do not think that any philosophical problems can be solved through scientific enquiry. We acknowledge that concepts sometimes need to be revised or augmented for scientific purposes, but deny that any philosophical problems can be *solved* thereby. Indeed, the suggestion that they can seems to us to be akin to claiming that knots can be untied in a piece of string by taking a fresh piece of string.

---

[4] Dennett, 'Setting off on the right foot', in *Intentional Stance*, p. 5.

[5] The observation is John Symons's, in his book *On Dennett* (Wadsworth, Belmont, CA, 2002), p. 12. Since the book appears to have Dennett's imprimatur, we presume he concurs.

[6] Dennett, quoted in ibid., p. 15.

[7] Dennett, 'Dennett, Daniel C.', p. 236.

[8] Symons, *On Dennett*, p. 8.

1 Dennett's Methodology and Presuppositions

Like the Churchlands, Dennett conceives of our common or garden psychological terms as the vocabulary of 'folk psychology', a theoretical edifice that is part of the intellectual legacy of Everyman. Unlike the Churchlands, however, Dennett holds folk psychology to be a true theory, and therefore to be a candidate for incorporation into 'science'. (TK 47f.). For, in his view, folk psychology works: it is 'thanks to folk psychology [that] we cooperate on multi-person projects, learn from each other and enjoy periods of local peace'.[9] Nevertheless, he argues, before we can incorporate such a proto-theory into a genuine science, we must separate the wheat from the chaff. We must discern what it is within the theory that accounts for its explanatory and predictive success. 'In this way we can criticize as we analyse, and it is even open to us in the end to discard folk psychology if it turns out to be a bad theory, and with it the presumed theoretical entities named therein' (TK 47).

Dennett holds that folk psychology 'can best be viewed as a sort of logical behaviourism': *what it means* to say that someone believes something is that he is disposed to behave in certain ways under certain conditions, namely, in ways in which it would be rational for him to behave given his other beliefs and desires (TK 50). However, he also claims that it is part of the theory of folk psychology that beliefs 'are information-bearing states of people that arise from perceptions and that, together with appropriately related *desires*, lead to intelligent action' (TK 46). He further holds that folk psychology is a 'rationalistic calculus of interpretation and prediction – an idealizing, abstract, instrumentalistic interpretation method that has evolved because it works' (TK 48). It is far from evident how the concept of belief can simultaneously signify or be thought to signify an information-bearing state, a mere behavioural disposition, and also no more than an instrumentalist predictive device. We shall revert to this point below.

As noted, Dennett aspired to contribute to a substantial, first-order, empirical theory about human psychology. So, 'from the outset', he avers, 'I worked from the third-person point of view of science'.[10] This methodological commitment was derived from the behaviourists, according to whom 'only facts garnered "from outside" count as data. . . . The idea at its simplest was that since you can never "see directly" into other people's minds, but have to take their word for it, any such facts as there are about mental events are not among the data of science, since they can never be properly verified by objective methods. This methodological scruple . . . is the ruling principle of *all* experimental psychology and neuroscience today (not just "behaviourist research")' (*CE* 70). Nevertheless, Dennett points out, even if mental events are not among the data of science, this does not mean that we cannot study them scientifically. The challenge, as he sees things, is to construct a theory of mental events, using the data that scientific method permits. 'Such a theory will have to be constructed from the third-person point of view, since *all* science is constructed from that perspective' (*CE* 70).

---

[9] Dennett, 'Setting off on the right foot', p. 11.
[10] Dennett, 'Dennett, Daniel C.', p. 237.

Dennett has no qualms about ascribing psychological properties to the brain. He thinks that the brain is conscious (*CE* 172), that it gathers information from the world and uses it to extract anticipations (*CE* 144). The brain, he avers, often makes simplifying assumptions, makes use of supporting information, arrives at conclusions, and interprets the information it receives (*CE* 142f.). This, as we have argued (see chapter 3), is incoherent.

Dennett also claims that the brain is *turned into a mind* as a result of being parasitized by what he calls 'memes' (*CE* 254). We shall investigate this claim below. Given that he believes that the brain *becomes* and then *is* the mind, it is surprising to find him also claiming that each of us is more intimately acquainted with our mind than with our brain. For if the mind is the brain, then to be acquainted with the mind *is* to be acquainted with the brain (even if one does not realize it). Dennett goes further: so intimately are we acquainted with our minds, he avers, 'that you might even say that you *are* your mind'. That thought suggests, in his view, that 'each of us knows exactly one mind from the inside, and no two of us know the same mind from the inside'.[11] It is beyond dispute, he claims, that we have minds (although it remains unclear how we can both *be* and also *have* a mind). Like Descartes, Dennett holds that we know that other people have minds because they can understand speech, and only things with minds can do that (*KM* 8). Wherever there is a mind, he claims, 'there is a point of view. *This is one of the most fundamental ideas we have about minds* − or about consciousness. . . . For most practical purposes, we can consider the point of view of a particular conscious subject to be just that: a point moving through space-time' (*CE* 101, our emphasis).

Before moving on to the substantive parts of Dennett's philosophy, we should pause in order to clarify our disagreements on two large methodological issues: folk psychology and points of view.

Folk psychology   As we have argued, our ordinary psychological vocabulary is not a theoretical vocabulary, and it is not part of a rudimentary proto-theory (§§13.2.1–13.2.2). Our ordinary use of words such as 'see', 'hear', 'know', 'believe', 'like', 'dislike', 'pain', 'pleasure', 'anger', 'joy' does not disclose a *theory* of psychology − it exhibits *the concepts* that characterize sentient creatures, in particular human beings. These concepts are not theoretical ones. The nominals 'perception', 'knowledge', 'belief', 'attitude', 'emotion', 'liking', 'pleasure', 'anger' are not names of theoretical entities, since they are neither names of *entities* nor *theoretical*. The idea that we could, in principle, discard this vocabulary (if 'folk psychology' turned out to be a 'bad theory') is, as we have argued, confused (§§13.2.3–13.2.4).

'Logical behaviourism' is a philosophical doctrine according to which sentences containing psychological terms are logically equivalent to, and translatable into, sentences about behaviour and dispositions to behave. It is, therefore, incoherent to characterize so-called folk psychology − that is, the vocabulary of the mental and the forms of explanation of action and emotion that invoke it − as a form of logical behaviourism. At most it might

---

[11]   D. Dennett, *Kinds of Minds*, (Weideufeld and Nicolson, London, 1996), p. 3. Subsequent references in the text to this book will be flagged '*KM*'.

be claimed that logical behaviourism gives a correct analysis of ordinary psychological predicates. That would be false. (It makes perfectly good sense to describe someone as thinking something but not saying or being disposed to say what they think, or to describe someone as saying something without believing what they say.) But, of course, it is not a claim made by so-called folk psychologists – that is, by the normal competent users of our common psychological vocabulary.

Dennett's suggestion that folk psychology conceives of beliefs as information-bearing states of people is misguided. In the first place, the logical grammar of the verb 'to believe' is not that of a verb signifying a state. Secondly, and consequently, ordinary ascriptions of belief and explanations of action by reference to beliefs do not imply that the person to whom beliefs are ascribed is in any kind of mental state. Our common or garden belief ascriptions are not mental state ascriptions (see §10.2).

Dennett's suggestion that folk psychology is 'a rationalistic calculus of interpretation and prediction – an idealizing, abstract, instrumentalistic interpretation method' is misconceived. When we teach children to prefix 'I think' or 'I believe' to sentences or sentence nominalizations (i.e. that-clauses) or to insert these phrases parenthetically within a sentence ('Daddy is, I believe, in town'), we are not teaching them an 'abstract instrumentalistic interpretation method'. We are teaching them, for example, to indicate the character, or degree of adequacy, of their grounds for assertion. When we report someone's assertion, and prefix or parenthetically interpolate 'she believes' or 'he thinks', we are not interpreting or predicting anything, but typically distancing ourselves from what that person is reported as having asserted ('She *believes* that NN is plotting – but (I know) he is not'). When we teach a child to say 'It hurts' and later 'I have a pain', we are not teaching it part of an instrumentalist predictive calculus, and when the child learns to ascribe pains to his mother, and to commiserate with her when she has hurt herself, he is not learning how to operate an 'instrumentalistic interpretation method'. And when we teach a child to replace his cries of fear with 'Mummy, I had a nightmare!', we have not taught him a method of interpretation – he can learn that when he studies psychoanalysis.

Finally, it is misconceived to think, as Dennett does, that 'it is thanks to folk psychology [that] we cooperate on multi-person projects, learn from each other, and enjoy periods of local peace'. We do not cooperate with each other because we share a theory about 'other minds', any more than members of a wolf pack cooperate in hunting because they share a theory about 'other [wolf] minds'. Babies do not learn from their parents because they have worked out a folk-psychological theory about their parents. And we do not enjoy periods of local peace, any more than we suffer periods of local strife, because we have mastered the vocabulary of the mental. There is no such thing as a theory of 'folk psychology', save for such dicta as 'Once bitten, twice shy' or 'Spare the rod and spoil the child' (see §§13.2–13.2.2). It is not that folk psychology 'works' – it is no theory that might work or fail to work, and such commonplace dicta are as often as not misguided. Rather, the *vocabulary* of the mental partly defines what it is to be human – but that is an altogether different matter. Of course, knowing what another person knows and believes, knowing what he wants or intends, and knowing his emotions and attitudes, enables modest degrees of prediction – but that is not because of any theory of human behaviour. It is because of the limited rationality we enjoy and the character of the practical reasoning we engage in.

Points of view   The expressions 'point of view', 'first-person point of view', and 'third-person point of view' are 'ready-mades' of current cognitive science and philosophy of mind. The thought that one of our most fundamental ideas about the mind is that wherever there is a mind there is *a point of view* dresses up distorted trivialities as profundities. At best all it amounts to is (a) that sentient creatures perceive whatever they perceive from a particular place, (b) that different people may have different opinions about certain things, and (c) that language-using creatures can give expression to their thoughts and experiences using the first-person pronoun. The last triviality does not signify that first-person expressions, or even reports, of thought and experience are made from 'a point of view'. 'I have a headache' or 'I think that Shakespeare died in 1616' is no more a statement made from 'a point of view' than is 'I am six foot tall'. Can one intelligibly say 'From my point of view, I have a headache', or 'From my point of view, I think Shakespeare died in 1616'?

The claim that 'science' works 'from a third-person point of view' is explained by reference to behaviourism. On that account, 'only facts garnered "from outside" count as data'. The metaphor is unfortunate. Outside *what*? The mind is no place, and the apparently locative phrases 'in one's mind', 'at the back of one's mind', 'crossed one's mind' are misleading forms of words that are readily unpacked into verb phrases that make no use of the nominal 'mind' (see §3.10) or of the apparently spatial expressions 'in', 'at the back of', and 'crossed'. To say that a thought *crossed* one's mind – that is, that one thought of something – or that something is fixed indelibly *in* one's mind – that is, that one will never forget something – is not to report 'from inside' anything, and to assert third-person sentences such as 'He thought of something' or 'He never forgot the searing experience' is not to report anything 'from outside'. The metaphor of 'inside' and 'outside' wreaks havoc with our thought if we misinterpret it (see §§3.5–3.7)

The putative contrast between the third-person point of view of 'science' and the first-person point of view is explained by reference to the claim that one can never see directly into another person's mind, but has to take their word for it, and therefore one can never properly verify what people say about their thought and experience. According to Dennett, this methodological scruple informs *all* contemporary experimental psychology and neuroscience. Such scruples are misconceived. It is wrong to think that one cannot properly verify whether another person knows or believes something – we do so all the time. (What, to take but one example, are examinations for?) It is mistaken to suppose that one cannot verify whether another is in severe pain – just try doubting the screams of a person badly injured in an accident. There is no difficulty at all in verifying that little Tommy likes ice-cream. Psychiatrists successfully verify whether someone has a depression, and opticians can readily check whether someone sees double. And much of what neuroscientists have discovered about functional localization in the brain involved the data provided by patients' avowals during brain operations (and, more recently, brain scans). The sense in which one cannot 'see directly' into another's mind is the sense in which one cannot see sounds or hear colours: namely, because *there is no such thing* – this is a senseless form of words (hence it cannot describe a condition for knowing what another person thinks or feels). Equally, of course, there is no such thing as 'seeing directly' into one's own mind – *that* notion incorporates a confused conception of introspection (see §3.6). A person's utterances 'I can hear such-and-such', 'I see such-and-such', 'I think it is thus', 'I fear that so-and-so', 'I wish you would go away', 'I am tired', etc. are not reports derived from his observations of a peep-show which only he can see. He cannot hear his hearing or see his seeing, although others can often observe that he sees or hears something and, indeed, see or hear *what* he sees and hears. Finally, if it were so difficult, or indeed impossible, to see, detect or find out another person's thoughts and feelings, then it would be a mystery that from time to time we have to make such an effort to *conceal* what we think and feel from our audience.

First-person psychological utterances may be *expressions* of thought or experience, or may be *reports* or *descriptions*. But they are not based on perceiving something that no one else can see, or on having 'access' to something to which others have no 'access'. They are respectable data for medical or psychological diagnosis, and for neuroscientific investigation. That is perfectly compatible with the thought that self-deception is possible, that people sometimes lie or are confused – and that we are accordingly sometimes deceived or mistaken in our judgements about them. It is quite wrong that we *have* to take others' word for what they know or believe, feel or intend – we *can* often detect confusion, deception and self-deception.

'Science' does not investigate a subject matter from *either* a first- *or* a third-person point of view. But one might say that meteorologists and climatologists investigate the melting of the polar ice-caps from a physical and climatological point of view, whereas zoologists investigate it from a zoological point of view, and ecologists study it from an ecological point of view. Doctors may investigate the so-called madness of George III from a medical point of view (the poor man, as has been discovered, suffered from porphyria); historians may study it from a political-historical or from a medical-historical point of view. There is no single, uniform subject called 'science' that is pursued by all scientists in their investigations, any more than there is a single subject matter called 'reality' that furnishes them with a subject matter. There are numerous sciences, each with different concerns. Scientists, at their best, are dedicated to the pursuit of truth within their subject. Their data are the facts that they establish within their domains. These are selected according to their *scientific* points of view – the relevant data for a physicist being very different from the data relevant to the interests or concerns of a palaeontologist, ecologist, zoologist or climatologist. In the psychological sciences, the evidential support required to establish data includes the subjects' avowals and averrals of thought and experience. These are not *mere words* – nor are they reports of a *private peep-show*.

2 The Intentional Stance

The expression 'the intentional stance' is introduced by Dennett to characterize a 'tactic'[12] or a 'strategy' (*KM* 27) of interpretation. He contrasts it with what he calls 'the physical

---

[12] Dennett, 'Dennett, Daniel C.', p. 239.

stance' and 'the design stance', the former being exemplified by physics, the latter by our descriptions of artefacts. It is a mode of interpreting 'entities' (people, animals, artefacts) *as if* they were rational agents with beliefs, desires and other mental states exhibiting what Brentano called 'intentionality'.[13] Dennett explains this term of art by equating it with what he calls 'aboutness'. Something is held to exhibit intentionality 'if its competence is in some way *about* something else'. In Dennett's view, 'A lock and key exhibit the crudest form of intentionality; and so do the opioid receptors in brain cells' (*KM* 35). Perceptual and emotional states, as well as 'states of memory' are intentional. A 'state of recognition' 'exhibits a very particular aboutness', inasmuch as one recognizes whatever one recognizes *as* something – for example, a horse as a horse. Had one recognized it as something else – for example, a moose or a motor cyclist – one's perceptual state would have had a different aboutness (*KM* 36f.).

The intentional stance is, he claims, the attitude or perspective we routinely adopt whenever we attribute intentional mental states to ourselves and to others. According to Dennett, the fundamental form of attributions of mental states 'are sentences that express what are called *propositional attitudes*'. Such sentences have the general form 'A *V*'s that *p*', where '*V*' holds a place for a verb signifying a 'propositional attitude', and the variable '*p*' is 'a term for a particular content or meaning of that attitude – the *proposition* denoted (e.g. 'Jack believes that it will rain'). Propositions, in Dennett's view, 'are the theoretical entities with which we identify and measure beliefs. For two people to share a belief is, by definition, for them to believe one and the same proposition' (*KM* 45f.). This is a misconception. The sentences 'A believes that it will rain', 'B fears that it will rain', 'C hopes that it will rain', and 'D suspects that it will rain' do not signify attitudes to propositions. It is, of course, possible to believe propositions, just as one can believe statements, stories and rumours. But since A may believe what B fears, and also what C hopes and D suspects, and since there is no such thing as fearing, hoping or suspecting a proposition, what A believes (in our example) is not *the proposition that it will rain*, but simply *that it will rain*. We do not *measure* beliefs, fears, hopes and suspicions by propositions, but we *individuate* them by specifying what is believed, feared, hoped or suspected – which cannot be a proposition in the latter three cases, and need not be one in the case of belief. Finally, propositions are not theoretical entities, any more than are statements, declarations, stories, fairy-tales or rumours.

The intentional stance, according to Dennett, is an *interpretative* stance.[14] We interpret an entity thus by adopting the presupposition that it approximates the ideal of an optimally designed (i.e. rational) self-regarding agent, governing its choices by reference to its beliefs and desires. We do so, Dennett claims, in order to predict and explain its actions or moves. Adopting the intentional stance toward something other than a human being, he

---

[13] Dennett,'True believers: the intentional strategy and why it works', repr. in *Intentional Stance*, p. 15. Subsequent references in the text to this article are flagged 'TB'.

[14] In this respect it seems to stand in contrast with what Dennett calls 'the physical stance'. When physicists describe and predict natural phenomena, they are not interpreting them *as if* they were correctly described by the laws of physics. Physics is not an interpretative stance.

observes, 'seems to be deliberately *anthropomorphizing* it' (*KM* 27). Nevertheless, he thinks, it is wholly warranted if that thing is an intentional system.

'Intentional systems' are entities whose behaviour is predictable and explicable from an intentional stance. Strikingly, Dennett thinks that such heterogeneous items as self-replicating macromolecules, thermostats, amoebas, plants, animals, people and chess-playing computers are intentional systems (*KM* 34). The strategy is to think of these things as rational agents: 'you figure out what beliefs that agent ought to have, given its place in the world and its purpose. Then you figure out what desires it ought to have on the same considerations, and finally, you predict that this rational agent will act to further its goals in the light of its beliefs' (TB 17). This strategy, according to Dennett, works

> with people almost all the time. . . . The strategy works on birds, and on fish, and on reptiles, and on insects and spiders, and even on such lowly and unenterprising creatures as clams. . . . It also works on some artefacts: the chess-playing computer will not take your knight because it knows that there is a line of ensuing play that would lead to its losing its rook, and it does not want that to happen. More modestly, the thermostat will turn off the boiler as soon as it comes to believe the room has reached the desired temperature. (TB 22)

Why does the strategy work? In the case of human beings, Dennett contends, it works because 'evolution has designed human beings to be rational, to believe what they ought to believe and to want what they ought to want' (TB 33). Nevertheless, attributions of what Dennett calls 'intentionality' are no more than '*interpretations* of the phenomena – a "heuristic overlay", describing an inescapably idealized pattern. Like such *abstracta* as centers of gravity and parallelograms of force, the beliefs and desires posited by the highest stance have no independent and concrete existence.'[15] But for all that, the intentional stance is held to be unavoidable, both with regard to oneself and with regard to one's fellow intelligent beings (TB 27).

There are multiple objections to these views. We shall first examine Dennett's conception of intentionality and then his idea of the 'intentional stance'.

Intentionality   Dennett misconstrues what modern philosophers since Brentano (who revived the medieval term 'intentio') have called 'intentionality'. Brentano held (wrongly) that intentionality is the mark of the mental. Mental attributes, he argued, have 'objects'. If a person *V*'s (e.g. believes, hopes, fears, suspects, expects, loves, hates), then there is something that he *V*'s. What he *V*'s need not exist, occur or be the case in order for it to be true that he *V*'s it. According to Brentano, mental phenomena are unique in respect of 'the intentional in-existence of [their] object' – one can believe, fear or suspect that something or other is going to happen, but it may never come to pass. But the non-occurrence of what one believed, feared or suspected would occur does not imply that one believed, feared or suspected nothing. The object of one's belief, fear

---

[15]   Dennett, 'Dennett, Daniel C.', p. 239.

or suspicion is an 'intentional object'. Somewhat differently, one may look for (but not find) Eldorado even though it does not exist, or fear (but not meet) ghosts even though there are none. Mental phenomena, Brentano held, 'contain an object intentionally within themselves', which is said to enjoy *immanent existence* within, for example, the belief, fear or suspicion.[16]

No doubt this was confused. First, there are psychological phenomena that are *not* intentional at all, such as objectless moods (e.g. cheerfulness) and sensations (e.g. pain). Secondly, it is arguably mistaken to suppose that there is any form of intentional in-existence about believing Jack or his story (by contrast with fearing God (or Zeus) and his wrath). For in so far as Jack must exist in order for one to believe *him*, and in so far as he must have told a story in order for one to believe *it*, these are not intentional objects of belief. They may be contrasted with *believing that Jack is guilty* or *suspecting treachery* (i.e. suspecting that there is treachery), the intentional objects of which are specified by nominalization accusatives (i.e. that-clauses or their equivalents), as well as *fearing Zeus* or *looking for Eldorado*. So not all forms of mental attributes (such as belief) that *can* intelligibly be said to be intentional *are* intentional in all occurrences. Thirdly, it was misleading to speak of the 'intentional in-existence' of intentional objects, when all that was necessary was to point out that for certain psychological attributes, one can *V* that *p* even though it is not the case that *p*, and one can *V* M even though there is no M. We need not delve further into the logical complexities here,[17] for this rough indication suffices to show deficiencies in Dennett's discussion of the matter.

It is unilluminating to characterize intentionality as 'aboutness': if one fears defeat and hopes for victory, one's fear is not *about* defeat, although its intentional object is *that one will be defeated*, and one's hope is not *about* victory, although its intentional object is *that one will be victorious*. The preposition 'about' and the barbaric nominal 'aboutness' are ill-suited to capture what Brentano and the scholastics meant by 'intentionality' or to pinpoint the intentional objects which they conceived of as 'existing immanently' in mental phenomena. For one cannot say 'My belief is about that it will rain tonight', and the answer to the question 'What do you fear? is not 'About defeat', but 'Defeat' or 'That we shall be defeated'.

It is incorrect to ascribe intentionality to human beings as such – they do not enjoy any 'aboutness' or 'contain objects intentionally within themselves'. To speak of human beings

---

[16] F. Brentano, *Psychology from an Empirical Standpoint* (Routledge, London, 1995; first published 1874), pp. 88f. What Brentano seems to have meant was as follows. When one, for example, believes falsely that *p*, then what one believes (viz. that *p*) does not obtain or exist. But it does not follow, of course, that one believes nothing. Moreover, one can *say* what one believes, even though what one believes does not exist 'in reality'. But then how can one say (and how can one know) what one believes? According to Brentano we can *know*, by means of 'inner perception', that we believe, and we can 'read off' what we believe *from our belief*. So our belief *contains* its object 'intentionally' within itself; or, again, the object of our belief enjoys 'immanent existence' within our belief.

[17] For an overview of the problems of intentionality, see P. M. S. Hacker, 'An orrery of intention-ality', *Language and Communication*, 21 (2001), pp. 119–41.

'enjoying intentionality'[18] can, at best, only mean that human beings have intentional attributes: for example, that they believe, hope, fear, suspect, etc. that something or other is or will be the case. What is intentional, if anything, is the psychological attribute that has an intentional object (e.g. believing *that p*, as opposed to believing Harry or his story).

One cannot intelligibly ascribe 'intentionality' to molecules, cells, parts of the brain, thermostats or computers. Not only is it a subclass of psychological *attributes* that are the appropriate bearers of intentionality and not animals or things, but, further, only animals, and fairly sophisticated animals at that, and not parts of animals, let alone molecules, thermostats or computers, are the subjects of such attributes. For, as we have argued at length (see chapter 3), it makes no sense to ascribe belief, fear, hope, suspicion, etc. to molecules, cells, the brain or its parts, thermostats or computers. There is no such thing as a thermostat *believing* that it is too hot, *thinking* that it is cold, *wondering* whether it will cool down, *being convinced* that it is hot enough, *deciding* that the temperature has fallen enough, *judging* or *misjudging*. Such an artefact cannot (logically cannot) satisfy the criteria for belief, thought, wonder, conviction, deciding, judging or misjudging. It makes no literal sense to ascribe such psychological attributes to artefacts – 'The thermostat thinks that it is too hot' is a form of words which has no use (other than as a joke). Thermostats can no more think than $\sqrt{-1}$ can get married. A very rich array of possible forms of behaviour in the circumstances of life is already presupposed before a creature can intelligibly (truly *or* falsely) be said to think.

It is equally misconceived to attribute intentionality (or 'aboutness') to locks and keys or to opioid receptors. The fact that a key fits a lock does not imply that there is any sense in which the key is 'about' the lock, let alone that the key has intentional attributes (such as the belief, hope or fear that it will or will not fit a lock) that have intentional objects possessing 'intentional in-existence'. Opioid receptors are no more *about* opioids than cats are about dogs or ducks are about drakes.

A different mistake (see p. 420) is to think that an attribute such as recognition is intentional. If Jack recognizes Jill going up the hill, there is nothing intentional about his recognition. His recognition is not *about* Jill (or anything else) – it is *of* Jill. But he could *recognize* Jill only if she exists and is there to be recognized – so Jill cannot be said to enjoy intentional in-existence or immanent existence within Jack's recognition. Similarly, he could recognize that Jill is there only if she *is* actually there; if it is false that she is there, then Jack did not recognize Jill but merely thought he did. In short, recognition is not an intentional attribute. Of course, Jack may recognize Jill, but not recognize her 'as Jill'. He may recognize her as the girl who used to go up the hill, but he may no longer remember her name. But this feature should not be confused with intentionality. They are connected, but distinct. And each has to be disentangled separately.

---

[18] Dennett writes that 'all the intentionality we enjoy is derived from the more fundamental intentionality of these billions of crude intentional systems [presumably macromolecules]' (*KM* 55). We do not 'enjoy intentionality', although we do believe that things are thus-and-so (even if they are not), fear or suspect that things will be so (even if our fears and suspicions are never realized). The intentionality of our beliefs is not 'derived' from anything, although we doubtless would have no beliefs at all if our brains were not functioning appropriately.

The intentional stance   The notion of an intentional *stance* is apt to characterize various forms of animism distinctive of pre-scientific thought. But to ascribe pain, liking, disliking, perceiving, misperceiving, anger, fear, joy, knowledge, belief, memory, imagination, desire, intention, and so on, to living beings, in particular to human beings, is not to adopt an interpretative stance. Dennett characterizes the intentional stance as a mode of interpreting entities *as if* they were rational agents with beliefs, desires and other intentional mental states. It is, he holds, a 'heuristic overlay' of a belief/desire calculus that is relative to given goals, and that assumes self-regarding rationality. It is a theoretical posit with neither more nor less reality than centres of gravity or parallelograms of force. Its warrant is its instrumentalist, predictive and explanatory success.

But, (i)   anthropomorphizing pet owners apart, we do *not* treat animals as if they were rational agents – since we know perfectly well that they are not. But we do ascribe a wide range of perceptual, affective, cognitive and volitional attributes to animals in a perfectly literal sense. Being a rational agent is not a precondition for the applicability of psychological attributes to a creature.

(ii)   We do not treat the higher animals *as if* they were, from occasion to occasion, angry, frightened, contented, or *as if* they could see and hear, feel and smell. For we *know* that eagles can see farther than we can, that dogs have a better sense of smell than we do, and that short-eared owls can hear far better than we can. We *know* that the fleeing fox is afraid of the hounds, that the snarling dog is angry, and that the purring cat is contented. There is no *as if* about it.

(iii)   Dennett claims that the intentional stance is unavoidable, 'with regard to [both] oneself and one's fellow intelligent beings' (TB 27). But to ascribe psychological attributes to oneself, to avow that one is in pain ('It hurts!', 'I have a terrible toothache!'), sincerely to express one's regret or remorse ('I am so very sorry!'), to manifest one's pleasure and joy ('I am so pleased!', 'I am overjoyed'), to voice one's beliefs, fears, hopes, suspicions ('I don't believe a word he said', 'I fear disaster', 'I hope it works', 'I suspect treachery'), to declare one's wants, likings, intentions and so forth, is not to adopt an *interpretative stance* of any kind towards oneself – it is to give expression to one's pain, regret, pleasure, hopes and fears. And the pain or joy one feels, the beliefs one passionately embraces, the fears and suspicions one harbours, are not *heuristic overlays*, and are not *theoretical posits* of any kind.

One may agree with Dennett that 'the beliefs and desires posited by the highest stance [i.e. the intentional stance] have no independent and concrete existence', if all one means thereby is that there are no beliefs without believers, no desires without desirers, and that belief and desire are not tangible objects. But it is evident that that is *not* what Dennett means when he writes of *positing* beliefs and desires, and compares the psychological attributes to centres of gravity or parallelograms of forces.

(iv)   The intentional strategy requires one to think of the subject as a rational agent, and to 'figure out what beliefs that agent ought to have, given its place in the world and its purpose'. But if so, the strategy could not possibly be applied to such things as molecules, brains and their parts, thermostats or chess-playing computers. For it makes no sense whatsoever to suppose that self-replicating molecules ought to believe anything, any more than it makes sense to suppose that negative numbers ought to believe that when multiplied by themselves they yield positive numbers. Given the place of thermostats in the world and their purposes, it is clear that there could be no such thing as thermostats believing anything, hence too, no such thing as something that they ought to believe. Of course, we tend to anthropomorphize our chess-playing computer. We might be inclined to say that the computer 'will not take your knight because it knows that there is a line of ensuing play that would lead to its losing its rook, and it does not want that to happen' (TB 22). But what does this amount to? It is no more than a *façon de parler*. We know that the computer has been designed to make moves that will (probably) lead to the defeat of whomever plays with it – and there is no such thing as the computer's knowing or wanting anything. And in order to predict its moves, we need not absurdly ascribe knowledge or wants to it, but need only understand the goals of its program and programmer (viz. to make a (mindless) chess-playing machine). For design is one form of teleology, and teleology is a basis for prediction.

(v)   It is surely misconceived to suppose that in 'adopting the intentional stance' – that is, in ascribing psychological attributes to other human beings – we are supposing that 'evolution has designed human beings to be rational, to believe what they ought to believe and to want what they ought to want', that in so doing we presuppose that we are 'optimally designed (i.e. rational) self-regarding agents' and that that is why our 'intentional strategy' works. Evolution has not *designed* anything – Darwin's achievement was to displace explanation in terms of design by evolutionary explanations.

More importantly, we do not, in our efforts to describe, understand and sometimes also to predict the behaviour and reactions of others, assume that they believe what they ought to believe and want what they ought to want. Alas, we know perfectly well that they often believe and want what they have been taught, told, brainwashed and cajoled into believing and wanting by parents, teachers, priests, gurus, governments and advertising agencies, much of which ought not to be believed or wanted.

In ascribing psychological attributes to human beings and in predicting or explaining their behaviour, we do not presuppose that they are uniformly self-regarding creatures. Our conception of rationality is not a self-regarding one. It is not irrational to sacrifice oneself or one's interests for the sake of a greater good, and deeds of quotidian generosity, common modest forms of selflessness, and heroic self-sacrifice are not unpredictable or unintelligible forms of deviance for not fitting into Dennett's market-oriented conception of rationality.

Even in the third person, our employment of the psychological vocabulary and the intentional idiom is not guided exclusively, or even largely, by a constant desire to predict the behaviour of others. Curious, interested observation, as well as sympathetic and empathetic participation in the affairs of others play at least as great a role; and that often involves a need to know about the beliefs and desires of others (and if we ask them, they often reveal their beliefs and wants to us), not in order to predict their behaviour, but to advise them on what would be for the best, or simply to understand what they have done. And since we are eyes and ears to each other, we commonly share our beliefs and fears, suspicions and hopes, or engage in painstaking discussion, not in order to predict each other's behaviour, but to discover the truth, or to share our knowledge or our prejudices, or to foster a common sense of identity and community.

(vi)   Dennett characterized the intentional stance as interpreting the behaviour of an entity (person, animal, part of an animal, or artefact) by treating it *as if* it were a rational agent with an array of beliefs and desires. In the case of things other than us, this involves anthropomorphizing the thing. But we are also supposed to interpret each other *as if* we had beliefs and desires – and the beliefs and desires that we thus ascribe to each other are mere theoretical posits (akin to centres of gravity). But this generates an incoherence.

In order to be able to treat a being *as if* it believed that *p* or wanted to *V*, we must know what it *is* to believe or to want something. We must know under what circumstances it is appropriate to judge that another person actually believes or wants something, and indeed when it is appropriate to avow a belief or desire in our own case. Only when we have grasped this – that is, when we have understood the use of the verbs 'to believe' and 'to want' (in both the first and the third person) – can we come to understand what it is to treat a being *as if* it believed this or wanted that. But on Dennett's account the adoption of the intentional strategy towards an intentional system, including human beings, is *never* other than an 'as if'. But if so, there is no actuality in terms of which we might intelligibly cash the pretence, no believing or wanting in terms of which to understand what we are to feign when we treat a being (including ourselves and others) *as if* they believed or wanted things. Moreover, there is no specification of what would *count* as actually believing or wanting. But if so, we can assign no content to the concepts of belief and desire that Dennett deploys.

(vii)   Dennett attempts to explain intentionality as an interpretative strategy. But 'to interpret something as . . .' is itself an intentional expression. To interpret something as something is to take it to be so, to believe or suppose it to be so. But now the 'intentional stance' patently involves an incoherence, for it cannot be applied reflexively.

Given Dennett's conception of the intentional stance, it is unclear what precisely he means by claiming that the brain gathers information, anticipates things, interprets the information it receives, arrives at conclusions, etc. Presumably *he* is 'adopting the intentional stance' towards the brain, and is treating it as if it were a rational agent that believes what it ought to believe and desires what it ought to desire and acts on its beliefs and desires. But this is not coherent. We know what it is to treat a young child as if it were an adult, rational human being, but do we have any idea what it would be to treat *a brain* as if it were a rational being? The brain, as we have argued, is not a possible subject of beliefs and desires; there is no such thing as a brain acting on beliefs and desires, and there is nothing that the brain does that can be predicted on the basis of its beliefs and desires.

Similar obscurity surrounds Dennett's remark that we are intimately acquainted with our own minds, that we know that we have a mind, and that we know our own mind from the inside. Does this mean that we should, for the sake of predictive efficiency, treat ourselves *as if* we had a mind, and *as if* we knew our own mind? To treat a creature *as if* it had a mind, one must know how to treat a creature that *does* have a mind. Moreover, if the mind is merely an instrumentalist calculating convenience, like the centre of gravity in mechanics, then there can be no such thing, even figuratively, as 'knowing, from the inside, that we have a mind'.

3 Heterophenomenological Method

It is against the backcloth of these ideas that Dennett aims to meet 'the challenge of constructing a theory of mental events', using the data that scientific method permits. 'Such a theory will have to be constructed from the third-person point of view, since *all* science is constructed from that perspective' (*CE* 70). The method by which he proposes that this should be done he has dubbed 'the heterophenomenological method'. This consists in the 'experimenter' letting 'subjects' recount their thoughts, beliefs and feelings, their perceptions and memories, their likings and dislikings, their wishes, wants and intentions.

The experimenter's raw data are mere noises emitted by organisms. But he must adopt the intentional stance, and 'treat the noise emitter as an agent, indeed a rational agent, who harbours beliefs and desires . . . the uttered noises are to be interpreted as things the subjects *wanted to say*, of *propositions* they meant to *assert*, for instance, for various reasons' (*CE* 76).

The subject's self-ascriptions of experience are held to constitute 'a text': a fiction on a par with a novel. This alleged fiction is referred to as the subject's 'heterophenomenological world'.[19] It is held to be a 'stable, intersubjectively confirmable, theoretical posit' (*CE* 81), having the same status as fictional objects.

In the subject's heterophenomenological world, Dennett explains, there are intentional objects, to which various things happen. But, he claims, these objects, like Mr Pickwick, are made of nothing – they are fictional objects. But they are also said to be *abstracta* – not idle fictions, but 'hardworking theorists's fictions' (*CE* 95f.). These fictional worlds are also claimed to be populated by 'all the images, events, sounds, smells, hunches, presentiments and feelings the subject sincerely believes to exist in his . . . stream of consciousness' (*CE* 98).

The subject is not authoritative about what is happening 'in him', 'but only about what seems to be happening in [him]' (*CE* 96).

Having extracted this 'heterophenomenology', Dennett explains that

> theorists can then turn to the question of what might explain the *existence* of this hetero-phenomenology in all its details. The heterophenomenology exists – just as uncontroversially as novels and other fictions exist. People undoubtedly do believe that they have mental images, pains, perceptual experiences, and all the rest, and *these* facts about what people believe, and report when they express their beliefs – are phenomena any scientific theory of the mind must account for . . . the question of whether items thus portrayed exist as real objects, events and states in the brain . . . is an empirical matter to

---

[19] It is unclear why it is not deemed to be the *subject's* 'autophenomenological' world, and the *experimenter's* 'heterophenomenological' one.

investigate. If suitable real candidates are uncovered, we can identify them as the long-sought referents of the subject's terms; if not, we will have to explain why it seems to subjects that these items exist. (*CE* 98)[20]

This programme of research is, in our view, a non-starter, and the 'heterophenomenological method' incoherent.

First, Dennett wishes to construct 'a theory of mental events' by means of his heterophenomenological method. But it is unclear what is supposed to count as *a mental event*. Many of the things he mentions are not events at all, and much of what he speculates about cannot be said to be mental. Is seeing the tree in the quad a mental event? Is hearing that the government has fallen a mental event? Are loving Maisy and respecting Daisy mental events? Knowing, believing, supposing, assuming, meaning something by what one said, hoping and fearing are clearly not mental *events*, since they are not events. Feeling cheerful or depressed are moods – that is, mental states – not *events*. Calculating in one's head and talking to oneself in one's imagination are mental activities or processes, not *mental events*. Is calculating on paper or proving a theorem aloud before an audience a *mental* event? It is doubtful whether there is any coherent subject matter here that could be the subject of scientific investigation.[21] So it is equally unclear whether there can be such a thing as a *general theory* of 'mental events'. To be sure, there can be no such a thing as a *general theory* of non-mental events.

Secondly, it is unclear who is supposed to undertake the challenge that Dennett envisages. Is it meant to be a research programme for cognitive neuroscience? Or for experimental psychology? Or for an imaginary 'science of consciousness'? The 'experimenter' who is supposed to take tape recordings or transcripts of experimental subjects' 'heterophenomenology' is supposed to investigate 'what might explain the *existence* of this heterophenomenology in all its details'. So, we may suppose that subject A declares that he is tired, that he has a toothache, that he is pleased that he won his bet with Jack, that he believes that the Ruritanian Party will win the election, and that he is afraid the economy is going into recession. But one does not need a scientist to explain the existence of this 'heterophenomenology'. A is tired, because he has worked hard all day long; he has a toothache because there is a cavity in his tooth; he is pleased to have won his bet, because he wanted My Love to win the 3.30; he believes the RP will win the election because he has seen the latest opinion polls; and he is afraid that the economy is going into recession because he just read the financial news. These are explanations of the existence of A's

---

[20] Elsewhere Dennett elaborates: 'if we were to find real goings-on in people's brains that had enough of the "defining" properties of the items that populate their phenomenological worlds, we could reasonably propose that we had discovered what they were *really* talking about – even if they initially resisted the identifications. And if we discovered that the real goings-on bore only minor resemblance to the heterophenomenological items, we could reasonably declare that people were just mistaken in the beliefs they expressed, in spite of their sincerity' (*CE* 85).

[21] Although we deny that the concept of the mental is obsolete (see below, p. 450), we agree with Searle to the extent that we think that it is quite useless for the kinds of purposes for which Dennett invokes it.

'heterophenomenology', and they need no science. What might call for science, more specifically for psychiatry, is why, for example, someone persists in believing something (e.g. that he has a terrible disease, or that everyone is 'out to get him') when *all* the evidence shows the groundlessness of his belief. Such abnormalities call for a psychiatric explanation (an explanation of why things are awry). But, of course, it does not follow that we need a comparable psychiatric (or any other 'scientific') explanation of why we believe well-founded beliefs.

Thirdly, the supposition that the raw data for a future science of consciousness are noises that are to be interpreted as speech is misconceived. Human utterances are no more mere noises which stand in need of an 'interpretation' than the sights we see are mere patches of colour and shapes that need to be interpreted as the multicoloured objects that surround us. It is mistaken to suppose that a respectably scientific investigation into human psychology must take its raw data to be the bare noises of human speech (this would be to confuse phonetics with psychology). For (a) the raw data which we are given consist of significant human speech, not of bare sounds (phonetics is an *abstraction* from what is given.); and (b) there is no such thing as *interpreting* bare noises, any more than there is such a thing as interpreting a coded message (one can only interpret the message *after* it has been deciphered).

Fourthly, the heterophenomenological method treats human avowals and reports of knowledge, belief, memory, perception, hopes and fears, pleasures and pains as *fictions* (like sentences in a novel). But this involves important inconsistencies.

(i) To treat a text as fiction is, roughly speaking, to treat it as if it were preceded by a 'Once upon a time'. If the 'theorist' reads a transcript and treats it as fiction, he cannot also treat it as a theoretical posit. 'Once upon a time' does not introduce theoretical posits – it precludes them.

(ii) The alleged heterophenomenological world is held to consist of intentional objects, to which various things happen. But that makes no sense, since intentional objects such as *that Maisy will come tonight*, which is what A expects, or *victory*, which is what he hopes for, or *treachery*, which is what he fears, are not objects to which anything could possibly happen.

(iii) Intentional objects such as *that Maisy will come tonight* are *not* fictions. Mr Pickwick, of course, is a fiction – a fictional character. It is not true that Mr Pickwick was made of nothing. Hamlet's father's ghost (also a fictional character) was made of nothing, but Mr Pickwick was made of flesh and blood. *That Maisy will come tonight*, unlike Mr Pickwick, is indeed not made of anything – but that does not make an intentional object much like a fictional ghost.

(iv) The subject, according to Dennett, is not authoritative about the denizens of his heterophenomenological world ('what is happening in him'), but only about what seems (to him) to be happening within him. But that makes scant sense.

First, if the subject avers that he believes, hopes, fears, expects this, that or the other, he is not reporting on anything that *happens in him*. Beliefs, hopes, fears and expectations don't 'happen in' people. But he does enjoy a *prima facie* authority on what he believes, hopes, fears and expects. His sincere avowal is a (defeasible) criterion for his so believing, hoping, fearing or expecting. In the absence of defeating evidence, his word goes.

Secondly, with respect to an array of mental phenomena, there is no such thing as 'seeming', and for a subject to enjoy 'authority' with respect to such items has nothing to do with anything that merely seems to him to be the case. So, for example, there is no such thing as a person seeming to himself to be in pain (*a fortiori* no such thing as its seeming to him that he is in pain and his not being in pain); and what goes for pain goes for other sensations too (e.g. tickles, tingles). Similarly, it cannot seem to one that one has a mental image before one's mind, even though one has none.

(v)   Dennett holds that there is a question as to whether the (intentional) denizens of people's heterophenomenological world *exist as real objects, events and states in the brain.* If not, then they exist only as fictions, and, he claims, we will have to explain why it seems to their subjects that they exist. This is confused.

First, it surely does not seem to anyone that such intentional objects 'in the subject's heterophenomenological world' as *that Maisy will come to dinner* exist as 'real objects, events or states in the brain'. Indeed, it is unclear what, if anything, could be meant by asking whether an intentional object exists *in* the brain or *as* an object, event or state of some kind in the brain. The very notion of an intentional object was introduced by Brentano as something which need not exist *at all* in order to be the object of an intentional attribute such as belief or fear *that* something or other is thus and so.

Secondly, it does not *seem* to people that their pains, beliefs, hopes and fears really exist. People really do have pains;[22] they really believe, hope and fear things. There is no seeming about it – no matter whether these items can, or cannot, be identified with neural states or events. If they cannot be so identified, it does not follow that the pains are mere sham (fictions), so that we can close down all our hospitals; or that people do not really believe, fear and hope the various things they say they believe, fear and hope.

Thirdly, Dennett confuses the intentional object of belief, hope or fear with the believing, hoping or fearing that is or may be intentional (and has an intentional object if it is). He claims that it is an empirical question whether someone's *believing, hoping* or *fearing* something or other 'exists' as an object, event or state in the brain. (Of course, *these* are not intentional objects at all, but intentional attributes.) He holds that if we find neural states or events in the brain that bear enough similarity to believing, hoping, etc., then the scientist could declare that these are neural states or events. If not, then people are just mistaken in thinking that they have any beliefs, hopes, fears, etc. But this is absurd. The properties that one's believing can have are, for example, being passionate (if one believes passionately that such-and-such) or tentative (if one believes tentatively) or justifiable (if one believes justifiably, i.e. is justified in believing what one believes). One's believings are essentially individuated by their object – that is, by what it is that is believed to be the

---

[22] It is striking that Dennett apparently conceives of pain not as localized sensations of varying degrees of intensity, but a matter of 'having one's life hopes, life plans, life projects blighted by circumstances imposed upon one's desires, thwarting one's intentions' (*CE* 448). Would that analgesics were so readily dispensable.

case. And one may believe correctly or incorrectly, truly or falsely, depending upon whether what one believes is so or not. But it is *not* an open (or a closed) empirical question whether neural states or events are passionate, tentative or justifiable, or whether they are essentially individuated by their intentional object (since they have none); or whether they are correct or incorrect, true or false (since there is no such thing as a correct or incorrect, true or false neural state.) Finally, it is wholly obscure what might be meant by the idea that neural states could 'bear enough similarity' to believing or hoping to warrant declaring believing and hoping to be brain states. How could a brain state bear any significant similarity to believing that the Battle of Hastings was fought in 1066 or to hoping for salvation?

It is important to realize that there is more in heaven and earth than is dreamt of in Dennett's philosophy. In particular, he offers us too few alternatives. The rejection of a Cartesian mind substance does not leave one with the dilemma that believing is either a state of the brain or a fiction. It is human beings who believe things, not their brains; and it is not a fiction, but a truth, that human beings do actually believe myriad things. So, if believing is neither a brain state nor a fiction, what is it? That is a bad question, for believing is not *an anything*; that is, there is no superior genus under which believing may be illuminatingly or fruitfully subsumed. (Why should there be? Our general categorial terms in psychology were not devised by a divine Linnaeus for the classificatory purposes of cognitive scientists.) But there is nothing mysterious about that. The concept of belief can be perfectly well elucidated by connective analysis, by displaying the logico-grammatical similarities and differences between believing and opining, thinking, gathering, supposing, assuming, accepting, knowing, being sure, being doubtful and so on.

4 Consciousness

Dennett's aim in his work on consciousness is to show how 'a genuinely explanatory theory of consciousness' can be constructed (*CE* 256). He rejects the philosophical conception of consciousness that he refers to as 'the Cartesian Theater' (an amalgam of Descartes and the British empiricists). In its place, he suggests an account that he calls 'the Multiple Drafts' model. According to this, 'all varieties of thought or mental activity are accomplished by the brain by parallel, multitrack processes of interpretation and elaboration of sensory inputs' (*CE* 111). Information entering the nervous system is under continuous 'editorial revision', and there are multiple channels in which special circuits try, in parallel pandemonium, to do various things, creating Multiple Drafts as they go (*CE* 252). We should, he claims, 'think of the brain as a computer of sorts', as an information-processing system (*CE* 433). And we should think of ourselves as the program that runs on our brain's computer (*CE* 430).

The central 'hypothesis' that Dennett defends is that 'Human consciousness is *itself* a huge complex of memes (or, more exactly, meme-effects in brains) that can best be understood as the operation of a "von Neumannesque" virtual machine implemented in the parallel architecture of a brain' (*CE* 210). (We shall explain what he means by 'memes' below.) Anything that has such a virtual machine as its control system 'is conscious in the fullest sense of the word, and it is conscious because it has such a virtual machine' (*CE* 281). According to Dennett, 'the concepts of computer science provide the crutches of imagination we need if we are to stumble across the terra incognita between our phenomenology as we know it by "introspection" and our brains as science reveals them to us. By thinking of our brains as information-processing systems, we can dispel the fog . . . discovering how it might be that our brains produce all the phenomena' (*CE* 433). He has, he claims, explained the phenomena of human consciousness 'in terms of the operation of a "virtual machine", a sort of evolved (and evolving) computer program that shapes the activities of the brain' (*CE* 431).

Having announced that his aim was to show how to construct a 'theory of consciousness', and having claimed that he has actually explained the phenomena of consciousness, on the very last page of his book Dennett observes that all that he has *really* done 'is to replace one family of metaphors and images with another, trading in [Cartesian and empiricist metaphors] for Software, Virtual Machines, Multiple Drafts, a Pandemonium of Homunculi' (*CE* 455). We think that this is a perfectly accurate summary of his achievement. Moreover, as we shall argue, the metaphors are poor ones, and serve no useful purpose in either neuroscientific discovery and theory or in philosophical clarification of the concept of consciousness.

The Multiple Drafts model amounts to little more than a series of metaphors concerning largely unknown neural processes. Neither the brain nor its parts engage in any 'editorial processes'; there are no texts to edit in the brain, and the various concurrent neural processes occurring in the brain at any given moment are not in the least like a series of drafts of a text. The various parts of the cortex that are involved in, for example, perception are not akin to more or less stupid homunculi, and there is nothing intentional about these neural processes. For parts of the cortex are not subjects of intentional attributes.

The suggestion that we should think of ourselves as computer programs is not coherent. Human beings are animals of a certain kind. They weigh so-and-so many kilograms, are of such-and-such a height, are either male or female; they are born, grow, fall in love, get married and have children, and so forth – none of which can intelligibly be said of computer programs. Perhaps Dennett means that our selves are computer programs – but that is no less absurd, for reasons we have explained (§12.4). The Cartesian self, understood as an immaterial substance, was a misconception; but that misconception is not rectified, but only exacerbated, by equating the 'self' with a computer program.

The suggestion that human consciousness is a complex of meme-effects in brains that constitutes the operation of a von Neumannesque virtual machine implemented in the parallel architecture of the brain is simply unintelligible. We can make little sense of the thought that there is a von Neumannesque virtual machine implemented in the parallel architecture of the brain. That many neural processes run parallel with each other is no warrant for assuming that the brain is a parallel processing computer, let alone that it is implementing a program run by a serial, von Neumann computer. We can find no argument in Dennett's writings to render intelligible, let alone to provide evidence for, such a bizarre suggestion. We shall focus instead upon the incoherence of Dennett's notion of a meme and its role in his account of consciousness.

The term 'meme' is derived from the writings of Richard Dawkins.[23] Memes are held to be *complex ideas*, which are readily memorable, and which 'replicate themselves' (just like genes) 'with reliability and fecundity' (*CE* 201). Examples of memes are such ideas as 'arch, wheel, wearing clothes, vendetta, right triangle, alphabet, calendar, the *Odyssey*, calculus, chess, perspective drawing, evolution by natural selection, impressionism, "Greensleeves", deconstructionism';[24] but also faith, tolerance, free speech, the conspiracy theory (*DDI* 349), and cooperation, music, writing, education, environmental awareness, arms reduction, *The Marriage of Figaro*, returnable bottles, and the SALT agreements, anti-Semitism and spray-can graffiti (*DDI* 363). Once our brains 'have built the entrance and exit pathways for the vehicles of language', Dennett explains, 'they swiftly become parasitized (and I mean that literally, as we shall see) by entities that have evolved to thrive in just such niches: *memes*' (*CE* 200). Elsewhere, Dennett contends that the mind is a 'meme nest' (*DDI* 349) in which memes find a temporary home (*DDI* 355). Memes compete to enter human minds, where they take up residence (*CE* 203) and come into contact with each other (*DDI* 355). When they come into contact with each other, they adjust to each other, changing their phenotypical effects to fit the new circumstances, and it is the recipe for the new phenotype that then gets replicated when the mind broadcasts or publishes the results of this mixing (*DDI* 355). Once our brains have been parasitized by memes, the memes transform the operating system or computational architecture of the brain (*DDI* 343), turning it into a mind (*CE* 252).

Dennett compares the invisibility of genes with the invisibility of memes (ideas), the 'vehicles' of genes (organisms) with what he takes to be the 'vehicles' of memes (pictures, books, utterances (*DDI* 347)), the reproduction of genes with the alleged reproduction of memes, the phenotypic expression of genes with the alleged phenotypic expression of memes, the causal effects of genes with the alleged causal effects of memes.

The notion of a meme is, as we shall show, incoherent.

(i)　The term 'idea' is confusingly multivalent. An 'idea' may be a concept, a thought, a proposition, a notion or a conception. It is, therefore, hardly surprising to find Dennett becoming entangled in his own terminology. For, while memes were introduced as 'complex ideas' which people communicate to each other, Dennett claims that such 'memes' as cooperation, music, education, *The Marriage of Figaro* and the *Odyssey*, not to mention the SALT agreements, 'are, all things considered, good from our perspective'

[23] According to Dawkins, 'Examples of memes are tunes, ideas, catch phrases, clothes fashions, ways of making pots or of building arches. Just as genes propagate themselves in the gene pool by leaping from body to body via sperm or eggs, so memes propagate themselves in the meme pool by leaping from brain to brain via a process which, in a broad sense, can be called imitation. If a scientist hears or reads about a good idea, he passes it on to his colleagues and students. He mentions it in his articles and his lectures. If the idea catches on, it can be said to propagate itself, spreading from brain to brain' (R. Dawkins, *The Selfish Gene* (Oxford University Press, Oxford, 1976), p. 206).
[24] D. Dennett, *Darwin's Dangerous Idea* (Penguin, Harmondsworth, 1996), p. 344. Subsequent references in the text to this book will be flagged '*DDI*'.

(*DDI* 363) – and it is evident that he does not mean that *the idea* of *The Marriage of Figaro* or of the *Odyssey* is 'good from our perspective'. He observes that other memes are controversial, but should be tolerated – for example, television advertising. Should we tolerate *the idea* or the advertising? Other memes, he claims, are pernicious, but extremely hard to eradicate – for example, spray-can graffiti, but is it the graffiti or the idea of such graffiti that is difficult to eradicate? The invitation to confusion evidently proved irresistible.

(ii)   Genes are invisible in so far as they are molecules too small to be seen. Ideas, concepts, propositions and conceptions are not too small to be seen.

(iii)   If organisms (as opposed to molecules) are vehicles of genes, then utterances, pictures, books and artefacts are not vehicles of ideas – but human beings are. Utterances, pictures, etc. are the means whereby we communicate ideas one to the other – hence they are analogous not to organisms, but to sperm and ova. But the analogy is poor.

(iv)   The distinction between genotype and phenotype has no intelligible application to ideas, concepts, propositions, etc. There is no analogue of statistical correlations between variations in genotype and variations in phenotype, or of the genuine explanatory force which these correlations have.

(v)   Ideas, concepts, propositions and conceptions, unlike genes, have no causal, but only logical, powers. But, according to Dennett, memes *manipulate* us (*CE* 203); they take up residence in our brains, shape its tendencies (*CE* 252), and transform its computational architecture (*DDI* 343). One may concede that acquiring ideas (in one or other of the numerous senses of this hopelessly ambivalent term) will affect various synaptic connections in the brain – but the idea acquired cannot. Yet it was supposed to be *the idea* that is the meme.

(vi)   To communicate an idea, a concept, a proposition or a theory to another human being is not to *replicate* anything. Einstein had a very good idea: he showed that $E = mc^2$, and he communicated this to other physicists. This did *not* multiply the number of ideas in circulation, only the number of people acquainted with the very same idea. Communicating an idea to other people, fortunately, is not at all like impregnating them. There are thousands of people who know Einstein's equation, but there are not thousands of Einstein's equations – only one. And the proposition that $E = mc^2$ undergoes no propagation by being communicated to thousands of people – they all understand the very same proposition. So, it is altogether unclear what *replication of memes* is supposed to be. If the *Odyssey* is a meme, is its replication the copies of it that are produced by printers? But they do not exist in people's minds, or indeed in their brains; they exist in libraries and bookshops. And copies of books do not replicate *themselves* – if they did, we should have no need for printers. Is it the *idea* of the *Odyssey* that is supposed to be a meme? If so, what *exactly* is this idea? Is it simply knowing what the *Odyssey* is? But surely, knowing what something is, is not a meme! If a thousand people know what the *Odyssey* is, no idea has replicated itself. And if a thousand people all read the *Odyssey* (no matter whether it is the same copy or a thousand different copies), neither the *Odyssey* nor an idea of the *Odyssey* has replicated itself.

We conclude that the alleged analogy between complex, memorable ideas and genes is a very poor one. It certainly is not strong enough to support an evolutionary theory of the 'survival of the fittest' ideas, parasitizing the human brain.

The account that Dennett offers is equivocal through and through. Memes, he claims, occupy minds, which are 'nests' or 'temporary homes' for them. Presumably this means that people acquire ideas, have ideas, believe such-and-such ideas. But belief and other intentional attributes that have ideas as their intentional objects are, according to Dennett, merely instrumentalist predictive devices on a par with centres of gravity or parallelograms of forces. It is far from clear how ideas can find a home in anything that has the ontological status of a centre of gravity. On the other hand, memes 'take up residence in an individual brain, shaping its tendencies and thereby turning it into a mind' (*CE* 252). But, presumably noting the incoherence of supposing that there are any ideas in the brain, Dennett cautions that 'human consciousness is itself a huge complex of memes (*or, more exactly, meme-effects in brains*)' (*CE* 211, our italics). So it is not, after all, memes that take up residence in the brain, but only their effects – or rather, the effects of having an idea communicated to one. But we were told that it is memes that *literally* parasitize the brain, thereby turning it into a mind! We can see no hope of extracting any coherent account from this confusion. And the confusion fatally affects what purports to be an explanation of consciousness.

The suggestion that consciousness is a complex of meme-effects in the brain is incoherent. Memes, we have been told, are complex ideas. Meme-effects in the brain are presumably meant to be the neural effects of acquiring certain complex ideas. Being awake, as opposed to being unconscious, and being conscious *of* something or other (e.g. of an object in one's perceptual field) are certainly not neural effects of the acquisition of ideas such as the idea of the wheel, of wearing clothes, of the *Odyssey* or of 'Greensleeves'. But states of consciousness – that is, mental states that one may be in while conscious, such as being cheerful or sad, being in pain, or enjoying oneself – are not complexes of neural effects of ideas either. The claim that human consciousness is a complex of meme-effects in brains that can best be understood as the operation of a von Neumannesque virtual machine implemented in the parallel architecture of the brain is, we suggest, quite literally meaningless.

We have argued that Dennett's account of intentionality rests on an inadequate conception of the logical character of the intentional phenomena to which Brentano drew attention, that it involves the misguided attribution of intentional attributes to kinds of things that could not logically possess any intentional attributes or behave as if they did. We have given reasons for thinking that Dennett's conception of an 'intentional stance' is confused, and that his claim that our normal employment of our psychological vocabulary is an instrumentalist predictive device on a par with such *abstracta* or *theoretical posits* as centres of gravity is incoherent. We have tried to demonstrate that the idea that a new science of consciousness, dependent upon the heterophenomenological method, is about to emerge is chimerical. For, we argued, the 'heterophenomenological method' is worthless. Finally, we have challenged Dennett's 'Multiple Drafts model' and his claim that consciousness is a huge complex of meme-effects in brains that can be best understood as the operations of a 'von Neumannesque' virtual machine implemented in the parallel architecture of the brain. If our arguments hold, then Dennett's theories of intentionality and of consciousness make no contribution to the philosophical clarification of intentionality or of consciousness. Nor do they provide guidelines for neuroscientific research or neuroscientific understanding.

Appendix 2

John Searle

John Searle has written extensively about philosophical problems that impinge upon cognitive neuroscience. In his 1984 Reith Lectures *Minds, Brains and Science* he addressed the lay public in a series of six lectures on topics that are relevant to our discussions in this book. These lectures were delivered with his customary panache and clarity. In *The Rediscovery of the Mind* (1992), writing primarily (but not exclusively) for professional philosophers, he confronted the large theme of consciousness. In that book he advocated his conception of biological naturalism, and criticized various misconceived doctrines that have dominated philosophy of mind, psychology and cognitive science in the twentieth century, such as behaviourism, identity theory, 'black box' functionalism, strong AI (i.e. 'Turing machine' functionalism) and eliminative materialism. Between 1995 and 1997 he contributed a series of critical reviews to the *New York Review of Books* of various books on consciousness, including works by Crick, Edelman, Penrose, Dennett, Chalmers and Rosenfeld. These reviews were published in book form in 1997 in *The Mystery of Consciousness*. In the 'Millennium' edition of *The Philosophical Transactions of the Royal Society* (vol. 354, 1999), he addressed scientists in general, and neuroscientists in particular, on the subject of 'The future of philosophy'; delineated the relationship between philosophy and science as he sees it; and, among other things, outlined his conception of the traditional mind–body problem and of the relations between philosophy of mind and cognitive science.

Searle's work is widely read by cognitive neuroscientists. It is admired for its lucidity and forceful argument. It addresses a multitude of issues that are of concern to them, and displays familiarity with current advances in cognitive neuroscience. Since we have disagreed with Searle on a variety of points, it is important to make explicit the rationale for differences between the conception we have advocated in this book and the views that Searle has defended in his writings. We shall focus upon methodological issues concerning the nature of philosophical investigation, the methods of philosophy, the boundaries between philosophy and science, and upon substantive issues pertaining to the philosophical investigation of consciousness.

1 Philosophy and Science

According to Searle, there is no sharp dividing line between science and philosophy. In this respect, Searle works within the received American tradition that has been influenced so much by W. V. O. Quine.

Both science and philosophy, according to Searle, are (a) universal in their subject matter and (b) aim at truth. Nevertheless, he asserts, there are important differences. Philosophical problems tend to have three related features that scientific problems lack. First, philosophy is in large part concerned with questions for the answering of which there is as yet no satisfactory and systematic method. Secondly, philosophical questions tend to be what Searle calls 'framework questions' – that is, questions that deal with large frameworks of phenomena, rather than with specific individual questions. Thirdly, philosophical questions are typically about conceptual issues.[1]

The first and second points are meant to explain why philosophy stands in a rather peculiar relation to science. For, Searle claims, as soon as we can revise and formulate a philosophical question to the point where we can find a systematic way of answering it, it ceases to be philosophical and becomes scientific (so, for example, the debate between vitalists and mechanists was rendered obsolete once we came to understand the molecular basis of living organisms). And he envisages something similar happening in the current debate concerning the nature of consciousness and its relation to brain processes.

This conception of the relationship between philosophy as the clarifier of confused questions and of science as the answerer of clear questions explains, according to Searle, why science appears to have such a good record of success and philosophy seems to be an irremediable failure. For, as soon as we find a systematic way to answer a question, and get an agreed answer from competent investigators, we cease calling the problem 'philosophical' and start calling it 'scientific'. So, philosophy cannot answer, solve or resolve questions, but only contribute to their clarification. Once it has done so, the question becomes a scientific one and is answered by science.[2]

It should be clear that the conception of philosophy defended by Searle is very different from the one advocated and implemented in this book. We hold that there is a radical dividing line between philosophy thus practised and the natural sciences. We agree with Searle that philosophical questions are typically about conceptual issues, and we hold that philosophical problems and puzzles are typically the result of conceptual entanglement or of one form or another of conceptual unclarity. These problems and puzzles cannot be solved, resolved or dissolved by scientific theory or by scientific experiment. Whatever light we have succeeded in shedding upon the conceptual problems and puzzles that patently concern cognitive neuroscientists has been the result of a priori connective analysis, not of scientific experiment or empirical theory.

The natural sciences aim to explain contingent phenomena of nature. They construct theories in terms of which the phenomena can be explained, typically hypothetico-deductively. The theories and hypotheses are confirmed or disconfirmed by observation and experiment. The predictions the validation of which confirm a scientific theory may be only approximations to the truth, the degree of acceptable approximation varying with subject matter and with the standards of accuracy of the science of the time. The natural sciences are typically hierarchical and progressive, the positive results achieved

---

[1] John R. Searle, 'The future of philosophy', *Philosophical Transactions of the Royal Society*, **B** 354 (1999), p. 2069.
[2] Ibid., p. 2070.

commonly being the basis for the construction of yet more complex, more encompassing theories.

By contrast, the connective-analytic enterprise of philosophy does not aim to explain natural phenomena at all. It is not a form of armchair science, that seeks, without the labour of experiment and observation, to find answers to the questions that are the proper province of the sciences. In the sense in which the natural sciences explain phenomena, analytic philosophy explains nothing. Rather, it describes conceptual structures and connections, disentangles conceptual confusions, and explains, without any *theory* or *hypothetico-deductive explanation*, why we become entangled in the web of concepts that we deploy in our thinking and theorizing about the world, and so fall into certain kinds of confusion. In the sense in which there are theories in the natural sciences, there are no licit theories in philosophy (any more than there are, *in this sense*, theories in mathematics). There are no hypotheses in philosophy, nor is there anything hypothetical about the answers which analytic philosophy offers to its problems: there is no 'if such-and-such, then things will turn out thus-and-so – as will be observed in an experiment'. And of course, there are no experiments, no experimental confirmation or disconfirmation of theories, and no predictions the truth or falsity of which might validate or falsify a theory.

The procedures of philosophy thus understood are wholly a priori, and its proposed solutions or resolutions of its problems are validated or refuted by a priori argument, as are the problems of mathematics.[3] But while mathematics is a matter of concept *formation* by constructing proofs, philosophy is a matter of concept *elucidation*. Mathematics is a synthetic, constructive activity, creating new conceptual connections, whereas philosophy is an analytic, descriptive activity, clarifying and elucidating existing conceptual connections.

The proper task of the natural sciences is to determine how things are in the world and why they are thus or otherwise. It is therefore concerned with what is true and what is

---

[3] It is widely believed by American philosophers that W. V. O. Quine, in his 'Two dogmas of empiricism' (*Philosophical Review*, 60 (1951) pp. 20–43), showed that the customary distinction between analytic and synthetic propositions is not viable, and hence too that the different distinction between a priori and empirical propositions is equally untenable. Consequently, he is thought to have shown that one cannot demarcate philosophy from science by reference to philosophy's concern with a priori questions in contradistinction to science's concern with empirical fact. But this is mistaken. At most Quine showed that the conception of analyticity propounded by his teacher Rudolf Carnap is untenable (although Carnap denied that he had succeeded in so doing). But even if Quine was right and Carnap wrong, the Carnapian conception of analyticity is not the only one; moreover, Quine never responded adequately to the powerful reply to him by P. F. Strawson and H. P. Grice which did articulate a defensible conception of analyticity in the face of Quine's criticism ('In defence of a dogma', *Philosophical Review*, 65 (1956), pp. 141–58). Furthermore, one may reject the notion of analyticity altogether, as Wittgenstein did, and still cleave to the distinction between what is a priori and what is empirical (see P. M. S. Hacker, *Wittgenstein's Place in Twentieth-Century-Philosophy Analytic* ch. 7, and H.-J. Glock, 'Wittgenstein vs. Quine on logical necessity', (Blackwell, Oxford, 1996), in S. Teghrarian (ed.), *Wittgenstein and Contemporary Philosophy* (Thoemmes Press, Bristol, 1994), pp. 185–222).

false, and its successes contribute to our knowledge about the world. Philosophy, by contrast, is not concerned with empirical truth and falsehood, but rather with questions of sense. It is concerned with the determination of the bounds of sense, and with the explanation (by *description*) of the ways in which they are transgressed, both in scientific conjecture (including parts of cognitive neuroscience that have been our concern) and in philosophical reflection itself. But there can be no approximations to sense (whereas there can be approximations to truth in scientific theory and prediction), for any deviation from sense is one form or another of nonsense. And there can be no *theories* that determine, with such-and-such margin of error, what does and what does not make sense. For there is no *margin of error* in the determination of sense.

Analytic philosophy, in the domain of the philosophy of logic and language, metaphysics, epistemology and philosophy of psychology,[4] above all clarifies concepts and conceptual networks. It is concerned not with the description and explanation of empirical facts, but with the elucidation of the forms in which we describe empirical facts – that is, *with the description of our conceptual scheme*. It does not add to our knowledge of the world, but contributes to our understanding, in the face of very special kinds of confusions – namely, conceptual confusions – of the knowledge we already have. For its results are not, and cannot be, startling new facts and theories, but only the clarification of the forms of thought we employ, yet find exceedingly difficult to bring into focus – especially in domains in which there is, for various reasons, a perennial danger of conceptual entanglement.

According to Searle, both science and philosophy are universal in their subject matter.[5] This, in our view, is mistaken.

First, natural science is not universal in its subject matter: its domain consists of the phenomena of nature. There is no natural science (or any other science) of literature or of art, although both are meet subjects for serious study. Nor is there a natural science of morality, politics or law, although these subjects are legitimate spheres for human investigation and for the achievement of knowledge. There is no science of history, although the study of history is pivotal to the humanities and to our understanding of the development of science. There are, of course, social sciences, but whether the methods and forms of explanation of the social sciences are akin to those of the natural sciences, whether we can hope to discover laws of human society on the model of laws of nature which the natural sciences aim to disclose, is a highly contentious issue. But even methodological monists who think that the social sciences may aspire to discover social laws should hesitate to conceive of the study of *history* as a domain of science.

Secondly, it is less than obvious what might be meant by saying that philosophy is universal in subject matter. It is surely false that philosophy and empirical science compete

---

[4] Our remarks henceforth will be restricted to these branches of philosophy. Our claims would require qualification if ethics and legal and political philosophy were under consideration. For these are concerned not only with describing and clarifying our conceptual framework but also with reflecting on how we ought to live.

[5] Searle, 'Future of philosophy', p. 2069.

over the very same (universal) subject matter. The natural sciences are restricted to the domain of nature, but philosophy, even philosophy of science, is surely not concerned with making empirical discoveries about nature, in competition with science. What is true is that there are domains that are very much of concern to philosophy which are of none to science. While there is no such thing as a science of history, there is philosophy of history; while there is no such thing as a science of art, there is such a thing as philosophy of art. But the question is: what is the nature of the concern that philosophy has within its universal domain? For philosophy of history is no more in competition with history than philosophy of physics is in competition with physics.

The sense in which philosophy, *unlike science*, is universal is that its concern is character-istically with *conceptual* structures and relations within *any* domain of human thought and experience in which conceptual questions and confusions arise – no matter whether in the proper domain of the natural sciences or in the domain of the a priori sciences of mathematics, in the social sciences, history, the arts, morality, law, politics, etc.

On the other hand, it is misleading to suggest that philosophy is primarily concerned with 'framework' questions. It is true that among the questions of philosophy, there are many that are characterized by the highest degree of generality (e.g. what are the most fundamental objects of reference in our conceptual scheme? what are the conditions of the possibility of knowledge of objective particulars? what is the nature of necessity?). But it is unhelpful to suggest that philosophical questions can be characterized by their generality or by their concern with 'frameworks of phenomena'. There are endless very particular philosophical questions, with many of which we have been concerned in this book (e.g. how are *knowledge how* and *knowledge that* related? are mental images rep-resentations of what they are images of? is thinking an activity? is memory exclusively of the past? is a voluntary movement a movement caused by an act of will?). But one may happily concede to Searle that even the most particular philosophical question may be connected with, and ramify into, the broadest and most general of 'framework ques-tions'. For we are moving within the web of words, examining the structure of our conceptual scheme, and – in a sense – everything is connected with everything else: each node within the web is linked with numerous adjacent nodes. So very specific questions lead immediately to more general ones. That is why local disagreements among philo-sophers rapidly ramify into global ones.

Searle claims that both science and philosophy aim at the truth – and in a sense that is obviously correct. But it can be misleading. The natural sciences aim to dis-cover truths about nature, to unify and explain them by means of ever wider and more powerful theories. The social sciences, such as economics and sociology, aim to discover truths about the functioning of human society or societies. Many of the truths that the sciences have discovered are, or were, exceedingly surprising and un-expected. This applies to the social (and psychological) sciences no less than to the natural sciences, irrespective of whether the logical forms of explanation in them are or are not the same. What are the truths that philosophy aims to disclose? They concern conceptual connections and relationships. These are normative – rule-governed connections within the web of words. So they are not so much truths about the world as truths about the modes in which we represent truths about the world to ourselves.[6] Moreover, although philosophy may point out a connection (an implication, a presupposition, a compatibility or incompatibility) that had escaped notice *in philosophical reflection* or *in scientific theorizing*, there is an important sense in which this *cannot* be a new discovery, but at most something which had not been *realized*. It cannot be a genuine novelty, like a scientific discovery that yields new knowledge. For if it *were* a novelty, then it could not be part of our existing conceptual scheme, but at most a modification of it that is being recommended.[7]

If philosophy aimed at the discovery of new truths *after the manner of the empirical sciences*, it would be puzzling that it has, in its long history, come up with so few results. Physics, chemistry and biology have a shorter history, but they can fill libraries with accounts of the knowledge they have achieved. It should be puzzling, or alternatively very depressing, that philosophy has so little to show by way of comparable achievement. For although it can fill libraries, these libraries are not repositories of philosophical knowledge.

One explanation favoured by some neuroscientists (see §14.4) is that the apparent poverty of the results of philosophy is to be explained by reference to the fact that its practitioners (e.g. Descartes, Locke, Hume, Kant, Russell, Wittgenstein) are incompetent and their armchair methods are inappropriate to their goal. Hence, as we saw, some neuroscientists think that philosophy should step aside and let neuroscience take over the problems concerning the mind, consciousness and self-consciousness with which philosophers have been struggling for the last three and a half centuries. But *this* explanation, we argued, is predicated upon a fundamental misunderstanding of philosophical problems.

Searle offers a quite different explanation. He claims that philosophy is concerned with 'questions that we have not yet found a satisfactory and systematic way to answer'. In his view, 'as soon as we can revise and formulate a philosophical question to the point that we can find a systematic way to answer it, it ceases to be philosophical and becomes scientific'. This is a view that Russell advanced,[8] and it was, in a more qualified manner,

---

[6] Indeed, they are 'truths' in a Pickwickian sense, since they are, in effect, norms of representation, which we present to ourselves in the misleading form of descriptions of fact. They are not *true* norms of representation (there is no such thing); rather, it is true that they are our *norms* of representation, and are partly constitutive of their constituent concepts.

[7] This is a complex and ramifying point. It turns on the claim that to possess a concept is to have mastered the use of a word (or phrase). To have mastered the use of a word is to know how it is to be employed, hence to know what counts as correct and what as incorrect use. So it is to know (explicitly or implicitly) the rules for the use of the word, and to use the word in accordance with those rules. But there can be no *hidden, unknown* rules for the use of words, for rules are guides to conduct and standards of correctness for conduct, and there can be no hidden, unknown guides to (or norms of) conduct which inform the actions of participants in a practice. For, if they are hidden, then they cannot be used as standards of correctness by reference to which mistakes are identified and corrected, and in terms of which learners of the language are instructed in the correct use of terms. There can be hidden regularities in normative, rule-governed practices – i.e. regularities of which the participants are wholly unaware – but there can be no hidden rules.

[8] In 1912, in his introductory book *The Problems of Philosophy* (Oxford University Press, Oxford, 1967), p. 90, Russell wrote, that 'as soon as definite knowledge concerning any subject becomes possible, this subject ceases to be called philosophy, and becomes a separate science'.

advocated by Searle's teacher, Austin.[9] It is a convenient way of explaining why there is no philosophical *knowledge* (comparable to the knowledge achieved by physics) and why there are no established philosophical *theories* (comparable to theories in chemistry) worth speaking of. But this conception can and should be challenged.

It is perfectly true that throughout its long history the term 'philosophy' has encompassed a multitude of different kinds of subject. It was, after all, only relatively recently, that physics ceased to be known as 'natural philosophy'. In the seventeenth century, a great philosopher, Descartes, did not sharply distinguish his philosophical investigations from his scientific ones, viewing his *Optics*, for example, as a straightforward application of the methods advocated in his *Discourse on Method*; and a great scientist, Boyle, did not distinguish his empirical investigations into the nature of matter from his metaphysical reflections on the ontology of secondary qualities. Physics split off from philosophy in the late seventeenth century, and throughout the eighteenth and nineteenth centuries there was a tendency to conceive of philosophy as an investigation into the nature of the human mind. But at the end of the nineteenth and beginning of the twentieth century, psychology split off from philosophy, and became an independent science.

Does this show that as soon as we can revise and formulate a philosophical question to the point at which we can find a systematic way to answer it, it ceases to be philosophical and becomes scientific? No. It merely shows that philosophy's perennial craving for a special, first-order subject matter has repeatedly been frustrated. That in turn shows two things.

First, that throughout the history of what is called 'philosophy', empirical questions were commonly interwoven with non-empirical, conceptual ones. Once they were sharply distinguished, the empirical questions moved into the province of science. To that extent, Searle is correct.

Secondly, it shows that the quest for a first-order subject matter is futile. What remain within the province of philosophy, correctly conceived, are *conceptual questions* (and conceptual confusions) that are not amenable to scientific, experimental treatment at all. It is not true that as soon as we can find a systematic way of answering *these* questions, they are *ipso facto* transformed into scientific questions – here Searle is quite mistaken.

Although questions about the empirical nature of material objects and matter belong to the province of science, what the *logical* features of substance concepts (of sortal nouns (such as 'man', 'dog', 'cabbage') and concrete mass nouns (such as 'water', 'steel', 'oxygen')) are is not a question for empirical science, but for conceptual analysis. Whether the

---

[9] J. L. Austin, 'Ifs and cans', repr. in his *Philosophical Papers* (Clarendon Press, Oxford, 1961), p. 180. He wrote: 'In the history of human inquiry, philosophy has the place of the initial central sun, seminal and tumultuous: from time to time it throws off some portion of itself to take station as a science, a planet, cool and well-regulated, progressing steadily towards a distant final state. This happened long ago at the birth of mathematics, and again at the birth of physics: only in the last century we have witnessed the same process once again . . . in the birth of mathematical logic, through the joint labours of philosophers and mathematicians. Is it not possible that the next century may see the birth . . . of a true and comprehensive *science of language*? Then we shall have rid ourselves of one more part of philosophy (there will still be plenty left) in the only way we ever get rid of philosophy, by kicking it upstairs.'

identity of substances is absolute or merely relative identity is not a question that is likely to be resolved by physics. Moreover, the autonomy of physics has added *new questions* to the philosophical agenda – questions in the philosophy of physics concerning, for example, the logical nature of explanation in the physical sciences, the ontology of theoretical entities in physics, the reducibility or non-reducibility of other sciences and scientific explanations to those of physics. Similarly, the autonomy of the psychological sciences has not bankrupted philosophy of psychology. It is not as if empirical psychology can discover by experiment whether belief is a mental state or a mental disposition or neither. Neuroscience is not going to resolve questions about the *concepts* of consciousness and self-consciousness, any more than questions concerning the neural basis of intransitive consciousness are going to be answered by the a priori methods of philosophy.

Searle claims that 'as soon as we find a systematic way to answer a question, and get an answer that all competent investigators in the field can agree is the correct answer, we stop calling it "philosophical" and start calling it "scientific"'.[10] This is questionable, on two counts.

First, it implies that there are no systematic ways of answering questions in philosophy. This is wrong. One may indeed claim that there is no single 'universal method', any more than there is in science. But there are methods, which we have exemplified again and again throughout this book. For example, the meticulous examination of the grammar of problematic expressions, of the rules for the use of the words in question; the investigation of the logical implications of the use of such an expression in certain sentences, its entailments, compatibilities and incompatibilities; the scrutiny of the presuppositions of the use of the problematic expression, of the behavioural contexts in which its use may be embedded from occasion to occasion; the examination of its semantic field – that is, its relations to other expressions in the same domain; the clarification of the ways in which we can confirm or verify the application of the expression; and so on and so forth.

Secondly, Searle's claim implies that once philosophical clarity with respect to any given question is achieved, the question ceases to be philosophical, and its answer is 'scientific'. But this is mistaken. Competent philosophers by and large agree that the five proofs of the existence of God propounded by Aquinas are all invalid – but does this make the disproofs 'scientific'? Hume argued, contrary to many seventeenth-century thinkers, that causal knowledge is to be obtained by empirical observation and not by a priori argument, and that causal generalizations are to be established by inductive methods. Most philosophers (and scientists) agree. Does this imply that Hume's claim is part of an experimental science, established by observation and experiment?

2 Searle's Philosophy of Mind

We are in complete agreement with Searle in his repudiation of Cartesian dualism and of behaviourism, identity theory, eliminative materialism and functionalism in its various

---

[10] Searle, 'Future of philosophy', p. 2070.

forms. Searle characterizes his conception of consciousness as 'biological naturalism', by which he means that consciousness is a natural biological phenomenon, which is to be studied by the biological sciences. With this we have no quarrel. Although we distinguish philosophical, conceptual questions about consciousness from empirical ones, it is our view that there are many aspects of intransitive and transitive consciousness that are investigable by neuroscience, which can investigate the neural concomitants of consciousness in its various forms and the neural aetiology of various conscious states. Of course, the scientific discoveries will not solve or resolve the conceptual questions, just as the answers to the conceptual questions will not provide answers to the empirical ones.

We part company with Searle, however, when he claims that 'mental phenomena are caused by neurophysiological processes in the brain and are themselves features of the brain'.[11] Consciousness, in his view, 'is a *feature* or *property* of the brain in the sense, for example, that liquidity is a feature of water'.[12]

The claim that consciousness 'is caused by lower-level microprocesses in the brain' is misleading, but fairly harmless. It is misleading inasmuch as it conflates a causal condition with a cause.[13] It is of course true that, but for a multitude of only partially understood processes in the brain, one would not be conscious at all, and that, but for a variety of even less well-understood processes, one would not be conscious *of* the various things of which one is transitively conscious. Equally, but for a variety of lower-level microprocesses in the brain, one would not walk or run, get up or sit down. Nevertheless, one would surely not say that the cause of A's running or of B's sitting down is a process in their brain. If asked what made A wake up (and, in this sense, regain consciousness), one might reply, 'The knock on the door', or 'The ringing of the telephone', but surely not 'The microprocesses in his brain'. Similarly, if one were asked what made one conscious of someone's being behind the curtain or of one's ignorance, one might reply, 'It was the sudden movement of the curtain' or 'It was the speaker's remarkable display of erudition', but, again, not 'Why, microprocess M in the brain, of course'. For the latter are standing causal conditions, which we normally distinguish from the operative cause.

The claim that consciousness is *a feature of the brain*, however, is more grievous. For, as we argued at length in chapter 3, to ascribe consciousness and experiences to the brain is to ascribe to a part of an animal properties which can intelligibly be ascribed only to the animal as a whole; that is, it is to commit the mereological fallacy in neuroscience. Consciousness is not, and could not be, a feature of a brain.[14] Brains are no more conscious than they can go for walks or climb trees, even though it is true that an animal cannot go for walks or climb trees unless its brain functions appropriately. It is animals, including human beings, that are conscious or unconscious, that lose and later regain

---

[11] J. R. Searle, *The Rediscovery of the Mind* (MIT Press, Cambridge, MA, 1992), p. 1.

[12] Ibid., p. 105.

[13] Of course, *sometimes* microprocesses in the brain may indeed be the cause, and not merely the causal condition, of some phenomenon of consciousness, e.g. of depression, or of the 'shattered mirror effect' of migraine.

[14] Unless all that is thereby meant is that an animal will be conscious only if appropriate brain processes are going on.

consciousness, and that may become conscious of this or that if their attention is caught and held by some feature of their environment. They would not do so, of course, but for certain processes occurring in their brains, but it does not (and could not) follow that their being conscious is *a feature* of their brains. Liquidity can indeed be said to be a feature or property of quantities of water at appropriate temperatures. There are criteria for whether water is in a liquid, solid or gaseous state. But there are no criteria for whether a brain is in a conscious or unconscious state, any more than there are, or could be, criteria for whether a molecule of water is in a liquid, solid or gaseous state. There are no criteria for whether the brain is conscious of this or that, only inductive correlations between brain states and the animal's being conscious, unconscious or transitively conscious of this or that feature of its environment, or in one or another state of consciousness.

According to Searle, the brain is a machine, a biological machine, and it can think. Human brains, he contends, sometimes compute; they add two and two and get four, for example.[15] Here too we part company with him. Whether brains are machines is a debatable matter that turns on the notion of a machine, which need not be debated here and is not decisive for our disagreements with Searle. However, our *brains* neither think nor compute – *we* do (although, of course, we would not be able to do so but for a variety of brain (and other) processes and states that make thinking and computing possible). The brain no more adds two and two to make four than does an abacus; it cannot intelligibly be said to possess the concept of addition or of identity (or any other concept), or to have grasped the use of numerals (or of any other symbol).[16] As we have argued, for a being to be able to think (beyond the rudimentary thinking of non-human animals), it must also be able to be thoughtless and inconsiderate, or thoughtful, introspective or reflective. It must be able to think before it speaks, to speak without thinking, or to think while it is speaking. It must be capable of idle speculation or of purposeful reflection. It must be able to reconsider what it previously pondered, and so on and so forth, through myriad nuances which we distinguish with respect to the cogitative activities of human beings, but which we do not predicate of their brains. That we do not do so is not a mark of correctable ignorance – of failure to recognize the facts for what they are – but of our assigning no sense to the form of words 'My brain is thinking things over', 'His brain is in a pensive mood to day', or 'Her brain is thoughtless'.

As we observed in §4.1, Searle holds that sensations such as toothache or stomach-ache occur not in one's teeth and gums or in one's midriff, but in the brain. He writes: 'Common-sense tells us that our pains are located in physical space within our bodies, that for example a pain in the foot is literally inside the area of the foot. But we now know that is false. The brain forms a body image, and pains, like all bodily sensations, are parts of the body image. The pain-in-the-foot is literally in the physical space of the brain.'[17] Pains 'in the physical space of the brain' – that is, in the head – are headaches, not pains

---

[15] J. R. Searle, *The Mystery of Consciousness* (Granta Books, London, 1997), p. 13.

[16] By the same token, of course, it cannot be said to *lack* the relevant concepts or to have *failed to grasp* the use of numerals. Only what *can* acquire concepts can be said to lack certain concepts.

[17] Searle, *Rediscovery of the Mind*, p. 63.

in the foot, and, of course, they are not *in* the physical space of the head as *pins* may be in the head.[18] For pains are not kinds of objects that may be inside or outside physical objects, or that may be inserted into objects and then taken out again, and they are neither smaller nor larger than the part of the body in which they are located. For one to have a backache is simply for one's back to ache; to have a pain in one's foot is for one's foot to hurt, not one's brain or head. The criterion for the location of a pain is where the sufferer naturally assuages, where he points when asked where it hurts, and where he says he feels the pain – that is not 'common sense', but logical grammar (§4.1). It is not an opinion, but an aspect of the meaning of the phrase 'pain location'. According to Searle, the phenomenon of pain in phantom limbs makes it evident that we experience bodily sensations in the body image. Moreover, 'many of us have a version of the phantom limb in the form of sciatic pain'.[19] But the phenomenon of pain in a phantom limb shows that we can have the kinaesthetic illusion of possessing a limb that we have in fact lost – that is, it feels just as if the limb were still there – and we can feel a pain where the limb is felt to be; but it does not show that the pain is in the brain or in something called 'a body image' allegedly in the brain. Furthermore, this phenomenon is not comparable to the phenomenon of sciatic pains that are felt in the foot, although their cause is in the spine. Here it really is one's foot that hurts, whereas in the case of pain in a phantom arm it is not actually one's arm that hurts, since one has no arm.

According to Searle, consciousness has what he calls 'a first-person ontology', by which he means that (i) conscious states exist only when experienced by a person, and (ii) they exist only from the first-person point of view of that person. The mark of conscious states, in his view, is that for any such state there is something that it qualitatively feels like to be in it. In this sense, all conscious states are qualitative, subjective experiences, and hence are qualia.[20] This is confused (§§10.3–10.3.5). It is correct that there are no experiences that are not someone's experiences, no pains that are not someone's pains. If that gives conscious states a 'first-person ontology', well and good. But then it also gives smiles and sneezes a 'first-person ontology', for, the smile of the Cheshire cat apart, there are no smiles that are not someone's smiles and no sneezes that are not someone's sneezes.

To be sure, smiles and sneezes cannot be said to exist 'only from the first-person point of view' of the smiler or sneezer – indeed, it is not clear what that claim would mean. Smiles and sneezes don't *exist* (or fail to exist) from any 'point of view', although they can be seen or heard by anyone in the vicinity. But it is equally unclear why Searle claims that conscious states exist only from a first-person point of view. It seems that his idea is that since every experience is necessarily someone's experience, therefore each person stands in a special relationship to his own experience.[21] That 'relationship', it seems, is conceived to

---

[18] As we argued, the grammar of the phrase 'in the head' varies (without ceasing to be a spatial, locative phrase), depending on whether the subject term is a material object, such as a pin, or a sensation, such as a pain. For the logical consequences of the resultant propositions, their implications, compatibilities and incompatibilities vary accordingly.

[19] Searle, *Mystery of Consciousness*, p. 182.

[20] Ibid., pp. xiv and 9.

[21] Searle, *Rediscovery of the Mind*, p. 95.

be a form of inalienable ownership, which guarantees the existence of the experience as long as this relationship obtains: for the experience, it seems, ceases to exist as soon as it ceases to be owned. *If* that is what Searle thinks (and we are not sure it is), then it is mistaken.

To have a headache is not to stand in a relationship to a headache – it is for one's head to ache. To love Maisy may be said to be a matter of standing in a certain emotional relation (viz. of loving) to Maisy, but to have the experience of loving her is not a matter of standing in a *further* relationship to the experience of loving. Experiences are not mental 'objects' (just like material objects, only immaterial), since they are not 'objects' of any kind. In particular, they are not relata that stand in a relation (of being had) to the subjects of the experiences. To have an experience is not to own or possess anything, and experiences are not kinds of private property. One might perhaps say that experiences are attributes of subjects of experience, but then one must add the proviso that one no more stands in a relationship to one's own attributes than coloured objects stand in relation to their colours. Different people may have the very same headache or, more generally, pain (and that may betoken the fact they are suffering from the same disease). One cannot say, 'But they must be different, since yours is yours and mine is mine', for the subject of pain (i.e. being *had* by such-and-such a person) is not an identifying characteristic of the pain, any more than a red curtain (i.e. being *of* the curtain) is an identifying property of the red colour it has (see §3.8).

It is, in our view, a misconception to think that experiences exist only from a first-person point of view. It is trivially true that A's headache exists only as long as A's head aches – which is a misleading way of saying that A has a headache only if his head aches. But that tautology gives no support to the thought that a person's headache exists only from his point of view. From A's point of view, it may be better to do X rather than Y. From a moral point of view, it may be better to do Y rather than X. And from an economic point of view it may be better to do nothing at all. Differently, X may be visible only from certain points of view or viewpoints – but then *anyone* can see it from that point in space if it is vacated.[22] But experiences are not visible objects that can be seen from certain positions and not from others, although A's fury may be perfectly visible, and B's cheerfulness may be manifest. However, there is no such thing as something's *existing* only from some person's point of view (let alone from a moral, political or economic point of view) or from some viewpoint that a person may occupy.

It is a further error to suppose that the subject of an experience has 'access' to it, that my pain 'is accessible to me in a way that it is not accessible to you'.[23] For to have a pain, as we have pointed out, is not to have access to anything (§3.7). What is true is that if I have a pain, it does not follow that you will have one too, let alone that you will have the same pain. But that humble truth does not imply that you *cannot* have the very same pain

[22] This does not apply to all the perceptual modalities. Things are not felt to be hot or cold, wet or dry, smooth or rough, from any point of view or viewpoint. Nor do they have such-and-such a taste from any 'viewpoint'.
[23] Searle, *Mystery of Consciousness*, p. 8.

as I, such as a splitting headache as a result of drinking too much at yesterday's party. In Searle's view, the accessibility of a pain to the sufferer 'has epistemic consequences – you can know about your pain in a way that others cannot'.[24] This is, in our view, misconceived. To have a pain is not *a way of knowing* anything. What is true is that the person who is in pain can say so, whereas others may not be able to say whether he is or is not. This is not because he has access to something to which others lack access. It is because he is in pain, but if he is not showing it, others will not be able to tell that he is.

It is mistaken to think that 'conscious states are qualitative in the sense that for any conscious state, such as feeling a pain or worrying about the economic situation, there is something that it qualitatively feels like to be in that state'.[25] Of course, there is, in a sense, a 'qualitative feel' to pains. One has an affective attitude towards them. They are, to say the least, very unpleasant to endure, and one would normally prefer not to have any. So there is an answer to the question 'What does it feel like to have migraine?': namely, 'Dreadful' or 'Extraordinarily unpleasant'. But, as we have argued (§§10.3–10.3.5), it would be quite wrong to suppose that every experience, let alone every thought or belief, is distinguished by some special feeling and is the subject of some attitudinal predicate. And it is misconceived to characterize 'all conscious phenomena' as 'qualia', since, as we have argued at length, the notion of a quale, of there being something which it is like to experience this or that, is not coherent.

Searle cleaves to what he calls 'The Principle of the Independence of Consciousness and Behaviour', according to which there is no 'conceptual or logical connection between conscious mental phenomena and external behaviour'.[26] The grounds for this principle are that we can imagine circumstances in which appropriate behaviour occurs – for example, pain-behaviour – but without the subject being in pain; and, conversely, we can imagine a person in pain, but without exhibiting any pain-behaviour (e.g. if he is paralysed, or if the pain is trivial). So behaviour is neither necessary nor sufficient for the presence of the relevant mental phenomenon. We agree that, for the most part, behaviour is neither necessary nor sufficient for a wide array of mental phenomena – pretence and deception are sometimes possible, and concealment, suppression and paralysis are also conceivable. But it does not follow that the mental is not conceptually connected to its behavioural manifestations, or, conversely, that the relevant behavioural manifestations are not conceptually bound up with the mental phenomenon they manifest. And it is incorrect to say that 'the phenomena in question can exist completely and have all of their essential properties independent of any behavioural output'.[27] What is possible some of the time may not (and in this case is not) possible all of the time. There is a *conceptual* link between inner and outer. Behaviour, in appropriate circumstances, is a *logical criterion* of the mental. Pretence is not *always* possible (it makes no sense to suppose that a neonate might be pretending); concealment and suppression of outward manifestations are not always

---

[24] Ibid., p. 98.
[25] Ibid., p. xiv.
[26] Searle, *Rediscovery of the Mind*, p. 69.
[27] Ibid.

options. And what mental phenomena can intelligibly be ascribed to a creature depends upon what that creature can in principle express within the constraints of its behavioural repertoire. We have argued this at length, both in chapter 3 and elsewhere, and shall not repeat the arguments.

3 The Traditional Mind–Body Problem

Searle contends that the traditional mind–body problem is amenable to scientific solution.[28] If that were so, it might indeed vindicate Searle's conception of the relationship between philosophy and science. Philosophers have indeed worried over the relationship between the mind and the body since the dawn of the subject. They have wondered what kind of entity the *psuchē*, mind or soul is: whether it is the 'form' of the body, a principle of life, an immaterial substance, a bundle of experiences causally related to the body, or just the brain itself. They have been baffled by the dilemma of accepting the intelligibility of a causal connection between an immaterial mind and the material brain or denying its intelligibility and thereby denying any causal interaction. They have struggled with the question of the relation between mental states and states of the brain. And so on.

Evidently Searle holds that philosophy has now progressed to the point at which it can formulate a sharp question and hand it over to neuroscience for empirical resolution. So, what is held to be the form that the 'mind–body problem' takes that is amenable to scientific solution? It breaks down into two questions:

How exactly do neurobiological processes in the brain cause conscious states and processes?

and

How exactly are those conscious states and processes realized in the brain?[29]

Searle admits that these questions look like empirical scientific ones. The task of philosophy is to clear away some obstacles to tackling them, obstacles such as the allegedly obsolete categories of mind and body, matter and spirit, mental and physical; or the thought that since science deals with objective phenomena, and consciousness is subjective, science cannot investigate consciousness; or the worry about the indirectness of the verifying procedures for hypotheses about consciousness.

We do not think that questions about the neurobiological causes of mental states are any part of the philosophical problems concerning the mind and the body. How and why imbibing excessive alcohol causes one to be first jocose, then bellicose, later morose and finally comatose can be of no concern to philosophy, and is not a sharpening of any philosophical question. Nor can an investigation of the neural antecedents and concomitants

---

[28] Searle, 'Future of philosophy', p. 2073.
[29] Ibid.

of voluntary movement resolve any philosophical questions about freedom of the will or voluntary action. There are, as we have seen, deep philosophical questions about the nature of self-consciousness, but, as we showed in chapter 12, they are not to be solved or resolved by neuroscience. And if one wants to discover whatever neural features make self-consciousness possible, one would search not for neural self-scanning mechanisms in the brain, but for the neural conditions for mastery and use of the psychological vocabulary in the first person. Neuroscience is still very far from achieving any such thing, but if it is ever able to investigate such matters, it seems to us unlikely that it will find anything distinctive about the neural correlates of the use of psychological verbs in the first person as opposed to their third-person employment. The solution to the traditional puzzles about self-consciousness is an analytical, not a neuroscientific, task.

We do not think that there is anything obsolete about the categories of mind and body, mind and matter, or the mental and the physical. What is true is that there is much confusion about these concepts. They are commonly misunderstood and misused in philosophical, psychological and cognitive-neuroscientific debate. This does not show obsolescence, but a pressing need for philosophical clarification. It is not as if these concepts should be abandoned, as the concept of phlogiston was jettisoned in chemistry, *élan vital* in biology, and a ether in cosmology. There is no reason why we should cease talking of having minds of our own, of making up our minds, changing our minds, and having something in mind. Nor is it either likely or necessary that we cease to speak of having a body, cease being proud or ashamed of the body we have, or cease to admire the beautiful bodies of the young. There is nothing awry with the category of matter, although it is true that its customary juxtaposition with the mind and with the category of the mental is typically confused. There is nothing wrong with the general concepts of the physical and the mental, although, again, it is perfectly true that these are vague categories that are neither mutually exclusive nor conjunctively exhaustive (see Preliminaries to Part II, §3). It is true that they are not very useful for scientific purposes, but they are none the worse for that. For they have perfectly decent common or garden uses.

Searle contends that 'In the case of humans, unless we perform experiments upon ourselves, individually, our only conclusive evidence for the presence and nature of consciousness is what the subject says and does, and subjects are notoriously unreliable.'[30] However, he contends that this 'is no more an obstacle in principle [to a science of consciousness] than the difficulties encountered in other forms of scientific investigation where we have to rely on indirect means of verifying our claims'. We agree that the evidence for the ascription of states of consciousness (and much else that is broadly speaking 'psychological') to other human beings consists of what people do and say. But three important points should be noted.

First, such evidence may be logical – as in the case of criterial support – or inductive. There is nothing *indirect* about criterial evidence: pain-behaviour or conative behaviour, for example, are not established as criterial evidence for pain and desire, respectively, as a result of an inductive correlation. It is correct that criterial evidence is defeasible in certain

---

[30] Ibid., p. 2074.

circumstances (though not all). But if it is not defeated, it is often (though not always) adequate to confer certainty.

Secondly, it would be altogether mistaken to suppose that what we observe are mere physical movements, or to think that what we hear are mere sounds, as opposed to intelligible human speech. What we observe are human actions and reactions – chortles of amusement, gestures of rage, cries of joy or grief. When we observe someone behaving thus, there is nothing indirect about the verifying evidence for our immediate judgement that the person is amused, angry, joyous or grieving (although, of course, *in certain circumstances* deception is possible). Similarly, if someone *tells us* what he hopes or fears, there is nothing indirect about our consequent knowledge. Indirect knowledge in such a case would be hearsay, by contrast with hearing from the horse's mouth, as it were.

Thirdly, although we often *justify* our ascription of mental states to others by reference to what they do and say, it does not follow (nor does Searle think it does) that our know-ledge is always or even typically inferential. On the contrary, we commonly recognize immediately, without any inference, that someone is in agony or overjoyed or tormented by grief (see §§3.3–3.5). Similarly, if someone *tells us* what he thinks, we do not *infer* what he thinks from what he said.

Consequently we agree with Searle that knowledge of the experiences of other people is not (normally) inferential, *a fortiori* not analogical. However, we hold it mistaken to suggest that the indirect means of verifying claims concerning black holes or atomic or subatomic particles 'should give us a model for verifying hypotheses in the area of the study of human and animal subjectivity'.[31] The states of consciousness of others, their beliefs and thoughts, their hopes and fears, are not the slightest akin, from a logical or epistemological point of view, to black holes or to atomic particles that can be observed only indirectly. To see someone writhing in agony, dancing with joy, or distraught with grief is not to observe their pain, joy or grief indirectly, any more than to hear from their own mouth what they think or believe is to come to know their thoughts and beliefs indirectly.

We are in agreement with Searle that it is confused to suppose that because conscious-ness is 'subjective' and science is 'objective', therefore science cannot investigate the neural basis of conscious mental states. But we do not think that what neuroscience may thus investigate goes any way towards solving or resolving philosophical problems pertaining to consciousness. It should be obvious from antecedent discussions (see Chapter 3) that such a question as 'How is the mind related to the body?' is primarily a philosophical question that needs conceptual, not empirical, investigation. But it is far from clear that the *question* makes good sense (and this is something which philosophical investigation must elucidate). It requires clarification of the concept of a mind, as a condition of clarifying whether the question of how the mind and the body are related makes any sense. So, for example, if, as we argued (§3.10), discourse about the mind is characteristically a *façon de parler*, then it makes no sense to talk of *a relation* between mind and body. For 'the mind' is not a kind of entity that can stand in relationship to anything.

---

[31] Ibid., p. 2074.

So, too, it is a conceptual question how the concepts of a mind and of a person's body are related to the concept of a person. We say that a person *has* a mind and *has* a body. Are there three different entities here – a person, a mind and a body? Or two – a mind and a body? Or only one – a person? What is it to *have* a body? Might a person cease to have a body, but retain his mind? Or vice versa? These are not scientific questions, and are not soluble by scientific means. They are conceptual questions, requiring an overview and description of a field of concepts.

There are numerous other philosophical questions in this domain, many of which have been touched upon in the course of this book. We see no reason to suppose that these kinds of question are ever likely to be answered by neuroscience. They are conceptual questions, not empirical ones, and they can be answered only by conceptual investigations. But we agree with Searle that many of these questions need to be answered antecedently to fruitful investigations in the neurosciences, if only to ensure that neuroscientists do not get enmeshed in webs of grammar and misconstrue the questions they are raising and mis-interpret the results of their own experiments. That was one reason for writing this book.

Index